IMPROVING READING SKILLS

Improving
Reading Skills

**SECOND
EDITION**

Deanne Milan

City College of San Francisco

McGRAW-HILL, INC.

New York St. Louis San Francisco Auckland Bogotá Caracas
Lisbon London Madrid Mexico Milan Montreal New Delhi Paris
San Juan Singapore Sydney Tokyo Toronto

Improving Reading Skills

1 2 3 4 5 6 7 8 9 0   DOC   DOC   9 0 9 8 7 6 5 4 3 2 1

ISBN 0-07-041906-X

This book was set in Stempel Garamond by General Graphic Services, Inc.
The editors were Lesley Denton, Lyn Beamesderfer, and Scott Amerman;
the designer was Joan Greenfield;
the production supervisor was Denise L. Puryear.
R. R. Donnelley & Sons Company was printer and binder.

Library of Congress Cataloging-in-Publication Data

Milan, Deanne K.
    Improving reading skills / Deanne K. Milan. — 2nd ed.
        p.   cm.
    Includes index.
    ISBN 0-07-041906-X
    1. Reading (Higher education)   2. College readers.   3. Vocabulary.
    I. Title.
    LB2395.3.M56   1992
    428.4'071'1—dc20   91-14503

FOR DAVID

CONTENTS

But in a technological society such as ours—and we boast that the United States is the most technologically advanced society in the world—why are learning and scholarship held in such contempt?

PART 1
GETTING STARTED: PRACTICING THE BASICS

Whatever opening line you use, keep it clean. "Do you know if asparagus goes well in a cream sauce?" is fine. References to vegetables, or even fondling vegetables while trying a pickup line, went out with the '70s.

When we took her to Hephzibah, we said to her, "You keep that beautiful smile," Marge Procopio said. "Every time we would see her there, she would have this big smile frozen on her face, as the tears poured down her cheeks. It was as if she believed that if she smiled as we had asked, then she wouldn't have to be turned over."

Next day many customers called to examine Freeman's "new lot." The latter gentleman was very loquacious. He would make us hold up our heads, walk briskly back and forth, while customers would feel of our hands and arms and bodies, turn us about, ask us what we could do, make us open our mouths and show our teeth, precisely as a jockey examines a horse which he is about to barter for or purchase.

The widow she cried over me, and called me a poor lost lamb, and she called me a lot of other names, too, but she never meant no harm by it. She put me in them new clothes again, and I couldn't do nothing but sweat and sweat, and feel all cramped up.

They spoke with the detached fatalism of people with limited choices and alternatives. Their lives were as raw and brutal as ghetto streets—something they accepted with an odd grace and resignation. I was appalled and deeply affected by these confidences. The injustices they endured enraged me; their personal struggles overwhelmed me. I knew I could do little but sympathize.

Terry's face was grim as he ran his hand along the cow's back. He was in his early twenties, had a wife and a small baby and was one of the breed who was prepared to labour all day for somebody else and then come home and start work on his own few stock. His two cows, his few pigs and hens made a big difference to somebody who had to live on thirty shillings a week.

Crotalus had not yet arrived for the autumn rendezvous. He came that night. The den's mouth was a shattered mass of rock, for the men had done their dynamiting well. Dead members of his tribe lay everywhere. Crotalus nosed among them, tongue flicking as he slid slowly along.

When the survivors of a plane crash are interviewed, some of them inevitably insist that they were saved by prayer. The chances are good that some who did not survive also prayed for all they were worth, but they are now unable to testify about the value of the procedure.

For the uninitiated, urban legends are apocryphal tales of the unexpected, bizarre or horrible that often—but not always—include a dead or exploding animal (usually something adorable and fluffy, like a cat or bunny rabbit), a microwave oven, a dead human, a naked woman, a surprised repairman, a jilted lover, a hitchhiker or a car.

Though neither the American nor the Chinese could speak a word of each other's language, within minutes they were in a two-on-two game. It was a familiar sequence for the American journalist, who had been getting into pickup basketba'' games with strangers in gyms and on playgrounds all over the world for 20 v

[Dominic] attempts to explain why shopping, endless shopping, holds such appeal for youngsters his age. "You want to fit in, you want to be in style," he says. His companions nod, and a heated debate about socially correct labels ensues. The consensus is that Reebok high-top sneakers have just been eclipsed by Nikes. Is there any real difference? "Yes," Dominic replies pointedly, "the brand name and the price."

The human inhabitants of the land were just as marvelous. Boys and girls who overcame their first fears traded jackknives and coffee for beadwork and moccasins, and in the bargain they got a taste of the exotic. "They amused us by eating grasshoppers," a girl of 12 told her diary. As another young girl puts it, "It was like traveling over the great domains of a lost world."

While some pack rats specialize in what they collect, others seem to save indiscriminately. And what they keep, such as junk mail, supermarket receipts, newspapers, business memos, empty cans, clothes or old Christmas and birthday cards, often seem to be worthless. Even when items have some value, such as lumber scraps, fabric remnants, auto parts, shoes and plastic meat trays, they tend to be kept in huge quantities that no one could use in a lifetime.

Today, blacks have returned to the new plantations to work as gardeners, waiters and maids, to tend golf courses and tennis courts and to clean private homes. . . . "I know it sounds farfetched, but it's almost like South Africa," said Campbell, 47, over breakfast at one of the island's exclusive hotels. "We need passes to go to places on the island. We work in the lowest jobs so white people can play. We arrive in these buses every morning, and then we're shipped out again."

PART 3
READING ABOUT ISSUES

Ellen Goodman

U.S. KIDS NEED MORE SCHOOL TIME

The six-hour day, the 180-day school year is regarded as somehow sacrosanct. But when parents work an eight-hour day and a 240-day year, it means something different. It means that many kids go home to empty houses. It means that, in the summer, they hang out.

Cathy Trost

WOMEN WHO'VE HAD ABORTIONS

Nearly one-third of pregnancies, excluding miscarriages, in the U.S. end in abortion. The experience cuts across lines of class, race and age. A recent Wall Street Journal/NBC News poll shows that the public, by a 2-to-1 margin, believes that abortion should be legal. But the actual abortion decision remains a deeply personal one, and it is one that many women haven't wanted to discuss publicly.

Elizabeth Marek

THE LIVES OF TEENAGE MOTHERS

I feel that the woman should just make up her own mind, make her own decision. But he said, "Oh, I love you, and I'll do this for you, I'll do that for you, and our baby will have this, and our baby will have that." Now she's two and a half years old, and all he ever got her was a big box of Pampers and socks and T-shirts and $20 and that was it. Suddenly the resentment in her voice changes to wistfulness. "She's two and a half. And he was going to buy her a baby crib and a bassinet and clothes. Everything . . ."

Patrick Welsh

SEX AND THE MODERN TEENAGER

Kids seem to agree that the idea of "modern" parents' being so open with their children is a gigantic myth. "The only kind of open discussion that parents want is one that ends with 'Gee, Mom and Dad, you're so right and I'm not sexually active and won't be at least until I get out of high school,'" says one 16-year-old boy.

myth. In the wild, dolphins are mean, moody and ornery. They can also be winsome, funny and gentle. In short, they're as complex and mysterious as any mammal with a big brain.

patience with the homeless. It was neighborhood tolerance that allowed the encampment of homeless men and women to swell to a shantytown of more than 300 indigents last summer. But it was the rising outcry from neighbors who claimed that the homeless had "taken the park hostage" that forced the city to finally tear the mess down.

lessons elsewhere and lent their hydraulic skills to other countries. Today the *Afsluitdijk,* or Zuider Zee road, is a normal thoroughfare. To drive across it between the sullen ocean on one side and new land on the other is for that moment to feel optimism for the human race.

PREFACE

The second edition of *Improving Reading Skills* is a textbook for college reading improvement courses. Like the first edition, it contains thirty-six reading selections drawn from a variety of sources, most of them contemporary, representing the sorts of reading students will encounter in their college courses and in their adult lives.

This new edition retains the underlying principles that made the first edition successful, while making some changes that should make the book more useful and appealing for both students and teachers. For an author, a second edition gives one the opportunity to clarify, to sort out what worked and what didn't, and to respond to and implement the many comments and suggestions from teachers, students, and reviewers gathered along the way.

Specifically, here are the changes incorporated in this new edition:

- An easier and more readable sample reading passage (class-tested)
- A clearer division among the book's five sections
- An introduction to each section, including brief suggestions for improving comprehension and for completing some of the more challenging exercises such as making inferences, distinguishing between levels of support, identifying transitional devices, and using context clues
- More emphasis on reading about contemporary controversial issues
- A consistent number of comprehension questions throughout the text and a simplified formula for students to calculate their comprehension scores
- Moving the comprehension score formula so that it now comes immediately after Exercises A and B
- Level of exercises more closely appropriate to the level of each reading
- The inclusion of either a paraphrasing or summarizing exercise following each selection in the Topics for Writing or Discussion

The book should help students read material of increasing difficulty with greater ease, understanding, and most important, confidence. My aim in revising *Improving Reading Skills* has been twofold: to choose readings on a variety of timely and interesting subjects that will engage students' attention and to provide a variety of exercises giving them the opportunity to practice all the skills needed for effective reading.

The readings throughout the text embrace a wide range of subjects: how American slaves were sold at auction, the phenomenon of superstitions, packrats who save useless things, the public's fascination with urban legends, the daily lives of teenage mothers, new teenage sexual mores, the rather surprising contents of toothpaste, the imprisonment of Japanese-American citizens on the West Coast during the Second World War, the increasingly thorny dispute over bilingual education, and the recent spate of Elvis sightings. While I have tried to present new materials not previously reprinted, inevitably I have also included some selections that many instructors will recognize as being effective in the classroom. A glance at the table of contents should identify these.

The readings are arranged by order of increasing difficulty. The shortest selection is about 800 words; the longest is 5900. However, the majority fall into the 1000- to 2000-word range, representing the length of the average newspaper or magazine article. Students should be able to read a selection and complete the exercises in one sitting. In addition, within each section the readings are arranged by difficulty according not only to vocabulary level and sentence length, but also the more subjectively defined criteria of subject matter and sentence structure. Students should, therefore, read them in order.

To introduce students to the organization of the text and to the types of exercises following each reading, the book begins with a short sample reading by Isaac Asimov, appropriately titled "Reading, Writing, and Technology," in which he expresses his concern over our increasing failure to educate our citizens. In addition to being a readable account of a serious issue, this sample reading introduces students to the skills they will be practicing during the course and, through sample exercises, shows them the process they must follow. Finally, it discusses the relative merits of the answer choices to the sample questions so that students learn to think through their responses carefully. Accordingly, the exercises require careful, concentrated reading and provide a structure to the reading process. Most crucial, as I have discovered in my own classes, students learn what to look for when they read.

As in the first edition, this new edition of *Improving Reading Skills* treats vocabulary extensively. In addition to two vocabulary exercises, each reading begins with a Vocabulary Preview. Using five or six words from the selection that might be unfamiliar to the reader, the preview acquaints students with word origins, word parts, and word families. These previews have the twin benefits of teaching readers the meanings of a few important words that they will encounter in the selection and, more important, showing them how to undertake a systematic study of vocabulary. Rather than being taught in isolation, the constituents of English vocabulary words—roots, prefixes, and suffixes—so useful for improving students' word attack skills, are taught only in the context of their reading.

The exercises following each selection are more extensive than those in most other textbooks, offering the student an opportunity to work on every aspect of reading. Step by step, each exercise provides practice on a particular skill at a level appropriate for the selection. Specifically, here is a description of the skills students will encounter in the readings:

- Determining the main idea and author's purpose
- Comprehending main ideas
- Distinguishing between main ideas and supporting details
- Making inferences
- Drawing conclusions
- Distinguishing between fact and opinion
- Understanding vocabulary and using new words
- Summarizing and paraphrasing

Instructors should note that not all the readings are followed by exercises in Drawing Conclusions or in Distinguishing between Fact and Opinion; these are included only where appropriate. Similarly, there are two kinds of exercises on levels of support. Instructors should consult the *Instructor's Manual* for a fuller explanation.

The text ends with two sections on using the dictionary and on study skills techniques. More specifically, there are suggestions for managing one's time and planning a study schedule, for putting into effect the SQ3R study skills method, along with instruction in how to annotate textbooks, how to write paraphrases and summaries, and how to take notes and outline textbook material. Each section includes a short excerpt from textbooks for students to practice with.

Instructors should refer to the *Instructor's Manual* for information on readability levels, brief summaries of each selection, suggestions for using the text, and answers to all the exercises.

I would like to thank Sheila Behr, City University of New York, City College; Joyce Crawford, Miami-Dade Community College; Ida Egli, Santa Rosa Junior College; Betty Perkinson, Tidewater Community College; Louise Tomlinson, University of Georgia; and Anne Willekens, Antelope Valley College, for their comments and suggestions on the manuscript. I would also like to thank Terry Alberigi, reference librarian at City College of San Francisco; and Lesley Denton, Lyn Beamesderfer, and Scott Amerman, my editors at McGraw-Hill.

Deanne Milan

TO THE STUDENT

THE AIMS OF THE TEXT

The thirty-six selections in the second edition of *Improving Reading Skills* are drawn from books, magazines, and newspapers. Most are nonfiction, representing both the kind of reading required of you in your other college courses and reading material you will encounter after you finish school for the rest of your life. The readings have been carefully chosen for their high interest level; they represent a variety of topics and writing styles. Some are entertaining; some are informative; some are persuasive. Many will give you something to think about. Since the selections are arranged by order of difficulty, as you work through the text, you will be able to sharpen and refine your comprehension, vocabulary, and analytical skills with increasingly harder readings.

The first aim of the text, then, is to help you improve those skills required to meet the demands of college work. The second aim, which actually overlaps with the first, is to help you discover that reading can be enjoyable. But first you have to know what to look for and know what is expected of you. Good reading involves a systematic approach, whether you read for an academic course or for pleasure. All the exercises in the text will show you, by means of consistent practice, what is involved in this process. Once you complete the selections, you should be better prepared to tackle all of your reading, from the daily newspaper, to the essay your English composition instructor assigns, to your psychology textbook.

IMPROVING YOUR VOCABULARY

A major premise of this book is that a good vocabulary is essential for good comprehension skills. Stated another way, if you don't know the meanings of many words a writer uses, you can't really understand accurately what he or she is saying. All you can hope is to come away with a hazy idea of the main point. This, clearly, is not reading.

The best way to improve your vocabulary is to commit yourself during the term to looking up unfamiliar words that you will encounter in your reading. At first this task may seem overwhelming. However, there are some ways you can learn the meanings of new words without turning to the dictionary. First, you can study the

Vocabulary Preview section that precedes each reading, each of which introduces you to several of the words you will encounter in the selection. Second, you can use context clues: often the meaning of a word is made clear by the way it is used in the sentence. Finally, you can break the word down into its component parts—prefix, root, and suffix—as a way of getting at its meaning.

However, if the word is still unclear to you after you go through these three steps, then you will probably have to go to the dictionary, especially if knowing the meaning of the word is essential for you to understand the passage. Furthermore, it is not cheating to look these words up, even though you are asked to do vocabulary exercises at the end of each selection.

Since your instructor may test you periodically on the vocabulary from these readings, you might also want to write new words and their definitions in a special notebook or on index cards. This way you can review quickly before tests, rather than having to hunt through the book to find them.

Good comprehension and good vocabulary skills are, therefore, interdependent. Unlike other reading improvement texts, this one attempts to integrate vocabulary study more closely with reading. The Vocabulary Preview sections, as mentioned above, introduce you to some of the words in the reading that may be unfamiliar to you.

To illustrate certain principles of the English language and to introduce you to these new words, each preview section is divided into three parts: Word Origins, Word Parts (prefixes, roots, and suffixes), and Word Families. The context of each new word—the way it is used in the reading—is always included to help you. These previews serve three functions: (1) They make your reading of the selection easier, giving you a "leg up"; you already know some of the meanings of the more difficult words. (2) They teach you word attack skills—how to break down and analyze new words. (3) Most important, they present many new words which you will add to your reading vocabulary. And you will be pleasantly surprised to find that words you meet in the earlier selections will turn up again in later ones and in your other reading, as well.

Before you begin the book, you may find it helpful to read the section on dictionary skills (pages 447–455) even if your instructor does not assign it at the beginning of the course.

ESSENTIAL READING SKILLS

The aims of the text, discussed earlier, are carried out in the organization of the exercise material. Each exercise focuses on a specific skill and builds on the preceding exercises. Taken together, they will help you read more systematically, they will show you what to look for when you read, and they will provide a structure for your reading. Here is a list of the specific skills you will work on during the term:

Determining the Main Idea and the Author's Purpose

Comprehending Main Ideas

Recognizing Supporting Details

Distinguishing between Main Ideas and Supporting Details

Making Inferences

Drawing Conclusions

Distinguishing between Fact and Opinion

Analyzing Organization and Seeing Relationships

Understanding Vocabulary

Using Vocabulary

Writing Paraphrases and Short Summaries

The first two exercises will help improve both your comprehension and your retention of reading material. The remaining exercises, excluding the two vocabulary exercises, are intended to challenge your mind and to help you learn to think more clearly.

Since there has been an increased emphasis nationally on promoting critical thinking skills, both in schools and colleges and in the workaday world, these activities are important for your intellectual development. For example, you will be asked to determine the logical relationships and connections between ideas, to distinguish between fact and opinion, to assess supporting evidence, to determine the writer's attitude toward the topic, and to determine the method of development a writer uses to support the main idea.

The vocabulary exercises are self-explanatory—to show you the meanings of new words and to give you an opportunity to use them. The last exercise, Topics for Writing or Discussion, takes various forms, depending on the selection. Sometimes you will be asked to paraphrase (put into your own words) three or four sentences from the passage. Other times you might be asked to paraphrase an entire paragraph from the selection. Finally, you may be asked to summarize the important points from the reading.

The purpose of this may not be readily apparent to you. After all, you are enrolled in a reading, not a writing, course. But there is no question that reading and writing skills go hand in hand, and the best way to determine if you have understood what you have read is to see if you can put it into your own words. Before you begin any of these paraphrasing or summarizing exercises, you should read the section on paraphrasing and summarizing at the end of the text.

CALCULATING YOUR COMPREHENSION SCORE

The instructions accompanying each set of exercises ask you to do Exercises A and B without looking back at the selection. This will force you to read with greater attention and concentration than you would if you knew you could look back at the passage to refresh your memory. When you are finished with all the exercises, figure your comprehension score by counting your correct answers for the first two exercises, according to the formula.

Since the two questions on determining the main idea and author's purpose are most crucial, each is worth 2 points, while comprehending-the-main-idea questions in Exercise B are each worth 1 point. By adding up the total number of points and multiplying by 10, you can arrive at your score, based on 100 as the total number of points possible. A score of above 70 percent is adequate. Since the selections become progressively more difficult, maintaining a score of 70 percent or higher indicates real improvement.

Before you begin the book, it is essential to read the sample reading selection that follows. Do the sample exercises in each section, and read through the explanation of the answers. In this way, you will become familiar with the organization of the text and its specific requirements.

IMPROVING READING SKILLS

Isaac Asimov

READING, WRITING, AND TECHNOLOGY

Born in the Soviet Union in 1920, Isaac Asimov is a biochemist, teacher, and science fiction writer. This article, first published in the Los Angeles Times, *takes a serious look at America's future. Using American children's poor showing in reading and writing as his point of departure, Asimov candidly discusses our role as world leader, our need for technological understanding, and, most importantly, the increasing importance of learning and scholarship.*

VOCABULARY PREVIEW

WORD ORIGINS

The Word Origins section presents the *etymology* of some of the words you will meet in each selection. *Etymology* means the historical development of words—the way they came into the language and their original meaning. If you understand a word's origin, you may be better able to remember it. And some words have interesting or unusual stories behind them.

Each Word Origins section shows you the remarkable diversity of the English language. More than 50 percent of the words in our language originally came from Latin, usually by way of French. Most of the remainder come from the other European languages, such as Greek, Spanish, German, Dutch, and Norwegian. However, many English words have their roots in such non-European languages as Hindi and Tamil (spoken in India), various American Indian languages, and African languages.

If you are curious about the etymology of a word, you can consult an unabridged dictionary. Word origins are usually listed in brackets after the last definition. Here is an explanation of the etymology of three words that appear in this selection:

DISTRESS

Asimov writes in paragraph 1, "A *distressingly* large proportion of children simply cannot read or write at a level considered appropriate for their age" (italics are mine). This is the adverb form of the noun *distress,* which means "suffering" or "anxiety." It comes from the Old French *destresse,* meaning "narrow passage," from the original Latin word *distringere,* "to draw tight," "to detain," or "to hinder." This etymology makes more sense if you consider that the Latin word referred to the legal holding of goods apart as a way to correct a wrong, which in turn suggests the sorrow a person whose goods were withheld undoubtedly felt.

FUNDAMENTAL

Fundamental is used twice in the selection: First, in discussing why we have so much difficulty teaching our children to read and write, Asimov writes in paragraph 6, "I think the problem is more *fundamental.*" And in paragraph 13, he writes, "It can be argued that the problems, even something as *fundamental* as the ever-increasing world population, have been caused by technological advance."

Coming from the Latin word for "bottom," *fundus, fundamental* means "basic" or "primary." Thus when we cite a fundamental reason for a problem, we are getting to the bottom of the issue.

WORD PARTS

This section focuses on the *prefixes, roots,* and *suffixes* that are useful for building your stock of new vocabulary words. Each section takes an important word from the selection, breaks it down into its component parts, and analyzes their meanings. By the end of the course, you will have been exposed to a fairly large number of these common word parts. Knowing them will also help expand your ability to know the meanings of new words you will encounter elsewhere in your reading.

-ABLE, -IBLE, -UBLE

A large number of words in English end with these common related suffixes. The only difference between them is spelling; they all mean the same thing—"capable of." This article contains five such words:

unemployables	("This, in turn, means a reservoir of *unemployables*"—paragraph 2): people who are incapable of being employed
bearable and **unbearable**	("And this in turn means we will have a large demand for drugs as the only means of making the *unbearable* seem *bearable*"—2): able to bear, put up with, or endure, and its opposite
reasonable	("All this sounds *reasonable,* but what do we do about it?"—4): rational
possible	("These are problems that for *possible* solutions require technological advance and understanding"—12): capable of happening or existing

insoluble   (". . . these apparently *insoluble* problems"—15): incapable of being solved

Notice, too, that three of these words—*unemployable, unbearable,* and *insoluble*—begin with two common negative prefixes, *un-* and *in-*.

WORD FAMILIES

This section of the Vocabulary Preview discusses one or two words from the selection that are part of a larger vocabulary "family," either because they share a common root or prefix or because the root can form several parts of speech by the addition of various suffixes.

TELEVISION

Television, which can bring the whole world into our living rooms by satellites, is so much a part of our lives today that we may forget that it is a fairly recent invention, dating to the 1920s. It does, however, have its critics; in paragraph 3 Asimov cites television as one of the causes of children's lack of reading ability. The word *television* is an example of a neologism, meaning a new word. It derives from the Greek prefix *tēle-* ("at a distance") and the Latin root *vidēre* ("to see"). Here are some other examples of words beginning with this prefix:

telegram   communication transmitted by wire [*tēle-* + *graphos* ("writing")]

telepathy   communication between two minds [*tēle-* + *pathos* ("feeling")]

telephone   a device to transmit sound over distances [*tēle-* + *phone* ("sound," "voice")]

telescope   an instrument for seeing distant objects [*tēle-* + *skopos* ("watcher")]

Teleprompter   a trademark name for a device used in television showing the script in large type for the actor or speaker to see, unseen by the audience [*tēle-* + prompter ("something that reminds or prompts")]

Here are some other words or terms you will encounter in the article that may be unfamiliar to you:

wheeler dealers   [paragraph 6]: from the expression "to wheel and deal"; referring to people who promote their own interests and make business deals

junk bonds   [6]: highly risky and speculative bonds issued by corporations offering high rates of return; these bonds were largely responsible for the collapse of many savings and loans institutions during the late 1980s

stoop-shouldered professors   [10]: a visual image suggesting that professors' shoulders slump forward, meaning

that they are weak and not true ''he-men''
like the pioneers who settled and built the
country

Now read the selection once through without stopping, to get an understanding of its content. Then read it a second time more carefully, looking up any unfamiliar vocabulary words.

ISAAC ASIMOV

READING, WRITING, AND TECHNOLOGY

1   A careful survey completed early in 1990 has shown that American school children have not improved their ability to read or write over the past 18 years. We're not talking math and science, or history and geography. We're talking reading and writing. A distressingly large proportion of children simply cannot read or write at a level considered appropriate for their age.

2   What this means is that we have built up, and are continuing to build up, a large reservoir of Americans who are only fit for unskilled labor in a technological society that has almost no use for unskilled labor. This, in turn, means a reservoir of unemployables or those who will be forced to work at rock-bottom wages in the most menial forms of labor. And this in turn means we will have a large demand for drugs as the only means of making the unbearable seem bearable.

3   But why can't we teach our children to read and write? The report lists three reasons: 1) too much television; 2) too little reading matter; books, magazines, newspapers in the home; 3) too little homework.

4   All this sounds reasonable, but what do we do about it? The report suggests that parents grow more involved in their children's work and progress.

5   Here I feel a little cynical. I'm afraid that the parents of children who are backward in reading and writing are themselves likely to be similarly backward and could not, even if they wished, be of much help.

6   I think the problem is more fundamental. American society knows very well what it desires and admires. It desires to be amused. Fame and fortune are showered on show business personalities, on sports stars, on rock singers, and so on. Americans also desire to make money, a great deal of money, preferably without working too hard for it. So we admire wheeler dealers who manipulate junk bonds and dubious investments in order to make vast sums of money. Many of the rest of us keep hoping to win a few million in the lottery.

7   All this is perfectly understandable, and I do not intend or even wish to fight the universe on such matters. Of course people want amusement and easy money.

8   But in a technological society such as ours—and we boast that the United States is the most technologically advanced society in the world—why are learning and scholarship held in such contempt?

9   We see movies in which college students who are actually interested in their studies are called "nerds" and are pictured—male and female—as dumpy, plain, weak, unattractive. Opposed to them are the glorious "jocks" and "pinup girls," who are all pictured as Hollywood starlets and whose pleasure lies in endlessly humiliating the nerds—to the laughter of the audience.

10   Why is this? I have heard some explain it by saying America arose as a pioneer society where strong arms and sturdy frames were needed to tame a wilderness, with no use for stoop-shouldered professors. But we are no longer a pioneer society and we are no longer taming a wilderness—we are despoiling an environment, and now we need professors.

11   I have also heard it said that our dismissal of scholarship and learning is purely a matter of money. Becoming a learned man is no way to get rich and that is the measure of its worth. Yet surely that is a rather sleazy way of setting a value on human activity. How much more ought we to respect a $60 billion drug lord than a $60,000 professor?

12   The fact is that America (and the whole world for that matter) desperately needs its scientists. We need only rapidly go through the litany of disasters that faces us—the pollution and poisoning of the environment, the destruction of the rain forests and wetlands, the disappearing ozone layer, the threatening greenhouse effect. These are problems that for possible solutions require technological advance and understanding.

13   It can be argued that the problems, even something as fundamental as the ever-increasing world population, have been caused by technological advance. There is truth to this. But these problems have resulted from the short-sighted use of technology by people who grabbed for the immediate short-term benefits of new discoveries and new techniques without sufficient consideration of long-term side effects.

14   What we need, you see, are not merely scientists, engineers, and technologists, but political and industrial leaders willing to try to understand the world of science and technology in depth and to avoid basing their judgments on the "bottom-line"—of instant profit or loss.

15   Consider the disputes that fill the minds of human beings today. The endless conflict of Catholics and Protestants in Northern Ireland, of Azerbijanis and Armenians in the Soviet Union, of Palestinians and Israelis in the Middle East, of Bulgars and Turks in Bulgaria. These and dozens of other such disputes are devils dancing at the lips of a volcano about to erupt. Money, effort and emotion are expanded endlessly on these apparently insoluble problems right when the earth is sliding down the chute to destruction for all the disputants alike.

16   And America's responsibility in all this? As the most advanced, the strongest, the richest nation in the world, we owe the world leadership. We can't solve the problems by ourselves, but we can show the way.

17   But we are also the freest nation in the world, so we have no dictator to pull us along. We have an elected president, an elected legislature, elected officials at every

governmental level. We must depend on them to understand the state of the world and the nature of the measures that must be taken.

18   Because we are a democracy, it is the people themselves who must choose adequate leaders. Smiles are not enough, nor is flag-waving oratory. We must have understanding, or if you want to put it in another way, scholarship and learning.

19   And for that we must turn to an electorate, many of whom cannot even read or write. Does this not make a mockery of democracy? Frankly, as the 1990s opens, the state of American education freezes my blood with fear for all humanity.   ■

From Isaac Asimov, "Reading, Writing and Technology," *San Francisco Chronicle*, "This World," February 28, 1990. First published in the *Los Angeles Times*. Reprinted by permission.

SAMPLE EXERCISES

When you work through the text, you should answer the questions in the first two exercises immediately after reading the selection without referring back to it. This will force you to read with greater attention and concentration. Your retention, meaning how much you remember, should improve, as well.

A.   DETERMINING THE MAIN IDEA AND PURPOSE

How to Find the Main Idea

This exercise is the most important one of all. To find the main idea, you should ask yourself two questions: (1) What is the subject or topic? and (2) What does the author want me to understand about the subject or topic? Although the author often may provide the reader with the main idea, called a *thesis statement* in an essay or article, some writers do not, and you may have to determine the main idea yourself. If there is a main idea, however, it will usually be placed somewhere near the beginning of the essay, often in the first, second, or third paragraph.

Look for a general statement, one that states a *proposition*, a statement to be defended, supported, or given evidence for. Now, think about the Asimov article, consider these choices, and decide which one seems to represent most accurately the thesis, or main idea.

1.   _____ The main idea of the selection is that (a) because the U.S. is a free nation with great technological and scientific capacities, we owe the world leadership; (b) America's educational system needs improvement; (c) Americans are too respectful of money and power, and we spend too much time seeking amusement; (d) the inability of a future electorate to read and write acceptably and our inability to choose good leaders may result in many serious consequences in the future.

Before you decide on an answer, let us review the questions stated earlier. What is the topic of this article? Asimov covers a lot of ground in this article, and you can't really point to one sentence that states the main idea. However, the title, "Reading, Writing, and Technology," provides you with a good clue. His chief concern is stated at the end of paragraph 1: "A distressingly large proportion of children simply cannot read or write at a level considered appropriate for their age." This is his starting point.

Now for the second question. Asimov wants us to understand that the poor quality of American education will have serious consequences or repercussions. We will need to use technology wisely to solve the "litany of disasters," as he puts it in paragraph 12, but an uninformed electorate will not respect the "scholarship and learning" politicians must have if we are to solve our problems. Humanity's very future is at stake.

When you work through the exercises, consider carefully each choice to find the one that is most accurate. Often you will find that an answer may be too narrow or too general or perhaps even irrelevant to the main idea because it represents a supporting idea rather than the central concern.

Let us now examine the choices. The first answer, (a), is certainly stated in the article, but it is not Asimov's central concern. Choice (b) represents an important conclusion that one could certainly draw, but again, not the main idea. Choice (c), like (a), is discussed in the article, but it represents support—a reason to explain why, according to him, we have contempt for learning, not the main idea. The best choice— the one that most accurately represents the thesis of the whole article—is (d).

How to Determine the Author's Purpose

To determine the purpose, ask yourself what the author might hope to accomplish with the selection. Why did he or she write it? Is the purpose to entertain or to amuse? to explain and to inform? to describe what something looks like? to criticize or to condemn some particular action? to persuade us to change our thinking? to poke fun at weaknesses or faults? to present both sides of a controversial issue (so that we can make up our own minds), or perhaps to argue for only one side of the issue? to analyze a trend, a scientific phenomenon, or the background of a problem?

As you can see, there are many possibilities. Consider this sample question.

2. _____ With respect to the main idea, the author's purpose is (a) to tell an entertaining story; (b) to convince us of the seriousness of an issue; (c) to argue for one side of a controversial issue; (d) to explain and to inform.

The best answer is (b). Choice (a) is way off the mark; (c) is inaccurate, because the issue of an uninformed electorate with weak reading skills is hardly a controversial matter (in other words, this is one issue that it would be foolish to oppose); and (d) is half right, but too vague.

B.   COMPREHENDING MAIN IDEAS

This text provides you with two kinds of comprehension questions: multiple choice and fill-ins. Here are some sample questions of both kinds for you to practice with:

Multiple-Choice

1. _____ Asimov believes that one reason we cannot teach our children to read and write at an appropriate level is that we are too interested in

(a) movie stars; (b) making business deals; (c) being amused; (d) winning the lottery.

2.   _____ The author states that Americans regard learning and scholarship with (a) respect; (b) contempt; (c) indifference; (d) embarrassment.

3.   _____ To solve the environment's problems, Asimov argues that we will need (a) computer whizzes; (b) more people with the pioneer spirit; (c) politicians; (d) professors.

Fill-Ins

1.   According to Asimov, what are the three reasons that we have difficulty

teaching our children to read? _____,

_____, and _____.

2.   Asimov states that one problem with our culture is that the movie industry fosters the idea that learning is not important, chiefly by portraying students who study hard as _____.

3.   To deal with the world's seemingly insoluble problems, America owes

the world _____.

Here are the answers:
Multiple Choice—(1) c; (2) b; (3) d.
Fill-Ins—(1) too much TV; too little reading; too little homework; (2) nerds; (3) leadership.
Notice that these questions deal with simple comprehension and retention of the key points from the selection. They demand that you read carefully and understand what you read, but they are not particularly tricky, nor are they "picky." They test your understanding of the important concepts, not on your remembering trivial or irrelevant details.

After you complete Exercises A and B, you may refer to the selection as you do the remaining exercises.

C.   DISTINGUISHING BETWEEN MAIN IDEAS AND SUPPORTING DETAILS

In this exercise you are provided with some sentences from the reading. You will then be asked to decide if they represent one of the several main ideas (MI) in the selection or a supporting detail (SD). The purpose of this exercise is to show you that not everything in your reading is equally important. Main ideas are more important, that is, more important to understand and remember, than the details or examples that support them. A writer gives details for clarification, for proof, for evidence, for a better understanding.

As you do this exercise, keep in mind that a main idea is a *general* idea. A supporting detail, on the other hand, is more *specific*. Look at these sentences from Asimov's article:

1.   _____ The fact is that America (and the whole world for that matter) desperately needs its scientists.

2.   _____ We need only rapidly to go through the litany of disasters that faces us—the pollution and poisoning of the environment, the destruction of the rain forests and wetlands, the disappearing ozone layer, the threatening greenhouse effect.

3.   _____ These are problems that for possible solutions require technological advance and understanding.

The answers are (1) MI; (2) SD; (3) MI. If you look back through the sentences, you will see that sentences 1 and 3 represent important ideas that Asimov emphasizes, whereas sentence 2 gives us *examples* of the problems that face us.

A variation of this exercise asks you to determine whether a series of statements supports a main idea or not, as in the following:

Place an X in the space for each detail that *directly* supports this main idea from the selection: **"Why are learning and scholarship held in such contempt?"**

1.   _____ We see movies in which college students who are actually interested in their studies are called "nerds" and are pictured—male and female—as dumpy, plain, weak, unattractive.

2.   _____ I have heard some explain it by saying America arose as a pioneer society where strong arms and sturdy frames were needed to tame a wilderness, with no use for stoop-shouldered professors.

3.   _____ I have also heard it said that our dismissal of scholarship and learning is purely a matter of money.

4.   _____ Because we are a democracy, it is the people themselves who must choose adequate leaders.

You should have marked numbers 1, 2, and 3 as directly supporting the main idea. Sentence 4 is relevant to the essay as a whole but does not directly relate to the idea that as a nation we have contempt for learning and scholarship.

D.   MAKING INFERENCES

Inferences require you to "read between the lines," to deduce information from what the author *implies,* rather than from what he or she states directly. If an author implies the idea from a sentence or paragraph in the selection, write Y (Yes). If the inference is not accurate or if the statement misrepresents an idea from the selection, write N (No). Finally, write CT (Can't Tell) if there is no evidence for the inference in the selection or if you would need more information before you could decide whether it was accurate or not.

Remember that inferences are not *stated* in the selection. Rather, they are *suggested* by the author's words. Try your hand at these sample inference questions.

1.   _____ Drug abuse is closely related to poor reading and writing skills.

2.   _____ American schools increasingly are being expected to solve our society's problems, such as poverty and crime.

3.   _____ The parents of poor readers should give them as much help at home as they possibly can.

4.   _____ The movie industry is a powerful tool for shaping public opinion and perception.

5.   _____ Americans have more respect for millionaires and celebrities than they do for teachers and scientists.

6.   _____ The other developed nations, especially the European nations, should band together with the U.S. to provide leadership for the rest of the world in solving the problems of pollution and the destruction of the environment.

Here are the answers. (1) Y; (2) CT; (3) N; (4) Y; (5) Y; (6) N.

Clearly, these inference questions require you to do some thinking about what you have read, so let us examine carefully the reasoning behind the correct answers.

1.   In the last sentence of paragraph 2, Asimov implies that there is a connection between poor reading and writing skills and drug use. Adults who do not read well will form a "large reservoir of Americans" who will be fit only for unskilled labor; as a result, they may turn to drugs "as the only means of making the unbearable seem bearable."

2.   In fact, the idea that Americans expect schools to solve our social problems does have some currency, but since Asimov does not mention anything about this, the correct answer is CT. When you make inferences, be sure to stay within the scope of what that particular author suggests.

3.   This inference is inaccurate because Asimov, in fact, says the opposite in paragraph 5. He confesses to the cynical view that parents of poor readers probably would not know how to go about helping their children even if they wanted to. Note that this statement represents Asimov's subjective *opinion*, rather than a fact that you could verify.

4.   We can infer that, at least in Asimov's view, the movie industry does influence public perception, for he claims that movies foster Americans' contempt for learning. For example, movies depict students who enjoy studying as "nerds" and objects of ridicule, while they depict starlet types and athletes as glamorous.

5.   Asimov implies in both paragraphs 6 and 11 that because Americans are money-conscious, they admire those who make money more than those who do not. We can infer that Americans somehow view millionaires as "better" than underpaid teachers.

6.   The last inference misrepresents what Asimov says, making the correct answer N. In paragraph 16 Asimov calls upon the U.S. alone, as the world's richest nation, to show the rest of the world the way.

E.   DRAWING CONCLUSIONS

Although not all the selections in the text lend themselves to this kind of question, the ability to draw accurate conclusions is important. Like making inferences, this exercise requires you to make accurate deductions from what the author has written. But conclusions go further than inferences. They represent suggestions or recommendations for the future, or in the case of this selection, warnings and predictions. In other words, they suggest *future* courses of action and consequences from the information given. Look at these statements and place an X in the space if it represents a conclusion that you can reasonably draw from the article.

1. _____ Educators should conduct more surveys to assess American children's reading and writing skills.

2. _____ American teachers should assign more homework.

3. _____ The American movie industry should be required to make movies depicting learning and scholarship as glamorous and desirable activities.

4. _____ American politicians should have a better understanding of technology than they do.

5. _____ If something isn't done to improve our educational system, our society is going to be in deep trouble in the future.

6. _____ If American teachers were paid more, more qualified people would become teachers.

You should have placed an X only before numbers 2, 4, and 5. Statement (1) is not a reasonable conclusion because Asimov says in the first paragraph that the survey of children's skills was "careful." What would be the point of conducting another one, which would probably come up with the same results? And, with regard to (3), although Asimov deplores the movie industry's stereotyping of people interested in intellectual pursuits, he does not go so far as to suggest that it should be censored. Finally, (6) might be true; more qualified people might become teachers if the pay were higher, but he does not say much about teachers or the teaching profession.

F. ANALYZING ORGANIZATION AND SEEING RELATIONSHIPS

The questions in this exercise deal with the structure of the selection, kinds of support, paragraph patterns, logical relationships between ideas, transitional devices, unusual uses of language (metaphors and similes), and the author's attitude toward the subject. Try these sample questions.

1. _____ This article has a clear beginning, middle, and end. Write the number of the paragraph where the body begins. _____ Then write the number of the paragraph where the conclusion begins. _____

2. _____ What is the logical relationship between paragraphs 1 and 2? (a) steps in a process; (b) important term to be defined and a definition of it; (c) contrast; (d) cause and effect.

3. _____ What kind of evidence does Asimov rely on primarily to support his thesis? (a) facts and statistics; (b) the testimony of educational authorities; (c) his own observations and opinions; (d) summaries of scientific research.

4. _____ With regard to the article as a whole, the function of paragraph 13 is to serve as (a) a transition; (b) a concession to the other side; (c) supporting evidence for the main idea; (d) an emotional appeal.

5. _____ Which method of development is evident in paragraph 15? (a) term and a definition of it; (b) short examples; (c) contrast; (d) analogy; (e) facts and statistics.

6. Paragraph 15 contains this metaphor: "These and dozens of other such disputes are devils dancing at the lips of a volcano about to erupt." In

your own words, explain what this imaginative comparison means. _____

_____

7. _____ Which of the following best describes the audience that Asimov is writing for? (a) the general public; (b) scientists and technologists; (c) parents; (d) teachers; (e) politicians.

8. _____ Asimov's attitude toward the subject can best be described as (a) bitter, angry; (b) neutral, objective; (c) sympathetic, compassionate; (d) seriously troubled, concerned; (e) mocking, sneering.

Here are the answers. (1) The paragraph that begins the body of the article is paragraph 2; the paragraph that begins the conclusion is paragraph 16. (2) d; (3) c; (4) b; (5) b; (6) The social conflicts in many countries are so severe that they may cause great destruction if they are not solved. (7) a; (8) d.

The last two questions might have posed some difficulty. When you are asked to determine the *audience* for a piece of writing, you have to consider the content, the level of vocabulary, and the author's purpose. In this selection, the writer uses a fairly general and standard vocabulary, so he is probably not writing for scientists or technologists. Another clue is his use of the pronoun *we,* by which he means Americans in general. In addition, although he has something to say about scientists and scholars, parents and politicians, his remarks are not directed toward any single group. Therefore, the general reading public seems to be the most appropriate choice.

Now let us return to question 8. When we refer to the writer's attitude, we mean his or her *tone,* the emotional feeling that he or she has toward the subject. When we speak to people, we can observe their facial expressions and gestures and we can listen to their tone of voice. But in print we have only the words on the page to help us. All the other clues are absent. Consider the author's choice of words, particularly in the conclusion. Because he voices so many subjective ideas, he can hardly be described as objective. In particular, the last sentence gives it away: ". . . the state of American education freezes my blood with fear for all humanity." Of the other choices, the only one that fits is "seriously troubled" and "concerned."

G. UNDERSTANDING VOCABULARY

Most selections in the text use the multiple-choice format for the Understanding Vocabulary section. This kind of exercise requires no explanation. The context, the way the word is used in the selection, is always provided, along with the number of the paragraph. After you read the selection through once and answer the first two sets of exercises, you should read it again. During your second reading you can pay attention to the selection's organization, look for inferences and conclusions to draw, and look up any vocabulary words whose meaning is not readily apparent to you. Although the process may seem tedious and slow at first, there is really no other way to ensure that you are understanding what you read.

To give you some variety, a few selections have a different kind of vocabulary exercise. You are provided with the definitions and are asked to find the word that matches them, working through two paragraphs at a time. Here are a few samples from the selection:

Look through the paragraphs listed below and find a word that matches each definition. An example has been done for you.

Ex. scornful, disbelieving [paragraphs 5–6] _____*cynical*_____

1. body, group—used figuratively [2–3] _____

2. doubtful as to quality, questionable [6–7] _____

3. not substantial or valid [11–12] _____

The answers are (1) reservoir; (2) dubious; (3) sleazy. Remember that it is *not* cheating to look unfamiliar words up in the dictionary. In order to do this exercise, look at the paragraphs the word is supposed to appear in, and if you can't determine the word that matches the definition on your own, look up any unfamiliar words in those two paragraphs. Then you will easily find the one that matches.

H. USING VOCABULARY

Briefly, in this section you will encounter one of three different kinds of exercises, all of which are intended to help you use new vocabulary words in a different way from their use in the reading. (Since research shows that good readers are better writers than people who seldom read, one way you can improve the quality of your own writing is to use some of these new words in your own papers, hence, the need to learn what are called the *variant* forms of vocabulary words.)

One kind of exercise in this section gives you a series of words with different grammatical endings and asks you to insert the correct one in a sentence. You may have to add noun or verb endings like -*s* or -*ed*. Try these three examples:

1. (*distress, distressing, distressingly*) Asimov is _____ over the poor performance of American schoolchildren in reading and writing.

2. (*cynic, cynicism, cynical, cynically*) When he discusses why parents of poor readers may not themselves be able to help their own children,

    Asimov proves himself to be a _____.

3. (*democracy, democratic, democratically*) In his conclusion, Asimov writes

    that because we are the richest _____ nation, we have a responsibility to the rest of the world to provide sound leadership.

The answers are (1) distressed; (2) cynic; (3) democratic.

A second exercise gives you a vocabulary word from the selection and asks you to use another grammatical form of it in a sentence. You may need to refer to a dictionary.

1.   (*humiliating*—use a verb)   According to Asimov, movies depict good students as "nerds," who are, in turn, constantly _____ for caring about school.

2.   (*contempt*—use an adverb)   The author attempts to answer the question of why Americans treat professors and scholars so _____.

3.   (*possible*—use a noun)   What is the _____ of finding workable solutions to the problems that face our society today?

The answers are (1) humiliated; (2) contemptibly; and (3) possibility. The best way to do these exercises, if you are not familiar with the variant form of the word or if you are a little shaky in grammar, is to look up the word you are given and then find the word that corresponds to the part of speech the sentence requires. For example, if you look up *contempt,* the variant adjective form *contemptible* and the adverb form *contemptibly* will be listed nearby. Also, refer to the section at the back of the book on using the dictionary for further information.

The most difficult exercise in this last vocabulary section gives you a list of several words from the selection and sentences with two or three spaces into which you must fit new words according to both meaning and grammatical form. Here is a short sample exercise for you to practice with:

bearable	unemployable	insoluble
despoiling	sleazy	democracy
fundamental	manipulate	contempt

1.   Asimov is concerned that America's poor educational system will cause serious problems in the future, namely, a large group of

_____ people who will be forced to work for very low wages and who will turn to drugs as a way of making their lives

more _____.

2.   Some of our problems seem truly _____, especially

our _____ of the environment and our limited understanding of technology.

3.   Asimov writes that there is a _____ wrong in this society; we admire a rich person, for example, a junk bond promoter,

who becomes wealthy by _____ means, yet we feel

_____ for a person who respects scholarship and learning.

And the answers are (1) unemployable, bearable; (2) insoluble, despoiling; (3) fundamental, sleazy, contempt.

Finally each reading selection ends with Topics for Writing or Discussion. The first item in this section requires you to paraphrase information from a particular section or to write a short summary. You should refer to the suggestions at the end of the text for writing paraphrases and summaries. The second topic can be used for class discussion or as the basis of an essay.

So now you have an overview of the organization of the book and of the kinds of skills you will be working to improve during the course. It should be apparent to you that these selections affect some very important skills simultaneously. In this way, not only will you find that you can tackle your college reading assignments with greater efficiency, but you will also read with greater confidence and enjoyment. You will know what is expected of you and what to look for.

Getting Started: Practicing the Basics

In this section, you will be asked to practice in more depth the basic reading skills introduced in the sample reading selection. At this point in the course, you should be most concerned with comprehension, inference, and vocabulary skills. Read through each selection once, underlining any unfamiliar words. Either you can stop to look up their meanings after your first reading, or you can wait until you complete Exercises A and B. However, if a particular word is crucial to your accurate understanding of the passage, it is probably better to look it up immediately.

Apply the suggestions made in the introduction by asking yourself what the writer's subject is and what he or she wants you to understand about that subject. Then think about the writer's purpose as you consider the choices carefully.

The seven readings in Part 1 are relatively easy and enjoyable to read. With the exception of the first one, which is lighthearted and humorous, they will all have an emotional impact on you. You will read about supermarket etiquette; about a little girl who was taken away from her adoptive parents because of a bureaucratic regulation; about the way American slaves were sold at auction; about Huckleberry Finn's failure at learning religion and manners; about the plight of migrant workers, Hispanic women, in this case, who work in vegetable-packing sheds; about a young man who stayed up all night with his sick cow to make sure that she didn't die; and about the life cycle of the diamondback rattlesnake.

1

Bill Adler, Jr., and Peggy Robin

HOW NOT TO BE AN OAF AT THE SUPERMARKET

In this newspaper article, Adler and Robin explain proper supermarket etiquette in a humorous, lighthearted way.

VOCABULARY PREVIEW

WORD ORIGINS

OAF
The word *oaf* in the selection title is one of a small number of English words derived from Old Norse. It originally came from *alfr*, meaning an "elf" or "goblin." In an earlier usage, an *oaf* referred to a deformed elfin child that elves substituted for a human one. Today the word has lost this meaning entirely, now simply referring to a stupid, clumsy person.

VICE VERSA
In paragraph 27 the authors write that you may ask the supermarket checker "to put the plastic bag in a paper sack, and *vice versa*," meaning that you may reverse the order, asking for a paper sack in a plastic bag. This phrase comes from a Latin phrase that literally means "the position being changed." It is broken down like this:

[*vice* ("position") + *versa*, past participle of *vertere* ("to turn or change")]

WORD PARTS

-ISH
In paragraph 6 the authors explain the proper way to overtake a *sluggish* cart. Meaning "slow" or "showing little movement," this word comes from the Middle English *slugge*, a slow-moving person. A slug is also a kind of mollusk (like a snail, but without the shell), also known for moving slowly. Since the suffix *-ish* means "having the qualities or

19

characteristics of," a person described as *sluggish* moves slowly, or like a slug.

Some other common words with this ending are *childish*, *mannish*, and *sheepish*.

MEGA-

In paragraph 17 Adler and Robin discuss the advantages of small, intimate markets over suburban *mega-marts* for singles who want to meet people. The prefix *mega-* has two meanings: first, "one million," as in the word *megaherz*, a radio term meaning one million cycles per second; and second, "large" or "great," as in *megabucks*, slang for a large amount of money, or *megalopolis*, a region made up of several large cities, like the New York City or Los Angeles area. The root *mart* means "market."

The prefix *mega-* can be attached to all sorts of words, as the authors do in this case. Therefore, a *mega-mart* is a very large supermarket, often containing a bakery, take-out food counters, a pharmacy, a nursery, and so forth.

WORD FAMILIES

ANARCHY

In the first sentence the authors establish their purpose in enumerating the rules for supermarket etiquette: "For too long *anarchy* has reigned at the supermarket." Meaning "absence of political rule" or "disorder," *anarchy* is most often used as a political term. It comes from the Greek:

[*an-* ("without") + *-archy* ("rule" or "government")]

English contains a fairly large number of words with the root *-archy*. Here are some of them:

matriarchy	rule by the female members of a group [*matri-* ("female" or "motherhood") + *-archy*]
patriarchy	rule by men [*patri-* ("father") + *-archy*]
monarchy	rule by a monarch or by a single person [*mono-* ("one") + *-archy*]
oligarchy	rule by a few [*oligo-* ("few") + *-archy*]

BILL ADLER, JR., AND PEGGY ROBIN

HOW NOT TO BE AN OAF AT THE SUPERMARKET

1 For too long anarchy has reigned at the supermarket. The same people who insist on driving precisely 55 miles an hour in the left lane of the freeway have no idea who has right of way turning into the canned-goods aisle. Can you park a cart in the frozen-food lane? (Yes.) In the dairy section? (No.) Many shoppers can't figure out

what constitutes an "item" for the express lane of their local market—are three tomatoes counted as one item when they're together in a bag?

2   Civilized behavior being a desired quality everywhere, here are suggested rules for supermarket behavior:

Driving a Cart

3   Supermarket carts are one of the few vehicles for which you don't need a license. That does not, however, mean you can pretend you're playing bumper cars.

4   Carts can be driven by rear-wheel drive (pushing) or front-wheel drive (pulling). Only carts that have all four wheels operating—and are in no danger of wobbling or jackknifing—may be pulled from the front.

5   There is no minimum driving age; however, cart drivers must be able to see clearly over the back handle of the cart.

6   Carts traveling straight have right of way over carts leaving or entering aisles. Carts turning right into an aisle have right of way over carts turning left into an aisle. When overtaking a sluggish cart, a polite "pardon me" is expected.

7   When several carts want to pass a slow cart at the same time, the cart that started first has the right of way.

8   Drive carts to the right, just as with cars. Being a diplomat with one of the Commonwealth countries does not exempt anyone from this rule.

PACKING THE AISLES

9   Carts may be parked in aisles while you gather foods in other parts of the market provided:

10   A) Your cart is not left in a highly traveled location;

11   B) Your cart is not in a narrow aisle;

12   C) Your cart is not left in front of common-purchase areas such as milk, cereal and bread;

13   D) Your cart is left flush against the shelf, not halfway in the aisle.

14   A cart may be moved by other shoppers only as far as necessary to clear a passage. If you see your cart being moved, the correct response is to rush over and offer to do the moving yourself.

15   Keep your eyes on the aisle and your feet on the ground at all times. Watch out for children and for slippery patches of road. If you do get into a collision, you don't have to exchange information—a simple apology will do (and you can offer to return their broken eggs to the shelf)—but if you are shopping for a date you may use this opportunity to engage the operator of the other cart in conversation.

Shopping for Dates

16   Some people go to the supermarket with the idea of picking up a dinner companion first, and dinner second. But you need to know which stores are apt to have what you're after.

17   Singles are not likely to have much luck, for example, at one of those plaza-sized mega-marts in the suburbs. There are just too many departments and it's too easy to be overlooked. A better bet is a more intimate urban store, one with a small parking lot—so you can check first that there are more sports cars than Volvo wagons in it.

18   Whatever opening line you use, keep it clean. "Do you know if asparagus goes well in a cream sauce?" is fine. References to vegetables, or even fondling vegetables while trying a pickup line, went out with the '70s.

The Check-Out Line

19   Generally speaking, it's first come, first served at the check-out line. There are, however, a few important exceptions.

20   If you're in line with 20 or so items, and the person behind you has a single can of cat food, it's polite to let him in front of you. This is especially true because one day the situation will be reversed—only you won't be in line with cat food, it'll be a bottle of aspirin, and as you wait in line the seconds will be ticking away . . . loudly.

21   Cutting in front is acceptable only if you ask first and it's a dire emergency. Having a crying baby and a cart full of disposable diapers is a good enough excuse. A six-pack of beer that you've got to get home before the end of halftime isn't.

22   Coupons must be assembled and ready. Checks should be written in advance except for the amount, and presented along with your check-cashing card.

23   Trying to pay by check in a cash-only line results in a loss of your place in line. Ditto for those who realize they need to go to the cash machine as they arrive at the register.

24   If you get in line and realize that you have acquired an item you don't want, you may rush back to the aisle where you found that item if there's enough time and you've explained to the person in line behind you that you're returning an item, not gathering new things.

25   Hunting for exact change is allowed, within a reasonable time limit. You may use the supermarket to relieve yourself of excess pennies.

26   It isn't rude to want to keep your order separate from someone else's. Either the person in front or the person behind may put the divider in place. You may not shove someone else's food aside while dividing orders.

27   Be prepared to say "paper" or "plastic." If you're too slow, you're allowed to ask the checker to put the plastic bag in a paper sack, and vice versa, but you may not ask the checker to empty the contents of one bag into another. And you must be willing to accept a lecture on recycling from other people in line.

Examining Food

28   We all know it's essential to feel fruit to tell which is ripe. But when does testing become squishing?

29   Corn on the cob: Peeling back the green leaves to peek at the kernels at the end is OK. Stripping the side and poking at the kernels is a no-no.

30   Pumpkins, cantaloupes and other fruits with rinds: A few thumps with the palm of your hand is OK. Dribbling them on the floor like a basketball is forbidden.

31   Tomatoes (the most popular food to squeeze): Gentle finger pressure only.

32   Grapes: Bunches may be split to create the size desired, but that doesn't mean you can pick off and leave behind every individual grape you don't like the look of.

33   Items in jars, bottles and boxes: No opening is allowed, but shaking is OK.

34   Bulk foods in bins: Free sampling is out.

35   Bakery items, chilled sodas and chips: You may eat certain supermarket foods while shopping, such as cookies, potato chips and sodas, provided you save the

wrapper so the checker can ring up the value of what you've consumed. This, strictly speaking, is not sampling, but is more accurately a form of short-term credit that the store extends to its valued customers.

Life in the Express Lane

36 Several-of-a-kind count as separate items for express-lane accounting purposes. For example, if you buy three bottles of water (even if it's three for $1), that counts as three items.

37   Purchases that come physically connected in some way count as one item. For example, a six-pack of cola counts as one item; a bunch of four bananas counts as one item. However, four individual bananas, not connected at the stem, are considered to be four items.

38   Items picked up at the counter, such as magazines, candy and tabloids, do not figure into the nine items or less. To be considered a counter item, you must be able to reach that item while at least one foot remains in line. You may put these items on the conveyer belt only after the cashier has started toting up your first purchases.

39   If you are shopping with a partner, you may purchase 18 items between the two of you (the "double and divide exemption"). However, you must each ring up the items separately and demonstrate to the people behind you in line that you are going to pay for them separately, by either using a plastic divider to split the 18 items into two sets or by pretending you do not know each other. One shopping partner is allowed to pay for the other's purchases.

40   Finally, remember what you learned in seventh grade: Don't buy dented ■ cans.

From Bill Adler, Jr., and Peggy Robin, "How Not to Be an Oaf at the Supermarket," *San Francisco Chronicle*, March 12, 1990. Reprinted by permission.

EXERCISES

Do not refer to the selection for Exercises A and B.

A.   DETERMINING THE MAIN IDEA AND PURPOSE
Choose the best answer.

1.   _____ The main idea of the article is that (a) the rules for supermarket shopping are just about the same as the rules of the road; (b) most supermarket shoppers are rude and need instruction about the proper way to behave; (c) civilized behavior can be found in the supermarket if customers follow a few simple, commonsense rules; (d) there are several rules to follow to ensure that the consumer gets the most for his or her money at the supermarket.

2.   _____ The authors' primary purpose in writing this article is (a) to poke fun at contemporary Americans' behavior at the supermarket; (b) to

show how rude and insensitive some shoppers can be; (c) to provide useful shopping tips so that shoppers can be more efficient at the supermarket; (d) to enumerate in a humorous way the rules for good supermarket shopping.

B. COMPREHENDING MAIN IDEAS
Choose the correct answer.

1. _____ According to the authors, when one cart is traveling straight and another is leaving or entering an aisle, the right of way belongs to (a) whichever cart gets there first; (b) the cart traveling straight; (c) the cart leaving the aisle; (d) the cart on the right side of the aisle.

2. _____ When traveling down an aisle, shoppers should push their carts (a) directly in the middle, so that other carts may pass on either side; (b) on the right, just like on American roads; (c) on the left, just like on British roads; (d) wherever they will cause the least traffic congestion.

3. _____ Parking your cart in aisles while you gather food in other parts of the market is (a) acceptable if you don't block other carts; (b) acceptable if you are in a hurry; (c) annoying to other shoppers who may be more methodical in their habits; (d) never acceptable under any circumstances.

4. _____ Singles looking for dates in supermarkets (a) are just wasting their time; (b) should patronize only mega-marts, which usually have more single customers than smaller markets do; (c) should stand around the produce section and ask intelligent questions; (d) should check out the parking lot first to see if there are more sports cars than station wagons.

5. _____ At the check-out line, the general rule is (a) do unto others as you would have them do unto you (the Golden Rule); (b) every man (or woman) for himself (or herself); (c) first come, first served; (d) the "double and divide exemption" rule.

6. _____ With regard to eating food in the store, the authors state that eating chips and bakery items is (a) acceptable as long as you don't drop crumbs on the floor; (b) acceptable as long as you save the wrappings so the checker can ring up the cost; (c) acceptable only when you are actually in the check-out line and are ready to pay; (d) never acceptable; you should eat before you go shopping.

COMPREHENSION SCORE

Score your answers for Exercises A and B as follows:

A. No. right _____ × 2 = _____

B. No. right _____ × 1 = _____

Total pts. from A and B _____ × 10 = _____%

C. DISTINGUISHING BETWEEN MAIN IDEAS AND SUPPORTING DETAILS
Label the following statements from the selection as follows: MI if the statement represents a *main idea* and SD if the statement represents a *supporting detail.*

1. ____ Several-of-a-kind count as separate items for express-lane accounting purposes.

2. ____ For example, if you buy three bottles of water (even if it's three for $1), that counts as three items.

3. ____ Purchases that come physically connected in some way count as one item.

4. ____ For example, a six-pack of cola counts as one item; a bunch of four bananas counts as one item.

5. ____ However, four individual bananas, not connected at the stem, are considered to be four items.

6. ____ Items picked up at the counter, such as magazines, candy and tabloids, do not figure into the nine items or less.

D. MAKING INFERENCES
For each of these statements write Y (Yes) if the inference is an accurate one, N (No) if the inference is an inaccurate one, or CT (Can't Tell) if you do not have enough information to make an inference.

1. ____ The probable reason that it is acceptable to park your shopping cart in the frozen-food lane, but not in the dairy section, is that the dairy section is more heavily patronized than the frozen-food aisle.

2. ____ The authors would probably support the idea of issuing licenses to operators of shopping carts.

3. ____ It is never permissible to move someone else's cart, even if it is blocking an aisle.

4. ____ Most customers won't mind if you take the time to sort through your coupons, write out a check, or dash back through the market for forgotten items while you are at the check-out counter.

5. ____ The authors would probably not approve of a customer who sorted through a box of strawberries to choose only the best ones.

6. ____ The rules for proper supermarket behavior generally involve being considerate of other customers.

E. ANALYZING ORGANIZATION AND SEEING RELATIONSHIPS

1. ____ Look again at the first two sentences of paragraph 1, from which we can assume that (a) people who are polite while driving become rude and pushy when they shop in a supermarket; (b) people who follow the

rules of the road precisely may be genuinely confused about how to behave in a supermarket; (c) there should be a national set of laws governing correct supermarket manners; (d) the authors are authorities who have studied supermarket behavior for many years.

2. _____ Throughout the article, the authors use the pronoun *you*, which makes their style (a) formal and serious; (b) informal and chatty; (c) objective, neutral; (d) sincere, trustworthy.

3. _____ Look again at pargaraphs 3 and 5, both of which contain the transitional word *however*. This word signals (a) an example; (b) a cause-effect relationship; (c) steps in a process; (d) a contrast.

4. _____ Paragraphs 20 and 21 are developed mainly by (a) facts and statistics; (b) short examples; (c) definitions of unfamiliar terms; (d) steps in a process.

5. _____ The authors' treatment of the subject matter can be best described as (a) critical, ridiculing; (b) serious, somber; (c) amusing, lightly humorous; (d) philosophical.

F. UNDERSTANDING VOCABULARY
Choose the correct definition according to the context.

1. _____ *anarchy* has reigned at the supermarket [paragraph 1]: (a) rudeness; (b) disorder; (c) rule by the majority; (d) rule by a single individual.

2. _____ what *constitutes* an "item" [1]: (a) represents; (b) dictates; (c) makes up; (d) contains.

3. _____ overtaking a *sluggish* cart [6]: (a) slow; (b) lazy; (c) lost; (d) abandoned.

4. _____ does not *exempt* anyone from this rule [8]: (a) bind; (b) isolate; (c) prevent; (d) release.

5. _____ which stores are *apt* to have [16]: (a) quick to learn; (b) likely; (c) allowed; (d) insisted.

6. _____ a more *intimate* urban store [17]: (a) secret, private; (b) essential, innermost; (c) personalized, individualized; (d) close, familiar.

7. _____ *fondling* vegetables [18]: (a) showing affection for; (b) tasting, sampling; (c) handling lovingly; (d) pushing, squeezing.

8. _____ a *dire* emergency [21]: (a) imminent, about-to-happen; (b) life-threatening; (c) disastrous, terrible; (d) real, authentic.

G. USING VOCABULARY
From the following list of vocabulary words choose a word that fits in each blank according to both the grammatical structure of the sentence and the context. Use each

word in the list only once and add noun or verb endings (such as *-s, -ing,* or *-ed*) if necessary. (Note that there are more words than sentences.)

anarchy	constitute	sluggish
exempt	however	collision
apt	intimate	exception
excess	physically	provide

1. Peeling back the green leaves on an ear of corn is all right;

    _____, stripping off the leaves and poking the kernels are not.

2. Small, _____ markets are more _____ to be good places to meet singles, whereas suburban mega-markets are patronized mostly by families.

3. Since _____ reigns at the supermarket, the authors have compiled a list of useful suggestions.

4. It is permissible to overtake a _____ cart,

    _____ that you are careful not to play bumper cars

    and avoid major _____.

5. Items, like bananas, that come _____ connected in

    some way _____ a single item for the express checkout lane.

H.   TOPICS FOR WRITING OR DISCUSSION

1. Read again paragraphs 38–39. Then paraphrase them by putting the information into your own words. (If necessary, read the section on how to paraphrase at the end of the text before attempting this exercise.)

    _____

    _____

    _____

    _____

    _____

    _____

2. Write a paragraph or two in which you present your own humorous rules for a kind of activity we all take for granted. Some suggestions are filling your tank at a self-service gas station, using your bank's automatic teller machine, or waiting in a doctor's or dentist's office.

2 ||||

Bob Greene

HOME IS WHERE THE HEART IS

This editorial describes the case of a little girl, here called "Sarah" to protect her privacy. Abandoned at birth, Sarah was ordered by the state of Illinois to be removed from her foster parents when she was three years old and returned to her natural mother. Sarah's case well illustrates an all-too-common problem in child welfare cases: the insensitivity of government bureaucracies.

VOCABULARY PREVIEW

WORD ORIGINS

MORASS
In paragraph 7 Greene describes Sarah's parents' dealings with the Illinois Department of Children and Family Services as "a bureaucratic *morass.*" Pronounced me răs', this word came into English from the Dutch *moeras* ("marsh" or "moorland"), which in turn came from the French word *mareis*. In English *morass* can refer either to a marsh, a soggy piece of land, or, as a figure of speech, to any difficult or perplexing situation. It is this second definition that Greene has in mind in this context.

DEVASTATE
In paragraph 13 the attorney for Sarah's foster parents is quoted as saying that taking Sarah away from her foster parents would *devastate* her. Originally derived from Latin, *devastate* means "to lay waste," and implies severe injury and desolation. In this word, the prefix *dē-* is called an intensifier because it makes the root *vāstāre* ("to lay waste") stronger.

WORD PARTS

RE-
Many English words begin with the prefix *re-*. In the word *rehabilitation* (see paragraph 6), *re-* indicates something that is "restored to a former position." In this case, Sarah's natural mother went through drug *rehabilitation*, a program that attempts to restore a person to a useful life

29

usually through education and/or therapy. Other words using the prefix *re-* to mean "restore" are *replace, reimburse, rejuvenate,* and *refresh.*

Re- as a prefix is also used to indicate a repeated action, as in these words: *rewrite, rebuild, rebroadcast,* and *redevelop.*

Pre-

Sarah was examined by a *preeminent* child psychiatrist (see paragraph 8). Meaning "superior to all others" or "outstanding," *preeminent* is derived from these Latin word parts:

[*pre-* ("in front of") + *ēminēre* ("to stand out")]

As a prefix, *pre-* more typically indicates an action coming "before," as in the words *prearrange* ("to arrange before"), *precede* ("to come before"), *predict* ("to tell before"), and *presuppose* ("to suppose or assume in advance").

WORD FAMILIES

Volunteer

In paragraph 3 Greene writes that Joseph and Marge Procopio had *volunteered* to be Sarah's foster parents. From the Latin *voluntārius,* the root of this word is *voluntās,* meaning "free will." This word can be either a noun ("a hospital *volunteer*") or a verb ("to *volunteer* one's time"). Whichever part of speech, the underlying meaning is the same—an action performed of one's own free will. Here are some other words in this family:

voluntary	acting from one's own free will
involuntary	not performed willingly
volition	an act of willing or choosing

BOB GREENE

HOME IS WHERE THE HEART IS

1 Somewhere in the Chicago area at the end of April, a little girl turned 6 years old. Because of privacy considerations, we cannot print her name here, which is just one more aspect in the string of indignities that have been forced upon her in her short life—indignities that have been carried out in the name of the citizens of Illinois, the state where she was born.

2 So for the purposes of this column, we will call her Sarah. Sarah was born on April 27, 1984, to a woman described by lawyers familiar with the case as being addicted to heroin and cocaine. Sarah reportedly was addicted at birth; the mother reportedly had never seen a doctor during her pregnancy.

3   Lutheran Child and Family Services contacted Joseph and Marge Procopio, of Bridgeview, Illinois, who had volunteered to be foster parents. They were told that the mother had left Sarah at the hospital and had not returned. They agreed to take her in.

4   "The baby's drug withdrawal was a terrible thing," Marge Procopio said. "She would shake, and then she would stiffen out. We would hold her and comfort her."

5   At one point, according to attorneys, Sarah's natural mother and her boyfriend expressed interest in seeing the child. "So the social services agency set up times for us to bring (Sarah) in to see her natural mother," Marge Procopio said. "We did. But for seven straight scheduled visits, we took (Sarah) and the mother did not show up."

6   Meanwhile, Sarah grew up in the Procopios' home. When she was 3 years old, the Illinois Department of Children and Family Services (DCFS) informed the Procopios that the "goal of the case" had been changed. The natural mother was in drug rehabilitation and had decided that she and her boyfriend wanted Sarah. Sarah had never slept a night in their home.

7   The next two years were a bureaucratic morass. Sarah was taken back and forth to visit her natural mother and the boyfriend. "(Sarah) would cry and scream and throw up in the car on the way to the visits," said Carol Amadio, an attorney who worked with the Procopios. "She would beg the Procopios not to take her. She didn't understand that they were required to."

8   DCFS requested one of the nation's preeminent child psychiatrists, Dr. L. David Zinn of Chicago's Northwestern Memorial Hospital, to examine Sarah and to observe the Procopios and the natural mother. "It was absolutely clear that (Sarah) was happy and content with the Procopios." Dr. Zinn said. "At their house, she would take me into her room and show me her scrapbooks. The Procopios demonstrated love and compassion for her. (The natural mother and her boyfriend) seemed to regard her as a piece of property to possess. There was no question—she loved and belonged with the family who had brought her up. I stated this."

9   For some reason not revealed, DCFS rejected the recommendation of Dr. Zinn. Instead, in court, the department recommended that Sarah be returned to the woman who had given birth to her. "We are mandated to seek to reunite the child with the natural family whenever possible," said David Schneidman, a spokesman for DCFS.

10   Sarah was placed in the Hephzibah orphanage in Oak Park, Illinois, for a state-supervised "grieving period." During that time Sarah, who by then was 5, was to be weaned from the Procopios and then given to the birth mother and the man with whom she lived.

11   "When we took her to Hephzibah, we said to her, 'You keep that beautiful smile,'" Marge Procopio said. "Every time we would see her there, she would have this big smile frozen on her face, as the tears poured down her cheeks. It was as if she believed that if she smiled as we had asked, then she wouldn't have to be turned over."

12   But last August 29, on the orders of a judge who had never seen her, Sarah was turned over to the birth mother. "This was like a death imposed on (Sarah)," Dr. Zinn said. "She was taken from the only parents she had ever loved."

13   Attorney Amadio: "It was as if the legal system was told, 'If you take this child away you are going to devastate her.' And the legal system in essence said, 'Who cares?' The child was regarded as property."

14   Mary Burns, assistant Cook County, Illinois, Public Guardian: "This is a tragedy. The child should never have been removed from the only home she ever knew."

15   So somewhere in the Chicago area on April 27, Sarah turned 6 years old. Whatever qualities, good or bad, the Procopios may have is not what all of this is about. Whether or not the natural mother was "rehabilitated" is not what all of this is about. This is about Sarah.

16   We have all read too many stories about children being horribly hurt. One could be excused for thinking that, in this case, a child was horribly hurt quite legally by the state of Illinois. Because of all the confidentiality regulations, the bureaucrats involved are all able to say that it's a sad situation, and that it's no one's fault, really, and that they cannot discuss it any further. But what was done to Sarah was done by the state.   ■

From Bob Greene, "Home Is Where the Heart Is," *San Francisco Chronicle*, "This World," May 13, 1990. Reprinted by permission.

EXERCISES

Do not refer to the selection for Exercises A and B.

A.   DETERMINING THE MAIN IDEA AND PURPOSE
Choose the best answer.

1. _____ The main idea of the editorial is that (a) the state of Illinois's insistence that Sarah be returned to her natural mother was foolish and insensitive; (b) the whole child welfare system in the U.S. needs to be overhauled; (c) the state of Illinois regards foster children as property to be disposed of in whatever manner it sees fit; (d) there is a great deal of controversy about the rights of natural parents vs. those of foster parents.

2. _____ With respect to the main idea, the author's main purpose is (a) to defend an unpopular opinion; (b) to present the background and facts of a case history; (c) to convince the reader that a serious wrong was committed in a particular case; (d) to argue both sides of a controversial issue.

B.   COMPREHENDING MAIN IDEAS
Choose the correct answer.

1. _____ During her pregnancy, Sarah's natural mother was addicted to (a) alcohol and marijuana; (b) heroin and cocaine; (c) speed and cocaine; (d) alcohol and crack cocaine.

2.   _____ The Procopios became foster parents because (a) they had made an agreement with Sarah's mother before the baby was born; (b) they found Sarah abandoned on their doorstep; (c) they were on an adoption agency's waiting list; (d) the hospital informed them that Sarah's mother had left the baby there.

3.   _____ The Illinois Department of Children and Family Services (DCFS) informed the Procopios that Sarah's natural mother wanted the child returned to her when she was (a) three months old; (b) three years old; (c) six months old; (d) six years old.

4.   _____ According to the selection, when Sarah was scheduled to visit her natural mother and her boyfriend, she (a) reluctantly agreed to go; (b) refused to go; (c) begged her foster parents not to take her; (d) had terrible nightmares the night before.

5.   _____ Illinois's policy in cases like this is (a) to accept the testimony of child psychiatrists and other experts; (b) to reunite the child with the natural family whenever possible; (c) to listen to both families—the foster parents and the natural parents—before arriving at a decision; (d) to respect the child's wishes about which parents he or she would prefer to live with.

6.   _____ According to the article, the main reason Sarah's case is such a tragedy is that (a) she was removed from the only parents she had ever loved; (b) she never saw the Procopios again; (c) the judge had never seen Sarah; (d) the state of Illinois was not interested in Sarah's welfare.

COMPREHENSION SCORE

Score your answers for Exercises A and B as follows:

A.   No. right _____ × 2 = _____

B.   No. right _____ × 1 = _____

Total pts. from A and B _____ × 10 = _____%

C.   RECOGNIZING SUPPORTING DETAILS

Place an X in the space for each statement that *directly* supports this main idea from the article: **"The next two years were a bureaucratic morass."**

1.   _____ Sarah was taken back and forth to visit her natural mother and the boyfriend.

2.   _____ "Sarah would cry and scream and throw up in the car on the way to the visits," said Carol Amadio, an attorney who worked with the Procopios.

3.   _____ "She would beg the Procopios not to take her."

4.   _____ "She didn't understand that they were required to."

D.   MAKING INFERENCES

For each of these statements write Y (Yes) if the inference is an accurate one, N (No) if the inference is an inaccurate one, or CT (Can't Tell) if you do not have enough information to make an inference.

1.   _____ Sarah's natural mother behaved irresponsibly.

2.   _____ Both the natural mother and the state of Illinois are correct in thinking that a child is a piece of property to possess.

3.   _____ Sarah's mother successfully completed her drug rehabilitation program.

4.   _____ The responsibility for Sarah's tragedy lies solely with the state of Illinois's bureaucracy.

5.   _____ The recommendation of Dr. Zinn, the child psychiatrist chosen to evaluate Sarah's case, was rejected because it did not conform to the state guidelines with respect to foster children.

E.   DRAWING CONCLUSIONS

Mark an X before any of the following that represent a reasonable conclusion you can draw from the selection.

1.   _____ The state of Illinois and the DCFS should revise their child welfare policies.

2.   _____ It is not necessary for a judge to interview a child before removing him or her from foster parental care.

3.   _____ The state of Illinois's policy regarding foster children is insensitive and potentially harmful to the child's long-range emotional health.

4.   _____ Sarah may suffer irreparable harm as a result of being removed from her foster parents' care.

F.   ANALYZING ORGANIZATION AND SEEING RELATIONSHIPS

1.   _____ The author's tone or attitude toward the Illinois Department of Children and Family Services (DCFS) can be best described as (a) neutral, objective; (b) sympathetic, understanding; (c) disappointed, sorry; (d) sharply critical.

2.   Throughout the article Greene relies extensively on direct quotations from Sarah's foster parents, from their attorney, and from a child psychiatrist. With respect to Greene's opinions, these quotations provide (a) emphasis; (b) drama; (c) authority; (d) accuracy.

3.   Look again at paragraph 7. Write the sentence that represents the main idea. _____

_____

4.   Greene's attitude toward Sarah's natural mother throughout the article can best be described as (a) indifferent; (b) sympathetic; (c) unsympathetic; (d) hostile.

5.   In your own words, explain Greene's primary criticism of Illinois's handling of Sarah's case. _____

_____

G.   UNDERSTANDING VOCABULARY
Choose the correct definition according to the context.

1.   the string of *indignities* [paragraph 1]: treatments or actions that (a) cause anger; (b) are difficult to understand; (c) are degrading or abusive; (d) are praiseworthy.

2.   drug *rehabilitation* [6]: a program designed to (a) provide good medical care; (b) restore the person to a drug-free life; (c) teach the person about the proper use of drugs; (d) teach useful work skills.

3.   a bureaucratic *morass* [7]: (a) a difficult situation; (b) a time of uncertainty; (c) a series of options or alternatives; (d) a series of official rules.

4.   a *preeminent* child psychiatrist [8]: (a) well-respected; (b) outstanding; (c) having great power; (d) trustworthy.

5.   we are *mandated* to reunite the child with the family [9]: (a) advised; (b) commanded; (c) suggested; (d) accustomed.

6.   to be *weaned* from the Procopios [10]: (a) taken away by force; (b) abducted, kidnapped; (c) given permission; (d) gradually detached.

7.   a death *imposed* on Sarah [12]: (a) demanded; (b) substituted; (c) required; (d) forced.

8.   to *devastate* her [13]: (a) injure severely; (b) confuse; (c) annoy; (d) cause slight harm to.

H.   USING VOCABULARY
In parentheses before each sentence are some inflected forms of words from the selection. Study the context and the sentence. Then write the correct form in the space provided. Be sure to add appropriate endings like -s, -ed, or -ing, if necessary.

1.   (*privacy, private, privately*)   To maintain her _____, Greene calls the child in this article "Sarah."

2.   (*volunteer, voluntary, voluntarily*)   The Procopios _____ took Sarah into their home.

3.   (*bureaucracy, bureaucrat, bureaucratic*)   Sarah's foster parents had to deal with the Illinois state _____.

4. (*reject, rejection*)   Greene was not able to determine why the court

   _____ the psychiatrist's evaluation.

5. (*tragedy, tragic, tragically*)   The most _____ outcome
   of Sarah's case was being taken away from the only parents she had ever
   known.

I.   TOPICS FOR WRITING OR DISCUSSION

1. In your own words, briefly summarize the issues in Sarah's case. _____

   _____

   _____

   _____

   _____

   _____

2. Describe another injustice or tragic situation you are familiar with, either
   from your reading or from personal observation.

3

Solomon Northrup

A SLAVE WITNESS OF A SLAVE AUCTION

Slave narratives were common before the Civil War. In fact, abolitionists, those in favor of abolishing slavery, often used them in their campaigns. This particular narrative was published in 1853 in a book entitled Twelve Years a Slave: Narrative of Solomon Northrup, a Citizen of New York, Kidnapped in Washington City in 1841, and Rescued in 1853, from a Cotton Plantation near the Red River in Louisiana. *(Books had long titles in those days.) Northrup was finally freed when he was able to get a letter sent to friends in New York. The governor arranged for his release, which enabled him to return to his family.*

VOCABULARY PREVIEW

WORD ORIGINS

CALICO

The first steps required of slaves at an auction were bathing and dressing. According to paragraph 2, women were given "frocks of *calico*," or cotton dresses. *Calico* is a shortened form of *Calicut cloth*, named after Calicut, the city in southwest India that originally exported it. Another widely used fabric also derives from its place of origin. *Denim*, the fabric in blue jeans, was made in Nîmes (pronounced nēm), a city in southern France. Eventually, *serge de Nîmes* was shortened to simply *denim*.

EXHORTED

In paragraph 2, Freeman, the slave keeper, *exhorted* the people about to be auctioned to appear smart and lively. This verb, meaning "to urge strongly," came into English first from Middle English by way of Old French, originally from the Latin verb *exhortārī*. Here it is broken down:

[*ex-* ("completely") + *hortārī* ("to encourage")]

To *exhort* someone to do something, then, means to urge them strongly.

37

ADROITLY

A buyer who lived in New Orleans showed some interest in buying Northrup, which pleased the writer enormously because he thought it would be easy to escape from there. However, as Northrup writes in paragraph 5, the potential buyer argued *adroitly* against the asking price, which he claimed was too high. *Adroitly*, which means "skillfully" or "adeptly," means "rightly" from the literal Latin:

[*a*- ("to") + *droit* ("right"), from Latin *directus* ("direct")]

It is interesting to note that while *droit* has a positive connotation ("right" or "dexterous"), its opposite, *sinister*, the Latin word for "left," originally meant evil or bad luck. It is sometimes thought that this original derivation is the source of the old superstition that being left-handed meant being evil.

WORD PARTS

EXTRA-

In English, many compound words are formed with the prefix *extra-*, meaning "outside" or "beyond." Northrup uses the word *extraordinary* ("beyond the ordinary") in paragraph 5. Here are some other words containing this prefix:

extramarital	literally, outside the marriage bonds, as when a married person has sexual relations with someone other than his or her spouse
extrasensory	beyond ordinary sensory experience
extracurricular	outside the regular school curriculum
extraterrestrial	describing an inhabitant of another world, literally "beyond earth" [*extra-* + *terra* ("earth")]

WORD FAMILIES

DUC-

The Latin verb *dūcere* ("to lead") forms the root for a large number of words in English. In this narrative, Northrup uses two such words: *conducted* and *inducements* (both in paragraph 2). *Conducted* in this context means "led" or "guided into," and *inducements* are "incentives," "things that influence people." Here are the derivations of these words:

[*com*- ("together") + *dūcere* ("to lead")]

[*in*- ("in") + *dūcere*, literally "a leading into"]

In English there are many common words that derive from the root "lead" (for example, *duke*), although in a few of the following words, that connection may be hard to see:

abduct	to carry away by force, kidnap [*ab*- ("away") + *dūcere*]
duct	a passage or tube that carries fluids
aqueduct	a passage carrying water [*aqua* ("water") + *dūcere*]

induce	to lead or move by influence or persuasion
induct	to install, admit, call into service, as in "being *inducted* into the army"
educate	to provide with knowledge or training, literally "to lead out of" (one's ignorance or the dark) [*e-* ("out of") + *dūcere*]
reduce	to lessen the amount of [*re-* ("back") + *dūcere*]

SOLOMON NORTHRUP

A SLAVE WITNESS OF A SLAVE AUCTION

1   The very amiable, pious-hearted Mr. Theophilus Freeman, partner or consignee of James H. Burch, and keeper of the slave pen in New-Orleans, was out among his animals early in the morning. With an occasional kick of the older men and women, and many a sharp crack of the whip about the ears of the younger slaves, it was not long before they were all astir, and wide awake. Mr. Theophilus Freeman bustled about in a very industrious manner, getting his property ready for the sales-room, intending, no doubt, to do that day a rousing business.

2   In the first place we were required to wash thoroughly, and those with beards, to shave. We were then furnished with a new suit each, cheap, but clean. The men had hat, coat, shirt, pants and shoes; the women frocks of calico, and handkerchiefs to bind about their heads. We were now conducted into a large room in the front part of the building to which the yard was attached, in order to be properly trained, before the admission of customers. The men were arranged on one side of the room, the women on the other. The tallest was placed at the head of the row, then the next tallest, and so on in the order of their respective heights. Emily was at the foot of the line of women. Freeman charged us to remember our places; exhorted us to appear smart and lively,—sometimes threatening, and again holding out various inducements. During the day he exercised us in the art of "looking smart," and of moving to our places with exact precision.

3   After being fed, in the afternoon, we were again paraded and made to dance. Bob, a colored boy, who had some time belonged to Freeman, played on the violin. Standing near him, I made bold to inquire if he could play the "Virginia Reel." He answered he could not, and asked me if I could play. Replying in the affirmative, he handed me the violin. I struck up a tune, and finished it. Freeman ordered me to continue playing, and seemed well pleased, telling Bob that I far excelled him—a remark that seemed to grieve my musical companion very much.

4   Next day many customers called to examine Freeman's "new lot." The latter gentleman was very loquacious, dwelling at much length upon our several good points and qualities. He would make us hold up our heads, walk briskly back and forth, while customers would feel of our hands and arms and bodies, turn us about, ask us what we could do, make us open our mouths and show our teeth, precisely as a jockey examines a horse which he is about to barter for or purchase. Sometimes a

man or woman was taken back to the small house in the yard, stripped, and inspected more minutely. Scars upon a slave's back were considered evidence of a rebellious or unruly spirit, and hurt his sale.

5   One old gentleman, who said he wanted a coachman, appeared to take a fancy to me. From his conversation with Freeman, I learned he was a resident of the city. I very much desired that he would buy me, because I conceived it would not be difficult to make my escape from New-Orleans on some northern vessel. Freeman asked him fifteen hundred dollars for me. The old gentleman insisted it was too much, as times were very hard. Freeman, however, declared that I was sound and healthy, of a good constitution, and intelligent. He made it a point to enlarge upon my musical attainments. The old gentleman argued quite adroitly that there was nothing extraordinary about the nigger, and finally, to my regret, went out, saying he would call again. During the day, however, a number of sales were made. David and Caroline were purchased together by a Natchez planter. They left us, grinning broadly, and in the most happy state of mind, caused by the fact of their not being separated. Lethe was sold to a planter of Baton Rouge, her eyes flashing with anger as she was led away.

6   The same man also purchased Randall. The little fellow was made to jump, and run across the floor, and perform many other feats, exhibiting his activity and condition. All the time the trade was going on, Eliza was crying aloud, and wringing her hands. She besought the man not to buy him, unless he also bought herself and Emily. She promised, in that case, to be the most faithful slave that ever lived. The man answered that he could not afford it, and then Eliza burst into a paroxysm of grief, weeping plaintively. Freeman turned round to her, savagely, with his whip in his uplifted hand, ordering her to stop her noise, or he would flog her. He would not have such work—such snivelling; and unless she ceased that minute, he would take her to the yard and give her a hundred lashes. Yes, he would take the nonsense out of her pretty quick—if he didn't, might he be d—d. Eliza shrunk before him, and tried to wipe away her tears, but it was all in vain. She wanted to be with her children, she said, the little time she had to live. All the frowns and threats of Freeman, could not wholly silence the afflicted mother. She kept on begging and beseeching them, most piteously, not to separate the three. Over and over again she told them how she loved her boy. A great many times she repeated her former promises—how very faithful and obedient she would be; how hard she would labor day and night, to the last moment of her life, if he would only buy them all together. But it was of no avail; the man could not afford it. The bargain was agreed upon, and Randall must go alone. Then Eliza ran to him; embraced him passionately; kissed him again and again; told him to remember her—all the while her tears falling in the boy's face like rain.

7   Freeman damned her, calling her a blubbering, bawling wench, and ordered her to go to her place, and behave herself, and be somebody. He swore he wouldn't stand such stuff but a little longer. He would soon give her something to cry about, if she was not mighty careful, and *that* she might depend upon.

8   The planter from Baton Rouge, with his new purchases, was ready to depart.

9   "Don't cry, mama. I will be a good boy. Don't cry," said Randall, looking back, as they passed out of the door.

10   What has become of the lad, God knows. It was a mournful scene indeed. I would have cried myself if I had dared. ■

From Solomon Northrup, "A Slave Witness of a Slave Auction," in *The Southern Reader*, Willard Thorp, ed., Alfred A. Knopf, New York, 1955. Reprinted by permission.

EXERCISES

Do not refer to the selection for Exercises A and B.

A. DETERMINING THE MAIN IDEA AND PURPOSE
Choose the best answer.

1. _____ The main idea of the narrative is that (a) Theophilus Freeman represented a typical slave keeper; (b) plans to escape were on every slave's mind; (c) the fear of being separated from one's family was the most tragic result of slave auctions; (d) the slave auction was a sad, mournful occasion for both observers and those who were sold.

2. _____ With respect to the main idea, the author's purpose is (a) to show the reader how most slave auctions were conducted; (b) to explain the traits slaveowners wanted in the slaves they bought; (c) to make the reader aware of the terrible hardships the auction created for the slaves; (d) to argue for the abolition of slavery as an institution.

B. COMPREHENDING MAIN IDEAS
Choose the correct answer.

1. _____ The scene described in the narrative took place in (a) Baton Rouge; (b) New Orleans; (c) Natchez; (d) Atlanta.

2. _____ The slaves were exercised so that (a) they would be in good physical condition for their future labors; (b) they would be kept busy before the auction began; (c) they would be able to compete in athletic events; (d) they would look sharp.

3. _____ The slaves were divided first by sex and then by (a) age; (b) physical ability; (c) work experience; (d) height.

4. _____ Scars on a slave's back were evidence of a rebellious or unruly spirit and, as a result, meant that (a) the slave would cost more money; (b) the slave would not be purchased by anyone; (c) the sale would be hurt; (d) the slave would have to be set free.

5. _____ The man who purchased Randall could not also purchase Eliza and Emily because (a) he needed only one slave; (b) he needed only a male slave; (c) he had room for only one slave; (d) he couldn't afford to buy them.

6. _____ Northrup emphasizes that these slaves' primary hope was (a) not to be separated from their loved ones; (b) to be purchased by a kind owner; (c) to live in a place from which they could easily escape; (d) to live in a pleasant environment.

COMPREHENSION SCORE

Score your answers for Exercises A and B as follows:

A. No. right _____ × 2 = _____

B. No. right _____ × 1 = _____

Total pts. from A and B _____ × 10 = _____%

You may refer to the selection for the remaining exercises.

C. RECOGNIZING SUPPORTING DETAILS

Place an X in the space for each statement that *directly* supports this main idea from the selection: **"Next day many customers called to examine Freeman's 'new lot.'"**

1. _____ The latter gentleman was very loquacious, dwelling at much length upon our several good points and qualities.

2. _____ He would make us hold up our heads, walk briskly back and forth, while customers would feel of our hands and arms and bodies, turn us about, ask us what we could do, make us open our mouths and show our teeth, precisely as a jockey examines a horse which he is about to barter for or purchase.

3. _____ Sometimes a man or woman was taken back to the small house in the yard, stripped, and inspected more minutely.

4. _____ Scars upon a slave's back were considered evidence of a rebellious or unruly spirit, and hurt his sale.

5. _____ One old gentleman, who said he wanted a coachman, appeared to take a fancy to me.

6. _____ From his conversation with Freeman, I learned he was a resident of the city.

D. MAKING INFERENCES

For each of these statements write Y (Yes) if the inference is an accurate one, N (No) if the inference is an inaccurate one, or CT (Can't Tell) if you do not have enough information to make an inference.

1. _____ Theophilus Freeman was a successful slave broker.

2. _____ Northrup, the author of the narrative, had studied the violin at a music conservatory.

3.   _____ The customers were not allowed to learn much information about slaves they were interested in purchasing.

4.   _____ Northrup had no intention of trying to escape after he was sold.

5.   _____ Eliza was eventually reunited with her children, Randall and Emily.

E.   DRAWING CONCLUSIONS
Mark an X before any statement that represents reasonable conclusions you can draw from the selection.

1.   _____ The slaves described in this particular narrative were treated more like animals than like people.

2.   _____ The institution of slavery resulted in the breakup of many families.

3.   _____ Conflict over the slavery issue was one of the main causes of the American Civil War.

4.   _____ Slavery was a cruel and inhuman practice.

5.   _____ The U.S. is still feeling the negative effects of slavery.

F.   ANALYZING ORGANIZATION AND SEEING RELATIONSHIPS

1.   _____ In paragraph 1, when Northrup describes Mr. Theophilus Freeman, keeper of the slave pen, as "amiable" and "pious-hearted," he is being (a) honest; (b) sarcastic; (c) complimentary; (d) forgiving.

2.   _____ Look again at paragraph 2. Consider these transitions: "in the first place," "then," "now," "during the day." These suggest that the method of development in the paragraph is primarily (a) example; (b) cause and effect; (c) general statement and examples; (d) contrast; (e) steps in a process.

3.   _____ The kind of order used throughout the narrative is (a) general to specific; (b) specific to general; (c) chronological; (d) spatial or space order.

4.   _____ Northrup describes his violin playing in paragraph 3 in order to emphasize (a) his desire to make himself look more desirable as a slave to be purchased; (b) his superiority to the other slaves; (c) the contrast between his position as a slave and his artistic ability; (d) his love of music.

5.   _____ From Northrup's description of Randall's behavior after he was sold, the boy acted (a) bravely; (b) childishly; (c) predictably; (d) cowardly.

6.   _____ Northrup dwells on the scene with Eliza and her son to show (a) the inhumanity of slavery as an institution; (b) Northrup's own un-

selfish efforts to act on Eliza's behalf; (c) how hard the times were, since the planter could not afford to buy the entire family; (d) the long-term effects of slavery on the family.

G.   UNDERSTANDING VOCABULARY
Choose the correct answer according to the context.

1. _____ the *pious*-hearted Mr. Freeman [paragraph 1]: (a) generous; (b) simple; (c) devoutly religious; (d) superstitious.

2. _____ *exhorted* us to appear [2]: (a) greatly encouraged; (b) demanded; (c) strongly urged; (d) threatened.

3. _____ holding out various *inducements* [2]: (a) incentives; (b) threats; (c) bribes; (d) instructions.

4. _____ the latter gentleman was very *loquacious* [4]: (a) kindly; (b) talkative; (c) generous; (d) trustworthy.

5. _____ inspected more *minutely* [4]: (a) closely; (b) specifically; (c) with more concern; (d) critically.

6. _____ a rebellious or *unruly* spirit [4]: (a) insensitive; (b) cruel; (c) prone to violence; (d) difficult to discipline.

7. _____ I was of a good *constitution* [5]: (a) state of health; (b) moral character; (c) family; (d) conscience.

8. _____ the old gentleman argued quite *adroitly* [5]: (a) cleverly; (b) impassionedly; (c) skillfully; (d) convincingly.

9. _____ a *paroxysm* of grief [6]: (a) sudden outburst, fit; (b) emotional crisis; (c) example; (d) loud wailing.

10. _____ weeping *plaintively* [6]: (a) quietly; (b) intensely; (c) mournfully; (d) bitterly.

H.   USING VOCABULARY
From the following list of vocabulary words, choose a word that fits in each blank according to both the grammatical structure of the sentence and the context. Use each word in the list only once and add noun or verb endings (such as -s, -ing, or -ed) if necessary. (Note that there are more words than sentences.)

precision	exhibit	extraordinary
amiable	fancy	unruly
flog	avail	plaintively
adroitly	excel	loquacious

1. Mr. Freeman, who is ironically described as being _____, exercised the slaves and made them move to their places with exact

_____.

2. Scars on a slave's back indicated both that he or she had an

    _____ spirit and that he or she had been

    _____ in the past.

3. Northrup _____ at playing the violin; however, the

    old gentleman, who had initially taken a _____ to

    him, argued _____ that there was nothing

    _____ about him and that the price was too high.

4. Eliza begged Freeman not to separate her from her son and cried

    _____, but her pleas were to no _____.

I.   TOPICS FOR WRITING OR DISCUSSION

1. Here are some sentences from the selection. Paraphrase them by re-
    writing each one in your own words in the space provided.

    a. Mr. Theophilus Freeman bustled about in a very industrious manner,
    getting his property ready for the sales-room, intending, no doubt, to
    do that day a rousing business.

    _____

    _____

    _____

    b. We were now conducted into a large room in the front part of the
    building to which the yard was attached, in order to be properly
    trained, before the admission of customers.

    _____

    _____

    _____

    c. David and Caroline were purchased together by a Natchez planter.
    They left us, grinning broadly, and in the most happy state of mind,
    caused by the fact of their not being separated.

    _____

    _____

    _____

    d. A great many times she [Eliza] repeated her former promises—how
    very faithful and obedient she would be; how hard she would labor
    day and night, to the last moment of her life, if he would only buy
    them all together.

_____

_____

_____

2. Northrup's narrative ends with a long anecdote, a little story about Eliza's distress at being separated from her children. This anecdote serves as a powerful argument against the institution of slavery. Write an essay about an issue that concerns you. Begin or end your essay with an anecdote that, like Northrup's, will convince the reader that you are right.

4

Mark Twain

SIVILIZING HUCK

This selection is the first chapter from Mark Twain's classic American novel Huckleberry Finn *(1885), the sequel to* Tom Sawyer, *published nine years earlier. Twain's intention in both novels was to recapture for adults the lost world of childhood. Huck narrates the story in the first person, using a Missouri backwoods dialect. The story is set on the Mississippi River, and the time is around 1830 or 1840.*

VOCABULARY PREVIEW

WORD ORIGINS

DISMAL

In paragraph 2 Huck describes the Widow Douglas as "dismal regular and decent." *Dismal* means "gloomy" or "dreary." Although it is not certain how the word came into English, one theory is that it was a telescoped word, a new word formed when one word slides into another, like the parts of a telescope. In this case, the Latin words for "evil days" (*diēs malī*) were telescoped to form a new word, *dismal*.

Two other examples of telescoped words can be seen in the words *brunch*, where *breakfast* and *lunch* slide together to form a new word, and *smog*, a blend of *smoke* and *fog*.

VICTUALS

Victuals [paragraph 3], pronounced *vittles* and sometimes spelled that way, means "food" or "food supplies." Today the word has an old-fashioned, rural, "down-home" flavor. It comes from Latin: from *victuālis* ("provision") and *victus* ("sustenance"), both of which come from the Latin word *vivere* ("to live"). That the connection between food and life, so apparent in our physical nature, also occurs in our language should not be surprising.

WORD PARTS

-IZE

In paragraph 2 Huck tells about the Widow Douglas's attempts to *civilize* him, although because of his poor education, he spells it *sivilize*.

47

The suffix *-ize* is one of the most common verb endings in English. It has several related meanings, but probably the most common meaning is "to cause to be" or "to make into." *Civilize,* then, means "to bring out of a primitive state," "to educate," or "to refine" (literally, to make civil or fit for polite society).

Many common English words end in *-ize,* such as *symbolize, personalize, standardize,* and *sympathize.* In addition, many new words, especially technical or scientific terms, have been added to English by adding *-ize* to nouns or adjectives, such as *computerize, randomize, galvanize,* and *oxidize.*

WORD FAMILIES

COMPANY

In paragraph 8 when Huck describes his loneliness, he says that he wishes he had some *company.* Associated with a related word, *companion, company* comes from the Latin "one who eats bread with another" [*com-* ("together") + *pānis* ("bread")]. This word's origin, then, reinforces the idea that friends socialize and eat together. Here are some other words in this family:

companionable	suited to be a good companion; sociable; friendly
accompany	to go along with or to join in company; also to play a musical instrument with
accompaniment	something that accompanies or adds to as decoration or for completeness
accompanist	a performer, like a pianist, who plays a musical accompaniment

MARK TWAIN

SIVILIZING HUCK

1   You don't know about me, without you have read a book by the name of "The Adventures of Tom Sawyer," but that ain't no matter. That book was made by Mr. Mark Twain, and he told the truth, mainly. There was things which he stretched, but mainly he told the truth. That is nothing. I never seen anybody but lied, one time or another, without it was Aunt Polly, or the widow, or maybe Mary. Aunt Polly— Tom's Aunt Polly, she is—and Mary, and the Widow Douglas, is all told about in that book—which is mostly a true book; with some stretchers, as I said before.

2   Now the way that the book winds up, is this: Tom and me found the money that the robbers hid in the cave, and it made us rich. We got six thousand dollars apiece—all gold. It was an awful sight of money when it was piled up. Well, Judge Thatcher, he took it and put it out at interest, and it fetched us a dollar a day apiece, all the year round—more than a body could tell what to do with. The Widow Douglas, she took me for her son, and allowed she would sivilize me; but it was rough living in the house all the time, considering how dismal regular and decent

the widow was in all her ways; and so when I couldn't stand it no longer, I lit out. I got into my old rags, and my sugar-hogshead* again, and was free and satisfied. But Tom Sawyer, he hunted me up and said he was going to start a band of robbers, and I might join if I would go back to the widow and be respectable. So I went back.

3   The widow she cried over me, and called me a poor lost lamb, and she called me a lot of other names, too, but she never meant no harm by it. She put me in them new clothes again, and I couldn't do nothing but sweat and sweat, and feel all cramped up. Well, then, the old thing commenced again. The widow rung a bell for supper, and you had to come to time. When you got to the table you couldn't go right to eating, but you had to wait for the widow to tuck down her head and grumble a little over the victuals, though there warn't really anything the matter with them. That is, nothing only everything was cooked by itself. In a barrel of odds and ends it is different; things get mixed up, and the juice kind of swaps around, and the things go better.

4   After supper she got out her book and learned me about Moses and the Bulrushers, and I was in a sweat to find out all about him; but by-and-by she let it out that Moses had been dead a considerable long time; so then I didn't care no more about him; because I don't take stock in dead people.

5   Pretty soon I wanted to smoke, and asked the widow to let me. But she wouldn't. She said it was a mean practice and wasn't clean, and I must try to not do it any more. That is just the way with some people. They get down on a thing when they don't know nothing about it. Here she was a bothering about Moses, which was no kin to her, and no use to anybody, being gone, you see, yet finding a power of fault with me for doing a thing that had some good in it. And she took snuff too; of course that was all right, because she done it herself.

6   Her sister, Miss Watson, a tolerable slim old maid, with goggles on, had just come to live with her, and took a set at me now, with a spelling-book. She worked me middling hard for about an hour, and then the widow made her ease up. I couldn't stood it much longer. Then for an hour it was deadly dull, and I was fidgety. Miss Watson would say, "Don't put your feet up there, Huckleberry;" and "don't scrunch up like that, Huckleberry—set up straight;"and pretty soon she would say, "Don't gap and stretch like that, Huckleberry—why don't you try to behave?" Then she told me all about the bad place, and I said I wished I was there. She got mad, then, but I didn't mean no harm. All I wanted was to go somewheres; all I wanted was a change, I warn't particular. She said it was wicked to say what I said; said she wouldn't say it for the whole world; *she* was going to live so as to go to the good place. Well, I couldn't see no advantage in going where she was going, so I made up my mind I wouldn't try for it. But I never said so, because it would only make trouble, and wouldn't do no good.

7   Now she had got a start, and she went on and told me all about the good place. She said all a body would have to do there was to go around all day long with a harp and sing, forever and ever. So I didn't think much of it. But I never said so. I asked her if she reckoned Tom Sawyer would go there, and, she said, not by a considerable sight. I was glad about that, because I wanted him and me to be together.

*A large barrel, emptied of its shipment of sugar. Huck's place of refuge behind the abandoned slaughterhouse.

8   Miss Watson she kept pecking at me, and it got tiresome and lonesome. By-and-by they fetched the niggers* in and had prayers, and then everybody was off to bed. I went up to my room with a piece of candle and put it on the table. Then I set down in a chair by the window and tried to think of something cheerful, but it warn't no use. I felt so lonesome I most wished I was dead. The stars was shining, and the leaves rustled in the woods ever so mournful; and I heard an owl, away off, who-whooing about somebody that was dead, and a whippowill and a dog crying about somebody that was going to die; and the wind was trying to whisper something to me and I couldn't make out what it was, and so it made the cold shivers run over me. Then away out in the woods I heard that kind of a sound that a ghost makes when it wants to tell about something that's on its mind and can't make itself understood, and so can't rest easy in its grave and has to go about that way every night grieving. I got so down-hearted and scared, I did wish I had some company. Pretty soon a spider went crawling up my shoulder, and I flipped it off and it lit in the candle; and before I could budge it was all shriveled up. I didn't need anybody to tell me that that was an awful bad sign and would fetch me some bad luck, so I was scared and most shook the clothes off of me. I got up and turned around in my tracks three times and crossed my breast every time; and then I tied up a little lock of my hair with a thread to keep witches away. But I hadn't no confidence. You do that when you've lost a horse-shoe that you've found, instead of nailing it up over the door, but I hadn't ever heard anybody say it was any way to keep off bad luck when you'd killed a spider.

9   I set down again, a shaking all over, and got out my pipe for a smoke; for the house was all as still as death, now, and so the widow wouldn't know. Well, after a long time I heard the clock away off in the town go boom—boom—boom—twelve licks—and all still again—stiller than ever. Pretty soon I heard a twig snap, down in the dark amongst the trees—something was a stirring. I set still and listened. Directly I could just barely hear a *"me-yow! me-yow!"* down there. That was good! Says I, *"me-yow! me-yow!"* as soft as I could, and then I put out the light and scrambled out of the window onto the shed. Then I slipped down to the ground and crawled in amongst the trees, and sure enough there was Tom Sawyer waiting for me.   ∎

*In slave states, "nigger" was not necessarily an abusive word, but merely the ordinary colloquial term for a slave.
From Mark Twain, "Sivilizing Huck," *The Adventures of Huckleberry Finn.*

EXERCISES

Do not refer to the selection for Exercises A and B.

A.   DETERMINING THE MAIN IDEA AND PURPOSE
Choose the best answer.

1.   _____ The main idea of the selection is that (a) Huck Finn was a neglected, impolite boy who needed to be taught some manners;

(b) Huck Finn was a rebellious boy who came under Tom Sawyer's bad influence; (c) because of Huck Finn's ignorance and poor upbringing, he was destined to live a life of crime with Tom Sawyer; (d) Huck Finn's mischievous and adventurous nature made the Widow Douglas's attempts to teach him manners and religion unsuccessful.

2. _____ In addition to introducing the novel's main characters, the author's purpose is to show the reader (a) Huck's love of nature and the outdoors; (b) the importance to Huck of freedom from restraints and social conventions; (c) the necessity for young people to have a strong religious upbringing; (d) a typical nineteenth-century American boyhood.

B.   COMPREHENDING MAIN IDEAS
Decide if these statements from the selection are true (T) or false (F).

1. _____ Mark Twain stretched the truth in his novels.

2. _____ Huck liked the new clothes that the Widow Douglas asked him to wear.

3. _____ One habit of Huck's that the Widow Douglas did not approve of was his use of snuff.

4. _____ Huck was interested in the Bible story about Moses and the "Bulrushers" until he found out that Moses was dead.

5. _____ Miss Watson and the Widow Douglas's attempts to teach Huck about manners and religion were largely successful.

6. _____ Huck thought it was a bad sign that the spider burned up in the candle flame.

COMPREHENSION SCORE

Score your answers for Exercises A and B as follows:

A.   No. right _____ × 2 = _____

B.   No. right _____ × 1 = _____

Total points from A and B _____ × 10 = _____%

You may refer to the selection for the remaining exercises.

C.   RECOGNIZING SUPPORTING DETAILS
Place an X in the space for each sentence from the selection that *directly* supports this main idea from the selection: **"The Widow Douglas, she took me for her son, and allowed she would sivilize me."**

1. _____ But it was rough living in the house all the time, considering how dismal regular and decent the widow was in all her ways.

2. _____ But Tom Sawyer, he hunted me up and said he was going to start a band of robbers, and I might join if I would go back to the widow and be respectable.

3. _____ She put me in them new clothes again, and I couldn't do nothing but sweat and sweat, and feel all cramped up.

4. _____ The widow rung a bell for supper, and you had to come to time.

5. _____ When you got to the table you couldn't go right to eating, but you had to wait for the widow to tuck down her head and grumble a little over the victuals.

6. _____ Pretty soon I wanted to smoke, and asked the widow to let me. But she wouldn't. She said it was a mean practice and wasn't clean, and I must try to not do it any more.

7. _____ That is just the way with some people. They get down on a thing when they don't know nothing about it.

8. _____ And she took snuff too; of course that was all right, because she done it herself.

D.   MAKING INFERENCES
For each of these statements write Y (Yes) if the inference is an accurate one, N (No) if the inference is an inaccurate one, or CT (Can't Tell) if you do not have enough information to make an inference.

1. _____ Huck Finn thought both Aunt Polly, Tom's aunt, and the Widow Douglas were honest and never told lies.

2. _____ When the widow used to "tuck down her head and grumble a little over the victuals," she was complaining about the quality of the food.

3. _____ The Widow Douglas was being hypocritical in not allowing Huck to smoke.

4. _____ The "good place" refers to school and the "bad place" to prison.

5. _____ Miss Watson probably thought that Tom Sawyer was not a suitable friend for Huck.

E.   UNDERSTANDING VOCABULARY
Choose the correct definition according to the context.

1. _____ how *dismal* regular and decent the widow was [paragraph 2]:
(a) gloomily; (b) tolerably; (c) genuinely; (d) ordinarily.

2. _____ the old thing *commenced* again [3]: (a) prayed; (b) began;
(c) criticized; (d) cried.

3. _____ She said it was a *mean* practice [5]: (a) unhealthy; (b) cruel; (c) low in quality; inferior; (d) immoral.

4. _____ no *kin* to her [5]: (a) relative; (b) business; (c) importance; (d) good.

5. _____ I was *fidgety* [6]: (a) unhappy; (b) dissatisfied; (c) restless; (d) full of anxiety.

F. UNDERSTANDING EXPRESSIONS OF A REGIONAL DIALECT

As you know from the headnote to the selection, Huck's speech represents a dialect spoken in backwoods Missouri in the early nineteenth century. Below are some expressions from the selection, with the dialect phrase in italics, along with the paragraph where they appear. Look at the context and rewrite the expression in modern English.

1. "You don't know about me, *without* you have read a book by the name of "The Adventures of Tom Sawyer," and "I never seen anybody but lied, one time or another, *without* it was Aunt Polly" [1]:

   _____

2. ". . . That book—which is mostly a true book; with *some stretchers*, as I said before" [1]:

   _____

3. "The Widow Douglas, she took me for her son, and *allowed* she would sivilize me" [2]:

   _____

4. "I was *in a sweat* to find out all about him" [4]:

   _____

5. "She worked me *middling* hard" [6]:

   _____

6. "I asked her if she *reckoned* Tom Sawyer would go there" [7]:

   _____

G. TOPICS FOR WRITING OR DISCUSSION

1. This first chapter of *Huckleberry Finn* shows that Huck has a strong moral sense and a realistic view of the world. In your own words, list some of the major ideas suggested in this excerpt that you think Twain might develop in the rest of the novel. To get you started, one possible idea has been done for you:

   Huck doesn't like proper clothing because it suggests good behavior and cleanliness. Paying

   so much attention to social conventions prevents him from being truly free.

   _____

   _____

_____

_____

_____

_____

_____

2.   Describe an incident from your childhood when one of your teachers or your parents tried to instill good manners in you, to "sivilize" you. What were your reactions to their efforts?

5 |||||

Rose Del Castillo Guilbault

HISPANIC, USA: THE CONVEYOR BELT LADIES

Rose Del Castillo Guilbault is director of editorials and public affairs at KGO-TV in San Francisco and an associate editor at Pacific News Service. In addition, she writes a monthly column for the San Francisco Chronicle *on the Hispanic experience. In this article, the author describes her summer experiences during college working with migrant women in the vegetable packing sheds.*

VOCABULARY PREVIEW

WORD ORIGINS

STIGMATIZE

In paragraph 10, Guilbault writes that she feared her Anglo friends would *stigmatize* her for working with the Mexican women in the packing sheds. This verb comes from the Greek word *stigma*, meaning a "tatoo mark."

The original meaning, now archaic, was a mark burned into one's skin to identify him or her as a criminal or slave. Today the word has a more metaphorical meaning, referring to "any mark of disgrace." The plural form, *stigmata*, means the marks or sores resembling Christ's crucifixion wounds that sometimes appear on people's hands or feet and that are attributed to miracles.

GREGARIOUS

Guilbault describes her female coworkers as a "*gregarious*, entertaining group." This word, derived from the Latin word *gregārius*, has as its root *grex*, meaning "herd" or "flock." *Gregarious* has two meanings: first, "tending to move in a group with others of the same kind," describing animals like sheep, and second, "enjoying the company of others of one's kind," "sociable." It is this second meaning that fits the context in this case.

MELANCHOLIC

As they worked, sorting tomatoes, the women described in this article talked about their lives, their husbands and children, their concerns and worries. Guilbault writes in paragraph 18 that "in unexpected moments, they could turn *melancholic*: recounting the babies who died because their mothers couldn't afford medical care."

Melancholic is the adjective form of the noun *melancholy*. Meaning "sadness" or "depression of the spirits," *melancholy* (or black bile) was one of the four humors. Medieval physicians believed that these humors, or bodily fluids, governed specific human emotions. Therefore, an excess of *melancholy* was thought to cause one to be sullen or extremely sad. An excess of choler (or yellow bile) was thought to cause anger and bad temper. Blood (*sanguin* in Latin) caused a ruddy complexion and meant that a person was dominated by passion. And finally, phlegm caused one to have a sluggish temperament.

In modern English we still have the words *melancholic, sanguine,* and *phlegmatic* to describe people's emotional states.

WORD PARTS

UN-, IR-

The article contains two words with common negative prefixes: in paragraph 2, *uninspiring* ("not inspiring") and in paragraph 10, *irrevocably,* from the adjective form *irrevocable* ("not able to be revoked or reversed"). This latter word is pronounced ĭ-rĕv'ə-kə-bəl.

Un- is the most common negative prefix in English, occurring in hundreds of words, among them *unhappy, undetermined, unimpressive,* and *uninhabited. Ir-* is the negative prefix used with words beginning with the consonant *r.* You can see this prefix in such words as *irrational, irresponsible,* and *irregular.*

WORD FAMILIES

MONOTONOUS

Sorting tomatoes is *monotonous* work, as Guilbault suggests in paragraph 12. The Greek prefix *mono-* ("one" or "single") precedes many common words in English. *Monotonous* ("having one tone," "repetitiously dull") can be broken down like this:

[*mono-* ("single") + *tonos* ("tone")]

Other words with this prefix:

monotheism	belief in one God [*mono-* + *the(o)* ("god") + *-ism*]
monologue	a long speech made by one person [*mono-* + *(dia)logue*—from *legein* ("to talk")]
monophobia	excessive fear of being alone [*mono-* + *phobia* ("fear")]
monopoly	economic control by one group [*mono-* + *pōlein* ("to sell")]

ROSE DEL CASTILLO GUILBAULT

HISPANIC, USA:
THE CONVEYOR BELT LADIES

1   The conveyor-belt ladies were the migrant women, mostly from Texas, I worked with during the summers of my teenage years. I call them conveyor-belt ladies because our entire relationship took place while sorting tomatoes on a conveyor belt.

2   We were like a cast in a play where all the action occurs on one set. We'd return day after day to perform the same roles, only this stage was a vegetable-packing shed, and at the end of the season there was no applause. The players could look forward only to the same uninspiring parts on a string of grim real-life stages.

3   The women and their families arrived in May for the carrot season, spent the summer in the tomato sheds and stayed through October for the bean harvest. After that, they emptied the town, some returning to their homes in Texas (cities like McAllen, Douglas, Brownsville), while others continued on the migrant trail, picking cotton in the San Joaquin Valley or grapefruits and oranges in the Imperial Valley.

4   Most of these women had started in the fields. The vegetable packing sheds were a step up, easier than the back-breaking, grueling work the field demanded. The work was more tedious than strenuous, paid better, provided fairly steady hours and clean bathrooms. Best of all, you weren't subjected to the elements.

5   The summer I was 16, my mother got jobs for both of us as tomato sorters. That's how I came to be included in the seasonal sorority of the conveyor belt.

6   The work consisted of standing and picking flawed tomatoes off the conveyor belt before they rolled off into the shipping boxes at the end of the line. These boxes were immediately loaded onto waiting delivery trucks, so it was crucial not to let imperfect tomatoes through.

7   The work could be slow or intense, depending on the quality of the tomatoes and how many there were. Work increased when the company's deliveries got backlogged or after rainy weather had delayed picking.

8   During those times, it was not unusual to work from 7 a.m. to midnight, playing catch-up. I never heard anyone complain about the overtime. Overtime meant desperately needed extra money.

9   I was not happy to be part of the agricultural work force. I would have preferred working in a dress shop or baby-sitting, like my friends. But I had a dream that would cost a lot of money—college. And the fact was, this was the highest-paying work I could do.

10   But it wasn't so much the work that bothered me. I was embarrassed because only Mexicans worked at packing sheds. I had heard my schoolmates joke about the "ugly, fat Mexican women" at the sheds. They ridiculed the way they dressed and laughed at the "funny way" they talked. I feared working with them would irrevocably stigmatize me, setting me further apart from my Anglo classmates.

11   At 16 I was more American than Mexican and, with adolescent arrogance, felt superior to these "uneducated" women. I might be one of them, I reasoned, but I was not like them.

12   But it was difficult not to like the women. They were a gregarious, entertaining group, easing the long, monotonous hours with bawdy humor, spicy gossip and inventive laments. They poked fun at all the male workers and did hysterical impersonations of a dyspeptic Anglo supervisor. Although he didn't speak Spanish (other than *"Mujeres, trabajo, trabajo!"* Women, work, work!), he seemed to sense he was being laughed at. That would account for the sudden rages when he would stamp his foot and forbid us to talk until break time.

13   "I bet he understands Spanish and just pretends so he can hear what we say," I whispered to Rosa.

14   *"Ay, no, hija,* it's all the buzzing in his ears that alerts him that these *viejas* (old women) are bad-mouthing him!" Rosa giggled.

15   But it would have been easier to tie the women's tongues in a knot than to keep them quiet. Eventually the ladies had their way and their fun, and the men learned to ignore them.

16   We were often shifted around, another strategy to keep us quiet. This gave me ample opportunity to get to know everyone, listen to their life stories and absorb the gossip.

17   Pretty Rosa described her romances and her impending wedding to a handsome field worker. Bertha, a heavy-set, dark-skinned woman, told me that Rosa's marriage would cause nothing but headaches because the man was younger and too handsome. Maria, large, moon-faced and placid, described the births of each of her nine children, warning me about the horrors of childbirth. Pragmatic Minnie, a tiny woman who always wore printed cotton dresses, scoffed at Maria's stupidity, telling me she wouldn't have so many kids if she had ignored that good-for-nothing priest and gotten her tubes tied!

18   In unexpected moments, they could turn melancholic: recounting the babies who died because their mothers couldn't afford medical care; the alcoholic, abusive husbands who were their "cross to bear"; the racism they experienced in Texas, where they were branded "dirty Mexicans" or "Mexican dogs" and not allowed in certain restaurants.

19   They spoke with the detached fatalism of people with limited choices and alternatives. Their lives were as raw and brutal as ghetto streets—something they accepted with an odd grace and resignation.

20   I was appalled and deeply affected by these confidences. The injustices they endured enraged me; their personal struggles overwhelmed me. I knew I could do little but sympathize.

21   My mother, no stranger to suffering, suggested I was too impressionable when I emotionally told her the women's stories. "That's nothing," she'd say lightly. "If they were in Mexico, life would be even harder. At least there's opportunities here, you can work."

22   My icy arrogance quickly thawed, that first summer, as my respect for the conveyor-belt ladies grew.

23   I worked in the packing sheds for several summers. The last season also turned out to be the last time I lived at home. It was the end of a chapter in my life,

but I didn't know it then. I had just finished junior college and was transferring to the university. I was already over-educated for seasonal work, but if you counted the overtime, no other jobs came close to paying so well, so I went back one last time.

24   The ladies treated me with warmth and respect. I was a college student, deserving of special treatment.

25   Aguedita, the crew chief, moved me to softer and better-paying jobs within the plant. I went from the conveyor belt to shoving boxes down a chute and finally to weighing boxes of tomatoes on a scale—the highest-paying position for a woman.

26   When the union's dues collector showed up, the women hid me in the bathroom. They had decided it was unfair for me to have to join the union and pay dues, since I worked only during the summer.

27   "Where's the student?" the union rep would ask, opening the door to a barrage of complaints about the union's unfairness.

28   Maria (of the nine children) tried to feed me all summer, bringing extra tortillas, which were delicious. I accepted them guiltily, always wondering if I was taking food away from her children. Others would bring rental contracts or other documents for me to explain and translate.

29   The last day of work was splendidly beautiful, warm and sunny. If this had been a movie, these last scenes would have been shot in soft focus, with a crescendo of music in the background.

30   But real life is anti-climactic. As it was, nothing unusual happened. The conveyor belt's loud humming was turned off, silenced for the season. The women sighed as they removed their aprons. Some of them just walked off, calling *"Hasta la próxima!"* Until next time!

31   But most of the conveyor-belt ladies shook my hand, gave me a blessing or a big hug.

32   "Make us proud!" they said.

33   I hope I have.   ∎

From Rose Del Castillo Guilbault, "Hispanic USA: The Conveyor-Belt Ladies," *San Francisco Chronicle*, "This World," April 15, 1990. Reprinted by permission.

EXERCISES

Do not refer to the selection for Exercises A and B.

A.   DETERMINING THE MAIN IDEA AND PURPOSE
Choose the best answer.

1.   _____ The main idea of the selection is that (a) summer jobs can offer rewarding experiences for college students; (b) working in the vegetable-packing sheds and picking vegetables are tedious, difficult jobs; (c) the conveyor-belt ladies faced daily hardships and injustices; (d) despite her initial misgivings, the author learned to respect the lives of the conveyor-belt ladies she worked with.

2.   _____ With respect to the main idea, the author's purpose is (a) to entertain the reader; (b) to describe her experiences and those of her coworkers; (c) to enumerate facts about migrant workers; (d) to argue for better working conditions in the agricultural industry.

B.   COMPREHENDING MAIN IDEAS
Choose the correct answer.

1.   _____ Guilbault's job during her first summers working with the conveyor-belt ladies was (a) picking beans; (b) sorting tomatoes; (c) packing strawberries; (d) trimming onions.

2.   _____ The author writes that the daily lives of the conveyor-belt ladies were (a) inspiring; (b) hard but profitable; (c) grim and tedious; (d) desperate, nearly hopeless.

3.   _____ At first, Guilbault was afraid that (a) she would not be physically able to do the work; (b) she would be stigmatized by her Anglo friends for working with Mexican women; (c) she would not earn enough money to attend college; (d) she would be ridiculed by the other workers for her arrogant manner.

4.   _____ The conveyor-belt ladies eased the monotonous hours by (a) playing jokes on the supervisors; (b) playing games; (c) listening to music; (d) talking and gossiping.

5.   _____ According to the author, the conveyor-belt ladies accepted their lives, which she describes as being raw and brutal, with (a) grace and resignation; (b) hostility and anger; (c) detachment and indifference; (d) good humor.

6.   _____ Because Guilbault was a college student, the conveyor-belt ladies (a) were envious of her education; (b) treated her with hostility; (c) treated her with warmth and respect; (d) complained when she was given an easier job.

COMPREHENSION SCORE

Score your answers for Exercises A and B as follows:

A.   No. right _____ × 2 = _____

B.   No. right _____ × 1 = _____

Total pts. from A and B _____ × 10 = _____%

You may refer to the selection for the remaining exercises.

C.   RECOGNIZING SUPPORTING DETAILS
Place an X in the space for each sentence that *directly* supports this main idea from the selection: **"In unexpected moments, they could turn melancholic. . . ."**

1. _____ Pretty Rosa described her romances and her impending wedding to a handsome field worker.

2. _____ They recounted the babies who died because their mothers couldn't afford medical care.

3. _____ They recounted the alcoholic, abusive husbands who were their "cross to bear."

4. _____ They recounted the racism they experienced in Texas, where they were branded "dirty Mexicans" or "Mexican dogs" and not allowed in certain restaurants.

5. _____ They spoke with the detached fatalism of people with limited choices and alternatives.

6. _____ Their lives were as raw and brutal as ghetto streets—something they accepted with an odd grace and resignation.

D. MAKING INFERENCES
Answer these inference questions in your own words.

1. What can you infer about the educational level of the conveyor-belt ladies? _____

_____

2. From what she writes in paragraph 10, why was Guilbault embarrassed to be working in the packing sheds? _____

_____

_____

3. Look again at paragraph 11. When Guilbault writes "I might be one of them, I reasoned, but I was not like them," what does she mean? _____

_____

_____

4. According to what Guilbault's mother states, why were the conveyor-belt ladies so resigned to their hard lives in America? _____

_____

_____

5. Guilbault eventually came to respect the women she worked with. What specific qualities did the conveyor-belt ladies display that she found admirable? _____

_____

E.   ANALYZING ORGANIZATION AND SEEING RELATIONSHIPS

1.   _____ In paragraph 2 Guilbault compares the lives of the conveyor-belt ladies to (a) working in a vegetable-packing shed; (b) going to the theater; (c) playing parts in a grim play; (d) auditioning for a role in a play.

2.   _____ The kind of writing that this selection represents is primarily (a) narrative, telling a story; (b) descriptive, showing what something looks like; (c) expository, explaining and discussing; (d) persuasive, trying to convince.

3.   _____ Look again at paragraph 11. Why does the author put the word "uneducated" in quotation marks? (a) She is being ironic, because the women were educated in the ways of the world, if not in school; (b) she is quoting someone directly; (c) she wants to emphasize the word; (d) she wants to keep the word separate from the rest of the text.

4.   _____ Paragraphs 16–18 are developed with (a) reasons; (b) short examples; (c) steps in a process; (d) definitions of important words.

5.   _____ Look again at paragraphs 19 and 20. What logical relationship exists between them? (a) cause and effect; (b) contrast; (c) key term and a definition of it; (d) steps in a process.

6.   _____ In paragraph 23 Guilbault uses a metaphor, an imaginative comparison that is not meant to be taken literally. Find the metaphor. What is she comparing to what? _____

_____

F.   UNDERSTANDING VOCABULARY
Look through the paragraphs listed below and find a word that matches each definition. An example has been done for you.

Ex.   moving from place to place [1–2]   _____migrant_____

1.   dull, having no excitement [1–2]   _____

2.   demanding, exhausting [3–4]   _____

3.   tiresome, monotonous, boring [3–4]   _____

4.   very important [6–7]   _____

5.   describing something that can't be reversed [10–11]   _____

6.   sociable, enjoying others' company [11–12]   _____

7.   calm, undisturbed [17–18]   _____

8.   about to happen [17–18]   _____

9. practical, dealing with facts [17–18]   _____

10. dismayed, filled with consternation [20–21]   _____

G. USING VOCABULARY

From the following list of vocabulary words, choose a word that fits in each blank according to both the grammatical structure of the sentence and the context. Use each word in the list only once and add noun or verb endings (such as -s, -ing, or -ed) if necessary. (Note that there are more words than sentences.)

migrant	grim	tedious
subject (verb)	desperately	stigmatize
arrogance	monotonous	lament
melancholic	barrage	anticlimactic

1. The author writes that when she first began working with the conveyor-

    belt ladies, she behaved with an icy _____ and felt
    that working with only other Mexicans would forever

    _____ her with her Anglo friends.

2. Because working in the vegetable-packing sheds was so

    _____, the women amused themselves gossiping and

    laughing; but often their talk would be _____, and

    they would _____ the hardships of their lives.

3. Most people who work in the fields are called _____
    workers because they follow the crops; however, the conveyor-belt ladies
    worked indoors in sheds, and as a result were not

    _____ to bad weather as pickers are.

H. TOPICS FOR WRITING OR DISCUSSION

1. In your own words summarize Guilbault's experience working with the

    women described in the selection. _____

    _____

    _____

    _____

    _____

    _____

_____

_____

2.   Recount an experience in which you learned something you didn't expect to, which taught you something about life or the real world that you didn't know before.

6

James Herriot

ALL CREATURES GREAT AND SMALL: "TERRY WATSON AND HIS COW"

James Herriot is a practicing veterinarian who grew up in Scotland where he attended Glasgow Veterinary College. He has worked as a practicing veterinarian in the Yorkshire Dales of northern England all his life. A gifted storyteller, Herriot has published several collections of stories describing his experiences, among them All Things Bright and Beautiful, The Lord God Made Them All, *and* All Creatures Great and Small, *from which this selection comes.*

VOCABULARY PREVIEW

WORD ORIGINS

MERCURIAL
In paragraph 7, Herriot mentions that he lived at Skeldale House with his boss, Siegfried, and with Siegfried's rather lazy brother, Tristan. He describes Siegfried as "gifted but *mercurial.*" This adjective is derived from the name of the Roman god Mercury, who served both as messenger to the other gods and as the god of commerce, travel, and thievery. The adjective *mercurial* describes the characteristics associated with the god Mercury, namely, being fickle or having a changeable temperament.

BEWILDERMENT
Toward the end of the selection, in paragraph 32, Herriot writes that he felt *bewilderment* as he considered the remarkable recovery made by Terry Watson's cow. Meaning a state of confusion or perplexity, this noun is derived from the verb *bewilder*. It can be broken down like this:

[*be-* + *wilder*, an archaic root meaning "to stray," probably derived from *wilderness*]

65

This current meaning is a logical extension from the original meaning, describing a state of confusion experienced when someone is lost in a wilderness.

WORD PARTS

-ITIS

This common suffix is a medical term meaning "inflammation of." Terry Watson's cow developed *mastitis*, in other words, inflammation of her udders. Many medical terms end with this suffix, for example, *bronchitis*, *appendicitis*, and *tonsilitis* (respectively, inflammation of the bronchial tubes, the appendix, and the tonsils).

-ABLE

This English suffix, meaning simply "able to" or "capable of," is used in hundreds of words to form an adjective from a stem. For example, in paragraph 10 Herriot says that summer mastitis in cows is nearly always *incurable* ("unable to be cured)." It can easily be broken down into prefix, root, and suffix: [*in-* (not) + *cure* + *-able*].

Some other words using this suffix are *debatable* (capable of being debated), *enjoyable* (capable of being enjoyed), *incomprehensible* (incapable of being comprehended), and *measurable* (able to be measured). *-Able* is also commonly tacked on to new words in the English language, as we see in *microwaveable*, *rechargeable*, and *programmable*.

WORD FAMILIES

BOVINE (and other words associated with animals)

The word *bovine* (see paragraph 29) can be either a noun referring to a cow or an adjective meaning "cowlike" or "resembling a cow." There are many words in the family of adjectives describing animals; all are formed from Latin roots plus the adjective suffix *-ine*, for example:

canine	characteristic of a dog [*canis*—dog]
feline	characteristic of a cat [*fēlēs*—cat]
lupine	wolflike [*lupus*—wolf]
equine	referring to a horse [*equus*—horse]
serpentine	like a serpent [*serpent*—"crawling thing"]
leonine	pertaining to a lion [*leō*—lion]
vulpine	resembling a fox [*vulpēs*—fox]
porcine	piglike [*porcus*—pig]

JAMES HERRIOT

ALL CREATURES GREAT AND SMALL: "TERRY WATSON AND HIS COW"

1   I had been away for only two weeks but it was enough to bring it home to me afresh that working in the high country had something for me that was missing elsewhere. My first visit took me up on one of the narrow, unfenced roads which join Sildale

and Cosdale and when I had ground my way to the top in bottom gear I did what I so often did—pulled the car on to the roadside turf and got out.

2   That quotation about not having time to stand and stare has never applied to me. I seem to have spent a good part of my life—probably too much—in just standing and staring and I was at it again this morning. From up here you could see away over the Plain of York to the sprawl of the Hambleton Hills forty miles to the east, while behind me, the ragged miles of moorland rolled away, dipping and rising over the flat fell-top. In my year at Darrowby I must have stood here scores of times and the view across the plain always looked different; sometimes in the winter the low country was a dark trough between the snow-covered Pennines and the distant white gleam of the Hambletons, and in April the rain squalls drifted in slow, heavy veils across the great green and brown dappled expanse. There was a day, too, when I stood in brilliant sunshine looking down over miles of thick fog like a rippling layer of cotton wool with dark tufts of trees and hilltops pushing through here and there.

3   But today the endless patchwork of fields slumbered in the sun, and the air, even on the hill, was heavy with the scents of summer. There must be people working among the farms down there, I knew, but I couldn't see a living soul; and the peace which I always found in the silence and the emptiness of the moors filled me utterly.

4   At these times I often seemed to stand outside myself, calmly assessing my progress. It was easy to flick back over the years—right back to the time I had decided to become a veterinary surgeon. I could remember the very moment. I was thirteen and I was reading an article about careers for boys in the Meccano Magazine and as I read, I felt a surging conviction that this was for me. And yet what was it based upon? Only that I liked dogs and cats and didn't care much for the idea of an office life; it seemed a frail basis on which to build a career. I knew nothing about agriculture or about farm animals and though, during the years in college, I learned about these things I could see only one future for myself; I was going to be a small animal surgeon. This lasted right up to the time I qualified—a kind of vision of treating people's pets in my own animal hospital where everything would be not just modern but revolutionary. The fully equipped operating theatre, laboratory and X-ray room; they had all stayed crystal clear in my mind until I had graduated M.R.C.V.S.

5   How on earth, then, did I come to be sitting on a high Yorkshire moor in shirt sleeves and wellingtons, smelling vaguely of cows?

6   The change in my outlook had come quite quickly—in fact almost immediately after my arrival in Darrowby. The job had been a godsend in those days of high unemployment, but only, I had thought, a stepping-stone to my real ambition. But everything had switched round, almost in a flash.

7   Maybe it was something to do with the incredible sweetness of the air which still took me by surprise when I stepped out into the old wild garden at Skeldale House every morning. Or perhaps the daily piquancy of life in the graceful old house with my gifted but mercurial boss, Siegfried, and his reluctant student brother, Tristan. Or it could be that it was just the realisation that treating cows and pigs and sheep and horses had a fascination I had never even suspected; and this

brought with it a new concept of myself as a tiny wheel in the great machine of British agriculture. There was a kind of solid satisfaction in that.

8   Probably it was because I hadn't dreamed there was a place like the Dales. I hadn't thought it possible that I could spend all my days in a high, clean-blown land where the scent of grass or trees was never far away; and where even in the driving rain of winter I could snuff the air and find the freshness of growing things hidden somewhere in the cold clasp of the wind.

9   Anyway, it had all changed for me and my work consisted now of driving from farm to farm across the roof of England with a growing conviction that I was a privileged person.

10   I got back into the car and looked at my list of visits; it was good to be back and the day passed quickly. It was about seven o'clock in the evening, when I thought I had finished, that I had a call from Terry Watson, a young farm worker who kept two cows of his own. One of them, he said, had summer mastitis. Mid-July was a bit early for this but in the later summer months we saw literally hundreds of these cases; in fact a lot of the farmers called it 'August Bag'. It was an unpleasant condition because it was just about incurable and usually resulted in the cow losing a quarter (the area of the udder which supplies each teat with milk) and sometimes even her life.

11   Terry Watson's cow looked very sick. She had limped in from the field at milking time, swinging her right hind leg wide to keep it away from the painful udder, and now she stood trembling in her stall, her eyes staring anxiously in front of her. I drew gently at the affected teat and, instead of milk, a stream of dark, foul-smelling serum spurted into the tin can I was holding.

12   'No mistaking that stink, Terry,' I said. 'It's the real summer type all right.' I felt my way over the hot, swollen quarter and the cow lifted her leg quickly as I touched the tender tissue. 'Pretty hard, too. It looks bad, I'm afraid.'

13   Terry's face was grim as he ran his hand along the cow's back. He was in his early twenties, had a wife and a small baby and was one of the breed who was prepared to labour all day for somebody else and then come home and start work on his own few stock. His two cows, his few pigs and hens made a big difference to somebody who had to live on thirty shillings a week.

14   'Ah can't understand it,' he muttered. 'It's usually dry cows that get it and this 'uns still giving two gallons a day. I'd have been on with tar if only she'd been dry.' (The farmers used to dab the teats of the dry cows with Stockholm tar to keep off the flies which were blamed for carrying the infection.)

15   'No, I'm afraid all cows can get it, especially the ones that are beginning to dry off.' I pulled the thermometer from the rectum—it said a hundred and six.

16   'What's going to happen, then? Can you do owt* for her?'

17   'I'll do what I can, Terry. I'll give her an injection and you must strip the teat out as often as you can, but you know as well as I do that it's a poor outlook with these jobs.'

18   'Aye, ah know all about it.' He watched me gloomily as I injected the Coryne pyogenes toxoid into the cow's neck. (Even now we are still doing this for summer mastitis because it is a sad fact none of the modern range of antibiotics has much

*anything

effect on it.) 'She'll lose her quarter, won't she, and maybe she'll even peg out?'

19   I tried to be cheerful. 'Well, I don't think she'll die, and even if the quarter goes she'll make it up on the other three.' But there was the feeling of helplessness I always had when I could do little about something which mattered a great deal. Because I knew what a blow this was to the young man; a three-teated cow has lost a lot of her market value and this was about the best outcome I could see. I didn't like to think about the possibility of the animal dying.

20   'Look, is there nowt† at all I can do myself? Is the job a bad 'un do you think?' Terry Watson's thin cheeks were pale and as I looked at the slender figure with the slightly stooping shoulders I thought, not for the first time, that he didn't look robust enough for his hard trade.

21   'I can't guarantee anything,' I said. 'But the cases that do best are the ones that get the most stripping. So work away at it this evening—every half hour if you can manage it. That rubbish in her quarter can't do any harm if you draw it out as soon as it is formed. And I think you ought to bathe the udder with warm water and massage it well.'

22   'What'll I rub it with?'

23   'Oh, it doesn't matter what you use. The main thing is to move the tissue about so that you can get more of that stinking stuff out. Vaseline would do nicely.'

24   'Ah've got a bowl of goose grease.'

25   'O.K. use that.' I reflected that there must be a bowl of goose grease on most farms; it was the all-purpose lubricant and liniment for man and beast.

26   Terry seemed relieved at the opportunity to do something. He fished out an old bucket, tucked the milking stool between his legs and crouched down against the cow. He looked up at me with a strangely defiant expression. 'Right,' he said. 'I'm startin' now.'

27   As it happened, I was called out early the next morning to a milk fever and on the way home I decided to look in at the Watsons' cottage. It was about eight o'clock and when I entered the little two-stall shed, Terry was in the same position as I had left him on the previous night. He was pulling at the infected teat, eyes closed, cheek resting against the cow's flank. He started as though roused from sleep when I spoke.

28   'Hello, you're having another go, I see.'

29   The cow looked round, too, at my words and I saw immediately, with a thrill of pleasure that she was immeasurably improved. She had lost her blank stare and was looking at me with the casual interest of the healthy bovine and best of all, her jaws were moving with that slow, regular, lateral grind that every vet loves to see.

30   'My God, Terry, she looks a lot better. She isn't like the same cow!'

31   The young man seemed to have difficulty in keeping his eyes open but he smiled. 'Aye, and come and have a look at this end.' He rose slowly from the stool, straightened his back a little bit at a time and leaned his elbow on the cow's rump.

32   I bent down by the udder, feeling carefully for the painful swelling of last night, but my hand came up against a smooth, yielding surface and, in disbelief, I kneaded the tissue between my fingers. The animal showed no sign of discomfort. With a feeling of bewilderment I drew on the teat with thumb and forefinger; the

†nothing

quarter was nearly empty but I did manage to squeeze a single jet of pure white milk on to my palm.

33 'What's going on here, Terry? You must have switched cows on me. You're having me on, aren't you?'

34 'Nay, guvnor,' the young man said with his slow smile. 'It's same cow all right—she's better, that's all.'

35 'But it's impossible! What the devil have you done to her?'

36 'Just what you told me to do. Rub and strip.'

37 I scratched my head. 'But she's back to normal. I've never seen anything like it.'

38 'Aye, I know you haven't.' It was a woman's voice and I turned and saw young Mrs. Watson standing at the door holding her baby. 'You've never seen a man that would rub and strip a cow right round the clock, have you?'

39 'Round the clock?' I said.

40 She looked at her husband with a mixture of concern and exasperation. 'Yes, he's been there on that stool since you left last night. Never been to bed, never been in for a meal. I've been bringing him bits and pieces and cups of tea. Great fool—it's enough to kill anybody.'

41 I looked at Terry and my eyes moved from the pallid face over the thin, slightly swaying body to the nearly empty bowl of goose grease at his feet. 'Good Lord, man,' I said. 'You've done the impossible but you must be about all in. Anyway, your cow is as good as new—you don't need to do another thing to her, so you can go in and have a bit of rest.'

42 'Nay, I can't do that.' He shook his head and straightened his shoulders. 'I've got me work to go to and I'm late as it is.' ■

From James Herriot, ''Terry Watson and His Cow'' [my title], from *All Creatures Great and Small*, St. Martin's Press, New York, 1972, pp. 215–221. Reprinted by permission.

EXERCISES

Do not refer to the selection for Exercises A and B.

A. DETERMINING THE MAIN IDEA AND PURPOSE
Choose the best answer.

1. _____ The main idea of the selection is that (a) Terry Watson's hard work resulted in a nearly miraculous cure of his cow's mastitis; (b) being a veterinarian is an unpredictable but rewarding occupation; (c) life in the Dales area of Yorkshire is quiet and peaceful; (d) summer mastitis is a potentially life-threatening disease affecting cows that is almost never curable.

2. _____ With respect to the main idea, the author's purpose is (a) to convince the reader about a controversial idea; (b) to describe an experience; (c) to explain and to inform; (d) to show the steps in a process.

B.   COMPREHENDING MAIN IDEAS

Choose the correct answer.

1.   _____ The moors, the broad expanses of open land associated with Yorkshire, always gave Herriot a feeling of (a) loneliness and isolation; (b)
peace and silence; (c) gloom and sadness; (d) happiness and exhilaration.

2.   _____ When Herriot decided to become a veterinarian, he initially wanted
to take care of (a) sheep and cows; (b) horses; (c) all farm animals; (d)
dogs and cats.

3.   _____ Summer mastitis, the inflammation that infected Terry Watson's
cow, (a) nearly always resulted in the cow's death; (b) was incurable and
usually resulted in the cow's losing one of her udders; (c) was easy to
cure with antibiotics; (d) was curable only by performing risky surgery.

4.   _____ Although Terry Watson kept a small number of livestock for his
own use, his regular occupation was as a (a) mine worker; (b) veterinarian's assistant; (c) farm worker; (d) office clerk.

5.   _____ The cow was important to Terry Watson because (a) he hoped to
sell the cow for a good price; (b) she was the first cow he had ever
bought, and he felt very attached to her; (c) she was a good milk-pro-
ducer; (d) he did not earn very much money, so she and his other livestock helped feed his family.

6.   _____ To help ease the cow's condition, Herriot recommended that Terry
Watson (a) sterilize the affected area; (b) cauterize the cow's affected
udder; (c) rub and strip the affected area; (d) put the cow to sleep to
avoid her suffering further pain.

COMPREHENSION SCORE

Score your answers for Exercises A and B as follows:

A.   No. right _____ × 2 = _____

B.   No. right _____ × 1 = _____

Total pts. from A and B _____ × 10 = _____%

You may refer to the selection for the remaining exercises.

C.   RECOGNIZING SUPPORTING DETAILS

Place an X in the space for each statement that *directly* supports this main idea
from the selection: **"Terry Watson's cow looked very sick."**

1.   _____ She had limped in from the field at milking time, swinging her
right hind leg wide to keep it away from the painful udder.

2.   _____ Now she stood trembling in her stall, her eyes staring anxiously in
front of her.

3. _____ I drew gently at the affected teat and, instead of milk, a stream of dark, foul-smelling serum spurted into the tin can I was holding.

4. _____ "It's the real summer [mastitis] all right."

5. _____ Terry's face was grim as he ran his hand along the cow's back.

6. _____ He was in his early twenties, had a wife and a small baby and was one of the breed who was prepared to labour all day for somebody else and then come home and start work on his own few stock.

D.   MAKING INFERENCES

For each of these statements write Y (Yes) if the inference is an acurate one, N (No) if the inference is an inaccurate one, or CT (Can't Tell) if you do not have enough information to make an inference.

1. _____ Herriot decided to establish his veterinary practice in Yorkshire because he had visited the region extensively in his youth.

2. _____ Initially, Herriot planned to work in Yorkshire only temporarily before fulfilling his real ambition of becoming a veterinary surgeon.

3. _____ Herriot's dream of an ultramodern veterinary hospital came true for him with the establishment of his Yorkshire practice.

4. _____ The normal temperature for a cow is 98.6 degrees, the same as it is for humans.

5. _____ Herriot was both bewildered by and impressed with the cow's quick recovery.

6. _____ Herriot admired Terry Watson's devotion to his cow.

E.   ANALYZING ORGANIZATION AND SEEING RELATIONSHIPS

Choose the correct answer.

1. _____ Look again at paragraphs 1–3. The dominant characteristic suggested by the descriptive details in this section is (a) Herriot's love of nature; (b) the special beauty and peacefulness of Yorkshire; (c) Yorkshire's unpredictable weather changes; (d) the loneliness and emptiness of the Yorkshire moors.

2. Near the end of paragraph 7, Herriot writes, ". . . this brought with it a new concept of myself as a tiny wheel in the great machine of British agriculture." Rewrite this sentence in your own words. _____

_____

_____

3. _____ In paragraph 6 Herriot mentions the change in his outlook after he moved to Yorkshire. With respect to this main idea, paragraphs 7 and 8

are developed by (a) contrasting ideas; (b) definitions of important words; (c) short examples; (d) reasons.

4.   In paragraph 9 the author writes that he was "driving from farm to farm across the roof of England." Explain what he means by this metaphor. ___

_____

_____

5.   _____ In paragraph 13 Herriot says that Terry Watson was "one of the breed who was prepared to labour all day for somebody else and then come home and start work on his own few stock"; and at the end of the essay he writes that Watson went to work despite his fatigue. By these examples Herriot means to emphasize Watson's (a) ambition and determination to succeed economically; (b) willingness to work hard to support his family; (c) trustworthiness and loyalty; (d) sensitivity to others' needs.

6.   _____ Herriot's tone, his emotional attitude toward the topic, can be best described as (a) neutral, objective; (b) skeptical, unbelieving; (c) admiring, laudatory; (d) emotionally sentimental.

F.   **UNDERSTANDING VOCABULARY**
Choose the correct definition according to the context.

1.   _____ fields *slumbered* in the sun [paragraph 3]: (a) glistened; (b) stirred; (c) became alive; (d) slept.

2.   _____ the peace filled me *utterly* [3]: (a) quickly; (b) completely; (c) joyfully; (d) quietly.

3.   _____ calmly *assessing* my progress [4]: (a) evaluating; (b) considering; (c) remembering; (d) estimating.

4.   _____ a surging *conviction* [4]: (a) guilty finding; (b) strong belief; (c) remembrance; (d) reluctance.

5.   _____ a *frail* basis on which to build a career [4]: (a) delicate; (b) fragile; (c) weak; (d) silly.

6.   _____ my gifted but *mercurial* boss [7]: (a) thieving; (b) moody; (c) unpredictable; (d) changeable.

7.   _____ Terry's face was *grim* [13]: (a) stern, rigid; (b) ghastly, gruesome; (c) evil, sinister; (d) unemotional, impassive.

8.   _____ didn't look *robust* enough [20]: (a) interested; (b) determined; (c) strong; (d) capable.

9.   _____ a smooth, *yielding* surface [32]: Inclined to (a) give way to pressure or touch; (b) surrender, give up; (c) be productive; (d) furnish, give in return.

10. _____ the *pallid* face [41]: (a) dull, lacking life; (b) abnormally pale; (c) creased, seamed; (d) weatherbeaten.

G. USING VOCABULARY

In parentheses before each sentence are some inflected forms of words from the selection. Study the context and the sentence. Then write the correct form in the space provided. Be sure to add appropriate endings like -s, -ed, or -ing, if necessary.

1. (*revolution, revolutionary, revolutionize*) Before he started his practice, Herriot thought that he would open up a small-animal hospital and

_____ the practice of veterinary medicine.

2. (*defiance, defiant, defiantly*) Terry Watson looked at Herriot almost

_____ before he began to work on his cow.

3. (*immeasurableness, immeasurability, immeasurable, immeasurably*) When Herriot returned to Watson's barn the next morning, he saw that the cow

had _____ improved.

4. (*bewilder, bewilderment, bewilderingly*) Herriot was completely

_____ by the cow's remarkable improvement.

5. (*exasperation, exasperate, exasperatedly*) Terry Watson's wife felt both con-

cerned and _____ with her husband.

H. TOPICS FOR WRITING OR DISCUSSION

1. Write a short paragraph in which you enumerate Terry Watson's good

qualities. _____

_____

_____

_____

_____

_____

2. Whom do you admire? Describe the good qualities of someone you ad-mire, either living or dead, famous or ordinary. Be sure to include specific examples to support these qualities.

7

Charles Finney

THE LIFE AND DEATH OF A WESTERN GLADIATOR

In this fictional account Charles Finney describes the life cycle of Crotalus, a diamondback rattlesnake, one of the most feared yet splendid creatures that inhabit the western United States.

VOCABULARY PREVIEW

WORD ORIGINS

NEMESIS

In paragraph 12 Finney says that the *nemesis* of Crotalus's sister was a kind of bird called a road runner, because the bird ate her. The Greek word *nemesis* ("just fate") comes from *nemein*, "to measure what is due," "to allot." In Greek mythology, ideas were often associated with gods and goddesses, and *Nemesis* was also the name of the goddess of vengeance. In *Thereby Hangs a Tale*, Charles Funk describes her role:

> She measured out happiness and unhappiness, and saw to it that any who were too greatly or too frequently blessed by fortune were visited in equal measure by loss or suffering. From this last she became looked upon as the goddess of retribution, as a goddess of vengeance and punishment.

In this context, *nemesis* means "an unbeatable rival" or "one who causes a downfall."

DIABOLICALLY

Finney describes Crotalus in his mature state as "*diabolically* beautiful and deadly poison" (paragraph 32). The adverb *diabolically* refers to the devil. The origin of the adjective form, *diabolic*, illustrates the historical route many words took before they came into modern English. *Diabolic* can be traced back to Middle English, to French, to Latin, and originally to the Greek word for *devil*—*diabolos*, which, in turn, came from a verb meaning "to slander or to accuse."

75

Apparently, the Greeks believed that the devil was the "accuser" of the soul, the enemy of mankind. However, in this context when Finney describes Crotalus as *"diabolically* beautiful," he is describing a kind of beauty that is extraordinarily dangerous.

WORD PARTS

DE-

The prefix *de-* has several meanings, one of which means removal of something. Therefore, *dehydration* (see paragraph 3) means the process of removing water from something. Here is how the word is broken down:

[*dē-* ("removal of") + *hydr* ("water") + *-ation*]

Incidentally, new words ending with the common noun suffix *-tion* will be easy to pronounce if you remember that the primary accent or stress mark always occurs on the syllable just *before* the suffix: dē hī drā' shen. Some other words with the prefix *de-*:

dehumidify	to remove moisture from
decapitate	to cut off one's head
decriminalize	to eliminate criminal penalties for possession and use, as in *decriminalizing* possession of marijuana
detoxify	to rid of poisons or their effects
deflate	to release gas or air from something inflated

WORD FAMILIES

SOMNOLENT

In paragraph 13 Finney describes Crotalus as *somnolent*, or sleepy, as he lies in his cave. Somnolent is from the Latin word *somnus*, meaning "sleep." English has a few words in this family that refer to sleep.

somnolence	sleepy
insomnia	the inability to sleep
insomniac	one who suffers from insomnia
somnambulate	to sleepwalk

In addition, this root can be seen in many sleep-inducing products available in drugstores, like *Sominex* and *Unisom*.

CHARLES FINNEY

THE LIFE AND DEATH OF A WESTERN GLADIATOR

1   He was born on a summer morning in the shady mouth of a cave. Three others were born with him, another male and two females. Each was about five inches long and slimmer than a lead pencil.

2   Their mother left them a few hours after they were born. A day after that his brother and sisters left him also. He was all alone. Nobody cared whether he lived or died. His tiny brain was very dull. He had no arms or legs. His skin was delicate. Nearly everything that walked on the ground or burrowed in it, that flew in the air or swam in the water or climbed trees was his enemy. But he didn't know that. He knew nothing at all. He was aware of his own existence, and that was the sum of his knowledge.

3   The direct rays of the sun could, in a short time, kill him. If the temperature dropped too low he would freeze. Without food he would starve. Without moisture he would die of dehydration. If a man or a horse stepped on him he would be crushed. If anything chased him he could run neither very far nor very fast.

4   Thus it was at the hour of his birth. Thus it would be, with modifications, all his life.

5   But against these drawbacks he had certain qualifications that fitted him to be a competitive creature of this world and equipped him for its warfare. He could exist a long time without food or water. His very smallness at birth protected him when he most needed protection. Instinct provided him with what he lacked in experience. In order to eat he first had to kill; and he was eminently adapted for killing. In sacs in his jaws he secreted a virulent posion. To inject that poison he had two fangs, hollow and pointed. Without that poison and those fangs he would have been among the most helpless creatures on earth. With them he was among the deadliest.

6   He was, of course, a baby rattlesnake, a desert diamondback, named Crotalus atrox by the herpetologists Baird and Girard and so listed in the *Catalogue of North American Reptiles* in its issue of 1853. He was grayish brown in color with a series of large dark diamond-shaped blotches on his back. His tail was white with five black cross-bands. It had a button on the end of it.

7   Little Crotalus lay in the dust in the mouth of his cave. Some of his kinfolk lay there too. It was their home. That particular tribe of rattlers had lived there for scores of years.

8   The cave had never been seen by a white man.

9   Sometimes as many as two hundred rattlers occupied the den. Sometimes the numbers shrunk to as few as forty or fifty.

10   The tribe members did nothing at all for each other except breed. They hunted singly; they never shared their food. They derived some automatic degree of safety from their numbers, but their actions were never concerted toward using their numbers to any end. If an enemy attacked one of them, the others did nothing about it.

11   Young Crotalus's brother was the first of the litter to go out into the world and the first to die. He achieved a distance of fifty feet from the den when a Sonoran racer, four feet long and hungry, came upon him. The little rattler, despite his poison fangs, was a tidbit. The racer, long skilled in such arts, snatched him up by the head and swallowed him down. Powerful digestive juices in the racer's stomach did the rest. Then the racer, appetite whetted, prowled around until it found one of Crotalus's little sisters. She went the way of the brother.

12   Nemesis of the second sister was a chaparral cock. This cuckoo, or road runner

as it is called, found the baby amid some rocks, uttered a cry of delight, scissored it by the neck, shook it until it was almost lifeless, banged and pounded it upon a rock until life had indeed left it, and then gulped it down.

13   Crotalus, somnolent in a cranny of the cave's mouth, neither knew nor cared. Even if he had, there was nothing he could have done about it.

14   On the fourth day of his life he decided to go out into the world himself. He rippled forth uncertainly, the transverse plates on his belly serving him as legs.

15   He could see things well enough within his limited range, but a five-inch-long snake can command no great field of vision. He had an excellent sense of smell. But, having no ears, he was stone deaf. On the other hand, he had a pit, a deep pock mark between eye and nostril. Unique, this organ was sensitive to animal heat. In pitch blackness, Crotalus, by means of the heat messages recorded in his pit, could tell whether another animal was near and could also judge its size. That was better than an ear.

16   The single button on his tail could not, of course, yet rattle. Crotalus wouldn't be able to rattle until that button had grown into three segments. Then he would be able to buzz.

17   He had a wonderful tongue. It looked like an exposed nerve and was probably exactly that. It was forked, and Crotalus thrust it in and out as he traveled. It told him things that neither his eyes nor his nose nor his pit told him.

18   Snake fashion, Crotalus went forth, not knowing where he was going, for he had never been anywhere before. Hunger was probably his prime mover. In order to satisfy that hunger he had to find something smaller than himself and kill it.

19   He came upon a baby lizard sitting in the sand. Eyes, nose, pit, and tongue told Crotalus it was there. Instinct told him what it was and what to do. Crotalus gave a tiny one-inch strike and bit the lizard. His poison killed it. He took it by the head and swallowed it. Thus was his first meal.

20   During his first two years Crotalus grew rapidly. He attained a length of two feet; his tail had five rattles on it and its button. He rarely bothered with lizards any more, preferring baby rabbits, chipmunks, and round-tailed ground squirrels. Because of his slow locomotion he could not run down these agile little things. He had to contrive instead to be where they were when they would pass. Then he struck swiftly, injected his poison, and ate them after they died.

21   At two he was formidable. He had grown past the stage where a racer or a road runner could safely tackle him. He had grown to the size where other desert dwellers—coyotes, foxes, coatis, wildcats—knew it was better to leave him alone.

22   And, at two, Crotalus became a father, his life being regulated by cycles. His cycles were plantlike. The peach tree does not "know" when it is time to flower, but flower it does because its cycle orders it to do so.

23   In the same way, Crotalus did not "know" when it was time for young desert diamondback rattlers to pair off and breed. But his cycle knew.

24   He found "her" on a rainy morning. Crotalus's courtship at first was sinuous and subtle, slow and stealthy. Then suddenly it became dynamic. A period of exhaustion followed. Two metabolic machines had united to produce new metabolic machines.

25   Of that physical union six new rattlesnakes were born. Thus Crotalus, at two,

had carried out his major primary function: he had reproduced his kind. In two years he had experienced everything that was reasonably possible for desert diamondback rattlesnakes to experience except death.

26   He had not experienced death for the simple reason that there had never been an opportunity for anything bigger and stronger than himself to kill him. Now, at two, because he was so formidable, that opportunity became more and more unlikely.

27   He grew more slowly in the years following his initial spurt. At the age of twelve he was five feet long. Few of the other rattlers in his den were older or larger than he.

28   He had a castanet of fourteen segments. It had been broken off occasionally in the past, but with each new molting a new segment appeared.

29   His first skin-shedding back in his babyhood had been a bewildering experience. He did not know what was happening. His eyes clouded over until he could not see. His skin thickened and dried until it cracked in places. His pit and his nostrils ceased to function. There was only one thing to do and that was to get out of that skin.

30   Crotalus managed it by nosing against the bark of a shrub until he forced the old skin down over his head, bunching it like the rolled top of a stocking around his neck. Then he pushed around among rocks and sticks and branches, literally crawling out of his skin by slow degrees. Wriggling free at last, he looked like a brand new snake. His skin was bright and satiny, his eyes and nostrils were clear, his pit sang with sensation.

31   For the rest of his life he was to molt three or four times a year. Each time he did it he felt as if he had been born again.

32   At twelve he was a magnificent reptile. Not a single scar defaced his rippling symmetry. He was diabolically beautiful and deadly poison.

33   His venom was his only weapon, for he had no power of constriction. Yellowish in color, his poison was odorless and tasteless. It was a highly complex mixture of proteids, each in itself direly toxic. His venom worked on the blood. The more poison he injected with a bite, the more dangerous the wound. The pain rendered by his bite was instantaneous, and the shock accompanying it was profound. Swelling began immediately, to be followed by a ghastly oozing. Injected directly into a large vein, his poison brought death quickly, for the victim died when it reached his heart.

34   At the age of twenty Crotalus was the oldest and largest rattler in his den. He was six feet long and weighed thirteen pounds. His whole world was only about a mile in radius. He had fixed places where he avoided the sun when it was hot and he was away from his cave. He knew his hunting grounds thoroughly, every game trail, every animal burrow.

35   He was a fine old machine, perfectly adapted to his surroundings, accustomed to a life of leisure and comfort. He dominated his little world.

36   The mighty seasonal rhythms of the desert were as vast pulsations, and the lives of the rattlesnakes were attuned to them. Spring sun beat down, spring rains fell, and, as the plants of the desert ended their winter hibernations, so did the vipers in their lair. The plants opened forth and budded; the den "opened" too, and

the snakes crawled forth. The plants fertilized each other, and new plants were born. The snakes bred, and new snakes were produced. The desert was repopulated.

37 In the autumn the plants began to close; in the same fashion the snake den began to close, the reptiles returned to it, lay like lingering blossoms about its entrance for a while, then disappeared within it when winter came. There they slept until summoned forth by a new spring.

38 Crotalus was twenty years old. He was in the golden age of his viperhood.

39 But men were approaching. Spilling out of their cities, men were settling in that part of the desert where Crotalus lived. They built roads and houses, set up fences, dug for water, planted crops.

40 They homesteaded the land. They brought new animals with them—cows, horses, dogs, cats, barnyard fowl.

41 The roads they built were death traps for the desert dwellers. Every morning new dead bodies lay on the roads, the bodies of the things the men had run over and crushed in their vehicles.

42 That summer Crotalus met his first dog. It was a German shepherd which had been reared on a farm in the Midwest and there had gained the reputation of being a snake-killer. Black snakes, garter snakes, pilots, water snakes; it delighted in killing them all. It would seize them by the middle, heedless of their tiny teeth, and shake them violently until they died.

43 This dog met Crotalus face to face in the desert at dusk. Crotalus had seen coyotes aplenty and feared them not. Neither did the dog fear Crotalus, although Crotalus then was six feet long, as thick in the middle as a motorcycle tire, and had a head the size of a man's clenched fist. Also this snake buzzed and buzzed and buzzed.

44 The dog was brave, and a snake was a snake. The German shepherd snarled and attacked. Crotalus struck him in the underjaw; his fangs sank in almost half an inch and squirted big blobs of hematoxic poison into the tissues of the dog's flesh.

45 The shepherd bellowed with pain, backed off, groveled with his jaws in the desert sand, and attacked again. He seized Crotalus somewhere by the middle of his body and tried to flip him in the air and shake him as, in the past, he had shaken slender black snakes to their death. In return, he received another poison-blurting stab in his flank and a third in the belly and a fourth in the eye as the terrible, writhing snake bit wherever it could sink its fangs.

46 The German shepherd had enough. He dropped the big snake and in sick, agonizing bewilderment crawled somehow back to his master's homestead and died.

47 The homesteader looked at his dead dog and became alarmed. If there was a snake around big enough to kill a dog that size, it could also kill a child and probably a man. It was something that had to be eliminated.

48 The homesteader told his fellow farmers, and they agreed to initiate a war of extermination against the snakes.

49 The campaign during the summer was sporadic. The snakes were scattered over the desert, and it was only by chance that the men came upon them. Even so, at summer's end, twenty-six of the vipers had been killed.

50 When autumn came the men decided to look for the rattlers' den and execute

mass slaughter. The homesteaders had become desert-wise and knew what to look for.

51   They found Crotalus's lair, without too much trouble—a rock outcropping on a slope that faced the south. Cast-off skins were in evidence in the bushes. Bees flew idly in and out of the den's mouth. Convenient benches and shelves of rock were at hand where the snakes might lie for a final sunning in the autumn air.

52   They killed the three rattlers they found at the den when they first discovered it. They made plans to return in a few more days when more of the snakes had congregated. They decided to bring along dynamite with them and blow up the mouth of the den so that the snakes within would be sealed there forever and the snakes without would have no place to find refuge.

53   On the day the men chose to return nearly fifty desert diamondbacks were gathered at the portals of the cave. The men shot them, clubbed them, smashed them with rocks. Some of the rattlers escaped the attack and crawled into the den.

54   Crotalus had not yet arrived for the autumn rendezvous. He came that night. The den's mouth was a shattered mass of rock, for the men had done their dynamiting well. Dead members of his tribe lay everywhere. Crotalus nosed among them, tongue flicking as he slid slowly along.

55   There was no access to the cave any more. He spent the night outside among the dead. The morning sun warmed him and awakened him. He lay there at full length. He had no place to go.

56   The sun grew hotter upon him and instinctively he began to slide toward some dark shade. Then his senses warned him of some animal presence near by; he stopped, half coiled, raised his head and began to rattle. He saw two upright figures. He did not know what they were because he had never seen men before.

57   "That's the granddaddy of them all," said one of the homesteaders. "It's a good thing we came back." He raised his shotgun.   ■

From Charles Finney, "The Life and Death of a Western Gladiator." Reprinted by permission of Barthold Fles, literary agent.

EXERCISES

Do not refer to the selection for Exercises A and B.

A. DETERMINING THE MAIN IDEA AND PURPOSE
Choose the best answer.

1. _____ The main idea of the story is that (a) the life of a diamondback rattlesnake is harsh; (b) Crotalus was well suited to survive and exist harmoniously in his environment until human civilization intruded; (c) diamondback rattlesnakes are a threat to human settlements; (d) diamondback rattlesnakes can adapt to even the most hostile environment by depending on their instinct to survive.

2. _____ The author's primary purpose in telling this story is to (a) encourage the reader to learn more about rattlesnakes; (b) persuade the reader that rattlesnakes are important to the environment; (c) describe those physical characteristics of the rattlesnake that enable it to survive so well; (d) make the reader aware of and sympathetic to the rattlesnake's life cycle and behavior.

B. COMPREHENDING MAIN IDEAS
Choose the correct answer.

1. _____ In describing the baby stage in a rattlesnake's life, Finney emphasizes its (a) dependence on its mother; (b) well-developed killing instinct; (c) deadly effect on its victims; (d) helplessness and susceptibility to danger.

2. _____ According to the selection, a baby rattlesnake (a) is immediately able to survive; (b) has a well-developed killing instinct; (c) must be taught by older snakes how to kill and fend for itself; (d) is almost totally helpless and susceptible to danger.

3. _____ This particular group of rattlesnakes described in the selection lived (a) in an abandoned farmhouse; (b) in a den or cave; (c) in a large underground cavern; (d) in a quarry.

4. _____ The rattlesnake "senses" the presence of other animals by using its (a) pit; (b) mouth; (c) eyes; (d) ears.

5. _____ Rattlesnakes molt or shed their skin (a) once a year; (b) twice a year; (c) three or four times a year; (d) three or four times in a normal life span.

6. _____ After the homesteaders found the rattlesnakes, they decided to (a) alert the authorities; (b) begin a campaign to decrease their numbers; (c) wage a war of extermination; (d) move them to a more isolated location.

COMPREHENSION SCORE

Score your answers for Exercises A and B as follows:

A. No. right _____ × 2 = _____

B. No. right _____ × 1 = _____

Total pts. from A and B _____ × 10 = _____%

You may refer to the selection for the remaining exercises.

C. RECOGNIZING SUPPORTING DETAILS
Place an X in the space for each statement that *directly* supports this main idea from the selection: "**. . . he had certain qualifications that fitted him to be a competitive creature of this world and equipped him for its warfare.**"

1. _____ The direct rays of the sun could, in a short time, kill him.

2. _____ Without moisture he would die of dehydration.

3. _____ He could exist a long time without food or water.

4. _____ He was eminently adapted for killing by means of the virulent poison contained in sacs in his jaws.

5. _____ To inject that poison he had two fangs, hollow and pointed.

6. _____ Without that poison and those fangs he would have been among the most helpless creatures on earth.

D.   MAKING INFERENCES
For each of these statements write Y (Yes) if the inference is an accurate one, N (No) if the inference is an inaccurate one, or CT (Can't Tell) if you do not have enough information to make an inference.

1. _____ The survival rate of baby rattlesnakes is high.

2. _____ Ironically, rattlesnakes are solitary creatures; they live communally, but they do not work together in any way.

3. _____ The "pit," the rattlesnake's main sensing device, is used to detect the presence of potential victims and enemies.

4. _____ A rattlesnake is severely handicapped without any sense of hearing.

5. _____ An adult male rattlesnake mates every two years.

6. _____ When a segment of a rattlesnake's tail breaks off, it is never replaced.

7. _____ The rattlesnake's best weapon is its power of constriction; that is, its ability to coil itself around an enemy.

8. _____ The homesteaders were familiar with the benefits of snakes on the natural environment.

9. _____ It was illegal for the homesteaders to exterminate the rattlesnake population.

10. _____ Crotalus did not survive the homesteaders' assault.

E.   ANALYZING ORGANIZATION AND SEEING RELATIONSHIPS
Choose the best answer.

1. _____ Finney delays identifying Crotalus as a diamondback rattlesnake until paragraph 6 because (a) he is a disorganized writer who should learn to state his subject at the beginning rather than delay it; (b) he wants to stimulate the reader's curiosity and sympathy; (c) he needs to get background information out of the way before he introduces his subject; (d) it is obvious even at the beginning of the story what kind of animal Crotalus is.

2. _____ The main pattern Finney uses to organize the entire selection is (a) steps in a process; (b) least important details to most important details; (c) chronological or time order; (d) general to specific order.

3. _____ Look again through paragraphs 1–8. Most of the sentences are short and simple. What do sentences like this lend to the story? (a) economy, saving space for more important information; (b) emphasis and dramatic effect; (c) suspense and mystery; (d) sincerity.

4. _____ Read paragraphs 22–25 again. In his description of Crotalus's mating he emphasizes that reproduction is largely the result of (a) intense sexual desire; (b) a romantic tendency; (c) the instinct to repopulate the species with new members; (d) the physical instinct to reproduce.

5. _____ In his description of the homesteaders' extermination campaign, Finney strongly implies that the white men (a) were ignorant of the principle of the balance of nature; (b) were genuinely concerned for the environment, since rattlesnakes are the enemy of all wildlife; (c) killed the snakes merely for sport or pleasure; (d) were seeking revenge for the German shepherd's death.

6. _____ From the author's description of the homesteaders' campaign and Crotalus's death, he intends the reader to feel (a) fear; (b) hostility; (c) anxiety; (d) sorrow.

F.   UNDERSTANDING VOCABULARY

Look through the paragraphs listed below and find a word that matches each definition. An example has been done for you.

Ex. changes, alterations [3–4]   _____modifications_____

1. actively poisonous [5–6]   _____

2. an unbeatable rival [12–13]   _____

3. sleepy [12–13]   _____

4. to plan cleverly, devise [20–21]   _____

5. not immediately obvious, cunning [24–25]   _____

6. active, forceful, energetic [24–25]   _____

7. awesome in strength, intimidating [26–27]   _____

8. dangerously, wickedly [32–33]   _____

9. dreadful, horrible [33–34]   _____

10. thorough, deep, pervasive [33–34]   _____

11. confusion, complete puzzlement [45–46]   _____

12. occurring irregularly [48–49]   _____

13. to begin [48–49]   _____

14. assembled; come together in a crowd [51–52]   _____

15. shelter or protection from danger [52–53]   _____

G. USING VOCABULARY
In parentheses before each sentence are some inflected forms of words from the selection. Study the context and the structure of the sentence and then write the correct form in the space provided. Add appropriate endings like -s, -ed, or -ing, if necessary.

1. (*formidableness, formidability, formidable, formidably*)   Because of Crotalus's

_____ size and strength, it became less likely that another animal could kill him.

2. (*bewilderment, bewilder*)   Crotalus was _____ by his first molting experience.

3. (*symmetry, symmetrical, symmetrically*)   As an adult rattlesnake, Crotalus had a body that was an example of perfect _____.

4. (*domination, dominate, dominant, dominantly*)   Crotalus

_____ that particular tribe of snakes.

5. (*sporadic, sporadically*)   At first the homesteaders carried out their extermination campaign only _____.

H. TOPICS FOR WRITING OR DISCUSSION

1. In the space below, write a short summary of the physical changes Crotalus underwent throughout his life, from his birth to adulthood.

_____
_____
_____
_____
_____
_____

2. Describe the life cycle of an animal or organism that you have studied or observed.

3. An imbalance between the native organisms in an environment is a common problem today. Sometimes these imbalances are a result of human interference with the population; sometimes they have natural causes. For example, in the West, the native deer population has grown to a point where the environment can often no longer support it, mainly because the deer's natural predators—the mountain lion and bobcat population—no longer exist. Do some investigating and gather evidence about an imbalance in the ecology in your area.

PART

2

Refining the Basics

Now that you have practiced some basic comprehension skills with some relatively easy readings, in this section you will read seven slightly more difficult selections. Before you tackle the first one, it might be a good idea to review the exercises you completed in the first section in case any particular one caused you some difficulty. If, for example, you had more trouble with the inference questions than with any of the others, you can study this explanation and then ask your instructor for help if necessary.

MAKING INFERENCES

When you are asked to label statements as Y (Yes), N (No), or CT (Can't Tell), it is essential—unless your memory is very good—to look back at the selection. Many of these inference questions are subtle, requiring you to look carefully at the writer's exact words to see what they imply or suggest before you can make a judgment.

Remember that the answer Y means that the statement is worded accurately; it states something the writer implied or suggested. You could "read it between the lines." The N answer means that the statement is either inaccurate or somehow distorted. Save the CT (Can't Tell) choice for a statement either that was not implied at all in the selection or that exists *outside* the selection.

For example, let us look again at three inference questions from selection 7, "The Life and Death of a Western Gladiator," which you have just completed:

2. _____ Ironically, rattlesnakes are solitary creatures; they live communally, but they do not work together in any way.

We can infer that this statement is an accurate inference, which you should have marked "Y" because of what Finney says in paragraphs 7, 9, and 10:

> That particular tribe of rattlers had lived there for scores of years. . . . Sometimes as many as two hundred rattlers occupied the den. Sometimes the numbers shrunk to as few as forty or fifty.
>
> The tribe members did nothing at all for each other except breed. They hunted singly; they never shared their food. They derived some automatic degree of safety from their numbers, but their actions were never concerted toward using their numbers to any end. If an enemy attacked one of them, the others did nothing about it.

4. ____ A rattlesnake is severely handicapped without any sense of hearing.

Finney writes in paragraph 15:

> He had an excellent sense of smell. But, having no ears, he was stone deaf. On the other hand, he had a pit, a deep pock mark between eye and nostril. Unique, this organ was sensitive to animal heat. In pitch blackness, Crotalus, by means of the heat messages recorded in his pit, could tell whether another animal was near and could also judge its size. That was better than an ear.

Therefore, you can infer that rattlesnakes are not handicapped by lacking ears; their eyesight, sense of smell, and the sensing device are all they need. You should have marked N.

Now look at this last inference:

9. ____ It was illegal for the homesteaders to exterminate the rattlesnake population.

Toward the end of the selection, after the homesteader's German shepherd has been killed by a rattlesnake, Finney writes in paragraphs 47 and 48:

> The homesteader looked at his dead dog and became alarmed. If there was a snake around big enough to kill a dog that size, it could also kill a child and probably a man. It was something that had to be eliminated.
>
> The homesteader told his fellow farmers, and they agreed to initiate a war of extermination against the snakes.
>
> The campaign during the summer was sporadic.

Notice that there is no mention of legality or illegality here. The homesteaders apparently decided to begin this extermination campaign themselves, but you *can't tell* from Finney's words whether or not they were doing something illegal. There is no mention of calling the sheriff or of getting permission from someone in authority. Therefore, this is a good example of an inference that should be marked CT.

Here are topics you will be reading about in this group of readings: superstitions and why we believe in them; the universal popularity of basketball, even in Beijing, China; teenage "mall rats"; urban legends, weird stories that sound too good to be true; the experiences of children who traveled west in wagon trains during the great overland migration of the nineteenth century; pack rats, people who accumulate junk; and the displacement of blacks from the Sea Islands off the coast of Georgia and South Carolina.

8

Paul Chance

KNOCK WOOD

If you think that breaking a mirror means seven years of bad luck or that stepping on cracks in the sidewalk will break your mother's back, you are superstitious. This article discusses the phenomenon of superstitions and the psychological motivation behind them. Paul Chance, a regular contributor to Psychology Today, *examines some studies that have been done on superstitions and explains why many people believe in them.*

VOCABULARY PREVIEW

**WORD
ORIGINS**

SUPERSTITIONS
Since the subject of this article is *superstitions*, it seems appropriate to explain its etymology. This word came into Middle English from Old French, originally from Latin, *superstitiō*, and meant "a standing over something (in amazement and awe)," from *super-* ("over") + *stāre* ("to stand"). A superstition is a belief that something we do will influence some event in the future, even if there is no logical connection between them.

SKEPTICS
Skeptics (see paragraph 8) habitually disagree with or doubt generally accepted ideas or conclusions. The word derives from the followers of the ancient Greek philosopher Pyrrho, who believed that human judgment is uncertain because nobody can be certain that things are what they seem to be. They were called the *skeptikoi* ("the hesitants") because they would not state anything positively.

**WORD
PARTS**

PSYCHOLOGY
Psychologists (see paragraph 7) study the human mind. The root of this word is *psyche*, the Greek goddess who personified the soul, and the

suffix is *-logy* ("science" or "study of"). Many words in English end with this Greek suffix, among them:

anthropology	the study of human culture
archeology	the study of antiquity, of man's past culture
etymology	the study of word origins
immunology	the medical study of immunity
pathology	the scientific study of the nature of disease
theology	the study of God, the study of divine truths

WORD FAMILIES

PREJUDICE

In paragraph 8 Chance writes, "Indeed, society is far more dedicated to noting evidence in favor of superstition than it is to observing contrary evidence. This *prejudice* goes a long way toward explaining our superstitious nature." The word *prejudice* comes from Latin: [*pre-* ("before") + *jūdicium* ("judgment")]. When one is prejudiced, he or she makes a negative judgment without having any knowledge of or without examining the facts.

Many other words in English are members of the family of words deriving from *jūdex* ("judge") or *jūdicium*, among them:

judgment	a formal decision; also the mental ability to make reasonable decisions
judge	one who sits in judgment in a court of law
judicial	pertaining to a court of law
judicious	describing someone who exercises sound judgment
adjudicate	to settle a case in court

PAUL CHANCE

KNOCK WOOD

1 Years ago I had a fountain pen that I always used for important things such as taking tests and filling out job applications. It was my lucky pen. It didn't have all the right answers, but with it I believed I could present my ignorance in the most favorable light. I was superstitious in those days, but I have reformed. I gave up all my superstitions, thanks largely to the work of psychologists, who showed me how foolish I was.

2 B. F. Skinner did what was probably the first superstition experiment. He had shown earlier that with a few grains of seed, you can get a pigeon to do nearly anything you want. You merely wait for the desired response, or a reasonable approximation of it, and then provide some food. Each time you do this, the rewarded response becomes stronger.

3 But Skinner wondered about the effect of offering food regularly regardless of what the bird did. One day he put a pigeon into a cage and provided grain every 15

seconds. The bird didn't have to lift a feather to earn these meals, but after awhile it began behaving oddly—it started turning in counterclockwise circles. Most other birds treated in this way also acquired unnecessary habits. One stretched its neck toward a corner; another made brushing movements toward the floor; a third repeatedly bobbed its head up and down, as if dancing to some imaginary drumbeat. Now, none of this activity had any effect; the food arrived every 15 seconds no matter what. Yet the birds behaved as if their actions made the food appear. They had become "superstitious," but why?

4   Skinner's explanation was quite simple. The first time food arrived, the bird had to be doing *something*. If the bird happened to be bobbing its head up and down (something that pigeons are wont to do), then that response was strengthened— that is, became more likely to occur again. This meant that the next time food arrived, the bird was likely to be bobbing its head. The second appearance of food further strengthened head-bobbing, and the cycle continued. Thus, argued Skinner, superstitious behavior is the product of coincidental reward.

5   There is evidence that coincidental reward plays a role in human superstition. In one study, researchers asked high school students to press one or more telegraph keys. If they pressed the third key from the left, a bell would sound, a light would go on and they would earn a nickel. However, the students made money only if they pressed the key a second time after a short interval. If they simply did nothing for a few seconds and then pressed key 3 again, they would be rewarded. But they didn't know that, so they spent the interval pressing keys. Eventually the delay period would end, the student would again press key 3, the bell would ring and the light would flash. Key presses that occurred during the delay were strengthened through coincidental reward.

6   The result was that each student worked out a pattern of key presses, such as 1-1-2-2-3-3 or 4-3-2-1-2-3, and stuck with it. None of this behavior, except pressing key 3, had any effect. But the students were convinced they had worked out the essential combination of key strokes.

7   Although superstition no doubt owes much to coincidental reward, some psychologists insist there is more to the study. If a boy finds a four-leaf clover and shortly afterward trips over a dollar, he may well believe that such clovers are lucky. But it is unlikely that the coincidental appearance of four-leaf clovers and dollars accounts for the popularity of this superstition. However, a boy may hear adults praise the four-leaf clover's power. And if the boy finds a four-leaf clover and something lucky happens to him a week later, the adult will undoubtedly say, "See, that's because of that four-leaf clover you found." If the boy finds another four-leaf clover and nothing good happens to him until puberty, no one points to the clover's failure.

8   Indeed, society is far more dedicated to noting evidence in favor of superstition than it is to observing contrary evidence. This prejudice goes a long way toward explaining our superstitious nature. When the survivors of a plane crash are interviewed, some of them inevitably insist that they were saved by prayer. The chances are good that some who did not survive also prayed for all they were worth, but they are now unable to testify about the value of the procedure. Arguing that evidence for superstitions is biased is unlikely to impress believers, who will point to someone who should have died six or seven times in a motorcycle

accident but was saved by a good-luck charm to endure the ecstasy of life in a coma. Skeptics might reason that if the charm were going to the trouble of making a miracle, it might have done a better job. But that logic won't disturb the faithful.

9   Of course, some superstitions probably have a measure of practicality. In the days of wooden ships and iron men, sailors believed that having a woman on board was bad luck. It doesn't take much imagination to find some sense in the idea that the combination of one woman and 30 or 40 men, isolated at sea for months on end, could prove volatile. Similarly, in some primitive societies hunters engage in a ritual bath before stalking their prey to make themselves pure in spirit. The bath also may make them harder to detect, thus improving their chances of success.

10   True superstitions are activities that have no effects on events but exist because of coincidental rewards and society's prejudices. Of course, I no longer have any superstitions. After I learned from my fellow psychologists how foolish superstitions are, I shed them all. A black cat means nothing to me now, nor does a broken mirror. There are no little plastic icons on the dashboard of my car, and I carry no rabbit's foot. I am free of all such nonsense, and I am happy to report no ill effects—knock wood. ■

From Paul Chance, "Knock Wood," *Psychology Today*, October 1988. Reprinted by permission.

EXERCISES

Do not refer to the selection for Exercises A and B.

A.   DETERMINING THE MAIN IDEA AND PURPOSE
Choose the best answer.

1.   The main idea of the article is that (a) psychologists have studied superstitions extensively; (b) every culture has its own set of superstitions; (c) even pigeons can develop superstitious behavior if they receive enough rewards; (d) superstitious behavior is probably a foolish, but natural, human phenomenon.

2.   With respect to the main idea, the author's purpose is (a) to explain the phenomenon of superstition; (b) to summarize current psychological research; (c) to convince the reader that superstitions are foolish; (d) to show his own experience and good fortune with lucky charms.

B.   COMPREHENDING MAIN IDEAS
Choose the correct answer.

1.   _____ The author begins the article by mentioning his lucky (a) horseshoe; (b) rabbit's foot; (c) pen; (d) coin.

2.   _____ Psychologist B. F. Skinner performed an experiment on pigeons in which he concluded that superstitious behavior is the product of (a) lack of religious faith; (b) coincidental reward; (c) cultural expectations; (d) an overly gullible personality.

3. _____ Another study performed to identify superstitious behavior among high school students rewarded them (a) only when they pressed a certain combination of keys; (b) every three seconds no matter what they did; (c) when they pressed the third key from the left; (d) when they pressed keys during a particular interval.

4. _____ The author cites the example of a four-leaf clover to show that (a) adults pass the idea on to their children that certain objects are lucky; (b) four-leaf clovers really do bring good luck to their finders; (c) four-leaf clovers are not inherently lucky, but owning one can do no harm; (d) people choose silly objects as lucky charms.

5. _____ The author cited two superstitions—women bringing bad luck aboard a ship in the old days and primitive hunters bathing before beginning the hunt—to show that superstitions are (a) occasionally practical; (b) usually foolish; (c) firmly entrenched; (d) based on ignorance.

6. _____ The author defines superstitious activities as those that (a) have some truth to them; (b) have no effect on events in our lives; (c) are the mark of primitive societies; (d) are the result of wishful thinking.

COMPREHENSION SCORE

Score your answers for Exercises A and B as follows:

A. No. right _____ × 2 = _____

B. No. right _____ × 1 = _____

Total pts. from A and B _____ × 10 = _____%

You may refer to the selection for the remaining exercises.

C. DISTINGUISHING BETWEEN MAIN IDEAS AND SUPPORTING DETAILS
Label the following statements from the selection as follows: MI if the statement represents a *main idea* and SD if the statement represents a *supporting detail*.

1. _____ Of course, some superstitions probably have a measure of practicality.

2. _____ In the days of wooden ships and iron men, sailors believed that having a woman on board was bad luck.

3. _____ It doesn't take much imagination to find some sense in the idea that the combination of one woman and 30 or 40 men, isolated at sea for months on end, could prove volatile.

4. _____ Similarly, in some primitive societies hunters engage in a ritual bath before stalking their prey to make themselves pure in spirit.

5.   _____ The bath also may make them harder to detect, thus improving their chances of success.

D.   MAKING INFERENCES

For each of these statements write Y (Yes) if the inference is an accurate one, N (No) if the inference is an inaccurate one, or CT (Can't Tell) if you do not have enough information to make an inference.

1.   _____ B. F. Skinner's study of superstitious behavior among pigeons showed that the birds developed odd and unnecessary habits so that they could be rewarded with food.

2.   _____ Superstitious behavior develops when the response to a coincidental reward is strengthened.

3.   _____ Other kinds of birds besides pigeons have been shown to behave superstitiously.

4.   _____ The research studies cited in the article suggest that superstitious behavior is learned, not inborn.

5.   _____ In the experiment on high school students, the researchers who conducted the study did not tell the students the real nature of the experiment.

6.   _____ The author strongly implies that prayer is a form of superstition.

E.   ANALYZING ORGANIZATION AND SEEING RELATIONSHIPS
Choose the correct answer.

1.   This article has a clear beginning, middle, and end. Write the number of the paragraph where the body begins _____. Then write the number of the paragraph where the conclusion begins _____.

2.   _____ Chance writes toward the end of paragraph 1 that he has reformed and has given up all his superstitions "thanks largely to the work of psychologists, who showed me how foolish I was." In this sentence he is being (a) candid; (b) humble; (c) facetious; (d) sarcastic.

3.   _____ Besides summarizing the findings of Skinner's research, paragraph 3 also uses *two* other methods of paragraph development: (a) cause and effect; (b) definition of a key term; (c) steps in a process; (d) facts and statistics; (e) contrast.

4.   _____ The method of development used in paragraph 7 is (a) definition of a key term; (b) illustration; (c) contrast; (d) steps in a process; (e) analogy—a figurative comparison.

5.   _____ Paragraphs 8 and 9 each begin with transitional words, "indeed"

and "of course." What do these transitions indicate? (a) emphasis; (b) steps in a process; (c) additional information; (d) contrast; (e) conclusions.

6. _____ Consider again this sentence from paragraph 8: "Arguing that evidence for superstitions is biased is unlikely to impress believers, who will point to someone who should have died six or seven times in a motorcycle accident but was saved by a good-luck charm to endure the ecstasy of life in a coma." How would you characterize the humor in this sentence? (a) sarcastic; (b) ironic; (c) lightly witty; (d) dry.

7. What is the purpose of the first sentence of paragraph 10?

    _____

8. _____ When Chance writes in the last sentence, "I am free of all such nonsense, and I am happy to report no ill effects—knock wood," he is being (a) ironic; (b) serious; (c) candid; (d) foolish.

F. **UNDERSTANDING VOCABULARY**
    Choose the correct definition according to the context.

1. _____ you wait for the desired *response* [paragraphs 2 and 4]: (a) answer; (b) reaction; (c) question; (d) activity.

2. _____ a reasonable *approximation* of it [2]: Something that is (a) a good guess; (b) a definite answer; (c) very similar; (d) unique, one of a kind.

3. _____ it started turning in *counterclockwise* circles [3]: (a) a direction that follows the sun's path; (b) a direction that goes the same way that a clock's hands move; (c) a direction that goes the opposite way that a clock's hands move; (d) a random, confused direction, going every which way.

4. _____ something that pigeons are *wont* to do [4]: (a) physically able; (b) physically unable; (c) accustomed; (d) likely.

5. _____ after a short *interval* [5]: (a) interruption; (b) period of time; (c) introduction; (d) break.

6. _____ to observing *contrary* evidence [8]: (a) completely different, opposite; (b) unfavorable, adverse; (c) perverse, willful; (d) illogical, confusing.

7. _____ *testify* about the value of the procedure [8]: (a) clarify; (b) swear; (c) declare as fact; (d) argue.

8. _____ evidence for superstitions is *biased* [8]: (a) favorable; (b) unfavorable; (c) opinionated; (d) prejudiced.

9. _____ one woman and 30 or 40 men could prove *volatile* [9]: (a) tricky; (b) potentially explosive; (c) threatening; (d) disturbing.

10. _____ *stalking* their prey [9]: (a) pursuing; (b) attacking; (c) looking for; (d) catching.

G. USING VOCABULARY

In parentheses before each sentence are some inflected forms of words from the selection. Study the context and the sentence. Then write the correct form in the space provided. Be sure to add appropriate endings like -s, -ed, or -ing if necessary.

1. (*psychology, psychologist, psychological, psychologically*) The author cites two experiments on superstitions conducted by leading

   _____.

2. (*imagination, imagine, imaginary*) It seems clear that superstitions arise

   from people's assumption that an _____ reward may result from a particular kind of behavior.

3. (*coincidence, coincide, coincidental, coincidentally*) Skinner's experiment

   with pigeons showed that the element of _____ plays a large role in superstitious behavior.

4. (*prejudice, prejudge, prejudicial*) Chance reports that people are

   _____ in favor of believing that lucky charms or particular objects actually work.

5. (*inevitability, inevitable, inevitably*) Chance also reports that people who

   are saved from death _____ point to their praying as the reason for their survival.

6. (*skepticism, skeptic, skeptical, skeptically*) There are, however, those people

   who are _____ of superstitions.

H. TOPICS FOR WRITING OR DISCUSSION

1. Here are some sentences from the article. Paraphrase them by rewriting each one in your own words in the space provided.

   a. You merely wait for the desired response, or a reasonable approximation of it, and then provide some food. Each time you do this, the rewarded response becomes stronger.

   _____

   _____

   _____

   b. If the bird happened to be bobbing its head up and down (something that pigeons are wont to do), then that response was strengthened—that is, became more likely to occur again.

_____

_____

_____

c. Indeed, society is far more dedicated to noting evidence in favor of superstition than it is to observing contrary evidence. This prejudice goes a long way toward explaining our superstitious nature.

_____

_____

_____

2. What superstitions do you have?

9

Gordon Monson

TALL TALES THAT GROW IN THE URBAN JUNGLE

This article, originally published in the Los Angeles Daily News, *discusses the phenomenon of urban legends, stories with a bizarre twist that are passed around as the gospel truth but that are probably fabricated. Jan Brunvand, a professor of English at the University of Utah, has published four collections of these tales. A few of them are recounted here.*

VOCABULARY PREVIEW

WORD ORIGINS

MEANDERING

One urban legend described in paragraph 15 is about a drunk man who was driving home late one night when a policeman spotted him *meandering* from lane to lane. The verb *meander* (pronounced mē·ǎn′dər) means to "wander aimlessly without direction." This word, of Greek origin, comes from the name of a river in Greece called *Maender*, known for its unusual number of twists and turns. Since Greece is a mountainous country, most rivers there flow down rapidly to the sea, but this river was different. So the Greek word *maiandros* became the term for anything that wandered from a straight course.

BIZARRE

As Monson writes in paragraph 28, urban legends are tales of the unexpected, the *bizarre*, or the horrible. Meaning "strikingly odd," "farfetched," or "grotesque," *bizarre* has completely changed its meaning from the original.

The word came into English from French, by way of the Spanish and Portuguese word *bizarro* ("handsome" and "brave"). It is thought that the word originally derived from *bizarra*, the Spanish word for "beard." Having a beard was the mark of a swashbuckler, meaning a dashing swordsman or adventurer (the role Errol Flynn played in so

101

many movies). Although in Spanish a beard indicated a spirited personality, foreigners turned the term into one of contempt.

This process, called *pejoration*, occurs when a word's meaning changes from a positive one to a negative one. In this case, *bizarre* became identified with extravagant, weird, or eccentric behavior.

APOCRYPHAL

Also in paragraph 28 Monson says that urban legends are *apocryphal* tales, meaning that they are of questionable authorship or authenticity. This word derives from the *Apocrypha*, fourteen books included in the Old Testament that Protestants and Catholics do not consider authentic or canonical (holy) because they were not part of the original Hebrew Scriptures.

This word was originally derived from Greek:

[*apokruphos*, from *apokruptein* ("to hide away"), from *apo-* ("away") + *kruptein* ("to hide away")]

WORD PARTS

-LESS

Fruitless used in paragraph 5 (literally "without fruit") means "having no results." The suffix *-less*, meaning "not having" or "without," is attached to many words in English, for example, *hopeless, joyless, fearless*, and *homeless*.

WORD FAMILIES

UNINITIATED

In paragraph 28 Monson defines the term *urban legend* for the *uninitiated*, which means "those who have not been introduced to a new field" or "those that have not been instructed." The Latin root of this word is *initium* ("beginning"). Here are some other English words in this family:

initial	in addition to the first letter of a name, this also means "occurring at the beginning," as in "an *initial* step"
initiate	the person who has been initiated; a beginner or novice
initiation	a ceremony, ritual, or test when a person is admitted into an organization; also the process of being instructed
initiative	This word has three meanings: (1) enterprise and determination to begin a project and see it through; (2) the first step, as in "to take the initiative"; (3) a proposal for a new law brought about by citizens.

PATHETICALLY

In paragraph 29 the author describes some urban legends as *"pathetically* disgusting." This adverb derives from the adjective *pathetic*, and it means here something that moves the feelings or evokes pity.

This word further connotes, at least in this context, a feeling of pity for something that is made helpless through misfortune. The Greek root of this word is *pathos*, "suffering" or "passion." Other words with this root include:

pathology	the study of diseases
pathos	a quality that arouses feelings of pity or sympathy in another
sympathy	the act of sharing another's feelings
empathy	an understanding so intimate that one's feelings and emotions are understood readily by another

GORDON MONSON

TALL TALES THAT GROW IN THE URBAN JUNGLE

1   These stories are true.

2   Honest.

3   In each case, they happened to a friend of a friend, or a friend of a sister's husband's friend's hairdresser.

4   A couple found a cute stray kitten and decided to keep it as a pet.

5   One day, it climbed to the top branch of a birch tree in their back yard and refused to come down. After a lot of fruitless coaxing, the couple looped a rope over the branch, hoping to pull the branch low enough for them to reach the stranded pet.

6   As they pulled, the rope broke and the kitten was launched into orbit. They were unable to find it.

7   A week later, while grocery shopping, they met one of their neighbors in the checkout line. The neighbor was carrying a bag of cat food.

8   "We didn't know you had a cat," one of them said.

9   "I didn't until last week," said the neighbor. "But Joe and I were sitting out on the patio the other day when this kitten dropped out of the sky, just like that. Fell right into Joe's lap."

10   A woman was taking a shower when the doorbell rang.

11   "Who is it?" she yelled.

12   "Blind man," shouted the visitor standing on her porch.

13   Thinking of a local charity, the woman stepped out of the shower, pulled some money out of her purse and, seeing no need to cover herself, swung open the door.

14   The man, looking a little surprised, said to her, "OK, lady, where do you want me to hang these blinds?"

15   A man, who earlier had had more than a few drinks, was driving home late one night when a police officer spotted him meandering from lane to lane and pulled him over to investigate.

16   As the officer walked toward the car, an accident took place on the other side of the highway. The cop told the man to stay put until he returned. The officer then crossed the median to see if he could help out.

17   The drunk, meanwhile, waited for a few minutes, then decided to get out of there. He jumped in the car and sped off toward his home. Upon arriving, he told his wife to tell the police, if they showed up, that he had been home all night.

18   The next morning, two state police officers knocked on the door, and when the man opened it, he explained that he hadn't left home all night. His wife would back him on the claim.

19   His wife went along with it, but the state troopers asked if they could look in the garage. Not knowing exactly what was going on, the man told them they could.

20   When they opened the garage door, there was a police cruiser, its lights still flashing.

LEGENDS IN OUR OWN TIME

21   Admit it.

22   You hear them, spread them and love them.

23   Sometimes, you believe them.

24   They make you laugh, they gross you out.

25   Urban legends have sunk deep enough into America's consciousness for folklorist Jan Harold Brunvand, a professor of English at the University of Utah, to write his fourth collection of the tales.

26   His latest book, "Curses! Broiled Again!" (Norton; $18.95), has just come out.

27   Besides the preceding stories, the work includes more than 70 others, divided into categories such as "Horrors," "Accidents and Mishaps" and "Sex and Scandal."

28   For the uninitiated, urban legends are apocryphal tales of the unexpected, bizarre or horrible that often—but not always—include a dead or exploding animal (usually something adorable and fluffy, like a cat or bunny rabbit), a microwave oven, a dead human, a naked woman, a surprised repairman, a jilted lover, a hitchhiker or a car.

29   Some are funny, some pathetically disgusting. And all are told as being the gospel truth. But few of them are.

30   Brunvand defines an urban legend as "a true story that's too good to be true."

31   "They are incidents that are too well-formed," he said. "They have varying versions from place to place. The details change, but the core remains.

32   "There's no set format for them, except that they usually have a bizarre twist and they are funny in a black-humor sort of way," he said.

33   For instance, remember the one about the carpet layer who could not find his pack of cigarets?

34   He had just finished putting a customer's carpet down when he reached for his pack of Marlboros. They were gone.

35   He then notices a small mound under the carpet in the middle of the room.

Darn, his pack must have slipped out of his pocket. Rather than rip up his day's work, the carpet layer hammers the lump flat and walks out to his van.

36   To his amazement, there, on the dash, are his cigarets.

37   Confused, he re-enters the house only to have the lady of the house ask if he has seen her precious pet parakeet that minutes ago crawled out of its cage.

38   "Usually, the stories are unfinished," Brunvand said. "You don't know what went on before and you don't find out what happens next."

THE HARE DRIER

39   One of the hottest urban legends Brunvand has collected recently is another animal-meets-its-destiny incident, a sorry episode—included in his book—called "The Hare Drier."

40   The story goes like this: A woman is horrified when she notices her dog chewing on a dead rabbit. She recognizes the bunny as the neighbor's pet, normally kept in a cage in their back yard.

41   She takes the rabbit from her pup, cleans it up with Woolite, hangs it by its ears in the shower and lets it drip dry. Or, in some versions, she blow-dries the bunny's fur. She then places it back in the neighbor's cage.

42   At a point shortly thereafter, the neighbor, aghast, discovers the blow- or drip-dried bunny. Turns out the bunny had died shortly before, and the neighbor had buried it in the back yard.

43   "The stories come and go," Brunvand said. "But, recently, I haven't heard any other (legend) as consistently as the Hare Drier. It's probably the hottest story going."

44   The professor, who has kept his ears open for urban legends for more than 20 years, collects them from the country's 1,500 folklorists, many of whom are professors of English, anthropology or history.

45   More important, he solicits them by listing an address to which his readers can send their favorites in each of his books, and as a part of his syndicated column, "Urban Legends."

46   Brunvand has run across thousands of legends, hundreds of which he files, studies and attempts to trace their origin and, sometimes, discover whether they really happened.

47   But to become a legend in its purest form, the incident has to have enough spinoff to make it so.

48   Brunvand was able to trace two legends in his current book to actual events.

ONE THAT ADDS UP

49   One legend involved a student who arrived late for a math test.

50   Upon settling in at his desk, he saw three math problems on the board. The student rushes to finish the first two and does so easily. But the third stumps him.

51   After numerous computations, the student solves the problem just as time runs out.

52   Later that night, he receives a phone call from his professor, who informs him that he was required to complete only the first two equations. The third was a problem that mathematicians since Einstein had been trying to solve without success.

53   "You just solved it," the professor tells the student.

54   Brunvand discovered that a similar incident actually happened to a student at the University of California at Berkeley, who solved two statistics problems thought to be unsolvable.

55   Truthful origin notwithstanding, there are enough versions of the story flying around for the versions to be considered urban legends.

TOO WELL-DONE

56   One of the more popular stories in Brunvand's book is the title urban legend, "Curses! Broiled Again!"—the tale of a woman who overzealously exposes herself to tanning rays in various tanning salons.

57   She's looking fine, tanned and trim when she notices a distinct, odd odor coming from her own body.

58   She goes to a doctor, who determines she cooked her insides and prognosticates certain death.

59   Such a thing never happened, as far as Brunvand knows.

60   Like most urban legends, the above stories have been passed by word of mouth across state and international borders.

61   Once the legends get rolling, according to Brunvand, who has an undergraduate degree in journalism and a master's degree in English from Michigan State University and a doctorate in folklore from Indiana University, they gain momentum and, eventually, lives of their own.

62   As for people's fascination with spreading the legends around, Brunvand said simply: "People enjoy having a good one to tell, especially in a social setting. A legend is less stressful to tell than a joke, where they have to get the punch line right. With these stories, they don't feel like they're performing. They just get a lot of pleasure out of knowing the latest story."

63   Black humor and all.   ■

"Tall Tales that Grow in the Urban Jungle," *San Francisco Chronicle*, September 26, 1989. Originally published in the *Los Angeles Daily News*. Reprinted by permission.

EXERCISES

Do not refer to the selection for Exercises A and B.

A.   DETERMINING THE MAIN IDEA AND PURPOSE
Choose the best answer.

1.   _____ The main idea of the article is that (a) gifted storytellers often exaggerate true stories to make them more entertaining; (b) Jan Brunvand has published four collections of urban legends; (c) urban legends are fabricated stories passed around that usually contain a bizarre or unexpected twist; (d) people enjoy relating urban legends, especially those that have a basis in reality.

2. _____ With respect to the main idea, the author's purpose is (a) to explain what urban legends are and to give a few examples; (b) to show us how ridiculous these stories are; (c) to trace the historical development of urban legends; (d) to review Jan Brunvand's book *Curses! Broiled Again!*

B.   COMPREHENDING MAIN IDEAS
Choose the correct answer.

1. _____ One urban legend claimed that a cat (a) had been dropped from an airplane and survived; (b) had been rescued from a tall tree by firemen; (c) had fallen out of the sky; (d) had climbed up a chimney and run away.

2. _____ One characteristic of urban legends is that they are usually told (a) by a storyteller in large gatherings; (b) as jokes rather than as real stories; (c) as if they were made up, not real at all; (d) as if they were the gospel truth.

3. _____ Which of the following was *not* mentioned as a characteristic of urban legends? (a) They may include something terrible happening to a cute, fuzzy animal; (b) they are funny in a black-humor sort of way; (c) they follow a formula, a set format; (d) there may be several versions of them as they are passed along; (e) they sound too good to be true; (f) they frequently are unfinished.

4. Brunvand, the English professor who has published four collections of urban legends, makes the point that (a) the practice of passing on urban legends is peculiar to the U.S.; (b) few of these stories are actually true; (c) most of these stories have a basis in fact; (d) a true urban legend has to take place in a city.

5. _____ In the story about the carpet layer, the reader is left to think that what he hammered into the carpet was (a) a little bunny; (b) his pack of cigarettes; (c) the lady's pet parakeet; (d) a little kitten.

6. _____ According to Brunvand, the hottest story going around is (a) "The New Einstein"; (b) "Curses! Broiled Again!"; (c) "The Case of the Exploding Bunny"; (d) "The Hare Drier."

COMPREHENSION SCORE

Score your answers for Exercises A and B as follows:

A.   No. right _____ × 2 = _____

B.   No. right _____ × 1 = _____

Total pts. from A and B _____ × 10 = _____%

You may refer to the selection for the remaining exercises.

C. RECOGNIZING SUPPORTING DETAILS

Label the following statements from the selection as follows: MI if the statement represents a *main idea* and SD if the statement represents a *supporting detail*.

1. _____ One legend involved a student who arrived late for a math test.

2. _____ Upon settling in at his desk, he saw three math problems on the board.

3. _____ The student rushes to finish the first two and does so easily.

4. _____ But the third stumps him.

5. _____ After numerous computations, the student solves the problem just as time runs out.

6. _____ Later that night, he receives a phone call from his professor, who informs him that he was required to complete only the first two equations.

7. _____ The third was a problem that mathematicians since Einstein had been trying to solve without success.

8. _____ "You just solved it," the professor tells the student.

9. _____ Brunvand discovered that a similar incident actually happened to a student at the University of California at Berkeley, who solved two statistics problems thought to be unsolvable.

10. _____ Truthful origin notwithstanding, there are enough versions of the story flying around for the versions to be considered urban legends.

D. MAKING INFERENCES

For each of these statements write Y (Yes) if the inference is an accurate one, N (No) if the inference is an inaccurate one, or CT (Can't Tell) if you do not have enough information to make an inference.

1. _____ The people who are the subjects of urban legends are usually not personally known to the storyteller.

2. _____ The phenomenon of urban legends is fairly recent, since the end of World War II.

3. _____ Dead or exploding animals are common occurrences in urban legends.

4. _____ The more bizarre or horrible the twist at the end of an urban legend, the better.

5. _____ Urban legends always start with a real event that happened to a real person, but as the legend is passed around, the details change and are distorted.

6.   _____ The story "The Hare Drier" is funny because the woman didn't know her neighbor's bunny had died.

E.   **ANALYZING ORGANIZATION AND SEEING RELATIONSHIPS**
Choose the correct answer.

1.   This article has a clear beginning, middle, and end. Write the number of the paragraph where the body begins _____. Then write the number of the paragraph where the conclusion begins _____.

2.   Look through the article again and find the sentence that best expresses the main idea. Write it in the blank. _____

_____

_____

_____

3.   _____ To provide support for the main idea, what method of development does the author rely on most throughout the article? (a) definition of important terms; (b) examples and illustrations; (c) cause and effect; (d) steps in a process.

4.   _____ When the author writes at the beginning of the article, "These stories are true. Honest. In each case, they happened to a friend of a friend, or a friend of a sister's husband's friend's hairdresser," he is being (a) candid; (b) abrupt; (c) humorous; (d) sarcastic.

5.   Look again at paragraph 61. What does Monson mean when he writes that "once the legends get rolling . . . they gain momentum and, eventually, lives of their own"? _____

_____

_____

_____

6.   From what the author implies, what does the term _black humor_ mean?

_____

F.   **UNDERSTANDING VOCABULARY**
Choose the correct definition according to the context.

1.   _____ a lot of _fruitless_ coaxing [paragraph 5]: (a) desperate; (b) producing no results; (c) making no effort; (d) helpless.

2.   _____ _meandering_ from lane to lane [15]: (a) wandering aimlessly; (b) dashing; (c) walking purposely; (d) strolling casually.

3.   _____ the officer then crossed the *median* [16]: (a) crosswalk; (b) center lanes; (c) center divider; (d) overcrossing.

4.   _____ urban legends are *apocryphal* tales [28]: (a) mythological; (b) probably authentic; (c) probably inauthentic; (d) tasteless, gross.

5.   _____ the neighbor, *aghast,* discovers the bunny [42]: (a) shocked; (b) embarrassed; (c) surprised; (d) amused.

6.   _____ he *solicits* stories [45]: (a) publishes; (b) seeks; (c) tracks down; (d) submits.

7.   _____ truthful origin *notwithstanding* [55]: (a) in addition; (b) in summary; (c) on the other hand; (d) nevertheless.

8.   _____ a doctor *prognosticates* certain death [58]: (a) advises; (b) predicts; (c) guards against; (d) prescribes a cure for.

G.   USING VOCABULARY

From the following list of vocabulary words, choose a word that fits in each blank according to both the grammatical structure of the sentence and the context. Use each word in the list only once and add noun or verb endings (such as *-s, -ing,* or *-ed*) if necessary. (Note that there are more words than sentences.)

bizarre	apocryphal	pathetically
urban	uninitiated	folklorist
horrify	anthropology	syndicated
notwithstanding	overzealously	momentum

1.   This article is concerned with a phenomenon known as _____

legends, which the author defines for the _____

reader as stories with _____ twists that are probably

_____, meaning that they are of doubtful authenticity.

2.   One story involves a woman who _____ exposed herself to tanning rays at a tanning salon and supposedly cooked her insides; another concerns a woman who was _____ to find her dog chewing on her neighbor's dead pet rabbit.

3.   According to Jan Brunvand, a _____ and professor of English at the University of Utah who also writes a

_____ column on urban legends, once these stories

get started, they gain _____ and take on a life of their own.

H.   TOPICS FOR WRITING OR DISCUSSION

1.   Here is a story that was circulating in the Bay Area during fall 1990 as I was preparing this book. After you read it, write a paragraph in which you consider whether this story represents a true urban legend as Monson defines the term in this article.

A young woman who is a student at City College of San Francisco has a friend, whom she calls Kathy to protect her identity. Kathy is twenty-four years old and comes from a fairly wealthy family. Her home is in San Jose, California, but she has traveled widely. A couple of years ago, she decided to spend a summer in Los Angeles. Kathy fell in love with the city and thought she might want to live there permanently some day.

A few days after she had arrived there, she went to a restaurant one night alone to eat dinner. She was sitting in a corner table when a very attractive man, also sitting alone, caught her eye. He looked over at her and winked; she blushed beet red. Finally, he asked if he could join her. He introduced himself to her as John. He was twenty-six years old and a college graduate; he worked as a claims adjuster for a major auto insurance company. Kathy was immediately attracted to him.

They talked and talked, and they discovered they had much in common. He asked her out, and they began seeing each other on a steady basis. Eventually, they became lovers. They spent as much time as they could together because they both knew that Kathy had to return to San Jose when the summer was over. Kathy loved him so much, and she thought he loved her, too.

The end of the summer came too quickly. John drove Kathy to the airport so they could be together in those last precious moments. Before she got on the plane, John gave her a card and specifically told her not to open the card until the plane left the ground. He was very insistent that she follow his instructions. Thinking that it was a love letter, Kathy did as he had asked. When she closed her eyes, she could still see him smiling at her.

As the plane rose in the air, she opened the card, and her ecstasy turned to shock. Written in the middle of the card, in block letters, were these words: WELCOME TO THE WORLD OF AIDS.

2.   Do you know any urban legends?

10 ||||

Timothy Harper

BASKETBALL SPOKEN HERE

Timothy Harper is a special correspondent for Newsday, *the Long Island, New York, newspaper. In this article, he discusses a game of pickup basketball he played in the Chinese capital, Beijing. Along the way, he makes some observations about basketball etiquette around the world.*

VOCABULARY PREVIEW

WORD ORIGINS

CALISTHENICS
In paragraph 2 Harper writes that he visited a recreational area in Beijing where a number of young Chinese men were doing *calisthenics.* As you probably already know, this word means "gymnastic exercises to improve one's health, strength, and grace." This definition is nearly an exact translation from the word's original meaning in Greek:

[*kallos-* ("beauty") + *sthenos* ("strength") + *-ics*]

You can see this same prefix in the word *calligraphy,* "beautiful writing."

BLATANT
Harper presents the reader with a number of rules for newcomers to a basketball court; among them is the rule that one shouldn't call a foul unless it's *blatant.* This word, which today means "offensively obvious or conspicuous," has changed meaning radically. Apparently, as coined by the English poet Edmund Spenser, it meant "bleating," as in "*blatant* herds of sheep." The root is similar to the Latin verb *blatīre* ("to babble," "to talk foolishly").

WORD PARTS

-GRESS
The root *-gress* comes from the Latin root *gradī* ("to step"). English has many words made from this root. *Aggression* (see paragraph 18) is one

113

such word. *Aggredi* in Latin comes from [*ad-* ("toward") + *gradī* ("to step")]. In English, the noun suffix *-sion* is added to the verb form (*aggressus*). The word *aggression* can imply hostile behavior (literally "to step up to" someone in a threatening manner), but in the context of the reading, it merely refers to a kind of strategy used by the offensive players.

Other common words in English with this root include:

progress	movement toward a goal; improvement [*prō-* ("forward") + *gradī*]
regress	to go back; to return to a previous condition, as in when a child regresses to an earlier stage by talking baby talk [*re-* ("back") + *gradī*]
digress	to stray from the main subject in writing or speaking [*dis-* ("aside" or "apart") + *gradī*]
egress	an exit [*ex-* ("out") + *gradī*]

WORD FAMILIES

SEQUENCE

In paragraph 5, Harper writes, "It was a familiar *sequence* for the American journalist, who had been getting into pickup basketball games with strangers in gyms and on playgrounds all over the world for 20 years." The word *sequence* means "a following of one thing after another." The root *sequī-*, which in Latin means "to follow," can be found at the heart of a large number of "relatives," among them:

consequence	something that naturally follows from an action or condition
consecutive	following successively without interruption, as in "a *consecutive* order of events"
consequent	describing something that follows as a natural effect, result, or conclusion, as in "The heavy floods caused huge losses for farmers and a *consequent* rise in food prices."
sequel	anything that follows or continues, as in the *sequel* to a popular movie, like "The Godfather"
subsequent	following in time or order, as in "a *subsequent* event"

CONFIDENCE

Confidence (see paragraph 19) means "trust in another person." Its root can be considered either the Latin verb *fidere* ("to trust") or the noun *fidēs* ("faith"). There are some other words in this family of words derived from these roots:

confide	to tell something in confidence
fidelity	faithfulness, loyalty
fiduciary	pertaining to someone who holds something in trust for another, as in a *fiduciary* responsibility
infidel	someone who has no religious beliefs

Fido a traditional name for a dog, probably from dogs' reputation as loyal pets

TIMOTHY HARPER

BASKETBALL SPOKEN HERE

1 Leaving his hotel Beijing for an early-morning run, the visiting American journalist found himself following the irregular beat of a bouncing basketball—an unmistakable sound for anyone who ever hung a hoop off a garage.

2 At a recreational area behind the Beijing Zoo, a number of young Chinese men who appeared to be soldiers and students were doing calisthenics. Three were shooting a basketball at an old metal backboard and rim.

3 What followed was part of a ritual that makes up the universal etiquette of pickup basketball. The American stood conspicuously alongside the court for a moment or two, just watching, and then moved near the basket. The three young Chinese glanced at him but continued shooting the ball, rebounding and shooting again.

4 When the ball bounced directly to the American, he tossed it to one of the Chinese, who shot again. The next time it bounced to the American, he put it up himself. One of the Chinese rebounded and, instead of shooting, passed it back to the American. They were willing to let him play with them.

5 Though neither the American nor the Chinese could speak a word of each other's language, within minutes they were in a two-on-two game. It was a familiar sequence for the American journalist, who had been getting into pickup basketball games with strangers in gyms and on playgrounds all over the world for 20 years.

6 In many ways, the new guy on a playground is like a gunfighter riding into Dodge City. All the regulars look him over—or her, since more and more women are playing pickup hoops—and decide whether he's good enough to play with them. Or, rarely, too good.

7 Assuming the new guy isn't too bad or too good, he'll get into a game almost immediately if he's needed. For instance, if five guys are looking for a sixth for three-on-three, almost any warm body will do. If regulars are waiting their turn to run, however, the newcomer may have to wait a few games.

8 Once into a game, the new guy's acceptance depends on how he plays, both his ability at the game itself and his ability to get along with the other players.

9 In New York's Central Park, for example, no one wants to be on the same team as the balding white guy with a slight beer belly. But if the guy makes a couple of jump shots and good passes to help his team win that game and stay on the court for the next game, he's in demand the next time he shows up.

10 No matter how good a newcomer is, however, if his on-court deportment is a problem, the regulars won't want to play with him again. If stuck on his team, they pass him the ball only as a last resort.

11 Rules for newcomers to a playground or gym:

12   • Keep your mouth shut. Attempts to joke and jive quickly become overfamiliar. Attempts to organize or instruct teammates, no matter how well-intentioned or sensible, are inevitably seen as pushy.

13   • Don't fight local custom, no matter how ridiculous. Examples include a gym in Des Moines where everyone who shows up plays at once, even if it's nine on eight, and the Milwaukee game where defensive players call the fouls. (That game is mostly lawyers, and sometimes it seems as if they argue more on the basketball court than they do in the other kind of court.)

14   • Pick up a few words of local terminology, if possible. In Harlem and Brooklyn, "J" is a jump shot, and "the rock" is the ball. "Bella" is a compliment for a nice play on the lone court between the canals in Venice, where offensive players holler "foulo" when hacked by opponents.

15   • Don't call a foul unless it's so blatant as to approach assault. On the South Side of Chicago the rule for new guys is "no autopsy, no foul."

16   • If calling a foul is necessary, don't do it in an angry tone. This rule must sometimes be broken, as when repeatedly confronted by a group of hard-hacking Israelis who prowl the gyms of London and have become known as "the Entebbe gang."

17   • If there is an argument, stay out of it. Every playground or gym has a pecking order of advocacy, and if teammates don't take up the case then it's not worth belaboring.

18   • Handle the ball as little as possible, except to go to the basket. Overdribbling, or "hogging," is a cardinal sin to regulars, but driving to the hoop—even when unsuccessful—is necessary to demonstrate the accepted offensive aggression.

19   • Shoot when open, pass when not. It's the simplest principle in the game, but doing it consistently is the only way to get the respect of opponents and the confidence of teammates.

20   • Work hard on defense. That also impresses playground regulars. Bumps and nudges with the body near the basketball are more acceptable than using the arms or hands to push or obstruct. Block out for rebounds.

21   The game in Beijing was "make it, take it," just as in most big-city playgrounds in America. Word went out that a Westerner was playing, and a crowd of perhaps 70 gathered to cheer every basket and laugh at every lost ball or blocked shot.

22   Pretty soon some of the big guys in the neighborhood, a couple of them 5-foot-8, joined the game and it was four-on-four.

23   The American, 6 feet tall and of admittedly marginal skills, found himself in the unaccustomed role of being not only the biggest but also the best player on the court—and thereby entitled to break the rules of deportment for newcomers.

24   The results were mixed.

25   He organized the two teams into shirts and skins and everyone smiled and nodded in seeming approval. After two baskets, two of the guys wearing shirts took them off.

26   When one of his teammates showed a marked reluctance to guard anyone—"matador defense," they call it in San Diego—the American grabbed the young man by the shoulders and positioned him in front of the opposing player he was supposed to guard. The teammate followed his man around for a while, but still played no defense.

27   The American, spurred on by his first applause from spectators, shot the ball far too much. "All China," he crowed to uncomprehending teammates. He tried to teach the smaller man guarding him to say "too tall," but the guy apparently thought it meant "nice shot," because he began saying it to everyone who scored.

28   The American tried to teach his teammates to high-five after good plays, but the Chinese, who don't ordinarily even shake hands, would have none of it at first. Every time the American approached with his palm upraised, they would wince and retreat as if he was about to cuff them around the head and shoulders.

29   At the end of the game, after a few tentative high-fives, it occurred to the American to ask the Chinese the word for basketball. They looked at each other, shrugged, and said, "Basketball."

30   It turned out they could speak a word of each other's language after all.   ■

From Timothy Harper, "Basketball Spoken Here," *Newsday*, September 21, 1987. Reprinted by permission.

EXERCISES

Do not refer to the selection for Exercises A and B.

A.   DETERMINING THE MAIN IDEA AND PURPOSE
Choose the best answer.

1.   _____ The main idea of the article is that (a) playing basketball in foreign countries is one way to promote good relations; (b) there is a certain ritual or a kind of etiquette that people follow when playing pickup basketball; (c) the Chinese version of basketball is remarkably similar to the American style; (d) the language of basketball is universal.

2.   _____ With respect to the main idea, the author's purpose is (a) to describe his experiences traveling overseas; (b) to contrast two styles of playing basketball; (c) to teach the reader the rules for basketball; (d) to enumerate some suggestions for playing pickup basketball, based on personal experience.

B.   COMPREHENDING MAIN IDEAS
Write the correct answer.

1.   The American knew it would be all right for him to play in the game in

Beijing when one of the players _____.

2.   A newcomer can get into a basketball game, according to the author, as

long as he or she is not either too _____ or too

_____.

3.   The author advises the newcomer to keep his or her mouth shut so as
      not to seem too _____.

4.   Harper also suggests that one should be particularly careful about calling
      _____.

5.   The author decided it was all right to break the rules of deportment
      when playing in China because he was both _____
      and _____.

6.   What American custom, done after good shots, made the Chinese players
      uncomfortable? _____

COMPREHENSION SCORE

Score your answers for Exercises A and B as follows:

A.   No. right _____ × 2 = _____

B.   No. right _____ × 1 = _____

Total pts. from A and B _____ × 10 = _____%

You may refer to the selection for the remaining exercises.

C.   DISTINGUISHING BETWEEN MAIN IDEAS AND SUPPORTING DETAILS

Label the following statements from the selection as follows: MI if the statement
represents a *main idea* and SD if the statement represents a *supporting detail*.

1.   _____ Once into a game, the new guy's acceptance depends on how he
      plays, both his ability at the game itself and his ability to get along with
      the other players.

2.   _____ In New York's Central Park, for example, no one wants to be on
      the same team as the balding white guy with a slight beer belly.

3.   _____ But if the guy makes a couple of jump shots and good passes to
      help his team win that game and stay on the court for the next game,
      he's in demand the next time he shows up.

4.   _____ No matter how good a newcomer is, however, if his on-court de-
      portment is a problem, the regulars won't want to play with him again.

5.   _____ If stuck on his team, they pass him the ball only as a last resort.

D.   MAKING INFERENCES

For each of these statements write Y (Yes) if the inference is an accurate one, N
(No) if the inference is an inaccurate one, or CT (Can't Tell) if you do not have enough
information to make an inference.

1. _____ The author traveled to China to observe and write reports about popular sports there.

2. _____ The author enjoys playing in pickup games.

3. _____ Despite his marginal skills as a player, the author was considerably better than any of the other players at the Beijing playground.

4. _____ The newcomer usually finds it hard getting into a pickup game even if there aren't enough players, because the regulars consider him or her an intruder.

5. _____ Although the author suggests that the newcomer pick up some local terminology, he also advises against seeming too familiar or helpful.

6. _____ In the Beijing game, the Chinese defensive players were timid about being aggressive.

E. **ANALYZING ORGANIZATION AND SEEING RELATIONSHIPS**
Choose the correct answer.

1. Who is the American journalist mentioned in paragraph 1?

_____

2. What are *two* methods of development the author uses in paragraphs 3 and 4? (a) general term and an example; (b) contrast; (c) important term to be defined and a definition of it; (d) cause and effect; (e) steps in a process.

3. Look again at the first sentence of paragraph 5. What is the logical relationship between the two parts? (a) cause and effect; (b) steps in a process; (c) general statement and a supporting example; (d) statement and a repetition of it; (e) contrast.

4. What does Harper mean when he writes at the beginning of paragraph 6, "In many ways, the new guy on a playground is like a gunfighter riding

into Dodge City"? _____

_____

_____

5. What is the method of development in the section comprising paragraphs 11–20? (a) steps in a process; (b) important term and definitions of it; (c) enumeration; (d) facts and statistics; (e) cause and effect.

6. Paraphrase this sentence from paragraph 24: "The results were mixed."

_____

F. **UNDERSTANDING VOCABULARY**
Look through the paragraphs listed below and find a word that matches each definition. An example has been done for you.

Ex.   prescribed form or ceremony [2–3]   _____ritual_____

1.   in an obvious way, attracting attention [3–4]   _____

2.   conduct, correct behavior [10 and 23]   _____

3.   a person finally turned to for help [10–12]   _____

4.   offensively obvious [14–15]   _____

5.   active support for a cause [17–18]   _____

6.   going over repeatedly for a long time, harping [17–18]   _____

7.   very serious [17–18]   _____

8.   urged, incited [27–28—look for two words]   _____

9.   not understanding [27–28]   _____

10.   shrink back, flinch [28–29]   _____

G.   USING VOCABULARY

Write the correct inflected form of the base word in each of the following sentences. Refer to your dictionary if necessary.

1.   (*inevitably*—use an adjective)   If a newcomer attempts to joke or jive too quickly or to organize teammates, it is _____ that the regulars will consider him too pushy.

2.   (*confront*—use a noun)   Calling a foul in an angry manner or arguing about a foul may result in a _____.

3.   (*aggression*—use an adverb)   The Chinese players were not able to play defense _____.

4.   (*confidence*—use an adjective)   The regular teammates will be _____ of a newcomer if he displays a couple of good jump shots.

5.   (*obstruction*—use another noun)   In defense, bumping and nudging are more effective and impressive than pushing or _____.

6.   (*admittedly*—use a verb)   The author readily _____ that his basketball skills are weak.

7.   (*marginally*—use an adjective)   For someone with only _____ skills, Harper was easily the best player among the Chinese.

8. (*tentative*—use an adverb)   At the end of the game the Chinese players

_____ gave each other high-fives.

H.   TOPICS FOR WRITING OR DISCUSSION

1. Write a paragraph in which you summarize the information stated in paragraphs 23–28.

_____

_____

_____

_____

_____

_____

_____

_____

2. Choose a sport you are familiar with and, either orally or in writing, discuss the rules of etiquette for newcomers who want to join in a pickup game (for example, tennis, pool, sandlot baseball, or football).

11 ||||||

Ellen Graham

BORN TO SHOP:
THE CALL OF THE MALL

The Wall Street Journal *is this country's leading newspaper for business and financial news. However, each issue also contains feature articles on topics of general interest, for example, the ways in which suburban shopping malls have changed Americans' shopping habits. This article describes the phenomenon of "mall rats," teenagers who hang out at malls because they have time to kill and money to spend.*

VOCABULARY PREVIEW

**WORD
ORIGINS**

SHROUD
In paragraph 2 the author briefly describes the Catskill Mountains of New York. The phrase "cloud-*shrouded* peaks" presents the reader with a visual image—the mountaintops are covered by clouds. *Shroud* literally refers to the winding sheet used to wrap corpses in, but it can also mean, as it does in this context, anything that hides or conceals. The derivation of this word does not suggest anything quite so specific. It comes from the Middle English word *schrud*, which had a much more general meaning—"a garment" or "article of clothing."

EMPORIUM
Paragraph 3 refers to a "scented-candle *emporium*," meaning simply a "store." This rather old-fashioned word came into English from Latin, although the Latin word derived from two Greek words: *emporion* ("market") and *emporos* ("merchant" or "traveler"). An *emporium* was originally a marketplace where merchants, who were traveling salesmen, could come together. The plural form is *emporia* or *emporiums*.

ECLIPSE
Paragraph 10 contains a rather unusual instance of the word *eclipse*. We typically associate this word with eclipses of the sun, for example, the

phenomenon that occurs when the earth passes in front of the sun, temporarily blocking it from view on earth. In this instance, however, Graham writes that, according to these teenagers, "Reebok high-topped sneakers have just been *eclipsed* by Nikes." Used here as a verb, it means "reduced in importance" or "overshadowed." The noun form is also *eclipse,* and it has a complicated history: from Middle English, from Old French, from Latin *eclipsis,* originally from Greek *ekleipsis,* meaning "cessation," "abandonment."

WORD PARTS

BE-

As a prefix, *be-* has several meanings. In the case of the word *bemused* (see paragraph 21), it conveys the idea of something done thoroughly or excessively. Therefore, *bemused* means "thoroughly confused" or "befuddled." Here are some other English words that begin with this verb prefix. As you can see, a few of them seem to have lost the idea of "thoroughly":

bedevil	to torment as a devil would
behave	[*be-* + *have,* literally "to hold oneself in a certain way"]
beseech	to request or beg earnestly [*be-* ("thoroughly") + *sechen* ("to seek")]
besmirch	to soil or to dishonor, as in "to *besmirch* one's name"
betray	to give aid or information to the enemy; commit treason [*be-* + the Latin verb *trādere, trans-* ("over") + *dare* ("to give")]
bespangle	to cover thoroughly with spangles

WORD FAMILIES

CHAPERONE

A *chaperone* (see paragraph 6) is a person, especially an older or married person, who accompanies a young woman in public or who supervises an activity where young people might congregate (for example, a high school dance). This word derives from the French word *chape,* the hood worn by the Knights of the Garter who were attendants of the queen. Besides *chape,* there are numerous words that derive from *caput,* the Latin word for "head." Here are a few of them:

cap	something worn on the head
capital	a capital letter, which stands at the head of a word; a capital city, which houses the head of the government; as an architectural term, the head of a column; or capital punishment
capitulate	to surrender or come to terms, from the Latin phrase, "to draw up under heads or chapters"
decapitate	to cut off someone's head
chapter	the main divisions (or heads) of a book

ELLEN GRAHAM

BORN TO SHOP:
THE CALL OF THE MALL

1   It could be anywhere, USA. But for teen-agers hereabouts with a Saturday to kill, the Hudson Valley Mall in Kingston, N.Y., is the only place to be.

2   Outside, from the shopping mall's parking lot atop a rocky plateau, the nearby Catskills beckon, their cloud-shrouded peaks beginning to show a faint haze of spring green. For the area's youthful "mall rats," however, the majestic vistas can't compete with the climate-controlled, neon-lit enticements inside.

3   There's Fluf n' Stuff, where fetching battery-powered stuffed animals bark, chirp and turn somersaults. And Rumford Pet Center, where fetching balls of living fluff mostly doze. And Wicks and Sticks, a scented-candle emporium that perfumes the entire mall with the cloying aromas of strawberry and musk. Pizza joints, record stores, a video arcade and a six-theater cinema all exert a pull, as do the boutiques offering a vast array of apparel—so long as it is denim.

4   The mall is a magnet for kids yearning to be free. Letty Larsen and Jennifer LeFevre, 13-year-old cheerleaders from the nearby village of Stone Ridge, N.Y., come nearly every weekend, and so do their friends. Their parents, they say, sometimes drop them at the mall for as much as six hours. "My parents are glad to get rid of me," says Letty, a curly-haired blonde. "They can go do what they want instead of listening to us complain about being bored." The mall, she adds, is never boring. "There are lots of good-looking guys here. You can walk up to people who look your age and introduce yourself."

5   Shopping is the other big draw. "It's fun to spend money," Letty says. "It feels good to get all the new clothes." She and Jennifer estimate that they each spend between $30 and $50 a weekend here.

6   What else is there for a 13-year-old to do around here? Letty is asked. Pretty much nothing, she answers. "School's no fun—you have to do work, and all the grown-ups are there." School dances are okay, "except for the chaperones."

7   Though the mall stands as a parentless playground, its denizens can't elude authority entirely. Indeed, when crowds of teens loiter too long around the arcade on Saturdays, security guards prod them to move on. Some of the surlier youngsters have dubbed this "Auschwitz Mall" for the rigor of its crowd control.

8   To Dominic Sagonis, a 12-year-old from Queens, N.Y., here on a weekend visit, Hudson Valley Mall is a tame country cousin to the two- and three-level city malls he frequents at home. Accompanied by his 13-year-old friend Heidi Schneider, whose parents have a weekend home in the area, he is eyeing a set of drums in the mall's music store. He plans to buy a set in a year and a half, when he has saved up half the $1,500 purchase price. "My parents will put in half," he says.

9   Their friends Christine and Sandra Wilson, willowy blonde sisters from Livingston, N.Y., say they could have spent the afternoon watching a donkey

basketball game at school, but "we saw it already." The Wilson girls are members of 4-H, and today they lead the group to the pet store, to check on a Chihauhua puppy they have noticed on previous visits. "He's been here for so many weeks," laments 12-year-old Sandra.

10   Dominic, whose dark good looks hint of a budding lady-killer, cadges a dollar from Heidi to play video games. He attempts to explain why shopping, endless shopping, holds such appeal for youngsters his age. "You want to fit in, you want to be in style," he says. His companions nod, and a heated debate about socially correct labels ensues. The consensus is that Reebok high-top sneakers have just been eclipsed by Nikes. Is there any real difference? "Yes," Dominic replies pointedly, "the brand name and the price."

11   For all their big-spending bluster, the group's haul at day's end is a meager one. Dominic has acquired a water pistol for his little brother, and Heidi is carrying a couple of plastic "Do Not Disturb" signs for her room.

12   After a late-afternoon lull, the mall again resonates with a high-energy buzz. Throngs of high-school kids—a sea of denim jackets—crowd the passageways. The shuffle of hundreds of pairs of sneakers beats a soft percussion to the throbbing rock issuing from the boutiques.

13   Laden with packages, Lisa Waddell, Lenchen Breitung and Kelly O'Brien wear matching sweatshirts that they purchased the previous weekend at a mall in nearby Poughkeepsie. They say they spend every weekend together, and to document their friendship, tonight have their photos taken with the Easter Bunny, who smiles mutely as they pile into his lap. They pay $5 for three shots, then return for a $5 retake because Lisa, 15, wasn't smiling in one picture. They move from store to store, scouting the current fashions. "You look for what you want and go back home and get the credit card," giggles Lenchen, 15. They, too, hit the pet shop, in search of T-shirts for their dogs. (They are out of stock.) "We don't eat dinner, we mostly just snack around," Lenchen says. Their boyfriends, they say, prefer to spend weekend nights gathered on a country road, where they build bonfires and "just hang out."

14   It is now near closing time, and the party drifts out into the night, to nearby music clubs, arcades, or even home to the VCR. Jeremy DuBois, a 17-year-old from Kingston with long hair and a crucifix in his ear, thinks he will drop by the Checkered Flag Lounge later on. Jeremy says he spends every night of the week at the mall, where he usually eats dinner. Money flies out of his pockets here. "I came with $30, and here it is 8:30 and I have $5 left," he says. "It just goes." His folks don't mind his spending so much time here, he says, adding: "If I'm home I'm just in my room on the phone."

15   There comes a time in every teen-ager's life, however, when even the mall begins to pall. Paul Hyatt, a 19-year-old from Port Ewen, N.Y., is at that awkward age. "I'm too young to go to bars and too old to stay at home," he says. "There's really no place else to go." Paul, who works full-time training to be an assistant manager of a drugstore, says the younger set "doesn't realize how dull this place is." He thinks they should get jobs, and scorns their lack of gumption. "Nobody wants to work anymore," he sighs, sounding older than his years.

16   He calls to a dark-haired girl padding by on her way to J.C. Penney: "Where's your purple hair?" She tells him that she had to give up her punk hairstyle when she

took a job at a local hospital. Paul, who says he once shaved his head, is incensed. "Why should a kid have to do that?" he sputters. "It's discrimination."

17   Youthful rebellion is a topic that comes up later at the mall's Youth Booth, an informal counseling center operated by the Ulster County Mental Health Association. Of outrageous hair styles and the like, Jacki Brownstein, the association's director of family and youth programs, says: "Who can blame them in this environment? They have a need to stand out in some way not created by the adult world."

18   For the past year, Youth Booth counselors Michael Johnan and Lorraine McGrane have spent their own Friday and Saturday nights at the mall, distributing pamphlets on topics like AIDS and stress, and giving pointers on everything from obtaining driver's licenses to the whereabouts of nearby resorts. Mostly, however, they are there to listen.

19   "We're here because the kids are here," says Mr. Johnan, who notes that some nights up to 500 teenagers converge on the mall. A core of perhaps 50 "regulars" drop by the booth nearly every week, and "if we don't see them, we worry about them," he says.

20   While many youngsters seek advice on nothing more pressing than which jacket to buy, booth counselors have dealt with drug and alcohol abusers, suicidal youths and some who appeared abused.

21   Mr. Johnan sees the mall as simply a "climate-controlled street corner," an updated version of the teen hangouts of yesteryear. Shopping, he insists, is less important than making the scene. "They say it's boring, dead," he grins. "But they're back the next week." In one respect, however, Mr. Johnan, a 31-year-old native of the area, contrasts today's teen behavior with his own. "When I was 16, 17, we liked to be outdoors. Now, it's out of the question to go on a hike." Bemused, he wonders aloud: "Why aren't they outside on a day like today?"   ■

From Ellen Graham, "Born to Shop: The Call of the Mall," *Wall Street Journal,* May 13, 1988, p. 7R. Reprinted by permission.

EXERCISES

Do not refer to the selection for Exercises A and B.

A.   DETERMINING THE MAIN IDEA AND PURPOSE
Choose the best answer.

1.   _____ The main idea of the article is that (a) for American teenagers, with time to kill and money to spend, shopping malls have become their favorite hangout; (b) shopping malls are an important feature of the suburban landscape; (c) shopping malls have changed Americans' shopping habits; (d) mall rats spend too much time and money hanging out at shopping malls.

2. ____ With respect to the main idea, the author's purpose is (a) to present two sides of a controversial issue; (b) to explain and discuss a current trend; (c) to criticize a new trend; (d) to trace the history of a new trend.

B.   COMPREHENDING MAIN IDEAS
Choose the correct answer.

1. ____ According to the article, the teenagers who hang out at the Hudson Valley Mall in Kingston, New York, pay no attention to (a) the boys who congregate there; (b) the nearby mountains and other outdoor attractions; (c) the advertised sales at the mall's various boutiques; (d) the security guards who patrol the mall.

2. ____ Letty Larsen and Jennifer LeFevre, two thirteen-year-old teenagers quoted in the article, nearly every weekend spend between (a) $5 and $10; (b) $10 and $20; (c) $30 and $50; (d) $75 and $100.

3. ____ The author describes a shopping mall as (a) a series of emporiums; (b) a convenient babysitter; (c) an example of sterile American architecture; (d) a parentless playground.

4. ____ According to the article, the main reason endless shopping in malls is so appealing to teenagers is that it provides (a) a way to escape from their parents; (b) a chance to socialize with other teenagers on neutral grounds; (c) the opportunity to keep up with current fads and styles; (d) a place where they can spend their allowance or earnings.

5. ____ The Hudson Valley Mall in Kingston, New York, provides (a) youth counseling; (b) a dating bureau; (c) a chaperone service; (d) a shuttle bus.

6. ____ Paul Hyatt, the nineteen-year-old assistant manager of a drugstore, is quoted as saying that young people (a) should spend more time reading and studying than hanging out at the mall; (b) should realize that the mall is really boring; (c) should save their money for college instead of spending it on faddy clothing; (d) should be more rebellious by dying their hair and wearing weird clothing.

COMPREHENSION SCORE

Score your answers for Exercises A and B as follows:

A.   No. right _____ × 2 = _____

B.   No. right _____ × 1 = _____

Total pts. from A and B _____ × 10 = _____%

You may refer to the selection for the remaining exercises.

C.   RECOGNIZING SUPPORTING DETAILS

Place an X in the space for each statement that *directly* supports this main idea from the selection. **"Mr. Johnan [one of the Youth Booth counselors] sees the mall as simply a 'climate-controlled street corner,' an updated version of the teen hangouts of yesteryear."**

1.   _____ For the area's youthful "mall rats," however, the majestic vistas can't compete with the climate-controlled, neon-lit enticements inside.

2.   _____ The mall is a magnet for kids yearning to be free.

3.   _____ Though the mall stands as a parentless playground, its denizens can't elude authority entirely.

4.   _____ After a late-afternoon lull, the mall again resonates with a high-energy buzz.

5.   _____ There comes a time in every teen-agers's life, however, when even the mall begins to pall.

6.   _____ Shopping, he [Mr. Johnan] insists, is less important than making the scene.

D.   MAKING INFERENCES

For each of these statements write Y (Yes) if the inference is an accurate one, N (No) if the inference is an inaccurate one, or CT (Can't Tell) if you do not have enough information to make an inference.

1.   _____ Some parents are not happy about the amount of time and money their teenagers spend at shopping malls.

2.   _____ The teenagers described in this article are fairly affluent.

3.   _____ Shopping mall store owners are unhappy about the hordes of teen-agers shopping in their stores after school and on weekends.

4.   _____ Aside from flirting and shopping, one other attraction of shopping malls is the absence of parents.

5.   _____ The students represented in this selection are not high academic achievers.

6.   _____ The teenagers mentioned in this article uniformly find the Hudson Valley Mall exciting.

E.   DRAWING CONCLUSIONS

Mark an X before any statement that represents a reasonable conclusion you can draw from the selection.

1.   _____ This particular area of New York needs more things for teenagers to do.

2. _____ The teenagers represented in this article seem materialistic.

3. _____ Teenagers often use socially correct labels as a way of fitting in and finding an identity.

4. _____ The parents of these teenagers apparently view the mall as a safe place to get rid of their children temporarily.

5. _____ The students described in the article spend more time shopping than studying.

F.   ANALYZING ORGANIZATION AND SEEING RELATIONSHIPS
Choose the correct answer.

1. This article has a clear beginning, middle, and end. Write the number of the paragraph where the body begins. _____ Then write the number of the paragraph where the conclusion begins. _____

2. _____ What is the method of development in paragraph 3? (a) steps in a process; (b) short examples; (c) cause and effect; (d) contrast; (e) definition of an important term.

3. Look again at paragraph 4. Write the sentence that represents the main idea. _____

   _____

4. The author emphasizes throughout the article that these teenagers (a) have a lot of money to spend; (b) are not representative of teenagers in the rest of the country; (c) do not get along very well with their parents; (d) are too willing to follow the crowd and cave in to peer pressure.

5. _____ Look again at paragraph 12, where Graham writes, "Throngs of high-school kids—a sea of denim jackets—crowd the passageways. The shuffle of hundreds of pairs of sneakers beats a soft percussion to the throbbing rock issuing from the boutiques." What does she strongly imply here? (a) Shopping malls should take steps to limit the number of teenagers allowed to shop at any one time; (b) The parents of these teenagers are too lenient with them; (c) The mall's store owners cater more to teenage shoppers than they do to adults; (d) These teenagers are rather conformist, all wearing the same thing.

6. _____ Which of the following best describes the author's attitude toward mall rats? (a) She is negative, critical; (b) she is sympathetic, understanding; (c) she is amused; (d) she is concerned, puzzled; (e) her attitude is not evident from the article.

G.   UNDERSTANDING VOCABULARY
Look through the paragraphs listed below and find a word that matches each definition. An example has been done for you.

Ex. level top of a mountain [1–2]   _____plateau_____

1. large assortment [2–3]   _____

2. excessively sweet [2–3]   _____

3. residents, inhabitants [6–7]   _____

4. stand about idly [7–8]   _____

5. avoid, escape from [7–8]   _____

6. playfully or facetiously named [7–8]   _____

7. gets by begging [10–11]   _____

8. general agreement [10–11]   _____

9. reduced in importance, overshadowed   _____
    [10–11]

10. become boring, wearisome [14–15]   _____

H.   USING VOCABULARY

Write the correct inflected form of the base word in each of the following sentences. Refer to your dictionary if necessary.

1. (*shroud*—use an adjective)   The beauty of the cloud-

    _____ peaks of the nearby Catskill Mountains can't compete with the attractions of the Hudson Valley Mall.

2. (*entice*—use a noun)   Mall rats are fascinated by the

    _____ for sale in the mall's various boutiques and emporia.

3. (*elusive*—use a verb)   Even though their parents are not with them at the

    mall, these teenagers can't _____ authority completely, for the mall is protected by security guards.

4. (*lamentable*—use a verb)   The Wilson sisters _____ that a Chihuahua puppy is still on display in the mall's pet store.

5. (*meagerly*—use an adjective)   By these teenagers' standards, their haul for

    this week is _____.

6. (*acquire*—use an adjective)   Although she does not state so directly, the author strongly suggests that these teenagers who hang out at the mall

    every weekend are basically _____.

7. (*resonate*—use a noun)   On a typical weekend, the noise of throngs of

high school kids creates a kind of _____ like a high-energy buzz.

8.   (*bemuse*—use an adjective)   Michael Johnan, a counselor at the mall's

Youth Booth, seems _____ by these teenagers' behavior; he wonders why they are in this climate-controlled mall when they could be outdoors enjoying themselves.

I.   TOPICS FOR WRITING OR DISCUSSION

1.   In your own words, write a paragraph in which you summarize the reasons teenagers find shopping malls so attractive and why they spend so much time and money in them.

_____

_____

_____

_____

_____

_____

_____

_____

2.   Certainly the shopping mall has forever changed the way Americans shop and spend money. What other institution or invention has had a profound effect on our daily lives or on the way we spend our time? What is its attraction?

12

Elliott West

WAGON TRAIN CHILDREN

Most of us have read of the hardships the nineteenth-century pioneers endured as they traveled west to California and Oregon, but for the children traveling overland, the experience must have been both exciting and unsettling. In this article the author recounts the experiences of several children on the Oregon Trail. Drawn chiefly from children's diaries and memoirs, the article speaks of encounters with Indians, of boredom and loneliness, and of the special adventure of moving west, not knowing what lay ahead of them.

VOCABULARY PREVIEW

**WORD
ORIGINS**

DISORIENTED

In paragraph 15 West writes of the possibility that children could get lost or stolen on the trail. He recounts the case of a seven-year-old boy who became *disoriented* and wandered away from his party. This word means "having lost one's sense of direction or location." Both the noun *Orient* ("the East"—as opposed to the Occident) and the verb to *orient* ("to place in a definite position") came into English from Latin. The Latin word *oriēns* meant "sunrise" or "east."

But as we use the word in English now, the meaning is broader, so that the reference to facing the east or the rising sun has been lost. Notice that this word contains the prefix *dis-*, so that *disoriented* is the antonymn of *oriented*.

CANNIBALISM

One of the memoirs quoted in paragraph 27 was written by a young girl who was a survivor of the Donner Party, a group of emigrants on their way to Oregon. Their guide foolishly decided to take a different route, supposedly a shortcut through the mountains. The group became completely lost and eventually was stranded in the Sierra Nevada mountains in northern California during an unusually harsh winter. Their supplies ran out, several people died, and the few survivors resorted to *cannibalism* to stay alive until help was found. (A fascinating account of the Donner Party is *Ordeal by Hunger* by George R. Stewart.)

The word *cannibal* is a corruption of *Caribales*, the name of a group of people living in Cuba and Haiti whom Christopher Columbus encountered when he landed in the New World. These tribes were fierce, and some were reported to be cannibals. European explorers used either word, *Canibales* and *Caribales*, to refer to the people of the West Indies. Somehow the incorrect name for the people became associated with their supposed reputation for eating people, and eventually the name *cannibal* came to be the English word for man-eaters.

WORD PARTS

EMIGRANTS

People often wrongly think that *emigrants* (paragraph 2) and *immigrants* mean the same thing. Although both words come from the same Latin root *migrāre* ("to move"), the prefixes make their meanings different. The prefix in *emigrate* comes from *ex-* ("away"), whereas the prefix in *immigrate* comes from *in-* ("in"). Thus, an *emigrant* is one who leaves ("moves from") one country or region, and an *immigrant* is one who enters ("goes into") and settles in a new country or region.

You will be able to remember the different meanings more easily if you think of the phrases *emigrate from* and *immigrate to*.

WORD FAMILIES

DOMAINS

One of the children wrote in her diary that the trip west "was like traveling over the great *domains* of a lost world." This word means "territory" or "realm." It derives from the French *domaine* ("property"), which in turn comes from the Latin word *dominus* ("lord"). This root, along with the related Latin word *domus* ("house"), is the source of a large family of English words, among which are the following:

dome	the hemispherical roof of a church or building; (from *domus Dei*, the "house of the Lord"), the most important feature of which was the domed roof
domestic	pertaining to the family or household
domesticate	to tame, to train to live with people in a household, as in a *domesticated* animal
domicile	one's legal residence or home
dominion	territory of sphere of influence or control

ELLIOTT WEST

WAGON TRAIN CHILDREN

1 The historian Francis Parkman, strolling around Independence, Mo., in 1846, remarked upon the "multitude of healty children's faces . . . peeping out from under the covers of the wagons." Two decades later, a traveler wrote of husbands

packing up "sunburned women and wild-looking children," along with shovels and flour barrels, in preparation for the journey West. In the gold fields of California in the 1850s, a chronicler met four sisters and sisters-in-law who had just crossed the Great Plains with 36 of their children. "They could," she wrote, "form quite a respectable village."

2   In the great overland migration that lasted from 1841 until the start of the Civil War, more than a quarter of a million people pushed their way from the Missouri valley to the Pacific coast. Probably at least 35,000 of them were young girls and boys; except during the Gold Rush, at least every fifth person on the trails was a child. Yet in all we read today, these thousands of young emigrants are infrequently seen and almost never heard.

3   The voices of many of them do survive, though. Some kept diaries along the way that have been preserved; many others wrote down their memories later. These records permit glimpses of a life that children of today might easily dream about—a child's life of adventure and purpose, of uncertainty and danger, albeit sometimes of sheer boredom. Once they reached their destinations and became settled, these children might well begin long years of isolation and monotony, but getting there was bound to be unpredictable and a challenge.

4   From Independence and St. Joseph and Council Bluffs their families packed into wagons usually no more than 5 feet by 10 feet and set out when the spring grass was up. For the next six months they would roll and lurch westward for more than 2000 miles—across plains and deserts, along the Platte, Sweetwater, Humboldt, Carson, Malheur, Snake and Columbia rivers, and through the Rockies, Blue Mountains and Sierra Nevada.

5   Children had little idea what to expect. For most of them the trip at first seemed a lark. "Every day was like a picnic," a young girl remembered of her earliest weeks on the trail. A 7-year-old had finished nearly half the trip when a question suddenly dawned on him. "I was looking far away in the direction we were traveling, across a dreary sage plain . . . and I got to wondering where we were trying to get to." "To Oregon," someone answered.

6   One boy had heard the fantastic names upon the land and waited eagerly for the show: "I was looking for the Black Hills. Hills I saw, but they were not black. Blue River had faded out, Chimney Rock was only a sharp pointed rock on the top of a hill, not a chimney at all. The 'Devil's Backbone' was only a narrow ridge."

7   Much of the passing scene measured up easily. Children gawked at giant whirlwinds, boiling springs, chasms hundreds of feet deep, wide rivers and dried desert streams. Some passed for hours at a stretch through land black with bison. There were antelope that bounded from sight before the dust was raised behind them, dogs that sang, squirrels that yipped like dogs. The human inhabitants of the land were just as marvelous. Boys and girls who overcame their first fears traded jackknives and coffee for beadwork and moccasins, and in the bargain they got a taste of the exotic. "They amused us by eating grasshoppers," a girl of 12 told her diary. As another young girl put it, "It was like traveling over the great domains of a lost world."

8   Children whose recollections survive rarely complained about the closeness of life in a wagon—they seem to have welcomed it in a time of uprooting—but food

was another matter. While they generally enjoyed antelope, bison and other new dishes of the Plains, there was much to rail at—like campside baking (bread "plentifully seasoned with mouse pills") and foul water ("drank red mud for coffee"). More than anything, they longed for fresh vegetables and fruit. Dried apples were brought along to ward off scurvy, but most youngsters found them a cruel mockery. An 11-year-old recommended them for their economy. "You need but one meal a day," he explained. "You can eat dried apples for breakfast, drink water for dinner and swell for supper."

9   Between the moments of excitement fell inevitable hours of boredom. Parents packed small libraries and organized school lessons to fill these hours; the children made up games. Many of the games would be instantly recognizable to both earlier and later generations—London Bridge, Run-Sheep-Run, Leapfrog, Button-Button. Girls and younger boys made wreaths and necklaces from wildflowers, a favorite pastime before the present century, and chanted handed-down rhymes and rounds.

10   By and large, they seemed to have preferred highly competitive games that stressed strategy. And they invented games of their own. One group of young boys found that when they dived onto a dead ox, its sun-bloated stomach would fling them back. This became a contest, with each competitor jumping harder and bouncing back farther. Finally a lanky boy sprinted, leaped head first—and plunged deep into the rotting carcass. Only with difficulty did his friends pull him out.

11   The same group of boys were expected to find fuel for the company's evening fires, and this, too, turned into a competition. At the end of the day they organized teams and divided the area around the night's camp into districts. Each group scoured its section and tried to amass the largest pile of buffalo chips, driving away all chip-rustlers and claim-jumpers with barrages of dried dung.

12   Most of the work was not so light. Children herded, cooked, hunted, gathered water, cared for babies and did other important tasks. And circumstances often left a boy or girl with graver responsibilities. When his fatherless family was abandoned by a hired hand, 11-year-old Elisha Brooks drove the animals, stood guard at night and generally took charge.

13   At 14, Octavius Pringle was sent on a lifesaving ride of 125 miles to fetch food for his group. Children of 10 and under sometimes drove ox teams, cared for herds and took part in difficult family decisions, and ones only a little older served on guard duty and chose camping sites. When the challenge of the road left her parents floundering, a daughter barely in her teens virtually took over her family of 12. "They all depend on her," wrote a fellow traveler. "The children go to her in their troubles and perplexities, her father and mother can rely on her, and she is always ready to do what she can."

14   Young girls in particular had chances to fill new roles—and to taste the complications that came with them. Mary Ellen Todd, 11, learned to drive the oxen pulling her family to Oregon. Later she recalled: "How my heart bounded . . . when I chanced to hear father say to mother, 'Do you know that Mary Ellen is beginning to crack the whip?' Then how it fell again, when mother replied, 'I am afraid it isn't a

very ladylike thing for a girl to do.' After this, while I felt a secret joy in being able to have power that sets things going, there was also some sense of shame. . . ."

15   Being lost or stolen could suddenly seem a real possibility on the trail. One 7-year-old sent to fetch a horse became disoriented and wandered for hours until he was found that night, miles from his party. Another, age 3, was found whimpering under some sagebrush a day after he walked away from camp.

16   "A dreadful fear of Indians was born and grown into me," remembered a girl who crossed the Plains at age 5 and had nightmares for years. Fed on stories of babies kidnapped by savages, children typically went into panic at their first sight of a Pawnee or Osage. An older boy recalled that the sight of scalps strung around a warrior's waist had "made me homesick"; many younger children, especially, never mastered their dread. Emma Shepherd wrote that every night on the trail was "full of terror" as she imagined that each breeze-blown bush was a skulking native.

17   But Indians were usually far more a help than a hindrance. Along the Sweetwater in 1852, a party of Crows took pity on a fatherless family and traveled with them for more than a week. It was quite a sight: Braves in panther robes rode before their favorite wives, tattooed and draped in mantles of bird skins, while behind them came the older women, dogs and finally an ox team with an exhausted white mother and her tattered brood of six. One of the boys remembered: "We were a wild West show."

18   Inevitably there were those who suffered terribly. An emigrant approaching the Sierra in 1850 would have passed children sitting on a wagon ruts sucking on pork rinds and eating rawhide. A widow of the trail recalled that near the end of her trip, her nine famished children "all would go out in the woods and smoke the wood mice out of the logs and roast and eat them."

19   Accidents were most common when a restless boy or girl, clambering around a rolling and pitching wagon, fell beneath its wheels. A woman told of such a tumble by her rambunctious grandson: "It did not quite kill him, but it made the little rascal holler awfully."

20   Although fewer than one in 20 emigrants died on the way West, most youngsters seem to have confronted death in some way. The wrote often of Indian burial platforms, with their decaying corpses and bleaching bones, and they hardly could have missed the hundreds of travelers' graves beside the trail.

21   In 1852 a boy and his mother methodically counted 32 in a stretch of 14 miles. One young girl told of seeing a baby's skeleton picked clean and lying beside the road. Another sat down only to discover the foot of an Indian's corpse poking from the sand next to her, and yet another glimpsed a woman's head, a comb still in its hair, pulled from a shallow grave by scavengers.

22   Sights like these could feed a child's basic fears. Mary Ackley had already lost her mother to cholera when her father disappeared for several hours. She wrote: "I never felt so miserable in my life. I sat on the ground with my face buried in my hands, speechless. . . . What would become of us children?"

23   A gold-seeker wrote in his diary of 1852: "I was one day traveling alone and in advance of our teams when I overtook a little girl who had lingered far behind her company. She was crying, and as I took her into my arms I discovered that her little

feet were bleeding by coming into contact with the sharp flint stones upon the road. I says why do you cry? Does your feet hurt you? See how they bleed. No (says she) nothing hurts me now. They buried my father and mother yesterday, and I don't want to live any longer. They took me away from my sweet mother and put her in the ground. . . ."

24   There is no indication that children died any oftener than adults on the road West, but parents probably buried more than 2000 of their young along the way. Only a tiny number were victims of Indians or wild beasts; most fell to diseases, especially cholera, which ravaged the travelers from 1849 to 1852. A far smaller number died from mishaps such as drownings, injuries by wagons and accidental poisonings or gunshots.

25   For a grim reminder of their vulnerability, children—those who could read— had only to look at the grave markers beside the road:

Our only child, Little Mary

Two children Killed by a Stampede, June 23, 1863

Jno. Hoover, died June 18. 49. Aged 12 yrs. Rest in peace, sweet boy, for thy travels are over

26   In October 1849, J. Goldsborough Bruff, a chronicler of the trail, rested just past the crest of the Sierra and watched the procession. Among the "rough-looking, hairy, dirty, ragged, jaded" emigrants were exhausted children of 10 carrying babies on their backs, and others leading cadaverous mules weighted with men and women wracked with scurvy and ague. But he shared his campfire with a pair of boys who cheerfully encouraged their weeping, despondent parents, and he met a cocky 6-year-old who bragged of his bravery and endurance: "I'm a great hand for walking." Along the soft, green sward of the Feather River, boys and girls laughed and played and napped.

27   As Bruff's observations suggest, children responded to the journey in countless ways. But a thread can be found: Most of these youngest pioneers seem to have come through with resilience and optimism, and many learned early of their own strengths. Nothing illustrates this better than a letter written from California in 1847 by Virginia Reed, at 13 a survivor of the tragic Donner party, whose terrible hardships in the snow of the Sierra Nevada had led them to cannibalism. "O Mary, I have not wrote you half of the truble [we have had] but I hav wrote you anuf to let you know what truble is," she told her cousin. She finished not with grief or self-pity but with a piece of offhand advice. "Don't let this letter dishaten anybody," she wrote. "Never take no cutof's* and hury along as fast as you can."   ■

*cutofs—Virginia Reed is referring to the cutoff the leader of the Donner Party took, supposedly a faster way through the Sierra Nevada mountains, which caused them to lose their way and become stranded for the winter.

From Elliot West, "Wagon Train Children," *American Heritage,* December 1985. Reprinted by permission of American Heritage, a division of Forbes, Inc.

EXERCISES

Do not refer to the selection for Exercises A and B.

A.   DETERMINING THE MAIN IDEA AND PURPOSE

1.   _____ The main idea of the selection is that (a) the diaries emigrant children kept of their journey west reveal that their lives were adventurous, uncertain, challenging, dangerous, and frequently monotonous; (b) in everything we read about the emigrants who moved west along the Oregon Trail, the experiences of the emigrants' children have been largely neglected; (c) for the children who migrated with their families, the trip west was only the beginning of a life of boredom and isolation, which would continue long after they reached their destination; (d) from 1841 until 1865 more than 250,000 people pushed their way west to the Pacific Ocean in a great overland migration.

2.   _____ The author's purpose is chiefly (a) to persuade the reader to accept his opinion on a controversial issue; (b) to relate a series of stories; (c) to describe the scenery of the western Plains states; (d) to inform the reader about a part of American history.

B.   COMPREHENDING MAIN IDEAS
Choose the correct answer.

1.   _____ Of the 250,000 emigrants who came west, the children probably numbered about (a) 10,000; (b) 35,000; (c) 50,000; (d) 100,000.

2.   _____ For the children, the greatest difficulty of the trip west was undoubtedly (a) the lack of companionship with other children; (b) the absence of a traditional schoolroom; (c) the uncertainty about what they would find when they reached their destination; (d) the close quarters they had to share with their families in the wagons.

3.   _____ What the children complained most about on the long journey was (a) the poor quality of the food; (b) the lack of privacy in the wagons; (c) the impossibility of making permanent new friends; (d) having to collect dried buffalo dung for fuel.

4.   _____ According to the author, the Indians that the emigrants encountered along the way were (a) generally savage and hostile; (b) terrified of the white travelers; (c) usually more of a help than a hindrance; (d) suspicious and distant in manner.

5.   _____ The most common danger for children along the route was (a) being kidnapped by Indians; (b) dying of starvation; (c) getting scurvy; (d) falling under the wagon wheels.

6. _____ The disease that caused the most deaths among the emigrants from 1849 to 1852 was (a) tuberculosis; (b) scarlet fever; (c) influenza; (d) cholera.

COMPREHENSION SCORE

Score your answers for Exercises A and B as follows:

A. No. right _____ × 2 = _____

B. No. right _____ × 1 = _____

Total pts. from A and B _____ × 10 = _____%

You may refer to the selection for the remaining exercises.

C. RECOGNIZING SUPPORTING DETAILS

Place an X in the space for each statement that *directly* supports this main idea from the selection. **"Most of the work was not so light. . . . And circumstances often left a boy or girl with graver responsibilities."**

1. _____ Boys who were expected to find fuel for the evening fires turned the work into a competition.

2. _____ Children herded, cooked, hunted, gathered water, and cared for babies.

3. _____ One 11-year-old boy took charge of his family after his fatherless family was abandoned by a hired hand.

4. _____ At 14 another boy was sent on a lifesaving ride of 125 miles to fetch food for his group.

5. _____ When Mary Ellen Todd learned to crack a whip at the age of 11, her mother complained that it wasn't a very ladylike thing for a girl to do.

6. _____ In 1852 a party of Crow Indians took pity on a fatherless family and traveled with them for more than a week.

7. _____ Some children suffered terribly from hunger and malnutrition.

8. _____ In one way or another, most youngsters learned to confront death on the way west.

D. MAKING INFERENCES

For each of these statements write Y (Yes) if the inference is an accurate one, N (No) if the inference is an inaccurate one, or CT (Can't Tell) if you do not have enough information to make an inference.

1. _____ The kind of life that the emigrant children experienced as they moved west would be nearly impossible for American children today to duplicate.

2. _____ Diaries kept by children during the journey would probably represent a more accurate account of their experiences than memoirs written when they were older.

3. _____ Even if the children were uncertain about what they would find when they reached their destination, their parents knew.

4. _____ Some of the place names, like Devil's Backbone or the Black Hills, were an exaggeration.

5. _____ By the time of the great migration west, the great herds of bison had nearly disappeared because of overhunting.

6. _____ Scurvy, caused by a vitamin deficiency, can be prevented by eating fruits and vegetables.

7. _____ The stories of savages kidnapping babies or killing children were completely made up and had no basis in fact.

8. _____ The author was impressed by the strength and good spirits the emigrant children apparently displayed.

E.   ANALYZING ORGANIZATION AND SEEING RELATIONSHIPS

1. This essay has a clear introduction, body, and conclusion. Write the number of the paragraph where the body begins. _____ Then write the number of the paragraph where the conclusion begins. _____

2. _____ To support the main ideas in the article, the author relies mainly on (a) personal opinion; (b) several examples and illustrations taken from firsthand accounts; (c) historical facts and statistics; (d) stories that have been handed down from generation to generation.

3. _____ Look again at paragraph 7. How does the author develop the main idea? (a) reasons; (b) definitions of unfamiliar terms; (c) descriptive examples; (d) contrasting statistics.

4. Read the first sentence of paragraph 8, which suggests a contrast between two things. What is the author contrasting? _____

    and _____

5. _____ In the section from paragraphs 9–12, the author emphasizes the children's (a) fears and concerns; (b) isolation and loneliness; (c) imagination and inventiveness; (d) ways of escaping from the harsh reality.

6. _____ The author intends the descriptive details in paragraph 21 to be (a) gruesome; (b) amusing; (c) unbelievable; (d) shocking.

7. Write the sentence from the article that represents West's conclusion and the number of the paragraph where it occurs.

    _____

_____

_____ in paragraph _____.

8.   _____ The author's attitude toward the emigrant children is (a) not evident from the essay; (b) neutral, impartial; (c) amazed, astonished; (d) admiring, sympathetic.

F.   UNDERSTANDING VOCABULARY

Choose the correct definition according to the context.

1.   _____ a child's life of uncertainty and danger, *albeit* sometimes of sheer boredom [paragraph 3—pronounced ôl-bē′ ĭt]: (a) although; (b) including; (c) in addition; (d) finally.

2.   _____ Children *gawked* at giant whirlwinds [7]: (a) were frightened of; (b) marveled at; (c) ran away from; (d) stared at.

3.   _____ *chasms* hundreds of feet deep [7—pronounced kăz′ əmz]: (a) valleys; (b) craters; (c) narrow cracks; (d) deep holes.

4.   _____ they got a taste of the *exotic* [7]: Referring to something that is (a) weird, bizarre; (b) foreign, unfamiliar; (c) usual, ordinary; (d) surprising, unexpected.

5.   _____ there was much to *rail* at [8]: (a) criticize harshly; (b) be grateful for; (c) long or wish for; (d) remember in a negative way.

6.   _____ to *ward off* scurvy [8]: (a) cure; (b) diagnose; (c) prevent; (d) cause.

7.   _____ left her parents *floundering* [13]: (a) acting in confusion; (b) wondering about the future; (c) feeling ill; (d) incapable of acting.

8.   _____ a grim reminder of their *vulnerability* [25]: (a) imminent death; (b) ability to withstand danger; (c) lack of sensitivity; (d) susceptibility to harm, danger.

9.   _____ encouraged their weeping, *despondent* parents [26]: (a) detested; (b) disheartened; (c) desperate; (d) devoted.

10.   _____ come through with *resilience* and optimism [27]: The ability to (a) look at the positive side of life; (b) keep a sense of humor; (c) learn a lesson from one's mistakes; (d) recover quickly from misfortune.

G.   USING VOCABULARY

From the following list of vocabulary words, choose a word that fits in each blank according to both the grammatical structure of the sentence and the context. Use each word in the list only once and add noun or verb endings (such as *-s, -ing,* or *-ed*) if necessary. (Note that there are more words than sentences.)

inevitable	domain	strategy
exotic	monotony	barrage
destination	disoriented	hindrance
dread	scour	skulk

1. It was _____ that life for the children on the Oregon
    Trail would be characterized by _____, but at the
    same time the Indians and the new scenery provided them with a taste of
    the _____.

2. Some children never overcame their _____ of In-
    dians, whom they imagined might be _____ around
    behind every bush or tree; in fact, however, the Indians the travelers en-
    countered were generally more of a help than a _____.

3. Emigrant children devised games that required some

    _____; even the task of _____
    the countryside for buffalo chips was turned into a competition.

H. TOPICS FOR WRITING OR DISCUSSION

1. Here are some sentences from the article. Paraphrase them by rewriting
    each one in your own words in the space provided.

    a. These records permit glimpses of a life that children of today might
    easily dream about—a child's life of adventure and purpose, of uncer-
    tainty and danger, albeit sometimes of sheer boredom. _____

    _____

    _____

    _____

    _____

    b. Children whose recollections survive rarely complained about the
    closeness of life in a wagon—they seem to have welcomed it in a time
    of uprooting—but food was another matter. _____

    _____

    _____

    _____

    _____

    c. For a grim reminder of their vulnerability, children—those who could read—had only to look at the grave markers beside the road. _____

_____

_____

_____

_____

2. Investigate what life was like for the immigrants after they arrived in the Gold Rush towns of California or in Oregon and report on your findings.

13 ||||||

Lynda W. Warren and Jonnae C. Ostrom

THEY'VE GOTTA KEEP IT: PEOPLE WHO SAVE EVERYTHING

This article, originally published in Psychology Today, *is about people who hoard stuff, otherwise known as pack rats. Lynda Warren is a counseling psychologist and professor of psychology at California State University, San Bernardino. Jonnae Ostrom is a licensed clinical social worker and a member of the staff at Hoag Memorial Hospital in Newport Beach, California.*

VOCABULARY PREVIEW

WORD ORIGINS

WINNOW

In paragraph 1, the authors write, "because they [pack rats] rarely *winnow* what they save, it grows and grows." Meaning in this context, "to sort" or "to eliminate," this verb indicates the practice of going through things carefully, separating out what to save and what to throw away.

Its meaning comes from agriculture. Although today we have machines to do this work, in earlier times farmers winnowed wheat by separating the chaff or grain husks from the grain itself by means of a current of air. The verb *winnow* comes from Middle English, *windowen,* from the Old English noun *wind.*

HAPHAZARDLY

The authors write in paragraph 3, "But pack rats tend to stockpile their possessions *haphazardly* and seldom use them." The adjective form *haphazard* means "characterized by lack of order," "done by chance." Because today we think of anything *hazardous* as being dangerous, we are apt to think that the root *hazard* has something to do with danger, but in fact, its original meaning had to do with chance, associated with throwing dice.

The prefix derives from the Old Norse word *happ* ("good luck," "chance"), but the root *hazard* has a more complicated history:

> Middle English *hasard* or *hazard*, from Old French *hasard*, from Spanish *azar* ("an unlucky throw of the dice"), from Arabic *yasara*, ("he played at dice")

As you can see, the current meaning suggests something a bit different, although the suggestion of chance is retained.

Joseph Shipley, in the *Dictionary of Word Origins*, offers a slightly different etymology for *hazard*:

> Roman soldiers tossed dice for the clothes of the crucified Jesus. The practice continued; at the time of the Crusades, William of Tyre tells us, a game of chance was played which the Spanish called *azar*, from the castle in Palestine called *Ain Zorba* or *Asart*. From the game, the word spread to anything *hazardous*.

ECCENTRICS

One theory about the reason people become pack rats is presented in paragraph 4: ". . . we, like most people, assumed that pack rats were all older people who had lived through the Great Depression of the 1930s—*eccentrics* who were stockpiling stuff just in case another Depression came along." An *eccentric* is a person who is odd in some fashion, one who deviates from the usual pattern.

This word's derivation, oddly, is from geometry, referring to planets or other spheres whose axis or support is not in the center. The word came into the language from Middle English *excentryke*, originally from Greek:

> [*ekkentros ex-* ("out") + *kentron* ("point," "center")]

In other words, an *eccentric* person is "off-center" or "different."

WORD PARTS

NEGATIVE PREFIXES: IN-, IM-, AND DIS-

The English language has a few prefixes indicating negation or "not," three of which are illustrated in this article:

1. *in-* (paragraph 2, "to save *indiscriminately*")
   (paragraph 12, "an *inordinate* fear")
   (paragraph 17, "the perfect way to avoid *indecision*")

2. *im-* (paragraphs 19 and 22, "I feel *impotent* about getting my bedroom cleaned")

3. *dis-* (paragraph 17, "the *discomfort* of getting rid of things")

Im- is a variation on the Latin prefix *in-*. It is used to make negative words beginning with the consonants *m* and *p*. The wisdom of this linguistic change is easily seen if you try to pronounce the nonword *inperfect* or *inmobile*.

Here are the definitions of these negative words:

indiscriminately	describing something done randomly or haphazardly
inordinate	exceeding normal limits, not regular or orderly
indecision	quality of not being able to make a decision
impotent	powerless, weak [pronounced ĭm′ pə-tent]
discomfort	distress, condition of being uncomfortable

These words containing negative prefixes also appear in the selection. Refer to your dictionary if you do not know their meaning: *insatiably* (paragraph 1), *intolerance* (paragraph 5), *disorder* (paragraph 12), *incredibly* (paragraph 13), *insensitive* (paragraph 14), *ineffective* (paragraph 19), *disarray* (paragraph 23), and *disapprove* (paragraph 25).

WORD FAMILIES

AVERT

In the conclusion of the article, the authors ask, "What predisposes people to become pack rats, and when does hoarding typically start? Can the behavior be *averted* or changed?" To *avert* means "to prevent," literally "to turn away." Here is its derivation from Latin:

[*ab-* ("away") + *vertere* ("to turn")]

Here are some other English words with the Latin root *vertere* at their heart:

advertise	to make known a product's or business's qualities, from *advert,* to call attention to, literally "to turn toward" [*ad-* ("toward") + *vertere*]
convert	to change into another form, from Latin, "to turn around," "transform"
divert	to turn aside from a course, to distract [*dis-* ("away") + *vertere*]
pervert	to turn away from what is considered morally right, corrupt, literally to turn the wrong way [*per-* ("completely") + *vertere*]
reverse	turned backward, moving backward, literally to turn back [*re-* ("back") + *vertere*]
vertigo	a sensation of dizziness, a feeling that one is whirling about, from Latin for "whirling" [*vertigo* ("a whirling"), from *vertere*]

LYNDA W. WARREN AND JONNAE C. OSTROM

THEY'VE GOTTA KEEP IT: PEOPLE WHO SAVE EVERYTHING

1   Most of us have more things than we need and use. At times they pile up in corners and closets or accumulate in the recesses of attics, basements or garages. But we sort through our clutter periodically and clean it up, saving only what we really need and giving away or throwing out the excess. This isn't the case, unfortunately, with people we call "pack rats"—those who collect, save or hoard insatiably, often with only the vague rationale that the items may someday be useful. And because they rarely winnow what they save, it grows and grows.

2   While some pack rats specialize in what they collect, others seem to save indiscriminately. And what they keep, such as junk mail, supermarket receipts, newspapers, business memos, empty cans, clothes or old Christmas and birthday cards, often seem to be worthless. Even when items have some value, such as lumber scraps, fabric remnants, auto parts, shoes and plastic meat trays, they tend to be kept in huge quantities that no one could use in a lifetime.

3   Although pack rats collect, they are different from collectors, who save in a systematic way. Collectors usually specialize in one of a few classes of objects, which they organize, display and even catalogue. But pack rats tend to stockpile their possessions haphazardly and seldom use them.

4   Our interest in pack rats was sparked by a combination of personal experience with some older relatives and recognition of similar saving patterns in some younger clients one of us saw in therapy sessions. Until then, we, like most people, assumed that pack rats were all older people who had lived through the Great Depression of the 1930s—eccentrics who were stockpiling stuff just in case another Depression came along. We were surprised to discover a younger generation of pack rats, born long after the 1930s.

5   None of these clients identified themselves during therapy as pack rats or indicated that their hoarding tendencies were causing problems in any way. Only after their partners told us how annoyed and angry they were about the pack rats' unwillingness to clean up the growing mess at home did they acknowledge their behavior. Even then, they defended it and had little interest in changing. The real problem, they implied, was their partner's intolerance rather than their own hoarding.

6   Like most people, we had viewed excessive saving as a rare and harmless eccentricity. But when we discussed our initial observations with others, we gradually came to realize that almost everyone we met either admitted to some strong pack-rat tendencies or seemed to know someone who had them. Perhaps the greatest surprise, however, was how eager people were to discuss their own pack-rat experiences. Although our observations are admittedly based on a small sample, we now believe that such behavior is common and that, particularly when it is extreme, it may create problems for the pack rats or those close to them.

7   When we turned to the psychological literature, we found surprisingly little about human collecting or hoarding in general and almost nothing about pack-rat behavior. Psychoanalysts view hoarding as one characteristic of the "anal" character type, first described by Freud. Erich Fromm later identified the "hoarding orientation" as one of the four basic ways in which people may adjust unproductively to life.

8   While some pack rats do have typically anal-retentive* characteristics such as miserliness, orderliness and stubbornness, we suspect that they vary as much in personality characteristics as they do in education, socioeconomic status and occupation. But they do share certain ways of thinking and feeling about their possessions that shed some light on the possible causes and consequences of their behavior.

9   Why do some people continue to save when there is no more space for what they have and they own more of something than could ever be used? We have now asked that question of numerous students, friends and colleagues who have admitted their pack-rat inclinations. They readily answer the question with seemingly good reasons, such as possible future need ("I might need this sometime"), sentimental attachment ("Aunt Edith gave this to me"), potential value ("This might be worth something someday") and lack of wear or damage ("This is too good to throw away"). Such reasons are difficult to challenge; they are grounded in some truth and logic and suggest that pack-rat saving reflects good sense, thrift and even foresight. Indeed, many pack rats proudly announce, "I've never thrown anything away!" or "You would not believe what I keep!"

10   But on further questioning, other, less logical reasons become apparent. Trying to get rid of things may upset pack rats emotionally and may even bring on physical distress. As one woman said, "I get a headache or sick to my stomach if I have to throw something away."

11   They find it hard to decide what to keep and what to throw away. Sometimes they fear they will get rid of something that they or someone else might value, now or later. Having made such a "mistake" in the past seems to increase such distress. "I've always regretted throwing away the letters Mother sent me in college. I will never make that mistake again," one client said. Saving the object eliminates the distress and is buttressed by the reassuring thought, "Better to save this than be sorry later."

12   Many pack rats resemble compulsive personalities in their tendency to avoid or postpone decisions, perhaps because of an inordinate fear of making a mistake. Indeed, in the latest edition of the psychiatric diagnostic bible (DSM-III-R), the kind of irrational hoarding seen in pack rats ("inability to discard worn-out or worthless objects even when they have no sentimental value") is described as a characteristic of people with obsessive compulsive personality disorder.

13   Some pack rats seem to have a depressive side, too. Discarding things seems to reawaken old memories and feelings of loss or abandonment, akin to grief or the

*A psychoanalytic term describing a type of personality who shows traits such as meticulousness (being overly precise), greed, and stubbornness; its origin is associated with infantile pleasure in retaining one's feces.

pain of rejection. "I feel incredibly sad—it's really very painful," one client said of the process. Another client, a mental-health counselor, said, "I don't understand why, but when I have to throw something away, even something like dead flowers, I feel my old abandonment fears and I also feel lonely."

14   Some pack rats report that their parents discarded certain treasured possessions, apparently insensitive to their attachment to the objects. "My Dad went through my room one time and threw out my old shell collection that I had in a closet. It devastated me," said one woman we interviewed. Such early experiences continue to color their feelings as adults, particularly toward possessions they especially cherish.

15   It's not uncommon for pack rats to "personalize" their possessions or identify with them, seeing them as extensions of themselves. One pack rat defiantly said about her things, "This is me—this is my individuality and you are not going to throw it out!"

16   At times the possessions are viewed akin to beloved people. For example, one woman said, "I can't let my Christmas tree be destroyed! I love my Christmas ornaments—I adore them!" Another woman echoed her emotional involvement: "My jewelry is such a comfort to me. I just love my rings and chains." Discarding such personalized possessions could easily trigger fears, sadness or guilt because it would be psychologically equivalent to a part of oneself dying or abandoning a loved one.

17   In saving everything, the pack rat seems to have found the perfect way to avoid indecision and the discomfort of getting rid of things. It works—but only for a while. The stuff keeps mounting, and so do the problems it produces.

18   Attempts to clean up and organize may be upsetting because there is too much stuff to manage without spending enormous amounts of time and effort. One pack rat sighed, "Just thinking about cleaning it up makes me tired before I begin." And since even heroic efforts at cleaning bring barely visible results, such unrewarding efforts are unlikely to continue.

19   At this point, faced with ever-growing goods and ineffective ways of getting rid of the excess, pack rats may begin to feel controlled by their possessions. As one put it, "I'm at the point where I feel impotent about getting my bedroom cleaned."

20   Even if the clutter doesn't get the pack rats down, it oftens irks others in the household who do not share the same penchant for saving. Since hoarding frequently begins in the bedroom, the pack rat's partner is usually the first to be affected. He or she begins to feel squeezed out by accumulated possessions, which may seem to take precedence over the couple's relationship.

21   At first, the partner may simply feel bewildered about the growing mess and uncertain about what to do, since requests to remove the "junk" tend to be ignored or met with indignation or even anger. One exasperated husband of a pack-rat client said: "She keeps her stuff in paper bags all over the bedroom. You can now hardly get to the bed. I tried talking to her about it but nothing seems to work. When she says she has cleaned it out, I can never see any change. I'm ready to hire a truck to cart it all away."

22   As the junk piles accumulate, the partner may try to clean up the mess. But that generally infuriates the pack rat and does nothing to break the savings habit. As the partner begins to feel increasingly impotent, feelings of frustration and irritation

escalate and the stockpiled possessions may become an emotional barrier between the two. This situation is even worse if the pack rat is also a compulsive shopper whose spending sprees are creating financial problems and excessive family debt.

23   Children are also affected by a parent's pack-rat behavior. They may resent having the family's living space taken over by piles of possessions and may hesitate to ask their friends over because they are embarrassed by the excessive clutter and disarray. One child of a pack rat said, "As long as I can remember, I've always warned people what to expect the first time they come to our house. I told them it was OK to move something so they would have a place to sit down." Even the adults may rarely invite nonfamily members to visit because the house is never presentable.

24   Children may also be caught in the middle of the escalating tension between their parents over what to do about all the stuff in the house. But whatever their feelings, it is clear that the children are being raised in an environment in which possessions are especially important and laden with complex emotions.

25   Our clients and other people we have consulted have helped make us aware of the problems pack rats can pose for themselves and those around them. Now we hope that a new study of excessive savers will provide some preliminary answers to a number of deeper questions: What predisposes people to become pack rats, and when does hoarding typically start? Can the behavior be averted or changed? Is excessive saving associated with earlier emotional or economic deprivation? Does such saving cause emotional distress directly or are pack rats only bothered when others disapprove of their behavior? Do pack rats run into problems at work the same way they often do at home?

26   Whatever additional information we come up with, we're already sure of at least one thing: This article will be saved forever by all the pack rats of the world.   ■

From Lynda Warren and Jonnae C. Ostrom, "They've Gotta Keep It: People Who Save Everything," *San Francisco Chronicle*, "This World," May 1, 1988. Originally published in *Psychology Today*. Reprinted with permission.

EXERCISES

Do not refer to the selection for Exercises A and B.

A. DETERMINING THE MAIN IDEA AND PURPOSE
Choose the best answer.

1.   _____ The main idea of the article is that (a) most pack rats are people who lived through the Depression and are stockpiling things in case there is another one; (b) excessive saving is a rare and harmless eccentricity, which has very little effect on the family; (c) the hoarding tendencies of pack rats is a relatively common phenomenon that can cause problems for both the pack rats and their families; (d) researchers who have studied pack rat behavior have uncovered some reasons to explain this phenomenon and some solutions for it.

2. _____ With respect to the main idea, the author's purpose is (a) to explain and to inform by discussing the behavior of pack rats; (b) to summarize current psychological studies done on pack rats; (c) to convince people not to become excessive savers; (d) to provide evidence in support of a controversial issue.

B.   COMPREHENDING MAIN IDEAS
Choose the correct answer.

1. _____ According to the authors, the problem with pack rats becomes worse and worse because they (a) do not specialize in what they collect; (b) refuse to get counseling; (c) become too emotionally attached to their possessions; (d) fail to go through their stuff and throw away or give away what they don't need.

2. _____ Not only do pack rats save stuff that is usually classified as worthless, but they may also (a) keep important items that they use every day; (b) save ridiculous amounts of useful items; (c) develop antisocial tendencies and become "loners"; (d) hoard money as if it were a possession.

3. _____ The authors state that hoarding tendencies in humans are (a) actually fairly rare; (b) actually quite common; (c) evident in all cultures; (d) a logical way of preparing for the next economic depression.

4. _____ The authors believe, from their interviews and observations, that pack rats (a) represent every personality trait, educational background, socioeconomic status, and occupation; (b) all share the same anal-retentive characteristics of miserliness, compulsiveness, stubbornness, and orderliness; (c) were raised in households where one member was a pack rat; (d) tend to be older people who endured deprivation during the Depression of the 1930s.

5. _____ Some pack rats feel physical distress or a terrible sense of loss when (a) their partner forces them to clean up; (b) they throw something away; (c) they see their clutter accumulating and filling all available space; (d) they are forced to confront their problem.

6. _____ Pack rats typically begin accumulating stuff in (a) the kitchen; (b) the living room; (c) the garage; (d) the bedroom.

COMPREHENSION SCORE

Score your answers for Exercises A and B as follows:

A.   No. right _____ × 2 = _____

B.   No. right _____ × 1 = _____

Total pts. from A and B _____ × 10 = _____%

You may refer to the selection for the remaining exercises.

C.   DISTINGUISHING BETWEEN MAIN IDEAS AND SUPPORTING DETAILS

Label the following statements from the selection as follows: MI if the statement represents a *main idea* and SD if the statement represents a *supporting detail.*

1.   _____ Some pack rats report that their parents discarded certain treasured possessions, apparently insensitive to their attachment to the objects.

2.   _____ "My Dad went through my room one time and threw out my old shell collection that I had in a closet."

3.   _____ "It devastated me," said one woman we interviewed.

4.   _____ Such early experiences continue to color their feelings as adults, particularly toward possessions they especially cherish.

5.   _____ It's not uncommon for pack rats to "personalize" their possessions or identify with them, seeing them as extensions of themselves.

6.   _____ One pack rat defiantly said about her things, "This is me—this is my individuality and you are not going to throw it out!"

7.   _____ At times the possessions are viewed akin to beloved people.

8.   _____ For example, one woman said, "I can't let my Christmas tree be destroyed!"

9.   _____ "I love my Christmas ornaments—I adore them!"

10.   _____ Another woman echoed her emotional involvement: "My jewelry is such a comfort to me."

11.   _____ "I just love my rings and chains."

12.   _____ Discarding such personalized possessions could easily trigger fears, sadness or guilt because it would be psychologically equivalent to a part of oneself dying or abandoning a loved one.

D.   MAKING INFERENCES

Choose the correct inference.

1.   _____ Look again at paragraph 1, from which we can infer that (a) pack rats would not save so much stuff if they only had more time to sort through things; (b) most people are basically pack rats at heart; (c) not sorting things out or giving things away compounds the pack rat's biggest problem of increasingly accumulating stuff; (d) the authors themselves are pack rats.

2.   _____ From paragraph 5 we can infer that (a) pack rats use denial, rather than admitting their faults or seeing the problems that result from their hoarding; (b) therapy can change pack rats' behavior; (c) the partners of pack rats should help them sort through and get rid of things; (d) pack rats do not enjoy hoarding but are powerless to stop.

3. _____ Paragraph 8 implies that (a) all pack rats are basically anal-retentive; (b) the authors do not have solid proof for their observation that pack rats vary in personality, education, and the like; (c) the authors do have solid proof for their observation that pack rats vary in personality, education, and the like; (d) pack rats are aware of their problem and the underlying causes for it.

4. _____ From the information contained in paragraphs 9, 10, and 11, we can infer that (a) pack rats really are thrifty and sensible people; (b) psychologists do not accept pack rats' explanations for their behavior; (c) there are deeper reasons underlying pack rats' behavior than the logical reasons they put forth; (d) pack rats do not readily learn from their past mistakes.

5. _____ Look again at paragraphs 17 and 18, from which we can infer that (a) even if a pack rat cleaned everything up, the clutter would just begin to accumulate again; (b) it is impossible for a pack rat to change his or her behavior; (c) being a pack rat involves a vicious circle: the more stuff accumulates, the harder the problem is to deal with; (d) nagging a pack rat is a good way to deal with the problem.

6. _____ The authors imply in paragraphs 22 and 23 that (a) pack rats need psychological counseling; (b) the children and spouse of a pack rat may suffer more than the pack rat from the pack rat's hoarding and spending habits; (c) the children of pack rats grow up to be compulsively neat and orderly, and are not hesitant about throwing stuff away; (d) nonfamily members of a pack rat may succeed in getting the pack rat to change his or her ways.

E.   ANALYZING ORGANIZATION AND SEEING RELATIONSHIPS
Choose the correct answer.

1. What is the function of the third sentence of paragraph 1 in relation to

the article as a whole? _____

2. _____ With respect to the topic of excessive hoarding, the authors' chief concern is (a) to illustrate this behavior from their experience with clients, friends, and relatives; (b) to analyze the research studies done on this behavior; (c) to explain some theories concerning the reasons for this behavior and the problems associated with it; (d) to explain the effects on the family; (e) to criticize psychiatrists for assuming that all compulsive savers exhibit anal-retentive characteristics.

3. Paragraph 3 uses contrast as its method of development. What two

things are being contrasted? _____ and

_____

4. _____ What is the method of development in paragraph 9? (a) a list of

rationalizations; (b) short examples; (c) facts and statistics; (d) comparison; (e) contrast.

5. What is the purpose of paragraphs 14–17 in relation to the article as a whole? _____

6. _____ Look again at the last sentence of paragraph 18. What is the relationship between the two parts? (a) contrast; (b) cause and effect; (c) term and a definition of it; (d) contrast; (e) general and specific.

_____

7. _____ What is the authors' attitude toward hoarders? They are (a) neutral, objective; (b) critical, deriding; (c) sympathetic, even empathetic; (d) confused, perplexed; (e) amused.

8. How would you describe the tone of the last paragraph?

_____ _____

F. UNDERSTANDING VOCABULARY
Choose the correct definition according to the context.

1. _____ those who collect, save or hoard *insatiably* [paragraph 1]: Describing someone incapable of being (a) understood; (b) criticized; (c) satisfied; (d) organized.

2. _____ others seem to save *indiscriminately* [2]: (a) haphazardly; (b) unconsciously; (c) uncontrollably; (d) with embarrassment.

3. _____ they are *grounded* in some truth and logic [9]: (a) prevented; (b) restricted; (c) planted; (d) based.

4. _____ an *inordinate* fear of making a mistake [12]: (a) irrational; (b) excessive; (c) absurd; (d) persistent.

5. _____ *akin* to grief or the pain of rejection [13; see also 16]: (a) different from; (b) identical to; (c) related to; (d) lessened by.

6. _____ I feel *impotent* about getting my bedroom cleaned [19; see also 22]: (a) uncertain; (b) insincere; (c) unfulfilled; (d) powerless.

7. _____ it often *irks* others in the household [20]: (a) irritates; (b) depresses; (c) saddens; (d) angers.

8. _____ the same *penchant* for saving [20]: (a) fondness; (b) responsibility; (c) inclination; (d) preference.

9. _____ the excessive clutter and *disarray* [23]: (a) state of disorder; (b) lack of harmony; (c) lack of cleanliness; (d) inconsistency.

10. _____ the *escalating* tension [24]: (a) annoying; (b) constant; (c) increasing; (d) isolated.

11. _____ possessions are *laden with* complex emotions [24]: (a) represented by; (b) associated with; (c) filled with; (d) weighed down by.

12. _____ Can the behavior be *averted* or changed? [25]: (a) abolished; (b) prevented; (c) controlled; (d) changed.

G.   USING VOCABULARY

In parentheses before each sentence are some inflected forms of words from the selection. Study the context and the sentence. Then write the correct form in the space provided. Be sure to add appropriate endings like *-s, -ed,* or *-ing* if necessary.

1. (*system, systematize, systematic, systematically*)   Based on the information presented in the article, it is probably a good idea for everyone who is not a pack rat and who doesn't want to become one to go through his or her possessions _____ every year and get rid of useless things.

2. (*haphazard, haphazardly*)   Rather than specializing in one object to save, pack rats tend to be _____ about the possessions they stockpile.

3. (*miser, miserliness, miserly*)   Although pack rats hoard things, there is no indication that they are _____ when it comes to hoarding money.

4. (*potentiality, potential, potentially*)   Pack rats often justify their saving by claiming that a possession may be _____ valuable.

5. (*distress, distressful, distressfully*)   Some hoarders actually claim that throwing things away increases their _____.

6. (*compulsion, compulsiveness, compulsive, compulsively*)   People who suffer from a _____ to save useless things may actually be incapable of making a decision.

7. (*obsess, obsession, obsessiveness, obsessive, obsessively*)   The authors explain that one characteristic of hoarders is an _____-compulsive personality disorder.

8. (*devastate, devastation, devastatingly*)   One woman interviewed for the article reported that she felt _____ when she discovered that her father had thrown out her cherished shell collection.

9. (*defy, defiance, defiant, defiantly*)   Some pack rats speak with _____ when they discuss their relationship with their possessions.

10. (*indecision, indecisiveness, indecisive, indecisively*) _____
may be one reason hoarders accumulate things; they just can't decide
what to keep and what to get rid of.

H.   TOPICS FOR WRITING OR DISCUSSION

1.   Here are some sentences from the article. Paraphrase them by rewriting
each one in your own words in the space provided.

a. None of these clients identified themselves during therapy as pack rats
or indicated that their hoarding tendencies were causing problems in
any way. Only after their partners told us how annoyed and angry
they were about the pack rats' unwillingness to clean up the growing
mess at home did they acknowledge their behavior.

_____

_____

_____

_____

_____

b. Such reasons are difficult to challenge; they are grounded in some
truth and logic and suggest that pack-rat saving reflects good sense,
thrift and even foresight.

_____

_____

_____

c. Many pack rats resemble compulsive personalities in their tendency to
avoid or postpone decisions, perhaps because of an inordinate fear of
making a mistake.

_____

_____

_____

d. Attempts to clean up and organize may be upsetting because there is
too much stuff to manage without spending enormous amounts of
time and effort. And since even heroic efforts at cleaning bring barely
visible results, such unrewarding efforts are unlikely to continue.

_____

_____

_____

_____

_____

2.   Do you know any pack rats? If so, write a short paper in which you describe their behavior. Do their behavior and their reasons for saving stuff correspond to those discussed in this article?

14

Ron Harris

SEA ISLANDS' SOUTH AFRICA

If you look at an atlas, you will see the Sea Islands lying just off the coast of Georgia and South Carolina. Untouched for 100 years, they were home to freed slaves, who settled there after the Civil War. They lived quietly and developed a unique culture. Now, however, the islands are being developed, threatening that culture, as this article, first published in the Los Angeles Times, *explains.*

VOCABULARY PREVIEW

WORD ORIGINS

FONDLY

One of the ironies of the Sea Islands' development into a resort area is that black residents now work in communities new residents *fondly* call "plantations." The work they do is *menial* (see the next section), and, according to the author in paragraph 9, is not very different from the work they did on the real plantations in pre-Civil War days. The word *fond* has undergone a radical change in meaning.

Today, in this context, it means "affectionate"; but in Middle English *fonned* meant "foolish." The dictionary labels as archaic this definition: "naively credulous (believing) or foolish." This process, when a word shifts in meaning from negative to positive, is called *amelioration*.

MENIAL

Menial refers to work that requires little skill or education or that is considered servile. This word illustrates *pejoration*, the opposite of amelioration that we saw in the case of *fond*. Pejoration occurs when a word's meaning changes from a neutral or positive meaning to a negative one, as you can see in this rather complicated etymology:

> [Middle English *meynial,* from Norman French *menial,* from Old French *mesne* ("servant"), from Latin *mānsiō* ("household," "dwelling").

159

In other words, the word originally had a neutral meaning, referring simply to a house, rather than to someone who performs menial work.

WORD
PARTS

DIS-

In selection 13 you read that the common English prefix *dis-* indicates negation, as in *distrust, disorder, discomfort,* and *disapprove.* But this prefix also has another meaning, "removal of" (see paragraph 1). Harris says that the original black inhabitants of the Sea Islands have been *displaced,* in other words, moved from their original location.

Here are some other common words having *dis-* as a prefix with this meaning: *dismiss, disappear, discard, dismount,* and *dispense.*

-IST

In paragraph 21 Harris quotes an *anthropologist* who has studied the inhabitants of the Sea Islands. Meaning "one who studies human culture," this word is composed of a Greek root and suffix and an English suffix:

[*anthropo* ("man" or "human") + *-logy* ("study of") + *-ist* ("one who does")]

The suffix *-ist,* which is commonly attached to English nouns, actually has three distinct meanings:

(a) A person who does, makes, studies, produces, or sells a particular thing, as in *motorist, dramatist, lobbyist, linguist.*
(b) A person who is skilled, trained, or employed in a particular field, as in *pharmacist, chemist, machinist, radiologist.*
(c) A person who believes or follows a particular doctrine, idea, or school of thought, as in *anarchist, romanticist, realist, hedonist.* This last word refers to a person who thinks that the pursuit of pleasure is the highest good.

WORD
FAMILIES

CEDED

According to paragraph 2, after the fall of the Confederacy, for 100 years, the land was *ceded* to the ancestors of the current island residents. Meaning to "yield" or "grant," this verb comes from the Latin *cēdere,* meaning "go," "withdraw," "yield." Here are some other common English verbs in the family of words stemming from this root:

recede	to move back or away [*re-* ("back") + *cēdere*]
secede	to withdraw or separate from [*se-* ("apart") + *cēdere*]
intercede	to come between as a mediator or to plead on someone's behalf [*inter-* ("between") + *cēdere*]
accede	to consent, to agree [*ad-* ("toward") + *cēdere*]
proceed	to come before in time [*pre-* ("before") + *cēdere*]
succeed	to win, to replace, literally "to come under someone" [*sub-* ("under") + *cēdere*]

RON HARRIS

SEA ISLANDS' SOUTH AFRICA

1   On these quiet, dreamy islands just off Georgia and South Carolina, a culture is being lost, a people displaced and, in an odd way, a part of America's most painful history is being replayed across a 20th-century stage.

2   For nearly 100 years, since the land was ceded to their ancestors after the fall of the Confederacy, children and grandchildren of freed slaves lived here in virtual isolation. Many thousands of them came to live undisturbed amid the pristine beaches, bountiful marshes and moss-laden live oaks, and to carve out a life rooted in the land and centered on customs and beliefs that closely resemble those of West African tribes such as the Ibo, Yoruba, Kongo and Mandinka, from whom they are probably descended.

3   Separated from the mainland, they came to be known as Gullahs and developed a unique lifestyle, culture and even their own language. Their life of subsistence farming, hunting and fishing was not easy, but at least it was their own.

4   Now their world has been turned upside-down. White retirees and vacationers increasingly are coming to claim this paradise as their own playground. As hotels, resorts, condominium projects and accompanying businesses have gone up, the original dwellers have been pushed aside.

5   As early as 1958, when Tom Barnwell got out of the Army and returned to Hilton Head Island, where his family had lived since slavery, the changes he found made him uneasy. "The bridge had been built from the mainland," said Barnwell, who heads the Hilton Head NAACP. "Electric lights were being put up. Telephones were coming. Roads were being paved. Things were really moving."

6   That was only the beginning.

7   By 1974, said Emory Campbell, another longtime resident of Hilton Head, "I realized that whites had taken over the island. At first it was a shock just watching the occupation, the occupation of land that was once black-owned, that was once vacant and commonly used, watching the access to various places closed off to you, like rivers and public roads and landings. Now we live with it every day."

8   Initially, many Sea Islanders sold their land cheaply, unaware of its real value. Later, some were happy to sell at very good prices as land values skyrocketed. But now, others who were determined to hold onto their homes often see them disappear at auctions as they struggle to keep up with rising property taxes. They find themselves bound by "pass" restrictions that will not allow them access to residential communities, shopping areas and even cemeteries on huge tracts of land that they once traversed freely.

9   They work in communities the new residents have fondly named "plantations." There, they are often given menial tasks not unlike those their slave forebears once performed on the real plantations that occupied these very grounds. The pay is so low and the cost of living so high that many have been forced to move off the islands, even though they still commute to work here. On island after island, residents tell the same tale of woe over lost land and a vanishing heritage.

10   On Daufuskie, a small island just south of Hilton Head, about 1,200 blacks farmed, crabbed, shrimped and harvested oysters until industrial wastes from Savannah, Ga., polluted the local oyster beds and forced most black families to flee the island in search of work in 1956. Now, three-quarters of Daufuskie has been earmarked for development over the next 20 years. Local government estimates are that the "build-out" will result in a permanent population of 10,000, while the remaining natives are forced off by escalating land values.

11   Although newcomers of nearby St. Simons Island think of all this development as progress, the islanders have watched sadly as pieces of their culture and history disappear. Ibo Landing, where Ibo warriors and their king marched into the ocean rather than be kept as slaves, has been fitted with a water-treatment facility. The Tree Stump, a town meeting site of the blacks for as long as anyone can remember, was torn up recently and covered with condominiums.

12   Nowhere is this rising tide of prosperity and its accompanying dismay more evident than on Hilton Head, a shoe-shaped island that hugs the South Carolina coast just above Savannah. At first, the stream of white retirees and vacationers, lured to the island by Fred Hacks' and retired General John Fraser's dream of turning timberland into a resort community, went almost unnoticed—that is, except by a few, such as Gene Wiley, whose first glimpse of a white person when he was 6 years old was a memorable experience.

13   "I thought it was a black person took sick," he recalled.

14   By the 1970s, however, the trickle of newcomers had become a torrent. Whites flooded down Highway 278 to the new golf courses, resort hotels and beachfront condominiums, followed closely by even more developers and land prospectors. Within 10 years, they outnumbered Hilton Head's 2,000 natives almost 6 to 1.

15   Under the name of planned communities, they cordoned off huge, private subdivisions and called them plantations—Sea Pines, Hilton Head, Port Royal and others—until four-fifths of the island was sealed off. To enter what are, in essence, residential neighborhoods, an islander must have a pass or special permission.

16   Land that was worth almost nothing shot up to $50,000 and $100,000 an acre as condominiums and hotels sprang up virtually in the islanders' back yards. Despite the attempts of local black organizations to prevent it, thousands of acres of black-owned land were sold to zealous real-estate dealers.

17   As property taxes soared, "a lot of people were being taxed off their property," said Mike Bell, a Hilton-Head planner, "especially the older blacks on fixed income. They still are."

18   Finally, five years ago, Hilton Head was incorporated, largely as a means of controlling the quality of development. The town quickly instituted sweeping zoning laws that, for all practical purposes, severely restricted land use on the remaining, native-owned property. Now, the natives complain, these new people—these white people—are telling them just what they can and can't do on their own land—their last valuable possession.

19   Blacks have been a fixture on the Sea Islands since slavery. When the Confederacy collapsed, freed blacks moved here in large numbers. On Jan. 16, 1885, after meeting in Savannah with a delegation of black clergymen who pleaded for land for former slaves, General William Tecumseh Sherman issued Special Field Order 15, ceding most of the Sea Islands off Georgia and South Carolina to the

slaves and declaring that no whites, apart from military officers and others present in helpful capacities, could live there.

20   Separated from the mainland by marshes, rivers and inlets, the native islanders created their own way of life, which included their own religion.

21   "They're as different from the mainland blacks as the Yoruba of Nigeria are from the Ashanti of Ghana," said Harris Mobley, a Georgia Southern College anthropologist and a native of Georgia's coastal low country.

22   One of the most distinctive aspects of the islanders' culture is Gullah, the lilting, African-influenced Creole language. It is understandable only to the initiated ear. Once derided but now a source of great pride, Gullah is a language of striking imagery. "Dayclean," for example, means dawn. "On rabel e mout" ("unravel his mouth") means talking a lot, and "tek e foot een e han" means to hurry away.

23   The islands, whose baseball-loving people have produced such stars as the New York Mets' Mookie Wilson and the Cincinnati Reds' Don Driessen, as well as football great Jim Brown, are rich in tradition. It was on St. Helena that the first school for blacks, Penn School, was established in 1861, and that the first black teacher, Charlotte Forten, taught. Dr. Martin Luther King Jr. made plans there for his march on Washington.

24   Today, blacks have returned to the new plantations to work as gardeners, waiters and maids, to tend golf courses and tennis courts and to clean private homes. Because of a shortage of labor on Hilton Head, almost half of them are bused in daily from as far as 90 miles away. They leave home at 5 a.m. for jobs that commonly pay a little more than minimum wage.

25   "I know it sounds farfetched, but it's almost like South Africa," said Campbell, 47, over breakfast at one of the island's exclusive hotels. "We need passes to go to places on the island. We work in the lowest jobs so white people can play. We arrive in these buses every morning, and then we're shipped out again." ■

From Ron Harris, "Sea Islands' South Africa," *San Francisco Chronicle*, "This World," October 2, 1988. Originally published in the *Los Angeles Times*. Reprinted by permission.

EXERCISES

Do not refer to the selection for Exercises A and B.

A.   DETERMINING THE MAIN IDEA AND PURPOSE
Choose the best answer.

1.   _____ The main idea of the article is that (a) the Sea Islands have recently been developed into resort communities; (b) the original residents of the Sea Islands are descendants of freed slaves who moved there after the Civil War; (c) Gullahs have a unique lifestyle, one completely different than that on the mainland; (d) development of the Sea Islands has resulted in many adverse changes for the Gullahs, descendants of freed slaves, who have lived there for over a hundred years.

2.   _____ With respect to the main idea, the author's purpose is (a) to tell a story; (b) to report and to inform; (c) to describe the Sea Islands; (d) to persuade and to incite the reader to action.

B.   COMPREHENDING MAIN IDEAS
Write the correct answer in the space.

1.   Which two U.S. states do the Sea Islands lie next to?

_____ and _____

2.   From which part of Africa were the original residents of the Sea Islands

descended? _____

3.   Vast tracts of land on the Sea Islands are now being developed primarily

for _____.

4.   The author mentions two reasons to explain why blacks who inhabited these islands for years are now being pushed off and forced to sell their

land: _____ and _____.

5.   To enter residential neighborhoods or certain shopping areas, an islander

must display a _____.

6.   According to one person interviewed for the article, the situation for blacks who are bussed in to do menial work on the Sea Islands is almost the same as it is for the residents of this country: _____

COMPREHENSION SCORE
Score your answers for Exercises A and B as follows:

A.   No. right _____ × 2 = _____

B.   No. right _____ × 1 = _____

Total pts. from A and B _____ × 10 = _____%

You may refer to the selection for the remaining exercises.

C.   RECOGNIZING SUPPORTING DETAILS
Place an X in the space for each statement that _directly_ supports this main idea from the selection. **"On island after island, residents tell the same tale of woe over lost land and a vanishing heritage."**

1.   _____ On Daufuskie, a small island just south of Hilton Head, about 1,200 blacks farmed, crabbed, shrimped and harvested oysters until industrial wastes from Savannah, Ga., polluted the local oyster beds and forced most black families to flee the island in search of work in 1956.

2. _____ Now, three-quarters of Daufuskie has been earmarked for development over the next 20 years.

3. _____ Local government estimates are that the "build-out" will result in a permanent population of 10,000, while the remaining natives are forced off by escalating land values.

4. _____ Ibo Landing, where Ibo warriors and their king marched into the ocean rather than be kept as slaves, has been fitted with a water-treatment facility.

5. _____ The Tree Stump, a town meeting site of the blacks for as long as anyone can remember, was torn up recently and covered with condominiums.

6. _____ Finally, five years ago, Hilton Head was incorporated, largely as a means of controlling the quality of development.

7. _____ Separated from the mainland by marshes, rivers and inlets, the native islanders created their own way of life, which included their own religion.

8. _____ "They're as different from the mainland blacks as the Yoruba of Nigeria are from the Ashanti of Ghana," said Harris Mobley, a Georgia Southern College anthropologist and a native of Georgia's coastal low country.

9. _____ One of the most distinctive aspects of the islanders' culture is Gullah, the lilting, African-influenced Creole language.

10. _____ Once derided but now a source of great pride, Gullah is a language of striking imagery.

D. MAKING INFERENCES

For each of these statements write Y (Yes) if the inference is an accurate one, N (No) if the inference is an inaccurate one, or CT (Can't Tell) if you do not have enough information to make an inference.

1. _____ One hundred years ago, whites and blacks coexisted peacefully together on these islands.

2. _____ Blacks are not allowed to buy land in the new condominium developments.

3. _____ Development of new resorts and communities has affected only Hilton Head Island.

4. _____ There are few opportunities for high-paying jobs for blacks on the Sea Islands.

5. _____ Many black landowners were cheated out of the rightful price for their land by unscrupulous or dishonest real estate brokers.

6. _____ Gene Wiley had never seen a white person until he was six years old.

7. _____ Blacks are not the only people on the islands who have to present passes; anyone who is not a property owner has to present one, as well.

8. _____ Most people from the mainland would not be able to understand Gullah the first time they heard the language spoken.

E. **ANALYZING ORGANIZATION AND SEEING RELATIONSHIPS**
Choose the correct answer.

1. _____ Throughout the article, the author is primarily concerned with (a) escalating land prices on the islands; (b) the loss of the Gullah lifestyle and culture; (c) the negative effects of overdevelopment; (d) lack of job opportunities for former island residents.

2. _____ Look again at paragraphs 3 and 4. What is the relationship between them? (a) steps in a process; (b) cause and effect; (c) term and its definition; (d) general and specific; (e) comparison.

3. _____ Paragraph 6 consists of only one sentence because (a) it is the main idea, and the author wants to be sure it is emphasized; (b) it acts as a transition between paragraphs 5 and 7; (c) the author wants to emphasize the idea contained within it; (d) the author is writing for a newspaper, where one-sentence paragraphs are routinely used.

4. _____ Mark any of the following that you can infer describes the author's attitude toward the newcomers' using the term *plantations* to describe their planned subdivisions. He thinks this term is (a) insulting; (b) funny; (c) ironic; (d) insensitive; (e) accurate.

5. _____ The method of development used in paragraph 11 is (a) steps in a process; (b) comparison; (c) contrast; (d) example; (e) cause and effect.

6. _____ The section from paragraphs 12–18 is developed mainly by (a) short examples; (b) steps in a process; (c) definitions of key terms; (d) analogy, a comparison between two unlike things; (e) contrast.

7. _____ What can you infer about the author's attitude toward the Gullahs and the changes that development on the islands has brought them? (a) He is unconcerned, almost indifferent; (b) he is angry and bitter; (c) he is sympathetic, almost sorrowful; (d) his opinion is not evident.

8. At the end of the essay, in paragraph 25, Harris quotes a longtime resident of Hilton Head Island, Emory Campbell, as saying that the islands are "almost like South Africa." What is the similarity he finds between these two places?

_____

F.   UNDERSTANDING VOCABULARY

Look through the paragraphs listed below and find a word that matches each definition. An example has been done for you.

Ex.   strange, peculiar [1–2]   odd

1.   moved from their original location [1–2]   _____

2.   yielded, granted [2–3]   _____

3.   in effect, though not completely [2–3]   _____

4.   in a pure state, untouched [2–3]   _____

5.   completely covered by [2–3]   _____

6.   providing sustenance or a meager
     existence [3–4]   _____

7.   traveled over, crossed [8–9]   _____

8.   describing unskilled work [9–10]   _____

9.   ancestors, forefathers [9–10]   _____

10.   loss of confidence, disheartenment [11–12]   _____

11.   enticed, attracted [11–12]   _____

12.   established a line to prevent people from
      coming in [15–16]   _____

13.   a group of people long established in
      [18–19]   _____

14.   abilities, positions, roles [18–19]   _____

G.   USING VOCABULARY

In parentheses before each sentence are some inflected forms of words from the selection. Study the context and the sentence. Then write the correct form in the space provided. Be sure to add appropriate endings like -s, -ed, or -ing if necessary.

1.   (*bounty, bountiful, bountifully*)   Harris describes the islands as having

     pristine beaches, _____ marshes, and moss-laden oak
     trees.

2.   (*uniqueness, unique, uniquely*)   According to the article, there is a

     _____ about the Gullah, who established their own
     way of life and culture apart from the mainland.

3.   (*initiate, initial, initially*)   Many Sea Islanders sold their land

     _____ for very little money, although at the time
     they were apparently happy.

4.   *(fondness, fond, fondly)*   Whites who live in planned subdivisions

   _____ refer to them as "plantations."

5.   *(woe, woeful, woefully)*   Island residents tell a _____
tale of lost land and a vanishing heritage.

6.   *(zeal, zealousness, zealot, zealous, zealously)*   During the 1980s, thousands of
acres of black-owned land were sold to real estate agents filled with

   _____ to make money for themselves.

7.   *(initiation, initiate, initial, initially)*   Only someone who has had experience

   with Gullah can understand it; someone who has no _____
experience with the language cannot understand it.

8.   *(derisiveness, deride, derisive, derisively)*   Although today Gullah is looked
upon with great pride, at one time, it was once treated

   _____.

H.   TOPICS FOR WRITING OR DISCUSSION

1.   Write a paragraph summarizing both the causes and the effects Harris
described in this article concerning the changes that have taken place for
the islands' black residents.

   _____

   _____

   _____

   _____

   _____

   _____

   _____

   _____

   _____

2.   Is progress good or bad? Think of a major change that has occurred in
your neighborhood or community. What particular effects has progress
had on the area's residents?

PART

3

Reading about Issues

The seven reading selections in Part III are all opinion essays or editorials. Each one takes up an issue or an idea about which there is a controversy or a wide variety of opinion. In four of these readings, there is no real attempt to persuade the reader: selection 16, which describes the experiences of women who have had abortions; selection 17, which describes the difficulties teenage mothers face; selection 19, which discusses the controversy about endangered species; and selection 21, which examines the white conspiracy theory regarding drugs. In each selection, the writer merely calls our attention to some significant issues of the day, and we are left to make up our own minds about the controversy.

However, in the other selections, the writers hope to convince the reader of the correctness of their opinions. For example, in selection 15 Ellen Goodman wants to convince us that year-round schools would benefit our children. In selection 18 Patrick Welsh questions the wisdom of teenagers' current sexual practices. And in selection 20 George Orwell attempts to convince us that capital punishment is terribly wrong.

When you read opinion essays, therefore, you should determine which kind of material you are reading—an article that presents conflicting points of view, thereby allowing you to consider the various points of view before you make up your own mind about where you stand; or an article that seeks to influence you, to make you change your mind or to convince you to adopt the writer's position.

With the second type, persuasive essays, you will need to determine the writer's central *argument,* the specific proposition or idea under discussion. Once you have located that—and in most persuasive pieces it comes at or near the beginning—then you can evaluate the kinds of evidence the writer uses to support this argument.

169

KINDS OF EVIDENCE

- Facts and statistics; these are verifiable because they can be looked up
- Examples drawn either from the writer's own experience or from personal observation
- "Good reasons"—sound or rational explanations to justify the author's opinion or point of view
- Quotations or the testimony from authorities or experts in the field, whose opinions and ideas on the subject we might be able to accept
- The author's own opinion, which is not as effective a way to support an opinion as the other kinds of evidence; recognizing the difference between fact and opinion is an important part of evaluating a writer's supporting evidence

Next, you should look to see if the writer includes what is called a *refutation* or *concession.* A good opinion writer usually will deal with the opposing side by examining one or two of its arguments and then *refuting,* or arguing against, them. In a *concession,* the author *concedes* or admits that there is some merit to the opposing side, but that the issue is serious enough that the author's own stand is more acceptable or perhaps that the opposing argument is somehow flawed.

Finally, when you read opinion essays or articles, look for evidence of *bias,* prejudices or preconceived ideas that may influence the writer's point of view. You can ask yourself if the writer seems to treat the issue fairly, whether there is sufficient evidence to support his or her opinion, and whether he or she appeals to your sense of reason or to your emotions. There is nothing wrong with appealing to your emotions, as long as you are aware that this is what the writer is doing.

You may recall from Part 1 Bob Greene's article, "Home Is Where the Heart Is," the story of Sarah, whom the state of Illinois removed from her foster parents' care. Greene is clearly biased in that article, because he strongly criticizes the state's role in Sarah's case, and he appeals—successfully, too—to our sense of outrage. Yet he offers facts and the testimony of experts, as well, to counteract his obvious bias.

If you know what to look for when you tackle persuasive prose, your reading will be at once more critical and more intelligent.

15

Ellen Goodman

U.S. KIDS NEED MORE SCHOOL TIME

Ellen Goodman is a syndicated columnist who writes on a wide variety of social and political issues. Her columns have been collected and published in a book titled Making Sense. *In this particular column, written during the summer of 1990, Goodman is concerned with the traditional American school calendar.*

VOCABULARY PREVIEW

WORD ORIGINS

SACROSANCT

Goodman writes in paragraph 4, "The six-hour day, 180-day school year is regarded as somehow *sacrosanct*." Pronounced săk'-rō-săngt, this word means "regarded as sacred and inviolable," which occurs when a particular custom, activity, or institution is treated as if it were sacred. This word, as you might imagine, is derived from Latin:

> [*sacrosanctus*, consecrated with religious ceremonies; from *sacrō* ("a sacred rite") + *sanctus*, from *sancīre* ("to consecrate")]

Sometimes, when a writer uses *sacrosanct* to refer to something nonreligious, he or she is using the word ironically, meaning that whatever is declared sacrosanct really doesn't deserve that status. It is this ironic use that Goodman intends when describing the school year calendar.

TOLL

Goodman writes in paragraph 8, "The long summers of forgetting take a toll." In English the phrase "to take a toll" does not mean literally to collect money. It has an idiomatic meaning, "to be negatively affected."

171

Originally, however, the word did have the literal meaning, and *toll* illustrates well the complicated path some words have taken before they came into English. Consider this derivation:

[Middle English *tol(le)*, Old English *toll*, from West Germanic *toln-*, from Late Latin *tolonium, telōnium*, a tollbooth, customhouse, from Greek *telōnion*, from *telōnēs*, from *telos*, tax]

WORD PARTS

MIS-
Goodman quotes Dr. Ernest Boyer in paragraph 5 as saying, "We have a huge *mismatch* between the school calendar and the realities of family life." The prefix *mis-* has two meanings: first, "error or wrongness," as in *misspell* and *misunderstand;* and second, "badness"," as in *misbehave* and *misuse.* In this context the prefix in *mismatch* has the first meaning.

SYN-
This common Greek prefix is used in many English words, most of them technical. Meaning either "the same" or "together," it occurs in paragraph 7 when Goodman writes, "Can they be asked now to *synchronize* our work and family lives?"

Synchronize means "to occur at the same time"; it can be analyzed as follows:

[*syn-* ("same") + *khronos* (Greek for "time")]

Here are some other common English words using the prefix *syn-*:

synonym	words that have the same or similar meanings
synopsis	a brief statement or summary [*syn-* ("together") + *opsis* ("view")]
synthesis	combining separate elements to form a whole [*syn-* ("together") + *tithenai* ("to put," "to place")]
synthetic	produced by synthesis, man-made, as in a *synthetic* fabric

WORD FAMILIES

CHRON-
You have already met the Greek root *khronos* ("time") in the preceding section. English has several words containing this root, among them:

chronicle	a record of the time
chronological	time order
chronometer	a mechanism for measuring time
chronic	occurring over a period of time, as in a *chronic* cough

ELLEN GOODMAN

U.S. KIDS NEED MORE SCHOOL TIME

1   The kids are hanging out. I pass small bands of once-and-future students, on my way to work these mornings. They have become a familiar part of the summer landscape.

2   These kids are not old enough for jobs. Nor are they rich enough for camp. They are school children without school. The calendar called the school year ran out on them a few weeks ago. Once supervised by teachers and principals, they now appear to be in "self care." Like others who fall through the cracks of their parents' makeshift plans—a week with relatives, a day at the playground—they hang out.

3   Passing them is like passing through a time zone. For much of our history, after all, Americans framed the school year around the needs of work and family. In 19th century cities, schools were open seven or eight hours a day, 11 months a year. In rural America, the year was arranged around the growing season. Now, only 3 percent of families follow the agricultural model, but nearly all schools are scheduled as if our children went home early to milk the cows and took months off to work the crops. Now, three-quarters of the mothers of school-age children work, but the calendar is written as if they were home waiting for the school bus.

4   The six-hour day, the 180-day school year is regarded as somehow sacrosanct. But when parents work an eight-hour day and a 240-day year, it means something different. It means that many kids go home to empty houses. It means that, in the summer, they hang out.

5   "We have a huge mismatch between the school calendar and the realities of family life," says Dr. Ernest Boyer, head of the Carnegie Foundation for the Advancement of Teaching.

6   Dr. Boyer is one of many who believe that a radical revision of the school calendar is inevitable. "School, whether we like it or not, is custodial and educational. It always has been."

7   His is not a popular idea. Schools are routinely burdened with the job of solving all our social problems. Can they be asked now to synchronize our work and family lives?

8   It may be easier to promote a longer school year on its educational merits and, indeed, the educational case is compelling. Despite the complaints and studies about our kids' lack of learning, the United States still has a shorter school year than any industrial nation. In most of Europe, the school year is 220 days. In Japan, it is 240 days long. While classroom time alone doesn't produce a well-educated child, learning takes time and more learning takes more time. The long summers of forgetting take a toll.

9   The opposition to a longer school year comes from families that want to and can provide other experiences for their children. It comes from teachers. It comes from tradition. And surely from kids. But the crux of the conflict has been over money.

10   But we can, as Boyer suggests, begin to turn the hands of the school clock forward. The first step is to extend an optional after-school program of education and recreation to every district. The second step is a summer program with its own staff, paid for by fees for those who can pay and vouchers for those who can't.

11   The third step will be the hardest: a true overhaul of the school year. Once, school was carefully calibrated to arrange children's schedules around the edges of family needs. Now, working parents, especially mothers, even teachers, try and blend their work lives around the edges of the school day.

12   So it's back to the future. Today there are too many school doors locked and too many kids hanging out. It's time to get our calendars updated. ■

From Ellen Goodman, "U.S. Kids Need More School Time," *San Francisco Chronicle,* "This World," October 2, 1988. Originally published in the *Los Angeles Times.* Reprinted by permission.

EXERCISES

Do not refer to the selection for Exercises A and B.

A.   DETERMINING THE MAIN IDEA AND PURPOSE
Choose the best answer.

1.   _____ The main idea of the article is that (a) the traditional school calendar is sacred and should not be tampered with; (b) American schools have a shorter school day than those in other industrialized nations; (c) the traditional school calendar does not match the needs of families today; (d) after-school programs and recreational programs would help solve the problem of children hanging out with nothing to do.

2.   _____ With respect to the main idea, the author's purpose is (a) to present facts and statistics; (b) to describe typical experiences; (c) to provide background information; (d) to convince us of the rightness of her opinion.

B.   COMPREHENDING MAIN IDEAS
Choose the correct answer.

1.   _____ Goodman describes the children she observes as (a) latchkey children; (b) being in a state of drift; (c) being in too many structured recreational programs; (d) being in self-care.

2.   _____ The current American school calendar was developed in the nineteenth century because of (a) the labor demands of the industrial age; (b) the growing season on the nation's farms; (c) school administrators' and teachers' demands for more vacation time; (d) parents' and children's demands for more time to spend together at home.

3.   _____ A mismatch results in the U.S. because the school year lasts only 180 days, whereas (a) school teachers are willing to work a longer year;

(b) American parents work an average of 240 days a year; (c) American children are behind children in other countries in important academic skills; (d) few children have enough activities to keep them occupied during the summer.

4. _____ According to the editorial, among women with school-age children, the percentage of women who work is (a) one-quarter; (b) one-half; (c) two-thirds; (d) three-quarters.

5. _____ Dr. Ernest Boyer, head of the Carnegie Foundation for the Advancement of Teaching, characterizes American schools as being both educational and (a) custodial; (b) inefficient; (c) unconventional; (d) traditional.

6. _____ Goodman's main concern is to synchronize the school year with (a) the educational needs of our children; (b) the school calendars of other industrialized nations; (c) the realities of parents' work schedules; (d) current theories about learning in the school environment.

COMPREHENSION SCORE

Score your answers for Exercises A and B as follows:

A.   No. right _____ × 2 = _____

B.   No. right _____ × 1 = _____

Total pts. from A and B _____ × 10 = _____%

You may refer to the selection for the remaining exercises.

C.   DISTINGUISHING BETWEEN MAIN IDEAS AND SUPPORTING DETAILS

Label the following statements from the selection as follows: MI if the statement represents a *main idea* and SD if the statement represents a *supporting detail*.

1. _____ It may be easier to promote a longer school year on its educational merits and, indeed, the educational case is compelling.

2. _____ Despite the complaints and studies about our kids' lack of learning, the U.S. still has a shorter school year than any [other] industrial nation.

3. _____ In most of Europe, the school year is 220 days.

4. _____ In Japan, it is 240 days long.

5. _____ While classroom time alone doesn't produce a well-educated child, learning takes time and more learning takes more time.

6. _____ The long summers of forgetting take a toll.

D.   MAKING INFERENCES

For each of these statements write Y (Yes) if the inference is an accurate one, N (No) if the inference is an inaccurate one, or CT (Can't Tell) if you do not have enough information to make an inference.

1. _____ Goodman has children of her own, and, thus, her concerns are based at least somewhat on personal experience.

2. _____ The children of rich or upper-middle-class parents probably do not spend as much time "hanging out" during vacation as children of less-well-to-do parents.

3. _____ The current American school calendar reflects an obsolete need for children to work on the family farm.

4. _____ In the fall when school begins, teachers have to spend valuable time reviewing the previous year's work with their students.

5. _____ The main reason that American schools have not extended the school calendar is the objections from teachers and students.

E. DRAWING CONCLUSIONS
Mark an X before any statement that represents a reasonable conclusion you can draw from the selection.

1. _____ Extending the school calendar would have more positive than negative effects, both socially and academically.

2. _____ The school calendar should reflect only students' academic needs, not their families' work schedules.

3. _____ One reason that American children are academically behind those in other industrialized nations is our emphasis on freedom and self-expression during the childhood years.

4. _____ If the U.S. wants to stay technologically competitive with other industrialized nations, sooner or later it may have to lengthen the school year.

5. _____ Schools should not be burdened with the responsibility of solving our country's social problems.

F. ANALYZING ORGANIZATION AND SEEING RELATIONSHIPS
Choose the correct answer.

1. _____ The main idea of the editorial represents (a) the concerns of teachers and school administrators; (b) the author's own opinion; (c) the result of research done by the Carnegie Foundation for the Advancement of Teaching; (d) the concerns of the nations' working parents.

2. In paragraph 1 Goodman writes that on her way to work she passes "small bands of once-and-future students." Explain in your own words why this phase is appropriate to the content.

_____

3. Goodman writes in paragraph 2 that many children "fall through the cracks of their parents' makeshift plans." Explain this phrase.

_____

_____

4. _____ Look again at paragraph 4. What is the logical relationship between the first sentence and those following it? (a) key term and a definition of it; (b) cause-effect; (c) contrast; (d) general idea and supporting examples.

5. _____ Paragraphs 10–11 take up (a) recommendations; (b) facts and statistics; (c) arguments from the opposing side; (d) statements in support of the main idea.

6. This selection has a clear beginning, middle, and end. Write the number of the paragraph where the body begins. _____ Write the number of the paragraph where the conclusion begins. _____

G. UNDERSTANDING VOCABULARY

Look through the paragraphs listed below and find a word that matches each definition. An example has been done for you.

Ex. directed, overseen [1–2]   _____supervised_____

1. something done as a temporary measure [1–2]   _____

2. sacred, inviolate [3–4]   _____

3. describing the country or agriculture [3–4]   _____

4. extreme, sweeping [5–6]   _____

5. incapable of being prevented [6–7]   _____

6. serving as a caretaker [6–7]   _____

7. powerful, forceful [8–9]   _____

8. critical point [8–9]   _____

9. adjusted, standardized [10–11]   _____

10. left to choice, not compulsory [10–11]   _____

H. USING VOCABULARY

From the following list of vocabulary words, choose a word that fits in each blank according to both the grammatical structure of the sentence and the context. Use each word in the list only once and add noun or verb endings (such as -s, -ing, or -ed) if necessary. (Note that there are more words than sentences.)

rural	mismatch	inevitable
routinely	synchronize	burden
merit	despite	toll
custodial	radical	sacrosanct

1.   There is currently a _____ between the American

school calendar and the needs of today's parents, and _____ the almost certain opposition from teachers and children, the author rec-

ommends a _____ overhauling of the school year.

2.   Schools have been _____ made to bear the

_____ of solving all of our social problems. The author questions whether it will be possible for schools to

_____ our work and family lives.

3.   The summer takes a _____ on children, who forget much of what they learned during the school year; accordingly, the au-

thor believes that there are substantial educational _____ to extending the school calendar.

I.   TOPICS FOR WRITING OR DISCUSSION

1.   In your own words, summarize the author's reasons for advocating a

longer school year. _____

_____

_____

_____

_____

2.   A few days after this editorial was published, Goodman wrote another piece on the same topic in response to the large amount of mail her ideas generated. In it, she quotes some parents' views:

"I suggest that we begin by updating the working-world's calendar about the personal lives of their workers and families," wrote an Oregon woman. "Let's give parents more time—not imprison our children in a year-long rat race," wrote a father from Nebraska. "We need more time with our children, not more time apart," added a mother from New Jersey.

Address the point that these three parents make. Weigh the advantages and disadvantages of Goodman's proposal and come to a conclusion of your own.

16 ||||

Cathy Trost

WOMEN WHO'VE HAD ABORTIONS

Abortion has been one of America's most divisive issues since the 1973 Supreme Court ruled in Roe vs. Wade *that abortion was legal. Over the past few years, antiabortion forces (often referred to as the "pro-life" movement) have gained strength and are attempting to challenge abortion laws in several states.*

The case mentioned in paragraph 5 involved a Missouri law that restricted certain women's access to abortion; the Supreme Court upheld some of these restrictions in a landmark ruling in 1989. Although that particular case has been settled, other cases from other states are pending before the Court. This article, published in the Wall Street Journal, *describes the personal stories of some women, both famous and ordinary, who have had abortions.*

VOCABULARY PREVIEW

WORD ORIGINS

REMORSE
The word *remorse* (see paragraph 8) has an interesting derivation. Meaning "moral anguish over past misdeeds" or "bitter regret," this word came into English from Middle English, from Old French, and originally from Latin. Its original meaning was "biting again" or "biting back," as you can see from its derivation:

[*re-* ("again") + *mordēre* ("to bite")]

In other words, when you feel remorse, you feel a constant gnawing inside about something you strongly regret.

IGNORANT
Journalist Linda Ellerbee describes her experience with an abortion at the age of nineteen or twenty, stating that she "wasn't prepared to be

179

shamed for being *ignorant*." To be *ignorant* is "not to know," the same meaning it had in Latin:

[*ig-* (from *in-*, "not") + gn$\bar{o}$r$\bar{a}$re ("to know")]

The verb *ignore* means "not to pay attention to" (or literally, not to know something), while the word for an ignorant person is *ignoramus* (Latin for "we do not know").

WORD PARTS

AMBIVALENCE

One of the main ideas in the article is the *ambivalence* many women feel about having an abortion (see paragraph 2). *Ambivalent* feelings are conflicting ones. Although the word parts come from Latin, the great twentieth-century Austrian psychiatrist Sigmund Freud put them together to coin the German word *Ambivalenz.*

The prefix *ambi-* means "both." The root *valence* comes from the Latin noun *valentia* ("strength," "capacity"). Therefore, ambivalent feelings are strongly conflicting, such as the strong love-hate feelings we may often feel for people or even for possessions.

Here are two other words with the prefix *ambi-:*

ambidextrous   describing a person who can use both hands equally well [*ambi-* + *dexter* ("right-handed")]

ambiguous   capable of having two or more meanings at once [*ambiguus* ("uncertain"), from *ambi-* + *agere* ("to drive," "to lead")]

SUB-

One woman quoted in paragraph 24 describes her experience seeking an illegal abortion: "She remembers how difficult it was to track down someone through the abortion *subculture*." A subculture is "a group distinguished by particular traits from the larger culture." In this context, however, the prefix *sub-* is important. It means "under" here, and in this context *subculture* has a strongly negative connotation. It suggests that such a group probably operated under cover, in secret, because anyone caught performing an abortion could be convicted of a crime.

Sub- as a prefix is easy to recognize in such words as *submarine* or *subsoil.* In more difficult words, however, the meaning of the prefix is less apparent, for example, in these words:

subvert   to ruin, to corrupt [*sub-* + *vertere* ("to turn")]
submit   to yield to someone's control [*sub-* + *mittere* ("to throw")]
subterranean   underground [*sub-* + *terra* ("earth")]

WORD FAMILIES

VOCAL

In paragraph 20 Linda Ellerbee asserts that abortion should be safe and available to women and that it should be kept out of the hands of state legislatures or small, *vocal* power groups. *Vocal* means "outspoken"; its root is Latin *vōx* ("voice"). English has a large number of words in the family with *vōx* or *vocāre* ("to call") at the root.

vocalize	to make vocal, to articulate
vocation	one's career or occupation; in other words, a calling
vociferous	making an outcry, speaking loudly and vehemently
advocate	one who supports or argues for a cause [*ad-* ("to" or "for") + *vocāre* ("to call")]
evoke	"to summon," "to call forth," as with memories [*e-*, from *ex-* ("out") + *vocāre*]
revoke	to cancel, to withdraw; literally to call back, as with a driver's license [*re-* ("back") + *vocāre*]

CATHY TROAST

WOMEN WHO'VE HAD ABORTIONS

1   Twenty-seven years ago, Barbara Corday, 18 and working in New York, became pregnant with little means to raise a child. Frightened and alone, she flew to Miami for an abortion. A Cuban claiming to be a doctor performed the illegal operation without an anesthetic in a walk-in closet converted to a primitive operating room.

2   Today Ms. Corday, the head of prime-time programs for CBS Entertainment, worries that the Supreme Court could change its 1973 ruling legalizing abortion, consigning others to repeat her dangerous experience. "I have no ambivalence about whose life is more important at that moment," says Ms. Corday, who now has four daughters. "I believe that it is the mother's."

3   Actress Patricia Neal also had an abortion when she was single. She was 25 and had become pregnant during an affair with the married actor Gary Cooper. She, however, now wants the Supreme Court to limit abortion rights.

4   "I wept over it for years and I still could," she says. Now 63 and the mother of four children, Ms. Neal says if she could do only one thing in her life over it would be to have the baby.

MOMENTOUS DECISION

5   In deciding a case that could revive the states' powers to restrict or even outlaw abortion, the Supreme Court will rule soon on an issue that has permanently affected millions of women. Nearly one-third of pregnancies, excluding miscar-

riages, in the U.S. end in abortion. The experience cuts across lines of class, race and age.

6   A recent Wall Street Journal/NBC News poll shows that the public, by a 2-to-1 margin, believes that abortion should be legal. But the actual abortion decision remains a deeply personal one, and it is one that many women haven't wanted to discuss publicly.

7   Driven by the urgency of the coming court decision, however, prominent women in business, the arts, the media and other professions who have had abortions increasingly are speaking out. This newspaper sought out such women, ranging from actress Polly Bergen and journalist Linda Ellerbee to a management consultant, a marketing director and a psychologist.

8   Some are swamped with remorse or anger and have become active in opposing abortion. Others see the freedom to choose abortion as essential to women's control over their lives and are striving to protect it. "I am not for abortion; nobody is for abortion," says Ms. Ellerbee. "I am for your right to make your own hard choices in this world."

YOUNG AND UNMARRIED

9 Of course, many women confronted with unwanted pregnancies have gone ahead and borne the baby because they opposed abortion or couldn't find or afford aid. Others who have had an abortion say it had little effect on their lives. But most of those interviewed feel otherwise. Many were young and unmarried when they became pregnant, often because of failed birth control, mistakes and ignorance. Many felt financially and emotionally incapable of raising a child. Some felt pressured by partners, parents or work.

10   Here is how some American women recall their abortion decisions and how those decisions affected their lives:

ALICE WALKER

11 The 45-year-old novelist, poet and Pulitzer Prize-winning author of "The Color Purple" was a senior at Sarah Lawrence College in 1965 who could envision "no way I could support a child and myself." Friends at school helped locate an abortionist who charged her $2,000, which she was "glad to pay because the alternative was to try to raise a child on no money." She says the abortion saved her life. "I had always suffered from depression and was really suicidal in the face of this new problem," she recalls.

12   The experience also influenced her writing career, shaping her first short story—called "To Hell With Dying." And it helped turn her into an outspoken feminist. "I never want anyone to go through the misery, suffering and anguish I endured. I felt so totally worthless and wrong and sinful," she says.

13   She didn't tell her mother for 10 years. Then, "it was the hardest thing I ever did."

14   But she says she isn't ashamed of her decision, and that out of it she grew to understand the hard choices women must make. She thinks repealing abortion rights would be "a terrible mistake," especially for her daughter's generation,

because "after years of relative freedom and feeling they control their own bodies, somebody is going to tell them they no longer do."

PATRICIA NEAL

15 The Academy Award-winning actress recalled in her autobiography that after her abortion in the early 1950s she continued working on the set of "Operation Pacific," a war movie in which she starred with John Wayne. "Life went on as usual," she wrote. "But for over 30 years alone in the night, I cried." She says now that the experience "broke my heart." But at that time, "I thought about only my mother, humiliating her. My family was a great part of it."

16   If she had it to over again, she hopes she would be like actress Ingrid Bergman, who had a child out of wedlock despite a public outcry. "She had guts," Ms. Neal wrote. "I did not. And I regret it with all my heart."

LINDA ELLERBEE

17 The 44-year-old journalist and author was 19 or 20 when she got pregnant, "mostly because sex education was a forbidden thing to teach in school and my family never talked about it." She didn't have $600 for an abortion so she appealed to her boss at the Chicago radio station where she was making $65 a week. "I got the money," she recalls, "but not before he made me stand there for an hour and shamed me by calling me the worst kinds of names."

18   She remembers the "pasty-faced man in the black trenchcoat" who came to her apartment at midnight and gave her a shot of sodium pentathol. "I was one of the lucky ones—I didn't bleed to death," she says, adding that she was "prepared for the damage to my soul, and my opinion of myself. I wasn't prepared to be shamed for being ignorant." She went on to have two children and a long career in network broadcasting and now runs her own production company.

19   Ms. Ellerbee has been active in the pro-choice movement, marching with her daughter in Washington this spring because she believes it is important that this "privacy issue" not be tampered with by the Justices. "Why you make this choice is a personal thing," she says. "What's of interest is *who* will make this choice."

20   Making abortion illegal won't stop it, she adds. "What we're talking about is keeping it safe and available to women who don't have a lot of money to fly to another state, and keeping it out of the hands of every state legislature or small, vocal power group."

STEPHANIE O'CALLAGHAN

21 Though she was "a super-liberal person" and a "real feminist" who felt that "anyone certainly had a right to do anything with their own bodies," the 46-year-old Westchester, N.Y., psychologist says she personally viewed abortion as "murder" and something she would never do. But the mother of four says she was pressured several years ago by her husband to end her fifth pregnancy.

22   Afterwards, she had "a very long episode of extraordinarily intense grief, exactly like if a mother's child had been run over by a truck." She says her marriage

was destroyed, and she still has regrets. Now she gives free abortion counseling, helps train other counselors, and speaks publicly on the issue.

23   She is angry that "the women's movement has completely neglected and rejected women in pain from this" and insists that women with ill-timed pregnancies can still advance in life. "I went to school and worked during all my children," she says. She doesn't see grounds for the Supreme Court to permit abortions even after rape or incest. "If my husband raped my daughter," she says, "I would know my daughter's life would be destroyed if she had an abortion," but that through love and therapy she could "be a mother to that baby."

BARBARA CORDAY

24   When she had her abortion, "I never thought about having the baby," says the CBS executive, "and I never even thought about adoption because I wasn't a school kid, I was working, and the idea of being pregnant for nine months in the early '60s would have been totally unthinkable." She remembers how difficult it was to track down someone through the abortion subculture: "getting phone numbers and skulking around and leaving messages and writing to post office boxes"—comparable to what it would be like buying drugs.

25   "Had I suddenly at age 19 or 20 stopped working to have a baby, I don't know how I would have ever gotten back to work again," says Ms. Corday, who as executive vice president of prime-time programs for CBS Entertainment is now the highest-ranking woman in network television.

26   She adds that the abortion "politicized me—it's always been for me the one issue that anyone could get me to do anything for," such as speaking and donating money. "If our right to abortion is taken away it won't be long before the government can tell us we *have* to have children," she argues.

27   An episode of the CBS series "Cagney & Lacey," which she co-created, was based on her experience. Mary Beth Lacey reveals a back-alley abortion she had as a teen-ager to her husband, who says that if abortion is outlawed, "It won't be like that again." To which she responds: "It will be exactly like that."

SUSAN STANFORDRUE

28   The 41-year-old San Diego-based management consultant became pregnant when she was estranged from her husband and finishing her degree in counseling psychology at Northwestern in 1975. She thought an abortion would "help me clear the way to make the other decisions in my life," but instead it was "just a nightmare of despair and loss."

29   She forged ahead, winning a faculty appointment at Northwestern University and later holding administrative posts at two other colleges. But her grief and guilt over the abortion didn't wane and she was "on the brink of suicide" before finding peace through prayer and spiritual study.

30   Ms. StanfordRue wrote a book, "Will I Cry Tomorrow?" to help women cope with the effects of abortion. Royalties go to fund abortion alternatives, and she speaks publicly several times a month on the issue. Now remarried and a manage-

ment consultant to hospitals, she would like to see a rolling back of the abortion decision. "There's almost no one who doesn't say there's a loss involved in this," she says.

POLLY BERGEN

31   The 58-year-old actress and businesswoman had just graduated from high school and moved to Hollywood to try to establish a singing career when she became pregnant at age 17. Those were the days "when Tampax and Kotex were wrapped in brown paper" and birth control wasn't something that her parents discussed, she says. Her partner fled. Financially and emotionally bereft, she felt she couldn't give birth to a child. In contrast to today, if you had a child out of wedlock in 1947-era Hollywood, she says, "your life was destroyed. Nobody remembers. Your life was destroyed!"

32   Her roommate "knew someone who knew someone," but the abortion was bungled and she "literally almost died." Complications later prevented her from bearing children. "I never carried guilt around concerning the illegal abortion I'd had," she says. "What I did carry around with me is the enormous guilt that I could not give birth to a child because I had a botched back-alley abortion."

33   She adopted two children and worked quietly with women's groups and children for years, but she never told anyone about her abortion until this year. She says she broke her silence to warn "young girls that their choices could be taken away" and to allow herself to "step forward out of the shame."

34   Now she speaks actively and raises money for pro-choice groups. "Women must be allowed to make a decision that affects their physical being, their health, their life, their ambitions, whatever it may be," she says.

MARCIA GOINS

35   The 29-year-old director of marketing at Comprehensive Nursing Agency in Los Angeles was reared in poverty by an unemployed welfare mother. Through hard work, she was preparing to enter college at age 16 when she became pregnant. Her mother took her to a gynecologist, who arranged an abortion the next day.

36   "I had a decision to make," she recalls now. "Was I going to go to college and get my education and be a professional person or was I going to start motherhood at age 16 with no husband, no money, go on welfare, be nobody—or end up being somebody later in life?"

37   She eventually married, had a son, began working and had another abortion when she became pregnant while in the midst of a divorce. "I'm a black woman and I strongly believe in freedom and equal rights," she says. If a court ruling "forces people to have children they don't want . . . it's going to extend the welfare role of anybody who had a chance to make it."

38   Though abortion was a painful, depressing experience, she says: "For people to say we are killing babies, what do they think we're going to do when they get older, when we can't feed them, when they're crying from hunger? Their concern should be for those children."

CAROL MUELLER

39 The 32-year-old sales representative for a commercial printer in Atlanta had her first abortion at age 21 after a man she had been dating forced himself on her. She was working as a service representative for International Business Machines, and after the abortion she went "totally wild for the next six years. I didn't care about anything or anybody." She subsequently had another abortion but this time she "nearly had a nervous breakdown. It hit me what I had done."

40 She became involved in a counseling group and, praying late one night, she says she had an experience that helped her deal with her grief. She saw "the children smiling at me. Their names came to me. The little boy who would be five, was Justin David. The girl was Jessica Lee, she'd be 11." Later, she became active with the anti-abortion group "Operation Rescue," standing in front of abortion clinics with a big sign that reads: "I've had two abortions. Talk to me before you do it."

41 An arrest once sent her to jail for seven days. She paid a $550 fine, is serving two years' probation, and can't go within 500 feet of an abortion clinic. She will be married next month to an Operation Rescue colleague and says of the Supreme Court decision: "Abortion is a horrible thing to wish on any woman. It should end." ■

From Cathy Troast, "Women Who've Had Abortions" [originally titled "Women Who've Had Abortions Speak Out, But Hardly in Unison"], *Wall Street Journal*, June 13, 1989. Reprinted by permission.

EXERCISES

Do not refer to the selection for Exercises A and B.

A. DETERMINING THE MAIN IDEA AND PURPOSE
Choose the best answer.

1. _____ The main idea of the article is that (a) the Supreme Court should look carefully at the abortion issue before upholding or reversing its 1973 decision; (b) abortion in the U.S. should remain legal; (c) abortion in the U.S. should not be legal; (d) the women's personal stories suggest that abortion is a highly complex, emotional issue.

2. _____ With respect to the main idea, the author's purpose is (a) to convince the reader to accept her personal opinion; (b) to present a wide variety of attitudes and opinions on a controversial subject; (c) to present background facts and statistics; (d) to set forth the findings of recent research.

B. COMPREHENDING MAIN IDEAS
Choose the correct answer.

1. _____ According to the article, the percentage of pregnancies, excluding

miscarriages, that end in abortion is (a) one-tenth; (b) one-quarter; (c) one-third; (d) one-half.

2.   _____ With respect to the women who seek out abortions, (a) most are poor, minority, and uneducated; (b) most are middle-class, educated, and white; (c) most are teenage girls; (d) they represent every age, class, and race.

3.   _____ A recent Wall Street Journal/NBC News poll shows that a majority of the American public (a) is confused about the issue of abortion; (b) believes that abortion should remain legal; (c) believes that the abortion law should be repealed; (d) believes that abortion should remain legal only when rape, incest, or potential birth defects are involved.

4.   _____ Linda Ellerbee, journalist and author, got pregnant at nineteen or twenty primarily because (a) she was rebelling against her parents; (b) her birth control measure failed; (c) her boyfriend said he would marry her; (d) she had not received any sex education at home or at school.

5.   _____ Polly Bergen, the actress and businesswoman, recently broke her silence and began speaking about her botched abortion because (a) she wants to warn young girls that their choices could be taken away; (b) her experience taught her that abortion is morally wrong; (c) she thinks the women's movement has not done a sufficient job in educating women about the issue; (d) she fears a return to unsafe, illegal abortions.

6.   _____ The women interviewed for this article reveal that, for them, abortion (a) was their only alternative to an unwanted pregnancy; (b) was illegal, dangerous, and left long-lasting scars; (c) had little effect on their lives; (d) was a deeply painful decision that had a great effect on their lives.

COMPREHENSION SCORE

Score your answers for Exercises A and B as follows:

A.   No. right _____ × 2 = _____

B.   No. right _____ × 1 = _____

Total pts. from A and B _____ × 10 = _____%

You may refer to the selection for the remaining exercises.

C.   DISTINGUISHING BETWEEN MAIN IDEAS AND SUPPORTING DETAILS

Label the following statements from the selection as follows: MI if the statement represents a *main idea* and SD if the statement represents a *supporting detail.*

1.   _____ Driven by the urgency of the coming court decision, however, prominent women in business, the arts, the media and other professions who have had abortions increasingly are speaking out.

2. ____ Some are swamped with remorse or anger and have become active in opposing abortion.

3. ____ Others see the freedom to choose abortion as essential to women's control over their lives and are striving to protect it.

4. ____ . . . says Ms. Ellerbee, "I am for your right to make your own hard choices in this world."

5. ____ Of course, many women confronted with unwanted pregnancies have gone ahead and borne the baby because they opposed abortion or couldn't find or afford aid.

6. ____ Others who have had an abortion say it had little effect on their lives.

7. ____ But most of those interviewed feel otherwise.

8. ____ Many were young and unmarried when they became pregnant, often because of failed birth control, mistakes and ignorance.

9. ____ Many felt financially and emotionally incapable of raising a child.

10. ____ Some felt pressured by partners, parents or work.

D.   MAKING INFERENCES

For each of these statements write Y (Yes) if the inference is an accurate one, N (No) if the inference is an inaccurate one, or CT (Can't Tell) if you do not have enough information to make an inference.

1. ____ Despite his claim, the Cuban who performed an abortion on Barbara Corday without an anesthetic was not a doctor.

2. ____ It is impossible to generalize about the background—ethnic, class, race, or age—of women who seek abortions.

3. ____ Most of the women interviewed in the article echo the opinions of Patricia Neal and Carol Mueller, who deeply regret their decision and think that abortions are too easy to obtain.

4. ____ In at least a few cases, abortion has allowed women to pursue their education so that they can support subsequent children.

5. ____ According to both Alice Walker and Linda Ellerbee, the central issue is whether the government should dictate what women do with their own bodies.

6. ____ Today a single woman who decides to keep her baby faces the same kind of stigma that women in the 1940s did, as, for example, Ingrid Bergman did as an unmarried woman when she decided to have her child.

7.   _____ The Supreme Court will probably hand down more decisions limiting women's access to abortion in the future.

8.   _____ Cathy Trost, the author of this article, was surprised at the opinions and reactions of the women interviewed for the article.

E.   ANALYZING ORGANIZATION AND SEEING RELATIONSHIPS

1.   Look again at paragraphs 1–4, which serve as the introduction to this article. In terms of the content of the remainder of the article, explain the function of this opening section.

_____

_____

2.   In summarizing the experiences of the various women she interviewed for the article, does the author present a balanced or a biased view? Explain. _____

_____

3.   _____ Look again at paragraph 8. What logical relationship is implied in the first two sentences? (a) steps in a process; (b) general statement and a supporting example; (c) term and its definition; (d) contrast.

4.   _____ Throughout the article, the women interviewed emphasize that abortion (a) is a deeply personal decision, a step not to be taken lightly; (b) is merely a sign of the times, a direct outgrowth of the feminist movement; (c) is an issue whose future the Supreme Court should resolve once and for all; (d) has become the rallying issue for many political groups.

5.   Look again at paragraph 23. What does Stephanie O'Callaghan imply about the women's movement's stand on abortion?

_____

6.   Look again at the last sentence of the article, in which Carol Mueller offers an emotional conclusion: "Abortion is a horrible thing to wish on any woman." Do you see anything illogical or inconsistent in that statement? _____

_____

F.   UNDERSTANDING VOCABULARY
Choose the correct definition according to the context.

1.   _____ with little *means* to raise a child [1]: (a) possibility; (b) experience; (c) desire; (d) financial resources.

2. _____ *consigning* others to repeat her dangerous experience [2]: (a) setting apart; (b) handing over; (c) allowing; (d) forcing.

3. _____ some are swamped with *remorse* [8]: (a) guilt; (b) a sense of loss; (c) bitterness; (d) deep regret.

4. _____ could *envision* no way to support a child [11]: (a) foresee; (b) determine clearly; (c) consider; (d) recommend.

5. _____ the suffering and *anguish* I endured [12]: (a) physical pain; (b) embarrassment; (c) sorrow; (d) torment.

6. _____ *repealing* abortion rights [14]: (a) reporting on; (b) restricting; (c) revoking; (d) clarifying.

7. _____ small, *vocal* power group [20]: (a) well-financed; (b) outspoken; (c) radical; (d) politically ambitious.

8. _____ She *forged* ahead [29]: (a) devised a plan; (b) ignored the problem; (c) worked hard to advance; (d) denied reality.

9. _____ her guilt over the abortion didn't *wane* [29]: (a) decrease gradually; (b) stop completely; (c) make sense; (d) matter significantly.

10. _____ financially and emotionally *bereft* [31—past tense of *bereave*]: (a) deprived of hope; (b) upset; (c) uncertain; (d) desperate.

G. USING VOCABULARY

In parentheses before each sentence are some inflected forms of words from the selection. Study the context and the sentence. Then write the correct form in the space provided. Be sure to add appropriate endings like *-s, -ed,* or *-ing* if necessary.

1. (*remorse, remorseful, remorsefully*) Some women interviewed for the article

    still feel _____ even years after the abortion.

2. (*ignore, ignorance, ignorant, ignorantly*) Linda Ellerbee confesses that she

    was naive and _____ about sex education and birth
    control.

3. (*ambivalence, ambivalent, ambivalently*) Barbara Corday states at the begin-

    ning of the article that she no longer has any _____
    feelings about whose life is more important, the mother's or the baby's.

4. (*alternate, alternative, alternatively*) Alice Walker had an abortion when

    she was a college student because she simply had no _____,
    no resources to care for a child.

5. (*vocalize, vocal, vocally*) Abortion has become a significant political issue

    since 1973, especially by _____ political groups.

H. TOPICS FOR WRITING OR DISCUSSION

1. On a sheet of paper list the effect abortion has had on each woman described in the article. A single sentence for each one should be sufficient.

2. What is your opinion on the abortion issue? Has your opinion changed as a result of reading this article?

17 ||||||

Elizabeth Marek

THE LIVES OF TEENAGE MOTHERS

Subtitled "Schoolbooks, Boyfriends, and Babies," this article, published in Harper's, *describes the day-to-day lives of teenage girls who became pregnant and kept their babies. Elizabeth Marek is the author of* The Children at Santa Clara.

VOCABULARY PREVIEW

WORD ORIGINS

MUSE

Muse (see paragraph 24) is a verb meaning "to ponder" or "to meditate on for a length of time." This word has a peculiar origin: from Middle English, then from the Old French verb *musen*, "to sniff around," "to cast about for a scent," which, in turn, was originally derived from the Medieval Latin root *mus* or "snout." This word illustrates well the strange and now unexplainable changes a word can take as the centuries pass.

ALIEN

The author was astonished to find in her meetings with these teenage mothers that a few of them did not know until relatively late that they were pregnant. She writes in paragraph 32, "Even their bodies rebel, growing *alien* creatures without their knowledge, the awareness of their pregnancy dawning only after the possibility for abortion has passed."

Alien means "unfamiliar" or "strange," and it derives from the Latin word for "other" (*alius*). The word *alias*, an assumed or "other" name for a person, comes from the same root.

WORD PARTS

-LESS

This useful suffix means "lack of," "free of," or "without," as in the words *sleepless* or *hopeless*. In this selection two words end with this suffix: *effortlessly* (paragraph 20) and *powerlessness* (paragraph 32). *Effortlessly* is an adverb, because of the *-ly* adverb ending; it means "describing something done without effort." On the other hand,

193

powerlessness is a noun because of the added noun suffix *-ness*, and it means the state of having no power.

These two words illustrate well the way English words can change grammatical function by adding various suffixes. Suffixes may indicate meaning in some cases, as, for example, in *-able* and *-less*. But more typically, suffixes simply indicate part of speech.

PERI-

In paragraph 20, Marek describes one of the mothers, April, a shy, withdrawn girl, "who seems to hover on the *periphery* of the discussion." The prefix *peri-* was originally a Greek prefix that also was used in Latin. Meaning "around," it occurs most commonly in scientific terms. The *periphery* is the outside boundary of a defined space.

[*peri-* + *pherein* ("to carry")]

Here are some other words with this prefix:

perimeter	the circumference or outer boundary of a circle or an enclosure
periscope	an instrument that allows one to look around [*peri-* + *scopein* ("to see")]
peritoneum	the membrane that lines the abdominal wall cavity that encloses the internal organs [*peri-* + *tenein* ("to stretch")]

WORD FAMILIES

SPECULATE

In paragraph 2 Marek writes that, concerning the issue of teenage pregnancy, "sociologists and psychologists *speculate* about social pressures and individual motivation." Coming from the Latin word *specere* ("to watch," "to observe"), to *speculate* means "to meditate or reflect on a subject." The connection with "seeing" is better shown in these related words:

speculate	a different usage: to engage in buying or selling a commodity with considerable risk (from the idea that one can never *see* into the future), as in one who *speculates* in real estate
spectacle	a public performance, an object of interest (in other words, something worth looking at)
spectator	one who attends and sees a show or an event
spectacles	eyeglasses, enabling one to see clearly

MOTIVATION

This word is used three times in the article (see paragraphs 2, 17, and 48). Here it is in one context, from paragraph 17: "part of the *motivation* for teenage girls to have babies is a wish to be reborn themselves, to re-create themselves as children." Meaning "the process of stimulating to action or providing with an incentive," this noun comes from the Latin root *movēre* (past participle *mōtus*), "to move." Here are some other words in the family of words derived from *mōtus:*

motion	process of change of position; the ability to move
motile	having the power to move, said of certain organisms
motive	an emotion, a desire, or similar impulse that incites to action, as in a motive for a crime

ELIZABETH MAREK

THE LIVES OF TEENAGE MOTHERS

1   At 2:30 on a Thursday afternoon in June, when most teenagers, done with school for the day, are hanging out with their friends, the girls I have come to meet are seated in a small office, reaching for cookies with one hand as they settle their babies on their laps with the other. We are at the Kingsbridge Heights Community Center in the Bronx. The center sits at the crossroads of several worlds. The spacious homes of Riverdale dot the rolling green hills to the west; to the south rise the housing projects that cast their shadow on the lower-middle-class single-family homes and the shops which line the blocks closest to the center. The Teen Parenting Program, which provides counseling, education, and health care to teenage parents and soon-to-be parents throughout the Bronx, was started in 1986 with a group of girls from the projects. Once a week the girls in the program, along with their babies and sometimes their boyfriends, crowd into a simply furnished room to drink Coke, munch on snacks, and talk about the difficulties of being a teenage parent.

2   On this particular Thursday, I have come too. For years I've read about the "problem of teenage parenthood"—children having children. In New York City, teen pregnancies make up 15 percent of all pregnancies and account for more than 13,000 births each year. Sociologists and psychologists speculate about social pressures and individual motivation. President George Bush, in his inaugural address, spoke of the need to help young women "who are about to become mothers of children they can't care for and might not love."

3   But despite the concern voiced by others, we've heard very little from the young women themselves. Are they ignorant about birth control, or are they choosing to get pregnant? What are the conditions of loneliness, poverty, and hopelessness in which having a baby might make sense? What happens to these girls and their babies? How does having a baby affect their lives? Where do the fathers fit in?

4   I've come to Kingsbridge because I want to get to know the mothers, most of whom are not much younger than I am. Sophie-Louise, the social worker in charge of the group, introduces me, and the room falls silent. "Well," she laughs, "here we

are. Ask away." Looking at the girls, as they tug at a baby's diaper or straighten a barrette, I am not sure where to begin.

5   "Tell me what it's like, having a baby at your age," I ask at last. As if on cue, all heads turn toward Janelle,* a heavyset black girl with short, blown-straight hair, who sits in an over-stuffed chair with her three-month-old son, Marc, draped across her lap. The baby, dressed in a pale green sleeper embroidered with a blue bunny, is drooling onto her stylish black skirt. She is eating a chocolate cookie and begins to talk about the logistical problems involved in getting to and from high school with an infant. She has just started summer school to make up credits from the classes she missed during her pregnancy. She is seventeen.

6   "Let's see," she begins. "I get myself up and get the baby up and get myself dressed and get the baby dressed, get my books, get the baby's bag, get the stroller . . ." She laughs. "Do you know how hard it is to get a stroller on the bus? That first day of school, I thought I wasn't going to make it."

7   Newspaper accounts of teen pregnancy tend to dwell on girls from welfare families. Janelle, however, is the daughter of a retired postal-service clerk and grew up in a small, one-family house in a lower-middle-class neighborhood in the North Bronx. Her childhood was relatively secure: her parents were together and could afford to send her to a Catholic school, where she made friends, got good grades, and dreamed about what she would be when she grew up. "I was gonna finish high school," she says. "Gonna go on to college, like my cousins did. I wanted to get married and have a baby someday, but, really, not now. All through high school I never cut classes, hardly was sick even . . ."

8   The turning point came when Janelle was fifteen and her parents divorced. "When my parents split, my family just fell apart. My mother only wanted my little sister, so she took her, and then my older sister, she left, too, so it was just me and my father all alone in the house." Feeling unwanted and unloved, Janelle moved into a room in the basement, and her father took over the upstairs. Sometimes they met at breakfast, but other times Janelle went for days without seeing him. "So I started hanging out with a bad bunch of kids," she says, "and cutting classes—I went through an entire year and only got three credits. And then I got pregnant and dropped out." She laughs bitterly. "One thing they don't teach you in high school is how to get a stroller on the bus."

9   Lynda, at twenty the mother of a three-year-old girl, nods sympathetically. She is a pretty, young Hispanic woman with long hair pulled away from her face in a ponytail. Three weeks earlier she had graduated from high school, having gone to classes in the evening and worked during the day as a cashier in a small store in Manhattan. Her daughter, Danielle, a small child with blonde hair and a dirty face, walks unsmiling around the edge of the room. There is little interaction between mother and daughter. They neither look at nor speak to each other.

10   Lynda's family, like Janelle's, could be classified as lower middle class. Unlike Janelle's, Lynda's parents are strict Roman Catholics. On the day Lynda told her father that she was pregnant, he left home. "I guess it was either that or throw me out," she says. A few months later he moved back, but even now, although he

*The names of the young women and their boyfriends and some identifying details have been changed.

allows her to live at home, she feels that he has not forgiven her. Lynda believes that her father, having worked hard to provide the best for her and her siblings, took her pregnancy as a slap in the face.

11   Leaning back in the circle of her boyfriend's arms, Lynda's large black eyes are ringed with dark circles. "My mother still talked to me, like, at the table, pass the salt and stuff. I think my father blamed her—'If you had brought her up right, this wouldn't have happened.'"

12   Janelle nods. "My father blamed my mother, too. I don't understand that, though, because he didn't even know that I was pregnant. Now he thinks it's my fault that he didn't know, and I think it's his fault. He was always telling me to stay downstairs, and we never talked. We never did anything. Now all he does is compare me to his sister's children, who are much older. They got jobs, finished college, and he says you make me look so bad, having babies, dropping out of school. But he didn't want to come back to my mother, he didn't want to try to help me. It was all just, 'Don't make me look bad. Don't make me look bad.'"

13   "So what did he do when he found out you were pregnant?" asks Lynda.

14   "He never found out! Not until I came home from the hospital. He found out when the baby was a week old."

15   Lynda's boyfriend, Tony, a construction worker in his early thirties, joins the discussion. "Maybe it's more that he didn't want to know. He wanted to keep it from himself." Tony is not Danielle's father, although he too was a teenage parent and has two boys of his own. He and Lynda have been going out for almost a year. "You know the parents, they blame themselves," he says. "Like maybe they did something wrong with your upbringing."

16   Janelle lets out her breath in a snort. "Yeah, well now he tells all his friends, 'She's so sneaky.' But I think that if he was really interested, he would have known. I mean, the last day, the day that I gave birth, he went out to the store and said, 'I'll be right back.' And I said, 'Fine, but I won't be here.' But he didn't hear me."

17   Later, riding home on the subway, I wonder whether, in part, Janelle got pregnant to get her father's attention. Or, perhaps, as one social worker I spoke with earlier suggested, part of the motivation for teenage girls to have babies is a wish to be reborn themselves, to re-create themselves as children, so they can get the love and attention they feel they were denied.

18   Nine girls, their babies, and a few of their boyfriends are officially enrolled in Sophie-Louise's group, but since the school year ended, only Janelle and Lynda have been coming regularly. The others, Sophie-Louise explains, have drifted away—to the beach, to parties—or are staying home, too overwhelmed by their lives as mothers to make the trip to the center. Janelle and Lynda represent what Sophie-Louise calls the "cream of the crop": the only ones able to structure their lives sufficiently to attend a regular weekly meeting. The others fade in and out.

19   At the next meeting, I notice that Lynda's boyfriend is missing. Sophie-Louise explains to me privately that Tony and Lynda have been having problems lately. Two new people are present, however: Janelle's boyfriend, Eron, and a new girl, April, a sad-looking black teenager, who brings her five-month-old daughter. April is thin, her ribs jut out below the orange halter top she wears. In contrast to the Calvin Klein jeans Lynda wears, April's jeans are frayed and stained. She sits with

her shoulders hunched, as though shielding herself from the vagaries of life. Glancing up, she notices my tape recorder on the table, and she stares at me for a moment before busying herself with the baby on her lap. The baby's dark eyes flicker across her mother's face, but neither of them registers a smile. Sophie-Louise has told me a few facts about April's life: She is the oldest child and lives with her mother, her two siblings, and her baby in a two-room apartment in a housing project in the East Bronx. Seemingly the least equipped to care for an infant, April appears to have been the most determined to have a baby: Kisha was the result of her third pregnancy, the other two having ended in abortions.

20   As the meeting starts, Janelle reaches across the table with one hand to grab some potato chips, while her other hand effortlessly settles baby Marc in a sitting position on her leg. April, sitting alone at the far end of the couch, shakes off Sophie-Louise's offer of a Coke and, grabbing a handful of Cheez Doodles, drapes a towel over her shoulder so that Kisha can nurse quietly at her breast. April seems to hover on the periphery of the discussion, offering tangential comments or staring fixedly at a spot on the wall. Sophie-Louise finds some rubber cows for Danielle to play with, but the little girl is more interested in building towers of checkers in the corner and knocking them down with excited squeals. Over the din, I ask the girls whether they had planned their pregnancies, and how they felt when they discovered they were pregnant.

21   As usual, Janelle begins. "At first, you know, I was real scared. I didn't want to have the baby," she says, smoothing her hand over Marc's diaper. "I was dead set against it. 'Cause you know, I'm just seventeen, and I didn't want to have a baby. I wanted to still go out and have fun with my friends and stuff. But now, you know, it's been three months, and I'm used to it." She pauses. "Of course, I haven't had too much time to myself. Just twice, in three months. I counted it. Twice. The father's family took care of him for a whole day. I couldn't believe it. I was outside and everything was so much fun. But I like being a mom now. I can handle it. All my friends keep telling me, 'Janelle, you're in a closet!' But I'm not in no closet. And if I am, well, they should leave me alone. It's fun in this closet now that I know what I'm doing and everything."

22   Lynda's mother takes care of Danielle during the day, when she is at work, and again in the evenings, when she attends classes. But Lynda also complains about a lack of freedom. "My mom says, 'Now you are a mother, you have responsibilities.' She will babysit when I go to work or to school, but otherwise, anywhere I go, Danielle goes."

23   "Did either of you ever think about having an abortion?" I ask.

24   "Abortion," muses Janelle. "Well, by the time I knew I was pregnant, I was already six months pregnant."

25   I wonder whether she has misspoken. Surely she can't mean that she had a baby growing inside her for six months before she was aware of its presence. But, shaking her head, she assures me that it was six months.

26   "Before that, I had no idea," she says.

27   Lynda backs her up. "By the time I knew I was pregnant, I was five months."

28   "Maybe," Sophie-Louise says, "it goes back to what we talked about before. Not knowing because you really didn't want to know."

29   Lynda is adamant. "No. There was no way I could know. I still had my regular monthly period until I was five months, and that's when I found out. And by then I didn't have much choice because they told me they only did abortions until twelve weeks, and I was way past that. And besides, I don't believe in doing abortions at five months. They say that at three months the baby is still not really formed into a baby, but after that the baby starts forming, and then I feel that it's killing . . ."

30   April reaches down to straighten Kisha's dress. She speaks for the first time, her voice so soft and low that the rest of us have to strain to hear her. "I didn't know I was pregnant until I was three months. I jumped in a pool and felt something move inside me, and that's when I knew." She pulls her daughter to a sitting position on her lap, pushing a Cheez Doodle into the baby's flaccid mouth.

31   Janelle pauses and then says quietly, "I don't think I knew, but then I wonder. Maybe somewhere in me I knew, but it was like I was saying, no, I'm not pregnant, I'm not pregnant . . . I was living day-to-day, one day at a time. I would just get up in the morning and do what I needed to do, and not think about it."

32   As the girls speak, their words reflect their sense of powerlessness. Even their bodies rebel, growing alien creatures without their knowledge, the awareness of their pregnancy dawning only after the possibility for abortion has passed. Does this reflect a yearning for a child? Or is it only a child's way of coping with something too terrifying to acknowledge?

33   Lynda glances at Danielle, who is still amusing herself with the checkers. She brings the group back to the abortion question. "I think that the girl should just make up her own mind, and then that's it," she says. "Because even if you don't let your boyfriend go, you are still going to get left."

34   "What do you mean?" Sophie-Louise asks. Like many working mothers, Lynda has an air of perpetual exhaustion. "Sometimes, if you're in love with a guy, and 'I love you' comes up, that's the one thing that always makes you weak. You say, 'Oh, I love you too.' But then it's time for you both to sit down and talk about the situation, you know, after you say, 'Well, I'm pregnant,' and he says, 'Oh, you are?' and he gets happy and everything. This happened to me. And I said, 'I want an abortion.' Then the brainwash would begin, the 'I love you and it's our baby and I'll give you support.' It was like, if I had an abortion, then I didn't love him. I feel that the woman should just make up her own mind, make her own decision. But he said, 'Oh, I love you, and I'll do this for you, I'll do that for you, and our baby will have this, and our baby will have that.' Now she's two and a half years old, and all he ever got her was a big box of Pampers and socks and T-shirts and $20 and that was it." Suddenly, the resentment in her voice changes to wistfulness. "She's two and a half. And he was going to buy her a baby crib and a bassinet and clothes. Everything . . ."

35   I have heard stories like this from other girls I talked with and from social workers as well. One fifteen-year-old mother told me that her boyfriend said that if she really loved him, she would have his baby. Despite her mother's urging, she decided against having an abortion. But by the time the baby was born, she and her boyfriend had broken up, and he was expecting another child by another girl in her school. As Sophie-Louise puts it, the guys like to have three or four "pots on different stoves" at the same time—visible proof of their virility.

36   Sophie-Louise turns to Eron, Janelle's boyfriend. He is seventeen and works

two jobs, one in a garage and the other as an attendant at Rye Playland. She asks him how he felt when he found out that Janelle was pregnant. He laughs. "I was scared."

37   "More scared than me!" Janelle adds. "I mean, you were chicken!" "Well my life was changing, too," says Eron. "I mean, I know guys who just say, oh no, a baby, and then walk off, but I'm not that type of person. My father was never there for me when I was little, so, you know, I don't want that to happen to my son. I don't want him to grow up and hate me and all that. I want to have somebody to love me. Even if me and Janelle don't end up together, I got him to remind me of her."

38   It interests me that Eron wants the baby as someone to love him. When I ask the girls what they think of this, April rejoins the discussion. Without raising her eyes from her baby, she says, "When my boyfriend found out I was pregnant, he just played it off. He would always play at my stomach, sort of punch me in the stomach.

39   "Now I don't even let him see her anymore. All he wants to do is play with her, and then give her back when it's time for changing."

40   "That's tough," Sophie-Louise says. "It [means] somewhere inside her she wished for a baby."

41   Janelle pauses to consider the question. "Well, I don't know. Maybe. You know, I was lonely. My parents had split, and I really didn't have anyone, just me and my father together in the house."

42   Sophie-Louise turns to April. Despite the fact that Kisha was the result of her third pregnancy, April is unwilling to admit that she had wanted the baby. "It was an accident," she insists. "I mean, I said that this isn't going to happen to me. I was using all kinds of protection. Most times I even had him use protection."

43   Sophie-Louise seems surprised. "You were using protection?" she asks. "What kind?"

44   Indignantly, April answers, "Well, I was taking the pill. I mean, I wasn't taking it all the time, but I was taking it. But I missed a couple of days, I guess. I think I took it on the day before my birthday, but not on my birthday, I don't think . . ."

45   "So for you it really was an accident," I say. I am surprised when she contradicts me.

46   "No. I wouldn't really say it was an accident. See, all the other times I got pregnant, my mother made me get rid of it. So I guess part of it was revenge against my mother, like I was gonna get pregnant but not let her know until she couldn't do nothing."

47   "Not with me," says Lynda. "With me it was just a pure accident. Just a pure accident. I wanted to get an abortion. I said that I was going to have one. But my boyfriend and my parents, my father especially . . . they wanted me to have it. That's when the brainwash began."

48   It occurs to me that I've been looking for a motivation, a reason why these girls, and others like them, might *choose* to become pregnant. But the more I listen, the more I wonder whether the question of choice is relevant. In all their stories, I hear again and again how little volition these girls feel they have, how little control over the events of their lives. The deadline for school admission passes and April shrugs. Sophie-Louise makes an appointment for Lynda with a job counselor, but Lynda forgets to go. Janelle knows about birth control but doesn't believe "it" will

happen to her. Sophie-Louise told me once that these girls exert no more control over their lives than a "leaf falling from a tree." Perhaps having a baby is less a question of ignorance or choice than one of inevitability. Once a girl is sexually active, it is not *having* a baby that requires choice and conscious action, but *not* having one.

49   Eron shifts in his chair. "You know, all this talk about we didn't want to have the baby, or it was an accident, or whatever . . . I just think it's a waste of time. I mean, now we have the baby. The question is, what are we going to do now?"

50   Sophie-Louise asks him what he means, and he explains that the cycle of babies having babies, single parents raising single parents, has haunted him as it has haunted most of the teens in the room, and that he feels it can end with them, but only if they are willing to face the realities of their situation. "My father was never there when I was little," he says, "but I don't want that to happen to my son. I don't want him to grow up and hate me and all that . . . That's why I'm going to finish school and do whatever I need to do."

51   His eyes shine as he speaks of his ambition, but he looks down shyly, as if afraid that someone will mock him. Janelle, however, backs him up with pride and speaks of her own ambition to become a social worker. "It's so easy to go on welfare," she says. "You just sit home and cash a check. But I'm not going to get on welfare, 'cause it makes you lazy. It's addictive."

52   "I couldn't do that," Eron says. "I'm the kind of person who needs to work." But then the realities of fatherhood seem to descend upon him. "I don't know, though. See, 'cause with a baby, it takes all the money that you don't even have . . ."

53   At the end of the session, the discussion shifts back to the problems that the girls will encounter when they return to school in the fall. Janelle is telling April that summer school really wasn't so bad. "It was hard leaving him at first," she says, "but I tried not to think about it. And I didn't think about it, because the classes were hard. And I was usually really tired. But I was happy. I just thought about the work, and the time flew by, and I was picking up the baby before I knew it."

54   Sophie-Louise presses April to consider how she will feel when she is separated from her daughter for the first time. "Have you thought at all about what it's going to be like?" Sophie-Louise asks. "How it's going to feel, emotionally, to be separated?"

55   April ignores her at first, and then shakes her head no. Sophie-Louise encourages her, suggesting she might feel relief or worry or sadness, but April clearly does not want to pursue the issue. Finally, in frustration, April says, "Look, I haven't thought about it yet. I haven't thought about it because it hasn't happened."

56   With that, the session ends. Having missed the deadline for entrance to summer school, April stays behind to talk to Sophie-Louise about starting a diploma-geared class in the fall. Danielle tugs at Lynda's arm, asking whether they can finally go to the zoo as she promised. I hear Eron and Janelle bickering about whose turn it is to buy diapers. And I head down the steep hill to the subway that will take me back downtown. ∎

From Elizabeth Marek, "The Lives of Teenage Mothers," *Harper's*, April 1989. Reprinted by permission.

EXERCISES

Do not refer to the selection for Exercises A and B.

A. DETERMINING MAIN IDEA AND PURPOSE
Choose the best answer.

1. _____ The main idea of the article is that (a) teenage pregnancy is not as serious a problem as the media have generally led the public to believe; (b) improved sex education courses and freer access to birth control would help solve the teenage pregnancy problem; (c) there are no easy answers for the problem of teenage pregnancy; (d) unmarried teenage mothers face many difficult obstacles in their daily lives.

2. _____ The author's main purpose in interviewing these young mothers was (a) to convince other young girls not to get pregnant; (b) to hear their own stories; (c) to discuss various psychological motivations; (d) to present her own views on a controversial topic.

B. COMPREHENDING MAIN IDEAS
Choose the correct answer.

1. _____ The Teen Parenting Program described in the article (a) dispenses birth control information; (b) provides a program for teenage parents to get together and discuss their experiences; (c) arranges for abortions for pregnant teenagers who want them; (d) provides a day-care center for teenage mothers while they are in school or at work.

2. _____ According to the article, the percentage of total pregnancies occurring among teenagers each year in New York City is (a) five percent; (b) ten percent; (c) fifteen percent; (d) twenty-five percent.

3. _____ The girls represented in Sophie-Louise's group come from (a) various races and social classes; (b) welfare families; (c) upper-middle-class families; (d) neighborhood housing projects.

4. _____ One of the girls' chief complaints about being a single mother is (a) their inability to complete high school; (b) their lack of freedom; (c) their inability to enjoy a normal social life; (d) the hostility they face from their parents.

5. _____ Lynda, the young Hispanic woman and the mother of Danielle, says that her father was very concerned about (a) her marrying the baby's father; (b) her ability to raise a child and finish school; (c) her refusal to get an abortion; (d) her making him look bad.

6. _____ The author concludes that these young mothers may have gotten pregnant (a) because they were deliberately rebelling against their parents; (b) because they were completely ignorant about sex and reproduc-

tion; (c) because they foolishly believed their boyfriends' professions of love and promises of marriage; (d) because they have little control over the events in their lives.

COMPREHENSION SCORE

Score your answers for Exercises A and B as follows:

A. No. right _____ × 2 = _____

B. No. right _____ × 1 = _____

Total pts. from A and B _____ × 10 = _____%

You may refer to the selection for the remaining exercises.

C.   DISTINGUISHING BETWEEN MAIN IDEAS AND SUPPORTING DETAILS
Label the following statements from the selection as follows: MI if the statement represents a *main idea* and SD if the statement represents a *supporting detail*.

1. _____ In all their stories, I hear again and again how little volition these girls feel they have, how little control over the events of their lives.

2. _____ The deadline for school admission passes and April shrugs.

3. _____ Sophie-Louise makes an appointment for Lynda with a job counselor, but Lynda forgets to go.

4. _____ Janelle knows about birth control but doesn't believe "it" will happen to her.

5. _____ Sophie-Louise told me once that these girls exert no more control over their lives than a "leaf falling from a tree."

6. _____ Perhaps having a baby is less a question of ignorance or choice than one of inevitability.

7. _____ Once a girl is sexually active, it is not *having* a baby that requires choice and conscious action, but *not* having one.

D.   MAKING INFERENCES
For each of these statements write Y (Yes) if the inference is an accurate one, N (No) if the inference is an inaccurate one, or CT (Can't Tell) if you do not have enough information to make an inference.

1. _____ The Kingsbridge Heights Community Center in the Bronx is surrounded by lower-class neighborhoods.

2. _____ The author came to Sophie-Louise's group with a set of preconceived ideas about the reasons for teenage pregnancy.

3. _____ It is possible that Janelle unconsciously got pregnant because she felt unwanted and unloved after her parents' divorce.

4. _____ All of the mothers described in the article display great love and affection toward their babies.

5. _____ The author was surprised that three of the mothers didn't know they were pregnant until it was too late for an abortion.

6. _____ For many young men, fathering a baby is a status symbol, proof of their manhood.

7. _____ The burden of teenage parenthood falls as much on the fathers as it does on the mothers.

8. _____ Single parenthood appears to be a cycle: babies having babies, who in turn produce more children who will be single parents in the next generation.

E.   ANALYZING ORGANIZATION AND SEEING RELATIONSHIPS

1. Look again at paragraph 3. How do the questions posed in this paragraph relate to the rest of the article? _____

_____

2. _____ How would you characterize the author's attitude toward these young women? (a) objective, neutral; (b) sympathetic, but questioning; (c) unsympathetic, unfeeling; (d) her attitude is not evident from the article.

3. _____ The body of the article is chiefly concerned with (a) an explanation of various psychological and sociological theories to explain the phenomenon of teenage pregnancy; (b) the author's opinions, observations, and conclusions; (c) facts and statistics that confirm the seriousness of the problem; (d) the young mothers talking about their experiences in their own words.

4. _____ Look again at paragraph 17. What is the relationship between the first and second sentence? (a) They represent contrasting ideas; (b) sentence 2 supports and explains the information in sentence 1; (c) sentence 1 introduces an important term, and sentence 2 defines it; (d) both sentences state steps in a process.

5. Sophie-Louise, the social worker in charge of this discussion group, is quoted in paragraph 48 as saying that these girls exert no more control over their lives than a "leaf falling from a tree." In your own words,

explain the meaning of this metaphor. _____

_____

6. _____ Look again at paragraphs 49–52. From his statements, Janelle's boyfriend, Eron, reveals (a) a sense of hopelessness; (b) pride and a great sense of responsibility; (c) feelings of ambivalence about his chances for success as a father; (d) confusion and bewilderment.

7. _____ In paragraph 48 Marek writes, "I hear again and again how little volition these girls feel they have, how little control over the events of their lives." Which of the following quotations from the people in the article *best* supports this statement? (a) Eron: "You know, all this talk about we didn't want to have the baby, or it was an accident, or whatever . . . I just think it's a waste of time. I mean, now we have the baby. The question is, what are we going to do now?" (b) Lynda: "He [her boyfriend] said, 'Oh, I love you, and I'll do this for you, I'll do that for you, and our baby will have this, and our baby will have that.' Now she's two and a half years old, and all he ever got her was a big box of Pampers and socks and T-shirts and $20 and that was it." (c) Sophie-Louise: "'How it's going to feel, emotionally, to be separated?'" April: "'Look, I haven't thought about it yet. I haven't thought about it because it hasn't happened.'" (d) Janelle: "'It's so easy to go on welfare. You just sit home and cash a check. But I'm not going to get on welfare, 'cause it makes you lazy. It's addictive.'"

8. _____ Look again at the last sentence of the article, which suggests (a) that the author's life is very far removed from the day-to-day struggles of these young mothers; (b) that the author thinks the problem of teenage pregnancy is far worse than anyone has imagined; (c) that the author felt drained and discouraged by these young parents' experiences; (d) that the author regretted gathering information for the article.

F.   UNDERSTANDING VOCABULARY

Look through the paragraphs listed below and find a word that matches each definition. An example has been done for you.

Ex.	brothers and sisters [10 and 19]	_____ siblings _____
1.	meditate on a particular subject [2–3]	_____
2.	concerned with managing time and equipment [5–6]	_____
3.	unpredictable occurrences [18–19]	_____
4.	the outside boundary of an area [20–21]	_____
5.	only slightly connected with the subject [20–21]	_____
6.	firm, unyielding [29–30]	_____
7.	soft, limp, flabby [29–30]	_____
8.	lasting for a long time [34–35]	_____
9.	manliness, masculine vigor [34–35]	_____
10.	conscious choice, the power to choose [47–48]	_____

G. USING VOCABULARY

In parentheses before each sentence are some inflected forms of words from the selection. Study the context and the sentence. Then write the correct form in the space provided. Be sure to add appropriate endings like *-s, -ed,* or *-ing,* if necessary.

1. (*relate, relative, relatively*)   Unlike many teenagers who become pregnant,

   Janelle says that as a child she lived in _____ security until her parents got a divorce.

2. (*alienate, alienation, alien*)   In at least two cases described in the article,

   the teenagers were seriously _____ from their parents as a result of their pregnancy.

3. (*yearn, yearning, yearningly*)   Marek wonders if these girls' ignorance about their pregnancy for so many weeks suggests that they uncon-

   sciously _____ for a child.

4. (*wistfulness, wistful, wistfully*)   Lynda _____ recalls her boyfriend's promises of things he was going to buy for their baby.

5. (*indignation, indignant, indignantly*)   When questioned about her birth

   control methods, April answers with _____.

6. (*relevance, relevant, relevantly*)   By the end of the session, Marek wonders

   about the _____ of asking whether or not these girls have any choice over their lives.

H. TOPICS FOR WRITING OR DISCUSSION

1. Look through the article again, and in your own words, state some of the motivations that appear to govern these young women's decision to keep

   their babies. _____

   _____

   _____

   _____

2. If you were in a position of authority in a high school, what measures would you suggest or implement to deal with the issue of teenage pregnancy?

18

Patrick Welsh

SEX AND THE MODERN TEENAGER

Patrick Welsh has taught English at T. C. Williams High School in Alexandria, Virginia, for nearly twenty years. He is the author of Tales Out of School. *This article, originally published in the* Washington Post, *examines sexual attitudes among this generation of teenagers.*

VOCABULARY PREVIEW

WORD ORIGINS

SOPHISTICATED

Although the spread of AIDS has changed single adults' sexual practices, the fear of this disease has not spread to high school students, according to the author. In paragraph 23 Welsh writes that high school students today are seemingly *sophisticated*. They belong to what he calls "one big family whose members have known each other since kindergarten." But they also forget that many members of that "family" may have outside sexual contacts.

Sophisticated means, in this context, "worldly-wise." Although the Greek word *sophos* meant "wise," the meaning of this word later changed completely. In the Middle Ages the word took on negative associations, since the verb *sophisticate* ("to devise") was used to describe the mixtures alchemists cooked up. (Alchemists were the medieval chemists who tried to change ordinary metals into gold.)

This negative association probably came about because the resulting mixture was considered impure. Today we use *sophisticated* to describe someone whose worldly knowledge makes him or her no longer innocent.

Incidentally, the word *sophomore*, which refers to a second-year student in an American high school or college, also derives from this root. Its etymology is similarly unflattering, since in Greek it means literally "wise fool": [*sophos* ("wise," "clever") + *moros* ("silly," "foolish")].

Naive

In paragraph 24 Welsh uses an antonym of *sophisticated.* He writes that high school girls are *naive* about what their older boyfriends do when they go away to college, because when they return home for vacations, they may sleep with their old girlfriends and pretend that they have been faithful.

The adjective *naive* means "lacking worldliness or sophistication," "simple or credulous" (believing in things as a child does). This connection can be seen in its derivation. It comes from the French word *naif,* "ingenuous" or "natural," which in turn came from Latin *nātīvus* ("native"), from *nāscī* ("to be born"). In other words, a *naive* person is as simple about the ways of the world as a newly born baby is.

Trysts

According to paragraph 48, "more kids today slip off to their parents' empty homes for afternoon *trysts* than ever did back then," meaning in the 1940s and 1950s. A *tryst* means a "meeting between lovers." This word has two possible derivations: from Old French *triste,* "an appointed station in hunting," or from Old Norse *treysta,* "to trust," "to make firm."

WORD PARTS

Trans-

In paragraph 24 Welsh uses the phrase "sexually *transmitted* disease." The prefix *trans-* means "over" or "across" before whatever root it precedes. To *transmit* means "to send from one person, thing, or place to another," from Latin: [*trans-* ("across") + *mittere* ("to send")].

Here are some other words with this prefix:

transcontinental	crossing a continent
transcribe	to write a copy of; to transfer information from one place to another, as in "to *transcribe* notes" [*trans-* + *scribere* ("to write")]
transplant	to uproot and replant; to transfer an organ from one body to another
transport	to carry from one place to another [*trans-* + *portare* ("to carry")]

WORD FAMILIES

Repentant

Toward the end of the article, Welsh writes, "I'd be dishonest not to admit that a part of me feels my students ought to be guilt-stricken—or at least a little *repentant.*" The root of this adjective, *repent,* means "to feel remorse," specifically, according to *The American Heritage Dictionary,* "to feel such remorse or regret for past conduct as to change one's mind regarding it." The root of this word came into Middle English from Old French *repentir,* which can be broken down like this:

[*re-* ("in response to") + *pentire* ("to be sorry")]

Here are some other words in this family:

penitent   feeling remorse for one's misdeeds
penance   an act intended to show one's sorrow for committing a sin
penalty   punishment established by law for a crime or offense
penalize   to impose a penalty on
penitentiary   a prison for those convicted of a crime

PATRICK WELSH

SEX AND THE MODERN TEENAGER

1   "It wasn't just sex. We were really involved with each other. I developed so much self-confidence from that relationship. I feel very comfortable about sex now. That relationship was one of the most important things in my growing up."

2   As I listened to the bright, accomplished young woman, a student at T. C. Williams High School in Alexandria, Va., I felt as though I were listening to a single or divorced woman in her 30s casually talking about a recent affair. But in the back of my mind I kept hearing the whisper of Monsignor Herlihy, the principal of the Catholic high school I attended: "Mortal sin! Mortal sin!"

3   I couldn't resist asking my student: "Don't you regret not waiting? Don't you think that this guy has used you? Don't you feel any guilt?" She replied that people my age don't realize how much a long-term relationship can mean to a teenager.

4   To be honest, I don't. Attitudes toward sex were just too different when I was a student at Notre Dame High School in Batavia, N.Y., in the mid-'50s. Maybe my high school experience was unusually repressive, even for the '50s. And granted, it's not easy for a 46-year-old English teacher to get a clear reading on just what is going on with kids. Still, I believe that the majority of my generation has difficulty understanding and coming to terms with the radically different sexual attitudes and habits of this generation of high school students.

5   Most of the recent public discussion of teenage sex has dealt with pregnancy among low-income students and its relationship to the cycle of poverty. But we often overlook the revolution in sexual attitudes—and the apparently ever-increasing amount of sexual activity—among middle- and upper-income kids.

6   "There's a feeling that it's OK for us to have sex because we're educated and know what's going on. We're not going to get pregnant and burden society with unwanted children. We're going to college and have a future. If we do slip up, we'll get an abortion," says one sexually active honors student.

7   When, in the course of getting material for this article, I first heard remarks like this, I thought that the kids were hiding something—that deep down they were feeling terribly guilty. (Guilt was a very familiar emotion when I was growing up. I remember a compulsory retreat in my senior year during which a Jesuit priest, imported from Buffalo, preached for two days that "French kissing" and "deliberately entertaining impure thoughts" would lead to eternal damnation.)

8   But I soon came to realize that I was reading my '50s attitudes about sex into these kids, and in fact that most of them may feel little if any guilt. "A lot of kids believe in God but just don't think God disapproves of their sex lives," says senior Will Peyton, a National Merit semi-finalist.

9   The general feeling among scores of middle-class kids I talked to is that as long as high school couples are "going together" and are faithful to each other—even if the relationship lasts only a few months—sexual intercourse is fine.

10   Even among those kids who are not sexually active there seems to be an amazingly tolerant and casual attitude toward friends who are. As school psychologist Roberta New says, "If sex is in the context of a serious relationship, they think it's perfectly natural. Even kids who have 'serially monogamous' relationships—two or three affairs a year—seem to feel little guilt. The sexual liberation that college students began experiencing in the '60s is now full-blown in high school. The only difference is that high school students still have parents around and have to be sneaky about it."

11   Said one high-achieving student at T. C. Williams: "I remember once when my mother suggested that it might be time for me to have my first gynecological exam. I told her that I didn't really need to see a gynecologist now. What I didn't tell her is that I had been seeing one to get birth-control pills already. I felt like my mother was probing to find out if I was sexually active. It made me uncomfortable."

12   Among the kids there is some disagreement as to just how much their parents do know about what's going on. "Parents are only around their own kids, and their own kids deceive them. I've one friend who has had 10 big parties in her house in the last year, and her parents, who've been out of town during each of them, have no idea about it. If they can't even find out about wild parties, how can they be expected to find out about their kid's private sex life?" says a top student. Senior Will Peyton thinks that parents may know more than they let on. "Most parents suspect what's going on, and many are even sure, but very few dare confront their kid," he says.

13   When it comes to confrontations about sex, it often seems that the "children" have the upper hand. "It's hilarious to watch my mother try to find out about my sex life. I've grown up with all these messages about being open—the 'You can tell me anything, dear—I'm from the '60s' kind of stuff. She's had 'The Joy of Sex' on the living-room bookshelf since I've been in sixth grade. But now that I'm 17 and have a boyfriend, she's getting desperate to know what's going on," says one of my favorite students, who admitted that in fact she isn't sexually active but doesn't think it's her mother's business either way.

14   Another girl sees that same desperation in her mother: "My parents . . . never punished me unfairly. But now that I'm serious about a guy, my mother is a different person. She makes all these nervous asides—'Now, don't jump into things, dear'—hoping she's getting her points across. But I really feel that it's none of her business. How can sex be personal and intimate if you go tell your mom about it? She doesn't tell me about her sex life," says this frank, charming and high achieving student.

15   Kids seem to agree that the idea of "modern" parents' being so open with their children is a gigantic myth. "The only kind of open discussion that parents want is one that ends with 'Gee, Mom and Dad, you're so right and I'm not sexually active and won't be at least till I get out of high school,'" says one 16-year-old boy.

16   Most kids say that their friends are bigger sources of psychological support than their parents. "Friends listen and understand. But most parents can't help being judgmental," says one student.

17   It's especially hard for divorced parents, who may be having affairs themselves, to give the "right values" to their teenagers. "When your mother has a Friday night date and he's in the kitchen eating breakfast Saturday morning, how can she preach about premarital sex?" another student asked me.

18   Jean Hunter, director of the Family Life program in the Alexandria schools and a recognized expert on adolescent sexuality, is concerned about what she sees as a tacit complicity going on between parents and their teenagers.

19   "Many parents agree to pretend that their kids are not sexually active, and in return the kids pretend for the parents' sake that they aren't," says Hunter. When these kids get pregnant and take the usual middle-class solution—abortion—they end up counseling themselves without the support of parents. Hunter feels that parents and other adults can no longer afford to ignore the increasing sexual activity among teens because of the growing risks of AIDS.

20   AIDS may have changed the sexual practices of single adults, but high school kids seem to act as if they are totally immune to the disease. The preferred method of birth control among middle-class high-school couples is the pill. Students say that no girl on the pill is going to ask her boyfriend to use a condom just to be safe about AIDS.

21   "It would be insulting to the guys, implying that they were cheating on you or were bisexuals," one senior girl says.

22   Another says that "it would break the mood" to ask a boy to wear a condom.

23   The main illusion that so many of these seemingly sophisticated kids have is that high school is one big family whose members have known each other since kindergarten. They tend to forget that some of that family are having outside sexual contacts on weekends, at college and on vacations.

24   "High school girls are very naive about what their older boyfriends are doing in college. Most of the guys I know are very sexually active in college and then come home and sleep with their old girlfriends and pretend that they've been faithful. Those girls are taking big chances," says Kellie Ray, now a college freshman. In a recent case in my school, an old boyfriend infected one of the girls with a sexually transmitted disease that he had picked up in college.

25   Jim Dawes, the valedictorian of my school's class of '87, says that for many kids "AIDS is kind of like nuclear war. It's too big to worry about." And the long latency period of the disease means that few students will show symptoms while still in high school.

26   There is still considerable reluctance on the part of high schools to face up to the prevalence of sexual activities and the associated risks. But as soon as a kid enters college, he or she is bombarded with warnings about AIDS and other diseases.

27   At Amherst College, for example, a student group puts condoms and informational packets with red crosses on them in student mailboxes. A former student of mine said she recently went to a "safe sex" party at Amherst where, in order to get a beer, a partygoer had to display a condom. At Vassar, a pink machine in a laundry room dispenses condoms.

28   But with all the openness about sex these days, it's easy to overlook the fact that a great number of kids still don't do it. There are really more virgins, male and female, in our high schools and colleges than generally assumed. Studies show that when students are asked what percentage of their classmates they think are sexually active, the numbers run as high as 80 percent. When individual students are asked if they are sexually active, however, the figure drops to around 50 percent, about the same rate that a 1986 Harris poll showed for 17-year-olds.

29   My students say it's not really "in" to come out and say you're a virgin. Recently, when I was talking to several kids to get ideas for this article, none of them said that they were sexually active—yet the impressions they seemed to leave with me and with one another was that they were. One of them returned later to tell me privately that she was a virgin but just felt funny saying so in front of the others.

30   Gary Alward says flat out that he doesn't believe in sex before marriage. He and his tall, attractive, blond girlfriend, Katherine Reilly, have been dating each other exclusively for almost three years. Gary says his belief in abstinence comes from his Baptist faith. Katherine, a Catholic, says: "I just don't feel ready for sex now. One of the reasons that Gary and I have such a good relationship is that he doesn't pressure me."

31   Family life teacher Jean Hunter says that adults have to help more kids to realize what Katherine and Gary have discovered: It's difficult but possible to have a meaningful, intimate relationship without sex. One thing that may make it easier for Katherine and Gary is that they are part of a group of about 20 kids, few of whom are paired off as couples. What the group members seem to have in common are high academic achievement, intelligence and a wide variety of interests. I am told that it is not "in" with these kids to be sexually active, although they seem tolerant of friends who are.

32   There are many bright kids at my school who are not part of this group. There are also many other kids not in the group who are not sexually active.

33   But other indicators suggest some relationship between academic achievement and virginity. A recent poll of 1,985 students who appear in "Who's Who Among High School Students" claims that only 26 percent of the males and 24 percent of the females surveyed say they have lost their virginity; those figures are well below the commonly accepted figures of 50 percent for all teens.

34   One very bright, sexually active girl says that with some of her high-achieving friends, virginity is less a matter of morality than of time. "Some of them are just too busy with schoolwork to form the kind of personal relationship that would lead to sex. Given enough time and the right person, they might change their minds fast."

35   (Certainly the priests and nuns I had in high school understand the time factor. Keeping busy was the saltpeter* of my generation. Young men were constantly encouraged to get into every kind of sport and other activity. The priests called it "avoiding temptation"; Freud called it sublimation.)

36   There may be argument about the correlation between academic achievement and virginity, but there's almost universal agreement that drinking goes hand in hand with teenage sex.

37   Almost every kid I talked to says that students who drink a lot tend to be more

*Potassium nitrate—a chemical thought to diminish sexual desire; here used metaphorically to mean vigorous activity.

sexually active—and more promiscuous—than those who do not. "I've seen couples who hardly know each other start drinking at a party and get so carried away they'll slip off somewhere and have sex. Sometimes it's really funny to see these girls who act like such prudes at school start coming on to guys after they have a few drinks," says one party observer.

38   As I look back on the vitriolic discussions I was part of as member of the Alexandria Mayor's Task Force studying the proposed school-based health clinic at my school, it seems that many adults on both sides, myself included, had no clear understanding of teenage sex today.

39   Those against the clinic described kids who have sex as "bad," or "corrupted." One elderly gentleman told the City Council that a clinic that dispensed condoms would turn our youth into "rubberized rabbits." A local pastor predicted that "our historic city would become a Sodom and Gomorrah."†

40   My side, the pro-clinic forces, didn't seem any more on target. The working assumption seemed to be that kids just couldn't control themselves and needed institutional intervention to protect them from pregnancy or sexually transmitted diseases.

41   Few of us adults seem able or willing to understand that there are some extraordinarily mature teenagers who make informed decisions to have sexual intercourse with someone they care deeply about.

42   I wonder how adults on my task force would react to the discussion that I described in the first paragraph of this article. Here was a highly respected and intelligent student—a girl I would be proud to have as my daughter—telling me that her long relationship with a fellow student had given her self-confidence and the deep enjoyment of a caring relationship. "I don't have a single regret about it," she concluded.

43   From other kids I've talked to, I don't think that her situation is that unusual.

44   What we may be seeing in the attitudes of these young people is not Sodom and Gomorrah revisited but an attempt to formulate an ethical code that judges sex in terms of individual personal relationships instead of absolute religious and moral codes.

45   The students' ethics condemn promiscuity as degrading, but approve of sex between teenagers committed to each other. Even many teenagers who come from staunch Catholic homes say that the church's strict teaching on premarital sex has little relevance.

46   "Our parents' beliefs about sex and religion just don't carry over to too many of us. Most kids make their decision based on their own conscience and on how committed to the other person they are," says a 16-year-old member of a local parish.

47   I'd be dishonest not to admit that a part of me feels my students ought to be guilt-stricken—or at least a little repentant—about their sexual attitudes and experiences. But another part of me recalls that teenagers in the '40s and '50s weren't as pure as we would like to remember.

48   Granted, more kids today slip off to their parents' empty homes for afternoon trysts than ever did back then. (Back seats of cars are now viewed as "not very

†Two cities in ancient Palestine that were destroyed by fire because the inhabitants were so depraved; see Genesis 19:24.

classy" venues for sex.) But teenage childbearing rates peaked in the '50s along with shotgun marriages. In those days, many kids dropped out of high school, went to work and got married, while many others married soon after graduation. Early marriages took care of many of the raging hormones of those times, but they often ended in early divorces—the source of so much turmoil in the lives of today's young people.

49   Is it surprising that this generation is forging its own moral code? Many more young people than ever before are encouraged to go on to college, postpone marriage for many years and at the same time not be sexually active. As psychologist Bruno Bettelheim observes, "This expectation cannot help creating severe emotional strains in the young, problems in their relations to each other, and difficulties in their relations to their parents."

50   Looked at in that perspective, perhaps we should be thankful that students are as responsible, and as well adjusted, as so many seem to be.   ■

From Patrick Welsh, "Sex and the Modern Teenager," *San Francisco Chronicle*, "This World," February 14, 1988. Originally published in the *Washington Post*. Reprinted by permission.

EXERCISES

Do not refer to the selection for Exercises A and B.

A.   DETERMINING THE MAIN IDEA AND PURPOSE
Choose the best answer.

1.   _____ The main idea of the selection is that (a) teenagers who engage in premarital sex should feel some remorse; (b) sexual attitudes are changing because of AIDS; (c) sexual attitudes are very different today from what they were in the 1940s and 1950s; (d) today's teenagers think sexual intercourse is permissible in a serious relationship.

2.   _____ With respect to the subject of teenage sexual activity, the author's purpose is (a) to investigate students' attitudes today and to inform the reader of them; (b) to present facts and statistics; (c) to convince students of the wrongness of their actions; (d) to relate the sexual experiences of a few representative students.

B.   COMPREHENDING MAIN IDEAS
Choose the correct answer.

1.   _____ According to the author, the majority of adults in his generation (a) readily accepts young people's attitudes toward sex; (b) has difficulty understanding the sexual attitudes of this generation of high school students; (c) thinks that birth control measures are too accessible; (d) realizes that not much has changed—today's teenagers have similar attitudes about sex to those that the adults did when they were young.

2.   _____ According to the article, high school students today believe that (a) being a virgin is synonymous with being cursed; (b) sex is all right in the context of a serious relationship; (c) being sexually promiscuous, i.e., sleeping around, is all right as long as the couple practices birth control; (d) sex is wrong, but peer pressure forces many teenagers to begin sexual activity when they might not actually be ready.

3.   _____ The term used in the article to define a series of relationships where the couple are faithful to each other is serial (a) polygamy; (b) abstinence; (c) sublimation; (d) monogamy.

4.   _____ The teenagers interviewed in this article suggest that, with regard to their sexual activity, their parents are (a) upset and angry; (b) suspicious, but afraid to confront them; (c) indifferent or ambivalent; (d) bewildered and confused.

5.   _____ In fact, the number of high school and college students who say that they actually are sexually active is about (a) twenty-five percent; (b) fifty percent; (c) sixty-five percent; (d) eighty percent.

6.   _____ The author concludes that today's generation of students (a) may regret their early sexual activity as AIDS and other sexually transmitted diseases spread through the population; (b) are formulating a new ethical code regarding sex; (c) represent a new age where total sexual awareness and freedom can flourish; (d) are sexually promiscuous and irresponsible, despite what they say.

COMPREHENSION SCORE

Score your answers for Exercises A and B as follows:

A.   No. right _____ × 2 = _____

B.   No. right _____ × 1 = _____

Total pts. from A and B _____ × 10 = _____%

You may refer to the selection for the remaining exercises.

C.   RECOGNIZING SUPPORTING DETAILS

Place an X in the space for each statement that *directly* supports this main idea from the selection: **"Few of us adults seem able or willing to understand that there are some extraordinarily mature teenagers who make informed decisions to have sexual intercourse with someone they care deeply about."**

1.   _____ What we may be seeing in the attitudes of these young people is not Sodom and Gomorrah revisited but an attempt to formulate an ethical code that judges sex in terms of individual personal relationships instead of absolute religious and moral codes.

2.   _____ The students' ethics condemn promiscuity as degrading, but approve of sex between teenagers committed to each other.

3.   _____ Even many teenagers who come from staunch Catholic homes say that the church's strict teaching on premarital sex has little relevance.

4.   _____ There may be argument about the correlation between academic achievement and virginity, but there's almost universal agreement that drinking goes hand in hand with teenage sex.

5.   _____ "Our parents' beliefs about sex and religion just don't carry over to too many of us."

6.   _____ "Most kids make their decision based on their own conscience and on how committed to the other person they are," says a sixteen-year-old member of a local parish.

D.   MAKING INFERENCES

For each of these statements write Y (Yes) if the inference is an accurate one, N (No) if the inference is an inaccurate one, or CT (Can't Tell) if you do not have enough information to make an inference.

1.   _____ The author initially believed that a teenage girl who has had sex has been exploited by her boyfriend.

2.   _____ Sexual attitudes among middle- and upper-income high school students are different from those of teenagers from low-income or very poor families.

3.   _____ The term *mortal sin* in the Catholic Church refers to a minor sin, one of little moral importance.

4.   _____ In the 1940s and 1950s only those people brought up in Catholic or in other strict religious homes felt guilty about sex.

5.   _____ Information about AIDS and AIDS prevention, for example, using condoms or abstaining from sex altogether, has made little impact on these high school students.

6.   _____ The AIDS virus has already afflicted several thousand high school students in this country.

7.   _____ Students who are virgins are reluctant to admit it publicly for fear of not seeming "cool."

8.   _____ Students who get good grades and who participate in extra-curricular activities are more likely to be virgins than to be sexually experienced.

9.   _____ The increase in the number of two-earner households is one possible reason for the increase in sexual activity among today's high school students.

10. _____ It is probably unrealistic to expect students to abstain from sex at the same time that they are encouraged to attend college and defer marriage.

E. ANALYZING ORGANIZATION AND SEEING RELATIONSHIPS
Choose the correct answer.

1. _____ Welsh is chiefly concerned in this article with (a) discovering teenagers' sexual attitudes, particularly the reasons for their lack of guilt about sexual relationships; (b) high school students' knowledge about sex; (c) contrasting sexual attitudes of today with those of the 1940s and 1950s; (d) finding evidence to support his observation that today's students are sexually promiscuous.

2. _____ To support his observation, Welsh relies mainly on (a) his own past experience; (b) information obtained from interviewing several high school students; (c) the opinions and judgments of health experts; (d) the results of recent research studies.

3. _____ Look again at paragraphs 4 and 48. The transitional word *granted* in these contexts means (a) in other words; (b) in contrast; (c) admittedly; (d) honestly.

4. What does Welsh mean when he writes in paragraph 8, "I soon came to realize that I was reading my '50s attitudes about sex into these kids"?

_____

_____

5. _____ Welsh strongly implies that many of today's parents (a) are unaware of the extent of their children's sexual activity; (b) are not fulfilling their responsibilities toward their children with regard to their sexual activity; (c) are worried about their children's sexual activity for nothing; (d) suspect their children may be sexually active, but are uncertain about how to deal with it.

6. _____ When one of Welsh's former students says in paragraph 25, "AIDS is kind of like nuclear war. It's too big to worry about," he is really suggesting that, like nuclear war, (a) there is no cure for AIDS; (b) getting AIDS is inevitable; (c) no one can do anything about the possibility of getting AIDS; (d) AIDS is preventable.

7. Look again at paragraph 48. What does the term *shotgun marriages* mean?

_____

_____

8. In your own words, explain the author's attitude toward high school students who are sexually active. _____

_____

_____

F. UNDERSTANDING VOCABULARY
Choose the correct definition according to the context.

1. _____ a *tacit* complicity [paragraph 18]: (a) strategic; (b) unhealthy; (c) unspoken; (d) unusual.

2. _____ a tacit *complicity* [18]: State of being (a) an accomplice in a wrongdoing; (b) a willing observer; (c) a forceful opponent; (d) a source of support and guidance.

3. _____ these seemingly *sophisticated* kids [23]: (a) innocent; (b) guilt-ridden; (c) complicated; (d) wordly-wise.

4. _____ High school girls are very *naive* [24]: (a) aware, realistic; (b) foolish, ignorant; (c) simple, credulous; (d) emotionally immature.

5. _____ the long *latency* period of the disease [25]: State of being (a) life-threatening; (b) hidden; (c) causing harm; (d) undetectable.

6. _____ Freud called it *sublimation* [35]: A psychological term meaning the process of (a) pretending that a feeling or urge doesn't exist; (b) condoning unacceptable behavior; (c) modifying an impulse in a socially acceptable manner; (d) engaging in numerous activities to keep busy.

7. _____ the *correlation* between academic achievement and virginity [36]: (a) relationship; (b) contrast; (c) similarity; (d) theory.

8. _____ look back on the *vitriolic* discussions [38]: (a) productive; (b) harsh; (c) angry; (d) honest.

9. _____ students' ethics condemn promiscuity as *degrading* [45]: (a) defensible; (b) embarrassing; (c) lowering in character; (d) ill-advised.

10. _____ this generation is *forging* its own moral code [49]: (a) counterfeiting; (b) devising; (c) rewriting; (d) perfecting.

G. USING VOCABULARY
From the following list of vocabulary words, choose a word that fits in each blank according to both the grammatical structure of the sentence and the context. Use each word in the list only once and add noun or verb endings (such as *-s, -ing,* or *-ed*) if necessary. (Note that there are more words than sentences.)

abstinence	illusion	bombard
prevalence	immune	transmit
promiscuity	repentant	venues
tryst	monogamous	turmoil

1.   Although teenagers today do not believe in sexual _____
     which they see as degrading, they do think that "serially

     _____" relationships are all right.

2.   Some students practice _____ because they don't be-
     lieve in sex before marriage; however, few students abstain from sex be-

     cause they are afraid of sexually _____ diseases.

3.   Although college students are _____ with informa-
     tion about AIDS and its prevention, high school students apparently

     operate under the _____ that they are

     _____ from this disease.

H.   TOPICS FOR WRITING OR DISCUSSION

1.   In your own words, summarize the differences in sexual attitudes be-

     tween adults and today's high school students. _____

     _____

     _____

     _____

     _____

     _____

     _____

     _____

2.   Just how representative of today's sexual activities are these students
     whom Welsh interviewed for this article? Based on your own assessment
     of high school students, do their attitudes—their ideas about "serial mo-
     nogamy," their lack of guilt or anxiety—seem common or unusual?

19

John Reid

IF IT'S CUTE ENOUGH, WE'LL SAVE IT

In 1990 the conflict between the campaign to save the northern spotted owl's habitat in California, Oregon, and Washington and the logging industry intensified. The government placed the spotted owl on the endangered species list, preventing timber companies from cutting down trees in forests where these owls live. The timber industry, on the other hand, complained that thousands of people's jobs would be affected. Using the spotted owl as an example, John Reid, a reporter at Pacific News Service, examines the increasingly troublesome issue of our disappearing animal species.

VOCABULARY PREVIEW

WORD ORIGINS

SAVVY

In paragraph 5, Reid writes that "conservationists have grown *savvy* about choosing simple, endearing symbols," in other words, about choosing which species to save from extinction. Most words derived from Latin came into English via French, because of the Norman Conquest of England in 1066. However, the word *savvy*, a slang term meaning "having practical knowledge" or "wise," derives from Spanish. Specifically, it is a corruption of *sabe usted* ("you know"), from *saber* ("to know"), from Latin *sapere*, "to be sensible or wise."

CHARISMATIC

The word *charisma* means "a rare quality applied to certain leaders who inspire devotion among their followers." It is most typically applied to political or religious leaders. For example, Adolf Hitler, John F. Kennedy, and Martin Luther King, Jr., were often described as *charismatic*. In this context, Reid uses the term *charismatic* a bit differently; according to paragraph 6, conservationists have chosen for media attention animals they call "'*charismatic* mega-vertebrates'—big, attractive animals with backbones." The origin of this word is from Greek, *kharisma*, meaning "favor" or "divine gift."

SYMBIOSIS

In paragraph 21 Reid writes, "Ultimately, the most important thing for many conservationists is creating a new kind of *symbiosis,* using spotted owls and their attractive ilk [their own kind] to save a broader range of living things." *Symbiosis* is a biological term meaning "a usually beneficial relationship between two or more different organisms." In this case, Reid means that saving the spotted owl's habitat will not only save that species but other species within the same environment. It is derived from Greek:

[*symbiosis* ("a living together"), from *syn-* ("together") + *bios* ("life")]

WORD PARTS

Co-

As a prefix, *co-* is attached to a large number of words in English indicating "together." In paragraph 12 Reid uses the term *co-inhabitants,* meaning organisms that inhabit an environment together. This prefix can be seen in many other ordinary words in English, among them *coworker, co-conspirator, coeducation,* and *cooperate.*

PHOBIA

Reid says in paragraph 19 that some conservationists attribute a species' success to a conflict between "*phobia* and fascination," meaning, "Would you instinctively save the animal or kill it?" *Phobia* is a common Greek word part often used as a suffix describing any abnormal or persistent fear. Here are some other common "phobia" words:

agoraphobia	an abnormal fear of open places [*agora* ("open space") + *phobia*]
claustrophobia	fear of confined spaces [*claustrum* ("enclosed place") + *phobia*]
hydrophobia	fear of water [*hydro-* ("water") + *phobia*]
xenophobia	fear of strangers or foreigners [*xeno-* ("foreigner") + *phobia*]

WORD FAMILIES

HABITAT

Occurring in paragraphs 9, 10, and 16, *habitat* means "a place or environment where a person or thing lives." This word followed the same route that so many words in English have taken: from Latin, into French, into Middle English. In Latin, *habitāre* means "to inhabit." Some other common words in this family include:

habitation	a dwelling place
inhabitant	one who lives in a specific place; a resident
habitable and **inhabitable**	both meaning suitable to live in
uninhabitable	not suitable to live in
uninhabited	not lived in

Other words you should know:

hype	[paragraph 3]—slang for an intense advertising or publicity campaign
sub-phylum	[6]—a *phylum* is a classification term used in the animal kingdom; a *sub-phylum* means a smaller division of a phylum
cause célèbre	[23]—French for a celebrated cause, meaning any controversy that attracts a lot of attention

JOHN REID

IF IT'S CUTE ENOUGH, WE'LL SAVE IT

1 This year's poster animal, by all odds, is the northern spotted owl. In attaining star status, the bird offers a glimpse into the reasons humans select one species over another for survival.

2 Facing possible extinction—it roosts in prized timberland—the northern spotted owl gained partial protection when the U.S. Fish and Wildlife Service recently listed it as No. 599 on the endangered species list of animals and plants.

3 Experts say there are between five and 100 million animal and plant species on Earth, of which only two percent have been inventoried. One to three species disappear every day, according to the Nature Conservancy. At this rate, why all the hype about one spotted owl?

4 "People respond to larger animals that we see or are part of our experience, like owls," says Daniel Taylor, a National Audubon Society biologist. "People know owls. People may not know spotted owls, but owls occupy an important place in our cultural psyche."

5 In a media age, conservationists have grown savvy about choosing simple, endearing symbols. Known as flagship species, symbols like the spotted owl tend to be "things that are large, things that are cute and cuddly," according to John Carr, research biologist at Conservation International in Washington, D.C.

6 Ironically, the new darlings of the jungle—and the press—are often the same species hunters once prized as game trophies. They form a new sub-phylum of animals known to conservationists as "charismatic mega-vertebrates"—big, attractive animals with backbones.

7 "Large vertebrates are more important to us as a society than small invertebrates," says Daniel Taylor of the National Audubon Society. He says this fact reflects our preoccupation with animals we eat and that eat us, or used to.

8 Carr puts it more simply: "It's easier to get people excited about a monkey than a spider."

9   Size is also a factor, because a species has to be seen to be saved. Strategically, Carr says, size is key because the larger the species protected, the larger its range is, and thus, the larger the habitat needed to preserve it.

10   Making the cover of *Time* magazine and garnering plenty of media attention, the northern spotted owl has also saved a flock of equally endangered, but less endearing, species that share its forest habitat.

11   One of these is the fisher, a sleek mammal that shares the northwestern forests with the owl and the unglamorous and obscure tailed frog.

12   Building a campaign around those co-inhabitants would be hard. Says the Audubon Society's Taylor, "I had a reporter for CBS News say, 'Do you have any footage of the fisher?' Well, we don't. There isn't any. So you're left with a still picture. It's harder to communicate the essence of the fisher if people in this television age can't see it."

13   But media images of the handsome spotted owl spurred a national audience into sympathizing with the rare bird.

14   Often, the more human traits an animal appears to have, the stronger its candidacy for stardom. A recent tuna commercial likened a dolphin group to a wholesome American family. Dolphins are seen as loyal, playful geniuses. Owls, of course, are wise.

15   But who sees anything humanlike about such little-known endangered species as the greasy Amazon tapir or the tailed frog?

16   With the cuteness, backbone-possession and "humanlike" tests to pass, a threatened species depends for survival not so much on its adaptation to climate and habitat as on its adaptation to the media marketplace of human causes.

17   The pioneering animal in "mediagenics" was the baby harp seal, whose big dark eyes and good television visuals helped galvanize the "Save the Seals" movement in the 1960s.

18   Other factors carry weight in piquing a positive public response. "We seem to have a fascination with black and white," says Bill Konstant, executive director of Wildlife Preservation Trust International, pointing to the popular panda and killer whale.

19   Some conservationists say a species' success may ultimately boil down to a visceral play between phobia and fascination in the human psyche: Would you instinctively save the animal or kill it?

20   "You won't sell snakes. The bushmaster (a 12-foot viper), for example; you're just not going to sell that," says Konstant.

21   Ultimately, the most important thing for many conservationists is creating a new kind of symbiosis, using spotted owls and their attractive ilk to save a broader range of living things.

22   "When you save the habitat for the spotted owl, what you're really doing is preserving biological diversity," says University of California at Berkeley biologist David Wake.

23   There is evidence, however, that the owl's charm is not universal. When rural Oregonians think about the spotted owl, they see it as a menace to the logging industry that is their lifeblood. The bird is widely seen as a cause célèbre of hot-tub liberals who backpack in the woods once a year.

24   Plastered to many pickup trucks around Oregon in recent months has been a bumper sticker reading: "I Love the Spotted Owl—Fried!"   ■

From John Reid, "If It's Cute Enough, We'll Save It," *San Francisco Chronicle*, "This World," July 15, 1990. Reprinted by permission.

EXERCISES

Do not refer to the selection for Exercises A and B.

A.   DETERMINING THE MAIN IDEA AND PURPOSE
Choose the best answer.

1.   _____ The main idea of the article is that (a) the government should make a stronger effort to save animals that are members of endangered species; (b) the case of the northern spotted owl reveals how scientists select one species over another for survival; (c) the conflict between environmentalists and industry will intensify as more and more animal species become endangered; (d) large "cute" vertebrates in danger of extinction should be saved over less attractive species.

2.   _____ With respect to the main idea, the author's purpose is (a) to explain and discuss a currently important issue; (b) to tell a story; (c) to convince us about a controversial idea; (d) to present the findings of recent scientific research.

B.   COMPREHENDING MAIN IDEAS
Write the correct answer.

1.   The article discusses "flagship species," those animals that are chosen to be saved. Two chief characteristics the author mentions that these species

generally have are _____ and _____.

2.   The spotted owl's habitat is _____.

3.   The author states that it is ironic that the species now considered worthy

of saving are the same ones that people used to _____.

4.   The specific technique that the media used to get the public's attention

and sympathy about the spotted owl's fate was _____

_____.

5.   According to Reid, the pioneering animal in "mediagenics," meaning the animal that had good visual appeal to the public, was the

_____.

6. The author concludes that the most important effect of saving the spotted owl will be _____

    _____.

COMPREHENSION SCORE

Score your answers for Exercises A and B as follows:

A. No. right _____ × 2 = _____

B. No. right _____ × 1 = _____

Total pts. from A and B _____ × 10 = _____%

You may refer to the selection for the remaining exercises.

C.   DISTINGUISHING BETWEEN MAIN IDEAS AND SUPPORTING DETAILS

Label the following statements from the selection as follows: MI if the statement represents a *main idea* and SD if the statement represents a *supporting detail.*

1. _____ Often, the more human traits an animal appears to have, the stronger its candidacy for stardom.

2. _____ A recent tuna commercial likened a dolphin group to a wholesome American family.

3. _____ Dolphins are seen as loyal, playful geniuses.

4. _____ Owls, of course, are wise.

5. _____ But who sees anything humanlike about such little-known endangered species as the greasy Amazon tapir or the tailed frog?

6. _____ With the cuteness, backbone-possession and "humanlike" tests to pass, a threatened species depends for survival not so much on its adaptation to climate and habitat as on its adaptation to the media marketplace of human causes.

D.   MAKING INFERENCES

For each of these statements write Y (Yes) if the inference is an accurate one, N (No) if the inference is an inaccurate one, or CT (Can't Tell) if you do not have enough information to make an inference.

1. _____ The northern spotted owl will become extinct if its natural habitat—northwestern forests—is destroyed.

2. _____ The main reason one to three species of animal and plant species disappear or become extinct every day is pollution.

3. _____ Conservationists have become both more realistic and more media-conscious in the past few years about their choice of animal species to save.

4.   _____ Unfortunately, fighting to save the habitats of large vertebrate animal species means that many smaller, insignificant invertebrates are doomed to extinction.

5.   _____ If the northern spotted owl is saved, then the fisher and tailed frog will be, too.

6.   _____ No one, not even scientists, is interested in saving the Amazon tapir or the tailed frog.

7.   _____ Owls are not really "wise"; wisdom is simply one of the "human" qualities we have ascribed to them.

8.   _____ We are more likely to promote saving an animal species that does not pose a physical threat to us than we are to save one that could possibly inflict harm.

E.   DISTINGUISHING BETWEEN FACT AND OPINION
    For each of the following statements from the selection, write F if the statement represents a factual statement that can be verified or O if the statement represents the writer's or someone else's subjective opinion.

1.   _____ Facing possible extinction—it roosts in prized timberland—the northern spotted owl gained partial protection when the U.S. Fish and Wildlife Service recently listed it as No. 599 on the endangered-species list of animals and plants.

2.   _____ Experts say there are between five and 100 million animal and plant species on Earth, of which only two percent have been inventoried.

3.   _____ One to three species disappear every day, according to the Nature Conservancy.

4.   _____ "People respond to larger animals that we see or are part of our experience, like owls," says Daniel Taylor, a National Audubon Society biologist.

5.   _____ Often, the more human traits an animal appears to have, the stronger its candidacy for stardom.

6.   _____ With the cuteness, backbone-possession, and "humanlike" tests to pass, a threatened species depends for survival not so much on its adaptation to climate and habitat as on its adaptation to the media marketplace of human causes.

F.   ANALYZING ORGANIZATION AND SEEING RELATIONSHIPS
Choose the correct answer.

1.   _____ In relation to the entire article, paragraphs 1 and 2 provide us with (a) a useful and necessary definition of an unfamiliar term; (b) an anecdote to entice the reader; (c) an introduction to the subject in the form of a relevant example; (d) the author's opinion about a controversial issue.

2. _____ Reid emphasizes throughout the article that conservationists (a) in the past foolishly attempted to save all animals from extinction; (b) have successfully used the media as a powerful tool to shape public opinion; (c) have persuaded the government to put more animal species on the endangered list; (d) have come into direct conflict with agricultural and industry forces over threatened species.

3. _____ To support the main idea, Reid relies primarily on (a) direct quotations from conservation experts; (b) facts and statistics from recent research studies; (c) his own observations and opinions; (d) quotation and observations from media experts.

4. _____ The author strongly implies that the animals whose numbers are easiest to save are (a) photogenic, that is, they photograph well; (b) dangerous to mankind; (c) black and white; (d) big, cute, and cuddly-looking.

5. _____ Look again at paragraphs 23–24. In relation to the rest of the article, they represent (a) a conclusion; (b) a contrasting point of view; (c) a recommendation for the future; (d) a threat, a warning.

6. _____ Consider this statement from paragraph 23: Rural Oregonians view the spotted owl as "a cause célèbre of hot-tub liberals who backpack in the woods once a year." What tone or attitude does this statement display? (a) anger; (b) sarcasm; (c) irony; (d) mild amusement.

G. UNDERSTANDING VOCABULARY
Choose the correct definition according to the context.

1. _____ the bird offers a *glimpse* [paragraph 1]: (a) an example; (b) a brief look; (c) a solution; (d) a thorough study.

2. _____ an important place in our cultural *psyche* [4; also 19]: (a) expectations; (b) ethical behavior; (c) important ideas; (d) spirit.

3. _____ conservationists have grown *savvy* [5]: (a) conscious; (b) cautious; (c) knowledgeable; (d) preoccupied.

4. _____ "*charismatic* mega-vertebrates" [6]: Describing animals that (a) inspire a following; (b) are in danger of extinction; (c) photograph well; (d) can adapt physically to a new habitat.

5. _____ *garnering* plenty of media attention [10]: (a) encouraging; (b) grabbing; (c) acquiring; (d) sharing.

6. _____ the fisher, a *sleek* mammal [11]: (a) well-groomed; (b) smooth and shiny; (c) well-fed; (d) declining in numbers.

7. _____ images of the handsome spotted owl *spurred* a national audience [13]: (a) stimulated; (b) excited; (c) involved; (d) created.

8. _____ Other factors carry weight in *piquing* a positive public response [18—pronounced like "peeking"]: (a) encouraging; (b) initiating; (c) reaching the highest point; (d) arousing.

9. _____ a *visceral* play between phobia and fascination [19]: (a) controversial; (b) incomprehensible; (c) uncertain; (d) intensely emotional.

10. _____ spotted owls and their attractive *ilk* [21]: (a) offspring, young; (b) type, kind; (c) relatives; (d) supporters.

H.   USING VOCABULARY

In parentheses before each sentence are some inflected forms of words from the selection. Study the context and the sentence. Then write the correct form in the space provided. Be sure to add appropriate endings like -s, -ed, or -ing, if necessary.

1. (*attainment, attain, attainable*)   According to the author, the northern spot-

   ted owl has already _____ star status among endangered species.

2. (*charisma, charismatic, charismatically*)   Conservationists now choose large

   vertebrates that also possess a special quality called _____,
   meaning a special appeal.

3. (*strategy, strategist, strategic, strategically*)   Proponents of saving animal

   species are turning to special _____ to raise the public's consciousness.

4. (*obscurity, obscure, obscurely*)   Conservationists believe that saving large,

   attractive animal species allows other unattractive, _____
   species that share the same habitat to be saved.

5. (*adaptation, adaptability, adapt, adaptable*)   Whether or not a threatened spe-

   cies survives depends not so much on whether it _____ to

   climate and habitat as it does on whether it _____ to media
   campaigns.

6. (*symbiosis, symbiotic, symbiotically*)   Conservationists predict a new kind of

   _____ relationship between the spotted owl and
   other animal species that live in the same habitat.

I.   TOPICS FOR WRITING OR DISCUSSION

1. Paraphrase the information in paragraphs 4 and 5.

   _____

   _____

   _____

   _____

   _____

_____   _____

_____   ___

_____

_____

2.   The controversy between preserving the northern spotted owl's habitat—
      prized northwest timberland—and saving jobs in the logging industry is
      a complicated and emotional issue. The lumber industry argues that
      denying loggers the right to clearcut forests where the owls live will re-
      sult in a severe economic downturn, costing the jobs of thousands of peo-
      ple. The conservationists, on the other hand, argue that preserving the
      owl's habitat is crucial to the area's ecology. Where do you stand on this
      issue?

20 ‖‖‖‖

George Orwell
A HANGING

George Orwell (1903–1950), the pen name of Eric Blair, was the author of Animal Farm *and* Nineteen Eighty-Four. *He is one of England's best known modern writers. During the 1930s he was a police officer representing the British imperialist system in Burma, a country in southeast Asia lying between India to the west and Thailand to the east. In this essay, which is widely considered one of the "classics" of English nonfiction writing, Orwell relates the hanging of a Hindu prisoner in Burma.*

VOCABULARY PREVIEW

WORD ORIGINS

PARIAH

As the group escorts the prisoner to the gallows where he is to be hung, it is interrupted by the appearance of a large dog, described as "half Airedale, half *pariah*" (paragraph 6). The word *pariah* (pronounced pe-ri′ə) refers here to a social outcast, usually describing a human being rather than an animal. It came into English from the word for "drummer" in Tamil, a language spoken in southern India.

As Charles Funk explains in *Thereby Hangs a Tale*, the Pariahs were a dark-skinned race of primitive people who inhabited southern India, who long ago were forced into menial positions. When the caste system was introduced in India, the Pariahs were regarded as one of the low castes; their duty was to beat the drums at festivals.

During the British rule of India, Pariahs became servants for white households. Today they still work in southern India and Burma as domestic and agricultural workers. Although they are not the lowest caste, they are considered to be "untouchables" by Brahmins, the highest caste in the Hindu religion.

WORD PARTS

-LY

Orwell uses many adverbs in this selection, so perhaps this is a good place to review what adverbs are, how they are formed, and how they are used. Probably 90 percent of the adverbs in English are formed by

231

adding the suffix *-ly* to an adjective root. Adverbs tell us "in what manner." An adverb's meaning is essentially the same as an adjective's, but adverbs and adjectives are used differently: Adjectives modify nouns, whereas adverbs modify verbs, adjectives, and other adverbs.

Here are some examples from "A Hanging." First, the most common way—adverbs that modify verbs:

In paragraph 9 the superintendent of the jail is anxious for the hanging to begin; Orwell writes that the prisoner "walked *clumsily* with his bound arms, but quite *steadily*. . . ." Here both italicized words indicate *how* the prisoner walked. Notice that the adverb may be separated by other words from the verb it modifies.

Next, adverbs that modify adjectives: "At that moment Francis' anecdote seemed *extraordinarily* funny" (paragraph 24). *Extraordinarily,* modifying *funny,* tells us again *how* humorous the men found his story.

Finally, adverbs modifying other adverbs: As the Hindu is led to his execution, Orwell writes, "he stepped *slightly aside* to avoid a puddle on the path" (paragraph 9). The adverb *aside* tells how and where the prisoner stepped, and *slightly,* in turn, modifies *aside,* again to tell us how far.

Although you do not really need to know whether an adverb is modifying a verb, an adjective, or an adverb, it is important, at least, to know which word the adverb is meant to go with. Here are some short excerpts from the essay, with the adverbs italicized for you. Underline the word that each adverb modifies.

1. He had a thick, sprouting moustache, *absurdly* too big for his body.
2. . . . yielding his arms *limply* to the ropes. . . .
3. Eight o'clock struck and a bugle call, *desolately* thin in the west air, floated from the distant barracks.
4. The superintendent . . . , *moodily* prodding the gravel. . . .
5. . . . the two warders, gripping the prisoner more *closely* than ever, half led half pushed him to the gallows and helped him *clumsily* up the ladder.
6. . . . he shouted almost *fiercely.* . . .
7. I let go of the dog, and it galloped *immediately* to the back of the gallows . . . it stood among the weeds, looking *timorously* out at us.
8. We all had a drink together, native and European alike, *quite amicably.*

(A word of caution: Not all words ending in *-ly* are adverbs. The word *lily,* for example, is a noun, the name of a flower. And in paragraph 1, when Orwell describes the Burmese morning as having "a *sickly* light," *sickly* is an adjective modifying "light," not an adverb.)

WORD FAMILIES

AMICABLY

As you have just seen, *amicably* is the adverb form of *amicable.* Meaning "in a friendly way" or "sociable," the root is the Latin word for

"friend," *amīcus.* Here are some other words in the family of words
with *ami-* at the root:

amiable   good-natured, agreeable
amigo   Spanish, for "friend"
amity   peaceful relations, for example, between nations; friendship
Bon Ami   a type of cleanser; French for "good friend"

GEORGE ORWELL

A HANGING

1   It was in Burma,* a sodden morning of the rains. A sickly light, like yellow tinfoil,
was slanting over the high walls into the jail yard. We were waiting outside the
condemned cells, a row of sheds fronted with double bars, like small animal cages.
Each cell measured about ten feet by ten and was quite bare within except for a
plank bed and a pot for drinking water. In some of them brown silent men were
squatting at the inner bars, with their blankets draped round them. These were the
condemned men, due to be hanged within the next week or two.

2   One prisoner had been brought out of his cell. He was a Hindu,† a puny wisp
of a man, with a shaven head and vague liquid eyes. He had a thick, sprouting
moustache, absurdly too big for his body, rather like the moustache of a comic man
in films. Six tall Indian warders were guarding him and getting him ready for the
gallows. Two of them stood by with rifles and fixed bayonets, while the others
handcuffed him, passed a chain through his handcuffs and fixed it to their belts, and
lashed his arms tightly to his sides. They crowded very close about him, with their
hands always on him in a careful, caressing grip, as though all the while feeling him
to make sure he was there. It was like men handling a fish which is still alive and
may jump back into the water. But he stood quite unresisting, yielding his arms
limply to the ropes, as though he hardly noticed what was happening.

3   Eight o'clock struck and a bugle call, desolately thin in the wet air, floated from
the distant barracks. The superintendent of the jail, who was standing apart from
the rest of us, moodily prodding the gravel with his stick, raised his head at the
sound. He was an army doctor, with a gray toothbrush moustache and a gruff voice.
"For God's sake hurry up, Francis," he said irritably. "The man ought to have been
dead by this time. Aren't you ready yet?"

4   Francis, the head jailer, a fat Dravidian‡ in a white drill suit and gold

---

*Burma—a country in southeast Asia lying between India to the west and Thailand to the east; at the time
of this essay Burma was part of the British Empire.
†Hindu—a native of northern India.
‡Dravidian—a person from southern India.

spectacles, waved his black hand. "Yes sir, yes sir," he bubbled. "All iss satisfactorily prepared. The hangman iss waiting. We shall proceed."

5   "Well, quick march, then. The prisoners can't get their breakfast till this job's over."

6   We set out for the gallows. Two warders marched on either side of the prisoner, with their rifles at the slope; two others marched close against him, gripping him by arm and shoulder, as though at once pushing and supporting him. The rest of us, magistrates and the like, followed behind. Suddenly, when we had gone ten yards, the procession stopped short without any order or warning. A dreadful thing had happened—a dog, come goodness knows whence, had appeared in the yard. It came bounding among us with a loud volley of barks and leapt round us wagging its whole body, wild with glee at finding so many human beings together. It was a large woolly dog, half Airedale, half pariah. For a moment it pranced round us, and then, before anyone could stop it, it had made a dash for the prisoner and, jumping up, tried to lick his face. Everyone stood aghast, too taken aback even to grab at the dog.

7   "Who let the bloody brute in here?" said the superintendent angrily. "Catch it, someone!"

8   A warder, detached from the escort, charged clumsily after the dog, but it danced and gamboled just out of his reach, taking everything as part of the game. A young Eurasian jailer picked up a handful of gravel and tried to stone the dog away, but it dodged the stones and came after us again. Its yaps echoed from the jail walls. The prisoner, in the grasp of the two warders, looked on incuriously, as though this was another formality of the hanging. It was several minutes before someone managed to catch the dog. Then we put my handkerchief through its collar and moved off once more, with the dog still straining and whimpering.

9   It was about forty yards to the gallows. I watched the bare brown back of the prisoner marching in front of me. He walked clumsily with his bound arms, but quite steadily, with that bobbing gait of the Indian who never straightens his knees. At each step his muscles slid neatly into place, the lock of hair on his scalp danced up and down, his feet printed themselves on the wet gravel. And once, in spite of the men who gripped him by each shoulder, he stepped slightly aside to avoid a puddle on the path.

10   It is curious, but till that moment I had never realized what it means to destroy a healthy, conscious man. When I saw the prisoner step aside to avoid the puddle I saw the mystery, the unspeakable wrongness, of cutting a life short when it is in full tide. This man was not dying, he was alive just as we are alive. All the organs of his body were working—bowels digesting food, skin renewing itself, nails growing, tissues forming—all toiling away in solemn foolery. His nails would still be growing when he stood on the drop, when he was falling through the air with a tenth of a second to live. His eyes saw the yellow gravel and the gray walls, and his brain still remembered, foresaw, reasoned—reasoned even about puddles. He and we were a party of men walking together, seeing, hearing, feeling, understanding the same world; and in two minutes, with a sudden snap, one of us would be gone— one mind less, one world less.

11   The gallows stood in a small yard, separate from the main grounds of the prison, and overgrown with tall prickly weeds. It was a brick erection like three sides of a shed, with planking on top, and above the two beams and a crossbar with the rope dangling. The hangman, a gray-haired convict in the white uniform of the prison, was waiting beside his machine. He greeted us with a servile crouch as we entered. At a word from Francis the two warders, gripping the prisoner more closely than ever, half led half pushed him to the gallows and helped him clumsily up the ladder. Then the hangman climbed up and fixed the rope around the prisoner's neck.

12   We stood waiting, five yards away. The warders had formed in a rough circle round the gallows. And then, when the noose was fixed, the prisoner began crying out to his god. It was a high, reiterated cry of "Ram! Ram! Ram! Ram!" not urgent and fearful like a prayer or a cry for help, but steady, rhythmical, almost like the tolling of a bell. The dog answered the sound with a whine. The hangman, still standing on the gallows, produced a small cotton bag like a flour bag and drew it down and over the prisoner's face. But the sound, muffled by the cloth, still persisted, over and over again: "Ram! Ram! Ram! Ram! Ram!"

13   The hangman climbed down and stood ready, holding the lever. Minutes seemed to pass. The steady, muffled crying from the prisoner went on and on, "Ram! Ram! Ram!" never faltering for an instant. The superintendent, his head on his chest, was slowly poking the ground with his stick; perhaps he was counting the cries, allowing the prisoner a fixed number—fifty, perhaps, or a hundred. Everyone had changed color. The Indians had gone gray like bad coffee, and one or two of the bayonets were wavering. We looked at the lashed, hooded man on the drop, and listened to his cries—each cry another second of life; the same thought was in all our minds; oh, kill him quickly, get it over, stop that abominable noise!

14   Suddenly the superintendent made up his mind. Throwing up his head he made a swift motion with his stick. "Chalo!" he shouted almost fiercely.

15   There was a clanking noise, and then dead silence. The prisoner had vanished, and the rope was twisting on itself. I let go of the dog, and it galloped immediately to the back of the gallows; but when it got there it stopped short, barked, and then retreated into a corner of the yard, where it stood among the weeds, looking timorously out at us. We went round the gallows to inspect the prisoner's body. He was dangling with his toes pointed straight downward, very slowly revolving, as dead as a stone.

16   The superintendent reached out with his stick and poked the bare brown body; it oscillated slightly. "*He's* all right," said the superintendent. He backed out from under the gallows, and blew out deep breath. The moody look had gone out his face quite suddenly. He glanced at his wrist watch. "Eight minutes past eight. Well, that's all for this morning, thank God."

17   The warders unfixed bayonets and marched away. The dog, sobered and conscious of having misbehaved itself, slipped after them. We walked out of the gallows yard, past the condemned cells with their waiting prisoners, into the big central yard of the prison. The convicts, under the command of warders armed with lathis, were already receiving their breakfast. They squatted in long rows, each man

holding a tin pannikin, while two warders with buckets marched round ladling out rice; it seemed quite a homely, jolly scene, after the hanging. An enormous relief had come upon us now that the job was done. One felt an impulse to sing, to break into a run, to snigger. All at once everyone began chattering gaily.

18   The Eurasian boy walking beside me nodded toward the way we had come, with a knowing smile: "Do you know sir, our friend [he meant the dead man] when he heard his appeal had been dismissed, he pissed on the floor of his cell. From fright. Kindly take one of my cigarettes, sir. Do you not admire my new silver case, sir? From the boxwalah, two rupees eight annas. Classy European style."

19   Several people laughed—at what, nobody seemed certain.

20   Francis was walking by the superintendent, talking garrulously: "Well, sir, all hass passed off with the utmost satisfactoriness. It was all finished—flick! like that. It iss not always so—oah no! I have known cases where the doctor wass obliged to go beneath the gallows and pull the prissoner's legs to ensure decease. Most disagreeable!"

21   "Wriggling about, eh? That's bad," said the superintendent.

22   "Ach, sir, it iss worse when they become refractory! One man, I recall, clung to the bars of hiss cage when we went to take him out. You will scarcely credit, sir, that it took six warders to dislodge him, three pulling at each leg. We reasoned with him. 'My dear fellow,' we said, 'think of all the pain and trouble you are causing to us!' But no, he would not listen! Ach, he wass very troublesome!"

23   I found that I was laughing quite loudly. Everyone was laughing. Even the superintendent grinned in a tolerant way. "You'd better all come and have a drink," he said quite genially. "I've got a bottle of whiskey in the car. We could do with it."

24   We went through the big double gates of the prison into the road. "Pulling at his legs!" exclaimed a Burmese magistrate suddenly, and burst into a loud chuckling. We all began laughing again. At that moment Francis' anecdote seemed extraordinarily funny. We all had a drink together, native and European alike, quite amicably. The dead man was a hundred yards away. ∎

George Orwell, "A Hanging," in *Shooting an Elephant and Other Essays*, Harcourt Brace Jovanovich, New York, 1950. Reprinted by permission of Harcourt Brace Jovanovich, Inc. and the estate of the late Sonia Brownell Orwell and Secker & Warburg Limited.

EXERCISES

Do not refer to the selection for Exercises A and B.

A. DETERMINING THE MAIN IDEA AND PURPOSE

1. _____ The main idea of the essay is that (a) conditions for Hindu prisoners in Burma during the 1930s were harsh; (b) capital punishment, es-

pecially when a dominant political group executes a member of a minority race, is wrong; (c) for the author the hanging of the Hindu prisoner emphasized the cruelty of the British imperialist rule in Burma; (d) the author's witnessing of the preparations for the prisoner's hanging made him realize the wrongness of putting to death a healthy, conscious human being.

2.   _____ The author's purpose is (a) to describe the hanging and his own participation in the preparations; (b) to persuade the reader, by describing one execution, of the wrongness of capital punishment; (c) to describe the prison conditions in Burma during the 1930s; (d) to show the reader the cruelty and insensitivity of the prison wardens and executioners.

B.   COMPREHENDING MAIN IDEAS

1.   _____ The superintendent was particularly concerned that the prisoner should be hanged quickly because (a) the other prisoners could not eat breakfast until the hanging was finished; (b) he found the prospect of executing a prisoner distasteful; (c) he was afraid that the prisoner might attempt to escape; (d) the warders were exhausted from working all night to prepare for the execution.

2.   _____ On the way to the gallows the solemn occasion was interrupted by (a) the pleas and cries of the prisoner's relatives; (b) the appearance of a large, friendly dog; (c) the author's loud protests that the hanging should not take place; (d) the prisoner's prayers to his god.

3.   _____ The prisoner gave Orwell a new insight when he (a) walked solemnly along and refused to look at anyone; (b) did not react to the dog; (c) sidestepped a puddle on the path; (d) allowed the warders to lead him without protest.

4.   _____ Orwell learned from watching the prisoner that (a) he was a human being despite the crime he had committed; (b) he had never realized what putting a man to death really meant; (c) capital punishment is an unfortunate, but sometimes necessary, institution; (d) death is unpredictable, coming when we least expect it.

5.   _____ Orwell writes that the prisoner's crying "Ram! Ram! Ram!" over and over represented (a) an abominable noise that should have been stopped much earlier than it was; (b) more seconds of life for the prisoner; (c) the prisoner's exercising his fundamental right to pray; (d) a last chance for the prisoner's life to be spared.

6.   _____ After the hanging, everyone felt (a) an enormous sense of relief; (b) a common bond of humanity; (c) a sense of moral outrage; (d) a feeling that justice had been done.

COMPREHENSION SCORE

Score your answers for Exercises A and B as follows:

A. No. right _____ × 2 = _____

B. No. right _____ × 1 = _____

Total pts. from A and B _____ × 10 = _____%

You may refer to the selection for the remaining exercises.

C.   DISTINGUISHING BETWEEN MAIN IDEAS AND SUPPORTING DETAILS

Label the following sentences from paragraph 10 of the essay as follows: MI if the sentence represents a *main idea* and SD if the sentence represents a *supporting detail.*

1. _____ It is curious, but till that moment I had never realized what it means to destroy a healthy, conscious man.

2. _____ When I saw the prisoner step aside to avoid the puddle I saw the mystery, the unspeakable wrongness, of cutting a life short when it is in full tide.

3. _____ This man was not dying, he was alive just as we are alive.

4. _____ All the organs of his body were working—bowels digesting food, skin renewing itself, nails growing, tissues forming—all toiling away in solemn foolery.

5. _____ His nails would still be growing when he stood on the drop, when he was falling through the air with a tenth of a second to live.

6. _____ His eyes saw the yellow gravel and the gray walls, and his brain still remembered, foresaw, reasoned—reasoned even about puddles.

7. _____ He and we were a party of men walking together, seeing, hearing, feeling, understanding the same world; and in two minutes, with a sudden snap, one of us would be gone—one mind less, one world less.

D.   MAKING INFERENCES

For each of these statements write Y (Yes) if the inference is an accurate one, N (No) if the inference is an inaccurate one, or CT (Can't Tell) if you do not have enough information to make an inference.

1. _____ The prisoner was being executed for committing a murder.

2. _____ The superintendent seemed more concerned with the other prisoners' breakfast than he was with the condemned man's fate.

3. _____ The probable reason that a convict served as hangman was that the prison officials considered it to be an extremely unpleasant job.

4. _____ The condemned man was made to wear a hood so that he would not be able to see the exact moment when the hangman pulled the lever.

5. _____ When the prisoner learned that his appeal had been dismissed, he acted calmly and impassively.

6. _____ It was most likely unusual for natives and Europeans to drink together as equals.

E. **ANALYZING ORGANIZATION AND SEEING RELATIONSHIPS**
Choose the best answer.

1. _____ Read paragraph 1 again. Taken together, Orwell's descriptive details are meant to convey a feeling of (a) solemnity, seriousness; (b) unease, tension; (c) gloom, depression; (d) uncertainty, suspense.

2. At the end of paragraph 2 Orwell compares the warders' handling of the prisoner to "men handling a fish which is still alive and may jump back into the water." Explain what this metaphor is meant to show about the

   warders. _____

   _____

3. _Irony_ is the deliberate contrast between what you might expect to occur and what actually does. Read paragraph 6 again and then explain what is ironic about the dog's behavior.

   _____

   _____

4. _____ Throughout the essay Orwell emphasizes that the prisoner's behavior was (a) impassive, almost indifferent; (b) fearful, tense; (c) hostile, contemptuous; (d) admirable, deserving to be imitated.

5. _____ Read the last sentence of paragraph 10. What relationship does Orwell suggest between "one mind" and "one world"? (a) These words are opposites; (b) these words are imaginative synonyms; (c) they represent a cause-and-effect relationship; (d) the mind represents part of the world, which represents the whole.

6. _____ Francis's anecdote about the doctor who had to pull the legs of an executed man elicited laughter from the group because (a) they thought that the incident was truly funny; (b) laughing lessened the tension they all felt; (c) the group understood the irony implied in the anecdote; (d) people like to laugh at other people's discomfort rather than their own.

F. **UNDERSTANDING VOCABULARY**
Choose the correct definition according to the context.

1. _____ a _sodden_ morning of the rains [paragraph 1]: (a) heavy with water; (b) miserable; (c) overcast; (d) gloomy.

2. _____ a _puny_ wisp of a man [2]: (a) weak; (b) inferior in size; (c) thin; (d) sad.

3. _____ a large woolly dog, half Airedale, half *pariah* [6]: (a) an un-identifiable breed; (b) wild; (c) outcast, stray; (d) scavenger.

4. _____ Everyone stood *aghast* [6]: (a) unmoving; (b) shocked; (c) uncomfortably; (d) silently.

5. _____ it danced and *gamboled* [8]: (a) frolicked; (b) slinked away; (c) groveled, crawled on the ground; (d) barked.

6. _____ all *toiling* away in solemn foolery [10]: (a) growing; (b) changing; (c) cooperating; (d) working hard.

7. _____ He greeted us with a *servile* crouch [11]: Describing the behavior of (a) an executioner; (b) a manual laborer; (c) a slave or servant; (d) a prisoner, convict.

8. _____ It was a high, *reiterated* cry [12]: (a) repeated; (b) mournful; (c) desperate; (d) heart-rending.

9. _____ looking *timorously* out at us [15]: (a) expectantly; (b) eagerly; (c) timidly; (d) humbly.

10. _____ one felt an impulse to *snigger* [17]: (a) carouse, get drunk; (b) run away; (c) jump for joy; (d) laugh lightly, snicker.

11. _____ Francis was talking *garrulously* [20]: Describing a way of talking that is (a) animated, lively; (b) stern, serious; (c) overly long, chattering; (d) pompous, overly self-important.

12. _____ it is worse when they become *refractory* [22]: (a) obstinate, difficult to manage; (b) quarrelsome, combative; (c) sentimental, overly emotional; (d) motionless, unable to act.

G.   USING VOCABULARY
Write the correct inflected form of the base word in each of the following sentences. Refer to your dictionary if necessary.

1. (*desolately*—use a noun)   There was an air of _____ in the sound of the bugle call.

2. (*glee*—use an adverb)   The dog danced _____ around the group of men.

3. (*oscillation*—use a verb)   After the condemned man died, his body _____ slightly.

4. (*genially*—use a noun)   The superintendent's invitation to the men was given with a feeling of great _____.

5. (*amicable*—use an adverb)   The men, European and native, drank together quite _____.

H.   TOPICS FOR WRITING OR DISCUSSION

1.   The most important paragraph in the essay is paragraph 10. Paraphrase it by putting the essential ideas into your own words.

_____

_____

_____

_____

_____

_____

_____

2.   One of the biggest controversies over capital punishment is the question of whether or not it deters other criminals, that is, whether it sets an example for other people who would then refrain from committing the same crime. Investigate this question, evaluate your findings, and come to a conclusion of your own.

21

Howard Kurtz

IS THE DRUG PLAGUE A RACIST CONSPIRACY?

Originally published in the Washington Post, *this article deals with one of the most critical issues facing the United States—the devastation caused by crack in our urban communities. One theory is that the white Establishment—the powerful people who run the country by private agreements and decisions—has tacitly encouraged or at least tolerated the epidemic of drugs and violence in the black communities. This theory is discussed at length in the article.*

VOCABULARY PREVIEW

WORD ORIGINS

CONSPIRACY

According to Pedro Noguera, a U.C. Berkeley professor quoted in paragraph 5, "Whether or not there is a real *conspiracy* is less important than whether people believe there to be a *conspiracy* . . . and in the black community, they do." The verb *to conspire*, meaning "to plan together secretly, especially to commit an illegal or evil act," has this etymology:

> [Middle English *conspiren*, from Old French *conspirer*, from Latin *conspīrāre* ("to breathe together"); agree, unite, or plot; from *com-* ("together") + *spīrāre* ("to breathe")]

The literal origin of this word suggests an activity we can see: conspirators, those people who plan conspiracies, sitting close together in a huddle and "breathing together."

GHETTOS

The word *ghetto* (see paragraph 17) derives from Italian. It originally referred to the section in European cities where Jews were forced to live, usually within a walled section of the city. In English the word also means a section of an American city, often a slum, that is occupied by members of a particular minority group who live there because of social or economic pressures. *The Random House Dictionary* provides this possible etymology:

> [Italian, perhaps an abbreviation of *borghetto*, a diminutive (short) form of *borgo*, a settlement outside the city wall]

WORD PARTS

-CIDE

At the end of paragraph 1 Kurtz writes that "the white Establishment has intentionally allowed narcotics to devastate their communities, even encouraged drug abuse as a form of *genocide.*" This word is composed of the root *geno* ("race") + the suffix *-cide* ("killing"), so that the word means the systematic destruction of a race of people. Here are some other words using the suffix *-cide:*

herbicide	an agent used to kill weeds
insecticide	an agent used to kill insects
patricide	killing one's father
matricide	killing one's mother
infanticide	killing of a baby
regicide	killing of a king
suicide	killing oneself

EPIDEMIC

In paragraph 3 Kurtz quotes Louis Farrakhan, the controversial and outspoken leader of the Nation of Islam, as saying that "the *epidemic* of drugs and violence in the black community stems from a calculated attempt by whites to foster black self-destruction."

The word *epidemic* can be broken down like this: *epi-*, a common Greek prefix meaning "among," and *dēmos*, the Greek root for "people." Although this literal derivation is not much help in determining the word's actual meaning, "a rapidly spreading disease," it does suggest that an epidemic, which is what crack cocaine is compared to in this article, can spread quickly among the entire population.

The prefix *epi-* can also be seen in these English words:

epidermis	the outer layer of skin [*epi-* + *dermis* ("skin")]
epigram	a short, concise poem expressing a thought, often a witty thought [*epi-* + *graphein* ("to write")]
epitaph	an inscription on a tombstone [*epi-* ("over") + *taphos* ("tombstone")]
epitome	a summary of a book or article, pronounced ĭ-pĭt'ə-mē [*epitemnein* ("to cut short")]

In addition, here are some common English words using *demos* ("people") as the root:

democracy	government by the people [*dēmos* + *kratein* ("to rule")]
demography	the study of human populations [*demos* + *graphein* ("to write")]
demagogue	a leader who appeals to the people's prejudices and emotions [*demagogos* ("popular leader"), from *dēmos* + *agōgos,* "leading")]

WORD FAMILIES

BENIGN

During the 1970s the term *benign neglect* came into fashion, indicating the government's refusal to solve the problems of ghetto residents. While the government did not openly oppose efforts at reform, neither did it do much constructive to help solve the problems of racism and poverty. The phrase *benign neglect* also occurs in paragraph 24 in the article.

Benign means "kind," "promoting well-being"; its root is *bene*, Latin for "well." There are several words in English with this root, among them:

benefit	something that promotes well-being
benefactor	someone who gives financial aid
benediction	a blessing, usually at the end of a religious service [*bene* + *dīcere* ("to speak")]
beneficence	the quality of kindness
beneficiary	someone who receives a benefit
benevolent	kindly, performing charitable acts [*benevolēns* ("wishing well")]

HOWARD KURTZ

IS THE DRUG PLAGUE A RACIST CONSPIRACY?

1 New York—Most people would dismiss the notion as little more than paranoia but, in neighborhoods from Harlem to Anacostia to Watts, a significant number of blacks believe that the white Establishment has intentionally allowed narcotics to devastate their communities, even encouraged drug abuse as a form of genocide.

2 "It's almost an accepted fact," said Andrew Cooper, publisher of the City Sun, a Brooklyn-based black weekly. "It is a deep-seated suspicion. I believe it. I can't open my desk drawer and say, 'Here it is [the evidence].' But there's just too much money in narcotics. People really believe they are being victimized by The Man. If the government wanted to stop it, it could stop it."

3 Louis Farrakhan, leader of the Nation of Islam, put it more graphically in a recent speech in Washington. He told an overflow crowd at the D.C. Armory that

"the epidemic of drugs and violence in the black community stems from a calculated attempt by whites to foster black self-destruction."

4   Many whites and blacks consider such statements examples of paranoia, and there is no concrete evidence to support the notion that white political leaders have actively perpetuated, or consciously tolerated, the drug scourge in the black community. But the conspiracy theory rings true to some blacks who are convinced that there must be an ominous explanation for the tragedy that has struck their community with particular force.

5   Pedro Noguera, a professor at UC Berkeley, said: "Whether or not there is a real conspiracy is less important than whether people believe there to be a conspiracy . . . and in the black community, they do. For years, when crack was first coming into the community, everybody knew where the crack houses were, including the police. So the police were either in on it or, if not in on it, they allowed it to exist."

6   Drug abuse and drug violence effectively subjugate blacks who might otherwise vent their frustrations on whites, while also allowing powerful whites to make enormous profits from narcotics, according to this theory. Moreover, it is said that white leaders became concerned only when drugs began to claim white, middle-class victims. Many argue that the government could stem the flow of drugs if it had the political will to do so.

7   Such sentiments are gaining currency at a time when many blacks are disillusioned with a society in which anti-poverty and civil rights efforts have clearly flagged, some scholars say.

8   Beginning with the Nixon Administration, they say, many blacks became convinced that a once-protective federal government was no longer concerned with their problems, and some grew more receptive to the self-help, black-separatist rhetoric of people such as Farrakham.

9   The Establishment news media, largely wedded to empirical facts, have taken only slight notice of these resurgent "conspiracy" charges.

10   In a recent discussion of racial issues on ABC's "Nightline," Brooklyn filmmaker Spike Lee said, "I think it is no mistake that a majority of the drugs in this country is being deposited in black and Hispanic and lower-income neighborhoods across the country."

11   Like many of those interviewed for this article, Lee mentioned a movie scene as evidence that organized crime had targeted blacks for drug addiction.

12   "I remember that one scene from 'The Godfather' where the dons are trying to decide where the drugs are going to go, and they said, 'Let's give it to the [blacks]; they're animals anyway, they're going to lose their souls.'"

13   Many black opinion leaders shy from such rhetoric.

14   "I don't believe in the 'white devil' theory," said Benjamin L. Hooks, executive director of the NAACP. "It's simply the anguished cry of people who really don't understand how it got started in the first place and why it's out of control."

15   At the same time, Hooks described the white attitude toward drug abuse among blacks as "absolute indifference bordering on criminal," likening it to the tolerance of official segregation in the District of Columbia during the 1940s.

16   "White people have never been anxious to fight a problem that they perceive to be . . . an all-black problem," he said. "It was only when it got to suburbia that it became a joint problem, a white problem, a national problem.

17   "If young white kids were shooting each other one a day like in the ghettos of Washington, there would be no question about taxes being raised, more policemen being hired. The people who control the money, if their sons and daughters were involved, it'd be different."

18   Although most users of illegal drugs in the United States are white, hard drugs that attract violence, such as crack cocaine, are largely a problem in black communities.

19   Russell Adams, chairman of the Afro-American Studies Department at Howard University, called the white-conspiracy theory "a minority opinion" favored by "folks who are paranoid about other racial matters, people who see a lot of conspiracies in routine racism. They would be less educated, borderline economic and probably prone to simplistic explanations of how things happen."

20   Still, variations on the conspiracy theory crop up in numerous conversations with blacks. Many say they regard the repeated federal declarations of war on drugs, including the $8-billion plan announced by President Bush, as laughable. Some of their criticisms echo those of white politicians, but the failures are frequently attributed to sinister motivations.

21   "There is an element that finds this a beautiful aspect of the genocidal attitude toward African American youth," said the Rev. Lawrence Lucas, a Harlem priest known for his acerbic criticism of the white Establishment. "You're killing them with drugs. You're killing them with the crime connected with drugs. You send them to jail and eliminate African-American males as fathers.

22   "White middle-class Americans are the ones who make the money on the billions spent on law enforcement necessary to keep feeding black and Hispanic youths through the jail mill," Lucas said. "It's a little too coincidental not to believe this was orchestrated by a group of people for other purposes."

23   Even some of those who reject such views agree with Hooks that the nation generally is unmoved by the plight of impoverished blacks.

24   "It's the same old thing of benign neglect," said Sterling Johnson, a special New York state narcotics prosecutor who is black.

25   "I've heard that this is a plot by the white Establishment to subjugate minorities, blacks and Hispanics, overtly and covertly. You'll hear that we don't solve the drug problem because too many higher-ups are involved."

26   Publisher Cooper said the conspiracy theory was born in the 1960s, when the FBI under J. Edgar Hoover frequently targeted blacks for investigation.

27   "The theory was that the white Establishment pushed heroin into the black community to divert young people from political action, so they'd be zonked out and wouldn't be a threat," he said.

28   "The addicts want treatment, and there is no treatment for them because all the slots are filled and we need the money for the B-1 bomber," prosecutor Johnson said.

29   One apparent inconsistency in the subjugation theory is the fact that drugs are

a major problem in many cities run by black politicians, with black police chiefs. Another is that numerous blacks are involved in the drug trade as sellers and buyers.

30   But William Hopkins, director of street research for New York state's Division of Substance Abuse, said most black customers "can only scrape together 10 bucks" for a bag of crack and that 70% of the drug money in minority neighborhoods comes from whites.

31   "They're the big customers, these people who drive in with their big cars," Hopkins said. "They're middle-class people, most of them white, and they buy a 100-pack. That's 100 $5 vials for $500. The attitude [black residents] take is, 'Why the hell isn't this happening in your neighborhood?'"

32   Johnson said blacks in New York are further penalized because most drug-treatment facilities are placed in their communities after noisy protests from white neighborhoods. This, he said, is another sign that middle-class society is protecting its own.

33   "You go to Bensonhurst or Howard Beach, and you don't see the crackheads out there selling crack, like on 145th Street," Johnson said. "It's not as visible."

34   Moreover, some blacks have not forgotten that the cocaine ravaging their communities was fashionable among white professionals and celebrities less than a decade ago.

35   "The people who are getting excited about it now are the very people who were socially using these kinds of drugs for years," Lucas said.

36   Some involved in drug treatment find such arguments counterproductive.

37   "I don't subscribe to the notion of blaming someone else for our short-comings," said James Allen, who runs the Addicts Rehabilitation Center in Harlem. "Certainly, we need more support from the white community, but we should not point the finger at any one group in the fight against drugs."   ∎

From Howard Kurtz, "Is the Drug Plague a Racist Conspiracy?" [originally titled "Drug Plague a Racist Conspiracy?"], *Los Angeles Times*, January 1, 1990. First published in the *Washington Post*. Reprinted by permission.

EXERCISES

Do not refer to the selection for Exercises A and B.

A.   DETERMINING THE MAIN IDEA AND PURPOSE
Choose the best answer.

1.   _____ Which of these excerpts from the selection *best* expresses the main idea? (a) "A significant number of blacks believe that the white Establishment has intentionally allowed narcotics to devastate their communities, even encouraged drug abuse as a form of genocide"; (b) "Drug abuse and drug violence effectively subjugate blacks who might otherwise vent their frustrations on whites, while also allowing powerful whites to make

enormous profits from narcotics, according to this theory"; (c) "The addicts want treatment, and there is no treatment for them because all the slots are filled and we need the money for the B-1 bomber"; (d) "the government could stem the flow of drugs if it had the political will to do so."

2. _____ With respect to the theory behind this issue, the author's purpose is (a) to convince the reader that it is valid; (b) to convince the reader that it is not valid; (c) to present the views of various black leaders and thinkers; (d) to argue both sides of the issue so that the reader can make up his or her own mind about the controversy.

B. COMPREHENDING MAIN IDEAS
Choose the correct answer.

1. _____ Some black leaders view the drug problems plaguing their communities as the white Establishment's attempt to foster (a) economic ruin; (b) dependence on white drug dealers; (c) genocide, black self-destruction; (d) conflict within the ghetto to diffuse their political power.

2. _____ According to Andrew Cooper, publisher of a Brooklyn black newspaper, the conspiracy theory (a) is almost an accepted fact in the black community; (b) is endlessly debated in the black community; (c) is not taken seriously by very many people in the black community; (d) is accepted by whites and blacks alike who deal daily with the nation's drug problem.

3. _____ Pedro Noguera, the U.C. Berkeley professor, as partial evidence to support the conspiracy theory, cites the fact that the police (a) routinely know when drug shipments are coming into a community; (b) know the names and addresses of major dealers in every community; (c) know the location of crack houses; (d) refuse to arrest known dealers until they have solid physical evidence.

4. _____ Benjamin Hooks, executive director of the NAACP, says that whites only became concerned about drug abuse when (a) the level of violence in the ghettos escalated; (b) gang activity got out of control; (c) drug lords began smuggling increasingly large amounts of drugs into the country; (d) drugs found their way into white suburbia.

5. _____ For the most part, blacks think that the federal war on drugs, including President Bush's $8-billion plan, (a) will help solve the problem; (b) is too expensive; (c) is laughable; (d) is shortsighted.

6. _____ The author quotes William Hopkins, director of New York's Division of Substance Abuse, as saying that the percentage of middle-class whites buying drugs in minority neighborhoods is (a) ten percent; (b) twenty-five percent; (c) fifty percent; (d) seventy percent.

COMPREHENSION SCORE

Score your answers for Exercises A and B as follows:

A. No. right _____ × 2 = _____

B. No. right _____ × 1 = _____

Total pts. from A and B _____ × 10 = _____%

You may refer to the selection for the remaining exercises.

C. RECOGNIZING SUPPORTING DETAILS

Place an X in the space for each sentence that *directly* supports this main idea from the selection: **"Hooks described the white attitude toward drug abuse among blacks as 'absolute indifference bordering on criminal.' "**

1. _____ "White people have never been anxious to fight a problem that they perceive to be . . . an all-black problem," Hooks said.

2. _____ "It was only when it got to suburbia that it became a joint problem, a white problem, a national problem."

3. _____ "If young white kids were shooting each other one a day like in the ghettos of Washington, there would be no question about taxes being raised, more policemen being hired."

4. _____ The people who control the money, if their sons and daughters were involved, it'd be different."

5. _____ Although most users of illegal drugs in the United States are white, hard drugs that attract violence, such as crack cocaine, are largely a problem in black communities.

D. MAKING INFERENCES

For each of these statements write Y (Yes) if the inference is an accurate one, N (No) if the inference is an inaccurate one, or CT (Can't Tell) if you do not have enough information to make an inference.

1. _____ Although there is no solid evidence to support the white conspiracy theory, the government's lack of serious commitment and the large amount of money whites make from the drug trade make many blacks suspect that the theory may be true.

2. _____ It is probably unrealistic to think that the government will ever put a complete stop to drug trade in this country.

3. _____ During Nixon's administration, the federal government made a concerted effort to curb the drug trade in the U.S.

4. _____ Movie director Spike Lee does not believe in the conspiracy theory.

5. _____ The scene from the movie "The Godfather," in which the Mafia dons decided to sell drugs to blacks, was based on the truth—organized crime deliberately targeted drugs to black communities.

6. _____ One tragic effect of drug abuse in black communities is the serious disruption to the structure of the black family.

7. _____ Many blacks resent whites coming into their neighborhood seeking to purchase drugs.

8. _____ There is unanimous agreement among all blacks that the conspiracy theory is not just a theory; it is a logical explanation for the problem of drug abuse in their communities.

E. **ANALYZING ORGANIZATION AND SEEING RELATIONSHIPS**
    Choose the correct answer.

1. _____ With respect to the article as a whole, paragraph 1 (a) states the thesis; (b) opens with a provocative anecdote; (c) defines an important term; (d) orients the reader to the subject by presenting background information.

2. _____ What is the relationship between the two sentences of paragraph 4? (a) general term to be defined followed by a definition; (b) main idea and supporting details; (c) contrast; (d) cause and effect.

3. _____ To support the main idea of the article, Kurtz relies primarily on (a) facts and statistics; (b) the observations of a variety of black political leaders and thinkers; (c) the results of polls and research studies; (d) his own opinions and observations.

4. _____ With respect to the conspiracy theory, what is the function of paragraphs 29, 30, and 37? (a) to provide support for it; (b) to provide arguments against it; (c) to state the author's personal opinion concerning it; (d) to present a solution to the problem.

5. _____ Look again at the second sentence of paragraph 29. Which of the following phrases would be an accurate opening for the second sentence? (a) Another inconsistency; (b) another theory; (c) another fact; (d) another problem.

6. _____ The transitional word *moreover* at the beginning of paragraph 34 means (a) in other words; (b) for example; (c) as a result; (d) in addition.

7. _____ In paragraphs 34 and 35, the author mentions that cocaine, which has caused so many problems in the black community recently, "was fashionable among white professionals and celebrities less than a decade ago." This statement is an example of (a) irony; (b) sarcasm; (c) evidence; (d) an unsupported opinion.

8. What is the author's own view of the theory that whites deliberately introduced drugs into the black community to keep its residents politically powerless? (a) He believes in the theory; (b) he does not believe in the theory; (c) he is unsure about the theory and has not yet made up his mind; (d) his opinion of this theory is not evident.

F.   UNDERSTANDING VOCABULARY

Look through the paragraphs listed below and find a word that matches each definition. An example has been done for you.

Ex. destroying, devastating [34–35]   _____ravaging_____

1. a psychological problem involving delusions of persecution [1 and 4]   _____

2. the destruction of a race of people [1–2]   _____

3. menacing, suggesting a bad sign [3–4]   _____

4. subdue, enslave, conquer [6 and 25]   _____

5. express, relieve by expressing [6–7]   _____

6. the persuasive use of language to influence [8–9]   _____

7. relying on practical experience rather than on theory [8–9]   _____

8. tending to occur or rise again [8–9]   _____

9. tending, leaning toward [19–20]   _____

10. suggesting an evil motive [19–20]   _____

11. sharp, severe [20–21]   _____

12. difficult situation [23–24]   _____

13. kindly, promoting well-being [24–25]   _____

14. a pair of adverb antonyms, openly and concealed [24–25]   _____

                                                               and _____

G.   USING VOCABULARY

Write the correct inflected form of the base word in each of the following sentences. Refer to your dictionary if necessary.

1. (*devastate*—use a noun)   There is no question that crack and other hard

    drugs have caused great _____ in many black communities.

2. (*graphically*—use an adjective)   In a _____ speech in
    Washington, Louis Farrakhan discussed the current epidemic of drugs
    and violence.

3. (*perpetuate*—use an adverb)   Since the 1970s, drugs have been a

    _____ serious problem in the U.S.

4. (*conspiracy*—use a verb)   According to one theory, people in power

    _____ to introduce drugs into urban ghettos.

5. (*disillusioned*—use a noun)   During the Nixon administration,

    _____ set in among many blacks who perceived
    that the government was not interested in helping solve their problems.

6. (*ravaging*—use an adjective)   For many drug-_____
    communities, the situation seems completely out of control.

H.   TOPICS FOR WRITING OR DISCUSSION

1. Look through the article once more and summarize the evidence to sup-
    port the conspiracy theory that Kurtz cites in the article.

    _____

    _____

    _____

    _____

    _____

    _____

2. Evaluate the evidence from question 1 above. How much credence do
    you give the conspiracy theory?

4

Tackling More
Difficult Prose

The seven selections in Part 4 are more difficult than those you have already completed, not so much because of the content, but because of more sophisticated vocabulary. Before you begin this section, read carefully through the following explanations and examples.

TRANSITIONS

Transitions are words or phrases that both connect a writer's ideas and show the logical relationships between them. You might think of them as signposts or markers, allowing you to move easily and smoothly from one idea to the next. Transitions are typically found at the beginning of sentences, but often they join the middle parts of sentences together, too. To show you how crucial transitions are, here is an excerpt from the last selection by Howard Kurtz, "Is the Drug Plague a Racist Conspiracy?" The excerpt is printed twice, once without transitions and then again with the transitions restored and italicized. Notice how difficult it is to read the first version, to make sense of the ideas.

> Many whites and blacks consider such statements examples of paranoia. There is no concrete evidence to support the notion that white political leaders have actively perpetuated, consciously tolerated, the drug scourge in the black community. The conspiracy theory rings true to some blacks who are convinced that there must be an ominous explanation for the tragedy that has struck their community with particular force.
>
> Pedro Noguera, a professor at UC Berkeley, said, "Whether or not there is a real conspiracy is less important than whether people believe there

to be a conspiracy . . . in the black community, they do. When crack was first coming into the community, everybody knew where the crack houses were, including the police. The police were either in on it. If not in on it, they allowed it to exist."

Drug abuse and drug violence effectively subjugate blacks who might otherwise vent their frustrations on whites, allowing powerful whites to make enormous profits from narcotics. It is said that white leaders became concerned only when drugs began to claim white, middle-class victims. Many argue that the government could stem the flow of drugs if it had the political will to do so.

*   *   *

Many whites and blacks consider such statements examples of paranoia, *and* there is no concrete evidence to support the notion that white political leaders have actively perpetuated, *or* consciously tolerated, the drug scourge in the black community. *But* the conspiracy theory rings true to some blacks who are convinced that there must be an ominous explanation for the tragedy that has struck their community with particular force.

Pedro Noguera, a professor at UC Berkeley, said, "Whether or not there is a real conspiracy is less important than whether people believe there to be a conspiracy . . . *and* in the black community, they do. *For years,* when crack was first coming into the community, everybody knew where the crack houses were, including the police. *So* the police were either in on it *or,* if not in on it, they allowed it to exist."

Drug abuse and drug violence effectively subjugate blacks who might otherwise vent their frustrations on whites, *while also* allowing powerful whites to make enormous profits from narcotics. *Moreover,* it is said that white leaders became concerned only when drugs began to claim white, middle-class victims. Many argue that the government could stem the flow of drugs if it had the political will to do so.

Here is a list of some common transitions and their functions, that is, the logical relationship they indicate:

To show additional information:
and, next, besides, in the same way, similarly, in like manner, in addition, further, furthermore, moreover, also, likewise, in the first place, too, again, equally important, first, second, at the same time

To contrast ideas:
but, yet, still, however, otherwise, nevertheless, on the contrary, on the other hand, conversely, nonetheless, notwithstanding, and yet, after all, in contrast, instead, whereas, unlike

To compare ideas:
similarly, likewise, in the same way, at the same time, to compare

To show time:
then, meanwhile, later, afterward, eventually, subsequently, thereafter, soon, immediately, after a few days, now, before, after, finally, in the meantime, next

To introduce an example:
for example, for instance, to illustrate, as a case in point, according to, consider the following

To show space or spatial order:
here, beyond, nearby, opposite to, adjacent to, where, next to, to the right (or left) of, on top of, on the bottom, above, below

To concede a different point:
true, indeed, granted, of course, there is no doubt that, admittedly, it is true that, no one disputes the fact that

To signal emphasis or intensification:
in fact, indeed, most of all, of course, truly, naturally, to be sure, certainly

To show result or conclusion:
finally, therefore, hence, thus, consequently, as a result, it follows that, thereupon, then, henceforth, in conclusion, all in all, from what has been said

To summarize ideas:
to sum up, in brief, in short, to summarize, as I have said, to conclude

TELLING THE DIFFERENCE BETWEEN MAIN IDEAS AND SUPPORTING DETAILS

Students who have used this text often find difficult the exercise asking them to distinguish between main ideas and supporting details. This skill is essential for several reasons: First, not all ideas are equally important. Some sentences contain essential information, important ideas worth remembering; others simply back up the main ideas, serving as examples, clarification, proof, or further explanation. Second, the ability to tell the difference between the two ensures that you can classify ideas according to their relative importance, in short, that you are *thinking* when you read. Finally, this skill will help you improve your own writing because you will see the importance of developing and supporting your assertions.

You may recall from the introduction that a main idea is a *general* idea, whereas a supporting detail is *specific*. To show you how this works, consider this paragraph from Elizabeth Marek's selection in Part 3, "The Lives of Teenage Mothers." The sentences have been numbered for easier reference.

(1) In all their stories, I hear again and again how little volition these girls feel they have, how little concern over the control over the events of

their lives. (2) The deadline for school admission passes and April shrugs. (3) Sophie-Louise makes an appointment for Lynda with a job counselor, but Lynda forgets to go. (4) Janelle knows about birth control but doesn't believe "it" will happen to her. (5) Sophie-Louise told me once that these girls exert no more control over their lives than a "leaf falling from a tree." (6) Perhaps having a baby is less a question of ignorance or choice than one of inevitability. (7) Once a girl is sexually active, it is not *having* a baby that requires choice and conscious action, but *not* having one.

On one hand, this is a fairly easy paragraph to use for analysis because it is organized according to a traditional pattern:

Main idea

    Support (three specific examples)

Conclusion (commentary and explanation)

If you examine the relationship between sentence 1 and sentences 2–4, you will see that the first one states the main idea and the next three represent supporting examples. The difficulty, however, is that the author does not use a transition like "for example" or "to illustrate" or "consider the following" to show you that she is moving from the general to the particular. You, as a careful reader, have to infer the relationship.

Sentence 5 represents the group leader's judgment about these teenage girls, and the last two represent the author's explanation and interpretation of their situation. Stated another way, it is much more important to know that these girls feel as if they have no control over their lives and that pregnancy during their teen years may be inevitable than it is to remember that April forgot the deadline for school admissions.

Here are the topics you will read about in Part 4: the 1906 San Francisco earthquake as experienced by Jack London; the importance of reading aloud to young children; a clever and witty discussion of the ingredients contained in a substance we use every day and take for granted—toothpaste; the random shooting of a young Milwaukee resident named Euclid Leslie, a civic activist who was shot for being in the wrong place at the wrong time; new experiments with animals and their ability to communicate and understand language; behavior in wild dolphins; and finally the internment of Japanese-Americans during World War II.

22

Jack London
THE STORY OF AN EYEWITNESS

In 1906 Jack London (1876–1916), one of America's best-known writers, was staying in San Francisco, building a boat called **The Snark,** *in which he hoped to make a seven-year tour of the world. At 5:15 a.m. on April 18, an earthquake of great magnitude struck San Francisco, destroying the entire downtown, the waterfront, and nearly all the residential areas. Scientists today estimate that the quake measured around 8.6 on the Richter scale, considerably stronger than the October 1989 Loma Prieta earthquake, which registered 7.0. This is London's eyewitness account.*

VOCABULARY PREVIEW

**WORD
ORIGINS**

NABOBS

London mentions the word *nabobs* three times in the course of the selection (paragraphs 2, 22, and 30). This word refers to the men of great wealth who built enormous houses (he calls them palaces) on what is now called the Nob Hill section of San Francisco. These men had made their fortune during the Gold Rush of 1849 or during the railroad-building era when the so-called Big Four—Mark Hopkins, Collis Huntington, Charles Crocker, and Leland Stanford—created the railroad monopoly in California.

The word *nabob* is of Indian origin. It is a corruption of the Hindi word *nawab,* the native title for the governors of provinces or districts when India was ruled by the Mongol Empire (before 1858, when the British took over). Some of these nawabs grew enormously wealthy. In the eighteenth and nineteenth centuries, Europeans used the word *nabob* to refer to an Englishman who returned from India having accumulated a large fortune. Today, however, it means any wealthy or influential person.

HYSTERIA

Despite the great destruction and the resulting chaos, London was surprised to observe (see paragraph 8) that "there was no *hysteria,* no disorder." This word is of Greek origin. It actually refers to a kind of neurosis, but it also can mean excessive fear or any other strong emotion.

The word's origin will very likely seem sexist to modern readers: The Greek word for *uterus* was *hustera,* and the Greek word *hysterikos* ("suffering in the womb") reflects the ancient belief that the disease was caused by disturbances in the uterus and that more women than men suffered from it.

WORD PARTS

REFUGEE

The word *refugee* (see paragraphs 17 and 31) comes from the French verb *réfugier,* "to see refuge or safety." It can be traced back to the Latin *re-* ("away" or "back") + *fugere* ("to flee"). The suffix *-ee* indicates "one who receives." This suffix occurs in certain legal words in English, for example, *addressee* ("one to whom something is addressed") or *grantee* ("one who is granted something").

It is sometimes added to nouns to make some rather silly-sounding new words, like *counselee* ("one who is counseled") or *tutee* ("one who is tutored"). You can also see that *-ee* is the opposite of *-or* ("one who does"), since a *counselor* is "one who counsels" and a *tutor* is "one who provides instruction."

WORD FAMILIES

COMPEL

London writes in paragraph 12 that thousands of refugees were *compelled* to abandon their possessions because of the advancing flames. The verb *compel* means "to force" or "to drive." It comes from Latin: [*com-* ("together") + *pellere* ("to drive")]. The noun form of *compel* is *compulsion.* English has three other word groups from the *pellere* and *puls-* Latin roots:

impel	to urge to action; to drive forward, as in the phrase "to be *impelled* to speak one's mind"
impulse	an impelling force or push; also a sudden urge or desire, as in "to give in to an *impulse*"
propel	to move or cause to move [*pro-* ("forward") + *pellere*]
propeller	a blade that causes a boat or plane to move
propulsion	a driving force, as in "jet *propulsion*"
repel	to drive back, to disgust
repellent	that which repels, as in "water-*repellent* fabric" or "insect *repellent*"
repulsion	a feeling of extreme dislike

JACK LONDON
THE STORY OF AN EYEWITNESS

1   The earthquake shook down in San Francisco hundreds of thousands of dollars worth of walls and chimneys. But the conflagration that followed burned up hundreds of millions of dollars worth of property. There is no estimating within hundreds of millions the actual damage wrought.

2   Not in history has a modern imperial city been so completely destroyed. San Francisco is gone. Nothing remains of it but memories and fringe of dwelling houses on its outskirts. Its industrial section is wiped out. Its business section is wiped out. Its social and residential section is wiped out. The factories and warehouses, the great stores and newspaper buildings, the hotels and the palaces of the nabobs, are all gone. Remains only the fringe of dwelling houses on the outskirts of what was once San Francisco.

3   Within an hour after the earthquake shock, the smoke of San Francisco's burning was a lurid tower visible a hundred miles away. And for three days and nights this lurid tower swayed in the sky, reddening the sun, darkening the day, and filling the land with smoke.

4   On Wednesday morning at quarter past five came the earthquake. A minute later the flames were leaping upward. In a dozen different quarters south of Market Street, in the working class ghetto and in the factories, fires started. There was no opposing the flames. There was no organization, no communication. All the cunning adjustments of a twentieth century city had been smashed by the earthquake. The streets were humped into ridges and depressions, and piled with the debris of fallen walls. The steel rails were twisted into perpendicular and horizontal angles. The telephone and telegraph systems were disrupted. And the great water mains had burst. All the shrewd contrivances and safeguards of man had been thrown out of gear by thirty seconds' twitching of the earth-crust.

5   By Wednesday afternoon, inside of twelve hours, half the heart of the city was gone. At that time I watched the vast conflagration from out on the bay. It was dead calm. Not a flicker of wind stirred. Yet from every side wind was pouring in upon the city. East, west, north, and south, strong winds were blowing upon the doomed city. The heated air rising made an enormous suck. Thus did the fire of itself build its own colossal chimney through the atmosphere. Day and night this dead calm continued, and yet, near to the flames, the wind was often half a gale, so mighty was the suck.

6   Wednesday night saw the destruction of the very heart of the city. Dynamite was lavishly used, and many of San Francisco's proudest structures were crumbled by man himself into ruins, but there was no withstanding the onrush of the flames. Time and again successful stands were made by the firefighters, and every time the flames flanked around on either side, or came up from the rear, and turned to defeat the hard won victory.

7   An enumeration of the buildings destroyed would be a directory of San Francisco. An enumeration of the buildings undestroyed would be a line and several addresses. An enumeration of the deeds of heroism would stock a library and bankrupt the Carnegie medal fund. An enumeration of the dead—will never be made. All vestiges of them were destroyed by the flames. The number of the victims of the earthquake will never be known. South of Market Street, where the loss of life was particularly heavy, was the first to catch fire.

8   Remarkable as it may seem, Wednesday night, while the whole city crashed and roared into ruin, was a quiet night. There were no crowds. There was no shouting and yelling. There was no hysteria, no disorder. I passed Wednesday night in the path of the advancing flames, and in all those terrible hours I saw not one woman who wept, not one man who was excited, not one person who was in the slightest degree panic-stricken.

9   Before the flames, throughout the night, fled tens of thousands of homeless ones. Some were wrapped in blankets. Others carried bundles of bedding and dear household treasures. Sometimes a whole family was harnessed to a carriage or delivery wagon that was weighted down with their possessions. Babybuggies, toy wagons and go-carts were used as trucks, while every other person was dragging a trunk. Yet everybody was gracious. The most perfect courtesy obtained. Never, in all San Francisco's history, were her people so kind and courteous as on this night of terror.

10   All night these tens of thousands fled before the flames. Many of them, the poor people from the labor ghetto, had fled all day as well. They had left their homes burdened with possessions. Now and again they lightened up, flinging out upon the street clothing and treasures they had dragged for miles.

11   They held on longest to their trunks, and over these trunks many a strong man broke his heart that night. The hills of San Francisco are steep, and up these hills, mile after mile, were the trunks dragged. Everywhere were trunks, with across them lying their exhausted owners, men and women. Before the march of the flames were flung picket-lines of soldiers. And a block at a time, as the flames advanced, these pickets retreated. One of their tasks was to keep the trunk-pullers moving. The exhausted creatures, stirred on by the menace of bayonets, would arise and struggle up the steep pavements, pausing from weakness every five or ten feet.

12   Often, after surmounting a heart-breaking hill, they would find another wall of flame advancing upon them at right angles and be compelled to change anew the line of their retreat. In the end, completely played out, after toiling for a dozen hours like giants, thousands of them were compelled to abandon their trunks. Here the shop-keepers and soft members of the middle class were at a disadvantage. But the workingmen dug holes in vacant lots and backyards and buried their trunks.

13   At nine o'clock Wednesday evening, I walked down through the very heart of the city. I walked through miles and miles of magnificent buildings and towering skyscrapers. Here was no fire. All was in perfect order. The police patrolled the streets. Every building had its watchman at the door. And yet it was doomed, all of it. There was no water. The dynamite was giving out. And at right angles two different conflagrations were sweeping down upon it.

14   At one o'clock in the morning I walked down through the same section.

Everything still stood intact. There was no fire. And yet there was a change. A rain of ashes was falling. The watchmen at the doors were gone. The police had been withdrawn. There were no firemen, no fire-engines, no men fighting with dynamite. The district had been absolutely abandoned.

15   I stood at the corner of Kearney and Market, in the very innermost heart of San Francisco. Kearney Street was deserted. Half a dozen blocks away it was burning on both sides. The street was a wall of flame. And against this wall of flame, silhouetted sharply, were two United States cavalrymen sitting their horses, calmly watching. That was all. Not another person was in sight. In the intact heart of the city two troopers sat their horses and watched.

16   Surrender was complete. There was no water. The sewers had long since been pumped dry. There was no dynamite. Another fire had broken out farther up town, and now from three sides conflagrations were sweeping down. The fourth side had been burned earlier in the day. In that direction stood the tottering walls of the *Examiner* Building, the burned out *Call* Building, the smouldering ruins of the Grand Hotel, and the gutted, devastated, dynamited Palace Hotel.

17   The following will illustrate the sweep of the flames and the inability of men to calculate their spread. At eight o'clock Wednesday evening I passed through Union Square. It was packed with refugees. Thousands of them had gone to bed on the grass. Government tents had been set up, supper was being cooked, and the refugees were lining up for free meals.

18   At half-past one in the morning three sides of Union Square were in flames. The fourth side, where stood the great St. Francis Hotel, was still holding out. An hour later, ignited from top and sides, the St. Francis was flaming heavenward. Union Square, heaped high with mountains of trunks, was deserted. Troops, refugees, and all had retreated.

19   It was at Union Square that I saw a man offering a thousand dollars for a team of horses. He was in charge of a truck piled high with trunks from some hotel. It had been hauled here into what was considered safety and the horses had been taken out. The flames were on three sides of the Square, and there were no horses.

20   Also, at this time, standing beside the trunk, I urged a man to seek safety in flight. He was all but hemmed in by several conflagrations. He was an old man and he was on crutches. Said he, "To-day is my birthday. Last night I was worth thirty thousand dollars. I bought five bottles of wine, some delicate fish, and other things for my birthday dinner. I have had no dinner, and all I own are these crutches."

21   I convinced him of his danger and started him limping on his way. An hour later, from a distance, I saw the truckload of trunks burning merrily in the middle of the street.

22   On Thursday morning, at quarter past five, just twenty-four hours after the earthquake, I sat on the steps of a small residence on Nob Hill. With me sat Japanese, Italians, Chinese, and Negroes—a bit of the cosmopolitan flotsam of the wreck of the city. All about were the palaces of the Nabob pioneers of forty-nine. To the east and south, at right angles, were advancing two mighty walls of flames.

23   I went inside with the owner of the house on the steps of which I sat. He was cool and cheerful and hospitable. "Yesterday morning," he said, "I was worth six hundred thousand dollars. This morning this house is all I have left. It will go in

fifteen minutes." He pointed to a large cabinet. "That is my wife's collection of China. This rug upon which we stand is a present. It cost fifteen hundred dollars. Try that piano. Listen to its tone. There are few like it. There are no horses. The flames will be here in fifteen minutes."

24   Outside, the old Mark Hopkins residence, a palace, was just catching fire. The troops were falling back and driving the refugees before them. From every side came the roaring of flames, the crashing of walls, and the detonations of dynamite.

25   I passed out of the house. Day was trying to dawn through the smoke-pall. A sickly light was creeping over the face of things. Once only the sun broke through the smoke-pall, blood-red and showing quarter its usual size. The smoke-pall itself, viewed from beneath, was a rose-color that pulsed and fluttered with lavender shades. Then it turned to mauve and yellow and dun. There was no sun. And so dawned the second day on stricken San Francisco.

26   An hour later I was creeping past the shattered dome of the City Hall. Than it, there was no better exhibit of the destructive force of the earthquake. Most of the stone had been shaken from the great dome, leaving standing the naked framework of steel. Market Street was piled high with the wreckage, and across the wreckage, lay the overthrown pillars of the City Hall shattered into short crosswise sections.

27   This section of the city, with the exception of the Mint and the Post Office, was already a waste of smoking ruins. Here and there through the smoke, creeping warily under the shadows of tottering walls, emerged occasional men and women. It was like the meeting of the handful of survivors after the day of the end of the world.

28   On Mission Street lay a dozen steers, in a neat row stretching across the street, just as they had been struck down by the flying ruins of the earthquake. The fire had passed through afterward and roasted them. The human dead had been carried away before the fire came. At another place on Mission Street I saw a milk wagon. A steel telegraph pole had smashed down sheer through the driver's seat and crushed the front wheels. The milk cans lay scattered around.

29   All day Thursday and all Thursday night, all day Friday and Friday night, the flames still raged. Friday night saw the flames finally conquered, though not until Russian Hill and Telegraph Hill had been swept and three-quarters of a mile of wharves and docks had been licked up.

30   The great stand of the firefighters was made Thursday night on Van Ness Avenue. Had they failed here, the comparatively few remaining houses of the city would have been swept. Here were the magnificent residences of the second generation of San Francisco nabobs, and these, in a solid zone, were dynamited down across the path of the fire. Here and there, the flames leaped the zone, but these isolated fires were beaten out, principally by the use of wet blankets and rugs.

31   San Francisco, at the present time, is like the crater of a volcano, around which are camped tens of thousands of refugees. At the Presidio alone are at least twenty thousand. All the surrounding cities and towns are jammed with the homeless ones, where they are being cared for by the relief committees. The refugees were carried free by the railroads to any point they wished to go, and it is estimated that over one hundred thousand people have left the peninsula on which San Francisco stood. The government has the situation in hand, and, thanks to the immediate relief given

by the whole United States, there is not the slightest possibility of a famine. The bankers and business men have already set about making preparations to rebuild San Francisco. ■

From Jack London, "The Story of an Eyewitness," *Jack London Reports.*

EXERCISES

Do not refer to the selection for Exercises A and B.

A. DETERMINING THE MAIN IDEA AND PURPOSE
Choose the best answer.

1. _____ The main idea of the selection is that (a) no other city in modern times had been so completely destroyed as San Francisco was in the 1906 earthquake; (b) a tragedy like the 1906 San Francisco earthquake brings out people's best qualities; (c) an eyewitness account of the 1906 San Francisco earthquake revealed terrible destruction to both people and property, not only by the quake itself but by the subsequent fires; (d) even the biggest palaces owned by the richest men could not be saved in the 1906 earthquake.

2. _____ With respect to the main idea, the author's purpose is (a) to provide a firsthand subjective account of events; (b) to offer emotional arguments about a controversial subject; (c) to present factual information; (d) to contradict previously published reports.

B. COMPREHENDING MAIN IDEAS
Choose the correct answer.

1. _____ The only part of San Francisco that was not destroyed by the 1906 earthquake was (a) the waterfront; (b) the residential areas on the outskirts of the city; (c) the industrial and business sections; (d) the main residential areas.

2. _____ The fire that broke out after the earthquake lasted for (a) two days and nights; (b) three days and nights; (c) five days and nights; (d) a week.

3. _____ Firefighters destroyed heavily damaged buildings by (a) knocking them down with bulldozers; (b) setting them on fire; (c) using dynamite; (d) using a wrecking ball.

4. _____ On the night of the earthquake the residents (a) panicked and caused near-riots; (b) fled the city in private cars, buses, and trains; (c) looted shops and rich people's mansions; (d) behaved calmly and sensibly.

5. ____ The main reason San Francisco was destroyed in 1906 was (a) the impact of the earthquake itself; (b) that the firefighters gave up and refused to work any longer; (c) that the city ran out of water to fight the fires; (d) that the rescue and disaster efforts were not well coordinated.

6. ____ The building that best showed the destructive force of the earthquake was (a) the Mint; (b) the Post Office; (c) the Mark Hopkins Hotel; (d) City Hall.

COMPREHENSION SCORE

Score your answers for Exercises A and B as follows:

A. No. right _____ × 2 = _____

B. No. right _____ × 1 = _____

Total pts. from A and B _____ × 10 = _____%

You may refer to the selection for the remaining exercises.

C. DISTINGUISHING BETWEEN MAIN IDEAS AND SUPPORTING DETAILS

Label the following statements from the selection as follows: MI if the statement represents a *main idea* and SD if the statement represents a *supporting detail.*

1. ____ Remarkable as it may seem, Wednesday night, while the whole city crashed and roared into ruin, was a quiet night.

2. ____ There was no shouting and yelling. There was no hysteria, no disorder.

3. ____ I passed Wednesday night in the path of the advancing flames, and in all those terrible hours I saw not one person who was in the slightest degree panic-stricken.

4. ____ Before the flames, throughout the night, fled tens of thousands of homeless ones.

5. ____ Some were wrapped in blankets.

6. ____ Others carried bundles of bedding and dear household treasures.

7. ____ Sometimes a whole family was harnessed to a carriage or delivery wagon that was weighted down with their possessions.

8. ____ Baby-buggies, toy wagons and go-carts were used as trucks, while every other person was dragging a trunk.

9. ____ Yet everybody was gracious.

10. _____ Never, in all San Francisco's history, were her people so kind and courteous as on this night of terror.

D. MAKING INFERENCES

For each of these statements write Y (Yes) if the inference is an accurate one, N (No) if the inference is an inaccurate one, or CT (Can't Tell) if you do not have enough information to make an inference.

1. _____ The flames destroying San Francisco's buildings produced a wind much stronger than any ordinary wind.

2. _____ Buildings were dynamited to prevent more fires from breaking out.

3. _____ London was impressed with the residents' calm and courteous behavior.

4. _____ Rich people fared better than middle-class or working-class people, since they had sufficient money to pay to be evacuated.

5. _____ Because of government and other relief efforts, there was never a shortage in the city's food supply.

6. _____ A house that survived the 1906 San Francisco earthquake would be somewhat unusual.

E. ANALYZING ORGANIZATION AND SEEING RELATIONSHIPS
Choose the best answer.

1. _____ What order does London use to organize the details in his account of the earthquake? (a) general to specific order; (b) specific to general order; (c) chronological or time order; (d) spatial or space order; (e) random or haphazard order.

2. _____ In describing the aftermath of the earthquake, which of our five senses does he rely on most? Our sense of (a) hearing; (b) smell; (c) touch; (d) sight; (e) taste.

3. _____ Look again at the verbs London uses in paragraph 4: *humped, twisted, disrupted, burst, twitching.* What are these verbs supposed to convey to the reader? (a) a tremendously destructive force or energy; (b) a feeling of respect and admiration; (c) the impossibility of controlling nature with technology; (d) the unpredictability of nature.

4. _____ In paragraphs 2 and 7 London repeats two phrases, "wiped out" and "an enumeration," several times. This repetition makes his discussion more (a) factual; (b) believable; (c) realistic; (d) emphatic.

5. _____ Read paragraph 11 again. The dominant impression conveyed is one of (a) fear; (b) exhaustion; (c) greed; (d) resignation.

6. _____ The description of the morning in paragraph 25 emphasizes (a) smells; (b) sights; (c) colors; (d) shapes.

7. _____ In the first sentence of paragraph 31 London compares San Francisco to the "crater of a volcano," by which he means that the city (a) was perched atop a high mountain; (b) would never be habitable again; (c) had sunk below sea level; (d) was utterly destroyed by the earthquake.

8. _____ The last sentence of the selection suggests a feeling of (a) doom; (b) optimism; (c) pessimism; (d) uncertainty.

F. **UNDERSTANDING VOCABULARY**
   Choose the correct definition according to the context.

1. _____ the *conflagration* that followed [paragraphs 1, 5, and 20]: (a) misery; (b) event; (c) large, destructive fire; (d) aftershock.

2. _____ The *cunning adjustments* of a twentieth century city; all the *shrewd contrivances* [4]: Both phrases refer to devices and equipment that are (a) expensive to build and maintain; (b) clever, devised with ingenuity; (c) technologically advanced; (d) handy, convenient to use.

3. _____ its own *colossal* chimney [5]: (a) easily seen; (b) destructive; (c) enormous; (d) sturdy.

4. _____ Dynamite was *lavishly* used [6]: (a) extravagantly; (b) finally; (c) reluctantly; (d) sparingly.

5. _____ An *enumeration* of the buildings [7]: (a) description; (b) summary; (c) published guide; (d) detailed list.

6. _____ All *vestiges* of them were destroyed [7]: (a) visible traces, signs; (b) memories, reminders; (c) examples, instances; (d) studies, examinations.

7. _____ stirred on by the *menace* of bayonets [11]: (a) threat; (b) presence; (c) signal; (d) display.

8. _____ thousands were *compelled* to abandon their trunks [12]: (a) encouraged; (b) forced; (c) obligated; (d) paid.

9. _____ the gutted, *devastated,* dynamited Palace Hotel [16]: (a) beautiful; (b) awesome, wondrous; (c) ruined; (d) crumbling.

10. _____ the smoke, creeping *warily* [27]: (a) slyly; (b) slowly; (c) invisibly; (d) cautiously.

G. **USING VOCABULARY**
   Write the correct inflected form of the base word in each of the following sentences. Refer to your dictionary if necessary.

1. (*estimating*—use a noun)   It is impossible to give a precise _____

   _____ of the damage caused by the 1906 earthquake.

2. (*disrupted*—use a noun) The _____ to both the telephone and telegraph system was immediate.

3. (*enumeration*—use another noun) _____ the buildings destroyed or the number of lives lost cannot be done.

4. (*hysteria*—use an adjective) To his surprise, London did not observe any _____ people on the first night.

5. (*courtesy*—use an adverb) The city's residents behaved calmly and _____.

6. (*possession*—use a verb) People were burdened carrying trunks with all they _____ up the city's steep hills.

7. (*menace*—use an adjective) The exhausted trunk-pullers were kept moving by the _____ police bayonets.

8. (*abandoned*—use a noun) By the middle of the night the _____ _____ of the center of town was complete.

9. (*refugee*—use another noun) Union Square served temporarily as a _____.

10. (*exhibit*—use a verb) The shattered dome of City Hall _____ well the earthquake's destructive force.

H. TOPICS FOR WRITING OR DISCUSSION

1. Here are some sentences from the article. Paraphrase them by rewriting each one in your own words in the space provided.

    a. All the shrewd contrivances and safeguards of man had been thrown out of gear by thirty seconds' twitching of the earth-crust.

    _____
    _____
    _____

    b. Often, after surmounting a heart-breaking hill, they would find another wall of flame advancing upon them at right angles and be compelled to change anew the line of their retreat.

    _____
    _____
    _____

c. An hour later I was creeping past the shattered dome of the City Hall. Than it, there was no better exhibit of the destructive force of the earthquake.

_____

_____

_____

2. If you have ever observed a tragedy, relate not only the events, but also the participants' subsequent behavior and reactions.

23 ||||

Jim Trelease

WHY YOU SHOULD READ TO YOUR KIDS

Jim Trelease is an artist, author, and lecturer who is best known for his book, The Read-Aloud Handbook. *This article, reprinted from* U.S. News & World Report, *summarizes his ideas about parents' responsibilities to read to their children.*

VOCABULARY PREVIEW

WORD ORIGINS

OBSESSION

In paragraph 6 Trelease questions the *obsession* some parents have with their children's achievement. An *obsession* today means "a compulsive preoccupation with a fixed idea." The verb *obsess* came into English from the Latin word *obsidēre* (past participle *obsessus*), meaning literally "to sit down before," "to occupy," or "to besiege." The archaic meaning was far more drastic than the current one we use—*obsessed* meant being harassed by an evil spirit, in addition to what it means today, which is to be haunted and troubled by a fixed idea.

EAVESDROP

Probably at one time or another, everyone has *eavesdropped*, or listened in on someone's conversation. Trelease writes in paragraph 13 that "reading aloud becomes a way to *eavesdrop* on history." This verb is of English origin, coming from *evesdrop* (the Old English was *yfesdrype*), which, according to the *Oxford English Dictionary*, referred to the dropping of rainwater from the eaves of a house. (The "eaves" refer to the overhang at the lower edge of a roof.)

An *eavesdropper*, then, could stand within the "eavesdrop" of a house and hear what was being said inside. Therefore, one who snooped like this ran the risk of getting a little wet.

WORD PARTS	**Dys-**

Dyslexia, mentioned in paragraph 19, is a reading disability, usually caused by a neurological problem, which results in severe difficulty in reading. The prefix *dys-* traveled a long route: through Middle English, through Old French, through Latin (where it was spelled the same way we spell it in English), and originally from Greek, where it was spelled *dus-*). This prefix always indicates "diseased," "difficult," or "bad." It is used in many scientific words. In the case of *dyslexia*, the prefix is added to the Greek word for speech, *lexis*. The dictionary lists some other common ones:

dysentery	infection in the lower intestinal tract [*dys-* + *enteron* ("intestine")]
dysfunction	the impaired functioning of a bodily system or organ
dyspepsia	indigestion [*dys-* + *pepsia* ("digestion")]

WORD FAMILIES	**Competence, Competency**

These two nouns have the same meaning: "the quality of being capable," "a skill," or "an ability." In many states, high school students are now required to take *competency* tests to determine if they have sufficient skills in basic subjects. The verb from which these nouns are derived is *compete*, which in Latin was formed like this: [*com-* ("together") + *petere* ("to seek or strive")]. Thus, when one *competes*, he or she strives with or contends with others for a prize or a reward. Here are some other words in this family:

competent	well qualified, capable
competition	striving with another for profit, position, or simply the necessities of life; a contest that measures skill or ability
competitor	one who competes; one's opponent
competitive	describing someone who likes to compete; or more generally, describing something determined by a competition, as in "a *competitive* sport"

Literacy

Trelease's subject is *literacy*, meaning "the ability to read and write." It derives from the Latin root for "letter" (*littera*). English has many words in this family, among them:

literate	able to read and write, and its opposite, *illiterate*
literal	in accordance with the primary meaning of a word, or word for word, as in "a *literal* translation" or "a *literal* interpretation"
literature	prose or verse writing; drama
obliterate	to destroy completely so as not to leave a trace [*ob-* ("off" or "away from") + *littera*], literally "to strike out words" or "erase"

Other words you should know:

syndrome   [6]—the complex of symptoms indicating an abnormal condition

osmosis   [10]—a gradual process of absorption

JIM TRELEASE

WHY YOU SHOULD READ TO YOUR KIDS

1   It's really never too early to start reading to a child. If a child is old enough to talk to—and parents talk to their children from Day 1—then he or she is old enough to be read to.

2   It doesn't matter if they cannot understand the words; the language inside the covers of books is frequently a whole lot more organized, colorful and coherent than "koochie, koochie, koochie."

3   Holding even a tiny child in front of a book and reading to him or her is intellectual stimulation. A visual competency is developing, too, because the child is being taught to focus attention on a picture on a page.

4   This visual literacy is just as important as print literacy, and it is usually achieved before print literacy. At 18 months old, a child can identify a picture of a puppy and understand the word—and that's long before he/she can read it.

THE "HURRIED CHILD"

5   I have strong reservations about trying to teach a child to read at too early an age.

6   While one school of thought claims that much is to be gained by developing a child's language abilities between birth and age 6, I am suspicious about the obsession some parents have with fostering an achievement syndrome in very young children. Too often, this is accomplished at the expense of a child's social and emotional skills.

7   One mother told me how vital it was to teach her child to read before first grade so that the youngster could get in a top reading group. If children aren't in the top reading group, she said, they won't get on the fast track or get into the right colleges.

8   The truth of the matter is that the country with the highest literacy rate and the greatest general affluence happens to be Denmark, which does not begin teaching reading until age 7. So why the hurry?

9   I recommend that every parent read David Elkind's book, "The Hurried Child." The professional parent—the career parent—is too often bringing his or her own career anxieties into the child-rearing process. They're in a big hurry to make their kids old before their time.

10   In contrast, several major studies on early fluent readers—those who learn to read before they ever set foot in the classroom—show that the overwhelming majority of these children were never taught how to read. They just picked it up by osmosis by being exposed to books and reading.

READING ALOUD

11   Next to hugging your child, reading aloud is probably the longest-lasting experience that you can put into your child's life. You will savor it long after they have grown up.

12   Reading aloud is important for all the reasons that talking to children is important—to inspire them, to guide them, to educate them, to bond with them and to communicate your feelings, hopes and fears. You are giving children a piece of your mind and a piece of your time.

13   They are more interested, really, in you than they are in the story—at least in the beginning. But it is not just you who are communicating but the author and illustrator. These are people who, in some cases, lived hundreds of years ago. So reading aloud becomes a way to eavesdrop on history.

14   Reading aloud to children on a routine basis improves their reading, writing, speaking, listening and imagining skills. And it improves their attitudes toward learning.

15   Today attitude is the major stumbling block to literacy achievement. But what we do in this culture is teach children how to read first; then we try and get them interested in it. That's putting the cart before the horse.

16   Reading aloud is the primary focus for the national report "Becoming a Nation of Readers." The first conclusion these people drew after two solid years of looking over all the research was: If you want to build readers, read aloud to children early and often.

17   Much the same conclusion was reached in another national study, released in late February, called "What Works: Research About Teaching and Learning."

WORKBOOK MENTALITY

18   For too many children, reading has become the leisure activity of last resort. They associate reading with ditto sheets, workbooks, homework, test scores. They develop a workbook mentality about reading, which carries on into adulthood.

19   Even if a child has a learning disability, such as dyslexia, the enjoyment from reading aloud will give him an incentive to work through that problem. Beyond that, the child with a learning difficulty linked to a visual defect needs to build his oral vocabulary so that he can understand words spoken in conversation. This vocabulary is developed by hearing the spoken word.

20   "Becoming a Nation of Readers" also pointed to the need within schools to give children the time to read by themselves—just for the fun of it.

21   There's a big difference between reading skills and reading enjoyment. Many children that have complete competence in reading don't read outside of school. You can teach them how to read, but if you don't also show them—at home and in the classroom—that reading is pleasurable, you have failed.

22   Look at all the adults who come home and relax by turning on the television

and letting a pretty man or a pretty woman in pretty clothes read the news to them every night.

WHERE THE BOYS ARE

23 The father who says he is too tired to read to his kids uses the same two eyes to watch a lot of television. There's always a shortage of men in the audience when I talk about reading aloud. But I'll tell you where there's no shortage of males in this country—in the remedial-reading classes.

24 Boys make up 75 percent of the remedial students.

25 I propose that an enormous percentage of those boys are in those classes not because of learning disabilities but because of father or male disabilities. They have been convinced by their fathers and males on TV that the really important things in life are the things we throw and the things we catch.

26 This is a colossal hoax! We have got to find a way to let the fathers know they can do both. They can be athletically *and* intellectually involved in their children's lives.   ■

From Jim Trelease, "Why You Should Read to Your Kids," *U.S. News & World Report,* March 17, 1986. Reprinted by permission.

EXERCISES

Do not refer to the selection for Exercises A and B.

A.   DETERMINING THE MAIN IDEA AND PURPOSE
Choose the best answer.

1.   _____ The main idea of the selection is that (a) visual literacy is just as important as print literacy; (b) children should not be taught to read at too early an age; (c) some parents are obsessed with fostering the idea of achievement in their children; (d) reading aloud to one's children is probably the most important and longest-lasting experience a parent can give them.

2.   _____ With respect to the main idea, the author's purpose is (a) to summarize current educational theories; (b) to convince the reader that his main idea is valid and correct; (c) to criticize the American educational system; (d) to present arguments on a highly emotional subject.

B.   COMPREHENDING MAIN IDEAS
Choose the correct answer.

1.   _____ According to the author, visual literacy (a) and print literacy mean the same thing; (b) develops before print literacy; (c) develops after print literacy; (d) is not as important as print literacy.

2.   _____ With respect to some parents' attempts to teach their children to

read at an early age, Trelease says that (a) he fully agrees; (b) he has not yet decided if they are right; (c) he has strong reservations; (d) he is firmly against it.

3. _____ According to the author, parents who foster the "achievement syndrome" in their children too early are making a mistake, because (a) it is too often accomplished at the expense of social and emotional skills; (b) the children will be so advanced when they begin school that they will be bored; (c) parents are not professional teachers, so teaching reading should be left to teachers; (d) it makes the children too concerned with status, for example, getting into the right college.

4. _____ The country with the highest literacy rate is (a) the United States; (b) the USSR; (c) Sweden; (d) Denmark.

5. _____ Trelease says that if parents want to make readers out of their children, they should (a) read "Becoming a Nation of Readers"; (b) teach their children to read at around age six; (c) read to their children early and often; (d) let their children develop at their own pace and not force books on them.

6. _____ Trelease criticizes the educational system for (a) tracking children by putting them into reading groups based on levels; (b) developing a workbook mentality about reading in children; (c) not demanding enough reading from students; (d) not encouraging parents to get more involved with their children's school.

COMPREHENSION SCORE

Score your answers for Exercises A and B as follows:

A.   No. right _____ × 2 = _____

B.   No. right _____ × 1 = _____

Total pts. from A and B _____ × 10 = _____%

You may refer to the selection for the remaining exercises.

C.   DISTINGUISHING BETWEEN MAIN IDEAS AND SUPPORTING DETAILS

Label the following statements adapted from the selection as follows: MI if the statement represents a *main idea* and SD if the statement represents a *supporting detail*.

1. _____ It is never too early to start reading to a child.

2. _____ The child develops a visual competency and learns to focus attention on a page.

3. _____ Visual literacy is just as important as print literacy, and it is usually achieved before print literacy.

4. _____ An 18-month-old child can identify a picture of a puppy and understand the word long before he or she can read it.

5.   _____ Trelease is suspicious about the obsession some parents have with fostering an achievement syndrome in very young children.

6.   _____ One mother told him how vital it was to teach her child to read before first grade so that the youngster could get in a top reading group.

7.   _____ If children aren't in the top reading group, she said, they won't get on the fast track or get into the right colleges.

8.   _____ Several major studies on early fluent readers (those who learned to read before they started school) show that they picked it up by osmosis, just by being exposed to books and reading.

D.   MAKING INFERENCES

For each of these statements write Y (Yes) if the inference is an accurate one, N (No) if the inference is an inaccurate one, or CT (Can't Tell) if you do not have enough information to make an inference.

1.   _____ It is a waste of time for parents to read to children before they are old enough to identify pictures on the page.

2.   _____ Reading aloud to one's children is more important than showing them physical affection.

3.   _____ One reason so many children are poor readers is that their parents devote too much time to their careers, leaving little time for reading to their children.

4.   _____ It would be better to get children to enjoy reading before we teach them to read.

5.   _____ The way schools teach children to read is too mechanistic, so that although children may become skilled readers, they derive little enjoyment from it.

6.   _____ In general, girls are better readers than boys.

7.   _____ American fathers are often more concerned with developing their sons' athletic abilities than fostering their sons' intellectual skills.

8.   _____ The author thinks that American children should be raised without a television in the house.

E.   DISTINGUISHING BETWEEN FACT AND OPINION

For each of the following statements from the selection, write F if the statement represents a factual statement that can be verified or O if the statement represents the writer's own subjective opinion.

1.   _____ One school of thought claims that much is to be gained by developing a child's language ability between birth and age 6.

2.   _____ The country with the highest literacy rate and the greatest general affluence happens to be Denmark.

3. _____ [Denmark] does not begin teaching [children] reading until age 7.

4. _____ I [the author] recommend that every parent read David Elkind's book, "The Hurried Child."

5. _____ Next to hugging your child, reading aloud is probably the longest-lasting experience that you can put into your child's life.

6. _____ Reading aloud is the primary focus for the national report "Becoming a Nation of Readers."

F.   DRAWING CONCLUSIONS
Place an X before each statement that represents a reasonable conclusion you can draw from the selection.

1. _____ The nation's educators should not be so concerned about our children's reading skills.

2. _____ More research still needs to be done before the best solution to our children's reading problems is discovered.

3. _____ Children do not really need to be taught how to read because most are able to pick it up by osmosis.

4. _____ The pressure for young children to compete and to succeed may result in emotional problems later.

5. _____ Parents should not be in such a rush to teach their children to read before they start school.

G.   ANALYZING ORGANIZATION AND SEEING RELATIONSHIPS
Choose the best answer.

1. _____ Throughout the selection Trelease seems to be most concerned with (a) the poor job the nation's schools have done in teaching children to read; (b) the responsibility parents have to provide their children with the best education possible; (c) the many advantages of early, frequent reading aloud to one's children; (d) the harm that can be done to children when they are pushed to read too early.

2. _____ To provide evidence for his ideas, Trelease uses both his own opinions and (a) examples from his own children's experience; (b) references to research studies published on teaching reading; (c) emotional and biased arguments; (d) explanations of exactly how parents should proceed if they want to teach their children to read.

3. _____ Look again at the first sentence of paragraph 6. What is the relationship between the two parts? (a) steps in a process; (b) term to be defined and a definition; (c) contrast; (d) general idea plus supporting idea.

4. _____ In paragraph 8 Trelease apparently finds a connection between (a) educational level and affluence; (b) literacy and affluence; (c) a postponement in teaching reading and affluence; (d) a postponement in teaching reading and well-adjusted children.

5. _____ Paragraphs 12–14 are developed by means of (a) effects; (b) short examples; (c) statistics; (d) definitions of terms.

H. UNDERSTANDING VOCABULARY
Choose the correct definition according to the context.

1. _____ the language of books is . . . more *coherent* [paragraph 2]: (a) interesting; (b) exciting; (c) logically connected; (d) mature.

2. _____ A visual *competency* is developing [3]: (a) skill, ability; (b) determination; (c) sophistication; (d) striving toward a goal.

3. _____ I have strong *reservations* [5]: (a) emotions; (b) doubts; (c) criticisms; (d) opinions.

4. _____ the *obsession* some parents have [6]: (a) illusion, false idea; (b) influence; (c) preoccupation with a fixed idea; (d) irrational concern over a moral issue.

5. _____ how *vital* it was [7]: (a) necessary to the continuation of life; (b) full of life, energetic; (c) immediately important, essential; (d) mentally challenging.

6. _____ the greatest general *affluence* [8]: (a) wealth; (b) educational level; (c) standard of living; (d) possession of material things.

7. _____ his or her own career *anxieties* [9]: (a) ambitions; (b) successes; (c) minor concerns; (d) worries, fears.

8. _____ early *fluent* readers [10]: Describing those who (a) enjoy reading; (b) have great confidence in their ability; (c) have great ease with reading; (d) were self-taught in reading.

9. _____ You will *savor* it [11]: (a) enjoy greatly; (b) remember fondly; (c) profit from; (d) learn from.

10. _____ This is a colossal *hoax* [26]: (a) misunderstanding; (b) youthful prank; (c) illusion; (d) deception, fraudulent act.

I. USING VOCABULARY
Write the correct inflected form of the base word in each of the following sentences. Refer to your dictionary if necessary.

1. (*organized*—use a noun) The language in books generally has more

_____ than spoken language.

2. (*competency*—use an adjective)   Making _____ readers out of their children requires parents to begin reading early to them.

3. (*literacy*—use an adjective)   Denmark has the highest number of

_____ adults in the world.

4. (*obsession*—use a verb)   Some parents are _____ with their children's achievement.

5. (*fluent*—use an adverb)   For children to read _____, they need constant exposure to reading aloud.

6. (*inspiration*—use a verb)   One advantage of reading aloud to children is

that they are _____ to learn more on their own.

7. (*routine*—use an adverb)   Reading aloud _____ to children improves their attitudes toward learning.

8. (*conclusion*—use a verb)   The national report, "Becoming a Nation of

Readers," _____ that parents can directly influence their children's reading habits.

9. (*enjoyment*—use an adjective)   Often students don't find reading

_____ because, to them, reading means workbooks.

10. (*relax*—use a noun)   Far too many adults find their only _____ in the television set.

J.   TOPICS FOR WRITING OR DISCUSSION

1. Write a brief summary, two or three sentences long, of paragraphs 1–4.

_____

_____

_____

_____

_____

_____

2. Describe a significant experience with reading you have had at some time in your life—a book or perhaps some other reading material that profoundly affected you.

24

David Bodanis
WHAT'S IN TOOTHPASTE

David Bodanis has a degree in mathematics from the University of Chicago. His book, The Secret House, *is subtitled "24 Hours in the Strange and Unexpected World in Which We Spend Our Nights and Days." It is a fascinating look at what really goes on in our homes, for example, what the common items that we use or eat consist of. In this excerpt, he shows us what's in toothpaste.*

VOCABULARY PREVIEW

WORD ORIGINS

LUCRATIVE

In paragraph 2 Bodanis writes that "Toothpaste manufacture is a very *lucrative* occupation." Meaning "producing wealth or profit," *lucrative* follows the path of so many English words: from Middle English *lucratif*, from Old French, and originally from Latin *lucrārī*, "to profit," "to gain," from *lucrum*, "gain." In English we also have a derived word *lucre*, meaning "money," most commonly seen in the phrase *filthy lucre*, confirming the old saying that money is the root of all evil.

CARNAGE

According to Bodanis, tooth enamel is the hardest substance in the body, requiring an even harder substance to clean it. Toothpaste, therefore, contains chalk, which acts as an abrasive and a polishing substance. In describing what this chalk does to teeth, Bodanis uses the word *carnage*, humorously referring to a "massacre" or "slaughter." *Carnage* comes from the Latin root *carō* ("flesh"); also a *carnāticum* or "slaughter of animals." Here are some related words derived from the root *caro:*

carnal	relating to the desires of the flesh; sensual
carnivore	a flesh-eating animal [*carō* + *-vorous* ("eating")]
carnival	any time of merrymaking and feasting [*carnem* + *vale* ("farewell to meat")]

281

carnation	a flower, from Old French for "flesh-colored"
chili con carne	chili with meat

WORD PARTS

-IVE, -OUS

These two word parts are common adjective endings in English, which are illustrated in the selection by these words: *lucrative*, which you saw in the preceding section; *abrasive* (paragraph 5), describing a substance that *abrades* (see *abrading*, paragraph 4), meaning "to wear away by friction"; and *cavernous* (paragraph 5), "cave-like," "like a cavern."

The suffix *-ive* means "having a tendency to," as in these adjectives: *disruptive, constructive, passive, connective*, and *corrosive*. The suffix *-ous* means "full of" or "like," as in *porous* ("full of pores"), *joyous, nervous*, and *miraculous*.

-IFY

This suffix is a common verb ending. It means simply "to make," as you can see in the word *rectify*, which usually means "to make right." However, in this context, Bodanis has the chemical meaning in mind. When he writes in paragraph 11 that toothpaste manufacturers use "double *rectified* peppermint oil," he means that the oil has been purified or refined by distillation.

These common verbs end with the suffix: *verify* ("to make real or true"); *falsify* ("to make false"); *purify* ("to make pure"); or *indemnify* ("to make compensation to for damages").

WORD FAMILIES

ERRANT

According to Bodanis, toothpaste apparently contains extra-abrasive chalk fragments, which he describes as *errant*, meaning that they don't conform to the prescribed standard. *Errant*, and its close cousin *error*, comes from the Middle English root *erren* and originally from the Latin root *errāre*, both meaning "to wander." Other words in English in this family include:

err	to go astray or to make a mistake
erroneous	containing an error; mistaken; false
erratic	wandering, without a fixed or regular course
errata	a list of errors found in published material
knights errant	medieval knights who wandered about the countryside in search of adventure

MANUFACTURE

The original meaning of *manufacture* (used throughout the selection) was literally "to make by hand," from Latin: [*manū* + *facere* ("to make")]. The root *manū* is the basis for a large number of English words, most of which no longer have any connection with doing things by hand:

maneuver	to make a change in position
manipulate	to operate or control by skilled use of the hands; also to influence or manage in a shrewd way
manuscript	a handwritten work in the traditional usage; now any typed work before publication
manual	done with the hands, as in a *manual* transmission
manumission	the act of freeing from slavery [*manū* + *ēmittere* (literally "to hand over," "to liberate")]

DAVID BODANIS

WHAT'S IN TOOTHPASTE

1   Into the bathroom goes our male resident, and after the most pressing need is satisfied it's time to brush the teeth. The tube of toothpaste is squeezed, its pinched metal seams are splayed, pressure waves are generated inside, and the paste begins to flow. But what's in this toothpaste, so carefully being extruded out?

2   Water mostly, 30 to 45 per cent in most brands: ordinary, everyday simple tap water. It's there because people like to have a big gob of toothpaste to spread on the brush, and water is the cheapest stuff there is when it comes to making big gobs. Dripping a bit from the tap onto your brush would cost virtually nothing; whipped in with the rest of the toothpaste the manufacturers can sell it at a neat and accountant-pleasing $2 per pound equivalent. Toothpaste manufacture is a very lucrative occupation.

3   Second to water in quantity is chalk: exactly the same material that schoolteachers use to write on blackboards. It is collected from the crushed remains of long-dead ocean creatures. In the Cretaceous seas chalk particles served as part of the wickedly sharp outer skeleton that these creatures had to wrap around themselves to keep from getting chomped by all the slightly larger other ocean creatures they met. Their massed graves are our present chalk deposits.

4   The individual chalk particles—the size of the smallest mud particles in your garden—have kept their toughness over the aeons, and now on the toothbrush they'll need it. The enamel outer coating of the tooth they'll have to face is the hardest substance in the body—tougher than skull, or bone, or nail. Only the chalk particles in toothpaste can successfully grind into the teeth during brushing, ripping off the surface layers like an abrading wheel grinding down a boulder in a quarry.

5   The craters, slashes, and channels that the chalk tears into the teeth will also remove a certain amount of built-up yellow in the carnage, and it is for that polishing function that it's there. A certain amount of unduly enlarged extra-abrasive chalk fragments tear such cavernous pits into the teeth that future decay bacteria will be able to bunker down there and thrive; the quality control people find

it almost impossible to screen out these errant super-chalk pieces, and government regulations allow them to stay in.

6   In case even the gouging doesn't get all the yellow off, another substance is worked into the toothpaste cream. This is titanium dioxide. It comes in tiny spheres, and it's the stuff bobbing around in white wall paint to make it come out white. Splashed around onto your teeth during the brushing it coats much of the yellow that remains. Being water soluble it leaks off in the next few hours and is swallowed, but at least for the quick glance up in the mirror after finishing it will make the user think his teeth are truly white. Some manufacturers add optical whitening dyes—the stuff more commonly found in washing machine bleach—to make extra sure that that glance in the mirror shows reassuring white.

7   These ingredients alone would not make a very attractive concoction. They would stick in the tube like a sloppy white plastic lump, hard to squeeze out as well as revolting to the touch. Few consumers would savor rubbing in a mixture of water, ground-up blackboard chalk and the whitener from latex paint first thing in the morning. To get around that finicky distaste the manufacturers have mixed in a host of other goodies.

8   To keep the glop from drying out, a mixture including glycerine glycol—related to the most common car anti-freeze ingredient—is whipped in with the chalk and water, and to give *that* concoction a bit of substance (all we really have so far is wet colored chalk) a large helping is added to gummy molecules from the seaweed *Chondrus Crispus*. This seaweed ooze spreads in among the chalk, paint and anti-freeze, then stretches itself in all directions to hold the whole mass together. A bit of paraffin oil (the fuel that flickers in camping lamps) is pumped in with it to help the moss ooze keep the whole substance smooth.

9   With the glycol, ooze and paraffin we're almost there. Only two major chemicals are left to make the refreshing, cleansing substance we know as toothpaste. The ingredients so far are fine for cleaning, but they wouldn't make much of the satisfying foam we have come to expect in the morning brushing.

10   To remedy that every toothpaste on the market has a big dollop of detergent added too. You've seen the suds detergent will make in a washing machine. The same substance added here will duplicate that inside the mouth. It's not particularly necessary, but it sells.

11   The only problem is that by itself this ingredient tastes, well, too like detergent. It's horribly bitter and harsh. The chalk put in toothpaste is pretty foul-tasting too for that matter. It's to get around that gustatory discomfort that the manufacturers put in the ingredient they tout perhaps the most of all. This is the flavoring, and it has to be strong. Double rectified peppermint oil is used—a flavorer so powerful that chemists know better than to sniff it in the raw state in the laboratory. Menthol crystals and saccharin or other sugar simulators are added to complete the camouflage operation.

12   Is that it? Chalk, water, paint, seaweed, anti-freeze, paraffin oil, detergent and peppermint? Not quite. A mix like that would be irresistible to the hundreds of thousands of individual bacteria lying on the surface of even an immaculately cleaned bathroom sink. They would get in, float in the water bubbles, ingest the ooze and paraffin, maybe even spray out enzymes to break down the chalk. The result would be an uninviting mess. The way manufacturers avoid that final

obstacle is by putting something in to kill the bacteria. Something good and strong is needed, something that will zap any accidentally intrudant bacteria into oblivion. And that something is formaldehyde—the disinfectant used in anatomy labs.

13   So it's chalk, water, paint, seaweed, anti-freeze, paraffin oil, detergent, peppermint, formaldehyde and fluoride (which can go some way towards preserving children's teeth)—that's the usual mixture raised to the mouth on the toothbrush for a fresh morning's clean. If it sounds too unfortunate, take heart. Studies show that thorough brushing with just plain water will often do as good a job.   ■

From David Bodanis, *The Secret House,* Simon & Schuster, New York, 1986, pp. 17–19. Reprinted by permission.

EXERCISES

Do not refer to the selection for Exercises A and B.

A.   DETERMINING THE MAIN IDEA AND PURPOSE
Choose the best answer.

1.   _____ The main idea of the selection is that (a) the toothpaste that we use every day contains many unappetizing ingredients, all of which are cleverly camouflaged; (b) the manufacture of toothpaste is a complicated and sophisticated process; (c) toothpaste is made from a combination of substances found in most households; (d) if we knew what really was in the toothpaste we use every day, we probably would stop using it.

2.   _____ With respect to the manufacture of toothpaste, the author's purpose is (a) to criticize; (b) to tell a story; (c) to describe the steps required to make toothpaste; (d) to analyze the ingredients.

B.   COMPREHENDING MAIN IDEAS
Choose the correct answer.

1.   _____ According to Bodanis, the primary ingredient in toothpaste is (a) chalk; (b) detergent; (c) peppermint flavorings; (d) ordinary tap water.

2.   _____ The chalk that is contained in toothpaste comes from the crushed remains of (a) blackboard chalk; (b) bones; (c) dead ocean creatures; (d) quarry rock.

3.   _____ Bodanis writes that tooth enamel (a) is easily subject to decay; (b) does not really need to be cleaned as often as we think; (c) is the hardest substance in the human body; (d) is easily damaged or scratched during brushing.

4.   _____ Titanium dioxide, the whitening substance contained in toothpaste, is also used (a) to make white paint white; (b) in laundry bleach; (c) to make blackboard chalk white; (d) in the manufacture of white paper.

5. _____ Adding seaweed, glycerine glycol, and paraffin oil makes toothpaste (a) effective in fighting tooth decay; (b) moist and smooth; (c) have a pleasant taste; (d) easier to squeeze from the tube.

6. _____ To kill any bacteria that might accidentally find their way into a toothpaste tube, manufacturers add (a) paint thinner; (b) very strong peppermint oil; (c) detergent; (d) formaldehyde.

COMPREHENSION SCORE

Score your answers for Exercises A and B as follows:

A. No. right _____ × 2 = _____

B. No. right _____ × 1 = _____

Total pts. from A and B _____ × 10 = _____%

You may refer to the selection for the remaining exercises.

C. DISTINGUISHING BETWEEN MAIN IDEAS AND SUPPORTING DETAILS

Label the following statements from the selection as follows: MI if the statement represents a *main idea* and SD if the statement represents a *supporting detail*.

1. _____ But what's in this toothpaste, so carefully being extruded out?

2. _____ Water mostly, 30 to 45 per cent in most brands: ordinary, everyday simple tap water.

3. _____ It's there because people like to have a big gob of toothpaste to spread on the brush, and water is the cheapest stuff there is when it comes to making big gobs.

4. _____ Dripping a bit from the tap onto your brush would cost virtually nothing; whipped in with the rest of the toothpaste the manufacturers can sell it at a neat and accountant-pleasing $2 per pound equivalent.

5. _____ Toothpaste manufacture is a very lucrative occupation.

D. MAKING INFERENCES

Choose the correct inference.

1. _____ From paragraph 2 we can infer that (a) toothpaste would be cheaper to manufacture if it didn't contain water; (b) accountants often advise businesses to begin manufacturing toothpaste; (c) toothpaste is a lucrative product because it does not require fancy packing or advertising; (d) toothpaste costs little to produce because its chief ingredient is water.

2. _____ Bodanis implies in paragraph 4 that the chalk particles in toothpaste (a) are so abrasive that they can actually damage tooth enamel; (b) are not as strong as tooth enamel; (c) are stronger than tooth enamel; (d) are not necessary for getting one's teeth clean.

3. _____ From paragraph 5 we can infer that (a) these large chalk particles ironically may create holes where bacteria can live, later causing decay; (b) the government should pass stricter legislation regulating the manufacture of toothpaste; (c) tooth enamel is virtually indestructible; (d) the chalk particles are completely effective in eliminating discoloration on the teeth.

4. _____ Look again at paragraph 6, from which we can infer that (a) the whitening agents in toothpaste really do make our teeth whiter; (b) the whitening agents in toothpaste do not really make our teeth whiter; (c) people should not be so concerned about having white teeth; (d) the whitening agents in toothpaste are harmful and should be prohibited.

5. _____ Paragraphs 10 and 11 strongly imply that (a) detergents in toothpaste do not work the same way they do in a washing machine; (b) consumers expect toothpaste to foam; (c) toothpaste doesn't work properly if it doesn't foam; (d) detergent is the only substance in toothpaste used to camouflage the appearance and taste.

6. _____ From the selection as a whole, we can infer that (a) the author refuses to use toothpaste himself; (b) we may think toothpaste is cleansing and refreshing, but these qualities are actually the result of a clever mix of chemicals and other ingredients; (c) we should stop using toothpaste; (d) toothpaste does more harm to our teeth than good.

E. **ANALYZING ORGANIZATION AND SEEING RELATIONSHIPS**
Choose the correct answer.

1. This selection has a clear beginning, middle, and end. Write the number of the paragraph where the body begins _____. Then write the number of the paragraph where the conclusion begins _____.

2. In this selection the author *analyzes* the contents of toothpaste, by breaking down and explaining each ingredient that goes into it. In your own words, explain the purpose of this analysis. _____

3. Look again at the first two sentences of paragraph 2. What is the relationship between them? (a) steps in a process; (b) cause and effect; (c) term and its definition; (d) general to specific; (e) contrast.

4. Find the irony in paragraph 5 and explain it in your own words.

5. From what Bodanis writes, what would you say are the two *main* concerns of toothpaste manufacturers? _____ and _____

6. _____ Consider again the first two sentences of paragraph 11. What is the relationship between them? (a) contrast; (b) steps in a process; (c) cause and effect; (d) general and specific.

7. _____ Look again at paragraph 11, in which Bodanis emphasizes that the flavoring in toothpaste (a) is there only to mask the foul-tasting substances like detergent and chalk; (b) is essential if the product is to do its job; (c) is probably dangerous to our health; (d) is present because Americans are overly concerned with the quality of their breath.

8. _____ Look through the selection again, this time paying careful attention to Bodanis's choice of words. Based on this, what is his tone, or emotional attitude, toward the topic? He is (a) neutral and objective, appropriate for a scientific article; (b) amusing, witty, and occasionally ironic; (c) hostile, sharply critical; (d) admiring, even laudatory.

F. DISTINGUISHING BETWEEN FACT AND OPINION

For each of the following statements from the selection, write F if the statement represents a factual statement that can be verified or O if the statement represents the writer's own subjective opinion.

1. _____ [Water] is there because people like to have a big gob of toothpaste to spread on the brush, and water is the cheapest stuff there is when it comes to making big gobs.

2. _____ Toothpaste manufacture is a very lucrative occupation.

3. _____ Second to water in quantity is chalk. . . . It is collected from the crushed remains of long-dead ocean creatures.

4. _____ The craters, slashes, and channels that the chalk tears into the teeth will also remove a certain amount of built-up yellow in the carnage, and it is for that polishing function that it's there.

5. _____ A bit of paraffin oil (the fuel that flickers in camping lamps) is pumped in with [the seaweed ooze] to keep the whole substance smooth.

6. _____ So it's chalk, water, paint, seaweed, anti-freeze, paraffin oil, detergent, peppermint, formaldehyde and fluoride (which can go some way towards preserving children's teeth)—that's the usual mixture raised to the mouth on the toothbrush for a fresh morning's clean.

G. UNDERSTANDING VOCABULARY

Choose the correct definition according to the context.

1. _____ like an *abrading* wheel [4]: (a) fast spinning; (b) grinding; (c) slow moving; (d) wearing away by friction.

2. _____ The *craters*, slashes, and channels [5]: (a) rivers; (b) pits; (c) mountains; (d) cuts.

3. _____ *unduly* enlarged chalk fragments [5]: (a) excessively; (b) inappropriately; (c) unbelievably; (d) undeniably.

4. _____ able to *bunker down* [5]: (a) bed down, rest; (b) lie in wait for a later attack; (c) fall back, retreat; (d) disappear from view.

5. _____ these *errant* super-chalk pieces [5]: (a) nearly invisible; (b) randomly distributed; (c) not conforming to the standard; (d) mistaken.

6. _____ even the *gouging* [6]: (a) polishing; (b) brushing; (c) digging holes into; (d) forcing.

7. _____ Few customers would *savor* [7]: (a) welcome; (b) find pleasure in; (c) attempt; (d) consider.

8. _____ that *gustatory* discomfort [11]: Pertaining to the sense of (a) hearing; (b) touch; (c) smell; (d) taste.

9. _____ other sugar *simulators* [11]: (a) enhancers; (b) substitutes; (c) imitations; (d) substances.

10. _____ *ingest* the ooze [12]: (a) inhabit; (b) eat; (c) multiply in; (d) enjoy.

H. USING VOCABULARY

From the following list of vocabulary words, choose a word that fits in each blank according to both the grammatical structure of the sentence and the context. Use each word in the list only once and add noun or verb endings (such as -s, -ing, or -ed) if necessary. (Note that there are more words than sentences.)

oblivion	irresistible	finicky
concoction	thrive	cavernous
abrasive	carnage	lucrative
virtually	quarry	rectified

1. To ensure that bacteria from the bathroom sink area don't multiply and _____ in the toothpaste, manufacturers add formaldehyde to zap these potentially harmful organisms into _____.

2. Consumers are _____ about toothpaste; they expect the product to taste pepperminty, to be foamy as they brush their teeth, and to be effective; little do they know what actually goes into this _____.

3. Because water costs _____ nothing in comparison to the other ingredients in toothpaste, toothpaste is a very _____ product to manufacture.

4. The chalk particles in toothpaste have an _____ ef-

fect on one's teeth; Bodanis compares this quality to a wheel grinding

down a boulder in a rock _____.

I. **TOPICS FOR WRITING OR DISCUSSION**

1. Paraphrase the information given in paragraph 2.

_____

_____

_____

_____

_____

2. Examine a product normally found in your household, for example, diet soda, laundry detergent, pudding mixes, or dog kibbles (or whatever else you can think of). Does knowing the ingredients it contains change your perception of the product? Explain.

25 ||||||

Lawrence W. Sherman
THE DEATH OF EUCLID LESLIE

Although the Wall Street Journal *is this country's best-known newspaper for business and financial affairs, each issue also contains feature articles and editorials on topics of general interest. The following piece appeared on the paper's editorial page. Lawrence Sherman, a professor of criminology at the University of Maryland, discusses the problem of random shootings of innocent bystanders, a phenomenon that began in America's cities during the 1980s.*

VOCABULARY PREVIEW

**WORD
ORIGINS**

PAROLE
Sherman writes in paragraph 11, "If bystander killers got life without *parole*, they wouldn't have another opportunity to shoot more innocents." Coming from the French word *parol*, meaning "word of honor," parole is a legal term referring to the early release of a prisoner, usually for good behavior, before his or her sentence has expired. The idea is that the parolee gives his word of honor that he will not get into trouble during the parole period.

RETALIATION
According to Sherman, few bystander killers get caught because "witnesses are understandably reluctant to risk *retaliation*." Meaning "to get back at" or "to return evil for evil," *retaliation* for a wrong was part of the Hebrew tradition. The Old Testament described the law of retaliation as *lex talionis*, or "an eye for an eye, a tooth for a tooth." The word *retaliate* came into English from Latin:

[*re-* ("back") + *tāliō* ("punishment in kind")]

The *lex talionis* principle still is followed to some degree in the American judicial system, as, for example, when a murderer is convicted of first-degree murder and is sentenced to death.

291

WORD PARTS

-FUL

This adjective suffix is attached to many English words, usually to convey the idea of fullness or abundance, as in *hopeful, joyful, doubtful,* or *playful.* Although this is the most common meaning, *-ful* has two other meanings: (1) "characterized by," as in *useful, shameful, wakeful,* or *harmful* or (2) "the amount that will fill," as in, for example, *armful, teaspoonful,* or *carful.*

Sometimes the meaning of the word cannot be determined directly from the root. See, for example, the adjective *watchful* in paragraph 3. "Full of watch," its literal meaning, doesn't make much sense; it actually means "tending to watch over," in other words, "alert."

-ER, -EST

The suffix *-er* is often added to nouns to indicate "one who does," as in *teacher, painter,* or *murderer.* It is also added to an adjective to make it comparative, that is, to indicate when only two things are being compared, as in *smaller, tougher,* and *stiffer* (see paragraphs 4, 10, and 11). When three or more things are compared, English words attach the suffix *-est,* as in *smallest, toughest,* or *stiffest.* Students often have difficulty with this rule because the language complicates the process by having another way to make adjectives comparative or superlative.

The rule is actually fairly simple. If the adjective is one or two syllables, we add the suffixes as described earlier. But if the adjective is three or more syllables, we add *more* for the comparative and *most* for the superlative. Thus, we say "the more interesting book" (if we are discussing only two) and "the most expensive restaurant" (if we are discussing all the restaurants in town).

WORD FAMILIES

HOMICIDE

You have already seen the suffix *-cide,* meaning "killing of", in selection 21. *Homicide,* used throughout the entire selection, means "the killing of a person," from the Latin:

[*homō-* ("man") + *cīdium* ("killing")]

Likewise, the Latin name for "human" is *Homo sapiens* ("thinking man"). But the Greek prefix *homo-* is different from the Latin, meaning "the same" or "like." It is used in many English words, among them:

homogeneous	composed of the same kind; similar; uniform
homogenize	to make homogeneous or uniform in consistency, especially used in milk
homonym	words that have the same sounds but that have different meanings
homosexuality	sexual desire for those of the same sex

LAWRENCE W. SHERMAN
THE DEATH OF EUCLID LESLIE

1   Euclid Leslie is dead. On June 17, the 55-year-old Milwaukee civic activist was killed by two of the 17 bullets fired from a semi-automatic handgun. The gun put an end to his long battle to get "drug houses" out of his neighborhood. But that's not why he died.

2   Mr. Lewis was an innocent bystander. In street slang, he was a "mushroom," someone who "popped up" in the line of fire. Standing with friends in front of their home when a gun battle started down the street, Mr. Lewis pushed everyone else inside. He was the last one still outside when two slugs hit his chest.

3   Milwaukee Police Lt. William Vogl called Mr. Lewis's death from stray bullets "an all-too-familiar story," which it has indeed become. So far this year, three of the 58 murder victims in Milwaukee have been innocent bystanders. Three-year-old Christopher Gray Jr. almost became the fourth fatality in May while playing under the watchful eyes of his grandmother, who was sitting on her front porch. Two men suddenly started shooting at each other, and hit Christopher three times in the crossfire.

4   Milwaukee is not alone. In 1988, at least 54 bystanders were shot in New York, 12 of them fatally. In Los Angeles, at least 77 people were shot, 21 of them fatally. Boston, Washington, Chattanooga, Tenn., and even smaller cities had bystander shootings in 1988.

5   But on one important point, Lt. Vogl is wrong. Bystander shootings are not a *long* familiar story. They appear to be a recent, rapidly growing and major problem for this country's underclass communities. Since there are no official statistics to test that theory, my colleagues and I went back through 1977 to examine newspaper indexes or data bases in four cities. We found very few published reports of bystanders shot anywhere except New York until about 1985, at which point the numbers began to explode.

6   In New York, for example, only 30 bystanders were reported shot in the three years from 1980 through 1982. By 1986–88, 128 bystanders were reported shot. In Los Angeles, the comparable numbers rose from zero to 105. In Boston, they rose from one to six, and in Washington from 0 to 11. While still a small part of the total homicide picture, the growth curve of bystander shootings seems as steep as the curve for AIDS. Yet unlike AIDS victims, there was very little the following residents of underclass neighborhoods could have done to avoid their deaths:

- A Washington woman washing dishes at her sink.
- A Los Angeles choir member singing in church.
- A New York woman sleeping in bed next to a baby.
- A Milwaukee girl walking home from a party.
- A New York college student eating in a crowded restaurant.

7   Residents of underclass communities have long suffered high homicide rates, but they could remain fairly safe by choosing their associates wisely. Now, their risk

of being murdered is increasingly a matter of being in the wrong place at the wrong time.

8   The random nature of such homicides makes them far more frightening than the more common murders among intimates and "business" associates. That conclusion is supported by the 1985 report of the National Survey of Crime Severity, which asked 50,000 Americans to rank the seriousness of over 100 types of crime. The survey did not ask about bystander shootings, since that type of crime was virtually unheard of when the survey was designed. But the survey did find that Americans ranked bystander murders from bombing as the most serious crime of all, far more serious than murder during rape or robbery.

9   Given those survey findings, our current policy seems perverse. Under some circumstances, prosecutors may treat bystander killings less severely than murder of intended targets. A prosecutor who finds a killer did not "intend" to harm a bystander can charge him with murder. But he can just as easily charge the killer with manslaughter or reckless endangerment. This wrongly puts shooting near crowds in the same category as driving too fast down a residential street.

10   It seems unlikely that tougher laws will deter drug dealers from shooting wildly near crowds. Many shooters take pride in taking risks. The greater the risk, the greater the "thrill."

11   But tougher laws would still be a good idea. If bystander killers got life without parole, they wouldn't have another opportunity to shoot more innocents. And even if prosecutors prefer plea-bargaining, stiffer sentences for bystander killings would give them a message to take this crime more seriously.

12   Criminal sentences mean little unless the killers get caught. Few of them are. Witnesses are understandably reluctant to risk retaliation. But if police could offer extra protection to witnesses in bystander killings, perhaps more witnesses would cooperate.

13   Giving special attention to bystander killers does not reduce the importance of intentional homicide. It just acknowledges the differences in causation. Most murders grow out of prior relationships in conflict, in which both parties may be equally blameworthy. But stranger murders in general, and bystander murders in particular, are like domestic terrorism: They destroy the assumption of safety that is the foundation of everyday life.

14   More Americans are dying from such domestic terrorism than from terrorism abroad. Legislators really interested in saving innocent victims should put by-stander killings high on their agendas. ■

From Lawrence W. Sherman, "The Death of Euclid Leslie," *Wall Street Journal*, July 10, 1989. Reprinted by permission.

EXERCISES

Do not refer to the selection for Exercises A and B.

A. DETERMINING THE MAIN IDEA AND PURPOSE
Choose the best answer.

1. _____ The main idea of the selection is that (a) urban violence, especially in underclass communities, is growing; (b) the victim of a bystander shooting was in the wrong place at the wrong time; (c) Euclid Leslie died because he lost the battle to get drug houses out of his neighborhood; (d) the laws concerning the murder of innocent bystanders need to be tougher than they currently are.

2. _____ With respect to the main idea, the author's purpose is (a) to tell a story; (b) to convince the reader to accept the author's opinion; (c) to explain the background of a social problem; (d) to present the findings of several major studies on crime.

B. COMPREHENDING MAIN IDEAS
Choose the correct answer.

1. Euclid Leslie, the civic activist who was the victim of random shooting, was called in street slang a "mushroom" because _____

   _____.

2. According to the author's research, the number of bystander shootings didn't increase sharply until the middle of which decade?

   _____

3. What makes bystander shootings more frightening than common murders by intimates or business associates is their _____.

4. When the National Survey of Crime Severity asked 50,000 Americans in 1985 to rank the most serious crime, they chose _____.

5. According to the author, few of these murderers are caught because witnesses _____.

6. Sherman says that shooting innocent bystanders is like domestic terrorism, because it destroys _____

   _____

   _____.

COMPREHENSION SCORE

Score your answers for Exercises A and B as follows:

A. No. right _____ × 2 = _____

B. No. right _____ × 1 = _____

Total pts. from A and B _____ × 10 = _____%

You may refer to the selection for the remaining exercises.

C.   RECOGNIZING SUPPORTING DETAILS

Place an X in the space for each statement that *directly* supports this main idea from the selection. **"[Bystander shootings] appear to be a recent, rapidly growing and major problem for this country's underclass communities."**

1.   _____ In New York, for example, only 30 bystanders were reported shot in the three years from 1980 through 1982.

2.   _____ By 1986–88, 128 bystanders were reported shot.

3.   _____ In Los Angeles, the comparable numbers rose from zero to 105.

4.   _____ In Boston, they rose from one to six, and in Washington from 0 to 11.

5.   _____ Residents of underclass communities have long suffered high homicide rates, but they could remain fairly safe by choosing their associates wisely.

6.   _____ Now, their risk of being murdered is increasingly a matter of being in the wrong place at the wrong time.

7.   _____ Under some circumstances, prosecutors may treat bystander killings less severely than murder of intended targets.

8.   _____ If bystander killers got life without parole, they wouldn't have another opportunity to shoot more innocents.

D.   MAKING INFERENCES

For each of these statements write Y (Yes) if the inference is an accurate one, N (No) if the inference is an inaccurate one, or CT (Can't Tell) if you do not have enough information to make an inference.

1.   _____ Lawrence Sherman, the author of this article, has himself witnessed a bystander shooting.

2.   _____ The person who killed Euclid Leslie, the Milwaukee civic activist, was probably associated with the neighborhood's drug houses.

3.   _____ The phenomenon of shooting innocent bystanders was almost unheard of before 1985.

4.   _____ Bystander shootings have been a problem in large cities like New York, Milwaukee, Washington, D.C., Boston, and Los Angeles, rather than in smaller cities.

5.   _____ Domestic terrorism commonly refers to airplane hijackings and bomb threats.

6.   _____ The increase in bystander shootings is a direct result of the increase in the nation's gang activity.

E.   ANALYZING ORGANIZATION AND SEEING RELATIONSHIPS

1. _____ The writer begins the article with Euclid Leslie's death because (a) he was a good friend of Leslie's; (b) he wants to begin with a single dramatic example to illustrate the problem; (c) Leslie was famous throughout the country and his death deserves special emphasis; (d) he wants to provide some general background for the subject.

2. _____ With regard to the phenomenon of bystander shootings, Sherman's main concern in this article seems to be (a) the reasons they have increased; (b) the means to prevent them; (c) the phenomenon itself; (d) the tragic consequences for underclass communities.

3. _____ To support the main idea, Sherman relies primarily on (a) statistics and examples from newspaper articles and surveys; (b) the testimony of authorities in the field; (c) his own opinion and observations; (d) the stories and experiences of firsthand witnesses and victims.

4. Besides the fact that they were the victims of random killings, what do the victims listed as evidence in paragraph 7 have in common?

_____

5. Look again at the first sentence of paragraph 8. Why does Sherman put quotation marks around the word "business" in the phrase "business associates." _____

6. _____ What is the relationship between the first sentence of paragraph 11 and the two sentences that follow it? (a) a key term and a definition of it; (b) steps in a process; (c) general idea and specific support; (d) contrast; (e) cause and effect.

7. _____ Read the first three sentences of paragraph 12 again. What is the relationship between the first two sentences and the third one? (a) steps in a process; (b) comparison; (c) contrast; (d) cause and effect; (e) general idea and specific support.

8. Paragraph 13 suggests a contrast. What is being contrasted?

_____ and _____

F.   DRAWING CONCLUSIONS
Mark an X before any of these statements that represent reasonable conclusions you can draw from the selection.

1. _____ Something is very wrong with our legal system if a bystander shooting that results in the death of an innocent person can be treated the same as involuntary manslaughter.

2. _____ More studies need to be done on the subject of bystander murders before any changes in the legal system should be made.

3. _____ Domestic terrorism affects all Americans equally, not just residents of the country's underclass communities.

4. _____ The law should probably be changed so that prosecutors would not be allowed to charge the murderer of an innocent bystander with reckless endangerment or manslaughter.

G.   UNDERSTANDING VOCABULARY
Choose the correct definition according to the context.

1. _____ death from *stray* bullets [paragraph 3]: (a) lost, misplaced; (b) isolated, alone; (c) going beyond a fixed course, errant; (d) unintended, accidental.

2. _____ The *random* nature of such homicides [8]: (a) occurring for a definite purpose; (b) frightening; (c) lacking uniformity; (d) haphazard, without reason.

3. _____ murders among *intimates* [8]: Those who (a) are casual acquaintances; (b) are well known to us; (c) are family relatives; (d) are in positions of authority.

4. _____ to *rank* the seriousness of over 100 types of crimes [8]: (a) classify in order; (b) evaluate, assess; (c) enumerate, list; (d) explain.

5. _____ that type of crime was *virtually* unheard of [8]: (a) occasionally; (b) obviously; (c) essentially; (d) purposefully.

6. _____ *prosecutors* may treat bystander killings [9]: Those who (a) defend criminals; (b) sit in judgment in a court of law; (c) conduct criminal proceedings against; (d) serve as legal advisors.

7. _____ *deter* drug dealers from shooting wildly [10]: (a) discourage through fear; (b) discover, detect; (c) cause to occur; (d) defend, guard against.

8. _____ reluctant to risk *retaliation* [12]: The process of (a) being responsible for; (b) paying back in the same way; (c) prejudging, deciding blame in advance; (d) being intimidated.

9. _____ It just *acknowledges* the differences [13]: (a) describes; (b) explains; (c) justifies; (d) recognizes.

10. _____ *prior* relationships in conflict [13]: (a) important, urgent; (b) bitter, divisive; (c) coming earlier in time; (d) destructive, dangerous.

H.   USING VOCABULARY
In parentheses before each sentence are some inflected forms of words from the selection. Study the context and the sentence. Then write the correct form in the space provided. Be sure to add appropriate endings like -s, -ed, or -ing if necessary.

1. *(fatality, fatal, fatally)*   In 1988 out of fifty-four bystander shootings in Milwaukee, twelve of them were _____.

2. (*watchfulness, watch, watchful, watchfully*)   A three-year-old boy in Milwaukee was almost another innocent victim despite the fact that he was playing under the _____ eyes of his grandmother.

3. (*perversion, perverseness, perverse, perversely*)   Sherman writes that there is a certain _____ in our laws when a murderer of an innocent person can be treated as leniently as a speeding driver.

4. (*endangerment, endanger, danger, dangerous, dangerously*)   Obviously, criminals who engage in random shootings _____ the lives of ordinary citizens; the author believes that charging them merely for reckless _____ is wrong.

5. (*causation, cause, causal*)   Different crimes have different _____: intentional murders should be treated differently from random murders of innocent people.

6. (*assumption, assume, assumable, assumably*)   We all have certain _____ about our daily life, one of which is that we expect to be safe going about our daily business.

I. TOPICS FOR WRITING OR DISCUSSION

1. Paraphrase the information presented in paragraph 13.

_____

_____

_____

_____

_____

2. Sherman maintains that stiffer crime rates would probably not deter other criminals from committing the same crimes. Other critics of the justice system say the opposite—if the punishments were meted out consistently and fairly, regardless of race, background, or quality of legal advice—that the crime rate would decrease. Do some research in the library on this matter, particularly in the area of first-degree murder, and come to a conclusion of your own.

26 ||||||

Sy Montgomery

CAN ANIMALS TALK?

In this article, Sy Montgomery, a free-lance writer from New Hampshire, discusses some of the research currently being conducted in California and Hawaii on marine mammals and language abilities.

VOCABULARY PREVIEW

**WORD
ORIGINS**

CRUCIAL

According to the article, Rocky, a female sea lion, can make distinctions between the relative sizes of objects. Montgomery calls this skill—the ability to classify and categorize—"*crucial* in the acquisition of language." Meaning "of supreme importance," *crucial* derives from the Latin word for cross, *crux*. This word also means "severe, difficult, or trying" and, more rarely, "cross-shaped." English has also retained the Latin word *crux*, referring to "a crucial or critical point."

RADICAL

Current research into animals' language abilities is "a *radical* departure from the bulk of previous language work with apes" (see paragraph 6). *Radical* comes from the Latin word *rādix*, meaning "root." *Radical* is a mathematical term (as in the radical sign) or, as it is in this context, an adjective meaning "favoring revolutionary changes." Thus, when we speak of a radical departure, for example, in politics, we mean something that is extreme, and when we use the radical sign in math, we find the square root.

**WORD
PARTS**

CONTRA-

In paragraph 7, one researcher is quoted as saying, "most of the cognitive abilities necessary for the comprehension of language are already present in most mammals and birds, *contrary* to current belief." Meaning "opposite in position," the root of this word, *contrā* ("against" in Latin) is also a common prefix, as you can see in these words:

contraband	material goods prohibited by law from being imported or exported [*contrā-* + *bando* ("proclamation")]
contraception	prevention of pregnancy
contradict	to speak against [*contrā-* + *dīcere* ("to speak")]
contravene	to act in opposition to, to oppose in an argument [*contrā-* + *venīre* ("to come")]
controversy	a lengthy dispute [*contrā-* + *vertere* ("to turn")]

WORD FAMILIES

COGNITIVE, RECOGNIZING

These two words (see paragraphs 7 and 25) both come from the same Latin root, *cognōscere* ("to know"). Specifically, *cognitive* is an adjective describing the mental process by which knowledge is acquired, and *recognize* means "to know again," from [*re-* ("again") + *cognōscere*]. In other words, we know something because we have seen it before. Here are some other words in this family:

cognizant (of)	fully informed, conscious
precognition	knowing something before it occurs
incognito	a person who does not want to be known or recognized, as in "traveling incognito" [*in-* ("not") + *cognōscere*]
cognoscenti	people with superior knowledge or taste; those who are "in the know"
connoisseur	a person with informed knowledge, especially in the arts, in matters of taste, or with food and wine

CREDIBILITY

One researcher mentioned in the article is Lou Herman, director of the Kewalo Basin Marine Mammal Laboratory in Honolulu. Montgomery writes in paragraph 14 that Herman's research "has given new scientific *credibility* to the field of animal-language experiments." Meaning "believability," *credibility* comes from the Latin root *crēdere* ("to believe"), which is the basis for many words in English:

creed	a statement of religious beliefs
incredible	describing something that is unbelievable
incredulous	describing someone who is disbelieving or skeptical
credit	belief or confidence in the truth of something; quality of being trustworthy; confidence in one's ability to repay money in the future
credulity	gullibility; a disposition to believe too readily

Other words you should know:

acoustic	[paragraph 15] pertaining to sound
semantics	[16] the study of the meaning of language
syntactic rules and syntax	[16] the rules governing the way words are put together to form phrases and sentences

Rubicon

[16] an allusion or reference to the river between Gaul and Italy crossed by Julius Caesar; here meaning a decisive or very important line of separation

synthesized

[24] several elements combined together; in
this case, synthesized sounds are used with
sea lions to represent objects, whereas hand
signals are used to represent actions

SY MONTGOMERY
CAN ANIMALS TALK?

1 With three hand gestures—each carrying its own meaning—Long Marine Laboratory researcher Ronald Schusterman signals "small ball fetch." This is old hat for
Rocky, a teenage female California sea lion that has been working with
Schusterman for more than five years. The sleek marine mammal reliably retrieves
the small ball—ignoring the large ball, the small bat and the black Clorox bottle,
also afloat in her tank—and brings it directly to the rubber-booted psychologist.

2 But then Schusterman tries a new experiment: He removes the small ball,
leaves the large ball in the tank and adds an even larger ball. Again he signals Rocky,
"small ball fetch."

3 Rocky begins to search the tank. Her dog-like head swivels, her liquid eyes
scan the water's surface. She circles. She even searches under water. No doubt about
it: The original small ball is not there. Finally, she appears to reach a decision about
Schusterman's odd request: She brings him the smaller of the two balls—the ball
that, only minutes before, had been the larger one.

4 Schusterman considers this an exciting finding. It demonstrates that not only
does Rocky understand the concept of "small," she also understands it in both
absolute and relative terms. And, he points out, "This kind of classification and
categorization is very crucial in the acquisition of language."

5 In studies here and in Honolulu, psychologists working with marine mammals are documenting language-like abilities that have never been so convincingly
demonstrated before.

6 Today, in a radical departure from the bulk of previous language work with
apes, these researchers are concentrating on probing the animals' language comprehension, rather than focusing on use of language. And by probing anew the
fundamental nature of language, learning and thinking, they are discovering that
humans and marine mammals appear to share remarkable similarities in the ways
that they gather, assimilate and make decisions about the information in their
world.

7 "I think we're living at a high point in terms of the study of these phenomena
in animals," Schusterman says. "I think (the observations) enable us to see a

powerful connection between ourselves and other animals." Perhaps, he ventures, most of the cognitive abilities necessary for the comprehension of language are already present in most mammals and birds, contrary to current belief.

8   In the 1960s and '70s, great apes were the stars of animal-language experiments. Koko, a female lowland gorilla, was tutored in American Sign Language. Her trainer, Penny Patterson, claimed the gorilla used this language to swear, joke, lie and even rhyme. Washoe, a female chimpanzee, used sign language to communicate her perceptions. Raised among humans, when she first saw another chimp and was asked what it was, she signed "black bug." A language-trained chimp named Lucy used known signs to create novel combinations to describe new objects: She called a watermelon a "candy-drink," citrus fruits "smell fruits." The first time she bit into a radish, she named it "hurt-cry food."

9   But these experiments were heavily criticized, and many were abandoned. As financial support disappeared and the powerful animals grew unmanageable, many of the apes ended up in zoos and medical laboratories.

10   While at times the apes seemed to have clearly understood what they were saying, often the humans could not. Critics pointed out that the apes often created mere "word salads." The apes could produce words, but how much did they understand about what they were saying? Could they process sentences using the grammatical features of a language?

11   By focusing instead on animals' understanding of language, the new studies can more carefully examine the thought processes and abilities that underlie language. It was difficult to understand what Koko was thinking when she signed "Please milk please me like drink apple bottle." But "if you issue a request and the animal carries it out," points out psychologist Lou Herman, "you can reasonably conclude that the animal understood it."

12   Child-language researchers have long believed that the ability to understand language and the ability to produce it evolve in the child as separate systems that are later integrated. (In fact, the two systems seem to be controlled by separate areas of the brain, as is indicated by the experience of certain stroke victims. Some, depending on the area of the brain affected, can understand language but not speak it; others can speak it but cannot understand it.)

13   In learning language, comprehension normally precedes and exceeds the actual production of language. And working with language comprehension provides a window into the language-like capabilities in which the animals are more likely to excel.

14   As director of Kewalo Basin Marine Mammal Laboratory in Honolulu, Herman was a pioneer of this approach. Many scientists agree that he has given new scientific credibility to the field of animal-language experiments.

15   For his work with dolphins, Herman devised two "dolphinized" artificial languages. One, created for Phoenix, a teenage female, was an acoustic language that referred to objects, actions and modifiers with computer-generated whistles played under water. The other, created for another female, Akeakamai (whose Hawaiian name means "lover of wisdom"), was composed of hand and arm gestures that the dolphin viewed in the air.

16   Language, Herman points out, is more than just the mental ability to pair symbols with their referents. There must also be syntactic rules—grammar—to

govern how the symbols are used and to dictate their meaning within a sentence. Semantics and syntax are the core attributes by which linguists define human language, separating language from other forms of communication. These features allow us to generate infinite meanings from a finite vocabulary—an ability long believed to be the Rubicon separating humans from animals.

17   In both of Herman's languages, the object word always precedes the action word. Modifiers always precede the object modified. In addition, Phoenix was taught a straightfoward grammar for the position of direct and indirect objects of a sentence: "Surfboard, take to Frisbee." Akeakamai was taught an inverse grammar: "To Frisbee, surfboard take."

18   With these rules and a vocabulary of about 50 "words," Herman has discovered that the dolphins will carry out the commands conveyed in literally thousands of sentences.

19   It is clear from the dolphins' performance, he says, that they understand the difference between the request. "To left Frisbee, right surfboard take," and "To right surfboard, left Frisbee take"—even though the two commands are made up of identical words.

20   Schusterman, who has obtained the same results with seals and sea lions, says this "tells us the animal is very sensitive to sequence. And we know that sequence is one of the important kinds of abilities in language."

21   This shows an ability that was obscured in the ape language experiments, which focused on production. For instance, to request an orange, the chimp Nim would typically signal a grammarless string of words: "Give orange me give eat orange me eat orange give me eat orange give me you."

22   Schusterman says he is not ready to call what his animals are doing "language." But then he admits that dolphins, sea lions, and seals "might not consider what we do swimming, until we can swim out 40 miles and stay under for 10 minutes." Herman is more confident. Although he stresses that the animals have not demonstrated the language comprehension abilities of even a young child, he concludes that "dolphins do take account of both the semantic and syntactic components of the sentences they receive when organizing a response."

23   Importantly, when known signals are combined in novel ways, the dolphins almost always understand them the very first time—an achievement so complex that linguist Noam Chomsky dubbed this, in humans, a "mysterious ability," central to language.

24   The animals spontaneously generalize meanings of symbols to apply beyond the contexts in which they were first taught. For instance, when Rocky was taught the symbol for "black," she could apply the concept of "blackness" to all the black items floating in her tank, and tell them apart from items that were white or gray. Schusterman has found that the seals and sea lions, like Herman's larger brained dolphins, are adept at processing symbols, whether they see them or hear them. Sprouts, a 2-year-old male harbor seal at the Santa Cruz lab, is now carrying out directions presented through "mixed media": Synthesized sounds signify objects, and hand signals represent actions.

25   And Herman's dolphins have proved so talented at recognizing and processing symbols that they will even correctly carry out gestural instructions signaled to them on a television screen viewed from an underwater window in their tank. They

can understand the symbols even when the image is degraded to show only two moving points of light where the trainer's white-gloved hands would be. Other work by Herman shows that dolphins can correctly report whether an object named by a trainer is present in the dolphin's tank. The dolphin responds by pressing one of two paddles to signal presence or absence.

26   Recent studies by Herman and research associate Palmer Morel-Samuels show that the dolphin brain appears to be similar to the human brain, in that complex instructions are processed faster by the left hemisphere, and simpler instructions by the right. Says Morel-Samuels: "Whatever the nature of this hemispheric specialization, it suggests that in the processing of information, humans and dolphins may be more alike than some people believe."   ■

From Sy Montgomery, "Can Animals Talk?" *San Francisco Chronicle*, "This World," August 26, 1990. Reprinted by permission.

EXERCISES

Do not refer to the selection for Exercises A and B.

A.   DETERMINING THE MAIN IDEA AND PURPOSE
Choose the best answer.

1.   _____ The main idea of the selection is that (a) researchers studying animals' linguistic ability now focus on their ability to use language; (b) marine mammals' ability to use and understand language is nearly as sophisticated as. humans; (c) the marine mammals have the same cognitive abilities and brain structure as humans do; (d) researchers working with marine mammals have discovered that they share remarkable similarities to humans in their ability to understand language and to process information.

2.   _____ With respect to the main idea, the author's purpose is (a) to present observations and conclusions based on his own research; (b) to summarize the findings and conclusions from current research; (c) to convince the reader to accept a controversial idea; (d) to explain the differences in research methods used to conduct animal-language experiments.

B.   COMPREHENDING MAIN IDEAS
Choose the correct answer.

1.   _____ What makes Rocky, the female California sea lion being studied in Santa Cruz, so remarkable is her ability (a) to distinguish between relative shapes of objects when they are changed; (b) to follow oral instructions; (c) to retrieve balls and Clorox bottles; (d) to respond so positively to praise.

2.   _____ According to Ronald Schusterman of the Long Marine Laboratory in Santa Cruz, (a) animals and birds will someday be taught to speak; (b)

current research is headed in the wrong direction; (c) cognitive abilities to comprehend language may be present in most mammals and birds; (d) more research needs to be done in the area of language acquisition and production.

3. _____ During the 1960s and 1970s, research with Koko, a female gorilla, and Lucy, a chimpanzee, showed that (a) experiments to teach apes language were a waste of time and money; (b) the apes could successfully be taught to speak, but that there was no point to it; (c) the apes could produce language, but it wasn't clear how much they actually understood; (d) the apes could quickly be taught American Sign Language, which allowed them to communicate with humans.

4. _____ Koko's signing of the sentence "Please milk please me like drink apple bottle" was cited as an example of (a) the confusion about the purpose of the experiments; (b) a "word salad" that the human researchers couldn't understand; (c) Koko's inability to understand what she herself was saying; (d) Koko's remarkable ability to ask for things in sign language.

5. _____ The experiments in Hawaii with dolphins' language ability show that, like humans, dolphins can (a) generate new sentences themselves from their stock of fifty vocabulary words; (b) understand and follow accurately many different oral commands; (c) understand several different languages, both real and artificial; (d) understand the meanings of an infinite number of sentences derived from a finite or limited set of vocabulary words.

6. _____ Research scientists now believe that dolphins, seals, and sea lions (a) can generalize meanings of symbols to apply in new situations; (b) have an inborn language ability that surpasses that of a young human child; (c) possess superior intelligence to that of humans; (d) will eventually provide the key to unlocking the secret of intelligence and language acquisition.

COMPREHENSION SCORE

Score your answers for Exercises A and B as follows:

A. No. right _____ × 2 = _____

B. No. right _____ × 1 = _____

Total pts. from A and B _____ × 10 = _____%

You may refer to the selection for the remaining exercises.

C. DISTINGUISHING BETWEEN MAIN IDEAS AND SUPPORTING DETAILS
Label the following statements from the selection as follows: MI if the statement represents a *main idea* and SD if the statement represents a *supporting detail.*

1. _____ In the 1960s and '70s, great apes were the stars of animal-language experiments.

2. _____ Koko, a female lowland gorilla, was tutored in American Sign Language.

3. _____ Her trainer, Penny Patterson, claimed the gorilla used this language to swear, joke, lie and even rhyme.

4. _____ Washoe, a female chimpanzee, used sign language to communicate her perceptions.

5. _____ Raised among humans, when she first saw another chimp and was asked what it was, she signed "black bug."

6. _____ A language-trained chimp named Lucy used known signs to create novel combinations to describe new objects: She called a watermelon a "candy-drink" and citrus fruits "smell fruits."

7. _____ The first time she bit into a radish, she named it "hurt-cry food."

8. _____ But these experiments were heavily criticized, and many were abandoned.

9. _____ As financial support disappeared and the powerful animals grew unmanageable, many of the apes ended up in zoos and medical laboratories.

10. _____ While at times the apes seemed to have clearly understood what they were saying, often the humans could not.

11. _____ Critics pointed out that the apes often created mere "word salads."

12. _____ The apes could produce words, but how much did they understand about what they were saying?

D. MAKING INFERENCES

For each of these statements write Y (Yes) if the inference is an accurate one, N (No) if the inference is an inaccurate one, or CT (Can't Tell) if you do not have enough information to make an inference.

1. _____ Rocky's ability to distinguish between the relative sizes of objects indicates that she processes information much the same way we do.

2. _____ Koko, Lucy, and Washoe ended up in medical laboratories as research subjects.

3. _____ Dolphins and other marine mammals are capable of language because they intuitively recognize that the sequence of words is crucial.

4. _____ Ape language experiments were flawed because they didn't take into account the importance of sequence or the rules of grammar.

5. _____ The string of words, "Give orange me give eat orange me eat or-

ange give me eat orange give me you," made sense in chimpanzee language because the subject was clearly asking for an orange, even if humans couldn't understand it.

6. _____ The author believes that the research done on apes' language abilities in the 1960s and 1970s was a waste of money.

7. _____ Researchers working with dolphins had to invent artificial languages because the dolphins cannot understand spoken commands.

8. _____ If Phoenix and Akeakamai, the dolphins who know artificial languages, were given the nonsense command, "to right left take Frisbee Surfboard," they would probably be confused and wouldn't know what to do.

9. _____ If dolphins could talk, they might tell us that what we call "swimming" is not really swimming.

10. _____ Studying marine mammals' language abilities is important primarily because it gives us clues about our own linguistic abilities—how we learn language and how our brains function.

E. ANALYZING ORGANIZATION AND SEEING RELATIONSHIPS
Choose the correct answer.

1. This article has a clear beginning, middle, and end. Write the number of the paragraph where the body begins _____. Then write the number of the paragraph where the conclusion begins _____.

2. _____ In summarizing the research on animals' language abilities, Montgomery is primarily interested in showing the reader that these experiments and their findings are (a) necessary; (b) fascinating; (c) ridiculous; (d) long overdue.

3. _____ Which method of development is used in the section comprising paragraphs 1–3? (a) steps in a process; (b) contrast; (c) cause and effect; (d) term and a definition; (e) main idea and supporting examples.

4. _____ Look again at the ideas discussed in the first sentence of paragraph 6. What is the relationship implied? (a) cause and effect; (b) steps in a process; (c) comparison—a discussion of similarities; (d) contrast—a discussion of differences.

5. _____ Now look at the ideas discussed in the *second* sentence of paragraph 6. What is the relationship implied? (a) cause and effect; (b) steps in a process; (c) comparison—a discussion of similarities; (d) contrast—a discussion of differences.

6. _____ What does the word "while" mean in the first sentence of paragraph 10? (a) still; (b) during that time; (c) at the same time; (d) although.

7. _____ With respect to the entire selection, the purpose of paragraphs 8–11

is (a) to ridicule early experiments done on animal language; (b) to show the change in direction research in animal language has taken; (c) to show the inherent cruelty of these early experiments; (d) to prove that the great apes have little ability to use or produce language.

8. _____ Paragraph 24 contains the transitional phrase "for instance," indicating that what follows is a (a) a conclusion; (b) a definition; (c) a supporting example; (d) a reason.

F. UNDERSTANDING VOCABULARY

Look through the paragraphs listed below and find a word that matches each definition. An example has been done for you.

Ex. the process of getting or learning [4–5]   _____acquisition_____

1. a pair of opposites, one meaning unqualified or unlimited; the other meaning compared to or interconnected with something else [4–5]   _____ and _____

2. showing an extreme change [6–7]   _____

3. studying, examining thoroughly [6–7]   _____

4. take in, absorb, incorporate [6–7]   _____

5. observable occurrences; also things that are remarkable [6–7]   _____

6. opposite in position [7–8]   _____

7. strikingly new and different [7–8]   _____

8. believability [14–16]   _____

9. distinctive features, qualities [14–16]   _____

10. reversed in order [16–17]   _____

11. named, described [23–24]   _____

12. highly skilled [23–24]   _____

G. USING VOCABULARY

In parentheses before each sentence are some inflected forms of words from the selection. Study the context and the sentence. Then write the correct form in the space provided. Be sure to add appropriate endings like -s, -ed, or -ing if necessary.

1. (*crux, crucial, crucially*)   According to one researcher quoted in the article, the ability to classify and categorize is _____ important in the acquisition of language.

2. (*acquisition, acquire, acquisitive, acquisitively*) _____ language is a fundamental process in humans.

3. (*document, documentation, documentary*)   Researchers in both California and Hawaii have _____ language-like abilities in marine mammals.

4. (*infinity, infinite, infinitely*)   One characteristic of human language ability is that we can generate an _____ number of expressions from a limited number of words.

5. (*obscurity, obscure, obscurely*)   The ape-language experiments _____ the importance of sequence in grammatical structures.

6. (*spontaneity, spontaneous, spontaneously*)   Dolphins can _____ generalize the meanings of symbols and apply them to new situations.

7. (*degradation, degrade, degradingly*)   Dolphins can carry out instructions even when the signals are _____ enough so that only two moving points of light are used to represent the trainers' white gloves.

8. (*synthesis, synthesize, synthetic, synthetically*)   Researchers have developed two _____ languages in training dolphins.

H.   TOPICS FOR WRITING OR DISCUSSION

1. Consider again the differences discussed in the article between the research done with apes and that done with marine mammals. Write a paragraph in which you summarize these differences, including both the ways in which the studies were conducted and their findings.

_____

_____

_____

_____

_____

_____

2. One criticism of the kind of research discussed in the article is that it costs an enormous amount of money that might be better spent trying to solve some of our serious social problems, for example, poverty, drug abuse, crime, and homelessness. Write a short paper in which you address this question and take a stand: Are experiments like those discussed in the article valuable or not?

27

J. E. Ferrell

WILD DOLPHINS OF MONKEY MIA

This selection is a good companion piece to the preceding selection. In it, J. E. Ferrell describes the behavior of wild dolphins in a remote area of Western Australia called Monkey Mia. Unlike their brothers and sisters in captivity, these dolphins exhibit some remarkable similarities with other mammals with large brains, namely chimpanzees, and humans, for that matter.

VOCABULARY PREVIEW

WORD ORIGINS

MURKY

At another wild dolphin community mentioned in the article, near Sarasota, Florida, scientists have observed the same behavior as researchers and visitors have at Monkey Mia. The difference, however, is that the Gulf water off Florida is *murky*, meaning in this context, "filled with sediment" or "not transparent." The noun *murk*, now labeled in the dictionary as archaic, comes from the Old English word for "darkness," *mirce*.

MYRIAD

You read about dolphins' ability to understand language in the preceding selection. However, scientists are also interested in studying the sounds dolphins make, here termed "vocalizations." In paragraph 22, Ferrell writes, "researchers are just beginning to analyze the *myriad* of sounds they've recorded."

Pronounced mîr'ē əd, this word, which means "a vast number," comes from the Greek word *myrias*, meaning "countless," or in its plural form *myrioi*, "ten thousand." Joseph Shipley writes in his *Dictionary of Word Origins*, "That the same word should mean 'countless' and 'ten thousand' to the ancients should not astonish us, who speak of the countless stars we see at night, when all the naked eye can behold on the clearest night is just over one thousand stars."

313

Captive, Captivity

Monkey Mia is a perfect environment for dolphins because they live freely, unlike those who live *captive,* or in *captivity* (see paragraphs 13 and 22). Meaning "forcibly confined or restrained," *captive* and the related noun form derive from Middle English *captif,* from Latin *captivus,* and ultimately from the Latin verb *capere,* "to seize." If a dolphin is held captive, then, it has been captured, literally moved by force to live in an aquarium or marine park.

Etiquette

Ferrell has some harsh things to say about people who come to Monkey Mia and behave badly; in his words, they "demonstrate a remarkable lack of dolphin *etiquette.*" This word, which means "prescribed social behavior," has an unusual etymology, which doesn't really explain today's usage. According to Charles Funk in *Thereby Hangs a Tale, etiquette* was a corruption of the French expression, "That's the ticket." But the *American Heritage Dictionary* includes another derivation: *etiquette* (French for "ticket") came from the Old French word *estiquiere* ("to attach"), which in turn came from Middle Dutch *steken.*

Ecstasy

The selection ends on a dramatic, touching note, and so as not to give the ending away, let us just say that the last word is *ecstasy.* Meaning "an emotion so intense that rational thought or self-control is impossible," this word is nearly a literal translation from its Greek root: [*ekstasis,* from *existanai,* "to displace, drive out of one's senses"].

WORD PARTS (REVIEW)

Telepathic

Although you have already met the word parts *tele-* and *pathy* (respectively in the sample reading selection at the beginning of the text and in selection 9), it doesn't hurt to review these common parts. In paragraph 25 one dolphin expert mentions that she must warn visitors to Monkey Mia not to expect a *telepathic* bond with dolphins. This word describes a kind of communication that occurs by scientifically unknown or mysterious means. *Tele-* means "distance" and the root *pathy* means "feeling." However, you can see that *telepathic* today doesn't have much connection with distance.

WORD FAMILIES

Terrain

Finally, we have the word *terrain,* which means simply "the character of land." The terrain of Monkey Mia is described in paragraph 9 as low and hummocky, meaning that it is covered with small ridges. *Terrain* is derived from the Latin word for "earth," *terra.* Here are some other words in this family:

subterranean	underground [*sub-* ("under") + *terra*]
terrestrial	pertaining to the earth and its inhabitants

territory	an area of land
terra cotta	ceramic clay used in pottery; from Italian, "cooked earth"
terra firma	solid ground; from Latin "firm land"
terrarium	a small enclosure or container for keeping plants or small animals

Other words you should know:

aboriginal	[8] describing people who are native or indigenous to an area
fission-fusion society	[16] this term describes the kind of society dolphins have: they live together in temporary groups (fusion), but the bonds aren't long-term (fission)
estrus	[19] the period of heat in animals

J. E. FERRELL

WILD DOLPHINS OF MONKEY MIA

1 A woman standing knee-deep in Australia's Shark Bay groped at a dolphin. She shrieked, yanking her arm high in the air. A deep red scratch curved from her thumb to her forearm. "It hurts," she said to a group of about 30 startled fellow waders.

2 Welcome to Monkey Mia, the only spot in the world where wild dolphins train humans. The first, and sometimes painful, lesson: Forget the friendly Flipper myth. In the wild, dolphins are mean, moody and ornery. They can also be winsome, funny and gentle. In short, they're as complex and mysterious as any mammal with a big brain.

3 The lessons that two-legged big-brained mammals are learning from these wild aquatic big-brained mammals have attracted a small group of U.S. primate biologists to this remote spot on the Australian west coast to watch how dolphins interact among each other. After several years of observing the dolphins, the researchers are doing their part to shatter the image of the happy-go-lucky ocean-going mammal. In addition, they have found striking similarities between the lives of dolphins and another species of big-brained mammal: chimpanzees.

4 Nearly every morning nine dolphins, part of a group estimated to number 200 in Shark Bay, swim to the beach at Monkey Mia to beg for fish from the people gathered in knee-deep water. The dolphins rush to newcomers, brace their pectoral fins against the sand as they lift their heads and tails out of the water, and open their mouths in a wide, endearing smile. If a person has no fish, some dolphins angrily shake their heads and swim away. Others linger to be stroked. As long as humans avoid the no-touch zones—blowhole, dorsal fin, head, tail or flippers—the dolphins may stay still for several moments.

5 Individual dolphins are recognizable by body scars and their dorsal fins,

which have been chipped and broken in unique patterns. Holey Fin, a female whose gray side is mottled with white splotches from sunburn she suffered when she beached herself, has frequented Monkey Mia for years. She also introduced her two daughters—Joy and Holly—to tourists, and recently brought in another tiny offspring who swims in tight circles out of tourists' reach while Mom asks for fish. Snubby, whose lower jaw protrudes significantly beyond his upper jaw, likes to have his belly rubbed. Rangers warn people away from Sickle Fin, the largest male at 7½ feet, who bites and whacks his tail at people who touch him. On the other hand, he loves babies, whose feet he nuzzles gently.

6   Dolphins began coming into the fishing camp in the 1960s, when anglers fed them fresh fish. Legend focuses on a dolphin named Charlie, who supposedly took the fish given to him to other dolphins too timid to come into shore.

7   "Whether Charlie was one dolphin or several dolphins isn't known," said Richard Connor, a University of Michigan graduate student who lives in a trailer at Monkey Mia, and has studied the dolphins off and on since 1982. More dolphins came in as more people fed them, and Monkey Mia evolved from a fishing camp to a tourist camp. Today six rangers staff a ranger station built three years ago. During Australian school holidays, up to 1,000 people visit daily; off season, 250.

8   If there were a spot at the end of the Earth, Monkey Mia would be it. Located about 500 miles north of Perth, near Hopeless Reach on the enormous Shark Bay that separates the Peron Peninsula from the Australian mainland, the remote beach is said to have derived its name from the aboriginal word for "home" (*mia*) and a rude term used by locals to describe Asian pearlers who camped there in the late 1800s.

9   Low, hummocky terrain—dotted with clay pans separated by sand ridges— stretches for hundreds of miles. A few short, sparse trees grow in the red dirt. Rainfall rarely exceeds seven inches a year. The heat is treacherous. An early explorer noted that the area was "abundant in flies." Little has changed in 150 years. A dozen flies hitch a ride on the backs of each resident or visiting human to drink their sweat.

10   The population is also sparse. The closest town, Denham, population 450, is 15 miles away. It attracts anglers, residents of the nearby smaller salt-farming town of Useless Loop, and tourists that drive or fly (by bush plane to a short dirt airstrip) by the thousands each year for the abundant aquatic life. Snapper, grouper, mackerel, mullet, bream, whiting, crabs, oysters, shark, rays and a large colony of dugong (a relative of the manatee) frequent the shallow grass-bottom bay.

11   The dolphins are by far the biggest attraction. Although the dolphin-human interactions can be fascinating, it is the dolphin-dolphin relationship that prompts scientists to stand knee deep in the water with the tourists. When they aren't asking for fish, the dolphins chase, play or fight with each other.

12   "It's a soap opera," said Connor of the dolphins' lives. "People are fascinated by the evolving social relationships portrayed in TV soap operas. That's very similar to Shark Bay. The dolphins have a very complex social relationship. I'm recording who's coming in with who, who's doing what with who, when Snubby and Nicky are having a tiff."

13   "It's a much richer environment for them," than the relatively sterile environments in which most captive dolphins live, said fellow University of Michigan

graduate student Rachel Smolker, who studies the dolphins' vocalization. "They know a tremendous number of dolphins, and events are constantly happening to change their feelings about each other." During their first trip to Monkey Mia, Connor and Smolker spent three months watching the dolphins from the beach. After he returned in 1986, Connor scraped together enough money to purchase a small skiff to follow the dolphins when they swam away.

14   "I found 60 to 70 dolphins who are regulars in the bay who are very tame," he said. "In part, that's due to their association with those who get fish. For example, if B. B. sees me, he comes over to the boat, and the others he's swimming with are more relaxed about having me around."

15   So far, the findings of the Shark Bay researchers corroborate nearly two decades of research done by Randy Wells off Sarasota, Florida, on a wild dolphin community that does not associate with humans. Although dolphins and chimpanzees are separated by 60 million years of evolution, scientists are interested in their similarities because both have evolved big brains while living in very different environments.

16   Both societies appear to be what scientists call a "fission-fusion" society, said Connor. A community of dolphins covers a home range. The females tend to stay in the middle, while the males roam the outside. Individuals join with others in temporary groups numbering two to five. Males tend to associate with males. Females are social butterflies that baby-sit for each other, or they are loners. Females and males don't form long-term bonds; they don't even associate much with each other, said Connor. The exception is the tight bond formed between mothers and offspring, which lasts three or four years.

17   Although Wells has been able to document who associates with whom, because the Gulf waters are so murky he has been less successful at seeing what identified dolphins are doing with one another. The clear waters of Shark Bay have enabled Connor and other scientists to watch the dolphins more closely, with fascinating results.

18   "We're seeing lots of social interaction that we haven't a clue if it's play or anger," said Connor, who is studying under University of Michigan primatologist Barbara Smuts. "We're listening to vocalization and beginning to tell. We can recognize a tiff, where two dolphins go head to head and shake their heads at each other. It doesn't seem like they fight too often, although they have lots of tooth rake marks over their bodies. They also hit each other with their tails."

19   Do the dolphins' clicks and whistles carry information as well as an emotional message? "A lot of their vocalizations are just expressions of their emotional state," said Smolker, who is studying the individual differences in dolphin sounds. "They are very emotional animals. But whether that's the only purpose of a certain sound, I don't know." As in some other species of mammals, sex has evolved into a recreational activity. Wells has reported males constantly mounting males, females not in estrus, even sailboats. Connor has watched "sexual herding," in which two or three males round up a female to keep her captive, sometimes for days. Because there's very little difference between the size of females and males, a lone male would have a difficult time dominating a female," he said, thus he suspects males capture females to mate with them.

20   Tiffs and fights alternate with flipper petting. "After a while you realize that

dolphins' flippers are like little hands," said Connor. "They do the petting because they want to maintain a social bond."

21   And what do dolphins do at night? No one knows, said Connor. They don't sleep, as humans know sleep, because they need to stay awake to breathe. "They sleep half their brain at a time," he said. "Russian scientists have reported that if you record brain waves in each side of the brain, you'll find a sleep wave in one side and not in the other, and then see a switch. Sometimes we'll see them with one eye closed near the shore, while they're waiting for fish."

22   "The things we've seen so far are very obvious and dramatic," said Connor. "We're just scratching the surface now." He and the other researchers still don't know such basics as the ratio of eating time to socializing. They don't understand some off-beat behaviors, such as why females carry sponges around so often. And because the dolphins make so many more different sounds than those in captivity, the researchers are just beginning to analyze the myriad of sounds they've recorded.

23   Because Connor and Smolker have spent hundreds of hours with the dolphins, they have developed strong relationships with them, as have the rangers and some of the people who live at Monkey Mia.

24   "They obviously come in to eat fish," said Connor. "But being intelligent social mammals, once there, if they're in the mood, they will play with you. You can have all sorts of fun with them." In the seaweed game, a dolphin will bring a human a piece of seaweed. The human's job is to run down the beach, trailing it in the water as one or more dolphins chase and snip the seaweed off with their teeth.

25   All who interact frequently with the dolphins have been bitten. But, according to Nikki Fryer, who works at the ranger station and has spent several years with the dolphins, it's nothing personal. She warns visitors against expecting some sort of telepathic bond with dolphins. "We humans tend to linger and cling," she said. "The dolphins are very detached. One day, they'll play with you. The next, they'll ignore you."

26   Smolker concurs. "Some people come here all starry-eyed thinking that the dolphins are from another planet and have come to Earth to teach humans how to love each other. A lot of those people get slapped in the face with reality. They see the dolphins bite each other. They see them being greedy about food. They're just being animals." On the other hand, some tourists who come to Monkey Mia demonstrate a remarkable lack of dolphin etiquette, said Connor. An "Ugly American" grabbed a dolphin by the fin, he said; an "Ugly Japanese" jumped on the back of a pregnant female; an "Ugly Australian" bitten by Sickle Fin is suing Monkey Mia.

27   "People need to deal with dolphins the way they deal with other people—act like you're talking to a person you don't know," said Connor. "With strangers, you don't put your fingers up their nose, grab their hair or pull their arm. There's a definite etiquette. It's the same with dolphins. It's a matter of treating them with respect."

28   When you treat dolphins with respect, the result can be pure magic. One quiet morning, Snubby slowly swam next to me. I opened my hands: No fish. No problem, he seemed to say, as he rolled on his side and looked at me with one huge sleepy eye. I touched his solid, smooth, rubber-like skin. He rolled a little further, to

expose more of his belly. As I stroked him gently, he bobbed in the tiny waves that lapped the shore, and closed one eye.

29   Dolphin nap. Human ecstasy.   ■

From J. E. Ferrell, "Wild Dolphins of Monkey Mia," *San Francisco Chronicle*, "This World," May 7, 1989. Reprinted by permission.

EXERCISES

Do not refer to the selection for Exercises A and B.

A.   DETERMINING THE MAIN IDEA AND PURPOSE
Choose the best answer.

1.   _____ The main idea of the selection is that (a) Monkey Mia is a richer environment for dolphins than the sterile environment most captive dolphins live in; (b) dolphins live in a complicated yet harmonious society, in which they form long-term bonds; (c) people who study wild dolphins and the way they interact have discovered that they exhibit the same complex and mysterious characteristics as other mammals with a big brain; (d) dolphin lovers are surprised to find that the dolphins of Monkey Mia behave quite differently from those animals kept in captivity.

2.   _____ With respect to the main idea, the author's purpose is (a) to tell a story; (b) to present his observations and those of dolphin researchers; (c) to offer emotional arguments about a controversial issue; (d) to contradict previously published reports of scientific research.

B.   COMPREHENDING MAIN IDEAS
Choose the correct answer.

1.   _____ Individual dolphins at Monkey Mia are recognizable by their (a) personality traits and behavior; (b) body scars and dorsal fins; (c) identification name bands that biologists have attached to them; (d) distinctive features on their heads and tails.

2.   _____ According to a legend, dolphins began coming to Monkey Mia, originally a fishing village, when a dolphin named Charlie (a) saved a fishing boat in trouble; (b) took the fish he begged to other dolphins who were too timid to come to shore; (c) performed tricks and other activities for fishermen and tourists; (d) led a large group of dolphins ashore each day who would beg for fish.

3.   _____ According to one researcher at Monkey Mia, the dolphins' lives are like a soap opera, meaning that (a) there is a large cast of characters, each with a specific role to play; (b) they are always having arguments; (c) their actions are melodramatic and sentimental; (d) they have complex social relationships that are always changing.

4. _____ Despite the fact that they evolved separately and lived in different environments, chimpanzees and dolphins have in common (a) the tendency to behave belligerently; (b) permanent mother-child bonds; (c) a large brain; (d) a repertoire of sounds.

5. _____ According to researchers, dolphins live in a "fission-fusion" society, which means that (a) adults live independently except to mate; (b) they form both short-term and long-term relationships; (c) they live together permanently, and strangers or outsiders are never allowed in; (d) females associate only with females, and males associate only with males.

6. _____ According to one researcher, people often come to Monkey Mia all starry-eyed about dolphins, and they get a rude shock when they see that (a) dolphins are always nasty and selfish; (b) dolphins do not observe a code of behavior; (c) some people are mean to dolphins; (d) dolphins behave pretty much like other animals, occasionally fighting and being greedy about food.

COMPREHENSIVE SCORE

Score your answers for Exercises A and B as follows:

A. No. right _____ × 2 = _____

B. No. right _____ × 1 = _____

Total pts. from A and B _____ × 10 = _____%

You may refer to the selection for the remaining exercises.

C. RECOGNIZING SUPPORTING DETAILS

Place an X in the space for each statement that *directly* supports this main idea from the selection. **"Both [dolphin] societies appear to be what scientists call a 'fission-fusion' society."**

1. _____ Although dolphins and chimpanzees are separated by 60 million years of evolution, scientists are interested in their similarities because both have evolved big brains while living in very different environments.

2. _____ A community of dolphins covers a home range.

3. _____ The females tend to stay in the middle, while the males roam the outside.

4. _____ Individuals join with others in temporary groups numbering two to five.

5. _____ Females and males don't form long-term bonds; they don't even associate much with each other.

6. _____ The clear waters of Shark Bay have enabled Connor and other scientists to watch the dolphins more closely, with fascinating results.

7. _____ "We're seeing lots of social interaction that we haven't a clue if it's play or anger," said Connor.

8. _____ "We can recognize a tiff, where two dolphins go head to head and shake their heads at each other."

9. _____ As in some other species of mammals, sex has evolved into a recreational activity.

10. _____ Wells [the researcher from Sarasota, Florida] has reported males constantly mounting males, females not in estrus, even sailboats.

D. MAKING INFERENCES
Choose the correct answer.

1. _____ Read paragraph 1 again. We can infer that the woman whom the dolphin scratched was (a) surprised; (b) angry; (c) confused; (d) outraged.

2. _____ From the information given in paragraphs 2 and 3, we can infer that (a) dolphins are more like chimpanzees than like humans; (b) dolphins and chimpanzees behave in similar ways because both have evolved large brains; (c) dolphins really are friendly and happy-go-lucky; (d) scientists were astonished to find that dolphins can be moody and ornery.

3. _____ From what Ferrell writes in paragraph 5, (a) it is ironic that Sickle Fin likes babies but not adults; (b) dolphins are fairly hard to tell apart; (c) only the female dolphins come to Monkey Mia's beach to beg for fish; (d) Holey Fin, the dolphin mother, wanted her baby to be petted by the assembled crowd.

4. _____ Ferrell strongly implies in paragraph 13 that dolphins who live in captivity (a) also display the same behavior traits as wild dolphins; (b) do not display the same behavior traits as wild dolphins; (c) should be freed; (d) are more appropriate for scientific research than wild dolphins.

5. _____ From the information provided in paragraph 16, we can accurately infer that (a) dolphins are monogamous; that is, they mate for life; (b) dolphin relationships have no fixed pattern; (c) both males and females can be loners, existing independent of the group; (d) dolphins migrate regularly and, therefore, have no fixed home territory.

6. _____ Paragraphs 15 and 17 imply that (a) Monkey Mia is a much better place to observe dolphins' behavior than Sarasota, Florida; (b) Monkey Mia allows interaction between dolphins and humans, while the area around Sarasota, Florida, does not; (c) Monkey Mia and Sarasota, Florida, are equally good places for observing dolphins; (d) tourists who are interested in observing dolphin behavior prefer Monkey Mia because it is so remote.

7. _____ We can accurately infer from paragraph 21 that (a) scientists still

are not sure exactly how dolphins sleep; (b) the Russian research experiments on dolphins' sleep habits were flawed; (c) dolphins and humans have similar brains, allowing them to sleep half a brain at a time; (d) dolphins can't sleep because they have to breathe.

8. _____ From the selection as a whole, we can infer that (a) the author is an expert in dolphin behavior; (b) Monkey Mia and Sarasota, Florida, are the only two places in the world where one can study dolphins in the wild; (c) dolphin behavior as observed by people at Monkey Mia has actually changed because of their interaction with humans; (d) dolphins are highly intelligent, social animals who are fascinating to study.

E. **ANALYZING ORGANIZATION AND SEEING RELATIONSHIPS**
Choose the correct answer.

1. _____ Ferrell begins the article with the short anecdote about the woman who was scratched by a dolphin because (a) it was the first thing he observed at Monkey Mia; (b) it illustrates well the idea that our image of dolphins as friendly Flippers is a myth; (c) the author thought it was funny; (d) it supports the main idea.

2. _____ The last sentence of paragraph 2 contains a transitional phrase, "in short," which means (a) in addition; (b) for example; (c) in brief; (d) in fact.

3. _____ What is the pattern of organization used in paragraph 4? (a) general to specific order; (b) specific to general order; (c) time or chronological order; (d) spatial or space order.

4. _____ The method of development used in paragraph 5 is (a) short examples; (b) comparison—a discussion of similarities; (c) contrast—a discussion of differences; (d) cause and effect; (e) analogy or imaginative comparison.

5. _____ In his description of the area around Monkey Mia in paragraphs 8 and 9, Ferrell emphasizes its (a) great beauty; (b) monotony and isolation; (c) scientific importance; (d) remoteness and bleakness.

6. _____ In addition to his own observations and experiences, Ferrell uses as support (a) summaries of scientific publications on dolphin behavior; (b) quotations and remarks from dolphin researchers and authorities; (c) testimony from tourists who have visited Monkey Mia; (d) his own subjective opinion.

7. _____ Read paragraph 16 again. In this paragraph Ferrell (a) defines a term that is likely to be unfamiliar to us; (b) explains the steps in a process; (c) compares and contrasts; (d) cites reasons.

8. _____ When Snubby allowed the author to stroke his belly gently while he took a nap, Ferrell felt (a) amused; (b) inferior; (c) elated; (d) astonished.

F.   UNDERSTANDING VOCABULARY

Look through the paragraphs listed below and find a word that matches each definition. An example has been done for you.

Ex.   stubborn and mean-spirited [2–3]   _____ornery_____

1.   charming, engaging [2–3]   _____

2.   be reluctant to leave, hang around [4 and 25]   _____

3.   covered with spots or streaks in different colors [4–5]   _____

4.   juts or sticks out [4–5]   _____

5.   petty quarrel [12, 18, and 20]   _____

6.   not stimulating, lacking in imagination [12–13]   _____

7.   confirm, attest to the truth of [15–16]   _____

8.   support a claim with evidence [17–18]   _____

9.   filled with sediment, unclear [17–18]   _____

10.   relation in degree between two things [22–23]   _____

11.   a vast number [22–23]   _____

12.   agrees, has the same opinion [25–26]   _____

G.   USING VOCABULARY

In parentheses before each sentence are some inflected forms of words from the selection. Study the context and the sentence. Then write the correct form in the space provided. Be sure to add appropriate endings like -s, -ed, or -ing if necessary.

1.   (*interaction, interact, interactive*)   By far, what was most interesting for the author about Monkey Mia was watching the dolphins _____ with each other.

2.   (*endearment, endear*)   When dolphins open their mouths wide, it looks as if they are smiling in an _____ way.

3.   (*sparseness, sparse, sparsely*)   The area around Monkey Mia is both remote and _____ populated.

4.   (*treachery, treacherousness, treacherous, treacherously*)   The climate in this part of western Australia is _____ hot.

5.   (*vocalization, vocalize, vocal*)   Scientists are only now beginning to study the large number of _____ wild dolphins make.

6. (*evolution, evolve, evolutionary*)   Researchers who observe dolphin behavior are most interested in their constantly _____ social relationships.

7. (*captivation, captivity, captivate, captive*)   Dolphins held in _____ apparently do not exhibit the same behavioral traits as those who live in the wild.

8. (*ecstasy, ecstatic, ecstatically*)   Ferrell felt _____ when Snubby allowed him to stroke his belly.

H.   TOPICS FOR WRITING OR DISCUSSION

1. In two or three sentences, summarize the information given in paragraphs 2 and 3.

2. We are apparently fascinated with dolphins and whales, perhaps because, like us, they are mammals, or perhaps because they make sounds that might represent a language. Think about this fascination, try to account for some other reasons to explain it, and come to some conclusions of your own.

28

Edward Iwata

BARBED-WIRE MEMORIES

In February 1942, President Roosevelt issued Executive Order 9066 authorizing the evacuation of West Coast Japanese Americans to ten different internment camps. In doing so, Roosevelt bowed to pressure from those who were convinced that Japanese Americans were committing treason by aiding Japan in its war effort. The Japanese were held in these camps until the war ended in 1945. "Barbed-Wire Memories" is the result of interviews that Edward Iwata, a newspaper reporter, conducted with his family, in which they described, for the first time to him, what life was like in Manzanar, the camp in the southern California desert where his family was sent.

VOCABULARY PREVIEW

**WORD
ORIGINS**

SCAPEGOATS

In paragraph 15 Iwata writes that the government ignored a study by one of its own agencies documenting that Japanese Americans were indeed loyal to the U.S. However, because wartime morale was low, "Japanese Americans became easy, visible *scapegoats*." This word occurs in the Old Testament book Leviticus, xvi, 10, which describes how Aaron, Moses's older brother, arbitrarily chose a live goat over whose head he confessed all the sins of the children of Israel. The goat was then sent to wander in the wilderness, where it symbolically carried their sins until the Day of Atonement. This day is celebrated as Yom Kippur, the holiest day in the Jewish religion.

Apparently, the biblical translator confused the Hebrew word in Leviticus, because the Hebrew word was incorrectly translated into English as "escape goat" (Hebrew for "goat that escapes"), which does not really make sense with respect to the biblical story. At any rate, a *scapegoat* refers to a person chosen at random to receive the punishment of an entire group.

GHETTO

Iwata writes (see paragraph 34) that before the war, Japanese Americans had been "*ghettoized* in Little Tokyos." The noun form *ghetto* (see also Selection 21) derives from Italian, and it originally referred to the section in European cities where Jews were restricted. In English, however, the word also means a section of a city, often a slum, that is occupied by members of a particular minority group, whether because of racial or ethnic segregation or economic circumstances. It is this second, more common, meaning that Iwata has in mind for the adjective form *ghettoized*.

WORD PARTS

-SHIP

Compared with the large number of Greek and Latin prefixes that are used in the English language, we have relatively few suffixes that show meaning. Typically, suffixes indicate grammatical function, as you have already seen in some of the preceding Vocabulary Preview sections.

One suffix, *-ship,* not only indicates that the root word is a noun, but also indicates three distinct meanings, as listed by the *American Heritage Dictionary:*

> (1) the quality or condition of, as in *friendship* or *scholarship;* (2) the status, rank, or office of, as in *professorship* or *authorship;* (3) the art or functioning of, as in *penmanship* or *leadership.*

This selection contains two words with this suffix: *citizenship* in paragraphs 3 and 12 and *relationship* in paragraph 5. Which of these three definitions do you think fits each word? After you consider the possibilities, look at the end of the Vocabulary Preview section for the answers.

MONO-

One reason Japanese Americans were distrusted and became scapegoats is their success as farmers, especially in California. Iwata mentions in paragraph 15 that "West Coast farmers were accusing 'treacherous' Japanese American farmers of stealing their land and *monopolizing* agriculture." Meaning "one" or "single," the verb *monopolize* can be broken down like this:

> [*mono-* + *pōlein* ("to sell") + *-ize* ("to make")]

This etymology is rather narrow, however, because today a monopoly need not be concerned only with selling. A monopoly means, essentially, "exclusive control by one group as a way of producing or selling a commodity." English has many other words beginning with this prefix, among them:

monochromatic	having only one color [*mono-* + *chrome* ("color")]
monophobia	excessive fear of being alone [*mono-* + *phobia* ("fear")]
monotheism	belief in one God [*mono-* + *the(o)* ("god") + *-ism* (noun suffix meaning "study of" or "belief in")]

monologue	a long speech made by one person [*mono-* + *(dia)logue*—from *legein* ("to talk")]
monotony	lack of variety, sameness
monogamy	custom of being married to one person at a time [*mono-* + *gamos* ("marriage")]

WORD FAMILIES

EVACUATION

Paragraph 11 uses three forms of this word: *evacuation* (noun), *evacuated* (verb), and *evacuees* (another noun meaning "those who are evacuated"). To *evacuate* in this context means to send inhabitants away from a particular area, as might be done, for example, when natural disasters like earthquakes or floods occur, or in wartime, as was the case here.

When this word is broken down from the Latin, you will see the root *vacuus* at the center: [*e-* ("out" or "from") + *vacuus* ("to empty") from *vacāre* ("to be empty")]. Besides the obvious words *vacation* and *vacuum*, here are two other relatives from the root *vacuus*:

| vacant | containing nothing, empty |
| vacuous | empty; also stupid or dull, as in "a *vacuous* remark" |

Answers: -ship in *citizenship* means the second usage. In *relationship*, the first usage governs.

EDWARD IWATA

BARBED-WIRE MEMORIES

> They had risen at dawn and boarded a yellow school bus in the cold, grey hours, determined to make the long pilgrimage to Manzanar, a place which no longer exists except in the memories of men's minds.
>
> —Edison T. Uno, 1929–1976

1   My parents rarely spoke about it, and I rarely asked them to.

2   Manzanar has emerged in recent years as a symbol of racial oppression for many Asian Americans, but it remained a painful subject in my family home.

3   For my parents, the very word "Manzanar" calls up shameful memories of a four-year period of their lives when their citizenship and patriotism, their simple belief in the unalienable goodness of America, meant nothing amid the flood of wartime racism.

4   I never asked them about it in any detail because a fearful part of me had refused to believe that my parents had been imprisoned by their own country. Their only crime was their color of skin and slant of eye.

5   It was as if too long a glimpse into their tragic past would shatter the rules of

our relationship, a relationship peculiar to Japanese people that relies heavily on unspoken but deeply understood values, emotions and expectations.

6   My knowledge of their stay in Manzanar was scant, a hazy mix of childhood tales and harmless anecdotes they told with a smile whenever their curious kids asked about "that camp in the desert."

7   Until recently, I did not know that my mother and father had met and fallen in love while behind barbed wires at Manzanar. I did not know that my grandmother cried daily the first two weeks in camp, hoping somehow that the tears would wash away the injustice of it all. I did not know that my mother's youngest brother, who later died in the Korean war, dreamed of fighting for the United States while he grew up as a little boy in Manzanar.

8   I learned all of this in what seems the most absurd, impersonal manner: while interviewing my parents for a newspaper story. In my role as a reporter, I was able for the first time to ask them about their concentration camp experience. In their roles as interview subjects, they spoke about Manzanar for the first time in an unashamed manner to their son.

9   Still, the going was shaky, the talk subdued.

10   "You don't have to write about all this, do you?" my father asked.

11   Japanese Americans learn the stark facts early: On February 19, 1942, President Roosevelt issued Executive Order 9066, sanctioning the evacuation of our people. One hundred ten thousand, most of them citizens, were evacuated to ten camps throughout the United States, where they would remain for four years. Most of the evacuees were given two to seven days to sell a lifetime of belongings, although some ministers and language instructors were arrested immediately with not even that much notice.

12   The sudden evacuation order shocked the Issei, the industrious first generation in this country, and the Nisei, their children. One Pismo Beach man shot himself in the head to spare his family from his shame. He was found clasping an honorary citizenship certificate from Monterey County, which thanked him for his "loyal and splendid service to the country in the Great World War."

13   In my own family, my uncle, a minister, was not even given the customary notice to evacuate. He was visited at his San Fernando home by two FBI agents at nine o'clock one evening. Within the hour, he was carted off, without his wife, for an undisclosed location.

14   Ironically, the evacuations came despite the fact that the only pre-war government study found a high degree of loyalty among Japanese Americans and concluded, "There is no Japanese 'problem' on the (West) Coast."

15   But the government ignored the study's findings. As historians later pointed out, U.S. wartime morale was sinking. West Coast farmers were accusing "treacherous" Japanese American farmers of stealing their land and monopolizing agriculture. Japanese Americans became easy, visible scapegoats. They looked like the enemy. They spoke and read Japanese. Their fishermen owned shortwave radios.

16   More important, they probably wouldn't fight back. The government was right; the Japanese Americans acquiesced without a struggle and filed silently into their prisons.

17   On her first trip to Manzanar in 1942, Komika Kunitomi stared bewilderedly

out the window as the bus rumbled past Mojave to the hastily constructed camp site eight miles north of Lone Pine.

18   "Look at the desert," she kept repeating in Japanese to her children. "They put us in the desert."

19   Grandma Kunitomi's husband had died in a truck accident five years earlier. Now she was forced to sell her car, her refrigerator and her grocery store in Los Angeles' Little Tokyo for a meager proportion of their original cost.

20   "Grandma was really upset, but she never talked about it," my mother explains softly. "You couldn't help it. It's war and there's nothing you can do about it."

21   As her sketchy recollections continue, my mother's long-buried thoughts grow fuller, more vivid.

22   The family was housed, she says, in wooden, tar-papered barracks that offered little protection against the furious desert winds. Seven people were crammed into a bare 12-foot by 20-foot room, with a hung sheet providing privacy for one of my aunts and her husband.

23   My mother worked for $19 a month as a secretary for the camp administrators: white secretaries there made $40. One of her sisters, Sue Kunitomi Embrey, edited the camp newspaper, The Manzanar Free Press.

24   During that same year, my father's parents lost their fruit and vegetable farm in the San Fernando Valley. The sudden evacuation to a prison camp, my father told me, "was hard to believe. It was kind of scary. I guess the older people, the parents, took it the worst.

25   "We went to Manzanar on red buses from Burbank. I thought, where are we coming to, all out in the desert with no trees. . . ."

26   My parents do not dwell on the bad parts. But they had to endure a riot, armed guards and fierce political factions—pro- and anti-American—among the residents. My mother recalls one night when her brother, a member of the camp's unarmed Japanese internal police, ripped off his uniform and dashed into their barrack, shouting, "I quit, I quit!"

27   A large mob of camp residents, fueled by rumors that the camp administrators were withholding sugar from them, had rioted. Two Japanese were shot and killed by white camp guards.

28   In one of those oppressive chapters of history that often give birth to monumental hope, the residents of Manzanar created a small, thriving, all-American town.

29   My parents prefer to talk about the high school, the social clubs and dances, the sports leagues they and their friends plunged into with enthusiasm.

30   They shined their shoes and fixed their hair so they could jitterbug to Glenn Miller and Tommy Dorsey records in the Manzanar gymnasium. They trudged through dust storms to see scratchy, black-and-white Laurel and Hardy movies. They watched boisterous baseball and basketball games that often erupted into bloody fights.

31   "You had fun there," my father says. "It was not a place to be, but you make the best of it."

32   Still versed in the old ways, the grandparents would sew, arrange flowers,

write haiku. They did not always understand that their children, prisoners of a crime not of their own making, were reacting to the camp in the only way they knew—as children of American culture.

33   As our family history unfolds, I see that every future move, every development, hinges on the war and evacuation in some way.

34   I find that the Japanese Americans, ghettoized in "Little Tokyos" before the war, embarked after their release on a lightning drive for middle-class respectibility unprecedented in U.S. immigration history. It was the surest way they could prove their worth again in the eyes of white America.

35   I learn that Manzanar, while a devastating psychological experience for my parents and their family, also gave them a mental resolve and emotional stamina that would surface again and again over the years.

36   The camp also spawned a curious brand of conservatism among Nisei that blends traditional Japanese values such as *enryo* (a quiet reserve) and *on* (loyalty and obligation) with America's aggressive, individualistic work ethic and love of material and cultural status.

37   The Sansei—my generation—are the children of that wartime tragedy. The spirit and gallantry, the shame and disillusionment of my parents and the Nisei are not lost upon us.

38   Forty years later, that legacy strengthens us, and it burdens us. . . .

39   Two weekends ago, under clear skies, a group of 250 Japanese Americans and a few blacks, whites and Hispanics journeyed from Los Angeles to what remains of the Manzanar site, a dusty one-mile-square swath of land in the heart of the Owens Valley.

40   In the shadow of Mt. Whitney, we drive slowly around the barbed-wire perimeter of the camp. We stop in the coolness of the barren stone guardhouses. We walk the deserted grounds littered with rusted pipes and rotting tree trunks.

41   At the western edge of Manzanar stands a large cemetery obelisk, its white marble form thrusting skyward. People throughout the warm day will circle it, touch it, as if its snowy mass and geometric purity could explain why they are there.

42   Etched deeply into the monument are stark black Japanese characters reading, "Rest Thy Soul." One by one, the pilgrims bow stiffly, adorning the broad base of the monument with roses and carnations and placing signs representing each of the ten concentration camps. Topaz. Heart Mountain. Tule Lake. One woman cries as she stumbled toward the monument. The cameras click, she averts her eyes. She bows quickly and hurries off, sharing a silent prayer with a harsh past that, on this day, rushes forward to greet her.

43   This is the first of the annual pilgrimages I am attending. Grandma Kunitomi made the trip frequently in the past; my mother accompanied her once. Their thoughts of the pilgrimage rarely came up in conversation.

44   Grandma often worried about the 200 people who died of illness and old age at Manzanar. Their spirits "are hot and thirsty in the desert," she would say, and she always left a cup or bowl of water for them in the cemetery.

45   Recently, I thumbed through a memorial book on Manzanar and chanced upon a picture of my grandmother and mother, their heads bowed low in prayer, their familiar faces taut and lined with sorrow. My eyes teared. An abstraction I had

only read about in historical texts abruptly, painfully, became a part of my own blood and family history.

46   I knew I had to speak with my parents about Manzanar. (I knew I had to make the pilgrimage myself.)   ∎

From Edward Iwata, "Barbed-Wire Memories," *San Francisco Chronicle*, 1982. Reprinted by permission.

EXERCISES

Do not refer to the selection for Exercises A and B.

A.   DETERMINING THE MAIN IDEA AND PURPOSE
Choose the best answer.

1.   _____ Which of the following sentences from the selection best represents the main idea? (a) "My parents rarely spoke about it, and I rarely asked them to"; (b) "Manzanar has emerged in recent years as a symbol of racial oppression for many Asian Americans, but it remained a painful subject in my family home"; (c) For my parents, the very word 'Manzanar' calls up shameful memories of a four-year period of their lives when their citizenship and patriotism, their simple belief in the unalienable goodness of America, meant nothing amid the flood of wartime racism"; (d) "Their only crime was their color of skin and slant of eye."

2.   _____ With respect to the main idea, the author's purpose is (a) to tell a story; (b) to inform and to recall a memory of a past event; (c) to criticize, to condemn; (d) to urge to action for the purposes of reform.

B.   COMPREHENDING MAIN IDEAS
Choose the correct answer.

1.   _____ According to the author, in his family home Manzanar (a) was a subject that was much discussed over the years; (b) symbolized a personal victory over governmental repression; (c) was a subject that was rarely discussed; (d) was a source of good memories where family relationships were cemented.

2.   _____ The author says that when President Roosevelt signed the evacuation order in 1942, the Japanese Americans were (a) shocked; (b) disbelieving; (c) not surprised; (d) rebellious.

3.   _____ According to a government study before the evacuation, (a) there was evidence that many Japanese Americans had been disloyal to the U.S.; (b) there was no way of proving whether Japanese Americans had been disloyal one way or another; (c) there was no evidence of Japanese American disloyalty; (d) the government was not sure about Japanese American loyalty and did not want to take any chances.

4.   _____ Manzanar, the camp where Iwata's family was interned, was located in California (a) in the mountains; (b) in the desert; (c) near the ocean; (d) in a metropolitan area.

5.   _____ According to Iwata, Manzanar grew to be just like (a) a Japanese American ghetto; (b) a prison where violence and brutality were everyday occurrences; (c) a center for strong anti-American sentiments; (d) a thriving, all-American town.

6.   _____ Iwata writes that he made the pilgrimage to Manzanar in order (a) to help refresh his memory about his childhood experiences; (b) to make a previously abstract idea real to him; (c) to report back to his parents on the conditions at Manzanar today; (d) to keep the memory of this example of racial oppression alive.

COMPREHENSION SCORE

Score your answers for Exercises A and B as follows:

A.   No. right _____ × 2 = _____

B.   No. right _____ × 1 = _____

Total pts. from A and B _____ × 10 = _____%

You may refer to the selection for the remaining exercises.

C.   DISTINGUISHING BETWEEN MAIN IDEAS AND SUPPORTING DETAILS

Label the following statements from the selection as follows: MI if the statement represents a *main idea* and SD if the statement represents a *supporting detail.*

1.   _____ In one of those oppressive chapters of history that often give birth to monumental hope, the residents of Manzanar created a small, thriving, all-American town.

2.   _____ My parents prefer to talk about the high school, the social clubs and dances, the sports leagues they and their friends plunged into with enthusiasm.

3.   _____ They shined their shoes and fixed their hair so they could jitterbug to Glenn Miller and Tommy Dorsey records in the Manzanar gymnasium.

4.   _____ They trudged through dust storms to see scratchy, black-and-white Laurel and Hardy movies.

5.   _____ They watched boisterous baseball and basketball games that often erupted into bloody fights.

6.   _____ "You had fun there," my father says. "It was not a place to be, but you make the best of it."

7.   _____ Still versed in the old ways, the grandparents would sew, arrange flowers, write haiku.

8. _____ They did not always understand that their children, prisoners of a crime not of their own making, were reacting to the camp in the only way they knew—as children of American culture.

D.   MAKING INFERENCES

For each of these statements write Y (Yes) if the inference is an accurate one, N (No) if the inference is an inaccurate one, or CT (Can't Tell) if you do not have enough information to make an inference.

1. _____ Iwata was afraid to bring up the subject of his family's experiences at Manzanar with his parents.

2. _____ For West Coast Japanese Americans, Executive Order 9066 was completely unexpected.

3. _____ President Roosevelt was not in favor of the evacuation order, but he signed it only because of political pressure from Congress and the media.

4. _____ Japanese American farmers had been prosperous before the evacuation order was signed.

5. _____ In general, after the evacuation order was signed ordering them to be transferred to internment camps, the evacuees were treated considerately.

6. _____ The United States was concerned that Japanese Americans would be more loyal to Japan, with whom it was at war, than to their adopted country.

7. _____ The accommodations at Manzanar were modern and comfortable.

8. _____ Japanese Americans who worked at Manzanar were discriminated against in their wages.

9. _____ Iwata's parents are justifiably bitter and even today harbor grudges about what they had to endure at Manzanar.

10. _____ Topaz, Heart Mountain, and Tule Lake are the names of other internment camps where Japanese Americans were sent.

11. _____ Japan was angry over the American decision to intern Japanese American citizens during the war.

12. _____ Our treatment of Japanese Americans during World War II remains a black mark in our history.

E.   DISTINGUISHING BETWEEN FACT AND OPINION

For each of the following statements from the selection, write F if the statement represents a factual statement that can be verified or O if the statement represents the writer's own subjective opinion.

1. _____ Manzanar has emerged in recent years as a symbol of racial oppression for many Asian Americans.

2. _____ I never asked [my family] about it in any detail because a fearful part of me had refused to believe that my parents had been imprisoned by their own country.

3. _____ On February 19, 1942, President Roosevelt issued Executive Order 9066, sanctioning the evacuation of our people.

4. _____ One hundred ten thousand, most of them citizens, were evacuated to ten camps throughout the United States, where they would remain for four years.

5. _____ As our family history unfolds, I see that every future move, every development, hinges on the war and evacuation in some way.

6. _____ The spirit and gallantry, the shame and disillusionment of my parents and the Nisei are not lost upon us.

F. **ANALYZING ORGANIZATION AND SEEING RELATIONSHIPS**
    Choose the best answer.

1. This selection has a clear beginning, middle, and end. Write the number of the paragraph where the body begins _____. Then write the number of the paragraph where the conclusion begins _____.

2. Look again at paragraph 6. What word suggests that Iwata's parents had never discussed their experiences openly before with their children?

    _____

3. _____ The purpose of paragraph 11 is (a) to provide a strong argument against the government's evacuation order; (b) to present the government's evidence against Japanese Americans; (c) to provide background information about the evacuation; (d) to relate a personal story connected with the evacuation.

4. _____ Read paragraph 15 again and consider the relationship between the first sentence and the remaining sentences. With respect to the evacuation order and the government's ignoring the study about Japanese American loyalty, the remaining sentences in the paragraph represent (a) steps in a process; (b) reasons; (c) conclusions; (d) definitions of key terms.

5. _____ Consider the two sentences in paragraph 16. What is the relationship between them? (a) general idea and specific example; (b) specific example and general idea; (c) reason and result; (d) term to be defined and its definition.

6. _____ In paragraphs 17–32, where Iwata describes his family's daily lives at Manzanar, he emphasizes their (a) rebelliousness and anger; (b) sullen, despondent attitude; (c) ability to have fun and to amuse themselves; (d) determination to make the best of a bad situation.

7. _____ Look again at paragraphs 33–38. In them, Iwata discusses (a) the negative effects of Manzanar; (b) the positive effects of Manzanar; (c)

both the negative and positive effects of Manzanar; (d) his own biased opinions.

8. _____ Iwata's attitude toward Manzanar and the internment of Japanese Americans during World War II can best be described as (a) critical; (b) neutral; (c) angry; (d) disbelieving.

G. UNDERSTANDING VOCABULARY
Choose the correct definition according to the context.

1. _____ the *unalienable* goodness of America [paragraph 3—usually spelled *inalienable*]: that which cannot be (a) taken away or transferred to another person; (b) examined in a court of law; (c) denied or rejected; (d) modified, changed.

2. _____ Japanese Americans learn the *stark* facts [11 and 42]: (a) incomprehensible; (b) blunt, grim; (c) true, verifiable; (d) awful, terrible.

3. _____ *sanctioning* the evacuation of our people [11]: (a) outlawing, prohibiting; (b) outlining, explaining in detail; (c) giving permission for or approval of; (d) establishing the punishment for.

4. _____ *Ironically,* the evacuations came despite [14]: Describing (a) a realistic situation; (b) the difference between what might be expected and what actually occurred; (c) a dramatic situation; (d) the tragic consequences of an event.

5. _____ U.S. wartime *morale* was sinking [15]: (a) mental condition, spirit; (b) sense of right and wrong; (c) physical courage; (d) success in battle.

6. _____ Japanese Americans became easy, visible *scapegoats* [15]: Those who (a) are suspected of committing a crime; (b) are guilty of a wrongdoing; (c) receive the punishment or blame for someone else; (d) receive scornful treatment from others.

7. _____ *acquiesced* without a struggle [16]: (a) endured a difficult period; (b) complied without protest; (c) resisted vigorously; (d) quietly dissented.

8. _____ to endure fierce political *factions* [26]: (a) anxieties, tensions; (b) internal conflicts within a larger group; (c) differences of opinions; (d) angry discussions, arguments.

9. _____ a small, *thriving* all-American town [28]: (a) prospering, growing vigorously; (b) closely knit, unified; (c) narrow-minded, intolerant; (d) well-organized, functional.

10. _____ *unprecedented* in U.S. immigration history [34]: (a) not having occurred before; (b) unrepresented; (c) not having been expected; (d) unparalleled, unmatched.

11. _____ a mental *resolve* and emotional stamina [35]: (a) attitude; (b) perspective; (c) energy; (d) determination.

12. _____ *spawned* a curious brand of conservatism [36]: (a) intensified, made worse; (b) produced, gave birth to; (c) changed, altered; (d) introduced, presented.

13. _____ America's aggressive, individualistic work *ethic* [36]: (a) a knowledge of right and wrong; (b) principle of good conduct; (c) dogmatic belief or principle; (d) attitude, behavior.

14. _____ The spirit and *gallantry* [37]: (a) drive, forcefulness; (b) chivalrous attention toward women; (c) showiness in appearance and manner; (d) nobility of action, courage.

15. _____ An *abstraction* I had only read about [45]: (a) memory; (b) experience; (c) emotion; (d) general idea.

H. USING VOCABULARY

In parentheses before each sentence are some inflected forms of words from the selection. Study the context and the sentence. Then write the correct form in the space provided. Be sure to add appropriate endings like -s, -ed, or -ing if necessary.

1. (*oppression, oppressor, oppressive, oppressively*) For Japanese Americans, Manzanar and the other internment camps have emerged in recent years

   as a symbol of racial _____.

2. (*absurdity, absurd, absurdly*) As _____ as it may seem, Iwata did not learn about Manzanar until he interviewed his own parents.

3. (*treachery, treacherous, treacherously*) West Coast farmers accused Japanese

   Americans of _____, saying that they were monopolizing agriculture.

4. (*monopoly, monopolizer, monopolize*) West Coast farmers claimed that Japanese Americans were creating a _____ in the agricultural industry.

5. (*meagerness, meager, meagerly*) When Japanese Americans were evacuated, they had to sell their belongings quickly, often at

   _____ prices compared to their worth.

6. (*aversion, avert, averse, aversely*) It is clear that until Iwata discussed the

   matter with his parents, they had an _____ to talking about their experiences in Manzanar.

7. (*evacuation, evacuee, evacuate*) One hundred ten thousand _____ were interned at ten camps throughout the United States.

8. (*industry, industriousness, industrious, industriously*) The first generation of

Japanese Americans, known as the Issei, were noted for their great

_____.

9. (*irony, ironic, ironically*)   Iwata finds it _____ that the
    government ignored its own study and ordered the evacuation despite
    the evidence it contained.

10. (*disillusionment, disillusion*)   The Issei and Nisei who were interned in the
    camps were _____ with the American government.

I.   TOPICS FOR WRITING OR DISCUSSION

1. Read paragraphs 14–16 again. Then write a short summary of the infor-
    mation contained in this section.

    _____

    _____

    _____

    _____

    _____

    _____

2. Iwata describes his family's life during their four years at Manzanar in
    the last years of World War II, information he learned only by inter-
    viewing his reluctant parents. Interview your own relatives about their
    wartime experiences (World War II, Korea, Vietnam, the Persian Gulf, or
    another conflict) and report on your findings.

5

Mastering Adult Reading Skills

You are now at the home stretch. By now you should be well equipped with a set of comprehension and analytical skills necessary for survival. These skills will carry over into your daily life, not just in college courses, but in your everyday reading as well—of magazines, news articles and editorials, and books. Once you become proficient and confident in your reading, there is no limit to what you can read. All that is left is continuing to acquire vocabulary words, something that you will do for the rest of your life.

Part 5 contains seven adult-level readings for you to practice the same skills you have been learning and refining through the course. As in Part 4, the selections contain both more complicated sentence structure and more difficult vocabulary words. It is fitting, therefore, to discuss some techniques for adding to your stock of reading vocabulary.

IMPROVING YOUR VOCABULARY

The best way to acquire new words is to read. Memorizing lists of words or studying vocabulary self-help books is really no substitute for reading. As you read, you will meet new words over and over, and eventually, you will intuitively figure out their meanings because of the several contexts in which you have seen them. This practice, however, takes years to accomplish. As a college student, you are confronted not only with large amounts of reading material, but also with material that will very likely contain many unfamiliar words, many of which you will need to look up in the dictionary if you are to understand what you are reading.

Before you turn to the dictionary, however, first, try to use context clues (see below) to determine the meanings of unfamiliar words. Then try to break the word down into its component parts—prefixes, roots, and suffixes—as you have learned in the Vocabulary Preview section. Most important, be sure you have an up-to-date dictionary. (For some recommendations, refer to the section on using the dictionary at the back of the book.) When you really cannot understand a word and its meaning seems to be crucial to your understanding the passage, look it up.

Begin writing down new words—especially those words that you have seen before but cannot readily define—in a vocabulary notebook or on a set of index cards. Last, develop an interest in and a curiosity about words. Play word games, like Dictionary, Boggle, Articulation, or Scrabble. Charles Funk and Richard Lederer both have published several humorous and readable books on words and their origins.

CONTEXT CLUES

The context is the way a word is used in a particular sentence or passage. Context clues are most useful when it is not essential to have a precise definition. Here are a series of short excerpts, one from each selection in Part 5. Read each one carefully; next, write your guess about the italicized word's meaning in the first blank, according to the way the word is used in the sentence or passage. Then look up the word in the dictionary to see how close your answer was and write the dictionary definition in the second blank.

Selection 29: William A. Nolen, "Deciding to Let Your Parents Die," Paragraphs 21–22:

For in the final analysis, after the doctor has fully explained what each choice will mean to the patient, it is often the family which is best qualified to say yes or no to prolonging life. There are some persons who, *anticipating* what may happen to them as they grow older, sign legal statements to the effect that, "If I am ever totally dependent on support systems for my life, I wish to have these supports discontinued."

_____   _____

Selection 30: Geoffrey C. Ward, "War on Polio," Paragraph 16:

Polio continued to be as *capricious* as it was crippling, settling lightly on the country one summer, storming through its cities the next. There were

13,624 cases in 1945, almost twice as many the next year, fewer than 11,000 in 1947, almost 28,000 in 1948, 42,033 in 1949.

Selection 31: Sarah Ferguson, "The Homeless: Us Against Them," Paragraphs 2–3:

It was neighborhood tolerance that allowed the encampment of homeless men and women to swell to a shantytown of more than 300 indigents last summer. But it was the rising outcry from neighbors who claimed that the homeless had "taken the park hostage" that forced the city to finally tear the mess down. Police raids on Tompkins Square Park over the past year, however, have done nothing to *abate* the flood of homeless people camped out in public spaces. Because, of course, the homeless keep coming back.

Selection 32: Dennis Meredith, "Day Care: The Nine-to-Five Dilemma," Paragraph 46:

"Children were not *randomly* assigned to the day-care programs in which we observed them," [Clarke-Stewart] points out. "Their parents deliberately selected these programs for them." Parents from more highly educated backgrounds may have chosen some programs because of the educational opportunities they offered.

Selection 33: Richard Bernstein, "A War of Words: Bilingual Education," Paragraph 20:

This class is the presumed end result of TBE—Transitional Bilingual Education—the program to teach children in their native languages while they master English. It illustrates another *tenet* of the bilingual philosophy: that once basic skills have been mastered, children can make the transition from their native language to English without losing ground.

Selection 34: Sue Hubbell, "The Vicksburg Ghost," Paragraph 2:

Promotion was what made Elvis Presley. In 1977, the year of his death, his likeness was more widely reproduced than any other save that of Mickey Mouse, and it has been reported that the news of his *demise* was greeted by one cynic with the words "Good career move!" According to Albert Goldman, the biographer who tells this story, Presley was by then a porky, aging, drug-befuddled Las Vegas entertainer and was getting to be a hard personality to promote.

Selection 35: Barbara Tuchman, "Mankind's Better Moments," Paragraph 17:

What of the founding of our own country, America? We take the *Mayflower* for granted—yet think of the boldness, the enterprise, the determined independence, the sheer *grit* it took to leave the known and set out across the sea for the unknown where no houses or food, no stores, no cleared land, no crops or livestock, none of the equipment or settlement of organized living awaited.

In this last section of the text, you will read about these topics and issues: the life-and-death decisions physicians and family members must often make about their terminally ill parents; the national fight, finally won by Jonas Salk, to find a cure for polio, a dreaded childhood crippling disease common during the 1940s and 1950s; the middle class's increased indifference and hostility to the growing number of homeless in American cities and the difficulty in finding solutions to the problem; the painful decision working parents must make about finding acceptable day care for their very young children; the growing controversy about the effectiveness of bilingual education in our schools; the recent phenomenon of Elvis Presley sightings, in this case, one that supposedly took place in a Vicksburg, Michigan, supermarket; and a recitation of some of mankind's most remarkable achievements, as a way of counteracting the pessimism so prevalent in the modern age.

29

William A. Nolen

DECIDING TO LET YOUR PARENTS DIE

In this article, William Nolen, a practicing physician for over thirty years, explores the dilemma that relatives of severely disabled and dying patients face: whether to provide extensive treatment which might prolong life or let nature take its course. He offers some practical solutions to a problem that will become common as technology offers more possibilities for prolonging our lives.

VOCABULARY PREVIEW

WORD ORIGINS

COMPASSION, COMPASSIONATE

Both the noun *compassion* and the adjective *compassionate* appear in the article (see paragraphs 19 and 26). The root *passion*, at the heart of both words, means either "any strong emotional feeling" or "an intense sexual desire." This context requires the first meaning. *Compassion* means "the deep feeling of sharing in another's suffering," and it is almost a direct translation from the original Latin root:

> [*com-* ("with") + *patī* ("to suffer"), from the Late Latin word *compassiō*]

Therefore, when people are *compassionate*, as Nolen suggests doctors must be when treating the terminally ill, they "suffer with" their patients by giving them help.

COLLABORATING

In paragraph 25 Nolen writes, "doctors and families have been quietly *collaborating* to decide what is best for the severely disabled and dying patient." This is one word in English that can have either a positive or a negative connotation, depending solely on the context. From the Latin, the word can be analyzed like this:

[*com-* ("together") + *labōrāre* ("to work")]

On the good side, to *collaborate* means the same as it does in Latin—"to work together in a joint effort." It is this definition that fits the context here. On the bad side, however, to *collaborate* can also mean "to cooperate so as to commit treason," as occurred for example, during World War II when some citizens of Nazi-occupied European nations collaborated with the enemy. This word, then, illustrates well the importance of paying attention to context.

**WORD
PARTS**

INTRA-, INTER-
One way to keep patients alive is to give them *intravenous* fluids (paragraph 9). Since the prefix *intra-* means "within" or "inside of," fluids given intravenously are given "inside the veins." However, to complicate matters, English also uses a similar Latin prefix, *inter-* ("between" or "among"), and the similarity in spelling and pronunciation makes the two prefixes easy to confuse.

What, then, is the difference, for example, between *interstate* and *intrastate* commerce? The preceding definitions will help you. *Interstate* commerce refers to trade *between* two or more states, whereas *intrastate* commerce refers to trade *inside* or *within* the same state. Another example comes from high school athletics. *Intramural* sports refers to athletic contests that take place "inside" or "within" a particular school (from the Latin root *murus* ["wall"], literally then, "inside the walls").

**WORD
FAMILIES**

DUCTS
The human body contains *ducts*, meaning passages or tubes carrying various fluids. As you have seen in earlier selections, most medical terms used in English come from either Latin or Greek. The Latin root *ductus* ("a leading") derives from the verb *dūcere* ("to lead"), so the medical connection is obvious. But English also has many common (nonmedical) words that derive from the root *dūcere* (for example, *duke*), although in a few of the following words, that connection may be hard to see:

abduct	to carry away by force; kidnap [*ab-* ("away") + *dūcere*]
induct	to install, admit, or call into service, as in "being *inducted* into the army"
induce	to lead or move by influence or persuasion, as in "trying to *induce* someone to stop smoking" or "to *induce* labor before childbirth"
reduce	the most common meaning in English is to lessen the amount of, as in "*reducing* the federal deficit" [*re-* ("back") + *dūcere*]
aqueduct	a passage carrying water [*aqua* ("water") + *dūcere*]

Other words you should know: *disinterested* (used in paragraph 27) means "not interested," "neutral," whereas *uninterested* means "not interested" in the sense of being bored.

WILLIAM A. NOLEN

DECIDING TO LET YOUR PARENTS DIE

1   Assume for a moment that your 90-year-old mother has recently suffered a stroke. She is right-handed, and her right arm and leg are now completely paralyzed. She can make sounds, but she can't make herself understood.

2   The condition has lasted two months and since there has been no sign of improvement, the doctor tells you she will never get appreciably better. Until this time your mother has always been an active, self-reliant person who lived on her own. Now she is completely dependent on others.

3   Recently she has been transferred from the hospital to a nursing home. An aide feeds her three times a day. The bill for keeping her there is $1500 a month. When you look into your mother's eyes, she seems to be pleading with you to help her in any way you can.

4   Next, your mother develops pneumonia—a frequent complication in stroke patients. The doctor then calls you, her only surviving relative.

5   "We can treat the pneumonia with penicillin and she'll probably get better in a week," he says. "When I say better, I mean she'll go on as she has—until she contracts pneumonia again. Or I can withhold the penicillin, in which case she'll probably die in three or four days. We can make those days comfortable by giving her pain killers and sedatives. Which course do you want me to follow?"

6   Tough question, isn't it? On the one hand, you cannot bear to see your once vivacious mother living the painful, limited life to which the stroke has condemned her. On the other hand, you hate to be the one to decide to let nature take its course. Until you are actually faced with such a decision, you probably won't be able to predict which course you would take.

7   I'll tell you which choice I would make. I'd say, "Don't give her any penicillin. Keep her as comfortable as possible and let's see what happens. Maybe she'll have the resistance to fight off the pneumonia on her own and if she doesn't, she'll die a peaceful death. I don't want to be responsible for condemning my mother to a living hell."

8   I can be decisive, with reasonable certainty, because I've gone down this road with patients many times. Recently I operated on an 87-year-old woman with a huge, unremovable cancer of the pancreas. There was nothing I could do surgically to relieve the obstruction to the bile ducts that this tumor had caused. She was an

intelligent woman, without any close relatives, and a couple of days after the operation I sat down with her and explained the situation.

9 "I can give you some anti-cancer drugs," I said, "but they will make you sick and cannot cure you. I can give you intravenous fluids every day, which will keep you nourished as your appetite slips away; the fluids might add a week or two to your life. Or I can do nothing except give you a vitamin pill, which may help you, and we can see what happens. Personally, I think I'd recommend that last choice. I'll keep you comfortable, and we'll see what happens."

10 The patient elected to follow my advice and died peacefully, pain free, three weeks later.

11 Sometimes such a clear-cut decision is more difficult to come by. Recently I had a patient who suffered a severe stroke. He was completely paralyzed and couldn't swallow anything. We gave him intravenous fluids for the first two weeks and then fed him through a tube which passed through his nose into his stomach.

12 After three weeks he was still completely comatose, and the nasogastric tube caused so much irritation that he had a constant, painful sore throat. I talked to his four grown children and told them I thought we should put a tube directly into his stomach through a small incision in his abdomen. Then we could transfer him to a nursing home where he could be fed without irritation.

13 The two sons and two daughters talked it over with their mother, but they couldn't agree. Two thought I should perform the operation, the other two wanted me to keep feeding him through the tube that went through his nose, even though it caused him pain. "Look," I explained, "there's a third alternative. I could remove the tube and just let him swallow whatever little bit he can. Chances are he won't live long, but he won't be in pain." I know I explained these alternatives to the children a dozen times but I could never get them all to agree. No one wanted to take the responsibility for permitting an operation, yet no one would give permission to stop feeding the patient entirely.

14 As a result, the poor man lingered for nearly three more months with a painful throat and frequent bleeding caused by ulcerations of the mouth. He died of overwhelming infection—a sad way to die.

15 So what should responsible persons do when confronted with the necessity of such an enormous decision?

16 I think they should listen very carefully to the doctor. Patients or families rarely have to make life-and-death decisions alone. The doctor has seen similar cases and can predict, with as much certainty as there ever is in medicine, what the results will be. The doctor has a legal and moral obligation to inform patient and family as best he can.

17 And it is my experience that if the doctor does his explaining job properly, family members are willing to accept his advice. I am not suggesting it is ever easy for a son or daughter to say, "Let my mother or father die," but there are times when this is the kindest thing one can do.

18 When there's division in the family, or when the doctor's explanation and advice don't satisfy one or more members of the family, then it's time to ask for a second opinion. If the second doctor agrees with the first, then family members have the peace of mind of knowing they've made a doubly-recommended decision. If the physicians differ, seek a third opinion.

19   Most doctors have compassion and will recognize when it is time to let a patient die with dignity. Certainly, now that we have advanced medical technology such as renal-dialysis machines, heart-lung machines and potent anti-cancer drugs, we've had to make the hard decisions more often.

20   However, to do this—to stop intravenous feedings or discontinue a life-support system—is a step most physicians are reluctant to take without the family's approval.

21   For in the final analysis, after the doctor has fully explained what each choice will mean to the patient, it is often the family which is best qualified to say yes or no to prolonging life.

22   There are some persons who, anticipating what may happen to them as they grow older, sign legal statements to the effect that, "If I am ever totally dependent on support systems for my life, I wish to have these supports discontinued." Or they may write, "If I ever have a stroke which deprives me of the ability to express myself and to dress and feed myself, I don't want any artificial means used to keep me alive."

23   Unfortunately, statements made when a person is in relatively good health are not entirely reliable. Consider that it is one thing when you are young and healthy to say you don't want to linger for years in a nursing home.

24   However, I visit these homes with some frequency, and I see long-term residents sitting in wheelchairs, watching television, eating dinner and playing cards despite strokes and partial paralyses. Once, when they were healthy, they couldn't imagine wanting to live this way. Now that it's the alternative to death, they accept it.

25   What it all comes down to is common sense. For the 30 years I have been a doctor, and for hundreds of years before that, doctors and families have been quietly collaborating to decide what is best for the severely disabled and dying patient.

26   In 95 percent of the cases the compassionate, reasonable decision can be made after appropriate discussion. In 5 percent of cases where such a decision cannot immediately be reached, the proper decision will become apparent after a few days or weeks of supportive treatment, observing the patient's progression or regression.

27   Let me sound one note of warning. Neither families nor doctors like to make life-death decisions. But there is no question that if either party insists on bringing in a third "disinterested" party (usually some representative of the state or legal profession), the process will not only be prolonged, in many instances it will be less well-reasoned and less compassionate.

28   What we are trying to avoid is disinterest; we want people who know the patient intimately and can put his or her interests first. If there's one place from which lawyers and government bureaucrats should be barred, it's from the bedside of critically ill patients. ■

From William A. Nolan, "Deciding to Let Your Parents Die." Reprinted by permission of Blassingame, McCauley, and Wood.

EXERCISES

Do not refer to the selection for Exercises A and B.

A.   DETERMINING THE MAIN IDEA AND PURPOSE
Choose the best answer.

1.   _____ The main idea of the article is that, in deciding the best treatment for a terminally ill patient, (a) new advanced medical technological equipment should be employed to prolong the patient's life for as long as possible; (b) the government should intervene by establishing clear and uniform guidelines for the doctor and the patient's family, to avoid confusion and mistakes; (c) decisions about proper medical care have become increasingly difficult for both doctor and family; (d) a reasonable and compassionate decision usually can be reached by the doctor and the patient's relatives working together.

2.   _____ With respect to the main idea, the author's purpose is (a) to summarize the results of recent medical research; (b) to explain a phenomenon by telling a story; (c) to persuade by presenting emotional arguments; (d) to inform by presenting a rational discussion of choices.

B.   COMPREHENDING MAIN IDEAS
Choose the correct answer.

1.   _____ According to Nolen, a frequent complication in stroke patients is that they develop (a) arthritis; (b) cancer; (c) pneumonia; (d) Alzheimer's disease.

2.   _____ In the case of terminally ill patients, Nolen most often suggests (a) immediate use of life-support systems; (b) penicillin or other antibiotics to fight infections; (c) giving intravenous fluids followed by surgery; (d) doing nothing beyond keeping the patient comfortable.

3.   _____ Sometimes doctors face immense difficulty dealing with the terminally ill, primarily because of (a) the inability of the patient's family to agree on the best way to proceed; (b) strict hospital regulations concerning the proper medical treatment; (c) government interference; (d) the patient's inability to afford good medical care.

4.   _____ Nolen's recommendation for the family members of a dying patient is (a) to ask for three or more opinions before reaching a decision; (b) to ask the patient what his or her wishes are and then to stick to them; (c) to listen very carefully to the doctor's explanation of the choices available and his or her recommendations; (d) to insist that the patient sign a statement rejecting life-support systems.

5.   _____ One reason that deciding how to treat terminally ill patients is harder today than ever before is (a) the constant threat of malpractice suits if the doctor makes the wrong decision; (b) confusion in medical circles over correct procedures; (c) the existence of life-prolonging medical technology; (d) the patient's own determination to cling to life, no matter how painful.

6.   _____ Nolen emphasizes that it would be a terrible mistake (a) not to take advantage of all available medical technology; (b) to bring in a disinterested third party to make decisions about treatment; (c) to ignore the patient's wishes, especially if he or she has signed a legal statement; (d) to allow doctors to commit euthanasia, by administering mercy-killing drugs.

COMPREHENSION SCORE

Score your answers for Exercises A and B as follows:

A.   No. right _____ × 2 = _____

B.   No. right _____ × 1 = _____

Total pts. from A and B _____ × 10 = _____%

You may refer to the selection for the remaining exercises.

C.   DISTINGUISHING BETWEEN MAIN IDEAS AND SUPPORTING DETAILS
Label the following statements adapted from the selection as follows: MI if the statement represents a *main idea* and SD if the statement represents a *supporting detail*.

1.   _____ Until people are actually faced with having to make a decision about treating a dying patient, they cannot predict what course they will take.

2.   _____ One choice is to let a stroke victim who develops pneumonia try to fight the infection without using antibiotics.

3.   _____ Sometimes a clear-cut way to deal with a terminally ill patient is hard to come by.

4.   _____ Because the family of one stroke victim could not agree on the best treatment, the patient developed severe infections and lingered painfully for three months.

5.   _____ When a doctor explains the patient's situation properly, family members are usually willing to accept the advice.

6.   _____ Some families cannot agree, and then a second or even a third opinion should be obtained.

7.   _____ After the doctor has fully explained what each choice will mean to

the patient, the family is often best qualified to decide whether to prolong life.

8. _____ Most doctors have compassion and recognize when it is time to let a patient die with dignity.

D. MAKING INFERENCES

For each of these statements write Y (Yes) if the inference is an accurate one, N (No) if the inference is an inaccurate one, or CT (Can't Tell) if you do not have enough information to make an inference.

1. _____ Nolen has extensive experience treating dying patients and counseling their families.

2. _____ Mercy killing, otherwise called euthanasia, should be made legal in this country.

3. _____ Twenty-five years ago the decision on how to proceed with terminally ill patients was much easier than it is today.

4. _____ The invention of life-saving medical technology simplifies the doctor's treatment of terminally ill patients.

5. _____ A doctor can always predict the exact outcome of a particular medical condition or illness.

6. _____ It is illegal in the U.S. to withhold food and water from patients, even terminally ill ones.

7. _____ The doctor has a legal and moral obligation to prolong a patient's life as long as possible, by whatever means are available, even at the risk of causing terrible suffering.

8. _____ Most doctors would prefer to avoid consulting a dying patient's family, since differences of opinion and conflict are inevitable.

9. _____ Doctors should never pay any attention to a legal statement that a patient has signed requesting that no artificial means be used to keep him or her alive.

10. _____ Often the best way to proceed when dealing with the terminally ill is to ask a neutral "third party," such as a state representative, to step in and decide on the best treatment.

E. ANALYZING ORGANIZATION AND SEEING RELATIONSHIPS

Choose the best answer.

1. _____ To support his ideas, Nolen relies primarily on (a) the most up-to-date scientific research on medical treatment; (b) the opinions of other

physicians; (c) examples of terminally ill patients he has treated; (d) highly emotional, biased statements.

2. _____ Look again at the information Nolen presents in the first five paragraphs, which (a) list symptoms, diagnosis, and treatment; (b) show the typical illnesses that older patients can develop; (c) show the reader what a wise decision he made; (d) provide a dramatic hypothetical case to show the dilemma a patient's family often has to face.

3. _____ Nolen discusses two cases in paragraphs 1–10 and later in 11–14 (a) to show us how different the two cases were; (b) to show us how similar the two cases were; (c) to prove the impossibility of reaching an intelligent decision that he could be comfortable with; (d) to show the kinds of obstacles that the relatives of patients can create.

4. Nolen organizes the article first by presenting some representative cases and then by offering suggestions. Where is the dividing line? That is, at what point in the article does Nolen begin to make these suggestions? Paragraph _____.

5. _____ The transitional phrase "as a result" in paragraph 14 signifies that what follows is (a) an example; (b) an explanation; (c) a conclusion; (d) a repetition for effect.

6. _____ Nolen begins paragraphs 16 and 17 with the phrases "I think" and "it is my experience," both of which suggest that what follows will be (a) his own personal opinion; (b) factual scientific information; (c) an emotional, prejudiced argument; (d) the thinking of physicians in general.

7. At the beginning of paragraph 20, Nolen writes, "However, to do this. . . . " What specific group of words does the pronoun "this" refer to? _____

8. _____ Read paragraphs 22–24 again. Concerning legal agreements drawn up by people who want to avoid being kept alive by life-support systems (actually, called living wills), we can accurately conclude that Nolen thinks that they (a) are a waste of time and money; (b) are useful guides for the patient's doctor and relatives; (c) should be required for every adult; (d) often do not represent the patient's true wishes after he or she becomes ill.

9. _____ Above all, Nolen emphasizes that his concern is for terminally ill patients (a) to have their last wishes fulfilled; (b) to be given every possible chance at living; (c) to die with dignity and without unnecessary pain; (d) to spare their families from having to make hard choices.

10. _____ With respect to terminally ill patients and their families, the author's attitude can best be described as (a) solemn, serious; (b) compassionate, sympathetic; (c) neutral, objective; (d) unsure, wishy-washy.

F.   UNDERSTANDING VOCABULARY
Choose the correct definition according to the context.

1. _____ she seems to be *pleading* with you [paragraph 3]: (a) appealing earnestly; (b) arguing persuasively; (c) addressing, speaking to; (d) suggesting a solution.

2. _____ your once *vivacious* mother [6]: (a) healthy; (b) spirited; (c) uncomplaining; (d) outspoken.

3. _____ to relieve the *obstruction* of the bile ducts [8]: (a) blockage; (b) infection; (c) disease; (d) painfulness.

4. _____ the bile *ducts* [8]: (a) producers; (b) tubes; (c) cavities; (d) cells.

5. _____ he was still completely *comatose* [12]: (a) indifferent; (b) anguished; (c) confused; (d) unconscious.

6. _____ *confronted* with the necessity [15]: (a) threatened; (b) confused; (c) faced with; (d) burdened.

7. _____ Most doctors have *compassion* [19]: (a) a feeling of helplessness; (b) strength, determination; (c) a feeling of shared suffering; (d) an intense feeling of desire.

8. _____ *potent* anticancer drugs [19]: (a) powerful; (b) revolutionary; (c) experimental; (d) unproven.

9. _____ some persons . . . *anticipating* what may happen [22]: (a) worrying about; (b) questioning; (c) eagerly awaiting; (d) foreseeing.

10. _____ doctors and families have been quietly *collaborating* [25]: (a) scheming, plotting together; (b) feuding, fighting; (c) exploring, investigating; (d) working together.

11. _____ bringing in a third *disinterested* party [27]: (a) uninformed, unknowledgeable; (b) impartial, unbiased; (c) indifferent, apathetic; (d) dishonest, corrupt.

12. _____ government bureaucrats should be *barred* [28]: (a) fired; (b) encouraged; (c) certified; (d) excluded.

G.   USING VOCABULARY
Write the correct inflected form of the base word in each of the following sentences. Refer to your dictionary if necessary.

1. (*assume*—use a noun)   Nolen begins with the _____ that the reader has a terminally ill mother.

2. (*reliant*—use a verb)   Until the hypothetical mother became ill, she had

   never _____ on anyone but herself.

3. (*condemning*—use a verb)   No one wants to be guilty of having

    _____ one's parent to a living hell.

4. (*paralyzed*—use a noun)   One stroke victim suffered from total

    _____.

5. (*responsible*—use an adverb)   Most relatives of terminally ill patients can

    act _____ with their doctor's advice.

6. (*obligation*—use a verb)   A doctor is legally and morally _____
    to inform the patient and the family as much as possible.

7. (*compassion*—use an adverb)   To deal with a patient's family

    _____, the doctor must present all their options.

8. (*dignity*—use an adjective)   A relatively painless, _____
    death is what most patients, relatives, and doctors hope for.

9. (*reliable*—use a verb)   Unfortunately, one cannot always _____
    on legal statements made when the patient was well.

10. (*collaborating*—use a noun)   _____ between doctors
    and the patient's family makes a difficult dilemma much easier.

H.   TOPICS FOR WRITING OR DISCUSSION

1. Here are some short passages from the article. Paraphrase them by re-
    writing and condensing each one in your own words in the space pro-
    vided.

    a. On the one hand, you cannot bear to see your once vivacious mother
    living the painful, limited life to which the stroke has condemned her.
    On the other hand, you hate to be the one to decide to let nature take
    its course. Until you are actually faced with such a decision, you prob-
    ably won't be able to predict which course you would take.

    _____

    _____

    _____

    _____

    b. So what should responsible persons do when confronted with the ne-
    cessity of such an enormous decision? I think they should listen very
    carefully to the doctor. Patients or families rarely have to make life-
    and-death decisions alone. The doctor has seen similar cases and can

predict, with as much certainty as there ever is in medicine, what the results will be. The doctor has a legal and moral obligation to inform patient and family as best he can.

_____

_____

_____

_____

c. Let me sound one note of warning. Neither families nor doctors like to make life-death decisions. But there is no question that if either party insists on bringing in a third "disinterested" party (usually some representative of the state or legal profession), the process will not only be prolonged, in many instances it will be less well-reasoned and less compassionate.

_____

_____

_____

_____

2. If appropriate, describe an experience you have had with health-care personnel (hospital administrator, physician, nurse, lab technician, etc.), whether positive or negative, that illustrates the state of health care in this country.

30

Geoffrey C. Ward

WAR ON POLIO

It is difficult for people born since the 1960s to understand how frightening the polio epidemic in the first half of the twentieth century was. Thousands of children were stricken, which often ended in their complete paralysis or in their having to exist in enormous breathing contraptions called iron lungs. This article, written by a former editor and columnist for American Heritage *magazine, describes the polio epidemic and the rush to find a cure for this crippling virus, which is now completely eradicated in the United States.*

VOCABULARY PREVIEW

WORD ORIGINS

QUACKS

Now that you have worked this far through the text, you know that the majority of English words come from Latin. However, occasionally there are some odd or unusual derivations. Such is the case with the word *quacks*, which has nothing to do with duck sounds as it is used in paragraph 3. Meaning "untrained people who pretend to have medical knowledge," *quacks* tried to peddle any number of worthless cures and preventive substances during the polio epidemic. It is a shortened form of the word *quacksalver*, which itself is derived from the Dutch word *quacsalven*, meaning "to cure with home remedies."

ATROPHIED

One characteristic of serious polio cases was, first, paralysis, and then *atrophy*, which occurred when affected limbs began to wither or waste away, becoming useless appendages. This word comes from the Greek: [*a-* ("without") + *trophe* ("nourishment")].

VIRULENCE

In paragraph 6 Ward writes, "Polio's growing *virulence* seems actually to have been a by-product of a new standard of middle-class cleanliness." When describing a disease or an epidemic, *virulence* means "the quality of being highly infective or deadly." Appropriately, this noun comes from the Latin *virus,* meaning literally "poison" or "slime."

PLACEBO

Pronounced plə sē' bō, *placebo* means in this context (see paragraph 25) "an inactive substance used as a control in a medical experiment." However, it can also refer to a harmless medication given merely to humor a patient, usually one who is complaining of imaginary illnesses. This word comes the Latin, "I please," from the verb *placēre,* "to please."

INOCULATED

In 1954 the first children were *inoculated* with the polio vaccine. This verb derives from Latin *inoculāre* and can be broken down like this: [*in* ("into") + *ocutus* ("eye" or "bud")]. The original term dealt with grafting, when a bud was inserted into a plant. Eventually it was used in medicine, meaning that the "bud" (actually the germ or virus) was implanted in a person, producing a mild case of the disease and making the patient immune from it.

WORD PARTS

INTERVENTION, INTERIM

This selection contains two words with the same Latin prefix: *inter-,* meaning "between." In paragraph 22 Ward quotes Jonas Salk as saying, "The polio vaccine came without any government intervention whatsoever." Today, vaccines and drugs are strictly regulated by various federal agencies; however, the polio vaccine was developed and tested independently, without government interference. Meaning "the process of coming between," *intervention* comes from this Latin word: [*inter-* ("between") + *venīre* ("to come")].

The Sabin oral live-virus vaccine was developed later, in 1962, and, according to the author, it largely superseded, or took the place of, the Salk vaccine. But, as Ward writes, "in the *interim,* Salk's discovery reduced the incidence of polio by 97 percent, saving thousands of lives and keeping hundreds of thousands more from being wrecked." The definition of *interim* is "an interval of time between one event and the next." Here are some other words using the prefix *inter-: international, interfaith, interracial, intermediary* ("one who serves as an agent between people"), and *interrupt* [*inter-* + *rumpere* ("to break")].

WORD FAMILIES

IMMOBILIZED

Strange it may seem to us now, probably because of the pervasive influence of television in our lives, few Americans knew that Franklin Roosevelt was himself a victim of polio, confined to a wheelchair, as Ward writes in paragraph 12, *immobilized* by the disease. This word can be broken down from the Latin like this: [*im-* ("not") + *mōbilus,* from *movere* ("to move") + *-ize* ("to make")]. Thus when one is *immobilized,* he or she cannot move. Besides the obvious words *movement* and *automobile,* here are some other words derived from the roots *mobilus* and *movere;*

mob	a large disorderly crowd (shortened form of *mobile*)
mobile	capable of moving; also a type of moving sculpture
automobile	a self-propelled vehicle
mobilize	to make capable of movement
motive	something that impels one to move or act

GEOFFREY C. WARD

WAR ON POLIO

1   Anyone who grew up in the 40's and early 50's remembers the panic that polio inspired each summer. Our Chicago newspaper carried two numbers on its front page each morning: The number of cases was printed in red, the number of deaths in black. Municipal swimming pools were closed. We were made to wash our hands incessantly, forbidden to go to the movies, to play with unknown children, to visit strange houses. Warm, wet, confined places were thought especially hazardous: I remember being stopped from entering the dark, close reptile house at the zoo.

2   "We were fighting ghosts," my mother remembers, and despite her best efforts, those ghosts caught up with me in July of 1950. A midnight headache and high fever and an inability to touch chin to chest sent me to the emergency room; I was diagnosed and admitted to the isolation ward within 10 minutes. At first my parents were told that I seemed to be one of the lucky ones: There would likely be no paralysis. Then, two days later, an evening call from the hospital: My parents had better come down; I was showing signs of crippling. The neurologist sat with them through that long night. "I *hate* this disease," he said again and again, holding my mother's hand, "I *hate* it." For all his training, he was no more able than she to halt the disease's steady progress from calves to thighs, hands to arms. For me, it stopped there, and I eventually regained full control of my hands and much of the strength in my legs, as well. But in others it went on to immobilize the body, or assault the lungs, so that patients were dependent for every breath on the great iron cocoon in which they were encased for what remained to them of life. That season more than 33,300 families went through some variant of our trauma.

3   Though polio is very old, the terror began for Americans in the summer of 1916, when 27,000 people in this country were affected. Seven thousand died, most of them children; there were 19,000 cases in New York City alone—2,448 of them fatal. No one knew what caused it. In Brooklyn, 215 stray cats were seized and destroyed on the chance that they might be responsible. Quacks flourished, peddling mustard plasters and the blood of frogs and oxen as preventives; a former

legislator was indicted for selling sacks of cedar shavings as a cure. When desperate New York parents tried to spirit their children out of town, they were turned back unless they had a certificate of good health signed by a physician. At small-town depots, hand-lettered signs greeted those who did manage to escape: NEW YORKERS KEEP OUT. WE SYMPATHIZE BUT WE HAVE CHILDREN.

4   The wife and children of the young Assistant Secretary of the Navy, Franklin D. Roosevelt, spent that summer on Campobello Island. From Washington, FDR begged Eleanor to *"please* kill all the flies"* that congregated on the sunny windows of their cottage for fear they might spread the dreaded virus. In a letter, Sara Delano Roosevelt, his ever-solicitous mother, offered him counsel on how best to greet his children at summer's end: "You ought not to kiss the children till you have washed & disinfected (nose & mouth especially) as it can be carried from people traveling."

5   In fact—although no one knew it then—the polio virus, too small for any available microscope to glimpse, was transmitted in fecal matter or secretions of the nose and throat. It traveled from the mouth to the stomach and then briefly into the bloodstream, overwhelming the body's natural antibodies and multiplying by the millions, before moving into the nerves and then the spinal cord. Nervous tissue died, limbs atrophied.

6   Polio's growing virulence seems actually to have been a by-product of a new standard of middle-class cleanliness. In the unsanitized past, infants and small children had been exposed to polio very early on, during a stage of life when paralysis was rare and lifelong immunity easily induced. But pristine bassinets, pure food and drink, freshly mopped floors had all helped to keep the virus at bay until children were older, when it was far more likely to cripple or kill.

7   Franklin Roosevelt's five children escaped polio. Their father did not. On August 10, 1921, FDR himself was stricken at Campobello. He was 39. The disease ravaged him more thoroughly than all but a few aides and family ever knew. Despite seven years spent trying to conquer its effects, he would never again be able to stand unaided, much less take a step. He could not even dress himself; his lower limbs, an examining physician wrote with pitiless candor, were utterly useless "flail legs."

8   A less resilient man would have admitted defeat, retreated inward. Instead, FDR, in characteristic fashion, sought a *solution* to polio; in 1924, he established what became the Warm Springs Foundation in Warm Springs, Ga. There, he hired physicians and therapists, converted a creaky resort into a treatment center, even conducted exercises in the pool himself.

9   In 1928, when FDR agreed to return to active politics and run for Governor of New York, his foundation was in financial trouble; by the time he was first inaugurated as President, in 1933, it was near bankruptcy. He was desperate to keep it from going under and to continue the battle against polio.

10   A series of President's Birthday Balls, held on January 30 of each year, seemed to provide the answer. These were gala evenings staged throughout the country to which celebrants paid to come, "Dancing So Others May Walk." All proceeds went to the cause. It's hard to imagine now how popular Franklin Roosevelt once was in Depression-wracked America; it evidently occurred to almost no one then how odd

it was in a Democracy for citizens to celebrate the birthday of their temporary sovereign.

11   The Birthday Balls provided enough funds both to keep Warm Springs functioning and to aid polio research elsewhere. But the President's popularity inevitably waned, and so did foundation funds. By 1937, the year of FDR's abortive purge of the Supreme Court, it was clear that the cause of polio must be separated from that of the increasingly controversial politician who had declared war upon it. In September, FDR announced the creation of an entirely independent National Foundation for Infantile Paralysis to "lead, direct, and unify the fight on every phase of this sickness." It was to begin functioning in January 1938. A new nonpartisan board of trustees was created to insure that Republicans could send in contributions without appearing also to support "That Man" in the White House.

12   FDR made his law partner, Basil O'Connor, president of the foundation without salary. The short, dapper, black-haired son of an Irish tinsmith, O'Connor was an able, self-made Wall Street lawyer—"one generation removed from servitude," he liked to boast—whose own weak eyes had interested him in medicine and earned him the nickname "Doc" while still at Harvard Law School. He was new at fund raising but willing to do almost anything to aid FDR. Roosevelt himself, not conquest of the disease that had immobilized him, was O'Connor's concern, at first. Later, victory over the disease would become something like an obsession.

13   First O'Connor needed to find a new way to raise funds. The radio comedian Eddie Cantor came up with the answer: On the night of the President's birthday, he suggested, all network programs originating in Hollywood would donate half a minute to the cause. "We could ask people to send their dimes directly to the President of the United States. Think what a thrill the people would get . . . and we could call it the March of Dimes!"

14   At first it seemed to be a disaster. "You fellows have ruined the President," a political aide told a foundation publicist the day after the first broadcast appeals. "All we've got is seventeen and a half dollars. The reporters are asking how much has come in. We're telling them we haven't had time to count it."

15   By the *next* morning, however, 30,000 envelopes had arrived at the White House and hundreds of thousands more waited in sacks at the Washington post office. The receipts that first year came to $1.8 million, and included 2,680,000 dimes—many of them wrapped in sticky tape or baked in cakes. The take rose with each succeeding campaign: By 1955, it fell just short of $67 million.

16   Polio continued to be as capricious as it was crippling, settling lightly on the country one summer, storming through its cities the next. There were 13,624 cases in 1945, almost twice as many the next year, fewer than 11,000 in 1947, almost 28,000 in 1948, 42,033 in 1949.

17   In 1950, "There were 16 or 17 new admissions every day," a nurse at Pittsburgh's Municipal Hospital remembered. "One of our resident physicians never went to bed for nights on end. . . . We nurses could never get home on time, either. To leave the place you had to pass a certain number of rooms, and you'd hear a child crying for someone to read his mail to him or for a drink of water or why can't he move, and you couldn't be cruel enough just to pass by. It was an atmosphere of

grief, terror, and helpless rage. It was horrible. I remember a high-school boy weeping because he was completely paralyzed and he couldn't move a hand to kill himself. I remember paralyzed women giving birth to normal babies in iron lungs. I remember a little girl who lay motionless for days with her eyes closed, and I can remember how we all cried when she went home. And I can remember how the staff used to kid Dr. Salk—kidding in earnest—telling him to hurry up and do something."

18   Dr. Jonas Edward Salk was hurrying as fast as he could, consonant with sound scientific caution. On July 12, 1950—just 14 days after I entered the hospital in Chicago, and 8 days before Bettyann O'Connor Culver, Basil O'Connor's own 30-year-old daughter, was stricken in Virginia—Salk formally applied to the foundation for a grant to undertake studies with the objective of developing a method for the prevention of paralytic poliomyelitis by immunologic means. The grant was awarded.

19   Jonas Salk, just 35 in 1950, was one of a score of researchers whose work was being underwritten by the foundation. He was an intensely private, serious, single-minded virologist from New York who had been doggedly performing the most painstaking and repetitious sort of laboratory work for three years—seeking to determine whether there were in fact three *and only three* types of polio virus. "My role in life," he decided early, "is to find out. If people do not like what I find out it is just too bad. They should then attack nature, not me."

20   In 1952, two scientists independently demonstrated that the polio virus did briefly enter the bloodstream, staying there long enough for antibodies to block it should they be present in large enough numbers. The question now became whether those antibodies would be placed there most effectively by a vaccine made from live or killed virus.

21   Dr. Albert Sabin of the University of Cincinnati was at work on a live vaccine to be administered by mouth, convinced that such a vaccine would be faster acting, longer, and more efficient to administer. Salk, now head of his own research institute and a team of some 50 equally dedicated researchers, was no less certain that a vaccine made from inactivated virus would be safer.

22   Salk moved faster: Working 18-hour days and following an infinitely painstaking series of steps, he and his team grew samples of all three strains of polio virus, killed them with formaldehyde and injected them, first into animals and then—in June of 1952 and in strict secrecy, to avoid the kind of press frenzy and subsequent letdown that followed every hint of progress—into human beings, 161 children living at the D. T. Watson Home for Crippled Children at Leetsdale, Pa. "I didn't have to ask permission of any regulatory groups," Salk has said. "They didn't exist at that time. The polio vaccine came without any government intervention whatsoever." Still, Salk remembered, he didn't "sleep well for two or three weeks," waiting for the results. None of the children whom Salk injected suffered any ill effects; more important, samples of their blood showed the presence of anti-polio antibodies. It was the worst polio summer in history: 57,879 people got the disease; 3,145 of them died.

23   Salk continued to test in the Pittsburgh area and continued to get good results—his own wife and three children were among his subjects. O'Connor's scientific advisers, impressed but cautious, recommended a 10-year field test.

Instead O'Connor gave the go-ahead for a crash one-year trial involving more than a million children.

24   There were last-minute hitches: The gossip columnist Walter Winchell warned over the radio that Salk's new vaccine "might be a killer"; an overeager press agent for the Parke-Davis pharmaceutical company trumpeted the company's role in manufacturing the vaccine, and—to Salk's fury—seemed to imply that the doctor was commercially connected with the firm; at least one batch of vaccine was falsely thought to have produced paralysis rather than immunity, in monkeys.

25   On April 26, 1954, the massive test began. Four hundred and forty thousand first-, second-, and third-graders in 217 communities were inoculated with the vaccine; another 210,000 were given placebo. It may have been the largest national mobilization short of war in our history, and government played no part in it. When it was suggested to O'Connor that professional clerks be hired to do the burdensome record-keeping, he refused; March of Dimes volunteers had proved over the past 17 years that they were *motivated*. "Our people will do it free and do it better," he believed. Twenty thousand doctors volunteered to help with the inoculations; so did 40,000 nurses, 220,000 civilians, 50,000 schoolteachers and a host of volunteer groups.

26   Just under a year later the announcement was made that the new vaccine was "safe, effective, and potent." Polio could be stopped.

27   The Federal Government licensed the vaccine's manufacture, and O'Connor provided funds to immunize nine million children the following year. (The Salk vaccine would largely be superseded after 1962 by the live-virus variety developed by Dr. Sabin, which could be administered by mouth and required no booster. But in the interim, Salk's discovery reduced the incidence of polio by 97 percent, saving thousands of lives and keeping hundreds of thousands more from being wrecked.)

28   Salk was an instant hero. He appeared on the cover of *TIME*, Marlon Brando asked to play him in the movies, he was offered a Broadway tickertape parade. The grateful citizens of Amarillo, Tex. sent him a brand-new automobile (he sold it and returned the money to Amarillo to buy more vaccine), and he was hideously embarrassed when two mothers recognized him on the New York subway and knelt to kiss his hands.

29   Ten days after the announcement of the vaccine's effectiveness, the reluctant hero was summoned for still another ceremony. Franklin Roosevelt was gone, of course; the announcement of Salk's triumph had come on the 10th anniversary of his death, a fact Basil O'Connor always stoutly insisted had been only a fortuitous coincidence. Dwight D. Eisenhower, who now occupied the White House, was no sentimentalist, but he was a fond grandfather. His own grandchildren had just been inoculated, and when he shook the scientist's hand there were tears in his eyes. "I have no words to thank you," he said, his voice breaking. "I am very, very happy."   ■

From Geoffrey C. Ward, "War On Polio," *Memories*, Spring 1988. Reprinted by permission of Diamandis Communications, Inc., 1515 Broadway, New York.

EXERCISES

Do not refer to the selection for Exercises A and B.

A.   DETERMINING THE MAIN IDEA AND PURPOSE
Choose the best answer.

1.   _____ The main idea of the selection is that (a) the development of the Salk and Sabin vaccines stopped the spread of polio, one of the most serious diseases to affect people in this country; (b) the spread of polio in the first half of this century was the result of improved standards of cleanliness; (c) polio is caused by a microscopic virus that overwhelms the body's natural antibodies, eventually causing paralysis and atrophy; (d) Franklin Roosevelt's own experience with polio was the decisive force behind the push to find a cure.

2.   _____ With respect to the main idea, the author's purpose is (a) to discuss and examine the causes and effects of a disease; (b) to trace the steps in the progression of a disease; (c) to argue in favor of a controversial opinion; (d) to summarize scientific research and evidence.

B.   COMPREHENDING MAIN IDEAS
Choose the correct answer.

1.   _____ When the author was a child, it was thought that the polio virus was especially contagious in (a) movie theaters; (b) warm, wet, and confined spaces; (c) the large animal cages in zoos; (d) public swimming pools and lakes.

2.   _____ When polio reached epidemic proportions, sanitary conditions were better than they had previously been, and (a) children were not as susceptible to diseases; (b) children had, therefore, not built up a lifelong immunity; (c) polio was virtually unknown; (d) there was no interest in finding a cure.

3.   _____ Franklin Roosevelt, himself a victim of polio, first founded the Warm Springs Foundation in Georgia, and then later, to keep it financially solvent, began a series of fund-raising (a) dance marathons; (b) fireside chats; (c) auctions; (d) birthday balls.

4.   _____ The author emphasizes that polio was a terrifying disease not only because it could cause permanent crippling, but also because (a) it appeared to strike its victims randomly and capriciously; (b) the government was uninterested in committing funds for research into a cure; (c) it affected adults more than children; (d) if one child contracted polio, the entire family was at risk.

5.   _____ To test the results of his inactivated polio virus, Dr. Jonas Salk injected first animals and then (a) the fifty researchers who worked with

him; (b) inmates from a nearby prison; (c) himself and his own family; (d) 161 crippled children.

6.   _____ The author emphasizes that the war against polio was won largely without (a) the government's intervention; (b) President Roosevelt's influence; (c) behind-the-scenes research by pharmaceutical companies; (d) the public's financial support.

COMPREHENSION SCORE

Score your answers for Exercises A and B as follows:

A.   No. right _____ × 2 = _____

B.   No. right _____ × 1 = _____

Total pts. from A and B _____ × 10 = _____%

You may refer to the selection for the remaining exercises.

C.   DISTINGUISHING BETWEEN MAIN IDEAS AND SUPPORTING DETAILS

Label the following statements from the selection as follows: MI if the statement represents a *main idea* and SD if the statement represents a *supporting detail*.

1.   _____ Polio continued to be as capricious as it was crippling, settling lightly on the country one summer, storming through its cities the next.

2.   _____ There were 13,624 cases in 1945, almost twice as many the next year, fewer than 11,000 in 1947, almost 28,000 in 1948, 42,033 in 1949.

3.   _____ In 1950, "There were 16 or 17 new admissions every day," a nurse at Pittsburgh's Municipal Hospital remembered.

4.   _____ "One of our resident physicians never went to bed for nights on end. . . . We nurses could never get home on time, either."

5.   _____ "To leave the place you had to pass a certain number of rooms, and you'd hear a child crying for someone to read his mail to him or for a drink of water or why can't he move, and you couldn't be cruel enough just to pass by."

6.   _____ "It was an atmosphere of grief, terror, and helpless rage."

7.   _____ "I remember a high-school boy weeping because he was completely paralyzed and he couldn't move a hand to kill himself."

8.   _____ "I remember paralyzed women giving birth to normal babies in iron lungs."

9.   _____ "I remember a little girl who lay motionless for days with her eyes closed, and I can remember how we all cried when she went home."

10.   _____ "And I can remember how the staff used to kid Dr. Salk—kidding in earnest—telling him to hurry up and do something."

D.   MAKING INFERENCES
For each of these statement write Y (Yes) if the inference is an accurate one, N (No) if the inference is an inaccurate one, or CT (Can't Tell) if you do not have enough information to make an inference.

1. _____ Polio has been almost completely eradicated in the U.S.

2. _____ In most cases, polio caused crippling and atrophy of the limbs, but few people died from it.

3. _____ Apparently, the polio virus struck its victims more in the winter months than during the summer.

4. _____ Stray cats carry the polio vaccine and were largely responsible for its spread in the U.S.

5. _____ Before the great polio epidemic, babies became immune to the virus both because it was present in the environment and because they developed a natural immunity to it.

6. _____ Before Roosevelt established an independent group to lead the fight against the polio epidemic, his efforts to combat the disease were seen by some as purely political.

7. _____ Polio apparently affected children in cities to the same degree as those who lived in rural areas or in small towns.

8. _____ The media were responsible for nearly ruining the national effort to combat polio.

9. _____ Jonas Salk was on the payroll of the Parke-Davis pharmaceutical company.

10. _____ Sabin's live-virus vaccine ultimately proved to be more effective in combating the polio virus than Salk's inactive variety.

E.   ANALYZING ORGANIZATION AND SEEING RELATIONSHIPS
Choose the correct answer.

1. _____ To support his ideas, the author relies both on his own experiences with the disease and on (a) his own opinions; (b) the testimony of medical experts; (c) historical facts and statistics; (d) the experiences of other polio victims.

2. Explain what the author means in paragraph 2 when he quotes his mother as saying, "We were fighting ghosts."

_____

_____

3. _____ Look again at the first sentence of paragraph 3. What is the relationship between "though polio is very old" and "the terror began for

Americans in the summer of 1916"? (a) steps in a process; (b) contrast; (c) comparison; (d) term and its definition; (e) general and specific.

4. ____ The transitional phrase "in fact" at the beginning of paragraph 5 indicates that the author is (a) emphasizing the idea that follows; (b) citing an example; (c) citing a fact; (d) drawing a conclusion.

5. ____ Look again at paragraph 6. The author apparently finds a connection between contracting polio and (a) unsanitary conditions; (b) increased awareness of the importance of sanitation; (c) middle-class values; (d) a healthier diet.

6. ____ In paragraph 11, the author also apparently finds a connection between a decrease in foundation funds to help polio research and (a) the Depression; (b) fewer polio cases; (c) political rivalry; (d) Roosevelt's growing unpopularity.

7. ____ In paragraph 8, the transitional word "instead" signals (a) contrast; (b) comparison; (c) a conclusion; (d) an example; (e) the first step in a process.

8. ____ The pattern of organization in the section comprising paragraphs 13–15 is (a) spatial or space order; (b) general to specific; (c) specific to general; (d) chronological.

9. ____ All of the following are dictionary definitions of the noun *take*. As it is used at the end of paragraph 15, which one best fits the context? (a) the amount of money collected; (b) the scene photographed; (c) a physical reaction indicating a successful vaccination; (d) any attempt or try.

10. ____ We can conclude that Jonas Salk produced a safe and effective vaccine earlier than Albert Sabin because (a) Sabin did not have a dedicated research staff; (b) Sabin's theory about live-virus vaccine was wrong; (c) Salk worked more quickly and took some big risks; (d) the government insisted on monitoring Sabin's research and refused to allow his vaccine to be tested.

F. UNDERSTANDING VOCABULARY
Choose the correct definition according to the context.

1. ____ parents tried to *spirit* their children out of town [paragraph 3]: (a) carry off secretly; (b) hide; (c) encourage; (d) establish a new life for.

2. ____ his ever-*solicitous* mother [4]: (a) domineering; (b) lonely; (c) attentive; (d) meddling.

3. ____ polio's growing *virulence* [6]: (a) lack of control; (b) resemblance to a virus; (c) strength; (d) great infectiousness.

4. ____ *pristine* bassinets, pure food and drink [6]: (a) shiny and new; (b) having its original purity; (c) glossy and white; (d) esthetically tasteful.

5. _____ the disease *ravaged* him [7]: (a) affected; (b) exhausted; (c) caused great damage to; (d) permanently influenced.

6. _____ with pitiless *candor* [7]: (a) straightforwardness; (b) lack of sympathy; (c) unpleasantness; (d) subjective opinion.

7. _____ a less *resilient* man [8]: Describing the ability to (a) remain calm; (b) resist defeat; (c) recover quickly from illness or misfortune; (d) withstand criticism and controversy.

8. _____ FDR's abortive *purge* of the Supreme Court [11]: (a) clearing of guilt or blame; (b) firing, getting rid of by cleaning out; (c) abolishment; (d) punishment.

9. _____ one generation removed from *servitude* [12]: (a) immigration; (b) slavery; (c) ignorance; (d) poverty.

10. _____ the disease that had *immobilized* him [12]: (a) frightened; (b) made immortal; (c) impaired, weakened; (d) made unable to move.

11. _____ as *capricious* as it was crippling [16]: (a) unpredictable; (b) exasperating; (c) difficult to eradicate; (d) uncontrollable.

12. _____ the Salk vaccine would largely be *superseded* after 1962 by the live-virus variety [27]: (a) used, implemented; (b) represented; (c) dominated; (d) replaced.

G. USING VOCABULARY

From the following list of vocabulary words, choose a word that fits in each blank according to both the grammatical structure of the sentence and the context. Use each word in the list only once and add noun or verb endings (such as *-s, -ing,* or *-ed*) if necessary. (Note that there are more words than sentences.)

trauma	fortuitous	quack
placebo	flourish	inoculate
indict	intervention	atrophy
doggedly	wane	inaugurate

1. According to the selection, until American children could be safely

   _____ against the disease, polio _____
   throughout the population, resulting in death or in crippled or

   _____ limbs.

2. Despite the fact that Franklin Roosevelt worked _____
   to keep it going, Warm Springs Foundation, founded by Roosevelt,
   eventually had trouble with its funding, and by the time he was first

   _____ as president, it was nearly bankrupt.

3. During the polio scare many remedies were peddled to unsuspecting par-

ents by various _____; one former legislator was even _____ for selling cedar shavings which he claimed worked as a cure.

4. The fight against polio was done with no _____ from the government, which today would almost certainly not approve an experiment in which schoolchildren are injected with viruses or even with

_____.

H. TOPICS FOR WRITING OR DISCUSSION

1. Here are some sentences from the article. Paraphrase them by rewriting each one in your own words in the space provided.

   a. In others [in other victims] it went on to immobilize the body, or assault the lungs, so that patients were dependent for every breath on the great iron cocoon in which they were encased for what remained to them of life.

   _____
   _____
   _____
   _____

   b. Polio's growing virulence seems actually to have been a by-product of a new standard of middle-class cleanliness. In the unsanitized past, infants and small children had been exposed to polio very early on, during a stage of life when paralysis was rare and lifelong immunity easily induced. But pristine bassinets, pure food and drink, freshly mopped floors had all helped to keep the virus at bay until children were older, when it was far more likely to cripple or kill.

   _____
   _____
   _____
   _____
   _____

   c. [Jonas Salk] was an intensely private, serious, single-minded virologist from New York who had been doggedly performing the most painstaking and repetitious sort of laboratory work for three years—seeking to determine whether there were in fact three *and only three* types of polio virus. "My role in life," he decided early, "is to find out. If people do not like what I find out it is just too bad. They should then attack nature, not me." [*Hint:* Paraphrase the quotation by making it into an *indirect* quotation, that is, by rewording it and removing the quotation marks.]

_____

_____

_____

_____

2.   Go to the library and do some research on another disease that you are interested in. Some examples are multiple sclerosis, AIDS, Lou Gehrig's disease, rheumatoid arthritis, Alzheimer's disease, and schizophrenia. Study its known causes, its symptoms and effects on the body, and any research currently being done to find a cure. Write a paper in which you summarize your findings.

31

Sarah Ferguson

THE HOMELESS: US AGAINST THEM

The plight of the homeless has reached serious proportions in America's cities, and there is some evidence that there is a backlash—an increasingly antagonistic reaction—by ordinary citizens who resent being accosted by panhandlers. This article discusses the problems associated with the homeless and some cities' efforts to deal with it. Sarah Ferguson, a correspondent for Pacific News Service, prepared this story, first published in the spring of 1990, for both the news service and the National Catholic Reporter.

VOCABULARY PREVIEW

WORD ORIGINS

CURFEW

In paragraph 29 Ferguson quotes a Manhattan resident who complains about conditions in Tompkins Square, apparently the only park in the city without a *curfew*. Today a *curfew* means a time when certain groups of people must be off the streets or out of an area. This word comes from medieval French. Since most houses were made of wood and had thatched roofs, the danger of fire was always great, especially at night. Every evening, therefore, residents had to put out their candles when a bell was rung, signaling the order "Cover fire." The French word *couvre-feu* was brought by the Norman conquerors to England, where eventually its pronunciation was changed to its present-day form.

BELLIGERENT

In paragraph 22 Ferguson writes, "The sometimes *belligerent* attitude of street people goes along with a growing shelter and welfare rebellion." *Belligerent*, describing openly hostile or aggressive behavior, has retained its original meaning from its Latin roots: [*belligerāre* ("to wage war"), from *bellum* ("war") + *gerere* ("to bear," "to carry")]. English also has a related word from the same root, *bellicose*, meaning "warlike in temperament."

STEREOTYPE

Ferguson writes in paragraph 13 that population shifts have created a new kind of panhandler with a different image from "the *stereotypical* image of the old skid row bum meekly extending his palm for change." This is the adjective form of *stereotype*, which can be defined in this context as "a standardized conception or image said to be held in common by people of a certain group."

Originally, however, this word was a printing term, referring to a metal printing plate containing fixed type. Probably because this plate always produced the same kind of type, the word *stereotype* eventually came to be identified with an unchanging pattern or image that could be applied to people.

WORD PARTS

A-, AN-

In selection 1 you learned that *anarchy*, meaning "an absence of government," comes from Greek: [*an-* ("without") + *archy* ("rule" or "government")]. The Greek prefix *a-* (occasionally *an-*) is often attached to a root word to indicate a complete lack or an absence of. Therefore, we have *apolitical* (having no interest in politics); *amoral* (having no sense of morality); *apathy* (having no feeling); *agnostic* (one who does not know whether God exists or not); *atheist* (one who does not believe in God); and *amorphous* (shapeless).

ADJECTIVE SUFFIXES

This selection contains several words ending with suffixes, which, when attached to a noun or verb root, change it into an adjective, a word that modifies a noun. The meaning often is quite clear—typically "having a tendency to" or "having the quality of"—so that the suffix indicates that something has the quality of the root. For example, if someone is described as *destructive*, he or she has a tendency to destroy things or relationships. Sometimes, however, the suffix serves only to change the word into an adjective and conveys no real meaning. For example, the word *potent*, used to describe a drink, means that it has the quality of being powerful, from the root *potere* ("to have power").

One special kind of adjective is called a participle, which is formed by adding either *-ing* or *-ed* to the verb stem. Although the resulting participle looks like a verb (and, in fact, is called a *verbal*), it functions like any other adjective. Look at paragraph 4 for several participles.

Here are some adjectives from the selection illustrating these various suffixes:

All of these words appear in the selection:

-al	(liberal, annual, constitutional)
-ant, -ent	(adamant, indigent, intransigent, belligerent, significant)
-ar	(popular)
-ate	(corporate)

-ed	(scorched, camped, plowed, huddled, squeezed, frightened, insulted, unguarded)
-en	(sodden)
-ial	(substantial, editorial)
-ic	(symbolic, public, periodic)
-ical	(stereotypical, polemical)
-ing	(sleeping, charging, requesting, enraging, shoving, spinning, revolving, overwhelming, degrading, condescending, protecting)
-ied	(intensified)
-ious	(precarious, obvious)
-less	(homeless)
-y	(preppy, angry)

In the next selection, you will be introduced to several common noun suffixes in English.

WORD
FAMILIES

Benign

One newspaper editorial advocated the *"benign* incarceration" of street people as a possible solution, meaning that they would be required to live in shelters as a kind of social kindness. English contains several words in the family of words containing the Latin prefix *bene-*, among them:

benefactor	one who benefits
benefit	anything that promotes or enhances well-being
beneficence	the quality of charity or kindness [*bene-* + *facere* ("to do")]
benevolence	a tendency to perform charitable acts; good will [from *benevolens* ("wishing well"): *bene-* + *volens,* from *velle* ("to wish")]
benediction	a blessing [*bene-* + *dicere* ("to speak")]

SARAH FERGUSON

THE HOMELESS: US AGAINST THEM

1   In streets and doorways across the country, a class war is brewing between angry indigents and disgruntled citizens forced to step out of their way.

2   Tompkins Square, the Manhattan park that spawned New York's first love-in in the '60s, has become symbolic of what happens when a liberal community loses patience with the homeless. It was neighborhood tolerance that allowed the encampment of homeless men and women to swell to a shantytown of more than 300 indigents last summer. But it was the rising outcry from neighbors who claimed

that the homeless had "taken the park hostage" that forced the city to finally tear the mess down.

3   Police raids on Tompkins Square Park over the past year, however, have done nothing to abate the flood of homeless people camped out in public spaces. Because, of course, the homeless keep coming back.

4   In Tompkins Square, construction crews have already plowed away the patches of scorched earth that remained after last December's raid, when many of the homeless burned their tents in open defiance. But you can still find a dozen or so homeless people, mostly black, huddled around the Peace, Hope, Temperance and Charity cupola. Another 15 are sprawled on piles of sodden blankets in the band shell, and maybe 20 more jammed in the bathrooms, sleeping in the stalls and sometimes charging fifty cents to move their bedding before you can enter.

5   Fed up with such seemingly intransigent masses, cities across the nation—budgets squeezed dry by the Reagan Revolution—are starting to adopt a closed-door attitude toward the displaced.

6   In Washington, D.C., the city council just slashed $19 million from the homeless budget and is seeking to roll back Initiative 17, the referendum that required the city to provide shelter to all those in need.

7   In Atlanta, Mayor Maynard Jackson has proposed a policy of licensing panhandlers as part of an intensified campaign to drive the homeless out of the center city business district.

8   In Berkeley, the University of California has ordered repeated police sweeps of People's Park, long a holdout for vagrants and the dispossessed, and has evicted the People's Cafe, a soup kitchen set up this winter by an organization called the Catholic Worker.

9   Of course, there have been periodic outcries against the homeless since the media first discovered the "problem" in the early 1980s. But today's growing disfavor bodes ill at a time when the economy worsens, and the line between the middle class and the poor becomes ever more precarious. The need to maintain an "us versus them" mentality seems all the more pressing.

10   "The tension level is definitely rising," says Wendy Georges, program director for Berkeley's Emergency Food Project. "With more homeless in the streets, people are starting to lose patience—even in Berkeley. If a city like this successfully attacks homeless people and homeless programs, it will set precedents. The homeless backlash will become a popular thing—so that nobody has to feel guilty about it."

11   Part of the reason for the growing backlash is simply sheer numbers. The U.S. Conference of Mayors' annual survey found that the demand for emergency shelter in 27 cities increased an average of 25 percent in 1989; by comparison, in 1988, the demand increased 13 percent. Some 22 percent of those requesting emergency shelter were turned away.

12   Public disfavor may also be spurred by changes in the makeup of the homeless population. Although figures are scarce, anyone who looks can see that the homeless population has grown younger. A 1960 survey of Philadelphia's skid row by Temple University found that 75 percent of the homeless were over the age of 45. And 87 percent were white. In 1988, 86 percent were under the age of 45, and 87 percent were minorities.

13   As the population shifts, the stereotypical image of the old skid row bum meekly extending his palm for change has been replaced by young African-American and Hispanic men, angry at the lack of well-paying jobs, often taking drugs or selling them—or demanding money with a sense of entitlement that passers-by find enraging.

14   In front of the Tower Records store on Manhattan's lower Broadway, a group of aggressive panhandlers confront shoppers with cardboard signs that read "Homeless Donations: $1 or token." "Cheap bastards," mutters one of the beggars, a black man named Flower, as he dumps a handful of pennies on the sidewalk that a passer-by just gave him. "What am I supposed to do with that?"

15   "Look, corporate criminals!" shouts his companion, Paradise, who sports preppy clothes and seashells woven in his short dreadlocks, pointing to a group of businessmen picking up their Lincoln Continental in the parking lot next door. "Hello, Mr. Executive, how you doing? You remember how to be human, don't you?" Paradise asks him mockingly, shoving a cardboard box in his face. "Come on, give me a dollar, man, I bet you make $50,000 in 10 minutes," he shouts. In response, the driver edges his window down a crack and mutters, "Get a job, will you?"

16   Meanwhile, Flower is chasing a frightened-looking man on the street. "Help me out. I know you're afraid of black people, but I won't bite."

17   "Get away from me," says John Kroeper, a young Jersey City resident in a business suit, who passes the panhandlers with contempt. "It's an invasion of my privacy. I don't want to be forced to give. Just because I have a suit on doesn't mean I'm a yuppie. I just lost my job."

18   "I'll give when they're just sitting there on the ground, but not when they come on to you like that," adds his sister Jean. "If you give money to people on the streets, you never know if they're really going to buy food with it or just buy liquor or drugs. I like to give to organizations where I know the money will go to good use, like the Salvation Army or Covenant House."

19   Back in front of the store, Guy Clare, a slight 29-year-old immigrant from Belize, seems caught up in his own angry monologue as he shakes a coffee cup at the shoppers spinning through the revolving doors. "The Japanese never help," he says watching a group of tourists pass him by. "They own over a quarter of New York, a quarter of Los Angeles, a quarter of Houston, and they can't help. They done bought up America, and they don't give nothing. F ----- white man."

20   Asked why he continues to panhandle, he responds, "I'm doing this cause I feel like it. I don't know, I'm lazy. You get insulted, you get disrespect, but it's better than a job. I don't want to rob somebody. I figure this is higher than that."

21   "It's just too overwhelming," says one woman, shaking her head. I ask her why she didn't give anything and she responds, "I think there's plenty of services in the city for people who want help."

22   The sometimes belligerent attitude of street people goes along with a growing shelter and welfare rebellion. In New York, the growth of a Tent City in Tompkins Square reflected the refusal by many homeless to enter New York's degrading shelter system. As many as 1,000 people are housed each night in armories where diseases such as AIDS and tuberculosis run rampant. Moreover, a substantial number of homeless people refuse to sign up for welfare and other entitlement

programs, preferring to fend for themselves on the streets rather than get caught up in a "dependency mentality" and suffer the degradation of long welfare lines and condescending case workers.

23   Instead, homeless people have begun banding together in support networks and tent encampments, demanding political recognition, and fighting back when they don't get it. Their resolve is seen in Santa Cruz, where a dozen vagrants have been arrested repeatedly for sleeping outside the local post office, or in San Francisco, where more than 100 people continue to camp in front of City Hall, adamantly protecting their belongings as police patrol the area daily to sweep away unguarded possessions.

24   "I see this as a form of anarchy," says Jake, a 30-year-old blond woman with tattoos decorating her chest, lying back in a bed of blankets and heavy metal tape cassettes next to her two companions, Red, 29, and Gadget, 24. "We're not going to hide somewhere. Just us being here is a protest." When pressed as to why they don't go out and get jobs, Gadget responds, "I'm not going to go flip burgers at some McDonald's so I can share a tiny apartment with a bunch of crazy a-----s. I've got friends and family here."

25   Such comments are grist for newspaper columnists, who are increasingly taking a hard-line approach toward the homeless, arguing that little can be done for people who don't want to help themselves. "Enough is enough," proclaims the editorial board of the Philadelphia Inquirer, which has called for a law to ban people from camping out in public places. The San Francisco Examiner recently ran an editorial calling for the "benign incarceration" of street people.

26   Even those cities that have made significant strides to shelter or house their homeless populations have begun to adopt closed-border policies. Although officials admit they cannot constitutionally restrict people from receiving assistance, both Philadelphia and Washington, D.C., have regulations stating that they need not provide shelter to people who come to their cities just for that purpose.

27   In San Francisco, Mayor Art Agnos recently announced that once his sweeping "master plan" to provide 6,000 units of homeless housing is implemented, homeless people from outside the county will be turned away. When questioned further, Agnos' homeless coordinator Bob Prentice explained the mayor was merely making a "polemical statement."

28   "Obviously we're not going to set up our own immigration service," Prentice said. "We're trying to draw some boundaries. How much can one city do in isolation? If we establish 6,000 units, at what point can you say we've done all that we can do?"

29   On Manhattan's Lower East Side, a group of merchants called BEVA (Businesses in the East Village Association) formed last year to respond to the growing number of street people and peddlers clogging the parks and sidewalks. "All of us are liberal people," says BEVA president Kathleen Fitzpatrick, owner of a local cafe. "Our doors are open. But many well-meaning acts, when they go unregulated, turn sour. Look at Tompkins Square—it's the only park without a curfew and that (allows) open fires (fire barrels). But look at what's happening. It's uncontrolled. It's a toilet. The other day they found 20 needles in the playground area."

30   "You can't say all homeless people are drug users—we know that," Fitzpatrick continues. "We want to do something to re-establish a community

presence in the park—not to kick the homeless out—to try and regulate it. I'm a victim of this. What happened to all the government programs? The states say they don't have any money; the cities don't have the money. It all filters down to the community—to me at Life Cafe or Bob at the bookstore—all of us little people who are now forced to contribute our income, our time, our energy and money to finally do something. I guess that's what Reagan wanted." ∎

From Sarah Ferguson, "The Homeless: Us Against Them" [original title, "Us Against Them"], *San Francisco Chronicle*, May 6, 1990. Reprinted by permission.

EXERCISES

Do not refer to the selection for Exercises A and B.

A.   DETERMINING THE MAIN IDEA AND PURPOSE
Choose the best answer.

1.   _____ The main idea of the article is that (a) tensions are escalating between the angry homeless and citizens, who are annoyed at being confronted by aggressive panhandlers; (b) many American cities are adopting workable solutions to solve their homeless problem; (c) some cities are closing their doors to the homeless by refusing to allow panhandlers to beg for money, to sleep in public places, or to move there simply to sleep in a shelter; (d) the homeless problem has accelerated in the U.S. because there aren't enough service agencies or shelters to provide help for them.

2.   _____ With respect to the main idea, the author's purpose is (a) to criticize, to find fault with the system; (b) to convince the reader about a controversial idea; (c) to relate her own personal experiences and observations; (d) to inform the reader and to provide background on a current problem.

B.   COMPREHENDING MAIN IDEAS
Choose the correct answer.

1.   _____ Tompkins Square, the New York City park where the police tore down the shantytown built by the homeless, is, according to the author, (a) a symbol of what happens when a liberal community loses patience with the homeless; (b) a model of the steps every city should take; (c) a blatant example of police brutality against a defenseless group; (d) the primary hangout for the homeless in the city.

2.   _____ The homeless situation and residents' rising intolerance of the problem are particularly troubling because (a) the government is not interested in solving the problem; (b) there are not enough adequate shelters to house them all; (c) the economy is worsening and city budgets are

being squeezed; (d) the nation is gradually becoming divided into "haves" and "have-nots."

3. _____ According to the author, the backlash against the homeless has occurred even in a tolerant and liberal city like (a) Washington, D.C.; (b) Atlanta; (c) Berkeley; (d) Philadelphia.

4. _____ Surveys taken in Philadelphia show that the homeless population has changed (a) from predominantly white to minority, and from old to young; (b) from predominantly minority to white, and from young to old; (c) from predominantly men to women and children; (d) from predominantly skid row bums to alcoholics and drug addicts.

5. _____ One reason cited for the number of homeless on the streets of New York City is that (a) there aren't enough shelters to house all the homeless; (b) the homeless think that being forced into a shelter is a violation of their civil rights; (c) the homeless often refuse to stay in shelters because conditions are degrading and unsanitary; (d) the shelters refuse to admit homeless people who come to the city only for welfare and a place to stay.

6. _____ Instead of going on welfare or signing up for entitlement programs, the author says that many homeless (a) are simply giving up all hope; (b) are moving into suburban and rural areas because of some cities' closed-border policies; (c) are banding together and demanding political recognition and support; (d) are advocating social and political anarchy.

COMPREHENSION SCORE

Score your answers for Exercises A and B as follows:

A. No. right _____ × 2 = _____

B. No. right _____ × 1 = _____

Total pts. from A and B _____ × 10 = _____%

You may refer to the selection for the remaining exercises.

C. DISTINGUISHING BETWEEN MAIN IDEAS AND SUPPORTING DETAILS

Label the following statements from the selection as follows: MI if the statement represents a *main idea* and SD if the statement represents a *supporting detail.*

1. _____ In streets and doorways across the country, a class war is brewing between angry indigents and disgruntled citizens forced to step out of their way.

2. _____ Fed up with such seemingly intransigent masses, cities across the nation—budgets squeezed dry by the Reagan Revolution—are starting to adopt a closed-door attitude toward the displaced.

3. _____ In Washington, D.C., the city council just slashed $19 million from the homeless budget and is seeking to roll back Initiative 17, the referendum that required the city to provide shelter to all those in need.

4. _____ In Atlanta, Mayor Maynard Jackson has proposed a policy of licensing panhandlers as part of an intensified campaign to drive the homeless out of the center city business district.

5. _____ In Berkeley, the University of California has ordered repeated police sweeps of People's Park, long a holdout for vagrants and the dispossessed, and has evicted the People's Cafe, a soup kitchen set up this winter by an organization called the Catholic Worker.

6. _____ Of course, there have been periodic outcries against the homeless since the media first discovered the "problem" in the early 1980s.

7. _____ But today's growing disfavor bodes ill at a time when the economy worsens, and the line between the middle class and the poor becomes ever more precarious.

8. _____ The need to maintain an "us versus them" mentality seems all the more pressing.

D. MAKING INFERENCES

For each of these statements write Y (Yes) if the inference is an accurate one, N (No) if the inference is an inaccurate one, or CT (Can't Tell) if you do not have enough information to make an inference.

1. _____ The encampment of homeless people in New York's Tompkins Square was finally leveled because the neighborhood residents no longer felt comfortable about using the park themselves.

2. _____ Citizens seem most upset and concerned about panhandlers' growing aggressiveness and belligerence when they are confronted with demands for money.

3. _____ Much of the nation's crime rate can be directly attributed to the rise of the homeless population.

4. _____ The "us-versus-them" mentality could have very serious consequences, suggesting escalating tensions and a class war.

5. _____ For those who want to help the homeless, it is definitely better to give to charities like the Salvation Army than to give panhandlers money outright.

6. _____ The 100-odd homeless who camped out nightly in front of San Francisco's City Hall were undoubtedly an embarrassment to the city's mayor and his "master plan" to help them.

7. _____ Organizing themselves into political units and demanding recognition have resulted in some significant gains for the homeless.

8. _____ The high cost of living is the primary cause of the increasing number of homeless in U.S. cities today.

E. **DRAWING CONCLUSIONS**

Mark an X before any of these statements that represent reasonable conclusions you can draw from the selection.

1. _____ Establishing a curfew or prohibiting sleeping in public places probably would not be a workable solution for the homeless problem unless there were a sufficient number of decent shelters and people were willing to go there voluntarily.

2. _____ A city that pledged to build or find shelter for all the homeless people who came there might soon find itself overwhelmed with newcomers.

3. _____ The growing number of younger people under forty-five who have adopted homelessness as a way of life indicates the need for improved educational and job-training facilities.

4. _____ Legalizing drugs and making them readily available at public clinics would help curb the large number of vagrants and indigents who panhandle for money.

5. _____ The homeless problem in this country is so complex that workable solutions seem nearly impossible.

F. **ANALYZING ORGANIZATION AND SEEING RELATIONSHIPS**

Choose the correct answer.

1. _____ Besides serving as an introduction, paragraph 1 also (a) acts as an attention-getter with an interesting anecdote; (b) states the thesis; (c) represents the author's personal views; (d) presents solutions for an important controversy.

2. _____ How would you characterize the information we are given in paragraph 4—that a dozen or so homeless people still congregate around the Peace, Hope, Temperance and Charity cupola in Tompkins Square? It is (a) ludicrous; (b) pathetically ironic; (c) predictable; (d) embarrassing.

3. Look again at paragraph 6–8. Then look at paragraph 5 and find a specific phrase—a group of words—that these short examples support.

_____

4. _____ Paragraph 9 opens with the transitional phrase "of course," which indicates (a) emphasis; (b) the author's personal point of view; (c) a contrast; (d) a concession.

5. _____ To support her discussion about the homeless and citizens' grow-

ing anger at their presence, Ferguson relies mainly on (a) the findings of research studies; (b) her own confrontations with panhandlers and the homeless; (c) the reports of government officials and civic leaders; (d) the testimony of residents, civic and social leaders, and the homeless themselves.

6. _____ What is the logical relationship implied in the first sentences of both paragraphs 11 and 12? (a) steps in a process; (b) cause and effect; (c) contrast—a discussion of differences; (d) comparison—a discussion of similarities.

7. _____ The author strongly implies that at least part of the blame for the homeless problem lies with (a) George Bush; (b) the Vietnam war; (c) the federal government; (d) Ronald Reagan.

8. _____ Which of these best characterizes the author's attitude toward the homeless and their plight? (a) She is sympathetic; (b) she is unsympathetic; (c) she is confused and perplexed; (d) her attitude is not evident from the article.

G.   UNDERSTANDING VOCABULARY

Look through the paragraphs listed below and find a word that matches each definition. An example has been done for you.

Ex.   the state of being held captive [look   _____held hostage_____
      for a phrase—paragraphs 1–2]

 1.   poor or destitute people [1 and 2]   _____

 2.   discontented, dissatisfied [1–2]   _____

 3.   reduce the amount of, lessen [3–4]   _____

 4.   uncompromising, inflexible [4–5]   _____

 5.   predicts, is a bad omen of [look for a   _____
      phrase—9–10]

 6.   past incidents that can serve as examples   _____
      for future actions [10–11]

 7.   humbly, patiently, submissively [13–14]   _____

 8.   a long speech made by one person [19–20]   _____

 9.   unchecked, unrestrained [22–23]   _____

10.   firmly, unyieldingly [23–24]   _____

11.   absence of government or rule [24–25]   _____

12.   harmless, displaying kindness [25–26]   _____

13.   imprisonment [25–26]   _____

14. put into effect, accomplished [27–28]   _____

15. describing a controversial argument   _____
       [27–28]

H.   USING VOCABULARY

In parentheses before each sentence are some inflected forms of words from the selection. Study the context and the sentence. Then write the correct form in the space provided. Be sure to add appropriate endings like *-s, -ed,* or *-ing* if necessary.

1. (*symbol, symbolism, symbolize, symbolic, symbolically*)   Tompkins Square in

New York City is a _____ of what happens when a liberal community loses patience over the homeless issue.

2. (*defiance, defy, defiant, defiantly*)   Many of the homeless who live in

Tompkins Square _____ the police's orders to move by burning their tents.

3. (*precarious, precariously*)   According to the author, the line between the

middle class and the poor in the U.S. is becoming _____ thin.

4. (*stereotype, stereotypical, stereotypically*)   The old _____
       image of a skid row bum meekly begging for money has been replaced by angry young men who demand money from passersby as if they are entitled to it.

5. (*aggression, aggressiveness, aggressive, aggressively*)   One reason citizens are upset over the rising number of homeless is that many panhandlers dis-

play open _____ when asking for money.

6. (*entitlement, entitle*)   Some panhandlers accost people on the sidewalk

and act as if they are _____ to get money from them.

7. (*mockery, mock, mocking, mockingly*)   Paradise, a young panhandler
       in New York, asks a young man driving a car for money in a

_____ tone of voice, which only antagonizes the driver.

8. (*belligerence, belligerent, belligerently*)   It is the increasing _____
       and anger displayed by the nation's homeless that has so many urban residents concerned and tense.

9. (*degradation, degrade, degrading, degradingly*)   According to the homeless,

both the shelters and social welfare system are seen as _____.

10. (*condescension, condescend, condescending, condescendingly*)   Many homeless

refuse to go on welfare because of social workers' _____
attitude toward them.

I.   TOPICS FOR WRITING OR DISCUSSION

1.   Here are some sentences and passages from the article. Paraphrase them
by writing each one in your own words in the space provided.

   a. It was neighborhood tolerance that allowed the encampment of
   homeless men and women to swell to a shantytown of more than 300
   indigents last summer. But it was the rising outcry from neighbors
   who claimed that the homeless had "taken the park hostage" that
   forced the city to finally tear the mess down.

   _____

   _____

   _____

   _____

   b. A substantial number of homeless people refuse to sign up for welfare
   and other entitlement programs, preferring to fend for themselves on
   the streets rather than get caught up in a "dependency mentality" and
   suffer the degradation of long welfare lines and condescending case
   workers.

   _____

   _____

   _____

   _____

   c. Such comments are grist for newspaper columnists, who are increasingly taking a hard-line approach toward the homeless, arguing that
   little can be done for people who don't want to help themselves.

   _____

   _____

   _____

   _____

2.   What do you do when you are confronted with panhandlers—aggressive
or otherwise? Do you give? Why or why not? What do you base your
decision on?

32

Dennis Meredith

DAY-CARE: THE NINE-TO-FIVE DILEMMA

*Dennis Meredith is a California-based science writer. In this article, originally published in
Psychology Today, he summarizes current research that psychologists have done on day-
care centers. With more than fifty percent of American families now classified as two-
income, it is especially important for parents to have confidence in their children's day-care
arrangements while they are at work. Meredith's article examines these findings and the
effects of day-care on children's emotional and intellectual development.*

VOCABULARY PREVIEW

**WORD
ORIGINS**

DILEMMA

The word *dilemma* [from Greek *di-* ("two") + *lēmma* ("proposition")],
which appears in the selection title, is a much-misused word. It is often
loosely used to mean simply any problem, but its meaning is more precisely, "a predicament or situation involving two equally balanced alternatives." In addition, the word usually connotes that neither of these
alternatives is attractive.

The *American Heritage Dictionary* lists a second definition: "a predicament that seemingly defies a satisfactory solution." For working
parents, for example, one alternative is to stay at home (and possibly
face economic ruin); the other is to put their children in day-care, with
potentially unknown or harmful effects.

SANGUINE

Edward Zigler is quoted in paragraph 19 as saying, "The first wave of
research made everybody feel pretty *sanguine*." Meaning, in this context, "cheerful" or "hopeful," *sanguine* has a rather odd derivation. In
Latin the root *sanguis* meant "blood," and the *Random House Dictionary*
lists two other definitions, "reddish" or "ruddy" (describing someone's

383

complexion) and "having blood as the predominating humor and consequently having a cheerful disposition."

Medieval physicians believed that four humors, or bodily fluids, governed human emotions. *Melancholy,* or black bile, for example, was believed to be the cause of a sullen disposition or extreme sadness. *Choler,* or yellow bile, was thought to cause anger and bad temper. *Phlegm* was the source of a sluggish temperament, and as you have seen, blood (or *sanguine*) was the source of cheerfulness or passion.

PSYCHOLOGIST, PSYCHIC

In Greek mythology, Psyche was a beautiful girl whom Eros fell in love with. Her name later become identified with the "soul" or the "spirit." A *psychologist* studies the human mind or spirit, and *psychic* (see paragraph 23) is an adjective that describes something pertaining to the mind or spirit.

WORD PARTS	

MIS-

University of Virginia psychologist Sandra Scarr is quoted in paragraph 12 as saying that business and government leaders believe that the traditional family still predominates, which she labels "a widespread *misapprehension.*" The prefix *mis-* indicates two separate meanings: (1) error or wrongness or (2) badness. *Misapprehension* means understanding incorrectly. Other words using *mis-* with this meaning are *misspell, misadventure, miscalculate, misdirect,* and *mislead.* For the second usage: *misfortune, mischief, mismanage,* and *misrule.*

NOUN SUFFIXES

In the previous selection, you learned some common adjective suffixes. Perhaps because this piece deals with social science, there are an unusually large number of nouns referring to abstractions—concepts or ideas. Therefore, this is a good place to list some of the more common suffixes that, when attached to verbs or adjectives, form nouns. Their meanings vary, but generally they mean "the quality or state of," so that, for example, *security* means the state of being secure, and *motherhood* means the state or condition of being a mother. Most important, they all indicate a noun function. All of these words appear in the selection:

-ance, -ence	(assistance, evidence, balance, consequences, difference, independence)
-cy	(emergency)
-er, -or	(babysitter, neighbor, employer, breadwinner, homemaker, childraiser, caregiver, researchers, factor, encounters)

-hood	(motherhood)
-ic, -ics	(statistics, public)
-ing	(settings, findings, socializing, meeting, beginning, training, engineering)
-ise	(compromise)
-ist	(psychologist)
-ity; -ities—pl.	(majority, university, quality, probability, security, abilities, activities, opportunities, sociability)
-ive	(alternatives, native)
-logy	(psychology)
-ment	(arrangement, development, government, commitment, equipment, enrichment, attachment, employment, environment, adjustment)
-ness	(business)
-ship	(relationship)
-tion, -sion	(corporation, alteration, predictions, situation, misapprehension, description, question, conditions, education, stimulation, functions, information, decisions, complications)
-ure	(nature)
-y	(worry, company, study, family, variety)

WORD FAMILIES

PREDICTIONS (DICT)

Meredith writes in paragraph 6, "Some *predictions* are that 80 percent of families will have two working parents by the end of the century." To *predict* means literally "to foretell," from the Latin: [*prae-* ("before") + *dīcere* ("to tell")]. Although some of them have only a vague connection with speaking or telling, here are some other words that are based on the root *dict:*

diction	choice of words in speaking or writing
benediction	a blessing [*bene-* ("well") + *dīcere*]
contradiction	speaking against
verdict	a jury's decision [*veir-* ("true") + *dīcere*]

Other words you should know:

Montessori	[paragraph 15] Founded in Italy by Maria Montessori, this method of early childhood education emphasizes the acquisition of intellectual skills at an early age and independent learning; many nursery schools in the U.S. use the Montessori method.
thalidomide	[25] a tranquillizer widely prescribed during the 1950s and 1960s that was found to cause severe birth defects and was withdrawn from the market.

DENNIS MEREDITH

DAY-CARE: THE NINE-TO-FIVE DILEMMA

1   Kathryn has a new baby, but she also has a challenging 9-to-5 job in a large corporation, and the combination is proving almost unmanageable. The corporation offers no day-care, so she and her husband must find their own. They have interviewed dozens of babysitters and still cannot find one who is reliable and capable. As a result Kathryn misses work often and when working is plagued by worries about her child.

2   Marie and Ken, with three children, have become master jugglers. After being on a waiting list for two years, they have managed to enroll their 3-year-old son in a church-run school three days a week. He spends the other two days with a neighbor who cares for children. The couple's daughters, ages 11 and 8, take care of themselves after school and sometimes watch the 3-year-old in emergencies. But just one sneeze and the juggling act is disrupted. The day-care center won't accept sick children, and if the older children are ill, the parents don't want to leave either of them at home alone.

3   These parents have problems, but at least they can afford day-care. Barbara, a maid, has to take her new baby to her employers' houses. Her older daughter used to come along to mind the baby and help with the work, but now that she's in school, Barbara has to combine housework with child-care. Some of her employers are not particularly happy with this arrangement, and Barbara fears losing her jobs.

4   All of these parents are caught up in a dramatic alteration in the way we rear our children. The majority of children no longer grow up in the traditional family of a male breadwinner and a female homemaker and child-raiser. Economic need and the desire for challenge outside the home have led unprecedented numbers of mothers of young children to join the work force during the past decade.

5   Almost half of all mothers with young children work, according to the Bureau of Labor Statistics. The current total is 8.2 million women, and nearly 200,000 more are joining the work force every year.

6   In surveys, most working women with young children say they would prefer to continue working, even if they didn't need the money. And many women at home with children say they would work if they could either find or afford child-care. Some predictions are that 80 percent of families will have two working parents by the end of the century.

7   As this trend continues, more and more working parents will be thrust into the frustrating and sometimes frightening business of finding day-care for their children. They can choose from a confusing number of alternatives, usually expensive and sometimes unreliable. And they must keep on re-solving their day-care problems, as underpaid, overworked sitters and day-care center workers leave and as children grow and change.

8   The compromises parents make in juggling careers and rearing children often cause them to worry that they are less fit parents. They have heard that they are

damaging their children's development, weakening the mother-child bond and even exposing their children to abuse or disease.

9   Both business and government are making some progress toward aiding working parents, but it's a "good news-bad news" situation. More than 2,000 companies now offer some form of day-care assistance, but this is still a very low percentage of companies in this country.

10   On the other hand, tax credits for child-care now total more than $3 billion annually. And there is a rising tide of interest in Congress. Approximately 20 child-care bills were submitted during the last session.

11   But the tax credit is threatened by changes in the income-tax code, and the federal government has not shown full-commitment to solving the problems of child-care.

12   The most fundamental problem is that leaders in business and government, as well as the public, still tend to believe that the traditional family predominates. It's a widespread misapprehension, says University of Virginia psychologist Sandra Scarr, author of *Mother Care/Other Care*. "The traditional family, which now makes up 11 percent of our families, is still a major myth," she explained at a recent symposium on day-care. "We believe that is what most American families are like. When we survey the general public [about] the typical American family, we still get a description that includes two parents, two children and a white picket fence." Americans' concept of the family doesn't include many of the current forms, including single-parent families and the working poor, Scarr says.

13   It is clear that for both financial and personal reasons the surge of women into the workplace is going to continue. So the question becomes not, is day-care more detrimental than parent-care, but what kind of day-care is the best.

14   Research on day-care itself has now entered a new phase, experts say. The first studies simply compared the effects of mother-care with high-quality center care, and concluded that day-care neither harms nor helps children. Now researchers are sharpening their focus, attempting to evaluate different forms of day-care.

15   At one end of the spectrum is the middle-aged woman down the block who cares for an infant and three toddlers in her home. At the other end is the nursery school that has three teachers with Montessori training, serves 25 children from 2 to 4 years old and boasts a well-equipped playground.

16   But parents cannot transfer the special warmth of the sitter's home to the nursery school nor bring the more elaborate play equipment and the staff of the nursery school to the conveniently located sitter's home. And these are only two of many options from which parents must choose. They may also find sitters willing to come to their home, or they may look into day-care centers that offer a variety of services.

17   For parents of children 2 years old and older, the results of day-care research offer both relief from guilt and some guidance. Psychologists have found clear evidence that older children of working parents can develop just as well socially and intellectually as those whose mothers are at home. In fact, in some cases day-care may be better than home care. For disadvantaged children it may offer enrichment they can't get at home.

18   Unfortunately, for parents of infants, day-care research offers neither such

certainty nor such comfort. So few studies have been done and their results are so controversial that the effects of infant day-care remain agonizingly murky.

19   "The first wave of research made everybody feel pretty sanguine," says Edward Zigler, a psychologist at Yale University who has just completed a review of the research with psychologist Tom Gamble.

20   Although early studies concluded that there were not many problems with day-care, the studies were all conducted in high-quality settings and were not very representative, Zigler says. "The second wave of studies shows that there seem to be some problems in mother-infant attachment with babies in day-care."

21   One such study was reported by psychologist Brian Vaughn of the University of Illinois at Chicago. He and his colleagues found that about 50 percent of babies in sitter-care were insecurely attached to their mothers, compared with 30 percent of babies under mother-care.

22   Attachment is "the degree to which the baby is able to use the mother or other caretaker as a source of support and security in unfamiliar settings," Vaughn explains.

23   "If there's a balance [between attachment and exploration] the child is motivated to find things out about the world and when his resources get exhausted, he returns to mother for a sort of psychic refueling."

24   Vaughn cautions that his findings "don't mean that all children in non-maternal or day-care groups have an insecure attachment, it's just that the probability is higher." He also points out there are consequences associated with any type of child-care, including mother-care.

25   Zigler, former head of the federal Office of Child Development, has called infant day-care "the psychological thalidomide of the '80s," a remark he now qualifies.

26   "When I said that, unfortunately people didn't hear what I was saying," Zigler explains. "They thought I was saying that mothers of infants were not to work. What I'm saying is that mothers are working, and they will continue to work, and we have to make sure that we have infant day-care of good quality."

27   Parts of the country permit a level of care that Zigler considers detrimental. For example, in many states a woman can take care of as many as eight babies in her home. Zigler believes any single adult trying to take care of the psychological and physiological needs of eight babies must in some way be neglecting the children.

28   For Scarr, the debate over infant care is colored by what she calls "the cult of motherhood." It's a cult that obscures the fact that high-quality day-care can yield happy, well-adjusted babies, she says.

29   Studies have shown that high-quality infant care is not necessarily damaging to either the child's emotional development or to the parent-child relationship, according to Scarr. What is crucial is that infants have a consistent and warm relationship with their caregivers.

30   "We know that children are attached to their fathers and most fathers are not home all day with their children. So, why should we be surprised that working mothers can have the same kinds of relationships with their children?" In fact, Scarr argues, an infant may thrive on intense relationships with more than one care-

giver. "After all, how bad can it be to have more than one person in this world that you can trust?"

31   If there is a consensus regarding infant day-care, it's that care of one baby by one sitter (the alternative most preferred by parents) is probably the most desirable. Since babies largely ignore other children, having playmates is not as important. Most vital, the experts agree, is that infants have warm, consistent, nurturing relationships with all their caregivers, both sitters and parents.

32   Once children are ready to begin socializing, parents have more day-care options open to them. Many psychologists believe that day-care for children older than 2 or 3 does no harm, and, in fact, can be very helpful.

33   One recent study claiming that children of working mothers can develop perfectly well was presented at last summer's meeting of the American Psychological Association. The psychologists, Adele Gottfried of California State University at Northridge, Allen Gottfried of California State University at Fullerton and Kay Bathurst of the University of California, Los Angeles, began their study of 130 children seven years ago when the children were 1 year old.

34   The children were mostly from white, middle-income families that included both employed and homemaking mothers. About one-third of the mothers were employed at the beginning of the study, and 56 percent were employed by the time the children reached the age of 5. While the California researchers did not include day-care as a specific factor in their study, children of employed mothers were far more likely to be in day-care.

35   After testing the children's intellectual, physical and social skills, the researchers concluded that the children of employed mothers developed no differently than the children of unemployed mothers. A child's development "really has nothing to do with maternal employment," Adele Gottfried says. "Mothers who are employed can provide the same kind of environment as mothers who are not employed. And they can be good environments or bad environments."

36   Psychologist Alison Clarke-Stewart, then at the University of Chicago, and her colleagues investigated what happens to children in various day-care environments. They studied 80 children in the Chicago area in a variety of day-care settings, including the children's homes, day-care homes, nursery schools and full-time day-care centers. The researchers interviewed each child's parents and caretakers, tested children's intellectual abilities and observed how the children reacted to their mothers, peers and strangers.

37   They also noted the physical environment, listing toys such as tricycles, adult objects such as plants, hazards such as razor blades and open stairways and dirty conditions such as unwashed dishes and open paint cans.

38   They recorded whom the children spent time with, what types of encounters these were (teaching, touching, kissing and hitting) and what caretakers said to children. For example, the command "Put the toy down" was listed as directive, while "Put the toy down because you're going to hurt somebody" was coded as explanatory. After analyzing the results, the researchers characterized each setting.

39   Sitter-care in the child's home, used by about one-third of working mothers in the study, was typically given by older women with no professional training and

limited education. The child's home was usually adult-oriented with fewer creative toys and more hazards than at a day-care center. While the children cared for at home were hugged, kissed, helped and talked to more often, they had little peer contact, particularly with more skilled older children. The only playmates were siblings, and there was little visiting with other children. More time was spent alone watching TV, and there were few structured activities.

40   Care at a sitter's house was used by another one-third of working mothers. The women who ran these day-care homes were younger, usually in their mid 30s. They were better educated than in-home sitters but had no professional child-care experience. These homes were similar to the child's home in that they were adult-oriented and contained hazards and messes.

41   "A day-care home is fundamentally a home, even when it is stretched to take in more children or to provide service for a fee," says Clarke-Stewart, now at the University of California, Irvine. The major difference was that day-care homes provided more social stimulation. Most had about five children, all around the same age.

42   The women who ran nursery schools were typically in their early 30s and were child-care professionals with formal college training in child development. As might be expected, there were few hazards, more adults and a wider variety of playmates for the children. There were fewer direct contacts between children and caretakers but more group and structured activities. Thus, the center offered more opportunities for education and socializing.

43   Full-time day-care centers were similar to nursery schools but included meals, naps and more free-play periods. The only difference was that the teachers were slightly younger and had held their jobs for less time than had teachers at nursery schools.

44   The researchers found that each type of day-care affected children differently. "Children attending nursery school programs scored consistently higher across the board, but especially higher on cognitive ability, social knowledge and sociability with the adult stranger," Clarke-Stewart says. "Least advanced were children with sitters in their own homes. These children never scored highest on a test and they were significantly more likely than children in day-care centers to avoid their peers. Children in day-care homes scored highest on sociability with the unfamiliar peer but lowest on independence from their mother."

45   Many parents choose home day-care because they are attracted to the idea of the warmer home environment, but Clarke-Stewart found that such warm environments may not challenge a child as much as other day-care alternatives do. "We found the greater the hugging and kissing, the worse the kids were doing," she says. "If you're helping and touching and cuddling 3- or 4-year-olds, it's not pushing them into developing faster."

46   Although day-care centers had many positive effects on children, Clarke-Stewart cautions that a super center won't automatically produce a super child. "Children were not randomly assigned to the day-care programs in which we observed them," she points out. "Their parents deliberately selected these programs for them." Parents from more highly educated backgrounds may have chosen some programs because of the educational opportunities they offered.

47   But in the end, Clarke-Stewart believes that the support, stimulation and good

genes parents give their children are as important as the type of day-care they are in. "Children do not live by day-care alone, no matter how fitting its form and fine its functions."

48   A recent study led by psychologist Kathleen McCartney at Harvard University also showed that center quality can have a positive effect on a child's development. She and her colleagues, Scarr and psychologists Deborah Phillips and Conrad Schwarz, studied 166 families with children in Bermuda day-care centers.

49   Bermuda was an ideal place to study day-care centers because the huge majority of Bermuda children are in day-care and the researchers were able to find nine centers that varied widely in quality, staffing and programs. The researchers tested and interviewed children in the centers to measure their intellectual, language and social skills, as well as their emotional adjustment. They also interviewed center directors and families, observed how children and teachers talked to one another and collected background information on the families.

50   Other concerns were how well the caregivers met the children's needs and interacted with them, how well the centers were furnished for the children and the quality and quantity of intellectual and social activities.

51   Neither the age at which the child began day-care nor the amount of time spent in group care affected intellectual or social development. However, children in the better centers did better on all tests of intellectual and language skills and showed better social development. And according to McCartney, "Both parents and caregivers agree that children in higher-quality day-care centers are more considerate and more sociable than children in lower-quality centers."

52   Quality, of course, will be an issue as parents make decisions about day-care, but much remains to be resolved. Legislators will continue the day-care debate and psychologists will do more studies. Their efforts, however, will be hindered by the moving nature of the target—the American family. The question of how our society should support its families in rearing their children is a devilishly complex issue of economics, government, social engineering, psychology and opportunities for women. But despite these complications, it is already clear that there are many ways to rear happy, effective children. Although all of them represent hard work and hard choices for parents, they can all be equally valid.   ■

From Dennis Meredith, "Day Care: The Nine-to-Five Dilemma," *Psychology Today*, February 1986. Reprinted by permission.

EXERCISES

Do not refer to the selection for Exercises A and B.

A.   DETERMINING THE MAIN IDEA AND PURPOSE
Choose the best answer.

1.   _____ The main idea of the article is that (a) the high cost of living in the U.S. has created a dilemma for working parents; (b) as the number of two-income families increases, more parents will have to go through the frustrating process of finding adequate day-care services for their children; (c) business and industry should begin providing low-cost day-care services for their employees; (d) there is no evidence that day-care harms young children either psychologically or intellectually.

2. _____ With respect to the main idea, the author's purpose is (a) to criticize, find fault with; (b) to present a number of alternatives for parents; (c) to present and summarize the findings of recent psychological research; (d) to present both sides of a controversial issue.

B.   COMPREHENDING MAIN IDEAS
Choose the correct answer.

1. _____ The author characterizes the current day-care alternatives as (a) inexpensive but sometimes inadequate; (b) expensive but usually reliable; (c) inefficient and always unreliable; (d) usually expensive and sometimes unreliable.

2. _____ The author writes that business and government leaders (a) are very interested in improving day-care facilities for working mothers; (b) are dominated by the erroneous idea that the traditional family still exists in the U.S.; (c) have consistently opposed legislation to improve day-care facilities and to provide child-care tax credits; (d) recognize the serious shortage of good day-care by sponsoring new on-site facilities.

3. _____ According to psychologist Sandra Scarr, the traditional family—two parents, two children, and a white picket fence—represents this percentage of the American population: (a) one percent; (b) eleven percent; (c) twenty-nine percent; (d) fifty percent.

4. _____ Although the first studies of day-care and its effect on children were positive, later studies have reported that some babies who have been cared for outside the home demonstrate (a) poor intellectual development; (b) an inability to socialize and interact with others; (c) a preference for the day-care personnel over their own parents; (d) an insecure attachment to their mothers.

5. _____ According to the author, there is a consensus that the best day-care for infants is (a) none at all, meaning that the mother should stay home with her child; (b) a one-on-one situation in which a baby is cared for consistently by one person; (c) a Montessori-type of preschool to stimulate intellectual development as soon as possible; (d) care by a grandmother in the infant's home.

6. _____ Several studies cited in the article—conducted in California, Illinois, and Bermuda—have produced evidence that for children over the age of two (a) the best day-care is that provided by a sitter in her own home; (b) day-care is harmful to the child's social and emotional development;

(c) a good-quality day-care center can have many positive effects; (d) day-care is the best way for them to learn independence and self-sufficiency.

COMPREHENSION SCORE

Score your answers for Exercises A and B as follows:

A. No. right _____ × 2 = _____

B. No. right _____ × 1 = _____

Total pts. from A and B _____ × 10 = _____%

You may refer to the selection for the remaining exercises.

C. DISTINGUISHING BETWEEN MAIN IDEAS AND SUPPORTING DETAILS
Label the following statements from the selection as follows: MI if the statement represents a *main idea* and SD if the statement represents a *supporting detail*.

1. ____ Parts of the country permit a level of care that Edward Zigler [a psychologist at Yale University] considers detrimental.

2. ____ For example, in many states a woman can take care of as many as eight babies in her home.

3. ____ Zigler believes any single adult trying to take care of the psychological and physiological needs of eight babies must in some way be neglecting the children.

4. ____ For [Sandra] Scarr [a psychologist at the University of Virginia], the debate over infant care is colored by what she calls "the cult of motherhood."

5. ____ It's a cult that obscures the fact that high-quality day-care can yield happy, well-adjusted babies, she says.

6. ____ Studies have shown that high-quality infant care is not necessarily damaging to either the child's emotional development or to the parent-child relationship, according to Scarr.

7. ____ What is crucial is that infants have a consistent and warm relationship with their caregivers.

8. ____ "We know that children are attached to their fathers and most fathers are not home all day with their children. So, why should we be surprised that working mothers can have the same kinds of relationships with their children?"

9. ____ In fact, Scarr argues, an infant may thrive on intense relationships with more than one caregiver.

10. _____ "After all, how bad can it be to have more than one person in this world that you can trust?"

D. MAKING INFERENCES
Choose the correct answer.

1. _____ Look again at paragraphs 1–3, from which we can accurately infer that (a) middle-class and upper-class families have just as much difficulty finding and paying for good day-care as poor or working-class families; (b) poor and working-class families have a harder time than middle-class families with day-care because of the expense; (c) eventually, working mothers become good at juggling career and children; (d) more fathers should take part in choosing day-care for their children.

2. _____ From paragraph 4 we can infer that (a) the women's liberation movement is responsible for women's desire to work outside the home; (b) the increasing number of divorces has resulted in more women working outside the home; (c) husbands generally do not approve of their wives working outside the home if they have young children; (d) the high cost of living rather than the desire for material possessions is responsible for mothers of young children entering the work force.

3. _____ Read paragraphs 9–11 again. We can infer that (a) abolishing the child-care tax credit would hurt middle-income families more than low-income families; (b) Congress should require companies with a certain number of employees to provide on-site day-care; (c) the government has no responsibility to help ease the child-care problem in this country; (d) the "bad news" in the "good news–bad news" situation is that the tax deduction for child care may be abolished.

4. _____ From what the author implies in paragraphs 13 and 14, we can infer that, because so many women with children are working, (a) it is no longer worth the effort to debate whether day-care is beneficial or harmful to children; (b) any kind of day-care is preferable to a bored mother staying at home all day; (c) no more expensive research studies on day-care should be done; (d) the direction of research into day-care and its effects needs to be completely different.

5. _____ The studies cited in paragraphs 21–27 and in paragraph 31 suggest that, with respect to the question of their emotional development, parents who put their infants into day-care (a) do not have anything to worry about; (b) may have some cause for concern; (c) should abandon the idea of day-care completely; (d) should find a day-care center that cares for large numbers of infants.

6. _____ From the information Meredith provides in paragraph 39, we can infer that an older woman with little professional training caring for children in their own home (a) is probably not as desirable as other kinds of day-care; (b) is probably the most desirable form of day-care for them;

(c) is just as good as any of the other alternatives; (d) fosters independence and good social skills.

7.   _____ The author probably intends us to interpret the information in
paragraph 45—that keeping a child in a warm environment where there
is lots of hugging and kissing actually retards their development—as
being (a) unrealistic; (b) untrue; (c) ironic; (d) logical.

8.   _____ From the article as a whole, we can accurately conclude that (a) the
parents' choice of a day-care center does not matter as much as a stable,
secure home environment; (b) with so many mothers now working,
choosing the best day-care environment for one's child is crucial; (c) with
so many good alternatives available today, parents should feel no guilt or
regret about using day-care services for their children; (d) if the economy
improves, fewer women with young children will be forced to seek work
outside the home.

E.   **ANALYZING ORGANIZATION AND SEEING RELATIONSHIPS**
Choose the correct answer.

1.   _____ The opening paragraphs of the essay, paragraphs 1–3, present short
examples, each of which illustrates (a) a national crisis; (b) the working
mother's dilemma; (c) the importance of mothers' working outside the
home; (d) the negative effects of day-care on young children.

2.   _____ The logical relationship implied in the last sentence of paragraph 4
is (a) contrast—a discussion of differences; (b) comparison—a discussion
of similarities; (c) general term and a supporting example; (d) cause and
effect.

3.   _____ To provide evidence for the conclusion that, at least for older children, day-care does not harm the child's intellectual or emotional development, Meredith relies mainly on (a) the experiences and observations
of several parents; (b) his own experiences and observations; (c) the
findings of several psychological studies; (d) the testimony of child development experts.

4.   _____ Look again at paragraphs 9–10. The relationship between the first
sentence of paragraph 9 and those that follow it is (a) general idea and
specific supporting examples; (b) contrast—a discussion of differences; (c)
comparison—a discussion of similarities; (d) analogy and an explanation
of it.

5.   Paragraphs 17 and 18 present a contrast. What is being contrasted?
_____ and _____.

6.   Edward Zigler apparently put his foot in his mouth when he was quoted
as characterizing infant day-care as "the psychological thalidomide of the
'80s," which he subsequently tried, unsuccessfully, to correct. What did

he mean by the original quotation? Refer to the definition of *thalidomide* at the end of the Vocabulary Preview section if necessary.

_____

_____

7.   _____ Concerning the somewhat negative effects of day-care on infants, Meredith presents the results of psychological research (a) confidently; (b) bluntly; (c) in a biased manner; (d) cautiously.

8.   _____ Meredith's tone—that is, his emotional attitude—toward the subject of day-care is (a) hostile, angry; (b) critical, fault-finding; (c) objective, neutral; (d) positive, optimistic.

F.   UNDERSTANDING VOCABULARY
Choose the correct definition according to the context.

1.   _____ "Day Care: The Nine-to-Five *Dilemma* [title]: (a) complex issue; (b) serious problem; (c) series of alternatives; (d) predicament involving two balanced choices.

2.   _____ when working is *plagued* by worries [1]: (a) tormented; (b) interrupted; (c) surrounded; (d) made physically ill.

3.   _____ *unprecedented* numbers of mothers [4]: (a) significantly large; (b) without previous example or parallel; (c) without any order or structure; (d) verifiable.

4.   _____ The *compromises* parents make [8]: (a) tough decisions; (b) definite plans; (c) settlements made by mutual concessions; (d) activities where one is in a dangerous situation.

5.   _____ to believe that the traditional family *predominates* [12]: (a) has authority or influence over; (b) is in a position of leadership; (c) is first in rank; (d) exists in greater numbers.

6.   _____ It's a widespread *misapprehension* [12]: (a) error; (b) illusion; (c) incorrect understanding; (d) lie.

7.   _____ the *surge* of women into the workplace [13]: (a) large increase, sudden onrush; (b) violent rising and falling action; (c) entry; (d) gentle, gradual movement.

8.   _____ is day-care more *detrimental* than parent-care? [13]: (a) expensive; (b) nurturing; (c) harmful; (d) unreliable.

9.   _____ At one end of the *spectrum* [15]: (a) broad range of varied but related ideas; (b) assortment of random items; (c) band of colors; (d) controversy, disagreement.

10.   _____ the effects of infant day-care remain agonizingly *murky* [18]: (a) dis-

turbing, unsettling; (b) unclear, confused; (c) negative, critical; (d) difficult to understand or accept.

11. _____ "The first wave of research made everybody feel *sanguine*" [19]: (a) cheerful, optimistic; (b) wildly enthusiastic; (c) gloomy, pessimistic; (d) sad, melancholy.

12. _____ an infant may *thrive* on intense relationships [30]: (a) be confused about; (b) survive; (c) compete for attention; (d) flourish, grow vigorously.

13. _____ If there is a *consensus* [31]: (a) a discussion; (b) a disagreement; (c) an agreement; (d) a debate.

14. _____ how the children reacted to their mothers [and] *peers* [36; also 39 and 44]: (a) brothers and sisters, siblings; (b) adult strangers; (c) equals; (d) caregivers.

15. _____ Children were not *randomly* assigned [46]: (a) hastily; (b) haphazardly; (c) finally; (d) impartially.

G. USING VOCABULARY

Write the correct inflected form of the base word in each of the following sentences. Refer to your dictionary if necessary.

1. (*disrupt*—use a noun)   Something as simple as a sore throat or the sniffles can cause great _____ to a working mother's schedule.

2. (*alteration*—use a verb)   The way we raise our children has dramatically _____ in the past two decades.

3. (*alternatives*—use a verb)   Although Meredith does not mention it, some families _____ their work schedules so that one parent is always home to care for the children.

4. (*commitment*—use an adjective)   According to the author, the government is not particularly _____ to solving the country's child-care problem.

5. (*psychologist*—use an adverb)   According to most studies, older children who receive quality day-care are not harmed _____.

6. (*obscure*—use a noun)   Unfortunately, the effects of day-care on babies remains somewhat in _____, since studies have produced contradictory findings.

7. (*crucial*—use an adverb)   It is _____ important for infants to have a consistent and warm relationship with their caregivers.

8. (*vital*—use an adverb)   Psychologists agree that it is _____ important that day-care centers have only a very few infants, if they are going to get the necessary attention.

9. (*hindered*—use a noun)   One _____ to better and more complete information about the effects of day-care on children will be the changing character of the American family.

10. (*valid*—use a noun)   There is some _____ to the theory that day-care has many advantages, especially for disadvantaged children.

H.   TOPICS FOR WRITING OR DISCUSSION

1.   This article presents the findings of three different research studies. Summarize these findings in a sentence or two for each.

---

2.   Should employers be required to give mothers and fathers automatic child-care leaves at full pay for a year after the birth of a baby?

33

Richard Bernstein

A WAR OF WORDS: BILINGUAL EDUCATION

This article is about bilingual education, a system of educating nonnative speakers of English in their own languages until they become proficient enough to take all of their classes in English. Begun in the 1970s, bilingual education has been widely praised for improving the educational level of immigrant children. On the contrary side, however, bilingual instruction has recently come under attack from critics who say that it prevents immigrant children from entering the mainstream and from becoming assimilated. At the heart of this issue is America's cultural identity, as increasing numbers of racial and ethnic minorities challenge the dominant white, Anglo culture.

VOCABULARY PREVIEW

WORD ORIGINS

PANACEA

Bernstein writes in paragraph 3 that supporters of bilingual education believe the system is "a kind of *panacea* for the generally poor performance of Hispanic children in public schools." Meaning "a cure-all," *panacea* is derived from *panakēs* ("all-healing"), which in turn derives from the common Greek prefix *pan-* ("all") + *akos* ("cure").

Here are some other English words beginning with this prefix:

panorama	an unlimited view [*pan-* + *horāma* ("sight")]
pantheon	a temple dedicated to all the gods; all the gods belonging to a people [*pan-* + *theos* ("god")]
pandemic	widespread, general; also describing a disease or epidemic spread over a wide geographic area [*pan-* + *dēmos* ("people")]
panegyric	a speech of praise, especially of the dead [*pan-* + *agora* ("assembly")]

ANATHEMA

As it is used in paragraph 3 ("bilingual education is *anathema*"), *anathema* means "something detested or loathed." *Anathema* is an example of a word that has done a complete about-face from its original etymology; it also illustrates the process of *pejoration*, which occurs when a word's meaning changes from positive to negative.

Anathema in Greek meant something set aside as an offering to a god. However, since this offering usually was sacrificed, the word took on the association of being doomed or accursed. The Catholic Church used this sense of the word to describe a formal curse involving being excommunicated from the church. Today, therefore, in common usage if something is described as *anathema*, it is shunned or despised.

UTOPIA

Bernstein quotes one writer, Rosalie Pedalino Porter, author of *Forked Tongue*, who became disillusioned with bilingual education. According to Porter, " 'Before the *utopia* arrives and everyone has equal access, we are going to have generations of children who are going to be in tough shape if they're not able to use the language of the majority.' "

The word *utopia* was made up by Sir Thomas More, whose *Utopia*, published in 1516, described an imaginary island where perfection reigned. However, his made-up word is a pun (a play on words). In Greek, the prefix *eu-* means "well," and *ou-* means "no" or "not." Therefore, *utopia* literally means "no place" [*ou-* ("no") + *topos* ("place")]. Today a *utopia* means any idealistic goal or situation.

WORD PARTS

BI-, CENT-

Both *bilingual* and *centuries* (see paragraph 10) begin with prefixes indicating number. *Bi-* indicates two, and *cent-*, one hundred. *Bilingual* means, literally, "having two languages," and a *century* is a period of one hundred years. Here are some of the common Latin and Greek prefixes that indicate number, along with some illustrative words:

half	Latin: *semi-* (semicircle, a semimonthly magazine is published twice a month); Greek: *hemi-* (hemisphere)
one	Latin: *uni-* (unicycle, unison, unicorn); Greek: *mono-* (monosyllable, monarchy, monotheism, monotone)
two	Latin: *bi-* (biannual, bimonthly, bisect); also *duo* (duet, duo-controls)
three	Latin: *tri-* (trimester, triplets, tricycle)
ten	Greek: *deca-* (decade, decathlon)
one hundred	Latin: *cent-* (centipede, cents, centigrade)
one thousand	Latin: *mille* [millennium ("a period of a thousand years"), millipede ("a thousand feet"), millimeter]

WORD FAMILIES

NATIVE

Bilingual education essentially instructs children in their *native* language, meaning the language they were born with. There are a fairly large number of words that derive from the same root, meaning "to be born." Most of them followed this journey: Middle English *natif*, from Old French, from Latin *nātīvus*, from *nātus*, ("to be born"). Here are a few of the more obvious ones: *nation, nationality, natural, nature, prenatal, postnatal, nativity.* Here are two less obvious ones:

naive	lacking worldliness and sophistication
née	from the French for "born," meaning the name a married woman was born with, for example, Mrs. Charlotte Spears, née Charlotte Grant.

CHRONICLES

The word *chronicle* can be either a noun, meaning "a record of events written in time order," or a verb, meaning "to record." It is the second form that Bernstein uses in paragraph 18. The root of this word *chron-* comes from the Greek root *khronos* ("time"); here are three English words in this family:

chronic	lasting a long time, as in "a *chronic* cough"
chronological	time order
chronometer	a watch, especially a very precise one

RICHARD BERNSTEIN

A WAR OF WORDS: BILINGUAL EDUCATION

1   In a well-worn classroom at the San Fernando Elementary School, 30 miles north of Los Angeles, Aracelis Tester, a second-grade teacher, is reading "Cuidado, un Dinosaurio!"—"Watch Out, a Dinosaur!"—with her diminutive pupils. This could just as well be Mexico City or San Salvador, Grenada or Seville: a roomful of Hispanic children and a Hispanic teacher speaking Spanish.

2   In downtown Los Angeles, at a school called the Wilton Place Elementary, Chan Hee Hong, a first-grade teacher, is talking in Korean with the children of recent immigrants about the wonderful world of frogs. There are public schools in Oklahoma where Cherokee is the language of instruction. In Astoria, in the borough of Queens in New York City, Greek is taught in Public School 122; Haitian Creole is a language of instruction in some 20 public schools in Brooklyn and Queens; in addition, New York offers schooling in Chinese, Korean, French, Italian, Russian, Vietnamese and Khmer.

3   In the San Fernando Elementary School, the teaching of non-English-speaking children in their native language enjoys a virtually religious status: It is seen as a kind of panacea for the generally poor performance of Hispanic children in public schools. But at the Glenwood Elementary School in the San Fernando Valley, in a

neighborhood of neatly kept stucco homes festooned with bougainvillea, bilingual education is anathema. The Glenwood teachers often conduct classes in Spanish, since they are given no choice by the Los Angeles School District. The school, a political model to some, is notorious to others. Hispanic demonstrators shouting ''racist'' and carrying signs printed ''KKK'' have picketed outside the school, where teachers have been outspoken in their view that teaching children in Spanish is a fraud, a trick played by tendentious adult theoreticians on innocent children. They say that bilingual education is a failure, a tactic that in the end will harm the chances of generally poor, non-English-speaking children ever having an equal share in the promise of American life.

4   The San Fernando school and the Glenwood school represent the two poles of a debate, already 20 years old, that has lately become more acrimonious than ever. This is a nation that has successfully absorbed millions of immigrants without creating a huge bureaucracy or spending tens of millions of dollars to teach them in the languages of their ancestors. But in the last few years, teaching children ''Watch Out, a Dinosaur!'' in Spanish and talking to them about frogs in Korean has become a matter of deep importance to an ever-growing minority.

5   Part of the reason for this is that in America today more people speak foreign languages than ever before. Neighborhoods like those in the San Fernando Valley, whose residents were largely white and English-speaking 10 to 20 years ago, today have a Hispanic population of at least 90 percent. In Los Angeles, school-district officials say there are, besides Spanish and English, seven other major languages spoken in their district—Korean, Cantonese, Armenian, Vietnamese, Filipino, Farsi and Cambodian.

6   Why aren't these students being taught only in the language of their newly adopted land? One reason is that organized minority groups are demanding that they be educated in their native language—and they have won allies within the local education establishments of a number of cities. For many of these minorities, the subject evokes deep emotions. Advocates of bilingual education believe that it represents the best chance for non-English-speaking children—who, not so coincidentally, often come from the lower-income groups—to enjoy the richness and opportunities of American life. ''We have found a way to achieve educational parity and, by the way, to have people who are competent in two languages,'' said Raul Yzaguirre, the director of the National Council of La Raza in Washington, an umbrella group of several hundred Hispanic organizations.

7   This argument, once a minority position, has acquired a new ally in Washington. The Bush administration has appointed an unequivocal advocate of bilingual education, Rita Esquivel, to take charge of federal programs in the Department of Education. ''We on the federal level like to leave it up to the districts to decide on their particular program,'' said Esquivel, the director of the Office of Bilingual Education and Minority Languages Affairs. ''But we certainly would like them to maintain their native languages. That's the president's point of view.''

8   If the forces in favor of bilingual education have gained an ally in the White House, there are still plenty of people on the other side of the issue—people who are convinced that teaching children in their native languages is bad, both for them and the country. Bilingual education, they argue, is more likely to prepare minority

children for careers in the local Taco Bell than for medical school or nuclear physics. "It doesn't work," said Sally Peterson, a teacher at the Glenwood School and the founder of Learning English Advocates Drive, or LEAD, a group of teachers and citizens that has quickly gathered adherents across the country. "It seemed to make a lot of sense, and I bought it at the beginning, but after a year, or so I saw that children were languishing in the program."

9   The other, more subterranean part of the argument is political. Ethnic pride is involved here on one side, a sense that what is sometimes called "white, Anglo" education is demeaning or psychologically harmful to minority groups. On the other side there is a deep-seated worry that more is involved than an educational program to help minority students.

10   Bilingual education is only one element in this picture, its opponents believe, a reflection of intensifying demands within the schools for courses that represent the interests of particular ethnic constituencies. It's no longer enough for children to learn who George Washington was. They have to learn to feel good about their own heritage. The much discussed "Curriculum of Inclusion," produced by a special minority task force in New York state last year, argued that "African Americans, Asian Americans, Puerto Ricans/Latinos and Native Americans have all been the victims of an intellectual and educational oppression that has characterized the culture and institutions of the United States and the European-American world for centuries."

11   The solution, the task force concluded, was a new curriculum that, by concentrating on contributions by members of minority groups to the culture, would ensure that minority children "have higher self-esteem and self-respect, while children from European cultures will have a less arrogant perspective of being part of the group that has 'done it all.' "

12   What's at stake, then, is nothing less than the cultural identity of the country. Those who argue that bilingual education is a right make up a kind of informal coalition with those who are pressing for changes in the way the United States is perceived—no longer as a primarily European entity to which all others have to adapt, but as a diverse collection of ethnic groups, each of which deserves more or less equal status and respect.

13   "The disagreement is whether a child has a right to have his native language developed—not just maintained but *developed*," said James J. Lyons, the executive director of the National Association for Bilingual Education, a professional organization that drafted much of the federal legislation on bilingual programs. "There is a racist xenophobia about Spanish in particular."

14   Those on the other side insist that diversity is all well and good, but they argue that bilingual education could lead to an erosion of the national unity, a fragmentation of the nation into mutually hostile groups. Leading the fight is a group called U.S. English, whose major objectives are to promote opportunities for people to learn English and to get a constitutional amendment adopted that would make English the official language of government. Founded by former Senator S. I. Hayakawa and including such eminent figures as Saul Bellow, Barry Goldwater and Eugene McCarthy on its board of advisers, U.S. English has seen its membership swell to 400,000 in just seven years of existence. "Language is so much a part of

our lives that it can be a great tool either for unity or disunity," said Kathryn S. Bricker, the group's former executive director. "And we are getting close to the point where we have a challenge to the common language that we share. Just look at what's going on in Miami, where a candidate to be school superintendent wanted everybody to have to learn Spanish.

15 "We are basically at a crossroads," she added. "We can reaffirm our need for a common language or we can slowly go down the road of division along language lines."

16 A volume called "Empowering Minority Students," written by Jim Cummins of the Ontario Institute for Studies in Education and printed by the California Association for Bilingual Education, so well sums up the underlying issues of the debate that it is cited by both sides: One side uses it to show the theoretical justification for bilingual education, the other to prove bilingual education's ulterior political motives. Cummins raises all the themes of the bilingual argument. It endorses multiculturalism; criticizes what he calls the "societal power structure" of white, English-speaking America; and claims that native-language teaching is not just an educational device, but a blow against an inherent injustice.

17 "Empowering Minority Students" does not argue that a child's inability to speak English is what leads him to fail if he is put into an English classroom. Children fail, Cummins says, because they are made to feel "shame" for belonging to a minority group, for not being a part of the "dominant group." The only way to "empower" such children, he argues, is for teachers to "consciously challenge the power structure both in their classrooms and schools and in the society at large." Bilingual education, he writes, is an "empowerment pedagogy." It is an act of rebellion against white, Anglo domination.

18 Another book, "Forked Tongue," written by Rosalie Pedalino Porter, a former educator from Massachusetts, chronicles her disillusionment with the bilingual-ed method. . . . "It's the old business of being a professional victim, of not admitting that anything good has ever been done for minorities. Otherwise you couldn't keep asking for special treatment," she says.

19 The idea of encouraging children who don't speak English to learn proficiency in their native language sounds like a plausible way to redress social inequality. But Porter is convinced that it could also have a negative effect. "Before the utopia arrives," she said, "and everyone has equal access, we are going to have generations of children who are going to be in tough shape if they're not able to use the language of the majority. Maintaining their language and their culture would be nice, but it's not as important as helping them learn to succeed in American life."

20 In a fifth-grade classroom at San Fernando Elementary School, Martha Ruiz, who is fluent in Spanish and English, sits at a low table with a group of a dozen or so little boys and girls, speaking to them only in English. She asks what a potion is, and a young girl with long hair and large black eyes replies in what sounds like perfectly mastered English: "It's something that could change you into a frog or something." This class is the presumed end result of TBE—Transitional Bilingual Education— the program to teach children in their native languages while they master English. It illustrates another tenet of the bilingual philosophy: that once basic skills have been mastered, children can make the transition from their native language to English without losing ground.

21   "Before," says Candida Fernandez-Ghoneim, San Fernando Elementary's principal, "in most bilingual programs, the kids were put into English so quickly that third graders would be reading at kindergarten levels and the students' self-esteem was damaged. Now we take the time to give the kids a real foundation, and they are really reading at their proper level."

22   It seems to make sense; certainly it does at Fernandez-Ghoneim's school, which imparts a warm feeling to a visitor, a sense that these kids—children of migrant families struggling economically—are learning. But Peterson's kindergarten class at Glenwood, where bilingual education is the enemy, also makes a favorable impression. The student constituency here is very similar to the one at San Fernando Elementary, with a high concentration of Hispanic children from migrant families, but Peterson concentrates on children whose parents have opted for virtually all-English instruction. She says that they are learning faster than the others.

23   Peterson and a junior colleague, Tracy Teitler, preside over 28 5- and 6-year olds sitting at two large tables in a gaily decorated classroom that has an air of controlled disorder about it. Hispanic children number about 20; there are a couple of Japanese; there is a Filipino; there are a few native English speakers. Over at San Fernando Elementary, they say Peterson is an advocate of what is pejoratively called "sink or swim"—just throwing foreign or Hispanic children into English-language classrooms and expecting them to absorb the language as if by magic.

24   Peterson replies that she gives special attention to the children who might have difficulty understanding English. You have to use drawings and act things out; you can speak a little Spanish here and there when it is necessary. You hug kids; you console them; you make sure they understand what you tell them. Within about two years, she says, those who started out with no English master it very well, illustrating the near-miraculous speed with which children will learn the language of their environment.

25   In his autobiography, "A Margin of Hope," the critic Irving Howe, speaking about the "ethnic" generation of the 1920s and 1930s, recalls his hunger for school as a child of Jewish immigrants growing up in the Bronx; for Howe, mastering the English language was a badge of Americanness. "The educational institutions of the city were still under the sway of a unified culture, that dominant 'Americanism' which some ethnic subcultures may have challenged a little, but which prudence and ambition persuaded them to submit to," he writes.

26   The question now is: What is the "dominant Americanism"? Can there even be such a thing in a country committed to a kind of ethnic self-realization that did not exist when Howe was growing up? The answers will be hammered out in the years ahead in classrooms such as Tester's and Peterson's, and they have to do with more than pedagogical philosophy. In the end, the way language is taught in this country will reflect where the country is going, its very identity.   ■

From Richard Bernstein, "A War of Words: Bilingual Education," *San Francisco Chronicle*, October 28, 1990. (Originally published in the *New York Times* in a slightly different version.) Reprinted by permission.

EXERCISES

Do not refer to the selection for Exercises A and B.

A.   DETERMINING THE MAIN IDEA AND PURPOSE
Choose the best answer.

1.   _____ The main idea of the article is that (a) American society is increasingly becoming a nation of immigrants who do not share a common culture or language; (b) bilingual education is the only way to help new immigrant children perform well in school and to prepare them for the future; (c) bilingual education is a controversial issue that raises serious questions about America's cultural identity; (d) bilingual education prevents immigrant children from becoming assimilated into American society.

2.   _____ With respect to the main idea, the author's purpose is (a) to present both sides of an issue; (b) to persuade the reader by presenting emotional and subjective arguments; (c) to inform and to explain; (d) to trace the history of a new educational method.

B.   COMPREHENDING MAIN IDEAS
Choose the correct answer.

1.   _____ Critics of bilingual education claim that it is a failure that ultimately will (a) result in a whole generation of illiterate children; (b) tear the schools apart and segregate ethnic groups even more than they already are; (c) deny these children the opportunity to go to college; (d) harm these children's chances for having an equal share in the promise of American life.

2.   _____ Bilingual education is offered in many school districts, and parents are demanding it for their children primarily because (a) more members of minority groups are becoming teachers; (b) more people speak foreign languages than ever before; (c) recent immigrants often refuse to learn English; (d) it has proved to be a sound educational policy.

3.   _____ According to Rita Esquivel, the director of the Office of Bilingual Education and Minority Languages Affairs, the Bush Administration (a) is opposed to bilingual education; (b) is in favor of bilingual education; (c) has changed its mind several times on the subject of bilingual education; (d) has no firm policy one way or the other concerning bilingual education.

4.   _____ Adherents of bilingual education say that the traditional "white Anglo" form of education for minority students is (a) demeaning and psychologically harmful; (b) inappropriate and obsolete in content; (c) appropriate only if the students have a facility for learning a language

quickly; (d) important if they are going to become full-fledged, assimilated members of American society.

5. _____ James J. Lyons, executive director of the National Association for Bilingual Education, says that whites demonstrate "a racist xenophobia" in particular toward (a) Vietnamese; (b) Chinese; (c) Spanish; (d) French.

6. _____ Bernstein says that the debate over the merits of bilingual education has brought to the forefront (a) divisions within the educational community that will probably never be healed; (b) the possibility of America as a diverse collection of ethnic groups, each of which deserves equal status and respect; (c) empowerment for minority group members; (d) increased racial and ethnic tensions.

COMPREHENSION SCORE

Score your answers for Exercises A and B as follows:

A.   No. right _____ × 2 = _____

B.   No. right _____ × 1 = _____

Total pts. from A and B _____ × 10 = _____%

You may refer to the selection for the remaining exercises.

C.   RECOGNIZING SUPPORTING DETAILS

Place an X in the space for each statement that *directly* supports this main idea from the selection. **"The idea of encouraging children who don't speak English to learn proficiency in their native language sounds like a plausible way to redress social inequality. But . . . it could also have a negative effect."**

1. _____ Rosalie Pedalino Porter, author of *Forked Tongue*, writes, "It's the old business of being a professional victim, of not admitting that anything good has ever been done for minorities. Otherwise you couldn't keep asking for special treatment."

2. _____ "Before the utopia arrives and everyone has equal access, we are going to have generations of children who are going to be in tough shape if they're not able to use the language of the majority."

3. _____ "Maintaining their language and their culture would be nice, but it's not as important as helping them learn to succeed in American life."

4. _____ Jim Cummins, author of *Empowering Minority Students*, says that children fail because they are made to feel "shame" for belonging to a minority group, for not being part of the "dominant group."

5. _____ James Lyons, the executive director of the National Association for Bilingual Education, writes, "The disagreement is whether a child has a

right to have his native language developed—not just maintained but *developed.''*

6. _____ They [opponents of bilingual education] argue that bilingual education could lead to an erosion of the national unity, a fragmentation of the nation into mutually hostile groups.

7. _____ This is a nation that has successfully absorbed millions of immigrants without creating a huge bureaucracy or spending tens of millions of dollars to teach them in the languages of their ancestors.

8. _____ Bilingual education . . . is more likely to prepare minority children for careers in the local Taco Bell than for medical school or nuclear physics.

D. MAKING INFERENCES

For each of these statements write Y (Yes) if the inference is an accurate one, N (No) if the inference is an inaccurate one, or CT (Can't Tell) if you do not have enough information to make an inference.

1. _____ The majority of America's bilingual education programs are located on either the West Coast or the East Coast.

2. _____ Opponents of the method have solid evidence that bilingual education is part of a white conspiracy to keep minority groups oppressed.

3. _____ Advocates of bilingual education believe that it is too hard for non-native children to struggle learning English during the years when they must also cope with learning basic skills like reading and math.

4. _____ Following the earlier waves of immigration to the U.S., one test of an immigrant's success in becoming assimilated was learning English.

5. _____ Children have a much easier time learning a new language than adults do.

6. _____ Bilingual education programs include, besides language study, information about children's cultural and ethnic heritage.

7. _____ Members of U.S. English and other opponents of bilingual education believe that linguistic diversity could erode national unity, which would ultimately result in more segregation and tension between ethnic groups rather than less.

8. _____ The bilingual education movement is as much a political doctrine as an educational one.

E. DISTINGUISHING BETWEEN FACT AND OPINION

For each of the following statements from the selection, write F if the statement represents a factual statement that can be verified or O if the statement represents the writer's own subjective opinion.

1. _____ In Astoria, in the borough of Queens in New York City, Greek is taught in Public School 122; Haitian Creole is a language of instruction in some 20 public schools in Brooklyn and Queens; in addition, New York offers schooling in Chinese, Korean, French, Italian, Russian, Vietnamese and Khmer.

2. _____ Advocates of bilingual education believe that it represents the best chance for non-English-speaking children—who, not so coincidentally, often come from the lower-income groups—to enjoy the richness and opportunities of American life.

3. _____ Ethnic pride is involved here on one side, a sense that what is sometimes called "white, Anglo" education is demeaning or psychologically harmful to minority groups.

4. _____ What's at stake, then, is nothing less than the cultural identity of the country.

5. _____ Those who argue that bilingual education is a right make up a kind of informal coalition with those who are pressing for changes in the way the United States is perceived—no longer as a primarily European entity to which all others have to adapt, but as a diverse collection of ethnic groups, each of which deserves more or less equal status and respect.

6. _____ Leading the fight is a group called U.S. English, whose major objectives are to promote opportunities for people to learn English and to get a constitutional amendment adopted that would make English the official language of government.

7. _____ Kathryn Bricker of U.S. English said, "We are basically at a crossroads. We can reaffirm our need for a common language or we can slowly go down the road of division along language lines."

8. _____ Within about two years . . . those who started out with no English master it very well, illustrating the near-miraculous speed with which children will learn the language of their environment.

F. ANALYZING ORGANIZATION AND SEEING RELATIONSHIPS
Choose the correct answer.

1. The author uses two kinds of evidence to support the main ideas,

    _____ and _____.

2. The relationship between the ideas expressed in paragraph 3 is contrast.

    What is being contrasted? _____ and

    _____

3. _____ Besides presenting the arguments for and against bilingual education, Bernstein is also particularly concerned with discussing (a) students'

poor performance in schools today; (b) the daily frustrations teachers face; (c) the contributions various minority groups have made to American culture; (d) the question of what constitutes a dominant Americanism today.

4. Sally Peterson is quoted in paragraph 8 as saying, "It seemed to make a lot of sense, and I bought it [the idea of bilingual education] at the beginning. . . . What is the meaning of the slang word "bought" in this context? _____

5. _____ Look again at paragraph 12. The transitional word "then" in the first sentence indicates that what follows will be (a) a conclusion; (b) an example; (c) a contrasting statement; (d) the next step in a process.

6. _____ Based on the author's discussion and the evidence he provides, how would you characterize Bernstein's own opinion about bilingual education? (a) He is definitely for it; (b) he is definitely against it; (c) he has not yet made up his mind about it; (d) his opinion is not evident from the article.

G. UNDERSTANDING VOCABULARY

Look through the paragraphs listed below and find a word that matches each definition. An example has been done for you.

Ex. small, tiny [paragraphs 1–2]   _____diminutive_____

1. a cure-all [2–3]   _____
2. something detested or shunned [2–3]   _____
3. done to promote a cause, biased [3–4]   _____
4. equality [6–7]   _____
5. clear, certain [7–8]   _____
6. weakening, continuing in a state of apathy [8–9]   _____
7. debasing, making one feel inferior [9–10]   _____
8. supporters, representatives [10–11]   _____
9. an alliance, especially a temporary one [12–13]   _____
10. fear of outsiders or foreigners [13–14]   _____
11. intentionally concealed so as to deceive [16–17]   _____
12. existing as an essential part [16–17]   _____

13. the art of teaching [16–17] _____

14. an idealistic goal, a state of perfection _____
    [19–20]

15. an opinion, principle, or doctrine [20–21] _____

H. USING VOCABULARY

In parentheses before each sentence are some inflected forms of words from the
selection. Study the context and the sentence. Then write the correct form in the space
provided. Be sure to add appropriate endings like -s, -ed, or -ing if necessary.

1. (*notoriety, notorious, notoriously*) San Fernando Elementary School has

   gained a certain _____ because its teachers dislike
   having to conduct bilingual classes.

2. (*acrimony, acrimonious, acrimoniously*) The debate over bilingual education, which has been going on for over twenty years, has been heating up

   and is now being argued even more _____ than it
   was in the past.

3. (*evocation, evoke, evocative, evocatively*) For many minorities the concept of

   bilingual education _____ deep emotions.

4. (*advocacy, advocate*) Some teachers who have _____
   that bilingual education is a fraud have been labeled "racist" by minority
   groups.

5. (*adaptation, adaptability, adapt, adaptive, adaptable*) In the late nineteenth

   century, recent immigrants eagerly _____ to Ameri-
   can life by becoming proficient in English, which was considered a badge
   of success.

6. (*proficiency, proficient, proficiently*) Some writers and teachers are con-

   cerned that if nonnative speakers don't become _____
   in English, their economic future will be in jeopardy.

7. (*plausibility, plausible, plausibly*) Proponents of bilingual education con-

   sider it a _____ way to ensure social equality and in-
   tegration.

8. (*option, opt, optional, optionally*) Some immigrant parents have ignored
   the arguments in favor of bilingual education and have, instead,

   _____ for their children to be instructed in English,

   apparently because bilingual instruction is _____ in
   the Los Angeles school district.

9. (*pejoration, pejorative, pejoratively*)   Advocates of bilingual education refer

_____ to the old "sink-or-swim" method of learning a language.

10. (*prudence, prudent, prudently*)   Irving Howe is quoted as saying that former immigrants _____ submitted to the dominant American culture because they were ambitious and wanted to become like other Americans as soon as possible.

I.   TOPICS FOR WRITING OR DISCUSSION

1.   In your own words and in a paragraph or two, briefly summarize the conflict over bilingual education; that is, list the arguments for each side as Bernstein explained them in the article.

_____

_____

_____

_____

_____

_____

_____

2.   Bilingual education is not only an educational issue; it is also both an emotional and a political issue with enormous long-term consequences for the future of the United States. What is your personal opinion about this issue? What assumptions and beliefs do you bring to it? To what extent has your background (your own education, your ethnic or cultural traditions) influenced your thinking? Examine your beliefs in some detail.

34 ||||||

Sue Hubbell

THE VICKSBURG GHOST

Since Elvis Presley's death in 1977, loyal fans make annual pilgrimages on the anniversary of his death to his Tennessee home, Graceland; a surprisingly large number of singers have made careers for themselves solely as Elvis-impersonators; and many communities sponsor Elvis look-alike contests. But in the late 1980s, a new phenomenon occurred: Elvis sightings.

This article, first published in The New Yorker *in 1989, describes one such incident—the case of a woman named Louise Welling who, like many Elvis fans, refuses to believe the King is dead and is convinced that she saw Elvis in a Vicksburg, Michigan, supermarket.*

VOCABULARY PREVIEW

WORD ORIGINS

NOSTALGIC, NOSTALGIA
The article contains the word *nostalgia* in paragraphs 1 and 49. The noun form *nostalgia* reflects the original Greek meaning, "a longing to return home": [*nostos* ("return home") + -*algia* ("pain")]. When we are *nostalgic* (the adjective form), we think of the past, specifically those elements—people, things, or events—that we have good memories about.

ALLUSIONS
This selection contains a few words that are allusions, that is, words that refer to things outside the text. Allusions can be difficult to understand unless you know what they are referring to. In order to find out, the dictionary is usually a good place to start. For example, in this article the author alludes to Greek history and mythology when he uses the words described below.

CYNIC
In paragraph 2 Hubbell quotes one *cynic* who exclaimed after Elvis's death, "Good career move!" A *cynic* is a person who believes that people are motivated by selfishness. The word derives from the name of a group of ancient Greek philosophers, the Cynics, who believed that sensual pleasure was contemptible and that virtue was the ultimate goal in

life, quite a different philosophy from the current meaning of the word. Although the original Cynics were not held in very high regard, linguists are not sure whether the name *Cynic* derives from *Cynosarges*, the name of the gymnasium where they congregated, or from *cynikos*, the Greek word for "dog," presumably because of their currish behavior.

TANTALIZING

Hubbell writes in paragraph 3: "In its year-end double issue, *People* ran a story featuring recent photographs of Elvis purportedly taken by readers around the country, each picture as vague and *tantalizing* as snapshots of the Loch Ness monster." Meaning "arousing interest or desire for something that is unobtainable," *tantalizing* derives from the name of a king, Tantalus. Charles Funk, in *Thereby Hangs a Tale*, explains both some theories about the crimes Tantalus supposedly committed and the etymology of the word:

> Whatever the crime he was punished by being placed in the lower world in the midst of a lake with clusters of fruit hanging over his head. Whenever he stooped to drink of the lake, however, the waters receded, and whenever he stretched up his hand for the fruit, the branches drew away. Thus, though water and fruit were apparently plentiful to relieve thirst and hunger, he was forever in torment by the withdrawal of that which he desired. *Tantalize,* formed from his name, commemorates the nature of his punishment.

DIONYSIAN, MAENADS

The author explains, also in paragraph 3, that she was too old during the 1950s "to respond to the *Dionysian* sexual appeal that he had for his teen-age *maenads*." Both allusions refer to Greek mythological figures. *Dionysus* was the Greek god of fertility and wine, and the adjective *Dionysian* refers to behavior that is frenzied, orgiastic, or recklessly uninhibited. A *maenad* was a woman who was a member of the original cult of Dionysus. Today, the word refers to any frenzied woman. Both words are apt terms to describe the behavior of Elvis's fans, who today would be called "groupies."

WORD PARTS

EPI-

This article, unlike the other selections in the text, begins with an *epigram*, a concise and cleverly worded quotation or saying that makes a pointed observation or effectively introduces a larger work. Novels often begin with epigrams. *Epi-*, a Greek prefix, can mean "on" or "around." In Greek an epigram meant an inscription, from: [*epi-* ("one") + *graphein* ("to write")].

And in paragraph 4, Hubbell writes that Vicksburg, Michigan, is *eponymously* named for John Vickers. An *eponymous* name refers to something named after a person, again from Greek, [*epi-* + *onoma* ("name")]. Some other examples of eponymous words are *mesmerize,* named after Friedrich Mesmer, an Austrian doctor who specialized in hypnosis, and *quisling,* a word referring to a traitor who serves an occupying enemy, named after Vidkun Quisling, a Norwegian traitor who supported the Nazis during their occupation. Here are some other English words that begin with *epi-:*

epicenter	the exact center of an earthquake
epidemic	a disease that spreads rapidly among a group of people [*epi- + dēmos* ("people")]
epidermis	the outer layer of skin [*epi- + derma* ("skin")]
epitome	a summary of a book or article; something that represents an entire class [*epitemnein,* "to cut upon the surface, cut short"]
epithet	a term used to characterize a person or thing [*epitheton* ("an addition")]

INTER-

To *interject* (see paragraph 34) means "to interrupt," "to say something in the middle of a conversation." The prefix *inter-* means "between" or "among," and it is used in literally dozens of English words, for example: *interrupt, intercept, interchange, interfere, intergalactic, interlude, intermarry, internal, international, intersperse,* and *intervene.*

WORD FAMILIES

MEMORABILIA

The word *memorabilia* means, literally, "things worthy of remembrance," in other words, "souvenirs." Hubbell writes in paragraph 1 that since his death, fans have collected Elvis *memorabilia.* This word comes from the Latin verb *memorare* ("to remember") and *memor* ("mindful"). Here are some other words in this family:

memento	a reminder of the past, a souvenir
memoir	a collection of remembered experiences
memorable	describing something worth remembering
memorandum or memo	a short note written as a reminder
memorial	something established to remember a person or an event
memory	the ability to remember

Other words you should know:

retro-Elvis	[paragraph 3]: The prefix *retro-* refers to "again"; in this case a reference to the phenomenon of keeping Elvis's memory alive
riposte	[11]: a quick, witty response
flotsam	[16]: literally, any wreckage floating on the ocean after a ship has sunk; here, any discarded bits and pieces of news
tabloid	[16]: illustrated newspapers that deal in sensational stories, such as are found at supermarket checkout counters

Amish	[29]: a branch of the Mennonites; a member of the Protestant sect that settled mainly in Pennsylvania, Ohio, and Iowa. They live simply, wearing dark clothing and farming with ox-drawn plows, since they do not believe in using gas-driven or electric tools or implements.
seánce	[51]: a meeting where people try to communicate with spirits

SUE HUBBELL

THE VICKSBURG GHOST

> The human predicament is typically so complex that it is not altogether clear which lies are vital and what truths beg for discovery.
>
> —*"Vital Lies, Simple Truths: The Psychology of Self-Deception,"* by Daniel Goleman

1   I guess most people found it hard to believe that Elvis Presley didn't die after all but instead is alive and well and shopping at Felpausch's Supermarket, in Vicksburg, Michigan. I know I did when I read about it in the New York *Times* last fall. The *Times* wasn't on record as saying, "THE KING LIVES," or anything like that, but it did report that a Vicksburg woman named Louise Welling had said she'd seen him the year before, in the supermarket's checkout line. Her sighting encouraged Elvins [Elvis fans] everywhere, many of whom believe that Presley faked his death. It also added an extra fillip to Elvismania, which is part nostalgia and part industry, the industry part consisting of the production of Elvis memorabilia, books, articles, tours, and prime-time TV "docudramas." Fans have made periodic demands for an Elvis postage stamp, and a multimedia musical—"Elvis: A Rockin' Remembrance"—had an Off-Broadway run this summer.

2   Promotion was what made Elvis Presley. In 1977, the year of his death, his likeness was more widely reproduced than any other save that of Mickey Mouse, and it has been reported that the news of his demise was greeted by one cynic with the words "Good career move!" According to Albert Goldman, the biographer who tells this story, Presley was by then a porky, aging, drug-befuddled Las Vegas entertainer and was getting to be a hard personality to promote. The Presley image shorn of the troublesome real man was easier to market. For example, after the King's death, Presley's manager, Colonel Thomas A. Parker, contracted with a vineyard in Paw Paw, Michigan—a town not far from Vicksburg—to produce a wine called Always Elvis. Its label bears a head shot of the entertainer, in a high-collared spangled white shirt, singing into a hand-held microphone. Colonel Parker's own four-stanza poem appears on the back of the bottle. Goldman has computed that the poem earned Parker twenty-eight thousand dollars in royalties, "making him, line for line, the best-paid poet in the world." Although the wine is no longer produced, I was able to find a dusty old bottle in my local liquor store. In the

interests of journalism, I sampled it. It was an adequate companion to the poem, which closes with the couplet

> We will play your songs from day to day
> For you really never went away.

3   In its year-end double issue, *People* ran a story featuring recent photographs of Elvis purportedly taken by readers around the country, each picture as vague and tantalizing as snapshots of the Loch Ness monster. While debate mounted over whether or not Elvis Presley was still alive, I got stuck back there in the part of the *Times'* story which said that he was shopping at Felpausch's. By the latter part of the nineteen-fifties, when Elvis arrived to sweep away the dreariness of the Eisenhower years, I was too old to respond to the Dionysian sexual appeal that he had for his teen-age maenads; consequently, I was also unmoved by retro-Elvis. But I did grow up near Vicksburg. My family lived in Kalamazoo, a bigger town (in which Elvis was also said to have appeared) twelve miles to the north, and we spent our summers at a lake near Vicksburg. My widowed mother now lives at the lake the year round, and when I visit her I often shop at Felpausch's myself. I know Vicksburg tolerably well, so when I read the account in the *Times* I strongly suspected that the reporter had been snookered by a group of the guys over at Mar-Jo's Café, on Main Street, half a block from Felpausch's, which is on Prairie Street, the town's other commercial thoroughfare. Last June, while I was visiting my mother, I decided to drive into Vicksburg and find out what I could about the Elvis Presley story.

4   Vicksburg is a pretty village of two thousand people, more or less. A hundred and fifty years ago, when it was first settled by white people, the land was prairie and oak forest. James Fenimore Cooper, who lived for a time in the nearby town of Schoolcraft, wrote about the area in his book "Oak Openings." It is in southern Michigan, where the winters are long and gray, and even the earliest settlers complained of the ferocity of the summertime mosquitoes. Vicksburg's one-block commercial section has been spruced up in recent years. There are beds of petunias at the curb edges, and new façades on the nineteenth-century buildings. The carefully maintained Victorian houses on the side streets are shaded by maples big enough to make you think elm. A paper mill, built near a dam that the eponymous John Vickers constructed on Portage Creek for his flour mill, has long provided employment for the local people, but today the village has become something of a bedroom community for commuters to Kalamazoo. Still, it seems very like the place I knew when I used to come to band concerts on Wednesday evenings at the corner of Main and Prairie, during the summers of the nineteen-thirties and forties. The band concerts are a thing of the past, but there are other homegrown entertainments, such as one going on the week I was there—the annual Vicksburg Old Car Festival, which is run by Skip Knowles, a local insurance man. The festival has a fifties theme, and last year, inspired by the commotion that Louise Welling's sighting of Elvis had produced, Knowles added an Elvis-look-alike contest to the roster of events. Knowles has his office in a storefront on Main Street which used to

be Matz's Confectionery, where I first discovered lime phosphates (known locally as "green rivers").

5   And the teen-agers are still bored. While I was in the library going through back issues of local newspapers, two high-school girls introduced themselves to me, saying that they had lived in Vicksburg all their lives and would be happy to talk to me about it. I asked them what they thought about Elvis Presley. They smiled patronizingly and informed me that no one they knew paid any attention to him. "But *everything* just stands still in Vicksburg," one of them confided. "We go to Kalamazoo on Saturday nights. I can't wait to get out of here and go to college."

6   Mar-Jo's has stayed the same, too. It has been in the same place for forty years. It was named after Marge Leitner and her partner, Josephine, whose last name no one at the café can remember. It is your basic tan place: tan floor, tan walls, tan tables, tan counter. The sign taped to the cash register was new to me. It said:

> THIS IS NOT
> BURGER KING
> YOU GET IT
> MY WAY
> OR YOU DON'T
> GET IT
> AT ALL

7   But the men having coffee together at the big round table near the front windows could have been the same ones sitting there the last time I was in, which was a couple of years ago.

8   "How's you-know-who?" gray crewcut asks feed-store cap. "Don't see her anymore."

9   The others guffaw, and one says, "He's taken her clothes."

10   "What clothes?" feed-store cap shoots back. A ripple of caffeine-fuelled laughter circles the table.

11   Shirley White, a small, wiry woman, has been a waitress at Mar-Jo's for eleven years. Her hair is dark and tightly curled. She is efficient and cheerful. She knows virtually all her customers by name and how they like their coffee, and she banters with all of them. She gets to work at four-forty-five every morning, so she is usually way ahead of the best of the town wits, giving as good as she gets. The coffee-club boys once arranged the kind of prank on her that made me suspect them of the Elvis Presley caper. One of the regulars was a big man whom she could deftly unsettle with a clever phrase or two. His invariable riposte was a mumbled "Paybacks are hell." A few years ago, he was on vacation in Florida when her birthday came around, and she had nearly forgotten about him. Mar-Jo's was jammed that day, and no one would tell her why. "Just as I was busiest, this really big monkey walked in," she told me. "At least, it was a big guy dressed in a monkey costume, and he kept following me around, getting in my way. I was real embarrassed, and everyone kept laughing. Then a messenger handed me something called an Ape-O-Gram. It had just three words: 'Paybacks are hell.' "

12   Nearly all the coffee drinkers thought that the Elvis Presley sighting was as funny as the Ape-O-Gram, but no one would own up to having had a hand in making up the story. Louise Welling, it seemed, was a real person, and well known in town. She lived to the east, a few miles outside the village, they told me. "She's different, that's for sure," one of the coffee drinkers said. "No one believes her about Elvis Presley, but we all enjoyed it. Kind of put Vicksburg on the map. Isn't it funny? Elvis Presley wasn't even a very good singer. But I don't think Louise thinks it's funny." They referred me to a woman in town who knew Louise Welling better than they did and lived not far from her.

13   I went over to see the woman, who had an office in town, and talked to her with the understanding that her name would not be used. "Yes," she said. "I guess you could say that Louise is different. Her whole family is different, except for her husband, who works at General Motors. He's real quiet. But she's not crazy or anything. In fact, I think she's real bright. I don't know what to make of her claim that she saw Elvis Presley. She was a big Elvis fan from way back, but she doesn't bring him up or talk about this stuff unless someone asks her. She's a kind woman. She's reliable, too, and I wouldn't hesitate to call her if I had trouble. I'm afraid that after the story came out a lot of people played jokes on her. Made Elvis phone calls. Sent her Elvis letters. I'm pretty sure she's not in it for money. She just seems to think it's an interesting story, and it makes her mad when people don't believe her. Of course, none of us do. I don't know anyone in this town who thinks she really saw Elvis Presley. She was furious with the Vicksburg newspaper because they wouldn't run her story."

14   It seemed odd to me that the Vicksburg *Commercial* had not used Louise Welling's story—a story that had made the New York *Times*—so I called up Jackie Lawrence, the owner of the *Commercial,* and asked her to meet me for lunch at Mar-Jo's. Jackie Lawrence, a former nurse, is a big woman with curly brown hair, and she smiles a lot when she talks about Vicksburg, her adopted town. There are, she said, perhaps a dozen loyal Elvis fans in town—people who make pilgrimages to Graceland and would *like* to believe Louise Welling even if they don't.

15   We studied the daily specials, which were posted on the wall, and I decided to order Ken's Homemade Goulash. Next to the list of specials were snapshots of Ken Fowler, a cheerful young man with a fine brushy mustache, who bought Mar-Jo's two years ago and does a lot of the café's cooking. Shortly after he bought the place, he had a birthday, and the regulars, the waitresses, and Ken's wife conspired to bring in a belly dancer. The event was captured on film, and the posted snapshots show Ken, in apparent embarrassment, on a chair in one corner of the café, surrounded by laughing customers as a woman in gold draperies writhes in front of him.

16   Jackie Lawrence told me that she remembered Louise Welling coming into the newspaper office, which is a few doors down from Mar-Jo's, in March, 1988, six months after the sighting at Felpausch's. At the time of her visit, Mrs. Welling knew that her story would soon be printed nationally, in the *Weekly World News*—and so it was, three months later. (According to Jim Leggett, who is the dean of free-lance tabloid photojournalists and once schemed to drill a hole in Howard Hughes' coffin

in order to photograph his face, the *Weekly World News* is not exactly esteemed in the trade. "It prints the flotsam left by the better tabloids," he told me.) Mrs. Welling had wanted the *Commercial* to run her story first, Lawrence said. "She stood right by my desk, trying to tell me all about it. I said to her, 'I'm sorry, I don't have time for this,' and showed her out the door. And if she came in again, I'd say the same thing."

17   There was only one mention in the *Commercial* of the stir caused by Louise Welling's encounter with Elvis. The winner of Skip Knowles' 1988 Elvis-look-alike contest, a truck driver named Ray Kajkowski, came into the newspaper office a few days after the event to ask for prints of any pictures that might have been taken. While he was there, he kissed Jean Delahanty, one of the *Commercial's* reporters, and she wrote a column about it, which concluded, "Some days are better than others!"

18   There is no chamber of commerce, as such, in Vicksburg. The town doesn't need one; it has Skip Knowles. I had telephoned Knowles before coming to Vicksburg. "Give me a jingle when you get in," he said. "Maybe we can do lunch." He is a handsome, trim, dark-haired man, and at our lunch a gold chain showed through the open collar of his shirt. There was another gold chain around his wrist. He was born in Atchison, Kansas, he told me, but spent his teen-age years—from 1962 to 1968—near Detroit, where he developed a passion for cars and for cruising, that cool, arm-on-the-window, slow patrolling of city streets which was favored by the young in those days. His dark eyes sparkled at the memory.

19   "We had what we called the Woodward Timing Association," he said. "It was made up of the guys that cruised Woodward Avenue. The Elias Big Boy at Thirteen Mile Road and Woodward was the place we'd go. But you know how the grass is always greener somewhere else? Well, my ultimate dream was to cruise the Sunset Strip. It wasn't until I got married, in 1969, and went out to California that I got to do that. And I talked to those guys cruising the Strip, and you know what they told me? It was *their* dream to cruise Woodward." He shook his head and laughed. "My wife and I still cruise when we go to a city." He hoped the local people had got cruising down pat for this year's festival, he said, handing me a packet of publicity material and a schedule of festival events. "I had to *teach* them how to cruise last year, which was the first time we closed off the streets for it."

20   The second annual Elvis-look-alike contest would be held at 9 P.M. Saturday, over on Prairie Street, in the parking lot of the Filling Station, a fast-food restaurant across the street from Felpausch's. Skip Knowles knew a good thing when he had it. Before last summer, he said, the festival had been drawing several thousand people, but each year he had had more trouble getting good publicity. "I can't understand the way they handled the Elvis business over at Felpausch's," he told me. "They even refused an interview with the New York *Times*. But I decided to play it for whatever it was worth."

21   After the first Elvis-look-alike contest, Knowles received a lot of calls from Louise Welling, who wanted to talk about Elvis Presley with him. "I put her off," he said. "She's *really* different. I think she really believes Presley never died." He also received other phone calls and visits. When his secretary told him last fall that a reporter from the *Times* was in his outer office waiting to talk to him, he thought it was just a hoax—a joke like the ones dreamed up at Mar-Jo's. But when he came out the man introduced himself as the paper's Chicago bureau chief and interviewed

him about the Elvis contest. Then a producer from Charles Kuralt's show, "Sunday Morning," called and said he was interested in doing a segment for the show on the impact of the Elvis sighting in Vicksburg, and would anything be going on in Vicksburg around Thanksgiving time? "I told him, 'Look, I'll do *anything* to get you here,'" Knowles recalled. "'If you want me to rent Cadillac limos and parade them up and down Main Street for you to film, I'll get them.' But the TV people never came."

22   I decided that it was time to talk to Louise Welling herself. I couldn't make an appointment with her by telephone, because she had recently obtained an unlisted number, but one midweek morning I took a chance on finding her at home and drove out to see her. The Wellings live in the country, in a modest split-level house on non-split-level terrain; this is the sandy, flat part of Michigan, too far south for the ice-age glaciers to have sculpted it. Mrs. Welling sometimes works as a babysitter, but this morning she was home, along with four of her five children—all of them grown—and Nathan, her four-year-old grandson. Mrs. Welling is a heavyset woman with closely cropped dark hair and a pleasant face. Her eyes stay sad when she smiles. She touched my arm frequently as we talked, and often interrupted herself to digress as she told me her story. She said that she grew up in Kalamazoo and for a time attended St. Mary's, a Catholic grammar school there. When she turned sixteen, she was given a special present—a ticket to a Presley concert in Detroit. "Somehow, the fellow who took tickets didn't take mine, so after the first show I was able to move up, and I sat in front during the second," she said. "And then, toward the end, Elvis got down on his knee right in front of me and spread his arms wide open. Well, you can imagine what *that* would be like for a sixteen-year-old girl." Her voice trailed off, and she fell silent, smiling.

23   I asked her if she had continued to follow his career.

24   "When I got married, I started having children, and I never thought much about Elvis," she said. "After all, I had problems of my own." But then, in 1973, she saw a notice in a throwaway shopping newspaper from Galesburg, a nearby town, saying that Presley would be in Kalamazoo and, although he would not be performing, would stay at the Columbia Hotel there.

25   "I didn't try to get in touch with him," Mrs. Welling said, adding, with a womanly smile, "I had a husband, and you know how that is." Three years later, however, Presley appeared in concert in Kalamazoo, and she sent flowers to him at the Columbia Hotel, because she assumed that he would be staying there again. She went to the concert, too, and, as she remembers it, Elvis announced in the course of it that he had a relative living in Vicksburg. "He said he liked this area," she recalled. "Kalamazoo is a peaceful place. He'd like that. And I think he's living at the Columbia right now, under another name. But they won't admit it there. Every time I call, I get a run-around. You know what I think? I think he has become an undercover agent. He was interested in that sort of thing."

26   "What year was it that you saw him in concert in Detroit?" I asked. I had read somewhere that Presley had not started touring outside the South until 1956.

27   "Oh, I don't remember," Mrs. Welling said. "I'm fifty-one now, and I had just turned sixteen—you figure it out."

28   The arithmetic doesn't work out—nor, for someone who grew up in

Kalamazoo, does the Columbia Hotel. The Columbia had its days of glory between the First World War and Prohibition, and it was growing seedy by the forties, when I used to ride by it on my way to school. Its decline continued after I left Kalamazoo, until—according to Dan Carter, one of the partners in a development company that remodelled the hotel to create an office complex called Columbia Plaza—it became "a fleabag flophouse and, for a while, a brothel." Carter also told me that in the mid-eighties a rumor arose that Elvis Presley was living there, behind the grand pink double doors on the mezzanine, which open into what was once a ballroom. The doors have been locked for years—the empty ballroom, its paint peeling, belongs to the man who owns Bimbo's Pizza, on the floor below—but that didn't deter Elvins here and abroad from making pilgrimages to Columbia Plaza. "You'd hear foreign voices out in the hallway almost every day," he said. "Then there was a visit from some people from Graceland—at least, they told us they were from Graceland, and they looked the part—who came by to see if we were making any money off this." They weren't, he said, and today the building's management denies that Elvis Presley, under any name, lives anywhere on the premises.

29   Mrs. Welling's next good look at Elvis Presley came at Felpausch's, in September, 1987. There had been, she told me, earlier hints. In 1979, she had seen a man in the back of the county sheriff's car when the police came to her house to check on the family's dog, which had nipped a jogger. "The man in the back seat was all slouched down, and he didn't look well," she said. "I'm sure it was Elvis." A few years later, black limousines began to appear occasionally on the road where she lives. "Now, who around here would have a limo?" she asked. Then she began seeing a man she believes was Elvis in disguise. "He looked real fake," she recalled. "He was wearing new bib overalls, an Amish hat, and a beard that didn't look real. I talked to a woman who had seen the same man, and she said he sometimes wore a false nose. Now, why does he have to bother with disguises? Why couldn't he have said that he needed a rest, and gone off to some island to get better?"

30   A note of exasperation had crept into Mrs. Welling's voice. She showed me a cassette that she said contained a tape that Presley made after he was supposed to have died; in it, she said, he explained why he had faked his death. But when she played it the sound was blurred and rumbly, and I couldn't make out the words. The tape had been issued in 1988, to accompany a book by a woman—with whom Mrs. Welling has corresponded—who put forward the theory that the body buried as Presley's was not his own. The book and another by the same author, which Welling said was a fictional account of a rock star who fakes his death, were lovingly inscribed ("It's hard to take the heat") to Mrs. Welling.

31   Here is what Mrs. Welling said happened to her in September, 1987. She had just been to eleven-o'clock Sunday Mass at St. Martin's Church. With grandson Nathan, she stopped at Felpausch's to pick up a few groceries. Having just celebrated one publicly accepted miracle, she saw nothing strange in the private miracle at the supermarket.

32   "The store was just about deserted," she said. "There wasn't even anyone at the checkout register when I went in. But back in the aisles I felt and heard someone behind me. It must have been Elvis. I didn't turn around, though. And then, when I got up to the checkout, a girl was there waiting on Elvis. He seemed kind of nervous.

He was wearing a white motorcycle suit and carrying a helmet. He bought something little—fuses, I think, not groceries. I was so startled I just looked at him. I knew it was Elvis. When you see someone, you know who he is. I didn't say anything, because I'm kind of shy and I don't speak to people unless they speak first. After I paid for the groceries, I went out to the parking lot, but no one was there."

33   I asked Mrs. Welling if she had told anyone at the time what she had seen. She replied that she had told no one except the author of the Elvis-isn't-dead book, who was "very supportive." After that, she and her daughter Linda started seeing Elvis in Kalamazoo—once at a Burger King, once at the Crossroads Shopping Mall, and once driving a red Ferrari. And she said that just recently, while she was babysitting and filling her time by listening to the police scanner, she heard a man's voice ask, "Can you give me a time for the return of Elvis?" and heard Presley reply, "I'm here now."

34   I asked her what her family thought about her experiences. Linda, a pale, blond woman who was sitting off to one side in a dining alcove smoking cigarettes while I talked to her mother, was obviously a believer, and occasionally she interjected reports of various Elvis contacts of her own. "But *my* mother thinks it's all nutty," Mrs. Welling said, laughing. "She says I should forget about it. My husband doesn't say much—he's real quiet—but he knows I'm not crazy."

35   It wasn't until the spring of 1988, Mrs. Welling said, that she started getting in touch with the media. She claims that she didn't bother talking to the people at the Vicksburg newspaper (although Jackie Lawrence remembers otherwise), because "it wasn't an important newspaper." Instead, she tried to tell her story to the Kalamazoo *Gazette* and people at the television station there. No one would take her seriously—except, of course, the author of the Elvis book. After Mrs. Welling had written to her and talked to her on the telephone, a writer for the *Weekly World News* phoned for an interview. Mrs. Welling asked him how he knew about her, but he declined to reveal his sources. In early May, the tabloid prepared the ground for Mrs. Welling's story by running one that took note of the rumor that Presley was living in Columbia Plaza, and gave Mrs. Welling's friend a nice plug for her book. Shortly after that, the syndicated columnist Bob Greene gave the rumor a push. By that time, the Kalamazoo *Gazette* realized that it could no longer ignore Mrs. Welling's phone calls, and in its May 15th issue Tom Haroldson, a staff writer, wrote a front-page story headlined " 'ELVIS ALIVE' IN KALAMAZOO, SAY AREA WOMAN AND NEWS TABLOID." That was the beginning of Mrs. Welling's fame, but it was not until June 28th that the *Weekly World News* told her whole story. In thousands of supermarkets, the issue appeared with a big front-page picture of Mrs. Welling and a headline in type an inch and a half high proclaiming "I'VE SEEN ELVIS IN THE FLESH!" The story began to be picked up by newspapers around the country as a brightener to the increasingly monotonous accounts of the pre-Convention Presidential campaigns. CBS investigated it for possible production on "60 Minutes." Radio stations from coast to coast and as far away as Australia called to interview Louise Welling and anyone else they could find. Kalamazoo's mayor, Edward Annen, reacted to all this by announcing to a *Gazette* reporter, "I've told them that everyone knows this is where he lives and that they should send their residents here to spend tourist dollars to find him."

36   Funny signs sprouted throughout Kalamazoo and Vicksburg in places of commerce. A rival market of Felpausch's posted one that said "JIMMY HOFFA SHOPS HERE." A dentist boasted, "ELVIS HAS HIS TEETH CLEANED HERE." At Mar-Jo's, the sign read "ELVIS EATS OUR MEATLOAF." The folks at Felpausch's, however, were not amused. Cecil Bagwell, then the store's manager, told the *Gazette*, "The cashier who supposedly checked out Elvis that day cannot remember anything about it," and characterized Mrs. Welling as "an Elvis fanatic." Bagwell no longer works at Felpausch's, but I spoke with Jack Mayhew, the assistant manager, who scowled when I brought up the subject. "I won't comment," he said, adding, nonetheless, "We've never given the story to anyone, and we're not going to. All I'll say is that the woman is totally—" and he rotated an extended finger beside his head.

37   Before I left Mrs. Welling that morning, I asked her why she thought it was that *she* had seen Elvis, when others had not—did not even believe her.

38   "I don't know, but the Lord does," she answered. "I'm a religious woman, and when things like this happen—that we don't understand—it just proves that the Lord has a plan."

39   The next day, a friend who had heard about my investigations telephoned to tell me that there had been an Elvis sighting just a week or so earlier, in Kalamazoo, at the delivery bay of the Fader Construction Company, which is owned by her family. She hadn't seen the man herself, she said, but the women in the office had insisted that the truck driver making the delivery was Elvis Presley. I suspected that it might have been Ray Kajkowski, winner of the Elvis-look-alike contest and kisser of Jean Delahanty. This turned out to be true. On Friday evening, at a run-through for the Old Car Festival's cruising event, I was introduced to Kajkowski by Skip Knowles, and Kajkowski confirmed that he had made quite a stir while delivering a shipment of concrete forms to Fader. He gave me his card—he has apparently made a second career for himself as an Elvis impersonator at parties and night clubs—and then he whipped out a pair of mirrored sunglasses, put them on, and kissed me, too. "Young, old, fat, skinny, black, white, good-looking, not so good-looking, I kiss them all," he said. "I'm a pretty affectionate fellow. I was raised in a family that hugged a lot."

40   Ray Kajkowski lives in Gobles, not far from Vicksburg. At forty-one, he is thick-featured, a bit on the heavy side, and looks like—well, he looks like Elvis Presley. He has big sideburns and dyed black hair, which he wears in a pompadour. He went down to Graceland recently with his wife and his two teen-age sons to study the Presley scene and recalls that while he was in the mansion's poolroom a couple came in and the wife took one look at him and collapsed on the floor in a faint.

41   "When I was growing up, I felt like an outsider," he told me. "I didn't think I was as good as other people, because my dad wasn't a doctor or a lawyer. We were just common folks. I knew about Elvis even when I was a little kid. I didn't pay much attention, though, except that some of my buddies had pictures of Elvis, so we'd trade those to our older sister and their friends for baseball cards." He laughed.

42   "I felt like we were invaded when the Beatles came over," he continued. By that time—1963—he was at Central High School in Kalamazoo, and had begun to

appreciate Presley's music and to defend it against foreign stars. "I mean, Elvis was a small-town boy who made good. He was just ordinary, and, sure, he made some mistakes, just like me or you or any of us. But he went from zero to sixty. He had charisma with a capital 'C,' and somehow people still know it."

43   After Presley's death, Kajkowski said, he felt sad and started reading about Elvis and studying his old movies. "Then, in September or October, 1987, right around then, I was at a nineteen-fifties dance in Gobles. My hair was different then, and I had a beard, but there was a fifty-dollar prize for the best Elvis imitator. Fifty bucks sounded pretty good to me, and I watched this one guy do an imitation, and he didn't move or anything, and I thought to myself, I can do better than that, so I got up and entered and won, beard and all. After that, I shaved off my beard, dyed my hair, and started building my act. I do lip-synch to Elvis tapes. I've got three suits now, one black, one white, one blue. My wife does my setups for me and runs the strobe lights. Evenings when we don't have anything else to do, we sit around and make scarves for me to give away. I cut them, and she hems them. When I'm performing, I sweat real easy, and I mop off the sweat with the scarves and throw them out to the gals. They go crazy over them. And the gals proposition me. They don't make it easy. Sometimes they rub up against me, and when I kiss them they stick their tongues halfway down my throat. Once, I went over to shake the guys' hands, because I figured it was better to have them on my side. But one big guy wouldn't shake my hand, and later he came over and grabbed me like a grizzly bear and told me to quit it. 'You don't sound like Elvis Presley. You don't look like Elvis Presley. Stop it.' I told him, 'Hey, it's all lip-synch! It's just an act! It's entertainment!' But I try to keep it under control. My wife's the woman I have to go home with after the act."

44   I asked Kajkowski if he had ever been in Felpausch's. As a truck driver, he said, he had made deliveries there; occasionally, he even shopped there. But although he owned a motorcycle, he said, he rarely drove it, and he never wore a white motorcycle suit.

45   I asked him what he made of Mrs. Welling's story.

46   "Well," he said thoughtfully, "when someone puts another person at the center of their life, they read about him, they think about him, I'm not surprised that he becomes real for that person."

47   Saturday night, at nine o'clock, Louise Welling is standing next to me in the Filling Station's parking lot—it is built on the site of John Vickers' flour mill—in a crowd that has just seen prizes awarded in the fifties dance concert and is waiting for the beginning of the second annual Elvis-look-alike contest. She is neatly dressed in a blue-and-white checked overblouse and dark pants. Her hair is fluffed up, and she is wearing pretty pink lipstick. She invited me to come to the contest, and told me that although many of the entrants in such affairs didn't come close to Elvis she was hoping that this one would draw the real Elvis Presley out from hiding. "If he came to me in the past, I believe he'll come again," she said. "I hope it will be before I die. If he comes, I'm going to grab him and hold on to him and ask him why he couldn't just be honest about needing to get away for a rest. Why couldn't he just tell the truth? Look at all the trouble he's caused those who love him."

48 Earlier in the day, I stopped in at Mar-Jo's for coffee. There were lots of extra visitors in the café. Ken Fowler had turned on the radio to WHEZ, a Kalamazoo station, which was broadcasting live from out on the street, acting as the festival's musical host. Rock music filled the café. Patrons were beating time on their knees, and the waitresses had begun to boogie up and down behind the counter. I asked one of them—a girl named Laurie, who was decked out fifties style with a white floaty scarf around her ponytail—what she made of Mrs. Welling's story. "I think it's kind of fun," she said. "I haven't met the lady, but, you know, maybe she's right. After all, if Elvis Presley never died he has to be someplace."

49 Mrs. Welling is subdued, as she stands next to me, but all attention—scanning the people, anticipatory. We are at the very back of the good-natured crowd, which has enjoyed the nostalgia, the slick cars, the dances, the poodle skirts, and the ponytails. She spots Kajkowski and says to me that he's not Elvis but "so far he's the only one here who even looks anything like him."

50 Skip Knowles is up on the stage, in charge of what has turned out to be a successful event. There have been record-breaking crowds. Six hundred and fifty cars were entered. He has had plenty of media coverage, and he seems to be having a very good time. He calls for the Elvis contest to begin. Ray Kajkowski's act is so good now that he has no competition—he is the only one to enter. I watch him play the crowd. He had told me, "When I first started, I really liked the attention, but now it's just fun to do the show, and, yeah, I do get caught up in it. I like the holding power I have over people. I know how it is to feel left out, so I play to everyone. But I like people in their mid-thirties or older best. I don't like to entertain for these kids in their twenties. The gals back off when I try to drape a scarf around them. I think that's an insult." Now he is dancing around the edge of the crowd, reaching out to kiss the women, who respond to him with delight and good humor, and then he launches into what Mrs. Welling tells me is "You're a Devil in Disguise." I look at her, and she seems near tears. Her shoulder slump. "I don't like to watch," she says softly, and walks away to gather her family together for the trip home.

51 On my own way home, on the morning after the festival, I made one final stop in Vicksburg, on the south side of town, at what is left of Fraser's Grove. For about forty years—up until the early nineteen-twenties—Fraser's Grove was one of this country's premier spiritualist centers. In 1883, Mrs. John Fraser, the wife of a well-to-do Vicksburg merchant, turned the twenty-acre woodland into a camp and gathering place for mediums, believers in mediums, and the curious. She had been inspired by a lecture on spiritualism given in a hall on Prairie Street by one Mrs. R. S. Lily, of Cassadaga, New York, a town in the spiritually fervent "burned-over" district of that state. In the years that followed, Mrs. Fraser became a national figure in séance circles, and another resident of Vicksburg, C. E. Dent, was elected president of something called the Mediums' Protection Union. A group calling itself the Vicksburg Spiritualists was formed shortly after Mrs. Lily's visit, and it met each Sunday. Its Ladies' Auxiliary held monthly chicken dinners (fifteen cents a plate, two for a quarter). On summer Sunday afternoons, people from around this country and abroad packed the campground at Fraser's Grove to talk of materialization and reincarnation and watch mediums go into trances to contact the dead. According to a 1909 issue of the Vicksburg *Commercial*, they debated subjects such as "Is the planet on which we live approaching final destruction, or is it

becoming more permanent?" (A follow-up article reports that the Spiritualists opted for permanency.)

52   Trees still stand in much of Fraser's Grove, although some of them have been cut down to make room for a small housing development. The campground itself has been taken over by the Christian Tabernacle, which makes use of the old camp buildings. Tazzie, my German shepherd, was with me, and I parked at the edge of the grove to let her out for a run before we drove onto the interstate highway. We headed down a dim path, where events passing strange are said to have taken place. The grove produced no Elvis, no John Vickers, not even a phantom band concert or the apparition of Mr. Matz––no spirits at all. But Tazzie did scare up a rabbit, and the oaks were still there, and, untamed through a hundred and fifty generations, so were the mosquitoes.   ■

From Sue Hubbell, "The Vicksburg Ghost," *The New Yorker*, September 25, 1989. Reprinted by permission.

EXERCISES

Do not refer to the selection for Exercises A and B.

A.   DETERMINING THE MAIN IDEA AND PURPOSE
Choose the best answer.

1.   _____ Louise Welling's sighting of Elvis at Felpausch's supermarket in Vicksburg, Michigan, (a) shows that his fans have remained loyal to his memory; (b) required an immediate investigation by the media; (c) was a joke played on her by some local pranksters; (d) reinforces the idea that people believe what they want to believe.

2.   _____ With respect to the main idea, the author's purpose is (a) to investigate and report on an unusual story; (b) to provide firsthand evidence based on her own observations; (c) to argue in favor of a controversial or unpopular view; (d) to satirize, to poke fun at.

B.   COMPREHENDING MAIN IDEAS
Choose the correct answer.

1.   _____ Many Elvis fans, otherwise known as Elvins, think that he (a) is hiding from the public because he suffers from a disfiguring disease; (b) is waiting to make a comeback on the twentieth anniversary of his death; (c) faked his own death; (d) is living in Vicksburg, Michigan, disguised as an Amish farmer.

2.   _____ According to the author, what made Elvis Presley was (a) clever promotion; (b) his remarkable talent; (c) the loyalty of his fans; (d) his sensual good looks and gyrating motions.

3.   _____ Most of the townspeople whom Hubbell interviewed for the article characterized Louise Welling as (a) publicity-hungry; (b) different; (c) harmless; (d) crazy.

4.   _____ After her initial sighting of Elvis at Felpausch's market, Louise Welling (a) saw him several more times; (b) never saw him again; (c) began to correspond with him; (d) contacted a medium who tried to put her in touch with Elvis's spirit.

5.   _____ Ray Kajkowski's regular job is driving a truck, but he has also made a second career as (a) a dealer in Elvis memorabilia; (b) a tour guide at Graceland, Elvis's home; (c) a news writer whose specialty is investigating Elvis sightings; (d) an Elvis impersonator.

6.   _____ The Kalamazoo *Gazette* (a) published Louise Welling's story immediately after she contacted the paper about the sighting; (b) published the story only after a national tabloid and a national columnist mentioned rumors of Elvis's whereabouts; (c) refused to publish the story because the rumors couldn't be verified; (d) refused to publish the story because it thought the publicity would be bad for Kalamazoo.

COMPREHENSION SCORE

Score your answers for Exercises A and B as follows:

A.   No. right _____ × 2 = _____

B.   No. right _____ × 1 = _____

Total pts. from A and B _____ × 10 = _____%

You may refer to the selection for the remaining exercises.

C.   DISTINGUISHING BETWEEN MAIN IDEAS AND SUPPORTING DETAILS

Label the following statements from the selection as follows: MI if the statement represents a *main idea* and SD if the statement represents a *supporting detail*.

1.   _____ Funny signs sprouted throughout Kalamazoo and Vicksburg in places of commerce.

2.   _____ A rival market of Felpausch's posted one that said "JIMMY HOFFA SHOPS HERE."

3.   _____ A dentist boasted, "ELVIS HAS HIS TEETH CLEANED HERE."

4.   _____ At Mar-Jo's, the sign read "ELVIS EATS OUR MEATLOAF."

5.   _____ The folks at Felpausch's, however, were not amused.

6.   _____ Cecil Bagwell, then the store's manager, told the *Gazette*, "The cash-

ier who supposedly checked out Elvis that day cannot remember anything about it," and characterized Mrs. Welling as "an Elvis fanatic."

7. ____ Bagwell no longer works at Felpausch's, but I spoke with Jack Mayhew, the assistant manager, who scowled when I brought up the subject.

8. ____ "I won't comment," he said adding, nonetheless, "We've never given the story to anyone, and we're not going to. All I'll say is that the woman is totally—" and he rotated an extended finger beside his head.

D. MAKING INFERENCES
Choose the correct inference.

1. ____ From the information we are given in paragraph 1, we can infer that (a) Elvins took Louise Welling's sighting seriously; (b) Elvins were skeptical about Louise Welling's sighting; (c) Elvis did, indeed, fake his own death; (d) "docudramas" about Elvis's life have been successful TV programs.

2. ____ The author implies in paragraph 2 that (a) Colonel Tom Parker made more money from publishing his Elvis poem than he did from promoting his singing; (b) Presley's drug problems were affecting his performance and his popularity; (c) as a singer Presley was washed up; (d) Presley should have retired years before his death.

3. ____ We can infer from paragraph 12 and elsewhere in the selection that the men at Mar-Jo's (a) definitely cooked up the Presley sighting as a prank; (b) had nothing to do with the Presley sighting; (c) bribed Ray Kajkowski to go to Felpausch's to impersonate Elvis; (d) might have had something to do with the Elvis sighting, but we can't be sure.

4. ____ From what we learn about Louise Welling throughout the article, we can conclude that she is (a) a reliable source of information; (b) mentally unstable; (c) more interested in making money from her Elvis stories than in getting at the truth; (d) an Elvis fanatic.

5. ____ We can infer that the writer of the Elvis-is-still-alive book was supportive of Louise Welling and her story because (a) she herself had seen Elvis, so the story was quite probable to her; (b) it enhanced her own reputation and potential for profit from her book; (c) she was a good friend of Welling's and knew she wouldn't make up such a story; (d) it confirmed the message on her cassette tape.

6. ____ From the epigram at the beginning of the article and from Kajkowski's characterization of Louise Welling in paragraph 46, we can infer that Louise Welling (a) wanted so much for the person she saw to be Elvis that he became Elvis to her; (b) actually did see Elvis; (c) deliberately lied about seeing Elvis just to attract attention; (d) was not really sure about Elvis's identity but was afraid to retract her story later.

E.   ANALYZING ORGANIZATION AND SEEING RELATIONSHIPS
Choose the correct answer.

1.   _____ The kind of writing this article represents is (a) an opinion piece, an editorial; (b) a summary of a research study; (c) a firsthand investigative report in narrative style; (d) a memoir, a collection of remembrances.

2.   This article has a clear beginning, middle, and end. Write the number of the paragraph where the body begins _____. Then write the number of the paragraph where the conclusion begins _____.

3.   _____ In paragraph 2 the author mentions her own background growing up in Kalamazoo because (a) it lends credibility and authority to her observations; (b) she is an authority on Elvis; (c) she has investigated other reports of Elvis sightings; (d) it is essential to understand the rest of the article.

4.   The word "still" is used once in the middle of paragraph 4 as a transitional word and twice in paragraph 5 as an adverb. Write the definition of each instance according to the context:

"*Still*, it seems very like the place I knew . . ." _____

"And the teenagers are *still* bored" _____

"But *everything* just stands *still* in Vicksburg" _____

5.   Why does Hubbell go into so much detail about the coffee-drinking group of men who gather at Mar-Jo's and the incident of the Ape-O-Gram?

_____

_____

6.   Read paragraphs 26, 27, and the beginning of 28 again. Then explain what is wrong with Louise Welling's math. (*Hint:* The article was published in 1989).

_____

_____

7.   The pattern of organization in the section comprising paragraphs 23–36 is (a) general to specific; (b) spatial—space order; (c) random order; (d) chronological order.

8.   _____ Which of these statements best describes the author's opinion of Louise Welling's alleged sighting of Elvis? (a) She is undecided about whether it actually happened; (b) she is skeptical about it; (c) she is certain that it did happen; (d) she thinks the whole story is preposterous.

F. UNDERSTANDING VOCABULARY

Look through the paragraphs listed below and find a word that matches each definition. An example has been done for you.

Ex. death [1–2]   _____ demise _____

1. a longing for the past [1–2]   _____

2. condition of being extreme, relentless [3–4]   _____

3. describing a condescending manner [4–5]   _____

4. teases playfully, good-naturedly [11–12]   _____

5. skillfully [11–12]   _____

6. twists, contorts [15–16]   _____

7. discarded bits and pieces [16–17]   _____

8. stray from the subject [21–22]   _____

9. prevent, discourage [28–29]   _____

10. interrupted, spoke in the middle of a conversation [33–34]   _____

11. someone with an excessive or irrational attachment to a cause, activity, or another person [35–36]   _____

12. looked at angrily [35–36]   _____

13. make an offer to have sexual relations [42–43]   _____

14. eagerly looking forward to [48–49]   _____

15. showing great emotion or warmth [51–52]   _____

G. USING VOCABULARY

From the following list of vocabulary words, choose a word that fits in each blank according to both the grammatical structure of the sentence and the context. Use each word in the list only once and add noun or verb endings (such as -s, -ing, or -ed) if necessary. (Note that there are more words than sentences.)

medium, media	memorabilia	befuddle
purportedly	tantalizing	facades
esteem	exasperation	nonetheless
charisma	cynic	apparition

1. A large industry has grown up around Elvis, specializing in

_____ and printing fuzzy, but _____
photographs of him to show that he is still alive.

2. There is no question that Elvis had a special quality, often attributed to great people, called _____; _____, the _____ found Elvis, in the years before his death, difficult to deal with because he was fat and aging, and was often in a drug-_____ state.

3. A note of _____ appeared in Louise Welling's voice when anyone suggested that the cassette tape made to show that Elvis was still _____ alive was unintelligible.

H. TOPICS FOR WRITING OR DISCUSSION

1. Here are some sentences from the article. Paraphrase them by rewriting each one in your own words in the space provided.

   a. The human predicament is typically so complex that it is not altogether clear which lies are vital and what truths beg for discovery.

   _____

   _____

   _____

   b. The Presley image shorn of the troublesome real man was easier to market.

   _____

   _____

   _____

   c. I asked him [Ray Kajkowski] what he made of Mrs. Welling's story. "Well," he said thoughtfully, "when someone puts another person at the center of their life, they read about him, they think about him, I'm not surprised that he becomes real for that person."

   _____

   _____

   _____

2. Elvis was clearly a folk hero who, despite his fame and talent, couldn't survive; yet his fans remain enthusiastic, even though he has been dead for nearly fifteen years. How do you account for the phenomenon of Elvis sightings? Are his fans merely misguided fanatics, are the sightings merely jokes ("ELVIS EATS OUR MEATLOAF"), or is there something more significant going on that is not mentioned in the article?

35 ‖‖‖‖

Barbara Tuchman

MANKIND'S BETTER MOMENTS

Barbara Tuchman was a noted American historian and the author of The Guns of August *and* Stillwell and the American Experience in China. *This selection is an excerpt from a Jefferson Lecture given in April 1980, in Washington, D.C., also printed in* Practical History. *As a way of counteracting the pessimistic way we view the world today, Tuchman recites some of man's most remarkable accomplishments, among them the Dutch project to reclaim land from the Zuider Zee, the building of Gothic cathedrals in medieval Europe, and explorations of the New World.*

Do not let the difficult vocabulary intimidate you, as the ideas are not hard to understand, but you should keep a dictionary next to you as you read this so that you will have a complete understanding.

VOCABULARY PREVIEW

**WORD
ORIGINS**

KNAVE

In the introductory paragraph Tuchman explains her purpose in writing. Paraphrased, she says that we are convinced that everything about the twentieth century is wrong; as she says, "we see our species—with cause—as functioning very badly, as blunderers when not *knaves.*" The word *knave*, which today has a rather old-fashioned flavor, refers to "a dishonest or unprincipled person." But its original meaning was far more positive, illustrating once again the process called *pejoration*, the process by which a word shifts from having a positive or neutral meaning to a negative one. Originally, the word meant simply "boy," closely related to the German *Knabe*, "male child." However, as Charles Funk notes in *Thereby Hangs a Tale*, its meaning gradually shifted:

> . . . People began to apply it to a boy who was employed as a servant, one who might be apprentice to a cook or to a groom, or who served as a potboy in a tavern or in any such form of work as a boy could perform. In those olden days, however, the life of any menial was hard; that of the boy doubly so. His sleeping place might be the stable or a drafty garret, without

433

mattress or blanket; his clothing any castoff garment that he could tie upon him; his food any scraps that might be tossed to him from his master's table. It is not surprising, therefore, that these boys, still called *knaves* as they became older, developed a high degree of rascality. They had to become crafty in order to survive. Thus the meaning of the term gradually came to apply only to such a person, boy or man who practiced dishonestly.

BLUNDERERS
Blunderers, quoted above, refers to people who make stupid mistakes. The verb *to blunder* came into modern English from Middle English, *blunderen* ("to proceed blindly"), originally from Old Norse *blunda* ("to shut the eyes"), probably following the idea that one makes mistakes if one's eyes are closed.

ANTAGONIST
Tuchman describes the Dutch miracle of making land out of sea in paragraph 5, concluding that the Dutch lost "as much to the revengeful ocean somewhere else, progressively developing methods to cope with their eternal *antagonist.*" Meaning an opposing force or an enemy, the verb *antagonize* comes from Greek:

[*antagonizesthai* ("to struggle against"), from *anti-* ("against") + *agōnizesthai* ("to struggle"), from *agōn* ("contest")]

WORD PARTS

EM-, EN-
These prefixes, used to form verbs from adjectives, indicate "becoming" or "causing to be." This selection uses two such words: *embodied* (paragraph 11) and *embellishment* (paragraph 14). *Embody* means "to cause to have bodily form," and *embellish,* the verb form, means "to adorn," literally, "to make beautiful." Other words with these prefixes include:

embolden	to make bold
empower	to give power to
enliven	to give life to
encourage	to give courage to
entrap	to catch in a trap

WORD FAMILIES

UNANIMOUSLY
Unanimously (see paragraph 6) describes a situation where everyone agrees or shares the same opinions. At its heart is the Latin root *animus* ("soul" or "mind"): [*ūnanimus* ("of one mind"), from *ūnus* ("one") + *animus*]. Besides the word *animal,* which shares this root, here are some other words in this family:

animate	living
inanimate	not living
animism	a primitive belief whereby both animate and inanimate things are believed to possess a soul
animosity	bitter hostility, hatred

BARBARA TUCHMAN

MANKIND'S BETTER MOMENTS

1   For a change from prevailing pessimism, I should like to recall some of the positive and even admirable capacities of the human race. We hear very little of them lately. Ours is not a time of self-esteem or self-confidence—as was, for instance, the nineteenth century, when self-esteem may be seen oozing from its portraits. Victorians, especially the men, pictured themselves as erect, noble, and splendidly handsome. Our self-image looks more like Woody Allen or a character from Samuel Beckett. Amid a mass of worldwide troubles and a poor record for the twentieth century, we see our species—with cause—as functioning very badly, as blunderers when not knaves, as violent, ignoble, corrupt, inept, incapable of mastering the forces that threaten us, weakly subject to our worst instincts; in short, decadent.

2   The catalogue is familiar and valid, but it is growing tiresome. A study of history reminds one that mankind has its ups and downs and during the ups has accomplished many brave and beautiful things, exerted stupendous endeavors, explored and conquered oceans and wilderness, achieved marvels of beauty in the creative arts and marvels of science and social progress; has loved liberty with a passion that throughout history has led men to fight and die for it over and over again; has pursued knowledge, exercised reason, enjoyed laughter and pleasures, played games with zest, shown courage, heroism, altruism, honor, and decency; experienced love; known comfort, contentment, and occasionally happiness. All these qualities have been part of human experience, and if they have not had as important notice as the negatives nor exerted as wide and persistent an influence as the evils we do, they nevertheless deserve attention, for they are currently all but forgotten.

3   Among the great endeavors, we have in our own time carried men to the moon and brought them back safely—surely one of the most remarkable achievements in history. Some may disapprove of the effort as unproductive, too costly, and a wrong choice of priorities in relation to greater needs, all of which may be true but does not, as I see it, diminish the achievement. If you look carefully, all positives have a negative underside—sometimes more, sometimes less—and not all admirable endeavors have admirable motives. Some have sad consequences. Although most signs presently point from bad to worse, human capacities are probably what they have always been. If primitive man could discover how to transform grain into

bread, and reeds growing by the riverbank into baskets; if his successors could invent the wheel, harness the insubstantial air to turn a millstone, transform sheep's wool, flax, and worms' cocoons into fabric—we, I imagine, will find a way to manage the energy problem.

4 Consider how the Dutch accomplished the miracle of making land out of sea. By progressive enclosure of the Zuider Zee over the last sixty years, they have added half a million acres to their country, enlarging its area by eight percent and providing homes, farms, and towns for close to a quarter of a million people. The will to do the impossible, the spirit of can-do that overtakes our species now and then, was never more manifest than in this earth-altering act by the smallest of the major European nations.

5 A low-lying, windswept, waterlogged land, partly below sea level, pitted with marshes, rivers, lakes, and inlets, sliding all along its outer edge into the stormy North Sea with only fragile sand dunes as nature's barrier against the waves, Holland, in spite of physical disadvantages, has made itself into one of the most densely populated, orderly, prosperous, and, at one stage of its history, dominant nations of the West. For centuries, ever since the first inhabitants, fleeing enemy tribes, settled in the bogs where no one cared to bother them, the Dutch struggled against water and learned how to live with it: building on mounds, constructing and reconstructing seawalls of clay mixed with straw, carrying mud in an endless train of baskets, laying willow mattresses weighted with stones, repairing each spring the winter's damage, draining marshes, channeling streams, building ramps to their attics to save the cattle in times of flood, gaining dike-enclosed land from the waves in one place and losing as much to the revengeful ocean somewhere else, progressively developing methods to cope with their eternal antagonist.

6 The Zuider Zee was a tidal gulf penetrating eighty miles into the land over an area ten to thirty miles wide. The plan to close off the sea by a dam across the entire mouth of the gulf had long been contemplated but never adopted, for fear of the cost, until a massive flood in 1916, which left saltwater standing on all the farmlands north of Amsterdam, forced the issue. The act for enclosure was passed unanimously by both houses of Parliament in 1918. As large in ambition as the country was small, the plan called for a twenty-mile dike from shore to shore, rising twenty feet above sea level, wide enough at the top to carry an auto road and housing for the hydraulic works, and as much as six hundred feet wide on the sea bottom. The first cartload of gravel was dumped in 1920.

7 The dike was but part of the task. The inland sea it formed had to be drained of its saltwater and transformed from salt to fresh by the inflow from lower branches of the Rhine. Four polders, or areas rising from the shallows, would be lifted by the draining process from under water into the open air. Secondary dikes, pumping stations, sluices, drainage ditches to control the inflow, as well as locks and inland ports for navigation, had to be built, the polder lands restored to fertility, trees planted, roads, bridges, and rural and urban housing constructed, the whole scheduled for completion in sixty years.

8 The best-laid plans of engineers met errors and hazards. During construction, gravel that had been painstakingly dumped within sunken frameworks would be

washed away in a night by heavy currents or a capricious storm. Means proved vulnerable, methods sometimes unworkable. Yet slowly the dike advanced from each shore toward the center. As the gap narrowed, the pressure of the tidal current rushing through increased daily in force, carrying away material at the base, undermining the structure, and threatening to prevent a final closing. In the last days a herd of floating derricks, dredges, barges, and every piece of available equipment was mustered at the spot, and fill was desperately poured in before the next return of the tide, due in twelve hours. At this point, gale winds were reported moving in. The check dam to protect the last gap showed signs of giving way; operations were hurriedly moved thirty yards inward. Suspense was now extreme. Roaring and foaming with sand, the tide threw itself upon the narrowing passage; the machines closed in, filled the last space in the dike, and it held. Men stood that day in 1932 where the North Sea's waves had held dominion for seven hundred years.

9   As the dry land appeared, the first comers to take possession were the birds. Gradually, decade by decade, crops, homes, and civilization followed, and unhappily, too, man's destructive intervention. In World War II the retreating Germans blew up a section of the dike, completely flooding the western polder, but by the end of the year the Dutch had pumped it dry, resowed the fields in the spring, and over the next seven years restored the polder's farms and villages. Weather, however, is never conquered. The disastrous floods of 1953 laid most of coastal Holland under water. The Dutch dried themselves out and, while the work at Zuider Zee continued, applied its lessons elsewhere and lent their hydraulic skills to other countries. Today the *Afsluitdijk*, or Zuider Zee road, is a normal thoroughfare. To drive across it between the sullen ocean on one side and new land on the other is for that moment to feel optimism for the human race.

10   Great endeavor requires vision and some kind of compelling impulse, not necessarily practical as in the case of the Dutch, but sometimes less definable, more exalted, as in the case of the Gothic cathedrals of the Middle Ages. The architectural explosion that produced this multitude of soaring vaults—arched, ribbed, pierced with jeweled light, studded with thousands of figures of the stone-carvers' art— represents in size, splendor, and numbers one of the great, permanent artistic achievements of human hands. What accounts for it? Not religious fervor alone but the zeal of a dynamic age, a desire to outdo, an ambition for the biggest and the best. Only the general will, shared by nobles, merchants, guilds, artisans, and commoners, could command the resources and labor to sustain so great an undertaking. Each group contributed donations, especially the magnates of commerce, who felt relieved thereby from the guilt of money-making. Voluntary work programs involved all classes. "Who has ever seen or heard tell in times past," wrote an observer, "that powerful princes of the world, that men brought up in honors and wealth, that nobles—men and women—have bent their haughty necks to the harness of carts and, like beasts of burden, have dragged to the abode of Christ these wagons loaded with wines, grains, oil, stones, timber and all that is necessary for the construction of the church?"

11   Abbot Suger, whose renovation of St.-Denis is considered the start of Gothic architecture, embodied the spirit of the builders. Determined to create the most

splendid basilica in Christendom, he supervised every aspect of the work from fund-raising to decoration, and caused his name to be inscribed for immortality on keystones and capitals. He lay awake worrying, as he tells us, where to find trees large enough for the beams, and went personally with his carpenters to the forest to question the woodcutters under oath. When they swore that nothing of the kind he wanted could be found in the area, he insisted on searching for them himself and, after nine hours of scrambling through thorns and thickets, succeeded in locating and marking twelve trees of the necessary size.

12   Mainly the compelling impulse lay in the towns, where, in those years, economic and political strengths and wealth were accumulating. Amiens, the thriving capital of Picardy, decided to build the largest church in France, "higher than all the saints, higher than all the kings." For the necessary space, the hospital and bishop's palace had to be relocated and the city walls moved back. At the same time Beauvais, a neighbor town, raised a vault over the crossing of transept and nave to an unprecedented height of 158 feet, the apogee of architects' daring in its day. It proved too daring, for the height of the columns and spread of the supports caused the vault to collapse after twelve years. Repaired with undaunted purpose, it was defiantly topped by a spire rising 492 feet above ground, the tallest in France. Beauvais, having used up its resources, never built the nave, leaving a structure foreshortened but glorious. The interior is a fantasy of soaring space; to enter is to stand dazed in wonder, breathless in admiration.

13   The higher and lighter grew the buildings and the slenderer the columns, the more new expedients and techniques had to be devised to hold them up. Buttresses flew like angels' wings against the exteriors. This was a period of innovation and audacity, and a limitless spirit of excelsior. In a single century, from 1170 to 1270, six hundred cathedrals and major churches were built in France alone. In England in that period, the cathedral of Salisbury, with the tallest spire in the country, was completed in thirty-eight years. The spire of Freiburg in Germany was constructed entirely of filigree in stone as if spun by some supernatural spider. In the St.-Chapelle in Paris the fifteen miraculous windows swallow the walls; they have become the whole.

14   Embellishment was integral to the construction. Reims is populated by five thousand statues of saints, prophets, kings and cardinals, bishops, knights, ladies, craftsmen and commoners, devils, animals and birds. Every type of leaf known in northern France is said to appear in the decoration. In carving, stained glass, and sculpture the cathedrals displayed the art of medieval hands, and the marvel of these buildings is permanent even when they no longer play a central role in everyday life. Rodin said he could feel the beauty and presence of Reims even at night when he could not see it. "Its power," he wrote, "transcends the senses so that the eye sees what it sees not."

15   Explanations for the extraordinary burst that produced the cathedrals are several. Art historians will tell you that it was the invention of the ribbed vault. Religious historians will say it was the product of an age of faith which believed that with God's favor anything was possible; in fact it was not a period of untroubled faith, but of heresies and Inquisition. Rather, one can only say that conditions were right. Social order under monarchy and the towns was replacing the anarchy of the

barons, so that existence was no longer merely a struggle to stay alive but allowed a surplus of goods and energies and greater opportunity for mutual effort. Banking and commerce were producing capital, roads were making possible wheeled transport, universities nourishing ideas and communication. It was one of history's high tides, an age of vigor, confidence, and forces converging to quicken the blood.

16   Even when the historical tide is low, a particular group of doers may emerge in exploits that inspire awe. Shrouded in the mists of the eighth century, long before the cathedrals, Viking seamanship was a wonder of daring, stamina, and skill. Pushing relentlessly outward in open boats, the Vikings sailed south, around Spain to North Africa and Arabia, north to the top of the world, west across uncharted seas to American coasts. They hauled their boats overland from the Baltic to make their way down Russian rivers to the Black sea. Why? We do not know what engine drove them, only that it was part of the human endowment.

17   What of the founding of our own country, America? We take the *Mayflower* for granted—yet think of the boldness, the enterprise, the determined independence, the sheer grit it took to leave the known and set out across the sea for the unknown where no houses or food, no stores, no cleared land, no crops or livestock, none of the equipment or settlement of organized living awaited.

18   Equally bold was the enterprise of the French in the northern forests of the American continent, who throughout the seventeenth century explored and opened the land from the St. Lawrence to the Mississippi, from the Great Lakes to the Gulf of Mexico. They came not for liberty like the Pilgrims, but for gain and dominion, whether in spiritual empire for the Jesuits or in land, glory, and riches for the agents of the King; and rarely in history have men willingly embraced such hardship, such daunting adventure, and persisted with such tenacity and endurance. They met hunger, exhaustion, frostbite, capture and torture by Indians, wounds and disease, dangerous rapids, swarms of insects, long portages, bitter weather, and hardly ever did those who suffered the experience fail to return, reenter the menacing but bountiful forest, and pit themselves once more against danger, pain, and death.

19   Above all others, the perseverance of La Salle in his search for the mouth of the Mississippi was unsurpassed. While preparing in Quebec, he mastered eight Indian languages. From then on he suffered accidents, betrayals, desertions, losses of men and provisions, fever and snow blindness, the hostility and intrigues of rivals who incited the Indians against him and plotted to ambush or poison him. He was truly pursued, as Francis Parkman wrote, by "a demon of havoc." Paddling through heavy waves in a storm over Lake Ontario, he waded through freezing surf to beach the canoes each night, and lost guns and baggage when a canoe was swamped and sank. To lay the foundations of a fort above Niagara, frozen ground had to be thawed by boiling water. When the fort was at last built, La Salle christened it Crèvecoeur—that is, Heartbreak. It earned the name when in his absence it was plundered and deserted by its half-starved mutinous garrison. Farther on, a friendly Indian village, intended as a destination, was found laid waste by the Iroquois with only charred stakes stuck with skulls standing among the ashes, while wolves and buzzards prowled through the remains.

20   When at last, after four months' hazardous journey down the Great River, La

Salle reached the sea, he formally took possession in the name of Louis XIV of all the country from the river's mouth to its source and of its tributaries—that is, of the vast basin of the Mississippi from the Rockies to the Appalachians—and named it Louisiana. The validity of the claim, which seems so hollow to us (though successful in its own time), is not the point. What counts is the conquest of fearful adversity by one man's extraordinary exertions and inflexible will.   ■

From Barbara Tuchman, "Mankind's Better Moments," *Practicing History*, Alfred A. Knopf, New York, 1981, pp. 227–233. Reprinted by permission.

EXERCISES

Do not refer to the selection for Exercises A and B.

A.   DETERMINING THE MAIN IDEA AND PURPOSE
Choose the best answer.

1.   _____ The main idea of the selection is that (a) with enough effort and energy, mankind will find a way to solve the energy problem; (b) despite the failures of the twentieth century, mankind has accomplished remarkable things; (c) the catalog of prevailing pessimisms is growing tiresome; (d) twentieth-century accomplishments look bad in relation to those of earlier periods.

2.   _____ With respect to the main idea, the author's purpose is (a) to complain about contemporary civilization; (b) to present a personal point of view about a serious controversy; (c) to trace the history of a particular phenomenon; (d) to catalog and illustrate the positive and admirable achievements of mankind.

B.   COMPREHENDING MAIN IDEAS
Choose the correct answer.

1.   _____ Tuchman states at the beginning of the selection that mankind's positive qualities are currently (a) under review; (b) nearly forgotten; (c) not worth remembering; (d) undermined by social and political problems.

2.   _____ Tuchman recounts the example of the Zuider Zee in Holland, which essentially involved (a) displacing long-time residents to make more farmland; (b) turning salt water into fresh drinking water; (c) making farmland and villages where a tidal gulf had been before; (d) building dikes for all of Holland's inlets and tidal gulfs.

3.   _____ The Zuider Zee project was particularly difficult to complete because of (a) labor union disputes; (b) conflicts in the Dutch Parliament; (c) storms and the daily tides; (d) objections from the area's residents.

4.   _____ Tuchman cites as the primary reason that the great cathedrals were built in medieval Europe (a) a never-before known religious fervor; (b)

the zeal of a dynamic age which sought to outdo; (c) competition among warring artisans; (d) the generosity of landowners who wanted to ensure a place in heaven for themselves.

5. _____ Contrary to what most people believe, the medieval age was not a period of untroubled faith, but of (a) heresies and the Inquisition; (b) intense rivalry between religious factions; (c) corruption at high levels of the Catholic Church; (d) a redefinition of the church's role in ordinary human affairs.

6. _____ La Salle was searching for (a) the inland passage between Canada and the U.S.; (b) the fountain of youth; (c) the Pacific Ocean; (d) the mouth of the Mississippi River.

COMPREHENSION SCORE

Score your answers for Exercises A and B as follows:

A.   No. right _____ × 2 = _____

B.   No. right _____ × 1 = _____

Total pts. from A and B _____ × 10 = _____%

You may refer to the selection for the remaining exercises.

C.   DISTINGUISHING BETWEEN MAIN IDEAS AND SUPPORTING DETAILS
Label the following statements from the selection as follows: MI if the statement represents a *main idea* and SD if the statement represents a *supporting detail.*

1. _____ The best-laid plans of engineers met errors and hazards.

2. _____ During construction, gravel that had been painstakingly dumped within sunken frameworks would be washed away in a night by heavy currents or a capricious storm.

3. _____ Means proved vulnerable, methods sometimes unworkable.

4. _____ Yet slowly the dike advanced from each shore toward the center.

5. _____ As the gap narrowed, the pressure of the tidal current rushing through increased daily in force, carrying away material at the base, undermining the structure, and threatening to prevent a final closing.

6. _____ In the last days a herd of floating derricks, dredges, barges, and every piece of available equipment was mustered at the spot, and fill was desperately poured in before the next return of the tide, due in twelve hours.

7. _____ At this point, gale winds were reported moving in.

8. _____ The check dam to protect the last gap showed signs of giving way; operations were hurriedly moved thirty yards inward.

9. _____ Suspense was now extreme.

10. _____ Roaring and foaming with sand, the tide threw itself upon the narrowing passage; the machines closed in, filled the last space in the dike, and it held.

11. _____ Men stood that day in 1932 where the North Sea's waves had held dominion for seven hundred years.

D. MAKING INFERENCES

For each of these statements write Y (Yes) if the inference is an accurate one, N (No) if the inference is an inaccurate one, or CT (Can't Tell) if you do not have enough information to make an inference.

1. _____ The Victorians were generally more optimistic about the world and their future than we in the twentieth century are.

2. _____ Two world wars are the main reasons that the twentieth century has fared so badly.

3. _____ Earlier attempts to reclaim land from the Zuider Zee had failed.

4. _____ The Dutch Zuider Zee project was necessary because the country is small and farmland was scarce.

5. _____ Without the impetus of the massive flood in 1916, the Zuider Zee project probably would not have been completed.

6. _____ The daily gale winds were the chief obstacle to the Zuider Zee project's completion.

7. _____ The construction of the great European cathedrals in the Middle Ages involved only the rich landowners and the poorer laborers and artisans.

8. _____ La Salle had been ordered by King Louis XIV to claim the land from the Rockies to the Appalachians.

E. DRAWING CONCLUSIONS

Mark an X before any of these statements that represent reasonable conclusions you can draw from the selection.

1. _____ We should have more opportunities for exploration, for example, to distant planets, to recapture the spirit shown by the Vikings and explorers like La Salle.

2. _____ Perhaps reminding us of mankind's "better moments" will make us see that our own era is not completely hopeless.

3. _____ Mankind is endowed with different intellect and mental capacities from our predecessors.

4. _____ We would do well to imitate the example of people who lived in the Middle Ages and build more religious monuments.

5. _____ Tuchman is most impressed with accomplishments successfully done under great adversity.

F. ANALYZING ORGANIZATION AND SEEING RELATIONSHIPS
Choose the correct answer.

1. _____ What is the purpose of the first sentence? It establishes (a) Tuchman's interest in the subject; (b) Tuchman's purpose in writing; (c) the central thesis of the essay; (d) Tuchman's opinion on a controversial subject.

2. _____ The predominant method of development used throughout the selection is (a) steps in a process; (b) analogy—an imaginative comparison; (c) illustrations; (d) cause and effect.

3. _____ What kind of order does Tuchman impose on her material? (a) chronological order; (b) least important to most important; (c) general to specific; (d) random order.

4. _____ Paragraph 4 begins with the sentence "Consider how the Dutch accomplished the miracle of making land out of sea." From this opening we can infer that she will use which _two_ of these methods of development? (a) steps in a process; (b) cause and effect; (c) example; (d) contrast—a discussion of differences; (e) comparison—a discussion of similarities.

5. Look again at paragraph 9; then write the sentence that states the main idea.

_____

_____

6. In paragraph 10 Tuchman writes, "What accounts for it [the building of the great cathedrals]? Not religious fervor alone but the zeal of a dynamic age, a desire to outdo, an ambition for the biggest and the best." What is the logical relationship between these sentences? (a) contrast; (b) comparison; (c) general and specific; (d) term and a definition of it; (e) cause and effect.

7. The last sentence of paragraph 15 and the first sentence of paragraph 16 contain, respectively, the words "tides" and "tide." In these contexts,

what do they mean? _____

8. _____ Tuchman's tone or emotional attitude toward the subject can be best described as (a) admiring, laudatory; (b) critical, negative; (c) neutral, objective; (d) sympathetic, compassionate.

G.   UNDERSTANDING VOCABULARY

Choose the correct definition according to the context.

1. _____ as blunderers when not *knaves* [paragraph 1]: (a) fools; (b) corrupt politicians; (c) unprincipled people; (d) pleasure-seekers.

2. _____ as violent, *ignoble,* corrupt [1]: (a) dishonorable; (b) unrepentant; (c) belligerent; (d) untrustworthy.

3. _____ played games with *zest* [2]: (a) intense rivalry; (b) added interest, charm; (c) wholehearted enjoyment; (d) discouragement.

4. _____ shown courage, heroism, *altruism* [2]: (a) concern for others' welfare; (b) bravery; (c) respect for others' opinions; (d) dedication to one's community.

5. _____ never more *manifest* [4]: (a) interesting; (b) justified; (c) understandable; (d) apparent.

6. _____ a *capricious* storm [8]: (a) destructive; (b) unpredictable; (c) unexpected; (d) violent.

7. _____ available equipment was *mustered* [8]: (a) purchased; (b) repaired; (c) made available; (d) collected.

8. _____ less definable, more *exalted* [10]: (a) acceptable, appropriate; (b) lofty, sublime; (c) reverent, devoted; (d) fervent, enthusiastic.

9. _____ the *zeal* of a dynamic age [10]: (a) main characteristic; (b) confusion, befuddlement; (c) enthusiastic devotion for a cause; (d) persecution of religious sect members.

10. _____ the *magnates* of commerce [10]: (a) powerful, influential people; (b) common laborers; (c) designers, inventors; (d) salespeople, promoters.

11. _____ have bent their *haughty* necks [10]: (a) proud; (b) willful; (c) arrogant; (d) intimidating.

12. _____ an *unprecedented* height [12]: (a) unusual; (b) unimaginable; (c) never before known; (d) unequaled.

13. _____ the *apogee* of architects' daring [12]: (a) the highest point; (b) the middle point; (c) the lowest point; (d) the most obvious point.

14. _____ Repaired with *undaunted* purpose [12—see also *daunting* in paragraph 18]: (a) undisguised; (b) unembarrassed; (c) unparalleled; (d) not disheartened.

15. _____ the new *expedients* and techniques [13]: (a) devices used to meet a need; (b) the final goals; (c) construction methods; (d) things eliminated for the sake of economy.

16. _____ exploits that inspire *awe* [16]: (a) imitation; (b) respect and wonder; (c) curiosity; (d) fear, intimidation.

17. _____ *shrouded* in the mists of the eighth century [16]: (a) remembered; (b) described; (c) sheltered; (d) hidden.

18. _____ What counts is the conquest of fearful *adversity* [20]: (a) misfortune, hardship; (b) anxieties, worries; (c) disease, pestilence; (d) lack of faith.

H.   USING VOCABULARY

In parentheses before each sentence are some inflected forms of words from the selection. Study the context and the sentence. Then write the correct form in the space provided. Be sure to add appropriate endings like *-s, -ed,* or *-ing* if necessary.

1. (*ineptitude, inept, ineptly*)   Tuchman begins the essay by stating that the human species in the twentieth century is characterized by violence, corruption, and _____.

2. (*decadence, decay, decadent, decadently*)   In sum, our civilization can be best described as _____.

3. (*exertion, exert*)   On the positive side, mankind has _____ remarkable endeavors throughout history, which we need to be reminded of.

4. (*antagonist, antagonize*)   For the Dutch the ocean was revengeful, eternally serving as their _____.

5. (*unanimity, unanimous, unanimously*)   Both houses of the Dutch Parliament voted _____ to pass the enclosure act in 1918.

6. (*embodiment, embody*)   For Tuchman, Abbot Suger was the main _____ of the spirit of medieval builders.

7. (*audacity, audacious, audaciously*)   The great European cathedrals represented _____ architectural designs and innovative construction techniques.

8. (*embellishment, embellish*)   Integral to the construction of the cathedrals were _____, like statues of saints, prophets, and animals.

9. (*tenacity, tenacious, tenaciously*)   Tuchman writes that never before in history did explorers persist so _____ against such terrible hardships.

10. (*perseverance, persevere, perseveringly*)   Through all the hardships and misfortune, La Salle _____.

I.   TOPICS FOR WRITING OR DISCUSSION

1.   Read paragraphs 1 and 2 again carefully. As an exercise in economy, summarize the information in these paragraphs in three sentences.

_____

_____

_____

_____

_____

2.   Describe in specific detail one of "mankind's better moments" that you have experienced, observed, or read about.

Using the Dictionary

The introduction to the text provided you with some suggestions for improving your reading vocabulary. To achieve this goal, it is essential that you have an up-to-date dictionary at home and that you learn how to use it correctly and efficiently. If possible, you should have two: an unabridged and an abridged version.

To *abridge* means to reduce or to condense. Therefore, an abridged dictionary, which is usually published in an inexpensive paperback format, is a short dictionary and does not contain as many words as an unabridged version. A standard college edition of an unabridged dictionary generally contains around 170,000 entries, whereas an abridged edition contains about 55,000 to 60,000 entries. But each has its own advantages. The light weight of the paperback dictionary makes it easy to carry to class, whereas the unabridged version is better used at home where you study.

Ask your instructor to recommend one, or choose one from this list of the three most widely used. Each comes in both an unabridged and an abridged version. In alphabetical order:

The American Heritage Dictionary of the English Language

The Random House Dictionary of the English Language

Webster's New World Dictionary of the American Language

No matter what dictionary you use, all contain the same features. Here is a brief outline of the important ones:

GUIDE WORDS

The guide words are printed in boldface type in the top margin of each dictionary page. They indicate the first and last words on that page, and they are used for locating words quickly. For example, to locate the word *incriminate,* you turn to the page with the guide words containing the first three or four letters that come before and after *incr*—in other words, the first letters of *incriminate.* In the three dictionaries listed previously, *incriminate* is located on the page with these guide words:

> *American Heritage:* between *in*corporate and *in*debted
>
> *Random House:* between *in*create and *in*deed
>
> *Webster's New World:* between *in*crassation and *in*decent

ENTRY

The word that you look up is called the *entry.* It is printed in boldface type against the left margin.

PRONUNCIATION SYMBOLS

Following the entry are the pronunciation symbols, printed in parentheses. English has a complicated pronunciation system, because the language has approximately seventy-five different sounds but only twenty-six letters to represent them. A single vowel letter like *a,* for example, can be pronounced seven ways, as in these words: *rat, rate, car, rare, raw, father,* and *alone.* Therefore, the pronunciation symbols represent a standardized system so that you know how each letter or combination of letters should be pronounced in a word.

Although most dictionaries use standard pronunciation symbols, there *are* slight variations, especially with the symbols used to represent vowel sounds. It is important that you become familiar with the pronunciation symbols that your dictionary uses. Here is a list of the pronunciation symbols used by *The American Heritage Dictionary.* Notice that the symbol carries the same sound as the way the boldface letter or combination of letters is pronounced in an easily recognized word:

Spellings		*Spellings*		*Spellings*	
pat	ă	**kick, cat, pique**	k	tight, stopped	t
pay	ā	lid, needle	*l (nēd′l)	thin	th
care	*âr	**mum**	m	this	th
father	ä	no, sudden	*n (sŭd′n)	cut	ŭ
bib	b	thing	ng	urge, term,	*ûr
church	ch	pot, *horrid	ŏ	firm, word,	
deed, milled	d	toe, *hoarse	ō	heard	

pet	ĕ	caught, paw,	ô	valve	v
bee	ē	*for		with	w
fife, phase	f	noise	oi	yes	y
gag	g	took	ŏŏ	zebra, xylem	z
hat	h	boot	o͞o	vision, pleasure,	zh
which	*hw	out	ou	garage	
pit	*ĭ	pop	p	about, item,	*ə
pie, by	ī	roar	*r	edible, gallop,	
pier	*îr	sauce	s	circus	
judge	j	ship, dish	sh	butter	*er

The pronunciation key for *The Random House College Dictionary* is conveniently printed in the hardback edition to the right of the cover page. It is also printed in the front matter:

a	act, bat, marry	ē	equal, seat, bee, mighty	i	if, big, mirror, furniture
ā	aid, cape, way				
â(r)	air, dare, Mary	ēr	ear, mere	ī	ice, bite, pirate, deny
ä	alms, art, calm				
		f	fit, differ, puff	j	just, badger, fudge
b	back, cabin, cab				
		g	give, trigger, beg	k	kept, token, make
ch	chief, butcher, beach				
		h	hit, behave, hear	l	low, mellow, all
d	do, rudder, bed	hw	white, nowhere		
				m	my, simmer, him
e	ebb, set, merry				
ng	sing, Washington	u	up, love	n	now, sinner, on
		û(r)	urge, burn, cur	ᵊ	occurs in unaccented syllables before l preceded by t, d, or n, or before n preceded by t or d to show syllabic quality, as in
o	ox, box, wasp				
ō	over, boat, no	v	voice, river, live		
ô	ought, ball, raw				
oi	oil, joint, joy	w	west, away		
oo	book, poor				
o͞o	ooze, fool, too	y	yes, lawyer		cra·dle (krād'ᵊl)
ou	out, loud, prow				red·den (red'ᵊn)
		z	zeal, lazy, those		met·al (met'ᵊl)
p	pot, supper, stop	zh	vision, mirage		men·tal (men't'ᵊl) and in accented syllables between ī and r to show dipthongal quality, as in
r	read, hurry, near				
		ə	occurs only in unaccented syllables and indicates the sound of a *in* alone e *in* system i *in* easily o *in* gallop u *in* circus		
s	see, passing, miss				
sh	shoe, fashion, push				fire (fī'ᵊr) hire (hī'ᵊr)
t	ten, butter, bit				
th	thin, ether, path				
th	that, either, smooth				

Finally, here is the pronunciation key for *Webster's New World Dictionary of the American Language:*

Symbol	Key Words	Symbol	Key Words	Symbol	Key Words
a	asp, fat parrot	u	up, cut, color	m	met, camel, trim
ā	ape, date, play	ur	urn, fur, deter	n	not, flannel, ton

Symbol	Key Words	Symbol	Key Words	Symbol	Key Words
ä	ah, car, father	e	a in ago	p	put, apple, tap
			e in agent	r	red, port, dear
e	elf, ten, berry		i in sanity	s	sell, castle, pass
ē	even, meet, money		o in comply	t	top, cattle, hat
			u in focus	v	vat, hovel, have
i	is, hit, mirror	ər	perhaps, murder	w	will, always, swear
ī	ice, bite, high			y	yet, onion, yard
		b	bed, fable, dub	z	zebra, dazzle, haze
ō	open, tone, go	d	dip, beadle, had		
ô	all, horn, law	f	fall, after, off	ch	chin, catcher, arch
oo	ooze, tool, crew	g	get, haggle, dog	sh	she, cushion, dash
oo	look, pull, moor	h	he, ahead, hotel	th	thin, nothing, truth
yoo	use, cute, few	j	joy, agile, badge	*th*	then, father, lathe
yoo	united, cure, globule	k	kill, tackle, bake	zh	azure, leisure
oi	oil, point, toy	l	let, yellow, ball	ŋ	ring, anger, drink
ou	out, crowd, plow				

As you can see by comparing these three keys, the only significant difference is in the vowel symbols. Short vowels in *The American Heritage* are printed with a special mark (˘), called a *breve* (pronounced brĕv′) from the French word for *short*. The *Random House* and *Webster's New World* do not use any mark over the short vowels.

One symbol that causes difficulty is the schwa, the funny-looking upside-down *e* that looks like this: ə. It is pronounced "uh" and can represent the sound of any vowel that occurs in an unaccented syllable, as you can see in these words: *about, system, edible, lemon,* and *focus.*

You can find a complete list of these symbols in the front matter of your dictionary. But since it is a nuisance to have to turn to this page every time you need to check on the pronunciation of a sound, all dictionaries provide a brief summary of the symbols—in particular the vowel symbols—with a familiar short word containing the sound that the symbol makes at the bottom of each dictionary page.

Using the pronunciation symbols in your dictionary, look up and pronounce these words: *brooch, capitulate, cicada, ethyl, exquisite, grimace, junta, machination, nuclear, sherbet, slough,* and *verbatim.*

STRESS MARKS

Stress or accent marks are as important for pronouncing words correctly as the pronunciation symbols. Referring to the relative degree of loudness of each syllable, stress marks are printed *after* the syllable to be stressed within the pronunciation symbols, as you can see in this word: sol′ id. In this case, the first syllable, *sol,* receives the stress or emphasis.

English has three kinds of stress. Primary or heavy stress is shown by a heavy boldface mark, like this: ′. Secondary or weak stress is shown by the same mark printed in lighter type, like this: ′. And unstressed syllables, such as those containing a schwa vowel, as you saw earlier, have no mark at all.

The word *magnification* is a good example of a word containing all three types of stress: mag′ nə-fə-kā′ shən. In this word, the fourth syllable (kā) receives primary stress; the second, third, and last syllables are unstressed (because the vowels in them are schwas, pronounced "uh"); and the first syllable (*mag*) receives secondary stress. It might help you to see the difference between them if the relative stresses are shown graphically, like this: mag nə-fə-K$\overline{\text{A}}$ shən.

If you have trouble pronouncing a word from the symbols, try this procedure: Find the primary stressed syllable first and pronounce it; then the rest of the syllables will fall into place more easily.

Use your dictionary to look up these multisyllable words to see where the stress or accent marks come: *choreography, demonic, idolatry, masquerade, phonetics, secretive, traverse.* Notice that *traverse* has two pronunciations: trav′ ərs and trə vûrs′. When two pronunciations are listed for the same part of speech, the first pronunciation is preferred.

But occasionally, a word may have two different pronunciations because they represent two different parts of speech. In this case you have to look at the context carefully to see which one to use. The word *convert*, for example, can be either a noun or a verb, depending on the way it is used. In the phrase "to *convert* dollars into pesos," *convert* is a verb, meaning "to change into a different form." It is pronounced kən vûrt′, with the stress on the second syllable. But in the phrase "a religious *convert*," it is a noun, meaning "a person who has been converted, as to a religion or an opinion," and it is pronounced kon′ vûrt, with the stress on the first syllable.

PARTS OF SPEECH

Following the dictionary pronunciation symbols is an abbreviation indicating what part of speech the entry word is. Here are the abbreviations and the grammatical terms they stand for. For examples and an explanation of how these parts of speech function in our language, refer to any grammar handbook:

n.	noun
v.	verb (*tr.* = transitive verb and *intr.* = intransitive verb)
adj.	adjective
adv.	adverb
prep.	preposition
conj.	conjunction
inter.	interjection

ETYMOLOGY

Etymology means the study of word origins. This information tells you the word's history or the way it came into the English language. The etymology of a word is printed in brackets, like this [ ], either before or after the definitions, depending on the dictionary. As you know, each Vocabulary Preview in this text introduces you to the word origins of two or three words in the reading. The abbreviations for each language can be found in the front pages of the dictionary.

Here is the etymology provided by the *Random House College Dictionary* for the English word *enchant,* which means "to subject to magical influence or to cast a spell over":

[ME *enchante*(n) < MF *enchante*(r) < L *incantāre* to bespell]

Enchant came into English during the Middle English period (ME). Originally, however, the word came into the language from the Middle French (MF) word *enchante,* but the word can be traced back to its initial origin, the Latin (L) word *incantāre.* In other words, the symbol < means "derived from." The last language mentioned in the etymological information is the original language from which the word was derived.

ORDER OF DEFINITIONS

The one significant way dictionaries differ is in the order of definitions if a word has more than one meaning. Let us compare the ways the three dictionaries mentioned at the beginning of this section list multiple definitions.

The American Heritage Dictionary explains its order of definitions in the front matter like this: The first definition is

the central meaning about which the other senses may be most logically organized. The organization seeks to clarify that, despite its various meanings, the entry is a single "word" and not a number of separate words that happen to be spelled the same.

The Random House College Dictionary uses a similar system:

The most common part of speech is listed first, and the most frequently encountered meaning appears as the first definition for each part of speech. Specialized senses follow, and rare, archaic, and obsolete senses are usually listed at the end of their part-of-speech group.

In other words, both of these dictionaries print the most common meaning first, followed by less common senses. However, *Webster's New World Dictionary* uses a completely different system when a word has more than one meaning:

The senses of an entry have, wherever possible, been arranged in semantic order from the etymology [word origin] to the most recent sense so that there is a logical, progressive flow showing the development of the word and the relationship of its senses to one another.

This means that the *Webster's New World* uses a historical approach: the first definition may be an archaic or obsolete usage. To find the current meaning or meanings of a word with many senses, then, you may have to look past the first definition or two. More important, you have to pay very special attention to the context to be sure that the definition matches the way the word is used.

If you are unsure about the order of definitions, you can find the information easily in the front matter of your dictionary. These are the pages preceding the A page that explain how to use the dictionary. You will find much useful information in these pages, and it is well worth your time to familiarize yourself with the special workings of your dictionary.

To give you some actual examples of dictionary entries, here are two sample entries from the three dictionaries mentioned in this section. Study each carefully and be prepared to explain the essential differences between the way each word is presented. The entries represent two typical examples. The first word, *benefit*, can be either a verb or a noun, depending on the context; the second word, *silly*, illustrates well the difference between the semantic and the historical way of ordering definitions.

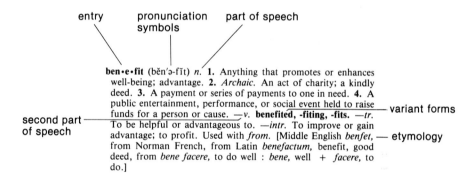

From *The American Heritage Dictionary*

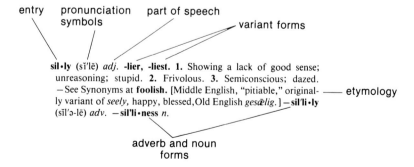

From *The American Heritage Dictionary*

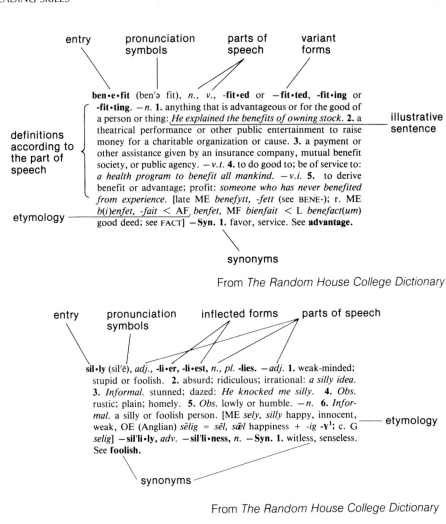

entry   pronunciation symbols   parts of speech   variant forms

ben·e·fit (ben′ə fit), *n., v.,* -fit·ed or −fit·ted, -fit·ing or -fit·ting. −*n.* **1.** anything that is advantageous or for the good of a person or thing: *He explained the benefits of owning stock.* **2.** a theatrical performance or other public entertainment to raise money for a charitable organization or cause. **3.** a payment or other assistance given by an insurance company, mutual benefit society, or public agency. −*v.t.* **4.** to do good to; be of service to: *a health program to benefit all mankind.* −*v.i.* **5.** to derive benefit or advantage; profit: *someone who has never benefited from experience.* [late ME *benefytt, -fett* (see BENE-); r. ME *b(i)enfet, -fait* < AF, *benfet,* MF *bienfait* < L *benefact(um)* good deed; see FACT] −**Syn. 1.** favor, service. See **advantage.**

definitions according to the part of speech

etymology

illustrative sentence

synonyms

From *The Random House College Dictionary*

entry   pronunciation symbols   inflected forms   parts of speech

sil·ly (sil′ē), *adj.,* -li·er, -li·est, *n., pl.* -lies. −*adj.* **1.** weak-minded; stupid or foolish. **2.** absurd; ridiculous; irrational: *a silly idea.* **3.** *Informal.* stunned; dazed: *He knocked me silly.* **4.** *Obs.* rustic; plain; homely. **5.** *Obs.* lowly or humble. −*n.* **6.** *Informal.* a silly or foolish person. [ME *sely, silly* happy, innocent, weak, OE (Anglian) *sēlig* = *sēl, sǣl, sǣl* happiness + *-ig* -Y¹; c. G *selig*] −**sil′li·ly,** *adv.* −**sil′li·ness,** *n.* −**Syn. 1.** witless, senseless. See **foolish.**

etymology

synonyms

From *The Random House College Dictionary*

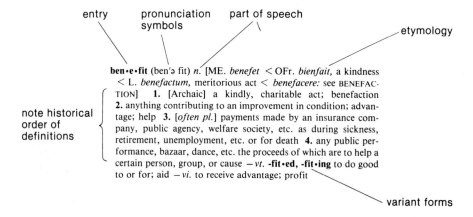

entry   pronunciation symbols   part of speech   etymology

ben·e·fit (ben′ə fit) *n.* [ME. *benefet* < OFr. *bienfait,* a kindness < L. *benefactum,* meritorious act < *benefacere:* see BENEFAC-TION] **1.** [Archaic] a kindly, charitable act; benefaction **2.** anything contributing to an improvement in condition; advantage; help **3.** [*often pl.*] payments made by an insurance company, public agency, welfare society, etc. as during sickness, retirement, unemployment, etc. or for death **4.** any public performance, bazaar, dance, etc. the proceeds of which are to help a certain person, group, or cause −*vt.* **-fit·ed, -fit·ing** to do good to or for; aid −*vi.* to receive advantage; profit

note historical order of definitions

variant forms

From *Webster's New World Dictionary*

entry   pronunciation   variant forms
symbols

etymology—
note complete
shift in
meaning

note historical
order of
definitions

synonyms—
subtle
differences
in meaning

sil·ly (sil'ē) *adj.* **-li·er, -li·est** [ME. *seli, sili* (with shortened vowel), good, blessed, innocent < OE. *sælig*, happy, prosperous, blessed (akin to G. *selig*, blessed) < *sæl*, happiness (sense development: happy → blissful → unaware of reality → foolish) < IE. base **sel-*, favorable, in good spirits, whence Gr. *hilasia*, propitiation, *hilaros*, gay, L. *solari*, to comfort] **1.** orig., *a)* simple; plain; innocent *b)* feeble; infirm; helpless **2.** [Now Rare] feebleminded; imbecile **3.** having or showing little sense, judgment, or sobriety; foolish, stupid, absurd, ludicrous, irrational, etc. **4.** trivial **5.** [Colloq.] dazed or senseless, as from a blow —*n., pl.* **-lies** a silly person —**sil'li·ly** (or **sil'ly**) *adv.* —**sil'li·ness** *n.* **SYN.** —**silly** implies ridiculous or irrational behavior that seems to demonstrate a lack of common sense, good judgment, or sobriety [it was *silly* of you to dress so lightly]; **stupid** implies a dullwittedness or lack of normal intelligence or understanding [he is *stupid* to believe that]; **fatuous** suggests stupidity, inanity, or obtuseness coupled with a smug complacency [a *fatuous* smile]; **asinine** implies the extreme stupidity conventionally attributed to an ass [an *asinine* argument] See also AB-SURD —**ANT. wise, intelligent.**

other parts of
speech

antonyms
(opposites)

From Webster's New World Dictionary

Study Skills: Techniques for Improving Your Study Habits

The final sections of the text explain and illustrate several practical study skills to help you learn the information in your textbooks more easily and efficiently. These techniques can be used singly or in combination, depending on what works best for you. Specifically, you will learn a study skills method called SQ3R and the related skills of annotating textbooks, paraphrasing and summarizing, and, finally, outlining and taking notes. Each skill is accompanied by a short selection reprinted from widely used textbooks. Each selection will give you an opportunity to practice with material from several disciplines and representing various levels of difficulty, the kinds of reading material that will be assigned in your classes.

Before introducing you to these skills, however, we should review the necessary steps to acquire good study habits, the most essential of which is learning to manage your time wisely. With the high cost of attending college today, many students need to work part time while they attend school, making sound time management even more crucial. You should start a study program, first, by taking an inventory of a typical week to see how you spend your time. Using the following grid, keep track of the way you spend your time for one week, being sure to account for each block. Use simple labels like *Class, Study, Work, Eat, Watch TV, Commute,* and so forth.

Now make a list of your courses and the number of class and lab hours per week. The standard formula that most colleges suggest is two hours of study time outside of class for every hour you spend in class. Using this formula, multiply the number of hours of class time by two to arrive at the minimal number of study hours you should be putting in each week. Naturally, some courses, especially science or writing courses, will require more time; others may require less, but this figure is a good starting place. For example, if you are taking twelve units of academic work, according to this formula, you should plan to spend about twenty-four hours per week studying outside of class.

457

	MON.	TUES.	WED.	THURS.	FRI.	SAT.	SUN.
8:00							
9:00							
10:00							
11:00							
12:00							
1:00							
2:00							
3:00							
4:00							
5:00							
6:00							
7:00							
8:00							
9:00							
10:00							

Next, if appropriate, calculate the number of hours you spend working. Be sure to include commute time. Now fill in a second grid, making a realistic schedule for your week. Begin with your classtime, work, and study hours. Include a sufficient amount of time for household tasks, relaxation, sports, recreation, or other outside activities.

By seeing where your time goes, or where it should be going, you may find that you will need to adjust your schedule. From my experience teaching freshmen and sophomores in a community college, I have seen that many students get into trouble by taking on too much because they overestimated what they could accomplish. Although there is no formula for a successful combination of study and work, by the end of the second week or so of classes, you should have a good idea of what your courses will require. With a little experience, you will know how to achieve a healthy balance between work and study.

However you arrange your schedule, stick to it as best you can. If you have a one-hour break between classes, study in the library. You can always review your notes or read while you wait for the bus or for an appointment.

Choosing a study place is also important. Wherever you decide is the best location, be sure that it is free of clutter and that is quiet, well-lighted, and not so comfortable that you will be tempted to doze off. Turn off the stereo or CD, radio, or

	MON.	TUES.	WED.	THURS.	FRI.	SAT.	SUN.
8:00							
9:00							
10:00							
11:00							
12:00							
1:00							
2:00							
3:00							
4:00							
5:00							
6:00							
7:00							
8:00							
9:00							
10:00							

television. Have everything you need for your study session at hand before you begin to work. Jumping up and down to find pencils or paper or notes or a dictionary only breaks your concentration, and you may be tempted to take unearned breaks.

Before you begin, make a list of what you can realistically accomplish in the amount of time you have set aside for that session. When you complete each major task, reward yourself by having a cup of coffee or taking a walk. And while you are studying, take short breaks every half hour or so. No one can concentrate fully for hours on end, and you should not expect it of yourself.

THE SQ3R METHOD

The SQ3R study skills method will help you tackle your college reading assignments systematically. Various study skills methods are taught in high school and college courses—PQ3R, PQ4R, SQ4R, SQ3R. All are variations on a system developed by Francis P. Robinson. All have in common previewing, reading purposefully, and reviewing. One might call these methods systems to "learn-as-you-go-along," because you learn the information *while* you are reading your assignment rather than saving up the "learning" part for the night before the test to cram.

Because these study skills techniques are so widely taught, today most textbook authors write their books and publishers produce them with these techniques in mind. As a result, the information in modern textbooks is usually very clear and well-organized.

The standard chapter begins with an overview or outline of the material. In the body of the chapter the relative importance of topics discussed is shown graphically by varying typefaces and type sizes. For example, main heads might be printed in large boldface capital letters, and subheads printed in smaller letters or in italicized type. Some college textbooks, especially for lower-division courses, are published with marginal annotations and main ideas underlined. In addition, most books contain graphs, charts, tables, illustrations, and maps that break up the page, and, more important, explain and reinforce important concepts. A chapter may also end with a summary, questions for review, a practice test, or a combination of these. All these devices are there to make your study time easier and more efficient.

SQ3R stands for the following steps:

S   SURVEY

Q   QUESTION

R   READ

R   RECITE

R   REVIEW

The SQ4R and PQ4R methods add an extra "R" step—"rite" (or "write"), meaning that you can take notes after the read step. If you prefer, you can substitute note taking for the recite step. (See the section on note taking for suggestions.)

Here is how the system works. Before you begin to read an assigned chapter, first *survey* its contents by briefly looking through the whole chapter. During the survey step, be sure to pay attention to these parts of the chapter:

- The chapter title
- The chapter outline
- The introduction
- The main head and subhead titles
- The chapter summary
- Any review questions or questions for discussion

The survey step gives you an overview of what the entire chapter is about *before* you start to read. In this way you can fit the various parts into a coherent whole during the next three steps—*question, read,* and *recite*—because the major points will already be familiar to you. For a typical textbook chapter the survey step should take no more than ten minutes.

Try the survey step now with this excerpt beginning on page 462 from Chapter 6 of a standard sociology textbook, *Sociology: The Core,* second edition, by James Vander Zanden. The chapter is titled "Social Stratification," and the entire chapter outline is reprinted here for you, even though you will be practicing with only one of the four main topics taken up in the chapter. As you look through the excerpt, notice that in the body of the chapter various kinds of typefaces are used to indicate main heads, subheads, and third-level heads:

The American Class System [main head is printed in boldface]

IDENTIFYING SOCIAL CLASSES [subhead is printed in capital letters, plain type]

The Objective Method [third-level heads are printed in boldface italics]

These typefaces, indicating the relative importance of the subjects, are also useful if you outline the chapter, as you will see later.

After you have completed your survey step, practice the next steps at the same time. To do this, go back to the beginning of the excerpt on page 462. The first main head, **"The American Class System,"** simply serves as an introduction to the section. The next subhead, however, IDENTIFYING SOCIAL CLASSES, might bring to mind these questions:

How do we identify social classes in America?

Which method is most valid?

For the next step, *read* through the excerpt to find the answers to them. When you come to the pertinent information, quickly *recite* it to yourself. Continue working through the excerpt in this way, first turning heads and subheads into questions, reading to find the answer, and then reciting the important information to yourself.

The final step in the SQ3R method, *review,* if done routinely and conscientiously and, most important, immediately after you finish each reading assignment, will greatly reduce your study time before tests, since the material will already be familiar to you. To review, look over the chapter once more, reading over the outline or introduction quickly; study the main points in each section; read the summary; and answer any review or discussion questions. Another effective technique is to review quickly all the accumulated chapters you have studied at the end of each week. This works especially well in preparing for major exams, where you are responsible for the material in several chapters.

After you practice with the SQ3R method for a while, you should feel free to modify it according to what works best for you. Some students find that they learn more easily if they annotate their textbook by writing in the margins. Others find that outlining or taking notes on their reading material is useful. These related skills are taken up in the next sections.

PRACTICE SELECTION
The American Class System

1 Sociologists may disagree regarding the sources of social stratification. However, they agree that social inequality is a *structured* aspect of contemporary life. When sociologists say that social inequality is structured, they mean more than that individuals and groups differ in the privileges they enjoy, the prestige they receive, and the power they wield. Structuring means that inequality is hardened or institutionalized, so that there is a system for determining who gets what. Inequality does not occur in a random fashion, but follows recurrent, relatively consistent and stable patterns. Further, these inequalities are typically passed on from one generation to the next. Individuals and groups that are advantaged commonly find ways to ensure that their offspring will also be advantaged.

2 Sociologists have borrowed the term "stratification" from geology. However, it is important to realize that it is somewhat more difficult to classify individuals within strata than it is to categorize rocks. Geologists usually find it rather easy to determine where one stratum of rocks ends and another begins. But social strata often shade off into one another so that their boundaries are dim and indistinct. All this raises the question of how we go about identifying classes.

IDENTIFYING SOCIAL CLASSES

3 In the course of our everyday conversations we talk about the "upper class," "middle class," and "lower class," referring to these social classes as distinct groups. Two views are found among sociologists concerning the accuracy of this popular conception. The first view holds that classes are real and bounded strata. Although this position has been a central element in Marxist formulations (Marx and Engels, 1848/1955; Anderson, 1971; Wright, 1979, 1985), it also emerges in the work of other sociologists who have identified a blue-collar–white-collar division in American life (Blau and Duncan, 1972; Vanneman and Pampel, 1977; Halle, 1984). The second view portrays American society as essentially classless, one in which class divisions are blurred by virtue of their continuous and uninterrupted nature. Seen in this manner, "social classes" are culturally quite alike and simply reflect gradations in rank, rather than hard-and-fast social groups (Hodge and Treiman, 1968; Rodman, 1968; Nisbet, 1970).

4 The differing conceptions derive in large measure from different approaches to identifying social classes: (1) the objective method, (2) the self-placement method, and (3) the reputational method. Although all the approaches produce some overlap in classes, there are appreciable differences in the results afforded by each (Kerbo, 1983). Moreover, each approach has certain advantages and disadvantages (see Table 1). Let us consider each method more carefully.

5 *The Objective Method* The **objective method** views social class as a statistical category. The categories are formed not by the members themselves, but by

TABLE 1 Identifying Social Classes

Method	Advantages	Disadvantages
Objective	A clear-cut method for studying the correlates of social class. It is commonly the simplest and cheapest approach since data can usually be obtained from government sources.	The method often does not yield divisions that people themselves employ in their daily lives.
Self-placement	The method can be applied to a large population since survey techniques can be employed for securing the data. A useful method for predicting political behavior since who people think they are influences how they vote.	The class with which people identify may represent their aspirations rather than their current associations or the appraisals of other people.
Reputational	The method provides a valuable tool for investigating social distinctions in small groups and communities. It is especially useful for predicting associational patterns among people.	The method is difficult to use in large samples where people have little or no knowledge of one another.

sociologists or statisticians. Most commonly people are assigned to social classes on the basis of income, occupation, or education (or some combination of these characteristics). The label "objective" can be misleading, for it is not meant to imply that the approach is more "scientific" or "unbiased" than either of the others. Rather, it is objective in that numerically measurable criteria are employed for the placement of individuals. Table 2 shows one way of depicting the distribution of Americans by family income.

6   The objective method provides a rather clear-cut statistical measure for investigating various correlates of class, such as life expectancy, mental illness, divorce, political attitudes, crime rates, and leisure activities. It is usually the simplest and cheapest approach since statistical data can be obtained from government agencies and the Census Bureau. But there is more to class than simply raw statistical data. In the course of their daily lives, people size one another up on a good many standards of excellence. Moreover, it is not only actual income, occupation, or education that matters, but also the meanings and definitions others assign to these qualities. For instance, a banker, while not falling below the middle class, is not necessarily accorded the highest social position in American communities (Warner and Lunt, 1941:82).

7   *The Self-Placement Method* The **self-placement method** (also known as the subjective method) has people identify the social class to which they think they belong. Class is viewed as a social category, one in which people group themselves with other individuals they perceive as sharing certain attributes in common with

TABLE 2   Family Incomes of Americans, 1986

Total income	Number of families (in thousands)	Percent
Less than $15,000	13,919	21.6
$15,000 to $24,999	12,619	19.6
$25,000 to $34,999	11,712	18.1
$35,000 to $44,999	9,403	14.6
$45,000 to $59,999	8,461	13.1
$60,000 to $74,999	3,918	6.1
$75,000 and over	4,461	6.9
Total	64,493	100.0

(SOURCE: *Census Bureau:* 1987 Current Population Survey.)

them. The class lines may or may not conform to what social scientists think are logical lines of cleavage in the objective sense. Researchers typically ask respondents to identify their social class, an approach reflected in Figure 1.

8   Within American life a family's class position historically derived from the husband's position in the labor market. But long-term social and economic changes, particularly the movement of many women into the workplace and declining family size, seem to be altering the way many women assess their class identity. The class identification of married men and women may be thought of as a continuum from "borrowing" (in which one's spouse's characteristics are more important than one's own) to "sharing" (in which equal weight is attached to one's own and one's spouse's characteristics) to "independence" (in which one's own characteristics outweigh those of one's spouse). Whereas in the 1970s, most employed women appraised their class position primarily in terms of the class position of their husbands, in the 1980s employed women had moved toward a sharing model. Husbands also moved in the direction of increasing independence. And single men and women now look increasingly to their own characteristics rather than those of their parents in assessing their class identities (Davis and Robinson, 1988). These trends seem linked to the growth of individualism that has permeated American life in recent years (Bellah et al., 1985).

9   The major advantage of the self-placement approach is that it can be applied to a large population, whereas, as we will shortly see, the reputational approach is limited to small communities. Table 3 shows how Americans rank the prestige of various occupations when asked to do so. The self-placement method is also an especially useful tool for predicting political behavior since who people *think* they are influences how they vote. However, the approach has its limitations. The class with which people identify may represent their aspirations rather than their current associations or the appraisals of other people. Further, when placing themselves in

Question: If you were asked to use one of four names for your social class, which would you say you belong in: the lower class, the working class, the middle class, or the upper class?

Answer: I belong in . . .

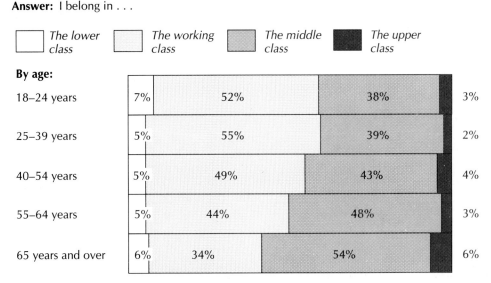

FIGURE 1   The Self-Placement Method for Identifying Class Membership

(Source: *Surveys by the National Opinion Research Center, General Social Surveys, 1982, 1983, and 1984 combined.* Public Opinion, 8 [February/March, 1985], p. 32.)

a national class structure, people commonly use fewer categories than they do when interacting with actual people and sizing them up in terms of subtle distinctions.

10   ***The Reputational Method***   In the self-placement method people are asked to rank themselves. In the **reputational method** they are asked how they classify *other* individuals. This approach views class as a social group, one in which people share a feeling of oneness and are bound together in relatively stable patterns of interaction. Thus class rests on knowledge of who associates with whom. The approach gained prominence in the 1930s when W. Lloyd Warner and his associates studied the class structure of three communities: "Yankee City" (Newburyport, Massachusetts), a New England town of some 17,000 people (Warner and Lunt, 1941, 1942); "Old City" (Natchez, Mississippi), a southern community of about 10,000 (Davis, Gardner, and Gardner, 1941); and "Jonesville" (Morris, Illinois), a midwestern town of about 6,000 (Warner, 1949). In Yankee City and Old City, Warner identified six classes: upper-upper, lower-upper, upper-middle, lower-middle, upper-lower, and lower-lower. In the more recently settled and smaller midwestern community of Jonesville he found five classes, since individuals made no distinction between the upper-upper and lower-upper classes (the former being

TABLE 3   Prestige Rankings of Occupations, 1972–1982

Occupation	Score	Occupation	Score
Physician	82	Reporter	51
College teacher	78	Bank teller	50
Lawyer	76	Electrician	49
Dentist	74	Police officer	48
Bank officer	72	Insurance agent	47
Airline pilot	70	Secretary	46
Clergy	69	Mail carrier	42
Sociologist	66	Owner of a farm	41
Secondary school teacher	63	Restaurant manager	39
Registered nurse	62	Automobile mechanic	37
Pharmacist	61	Baker	34
Elementary school teacher	60	Salesclerk	29
Accountant	56	Gas station attendant	22
Librarian	55	Waiter and waitress	20
Actor	55	Garbage collector	17
Funeral director	52	Janitor	16
Athlete	51	Shoeshiner	12

Note: *Americans ranked a number of occupations in terms of prestige in national surveys conducted between 1972 and 1982. The highest possible score an occupation could receive was 90 and the lowest 10. The table shows the ranking of a number of the occupations.*
(SOURCE: *National Opinion Research Center, 1982:299–314.*)

an "old-family" class representing "an aristocracy of birth and wealth" and the latter a class composed of the "new rich") (see Figure 2).

11   The reputational method is a valuable tool for investigating social distinctions in small groups and small communities. And it is particularly useful in predicting associational patterns among people. But it is difficult to use in large samples where people have little or no knowledge of one another.

12   ***Combining Approaches***   Warner undertook most of his research prior to World War II. Recently sociologists Richard D. Coleman and Lee Rainwater (1978) have updated our understanding of the class structure of urban America by combining the self-placement and reputational methods. They interviewed residents of Kansas City and Boston, querying them about their perception of the levels of contemporary living. The urbanites ranked each other and themselves in the following manner:

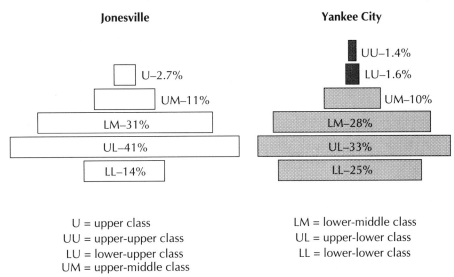

U = upper class   LM = lower-middle class
UU = upper-upper class   UL = upper-lower class
LU = lower-upper class   LL = lower-lower class
UM = upper-middle class

FIGURE 2 Stratification in Jonesville and Yankee City.

In Jonesville, a midwestern community, W. Lloyd Warner and his associates found five classes: one upper class, two middle classes, and two lower classes. In Yankee City, a considerably older eastern seaboard community, they identified six classes, the upper class being divided by an "old family"–"new family" chasm. Birth was crucial for membership in the "old family" (upper-upper) class. Its members could trace their lineage and wealth through many generations. In terms of wealth, the "new-family" (lower-upper) class could meet the means *test, but its members failed to meet the* lineage *test so essential for upper-upper class membership.*

(Source: *Adapted from W. Lloyd Warner, 1949.* Democracy in Jonesville. *Copyright 1949 by Harper & Brothers. Reprinted by permission of HarperCollins, Publishers, Inc.)*

1. *People who have really made it.* At the very top of the American class structure is an elite class of wealthy individuals. Some of these are old rich (the Rockefellers); others the celebrity rich (Paul Newman); still others the anonymous rich (a millionaire shopping center developer); and yet another group made up of the run-of-the-mill rich (a well-heeled physician).

2. *People who are doing very well.* Corporate executives and professional people make up this class. These individuals reside in large, comfortable homes, belong to relatively exclusive country clubs, occasionally vacation in Europe and places known for their elite clientele, and send their children to private colleges or large, reputable state universities.

3. *People who have achieved the middle-class dream.* These individuals enjoy the "good life" as defined in material terms, but they lack the luxuries of those in the higher classes. More often than not they are subordinates who reside in a three-bedroom home with a family-TV room.

4. *People who have a comfortable life.* While enjoying a "comfortable" life, the members of this class have less money at their disposal than the people above them and they live in less fashionable suburbs.

5. *People who are just getting by.* Some Americans enjoy "respectable" jobs, but "the pay is not the greatest." The husband may be employed as a blue-collar worker and the wife as a waitress or store clerk. The couple may own or rent a small home, but they find that "getting by" puts a strain on their joint income.

6. *People who are having a difficult time.* Members of this group find "the going tough." Both the husband and the wife work (although periodically they may experience unemployment), but their income is low. Much of their leisure time is spent viewing television. They do, however, have one consolation: "They are not on welfare."

7. *People who are poor.* At the "bottom of the heap" are "people who are down and out." Many of them receive government assistance and benefits.

13   The Coleman-Rainwater divisions are somewhat unwieldy. For the most part, sociologists as well as laypeople find it easier to employ the labels "upper class," "middle class," "working class," and "lower class" (poor people) when considering class distinctions. Research suggests that these terms correspond reasonably well with objective class indicators such as income, education, occupational skill level, and manual versus nonmanual jobs (Kerbo, 1983). However, the terms mask important divisions and interests among groups in our society. Moreover, they do not necessarily correspond with self-placement identifications. Even so, these class terms remain useful both because they have the most meaning for the most people and because they are significantly related to major occupational and property divisions.   ■

From James W. Vander Zanden, from *Sociology: The Core,* 2d edition, McGraw-Hill, New York, 1990, pp. 165–170.

ANNOTATING TEXTBOOKS

Annotation is another study technique that involves making notes of important ideas or writing explanatory notes in the margins of a text. Annotating is not the same as highlighting or underlining words and phrases with a brightly colored felt-tip pen. Although many students use this system, such a practice suggests that the material marked is important enough to learn in the future. Therefore, instead of helping you learn, it actually delays learning. Further, highlighting is a *passive* activity because you are not actively involved with the text, whereas careful annotating means that you are both *actively* reading and learning important concepts at the same time.

The following Practice Selection is reprinted from a music appreciation text. It is taken from Chapter 4, entitled "The Classical Period." Only paragraphs 2–7 have been briefly annotated for you. Before you practice your own annotations with the remaining paragraphs, read through this section, paying particular attention to these items:

- The notations are neat and brief. You don't want to clutter up the margins with too many notes, and it is imperative that they are legible.
- Only main points are annotated.

PRACTICE SELECTION
THE CLASSICAL SYMPHONY

The great contribution of the classical period to orchestral music is the symphony. Haydn wrote at least 104 symphonies, Mozart over forty, and Beethoven nine. Most of Haydn's symphonies were composed for his employers, who required a steady flow of works for their palace concerts. Beethoven, on the other hand, wrote a symphony only when inspired. His symphonies are longer than Haydn's or Mozart's and were conceived for performance in large concert halls.

Symphony—an extended composition using tone color; usually 4 movements with varying emotions, moods, and tempos.

A *symphony* is an extended, ambitious composition typically lasting between 20 and 45 minutes, exploiting the expanded range of tone color and dynamics of the classical orchestra. A classical symphony usually consists of four movements which evoke a wide range of emotions through contrasts of tempo and mood. A typical sequence is (1) a vigorous, dramatic fast movement; (2) a lyrical slow movement; (3) a dancelike movement (minuet or scherzo); and (4) a brilliant or heroic fast movement.

1) Opening—fast, vigorous, in sonata form

The opening movement is almost always fast and in sonata form. It is usually the most dramatic movement and stresses an exciting development of short motives. Sometimes a slow introduction leads to the opening fast movement and creates a feeling of anticipation.

2) Pace is slow, in sonata form, in a new key (not tonic key)

It is in the slow second movement that we are most likely to find broad, songlike melodies. This movement, by and large, is either in sonata form, A B A form, or theme-and-variations form. Unlike the other movements in the symphony, the slow movement is generally *not* in the tonic key. For example, if the first, third, and fourth movements are in the tonic key of C major, the second movement may be in F major. The new key points up the expressive contrast of the slow movement.

3) May represent many forms—a minuet or trio, a courtly dance or peasant romp

In the symphonies of Haydn and Mozart, the third movement is generally a minuet and trio, which may be in a moderate or fairly quick tempo. This movement varies in character from a courtly dance to a peasant romp or a vigorous piece that is hardly dancelike. Beethoven liked fast, energetic scherzos for his third movements.

4) Fast & lively, lighter in mood than opening

The fourth, concluding movement of a Haydn or Mozart symphony is fast, lively, and brilliant, but somewhat lighter in mood than the opening movement. (The agitated final movement of Mozart's Symphony No. 40 in G Minor is not typical.) Beethoven's concluding movement tends to be more triumphant and heroic in character and sometimes is meant as the climax of the whole symphony. The final movement of a classical symphony is most often in sonata or sonata-rondo form.

Each movement can stand alone; themes may be repeated; unity comes from using same key in 3 of 4 movements.

In most classical symphonies, each movement is a self-contained composition with its own set of themes. A theme in one movement will only rarely appear in a later movement. (Beethoven's Fifth and Ninth Symphonies are exceptions.) But a symphony is unified partly by the use of the same key in three of its movements. More important, the movements balance and complement each other both musically and emotionally.

The importance of the symphony has lasted into the middle of the twentieth century. Its great significance is reflected in such familiar terms as *symphonic music*, *symphony hall*, and *symphony orchestra*. ■

THE CLASSICAL CONCERTO

1   A classical *concerto* is a three-movement work for an instrumental soloist and orchestra. It combines the soloist's virtuosity and interpretive abilities with the orchestra's wide range of tone color and dynamics. Emerging from this encounter is a contrast of ideas and sound that is dramatic and satisfying. The soloist is very much the star, and all of his or her musical talents are needed in this challenging dialogue.

2   The classical love of balance can be seen in the concerto, for soloist and orchestra are equally important. Between them, there's an interplay of melodic lines and a spirit of give-and-take. One moment the soloist plays the melody while the orchestra accompanies. Then the woodwinds may unfold the main theme against rippling arpeggios (broken chords) played by the soloist. Mozart and Beethoven—the greatest masters of the classical concerto—often wrote concertos for themselves to play as piano soloists; the piano is their favored solo instrument. But other solo instruments used in classical concertos include violin, horn, trumpet, clarinet, bassoon, and cello.

3   Like symphonies, concertos can last anywhere from 20 to 45 minutes. But instead of the symphony's four movements, a concerto has three: (1) fast, (2) slow, and (3) fast. A concerto has no minuet or scherzo.

4   In the first movement and sometimes in the last movement, there is a special unaccompanied showpiece for the soloist, the *cadenza* (Italian for *cadence*). Near the end of the movement, the orchestra suspends forward motion by briefly sustaining a dissonant chord. This is indicated in the score by a *fermata* ($\frown$), a sign meaning *pause*, which is placed over the chord. The suspense announces the entry of the soloist's cadenza. For several minutes, the soloist, *without orchestra*, displays virtuosity by playing dazzling scale passages and broken chords. Themes of the movement are varied and presented in new keys. At the end of a cadenza, the soloist plays a long trill followed by a chord that meshes with the reentrance of the orchestra.

5   In the classical era, the soloist, who was often the composer, generally improvised the cadenzas. In this case, the score contained only the fermata, indicating where the cadenza should be inserted. But after the eighteenth century, the art of improvisation declined, and composers began to write cadenzas directly into the score. This gave them more control over their compositions.

6   A classical concerto begins with a movement in sonata form of a special kind, containing *two* expositions. The first is played by the orchestra, which presents several themes in the home key. This opening section sets the mood for the movement and leads us to expect the soloist's entrance. The second exposition begins with the soloist's first notes. Music for the solo entry may be powerful or quiet, but its effect is dramatic because suspense has been built. Together with the orchestra, the soloist explores themes from the first exposition and introduces new ones. After a modulation from the home key to a new key, the second exposition then moves to a development section, followed by the recapitulation, cadenza, and coda. The slow middle movement may take any one of several forms, but the finale is usually a quick rondo or sonata-rondo. ■

From Roger Kamien, *Music: An Appreciation*, brief edition. McGraw-Hill, New York, 1990, pp. 132–134.

PARAPHRASING AND SUMMARIZING

The last exercise following each selection in the text contains an exercise in which you are asked either to paraphrase particular sentences or to summarize the information in a short passage. When you paraphrase, you put someone else's words into your own words, meaning that you restate the original ideas without changing their meaning. When you summarize, you condense the original so that only the essential information is conveyed. Although paraphrasing and summarizing go together, actually one leads to the other. In order to write a good summary, you have to paraphrase by putting some of the ideas from the original into your own words.

Besides their obvious usefulness in note taking, which you will see in the next section, these skills will serve you well in other ways throughout your life. From preparing a report that includes information from many sources for your boss, to writing college research papers, to condensing the members' discussion at a meeting to write the minutes—each of these activities requires the ability both to change the wording and to eliminate the nonessential so that only the main points stand out.

Finally, writing a summary of a passage or longer selection is an excellent test of how well you have understood it. If you can strip away the supporting ideas, condense the main ideas, and restate them in your own words without introducing distortions or inaccuracies, then you can safely say that you have a good grasp of the content.

Let us first examine some techniques for paraphrasing:

- Substitute synonyms for a key word or words in the original.
- Change the order of ideas within sentences.

- Combine ideas.
- Omit supporting or unimportant ideas.

Notice that the first three techniques are concerned with both paraphrasing and summarizing, while the last one pertains more to summarizing.

To demonstrate the first three techniques, read these three paragraphs from an excerpt, "The Improbable Giraffe," part of a chapter on circulation in a college biology textbook:

Giraffes have always aroused irresistible curiosity in people. These strange African mammals are the third heaviest land animals after the elephant and rhinoceros, and of course they are by far the tallest: An adult male stands 5.5 m (18 feet) high, and a female 4.5 m (15 feet). Three basketball players standing feet to shoulders could scarcely look a male giraffe in the eye, yet a young giraffe just a few months old can easily browse tender leaves from the high branches of an acacia tree. . . . The Roman emperor Julius Caesar had the graceful beasts captured and paraded in the Roman Colosseum. And to satisfy the same public fascination, most major zoos since earliest times have kept giraffes on display.

Curiosity in the twentieth century has come from the scientific sector as well. As physiologists learned more about how animals function, they realized that a giraffe's body is even more enigmatic than it looks. The giraffe has, for example, a massive, muscular heart and thousands of miles of blood vessels. Yet, compared to the way these same vital organs operate in smaller, shorter animals, the giraffe should be on its last legs: It has very high blood pressure. With its heart 2.5 m above the ground yet 2–3 m below the head, the animal's legs and feet ought to swell with blood fluids, and upon standing up, the beast should faint from lack of blood to the brain. When a giraffe lowers its head 4 or 5 m to drink from a water hole, blood should come flooding down and blow out delicate vessels in the eyes and brain. Yet, none of these things happen. A giraffe can rise (albeit slowly) from a prone position, gallop away at 48 km (30 miles) per hour, then stop to drink water with no ill effects whatsoever. The giraffe is indeed a physiological marvel and makes a good case study for the functioning of the circulatory system—the heart and blood vessels.

Physiologists have found that giraffes show numerous evolutionary adaptations of the circulatory system that help them survive on land despite their height and massive weight. High blood pressure helps distribute blood with its cargo of oxygen, nutrients, and other materials throughout the lanky body. High-pressure fluid outside the thick-walled blood vessels counteracts the pressure inside and prevents leakage and swelling in the extremities. And in the head, large blood vessels branch out into a network of tiny channels before reaching the brain and eyes, and this *rete mirabile,* or "wonderful net," lowers and regulates the blood pressure reaching those delicate organs so that "blow-outs" are prevented.*

Here is a paraphrase of the first two sentences of paragraph 2:

Modern physiologists are curious about the way the giraffe's body, with its puzzling appearance, functions.

Notice that the wording has been changed completely without distorting the meaning of the original. *Curiosity* has been changed to *curious; twentieth century* has been replaced by *modern,* and *enigmatic* has been changed to *puzzling;* the order of ideas has been reversed; and the two original sentences have been combined into one.

Now to demonstrate the last technique, eliminating nonessential information. Here is paragraph 1 reprinted again, this time with the unimportant words and phrases crossed out:

Giraffes ~~have always~~ aroused irresistible curiosity ~~in people.~~ These strange African mammals are the third heaviest land animals ~~after the elephant and rhinoceros,~~ and ~~of course they are by far~~ the tallest: ~~An adult male stands 5.5 m (18 feet) high, and a female 4.5 m (15 feet). Three basketball players standing feet to shoulders could scarcely look a male giraffe in the eye,~~ yet a young giraffe ~~just a few months old~~ can easily browse tender leaves from the high branches of an acacia tree. . . . ~~The Roman emperor~~ Julius Caesar had the graceful beasts captured and paraded in the Roman Colosseum. ~~And to satisfy the same public fascination,~~ most major zoos since earliest times have kept giraffes on display.

Here is a sample summary of this paragraph:

People have long been curious about giraffes, the strange African mammal that is the third heaviest and tallest land animal. Giraffes are so tall that even a young one can eat the leaves from a tree's highest branches. From the time of Julius Caesar, who paraded giraffes in the Roman Colosseum, to our own time, giraffes have long fascinated the public.

To write a good summary, follow these suggestions:

- Read through the passage twice so that you have a good understanding of the content. Look up any unfamiliar words.
- Underline important words, phrases, and sentences. Cross out unimportant material, as shown above.

*John L. Postlethwait and Janet L. Hopson, "The Improbable Giraffe," *The Nature of Life.* McGraw-Hill, New York, 1989, pp. 460–461.

- Copy the material you underlined onto a sheet of paper. Double- or triple-space to give yourself plenty of room.
- Study the material. You may need to add information from the original or delete what you don't have room for.
- Condense and rewrite the material in your own words as much as possible.
- Insert transitional words or phrases if necessary to show the relationship between ideas.
- Rewrite the summary on another sheet of paper. Check to see that your summary is accurate and does not introduce your own ideas or opinions.

A general rule of thumb is that a summary is about twenty-five percent of the original length. These three paragraphs total around 400 words; therefore, a summary of them should be around 100 words. Here is a sample summary of the paragraphs we have been examining.

> The giraffe, the strange African mammal, is the third heaviest and tallest land animal. Modern physiologists are curious about the way the giraffe's body, with its puzzling appearance, functions. In particular, they are curious about its circulatory system, with its large, muscular heart, enormous system of blood vessels, and high blood pressure. Because its heart is so far below the head, it should experience many circulatory problems.
>
> Apparently, the giraffe's circulatory system has undergone evolutionary adaptations that enable it to survive on land despite its height. Its high blood pressure distributes blood and nutrients throughout the body, and the blood vessel system protects the brain and eyes from "blow-outs." (109 words)

Forcing yourself to limit a summary to an arbitrary number of words is an intellectually rigorous and challenging exercise. It requires you to think about what to save and what to omit, about how to retain the meaning of the original, using the fewest possible words, and yet about how not to distort the meaning or introduce inaccuracies.

For example, in preparing this summary, on the first go-around, I cut the original 400 words to about 180—clearly too long. I therefore had to omit many seemingly important details: people's long fascination with these marvelous creatures, specific dimensions, the potential ill effects of such high blood pressure, the way the blood vessel system functions. Yet I finally decided that these details—interesting as they were—were secondary to the main idea: that the giraffe's circulatory system has evolved, enabling it to survive despite its height and weight.

The second draft was around 150 words. From that point, it was fairly easy to rewrite and condense the important points for the final version. The trick, then, to writing a good summary is the ability to see the difference between main ideas and supporting details.

TAKING NOTES AND OUTLINING

You will recall that the fourth step of the SQ3R method is to recite the key points in each section. However, some students prefer substituting a combination of outlining and note taking for the recite step. As you work through this section, you will see that good notes require you both to paraphrase and to summarize, the two skills you practiced in the previous section. In other words, note taking really involves condensing large amounts of information so that only the most essential remains.

First, we should distinguish between *outlining* and *note taking*. When you outline, you make a schematic plan showing the overall organization and the main features of a chapter. When you take notes, you fill in the outline with the information contained within each section. You can also take notes in a free-form, nonschematic way, as will be illustrated below. To outline a chapter, you first need to survey its pages to look at the way the author has distinguished between the various levels of ideas.

Recall in "The American Class System" excerpt in the SQ3R section that main ideas were printed in boldface, whereas subheads were printed in capital letters with plain type, and third-level heads were printed in boldface italics. If we were to write a traditional outline that duplicated the author's way of displaying heads in that text, it would look like this:

I. **Main Head**

   A. SUBHEAD

   B. SUBHEAD

     1. *Third Head*

     2. *Third Head*

II. **Main Head**

   A. SUBHEAD . . . and so forth

Of course, not all books use this same graphic representation for classifying material. There are many possibilities, for example:

I. **MAIN HEAD**

   A. Subhead

   B. Subhead

     1. *THIRD HEAD*

     2. *THIRD HEAD* . . . and so forth

Outlining a chapter gives you an overview of the contents. When the chapter uses a graphic representation to indicate the relative importance of ideas, an outline indicates this importance by the slots. In other words, the roman numerals I, II, and III, and so on, represent main ideas; capital letters A, B, and C, and so on, represent subheads; and 1, 2, and 3 represent third-level heads. Therefore, it is imperative that your outline is consistent with the way the author classifies the material.

However, the two sample outlines printed earlier are only skeletons to demonstrate the possibilities of form. A real outline consists of a basic scheme or skeleton along with notes—a brief condensing of the important concepts. Before you practice taking notes with the practice selection that follows, here are some practical suggestions for making the job easier:

- Keep your notes brief. Many students make the mistake of taking overly long notes that include too much information. On a chapter quiz or even on a midterm exam covering several chapters, your instructor can ask only so much. The questions will very likely cover main concepts and principles, not trivial or explanatory information. Try to confine your notes for a standard-length textbook chapter to two or three pages at the most.
- As discussed earlier, be sure to duplicate the author's organizational scheme.
- Underline key terms and define each clearly. This is particularly important if the text contains many technical or scientific terms that you are likely to be tested on.
- Use the author's terms rather than your own. For example, the section from "The American Class System" uses the terms "reputational method" and "self-placement method." These should not be paraphrased. You may, however, paraphrase general material as long as you take care to do so accurately.
- To save space and time, use abbreviations, like these:
  info—information
  govt—government
  lit—literature
  c—century; also short for "circa" ("around"), as in "circa 19th century"
  org—organism
  intl—international
  pol—political
  econ—economics
  w/ or *w.*—with
  ex.—example

Turn now to page 477 and look at the way the headings are printed in this excerpt from Chapter 4, "Ethical and Social Responsibilities of Business," from a leading introduction to a business text. Reprinted here is the section called "Business and the Environment." In the original text, the main heads are printed in dark-brown *large*-type boldface print; subheads are printed in dark-brown *smaller*-type boldface print; and third-level heads are printed in even smaller black boldface print. An outline of this excerpt, including all the heads, follows. Read the excerpt, filling in the outline according to these heads, and then take notes following each third-level head where space has been left for you:

I.

   A.

      1.

      2.

   B.

      1.

      2.

      3.

Business and the Environment

1   . . . For the past 30 years, [Bofors Nobel Inc.] has manufactured paint pigments in Muskegan, Michigan. Waste from the manufacturing process has been disposed of in a company-owned dump site on 68 wooded acres behind the plant. Last year, the government ordered the firm to clean up the site, an undertaking with a $60 million price tag. With annual sales of only $30 million, Bofors opted to close its doors. Now the company is out of business, its customers are scrambling to line up new sources of pigment, the employees are out of work, and the toxic waste remains. In a situation like this, there are no winners.

The pervasiveness of pollution   2   Toxic wastes are not the only form of **pollution** threatening our environment. Our air, our water, and our land are all subject to abuse as a consequence of industrial activity.

Air pollution

3   The air we breathe is threatened by two forms of pollution: gaseous discharges and dust particles. About 155 million tons of pollutants spill into the air each year, and each type of pollutant has a different effect. For example, hydrocarbons (gases released when fossil fuels are burned) combine with sunlight under certain atmospheric conditions to produce smog, which burns the eyes, sears the throat, and distresses those who suffer from asthma, bronchitis, and emphysema. Such far-reaching health consequences have made fighting smog a priority in many areas.

4   Another sort of air pollutant is rain with a high acid content, which is created when nitrous oxides and gaseous sulfur dioxide react with air. This "acid rain" has

been blamed for damaging lakes and forests in southeastern Canada and the northeastern United States. Most of the harmful emissions come from coal-burning factories and electric utility plants.

5   Apart from contributing to acid rain, coal emissions have another disadvantage: They may contribute to a "greenhouse effect." The heated gases form a layer of unusually warm air around the earth, which traps the sun's heat and prevents the earth's surface from cooling. Some scientists believe that the greenhouse effect will eventually cause dramatic changes in the earth's climate, including a general increase in temperature, changes in rainfall, and a rise in the level of the oceans. If and when this will happen, no one knows for sure. But the threat serves as a warning about letting air pollution continue unchecked.

6   An air-pollution problem with more immediate implications is posed by the airborne carcinogens (cancer-causing agents) that are emitted into the atmosphere during some manufacturing processes. These toxins, according to environmentalists, are responsible for up to 20,000 cancer deaths each year.

Water pollution

7 Our air is not the only part of our environment to suffer. Approximately 11 percent of our river water and 30 percent of our lake water is polluted. The harbors and coastal waters are in trouble as well. This pollution comes from a variety of sources: municipal industrial facilities, oil spills, and runoff from farmlands, mining and construction sites, and urban areas.

8   In areas that are heavily industrialized, water-pollution levels are very high. Boston Harbor is a 50-square-mile soup of arsenic, chromium, lead, and PCBs, dumped there by some 6,000 factories. Fishing in the harbor is now outlawed; the flounder pulled from the water have tumors and cancerous sores.

9   Even if all wastewater were purified before being discharged, our ground water would still be endangered by leakage from the millions of tons of hazardous substances that have been buried in the ground or dumped in inadequate storage sites. Already, several hundred cases of ground-water pollution have been reported.

Land pollution

10 The disposal of industrial wastes directly into the ground is probably the single greatest threat facing the environment today. Two-thirds of the hazardous waste produced in the United States is disposed of in or on the land. And a large portion of this waste—some estimates reach as high as 90 percent—is disposed of unsafely. The government has identified some 20,000 dump sites around the country that are seriously contaminated. Almost half of the population lives in counties that contain one of these sites.

Government and industry response

11 Pollution problems became the subject of widespread public concern in the 1960s, when **ecology,** or the balance of nature, became a popular cause. In 1963, federal, state, and local governments began to enact laws and regulations aimed at reducing pollution. But the bedrock legislation underlying federal efforts to control pollution

is the National Environmental Policy Act of 1969, which established a structure for coordinating all federal environmental programs. This act was followed by a presidential order in December 1970, which established the Environmental Protection Agency (EPA) to regulate air and water pollution by manufacturers and utilities, supervise auto-pollution control, license pesticides, control toxic substances, and safeguard the purity of drinking water.

12   After some initial conflict, the EPA and industry established a relatively smooth working relationship; their willingness to work together brought advances in pollution control. During the past decade, however, the influence of the EPA has diminished. The political climate has favored deregulation and a relatively relaxed approach to the enforcement of environmental regulations. Much of the burden of environmental protection has shifted to state and local governments and to industry itself.

13   The current approach to pollution control recognizes that the health threat posed by a given industrial pollutant must be weighed against the economic cost of limiting or eliminating its use. Many activities that cause pollution also produce socially desirable results. As Frederick Krupp, director of the Environmental Defense Fund, points out, "Behind the waste dumps and dams and power plants and pesticides that threaten major environmental harm, there are nearly always legitimate social needs . . . long-term solutions lie in finding alternative ways to meet those underlying needs."

14   One of the most promising new directions is to emphasize prevention as opposed to correction. Pioneering companies are reducing the flow of pollutants into the environment—and lowering their cleanup bills—by using alternative materials, changing production techniques, redesigning products, and recycling wastes. In one year, du Pont reduced its output of waste by 50 percent in one division and by 35 percent in another.

Slow progress toward cleaner air

15   The fight against air pollution has been spotty at best. Despite nearly two decades of effort to improve air quality, 80 million Americans still breathe unhealthy air. The summer of 1988 was the worst in ten years in terms of ozone pollution.

16   Regulators and politicians are currently debating whether to ease federal air-quality goals or get tough in enforcing them. Federal law requires states and municipalities to meet air-quality goals or face economic penalties such as the loss of federal funding for new highways. Yet the Environmental Protection Agency has been reluctant to impose such sanctions. Deadlines for compliance are consistently extended, giving cities more time to clean up their air. With the federal pressure off, many cities ease up on businesses that have air-pollution problems.

17   The EPA has also been relatively flexible in dealing with industrial polluters. Rather than forcing individual businesses to curtail air pollution, the EPA allows groups of companies in certain urban areas to average their emissions. Thus, if one company can cut its pollution, it can sell or trade its "excess" clean air to another company that cannot meet the air-quality requirements. The businesses within a so-called air bubble can work together to plan the cheapest way to control pollution within the bubble as a whole.

18   But while overall progress has been slow, real strides have been made in dealing with some of the most serious air-pollution problems. Representatives of 24 nations have agreed to limit the production of chlorofluorocarbons (CFCs), which are responsible for damaging the upper layer of ozone that protects the earth from ultraviolet rays. This agreement should prevent a dramatic increase in skin cancer and cataracts that scientists claim would result if the ozone layer were depleted.

19   Meanwhile, the fight against toxic chemical emissions is getting a boost from the passage of the Emergency Planning and Community Right-to-Know Act of 1986, which requires businesses to report on the amount of toxic chemicals that they release into the air, land, and water. The publication of this information puts the spotlight on companies that pose a health hazard and encourages municipalities to press for safety controls.

20   In addition, some states and cities have established standards for toxic chemical emissions, but the substances controlled and the levels allowed in the air vary widely. The chemical industry itself, seeking to make order out of chaos, has called on members of Congress to impose uniform, nationwide controls over toxic air pollutants.

The battle for cleaner water

21   Since the passage of the Water Quality Act of 1965, the federal government has invested over $40 billion in the fight against water pollution, while state and local governments have contributed an additional $25 billion. The results have been mixed. Many lakes and rivers have improved dramatically; others are still mired in filth.

22   The EPA has established standards for sewage treatment, but only about 30 percent of all municipal sewage systems have complied, mostly because they lack the funds to do so. The EPA has also established clean-water rules aimed at chemical and plastics manufacturers, who are the leading dischargers of toxic wastes into the nation's waterways. These rules require manufacturers to install pollution-control equipment capable of treating wastewaters before they are dumped into public sewers.

23   Until recently, these rules were not stringently enforced, but the picture may be changing. A federal grand jury recently charged Ocean Spray Cranberries Inc. with 6 felony counts and 72 misdemeanor counts for discharging millions of gallons of polluted wastewater into the Nemasket River in violation of the federal Clean Water Act. Total fines in the case could exceed $2 million. As the U.S. attorney in charge of the case pointed out, this "should send a signal to all companies, no matter how large, that they cannot pollute the nation's waters and hope to pay small fines as a cost of doing business." The case is indicative of a growing trend to use criminal charges and steep fines as tools in prodding companies to behave responsibly.

The war on toxic waste

24   For years, most wastes were routinely dumped in landfills, whose protective barriers (if any) could not be counted on to prevent dangerous chemicals from leaking into the soil and eventually into the water supply. In 1980, Congress established the so-called Superfund to clean up the most hazardous of these old

dumps by taking the wastes to new sites that are supposed to be safe and stringently regulated. So far, 13 sites have been completely cleaned up; another 20,000 remain. According to toxic-waste experts, permanently cleaning up the worst sites would take about 50 years and cost $100 billion.

25   Although old sites will be a continuing problem far into the future, industry has begun to take steps to reduce new hazardous-waste contamination. For one thing, more companies are now dumping wastes in their own controlled and environmentally sound sites, and fewer are leaving their wastes to independent disposal firms, which are notorious for illegal dumping. In addition, manufacturers are trying out several other methods of eliminating or neutralizing their hazardous by-products. Some use high-temperature incineration, some recycle wastes, some give their wastes to other companies that can use them (sometimes getting in return wastes *they* can use), some neutralize wastes biologically, and some have redesigned their manufacturing process so as not to produce the wastes in the first place.   ∎

From David J. Rachman et al., *Business Today,* 6th edition, McGraw-Hill, New York, 1990, pp. 86–91.

Reading Comprehension Progress Chart

To calculate your progress find the number of the selection at the top and the number representing your percentage of correct answers at the left. At the square where the two numbers meet, shade it in with a pencil. This will allow you to keep track of the progress you make during the term. Remember that a score of 70 percent or above is considered acceptable and that since the selections become progressively more difficult, a constant score of 70 percent throughout the text indicates improvement.

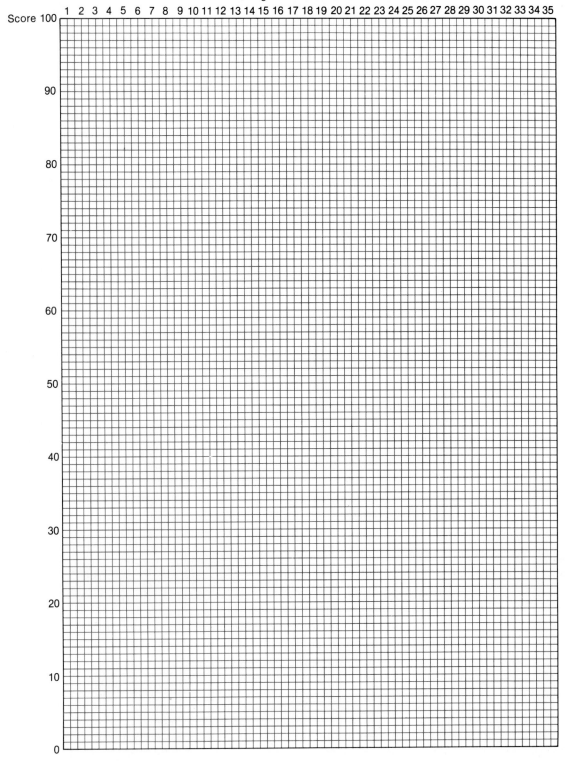

INDEX